Cato
Handbook
for
Policymakers

Cato
Handbook
for
Policymakers

7TH EDITION

CATO
INSTITUTE
WASHINGTON, D.C.

Previous editions of this book appeared under the titles *Cato Handbook for Congress* and *Cato Handbook on Policy*.

ISBN 978-1-933995-91-5

Printed in the United States of America.

Cato Institute
1000 Massachusetts Ave., N.W.
Washington, D.C. 20001
www.cato.org

Contents

FOREIGN AND DEFENSE POLICY

INTERNATIONAL ECONOMIC POLICY

1. Introduction

It's been a long time since a U.S. election generated feelings of actual joy beyond the ranks of partisan activists. If Barack Obama hasn't yet ushered in a new "era of good feelings," all Americans can take pride in the demise of yet another glass ceiling in a nation born in the idea that all of us are created equal, entitled to the inalienable rights of life, liberty, and the pursuit of happiness.

Indeed, we can take some satisfaction in observing that something normal happened: A party that had given Americans a long war and an economic crisis, led by a strikingly unpopular president, was defeated. Republican government requires that failed parties be turned out of office. The American Founders believed firmly in the principle of rotation in office. They thought that even successful officeholders should go back home to live under the laws after a short period in office. No doubt more members of the 110th Congress would have been given that privilege were it not for the vast incumbent protection complex of laws and regulations and subsidies.

George W. Bush and the Republicans promised choice, freedom, reform, and a restrained federal government. As far back as the Contract with America in 1994, congressional Republicans pledged "the end of government that is too big, too intrusive, and too easy with the public's money." But over the past eight years they delivered massive overspending, the biggest expansion of entitlements in 40 years, centralization of education, a war that has lasted longer than World War II, an imperial presidency, civil liberties abuses, the intrusion of the federal government into social issues and personal freedoms, and finally a $700 billion bailout of Wall Street that just kept on growing in the last month of the campaign. Voters who believe in limited government had every reason to reject that record.

At the Cato Institute we stand firmly on the principles of the Declaration of Independence and the Constitution, on the bedrock American values of individual liberty, limited government, free markets, and peace. And throughout our 32 years we have been willing to criticize officials of both

1

parties when they sought to take the country in another direction. We published papers critical of President Clinton's abuse of executive authority, his administration's misguided antitrust policies, his nation-building experiments, and his unwillingness to take on corporate welfare. Our analysts were among the first to point out the Bush administration's profligate spending, as well as the administration's policies on executive power, habeas corpus, privacy, expansion of entitlements, the federal marriage amendment, and the misbegotten war in Iraq.

But we have also been pleased to work with administrations of both parties when they seek to expand freedom or limit government—with the Clinton administration on free trade, welfare reform, and a few tentative steps toward Social Security reform; with the Bush administration on tax cuts, the initial response to the 9/11 attacks, health savings accounts, immigration reform, and Social Security accounts. We look forward to opportunities to work with the Obama administration when it moves to reverse the worst mistakes of the Bush years or otherwise to advance policies that would enhance peace, freedom, and prosperity.

The Current Crisis

In the current economic crisis, our first task is to understand it and its causes. This was a crisis caused by regulation, subsidization, and intervention, and it won't be cured by more of the same. Christopher Hitchens had a point when he wrote, "There are many causes of the subprime and derivative horror show that has destroyed our trust in the idea of credit, but one way of defining it would be to say that everybody was promised everything, and almost everybody fell for the populist bait."

The backdrop is central banking and implicit federal guarantees for risky behavior. The Federal Reserve Board creates money and adjusts interest rates, so any notion that our financial system was an example of laissez-faire fails at the start. Meanwhile, Congress and regulators encouraged Fannie Mae and Freddie Mac to become a vast duopoly in the mortgage finance industry. Their debt was implicitly backed by the U.S. Treasury, and they were able to expand their debt and engage in risky transactions. As Lawrence Summers wrote, "Little wonder with gains privatized and losses socialized that the enterprises have gambled their way into financial catastrophe."

There was substantial agreement in Washington that homeownership was a good thing and that more homeownership would be even better. Thus Congress and regulators encouraged Fannie, Freddie, and mortgage lenders to extend credit to underqualified borrowers. To generate more mortgage lending to low- and moderate-income people, the federal government loosened down-payment standards, pressured lenders to increase their percentages of "affordable" loans, and implicitly guaranteed Fannie and Freddie's dramatic expansion. All that hard work paid off: The share of mortgages classified as nonprime soared, and the quality of those loans declined.

Federal Reserve credit expansion helped to make all of this lending possible. As Lawrence H. White writes in a Cato study,

> In the recession of 2001, the Federal Reserve System, under Chairman Alan Greenspan, began aggressively expanding the U.S. money supply. Year-over-year growth in the M2 monetary aggregate rose briefly above 10 percent, and remained above 8 percent entering the second half of 2003. The expansion was accompanied by the Fed repeatedly lowering its target for the federal funds (interbank short-term) interest rate. The federal funds rate began 2001 at 6.25 percent and ended the year at 1.75 percent. It was reduced further in 2002 and 2003 and by mid-2003 it reached a record low of 1 percent, where it stayed for a year. The *real* Fed funds rate was negative—meaning that nominal rates were lower than the contemporary rate of inflation—for two and a half years. In purchasing-power terms, during that period a borrower was not paying but rather gaining in proportion to what he borrowed. Economist Steve Hanke has summarized the result: "This set off the mother of all liquidity cycles and yet another massive demand bubble."

"Everybody was promised everything"—cheap money, easy lending, and rising home prices. All that money and all those buyers pushed housing prices up sharply. But all good things—at least all good things based on unsustainable policies—must come to an end. When housing prices started to fall, many borrowers ran into trouble. Financial companies threatened to fall like dominos, and an ever-expanding series of bailouts began issuing from the Federal Reserve and the Treasury department. And instead of the usual response to businesses that make bad decisions—let them go into bankruptcy or reorganization and let their workers and assets go to more effective companies—the federal government stepped in to keep every existing enterprise operating.

At this point it is important that the recent emergency measures be recognized as just that: emergency—if not panic—measures and not long-term policy. Congress should turn its attention to extricating the government from financial firms and basing long-term policies on a clear diagnosis of what went wrong. As William Niskanen writes in Chapter 36, Congress should repeal the Community Reinvestment Act and stop pressuring lenders to make loans to underqualified borrowers. The Treasury should use its authority as conservator to liquidate Fannie Mae and Freddie Mac. The federal government should refrain from using its equity investments in companies to exercise power over their operations and should move with all deliberate speed to withdraw from corporate ownership.

One lesson of the credit crisis is that politicians prefer to "promise everybody everything"—low interest rates, affordable mortgages, higher housing prices, lower gas prices, a chicken in every pot. That's why it's important to keep politics out of such matters.

The End of Libertarianism—or a New Beginning?

Various pundits and public figures have claimed that the credit crisis means "the end of libertarianism" or even more dramatically "the end of American capitalism." As noted above, the crisis can hardly be considered a failure of laissez-faire, deregulation, libertarianism, or capitalism, since it was caused by multiple misguided government interventions into the workings of the financial system. It was and is precisely a failure of interventionism.

But could capitalism or libertarianism come to an end despite the facts? After all, the Great Depression was primarily caused by poor Federal Reserve policy and high tariffs. But a false impression that it was somehow caused by laissez-faire led to New Deal policies (pursued first by Herbert Hoover and then by Franklin D. Roosevelt) that turned a contraction into the Great Depression. What policies? Restrictive banking regulations, increases in top marginal tax rates, interventions to keep wages and prices from adjusting, and government rhetoric and activism that created (in the words of historian Robert Higgs) "pervasive uncertainty among investors about the security of their property rights in their capital and its prospective returns." That set of policies lengthened the Great Depression by eight years or more and is uncomfortably similar to recent and proposed policy responses to the 2008 credit crisis.

Jacob Weisberg of *Slate* declares "the end of libertarianism" in the wake of the financial crisis. But it was in fact "progressive" interventionism that caused the crisis—just the economic philosophy that Weisberg supports. So if one big failure can kill an ideology, then let's hear it for "the end of interventionism."

If this crisis leads us to question "American-style capitalism"—the kind in which a central monetary authority manipulates money and credit, the central government taxes and redistributes $3 trillion a year, huge government-sponsored enterprises create a taxpayer-backed duopoly in the mortgage business, tax laws encourage excessive use of debt financing, and government pressures banks to make bad loans—well, it might be a good thing to reconsider *that* "American-style capitalism." Or indeed, as a *Washington Post* editorial put it in October, "Government-sponsored, upside-only capitalism is the kind that's in crisis today, and we say: Good riddance."

Libertarianism calls for freedom and responsibility, free markets and civil liberties, a minimal government that stays out of both boardrooms and bedrooms. Obviously libertarianism wasn't in the driver's seat in either the Clinton or the Bush administration.

Even if there are misperceptions about the causes of the crisis, both the system of capitalism and the idea of libertarianism are going to have more staying power than pundits like Weisberg would like. There was a time when half the world rejected capitalism, and leading intellectuals in the "free world" worried that the centrally planned economies would obviously outcompete the capitalist countries and that "convergence" on some sort of half-capitalist, half-socialist model was the wave of the future. But after the world got a look at the results of the two systems in East and West Germany, North and South Korea, Hong Kong and Taiwan and China, the United States and the Soviet Union, it became clear that socialism is a clumsy, backward-looking prescription for stagnation at best and tyranny at worst.

Meanwhile, the half-planned economies of the West—Great Britain, New Zealand, the United States, and more—developed a milder version of economic sclerosis. Starting in the 1970s many of those countries began eliminating price controls, removing restrictions on market competition, opening up the economy, cutting tax rates, and reducing trade barriers. It came to be widely recognized—eventually on both sides of the Iron Curtain—that private property and markets are indispensable in organizing a modern economy. A nearly simultaneous cultural revolution opened up society. Women, racial minorities, and gays and lesbians entered the mainstream of society throughout the Western world. Art, literature, and lifestyles became more diverse and more individualized. The Sixties and the Eighties both led us to what Brink Lindsey in *The Age of Abundance* called "the implicit libertarian synthesis" of the United States today.

5

Some people see a future of ever more powerful government. Others see a future of greater freedom. *Reason* editors Nick Gillespie and Matt Welch write, "We are in fact living at the cusp of what should be called the Libertarian Moment, the dawning of . . . a time of increasingly hyper-individualized, hyper-expanded choice over every aspect of our lives. . . . This is now a world where it's more possible than ever to live your life on your own terms; it's an early rough draft version of the libertarian philosopher Robert Nozick's 'utopia of utopias.' . . . This new century of the individual, which makes the Me Decade look positively communitarian in comparison, will have far-reaching implications wherever individuals swarm together in commerce, culture, or politics."

Is it possible that Congress will choose to pursue policies—tax increases, yet higher spending, continued subsidies for risky decisions, intrusion into corporate decision making—that would slow down U.S. economic growth, perhaps make us more like France, with its supposedly kinder, gentler capitalism and its GDP per capita of about 75 percent of ours? Yes, it's possible, and clearly there are proposals for such policies. But if we want economic growth—which means better health care, scientific advance, better pharmaceuticals, more leisure opportunities, a cleaner environment, better technology; in short, more wellbeing for more people—there is no alternative to market capitalism. And if we want more growth, for more people, with wider scope for personal choice and decisionmaking, libertarian policy prescriptions are the roadmap.

Liberty Is More than Economics

The economic crisis grabbed the headlines last fall, and advocates of liberty and limited government can find much to criticize in the economic agenda advanced by President Obama and other Democrats on the campaign trail. But there is more to liberty than economic policy. In some of President Obama's other positions we find much to admire and many opportunities for cooperation.

President Obama first found favor on the campaign trail for his early and firm opposition to the war in Iraq. He spoke out against the war in 2002, as did Cato Institute analysts. We encourage him to move promptly to extricate American troops from Iraq and begin a process of military disengagement from the Middle East. In Chapter 49, Ted Galen Carpenter recommends that as we withdraw our troops we convene a regional conference to encourage a stable peace. We may hope that the experience with the Iraq war has led to a greater skepticism about military force, and

Chapters 46 on strategy and 50 on Iran offer further thoughts in that direction.

We see the potential for common ground in other areas as well:

- Executive power. During his campaign President Obama promised to reverse the sweeping claims of executive authority made by the Bush-Cheney administration. He said, for instance, "The President does not have power under the Constitution to unilaterally authorize a military attack in a situation that does not involve stopping an actual or imminent threat to the nation. . . . I will not assert a constitutional authority to deploy troops in a manner contrary to an express limit imposed by Congress and adopted into law. . . . I will not use signing statements to nullify or undermine congressional instructions as enacted into law. . . . I reject the Bush Administration's claim that the President has plenary authority under the Constitution to detain U.S. citizens without charges as unlawful enemy combatants. . . . The President is not above the law, and the Commander-in-Chief power does not entitle him to use techniques that Congress has specifically banned as torture." Campaigning in the Mountain West, he declared that libertarians and even conservatives would support him on the basis of concerns about such policies as warrantless wiretaps. We welcome his commitment on these issues. In Chapter 10, Gene Healy discusses the excesses of presidential war powers.
- Immigration. Immigrants are a source of economic and social vitality for the United States, as they have been throughout our history. But it will take real political skills to find a path forward to secure borders, legalization of people already living and working here, and a workable system for continued labor flows amid the political furor over illegal immigration. However, with the economy slowing and media attention focused elsewhere, the vocal hostility to immigration seems to have ebbed. This might be an opportunity for thoughtful debate in Congress on finding a sensible policy, and Dan Griswold offers some useful advice in Chapter 60.
- Guantanamo. In Chapter 27, Timothy Lynch calls on Congress to restore habeas corpus, close the Guantanamo prison, and repeal the Military Commissions Act. Congress and the new administration should repudiate the claim that America is a battlefield. Congress should abolish "national security letters" and require federal agents to conduct their searches within the American constitutional framework.

7

The Founders knew that habeas corpus, the "Great Writ," is one of the primary safeguards of individual liberty.

- Drug policy reform. It is long past time that we recognized the failure of drug prohibition. Voters are ahead of elected officials on this issue. In more than a dozen states, most recently in Michigan and Massachusetts, the people have voted to allow the use of marijuana for medical purposes or even to decriminalize marijuana. Those initiatives have usually won by a larger percentage than the winning presidential candidate in the state. Congress and the administration should stop federal interference with state marijuana law initiatives, stop treating pain doctors as drug dealers, and reform or better yet repeal mandatory minimum sentences. Beyond that, Sen. Barack Obama was not the only member of the 110th Congress who had acknowledged youthful drug use. Presumably neither he nor his colleagues thought that their lives or their communities would have been improved had they been incarcerated. Could we not now have a thoughtful debate on whether prohibition is working? Perhaps both liberals and conservatives could begin by agreeing that in a federalist system drug law should be a matter for the states and the federal Controlled Substances Act should be repealed, as recommended in Chapter 33.

Private property, free markets, and fiscal restraint are important foundations for liberty, and the party that claims to uphold those values has done a poor job of it lately. But there are restrictions on liberty beyond the realm of taxes and regulations. We hope that elected officials of both parties will recognize the dangers of censorship, drug prohibition, entanglement of church and state, warrantless wiretapping, indefinite detention, government interference with lifestyle and end-of-life choices, and other such policies. Americans declared in 1776 that life, liberty, and the pursuit of happiness are inalienable rights, and in 1787 they wrote a Constitution that empowers a limited government to protect those rights.

Conclusion

As this *Handbook* demonstrates, there are many more issues that demand the attention of Congress than we've been able to touch on here. Fiscal reform, for instance. Federal spending increased by more than a trillion dollars during the Bush years, or more than 70 percent (even before the budget-busting bailout and stimulus packages). The national debt rose even more sharply, from $5.727 trillion to more than $10.6 trillion, or an increase of more than 85 percent. The 2009 budget deficit may approach $1 trillion. Trends like this are unsustainable, yet elected officials continue to promise more spending on everything from new weaponry to college tuitions. Congress and the administration must find a way to rein in this profligacy. There are budget-cutting ideas throughout this *Handbook*, most notably in Chapter 4.

The current rates of spending don't yet reflect the acceleration of entitlement spending as the baby boomers start retiring. Entitlements are already about 40 percent of the federal budget. In 20 years they may double as a share of national income. The unfunded liability of Social Security and Medicare is now over $100 trillion, an unfathomably large number. Within barely a decade, the two programs will require more than 25 percent of income tax revenues, in addition to the payroll taxes that currently fund them. Congress needs to think seriously about this problem. Are members prepared to impose the tax burden necessary to fund such levels of transfer payments? Do we want that many Americans dependent on a check from the federal government? Eventually, the projected level of entitlements will not be feasible. It would be best to start now to make changes rationally rather than in a panic a few years from now. Chapters 12 through 17 discuss health care and Social Security reform.

Fidelity to our founding principles of respect for civil liberties and limited government may be easy when times are easy. The true test of our faith in those principles comes when we are beset by diabolical assaults from without and economic turmoil within, when public anxiety may temporarily make it seem expedient to put those principles aside. The importance of paying scrupulous deference to the Constitution's limits on federal power, of respecting its careful system of checks and balances, is greatest precisely when the temptation to flout them is strongest.

For those who go into government to improve the lives of their fellow citizens, the hardest lesson to accept may be that Congress should often do nothing about a problem—such as education, crime, or the cost of prescription drugs. Critics will object, "Do you want the government to just stand there and do nothing while this problem continues?" Sometimes that is exactly what Congress should do. Remember the ancient wisdom imparted to physicians: First, do no harm. And have confidence that free people, left to their own devices, will address issues of concern to them more effectively outside a political environment.

Suggested Readings

Bastiat, Frederic. *The Law*. 1850. Irvington, NY: Foundation for Economic Education, 1998.

Boaz, David. *Libertarianism: A Primer.* New York: Free Press, 1997.

Constitution of the United States of America.

Crane, Edward H. *Defending Civil Society.* Cato's Letter no. 8. Washington: Cato Institute, 1994.

Friedman, Milton. *Capitalism and Freedom.* Chicago: University of Chicago Press, 1962.

Murray, Charles. *In Pursuit: Of Happiness and Good Government.* New York: Simon & Schuster, 1988.

Higgs, Robert. "Regime Uncertainty: Why the Great Depression Lasted So Long and Why Prosperity Resumed After the War." In *Depression, War, and Cold War.* New York: Oxford University Press, 2006.

Powell, Jim. *FDR's Folly: How Roosevelt and His New Deal Prolonged the Great Depression.* New York: Crown Forum, 2003.

"Is Capitalism Dead?" *Washington Post,* Monday, October 20, 2008; Page A14.

Lindsey, Brink. *The Age of Abundance.* New York: Collins, 2007.

Gillespie, Nick, and Matt Welch. "The Libertarian Moment." *Reason,* December 2008.

Kling, Arnold. "Freddie Mac and Fannie Mae: An Exit Strategy for the Taxpayer." Cato Institute Briefing Paper no. 106, September 8, 2008.

White, Lawrence H. "How Did We Get into This Financial Mess?" Cato Institute Briefing Paper no. 110, November 18, 2008.

—Prepared by David Boaz

2. Limited Government and the Rule of Law

> **Congress should**
>
> - live up to its constitutional obligations and cease the practice of delegating legislative powers to administrative agencies—legislation should be passed by Congress, not by unelected administration officials;
> - before voting on any proposed act, ask whether that exercise of power is authorized by the Constitution, which enumerates the powers of Congress;
> - exercise its constitutional authority to approve only those appointees to federal judgeships who will take seriously the constitutional limitations on the powers of both the states and the federal government; and
> - pass and send to the states for their approval a constitutional amendment limiting senators to two terms in office and representatives to three terms, in order to return the legislature to citizen legislators.

Limited government is one of the greatest accomplishments of humanity. It is imperfectly enjoyed by only a portion of the human race, and, where it is enjoyed, its tenure is ever precarious. The experience of the last century is surely witness to the insecurity of constitutional government and to the need for courage in achieving it and vigilance in maintaining it.

Advocates of limited government are not anti-government per se, as some people would charge. Rather, they are hostile to concentrations of coercive power and to the arbitrary use of power against right. With a deep appreciation for the lessons of history and the dangers of unconstrained government, they are for constitutionally limited government, with the delegated authority and means to protect our rights, but not so powerful as to destroy or negate them.

The American system was established to provide limited government. The independent existence of the United States was based on certain truths:

> that all Men are created equal, that they are endowed by their Creator with certain unalienable Rights, that among these are Life, Liberty, and the Pursuit of Happiness—That to secure these Rights, Governments are instituted among Men, deriving their just Powers from the Consent of the Governed, that whenever any Form of Government becomes destructive of these Ends, it is the Right of the People to alter or to abolish it, and to institute new Government, laying its Foundation on such Principles, and organizing its Powers in such Form, as to them shall seem most likely to effect their Safety and Happiness.

On that foundation, the American Founders established a system of government based on delegated, enumerated, and thus limited powers.

The American Founders did not pluck those truths out of thin air, nor did they simply invent the principles of American government. They drew from their knowledge of thousands of years of human history, during which many peoples struggled for liberty and limited government. There were both defeats and victories along the way. The results were distilled in the founding documents of the American experiment in limited government: the Declaration of Independence, the Articles of Confederation, the state constitutions, and the Constitution of the United States.

The American Founders were careful students of history. It was Thomas Jefferson, in his influential *A Summary View of the Rights of British America*, prepared in 1774, who noted that "history has informed us that bodies of men as well as individuals are susceptible of the spirit of tyranny." Another Founder, Patrick Henry, devoted great attention to the study of history. He summed up the importance of history thus: "I have but one lamp by which my feet are guided, and that is the lamp of experience. I know of no way of judging the future but by the past." History—the lamp of experience—is indispensable to understanding and defending the liberty of the individual under constitutionally limited, representative government.

Through the study of history the Americans learned about the division of power among judicial, legislative, and executive branches; about federalism; about checks and balances among divided powers; about redress and representation; and about the right of resistance, made effective by the legal right to bear arms, an ancient right of free persons. Liberty and limited government were not invented in 1776; they were reaffirmed and strengthened. The American Revolution set the stage for the benefits of liberty and limited government to be extended to all. As John Figgis, professor of modern history at Cambridge University, noted at the beginning of the 20th century:

> The sonorous phrases of the Declaration of Independence . . . are not an original discovery, they are the heirs of all the ages, the depository of the emotions and the thoughts of seventy generations of culture.

The roots of the history of limited government stretch far back, to the establishment of the principle of the higher law by the ancient Hebrews and by the Greek philosophers. The story of the Golden Calf in the Book of Exodus and the investigations of nature by Aristotle both established— in very different ways—the principle of the higher law. Law is not merely an expression of will or power; it is based on transcendent principles. The legislator is as bound by law as is the subject or citizen; no one is above the law.

Many strands have been entwined to form the fabric of liberty:

- The struggle between church and state, which was put into high gear in the Latin West by Pope Gregory VII in the 11th century under the motto, "freedom of the church." That movement, which created an institutional distinction between the church and the secular authorities, could be seen as the first major "privatization" of a state-owned industry (the church) and provided the foundation for such important institutions as the rule of law and legal accountability, federalism, and the independent and self-governing associations that make up civil society.
- The growth of civil society in the self-governing chartered towns of Europe, in which the guiding principle was "city air makes one free." The independent cities of Europe were the seedbeds of modern civil society—of the market economy, of personal liberty, and of the security of person and property.
- The fixing of limits on the powers of monarchs and executives through written constitutions. The Magna Carta of 1215 is the most memorable of those documents to inheritors of the Anglo-Saxon political tradition. It included the requirement that taxes could not be imposed without the consent of the "general council of the realm," which provided the origin of the English parliament, as well as other very specific limitations on the king's power, including the stipulations that no

13

one be imprisoned or outlawed or exiled or his estate seized "except by the lawful judgment of his peers or the law of the land" and that "merchants shall have safe conduct in and out of England." That was the precursor of the Petition of Right of 1628, the Bill of Rights of 1689, the American Declaration of Independence, and the American Constitution and Bill of Rights.

Those various movements reinforced each other in a multitude of ways. The assertion of the freedom of the church and even of its supremacy over the secular powers was bound up with the idea of the higher law, by which all are judged—emperor, pope, and peasant alike. As legal scholar Henry Bracton, a judge during the reign of Henry III, noted of the royal authority, "The law makes him king. Let the king therefore give to the law what the law gives to him, dominion and power; for there is no king where will, and not law, bears rule." Were the king to consider himself above the law, it was the job of the king's council—the precursor of parliament—to rein him in: "if the king were without a bridle, that is, the law, they ought to put a bridle upon him." Not only was the nascent parliament above the king; the law was above the parliament, as Sir Edward Coke noted in the 17th century:

> when an act of Parliament is against common right and reason, or repugnant, or impossible to be performed, the common law will controul it, and adjudge such Act to be void.

The supremacy of the law over the exercise of power is a hallmark of the Western legal tradition. The rule of law is not satisfied by merely formal or ceremonial exercises, such as the publication of edicts in barely understandable form, whether in the archaic "Law French" of the king's courts or the pages of the *Federal Register*; the laws must be understandable and actually capable of being followed.

There was also widespread recognition of the principle of reciprocity between the holders of power and the general populace. Rights were spelled out in contractual form in constitutions and charters. Those rights were not gifts from the powerful, which could be taken away on a whim, but something on which one could take a stand. Tied up in the notion of a chartered right was the ancillary right to defend that right, even to the point of resistance with force of arms. The higher law, reciprocity and mutuality of obligations, written charters of rights, the right to be consulted on policy and to grant or refuse one's consent, and the right of resistance in defense of those rights are the foundations of constitutionally limited government. They were won over many centuries at great sacrifice.

Just how precious that heritage is can be gleaned from comparing it with the history of Russia, where, until very recently, there was no reciprocity between rulers and ruled and no independent power able to challenge the rulers. The principality of Muscovy and its successors were despotic to a high degree, with no charters of liberty, no power higher than the tsar (or his successor, the Communist Party), no limits on power—in effect, no law. As Harvard University historian Richard Pipes noted in his book *Russia under the Old Regime*, "There is no evidence in medieval Russia of mutual obligations binding prince and his servitor, and, therefore, also nothing resembling legal and moral 'rights' of subjects, and little need for law and courts." The immense difficulties in establishing the rule of law, a system of well-defined and legally secure property, and a market economy are testimony to the great and vital importance of building on a tradition of stable, constitutionally limited government. They also remind us how important it is for us to maintain our heritage of limited government and the rule of law.

The struggle for limited government was a struggle of liberty against power. The demands for religious liberty and the protection of property were fused in the heroic resistance of the Netherlands to the Empire of Spain in their great revolt. The Dutch inspired the English to rise up against the Stuart kings, who sought to fasten upon the English the absolutism that had made such headway on the Continent. The American Revolution was one link in a long chain of revolutions for liberty. The historian John Lothrop Motley opened his magisterial history *The Rise of the Dutch Republic* by connecting the Dutch Republic with the United States of America:

> The rise of the Dutch Republic must ever be regarded as one of the leading events of modern times. . . . The maintenance of the right by the little provinces of Holland and Zealand in the sixteenth, by Holland and England united in the seventeenth, and by the United States of America in the eighteenth centuries, forms but a single chapter in the great volume of human fate; for the so-called revolutions of Holland, England, and America, are all links of one chain.

Motley continued,

> For America the spectacle is one of still deeper import. The Dutch Republic originated in the opposition of the rational elements of human nature to

sacerdotal dogmatism and persecution—in the courageous resistance of historical and chartered liberty to foreign despotism.

The Dutch, like the British and the Americans after them, became a shining example of what was possible when people were free: prosperity was possible without the guiding hand of the king and his bureaucrats; social harmony was possible without enforced religious conformity; and law and government were possible without an unlimited and absolute sovereign.

The story of the attempts to institute absolutism in the Netherlands and in England was well known by the American Founders, who were, after all, British colonists. One cannot understand the American attempt to institute limited, representative government without understanding the history of England. What they were struggling against was the principle that the powers of the state are "plenary," that they fill up the whole space of power. King James I of England (then King James VI of Scotland) had written in 1598 that "the King is above the law, as both the author and giver of strength thereto." In 1610, James made *A Speech to the Lords and Commons of the Parliament at White-Hall* in which he railed against the notions of popular consent and the rule of law and stated that "as to dispute what God may do is blasphemy . . . so it is sedition in subjects to dispute what a king may do in the height of his power."

In other words, there are no limits to power. Distinct echoes of that view are still heard today. For example, the solicitor general of the United States, Drew Days, arguing in the 1995 case of *United States v. Lopez* before the Supreme Court, was unable to identify a single act of Congress, other than those expressly prohibited by the Constitution, that would be impermissible under the Clinton administration's expansive view of the commerce clause. Solicitor Days contended that the powers of Congress are plenary, that is, unlimited, unless, perhaps, specifically prohibited. That all-too-common view turns the notion of limited government on its head. Limited government means that government is limited both in the exercise of its delegated powers and in the means it can employ, which must be both "necessary and proper." The English Revolution of 1640, the Glorious Revolution of 1688, and the American Revolution of 1776 were fought precisely to combat unlimited government. What Americans need is not unlimited government, as Days proposed, but limited government under law, exercising delegated and enumerated powers. That is how the equal liberties of citizens are protected. As the philosopher John Locke, himself an active participant in the struggles for limited government in Britain and the primary inspiration of the American revolutionaries, argued in his *Second Treatise on Government*:

> *the end of Law* is not to abolish or restrain, but *to preserve and enlarge Freedom*: For in all the states of created beings capable of Laws, where *there is no Law, there is no Freedom*. For *Liberty* is to be free from restraint and violence from others, which cannot be, where there is no Law: But Freedom is not, as we are told, *A Liberty for every Man to do what he lists*: (For who could be free, when every other Man's Humour might domineer over him?) But a *Liberty* to dispose, and order, as he lists, his Person, Actions, Possessions, and his whole Property, within the Allowance of those Laws under which he is; and therein not to be subject to the arbitrary Will of another, but freely follow his own.

The American experiment in limited government generated a degree of liberty and prosperity that was virtually unimaginable only a few centuries before. That experiment revealed flaws, of course, none of which was more striking and repugnant than the toleration of slavery, or "man-stealing," as it was called by its libertarian opponents, for it deprived an individual of his property in his own person. That particular evil was eliminated by the Thirteenth Amendment to the Constitution, showing the self-correcting nature and basic resilience of the American constitutional system, which could survive such a cataclysm as the Civil War.

Other flaws, however, have been revealed or have surfaced since. Among them are the following:

- An erosion of the basic principles of federalism, as the federal government has consistently encroached on the authority of the states. Federal criminalization of acts that are already criminalized by the states, for example, usurps state authority (as well as circumventing—opinions of the Supreme Court notwithstanding—the prohibition of double jeopardy in the Fifth Amendment to the Constitution: "nor shall any person be subject for the same offense to be twice put in jeopardy of life or limb"). An even more striking contemporary example of the overreach of federal law is the continued exercise of federal controls over marijuana use in states, such as California and Arizona, that have legalized the medical use of that drug. The Tenth Amendment is quite explicit on this point: "The powers not delegated to the United States by the Constitution, nor prohibited by it to the States, are reserved to the States respectively, or to the people."
- Violation of the separation of powers between the various branches of government. In Article I, section 8, for example, the Constitution

explicitly reserves the power to declare war to the Congress, a power that the Congress has allowed to be usurped by the executive branch and which it should retake to itself.

- Failure of the legislative branch to fulfill its responsibilities when it delegates its legislative powers to administrative agencies of the executive branch, such as the Food and Drug Administration and the Federal Trade Commission. In addition to violating the Constitution, that failure has led to the erosion of the rule of law, as such administrative agencies have burdened the population with an unimaginably complex welter of edicts; the *Federal Register* ran 72,090 pages in 2007, reflecting a degree of minute regulation that is unreasonable and burdensome and that virtually guarantees that any citizen involved in a commercial transaction, for example, will run afoul of some part of it, no matter how well intentioned or scrupulous he or she may be. Such a situation is an invitation to the arbitrary exercise of power, rather than the application of law. That illegal delegation of powers is an abdication of the representative function described in the *Federalist Papers* and elsewhere by the Founders. Members of Congress are thereby converted from representatives of their constituents into "fixers," who offer to intercede on behalf of constituents with the agencies that are illegally exercising the authority of the legislative branch. Thus, members of Congress can avoid responsibility for onerous laws but can take credit for gaining special treatment for their constituents. That system may be thoroughly congenial to the interests of the existing officeholders of both the executive and the legislative branches, but it is directly contrary to the doctrine of the separation of powers and to the very concept of representative government.
- Inattention to the important role of the federal judiciary as a check on arbitrary and unauthorized exercises of power. Especially since the Court-packing "constitutional revolution of 1937," there has been too little attention by the federal judiciary—and by the Congress in ratifying judicial nominees—to fulfilling the role of the courts in enforcing constitutional restraints on both the federal and the state governments, as set out in Article III, section 2, of the Constitution. Sections of the Constitution that have suffered from relative neglect include Article I, section 1 ("All legislative Powers herein granted shall be vested in a Congress of the United States"); Article I, section 8 (enumerating and thus limiting the powers of Congress); Article I, section 10 ("No state shall ... pass any ... Law impairing the

Obligation of Contracts''); the Fifth Amendment (''No person shall be . . . deprived of life, liberty, or property, without due process of law; nor shall private property be taken for public use without just compensation''); the Ninth Amendment (''The enumeration in the Constitution of certain rights shall not be construed to deny or disparage others retained by the people''); the Tenth Amendment (''The powers not delegated to the United States by the Constitution, nor prohibited by it to the States, are reserved to the States respectively, or to the people''); and the Fourteenth Amendment (''No state shall make or enforce any law which shall abridge the privileges or immunities of citizens of the United States''). Although the First and Fourteenth Amendments have indeed been the source of significant judicial activity, the Court has not consistently applied the prohibitions of the First Amendment to either commercial speech or political speech (the latter in the context of campaign finance), nor has the Court rectified the novel (and specious) distinction between personal liberties and economic liberties drawn by Justice Harlan F. Stone in *United States v. Carolene Products Co.*

- The failure to pass a constitutional amendment limiting members of the Senate to two terms and members of the House of Representatives to three terms. Just as the president is limited in the number of terms he or she can serve, so should be the other elected branch of government, to guarantee the rotation in office that the Founders believed essential to popular government.

Those flaws can, however, be corrected. What is needed is the courage to place the health of the constitutional order and the future of the American system above short-term political gain. The original American Founders were willing ''to mutually pledge to each other our Lives, our Fortunes, and our sacred Honor.'' Nothing even remotely approaching that would be necessary for today's members of Congress to renew and restore the American system of constitutionally limited government.

In defending the separation of powers established by the Constitution, James Madison clearly tied the arrangement to the goal of limiting government power:

It may be a reflection on human nature that such devices should be necessary to control the abuses of government. But what is government itself but the greatest of all reflections on human nature? If men were angels, no government would be necessary. If angels were to govern men, neither external nor internal controls would be necessary. In framing a government which

19

is to be administered by men over men, the great difficulty lies in this: you must first enable the government to control the governed; and in the next instance oblige it to control itself. A dependence on the people is, no doubt, the primary control on the government; but experience has taught mankind the necessity of auxiliary precautions.

What is needed for the survival of limited government is a renewal of both of the forces described by Madison as controls on government: dependence on the people, in the form of an informed citizenry jealous of its rights and ever vigilant against unconstitutional or otherwise unwarranted exercises of power, and officeholders who take seriously their oaths of office and accept the responsibilities they entail.

Suggested Readings

Barnett, Randy. *Restoring the Lost Constitution.* Princeton, NJ: Princeton University Press, 2004.

Berman, Harold. *Law and Revolution: The Formation of the Western Legal Tradition.* Cambridge, MA: Harvard University Press, 1983.

Boaz, David. *Libertarianism: A Primer.* New York: Free Press, 1997.

————, ed. *The Libertarian Reader: Classic and Contemporary Readings from Lao-tzu to Milton Friedman.* New York: Free Press, 1997.

Bramsted, E. K., and K. J. Melhuish, eds. *Western Liberalism: A History in Documents from Locke to Croce.* New York: Longman, 1978.

Brooks, David L., ed. *From Magna Carta to the Constitution: Documents in the Struggle for Liberty.* San Francisco: Fox & Wilkes, 1993.

Ely, James W., Jr. *The Guardian of Every Other Right: A Constitutional History of Property Rights.* New York: Oxford University Press, 1998.

Epstein, Richard A. *Simple Rules for a Complex World.* Cambridge, MA: Harvard University Press, 1997.

Hamilton, Alexander, James Madison, and John Jay. *The Federalist Papers.* New York: Mentor, 1961.

Hayek, Friedrich A. *The Constitution of Liberty.* Chicago: University of Chicago Press, 1960.

Higgs, Robert. *Crisis and Leviathan: Critical Episodes in the Growth of American Government.* New York: Oxford University Press, 1987.

Jefferson, Thomas. ''A Summary View of the Rights of British North America.'' In *The Portable Jefferson.* New York: Penguin Books, 1977.

Locke, John. *Two Treatises of Government.* 1690. Cambridge: Cambridge University Press, 1988.

—Prepared by Tom G. Palmer

3. Congress, the Courts, and the Constitution

> ## Congress should
>
> - encourage constitutional debate in the nation by engaging in constitutional debate in Congress, as was urged by the House Constitutional Caucus during the 104th Congress;
> - enact nothing without first consulting the Constitution for proper authority and then debating that question on the floors of the House and Senate;
> - move toward restoring constitutional government by carefully returning power wrongly taken over the years from the states and the people; and
> - reject the nomination of judicial candidates who do not appreciate that the Constitution is a document of delegated, enumerated, and thus limited powers.

In a chapter devoted to advising members of Congress about their responsibilities under the Constitution, one hardly knows where to begin—so far has Congress taken us from constitutional government. James Madison, the principal author of the Constitution, assured us in *Federalist* No. 45 that the powers of the federal government under that document were "few and defined." No one believes that describes Washington's powers today. That circumstance raises fundamental questions about the constitutional legitimacy of modern American government.

For a while after the realigning election of 1994, it looked like Congress was at last going to rethink its seemingly inexorable push toward ever-larger government. In fact, the 104th Congress saw the creation in the House of a 100-strong Constitutional Caucus dedicated to promoting the restoration of limited constitutional government. And shortly thereafter, President Clinton announced that the era of big government was over.

21

But the spirit of that Congress waned in relatively short order. Today, it is hardly to be found.

The principles of the matter have not gone away, however, and nor, of course, has the Constitution itself. It is still the law of the land, however little Congress heeds it. And the moral, political, and economic implications of limited constitutional government have not changed either. That kind of government is the foundation for liberty, prosperity, and the vision of equality that many Americans still cherish—to say nothing of those around the world who in recent years have taken their inspiration from America's Constitution for limited government.

Yet all too many members of Congress seem still to believe that the good life is brought about primarily by government programs, not by individuals acting in their private capacities. And they believe equally that the Constitution authorizes them to enact such programs, even as many Americans know better. Below the level that polling usually reaches, those Americans understand that government rarely solves the problems it purports to solve; in fact, it usually makes those problems worse. More deeply, they understand that a life dependent on government is too often not only impoverishing but impoverished.

Reduce Government

If we are to move, then, toward restoring constitutional government— toward a world in which government is no longer expected to solve our problems; a world in which individuals, families, and communities assume that responsibility, indeed, take up that challenge—the basic questions are how much and how fast to reduce government. Those are not questions about how to make government run better—government will always be plagued by waste, fraud, and abuse—but about the fundamental role of government in this nation.

How Much to Reduce Government

The first of those questions—how much to reduce government—would seem on first impression to be a matter of policy. Yet in America, if we take the Constitution seriously, it is not for the most part a policy question, a question about what we may or may not want to do. For the Founding Fathers thought long and hard about the proper role of government in our lives, and they set forth their thoughts in a document that explicitly enumerates the powers of the federal government.

Thus, setting aside for the moment all practical concerns, the Constitution tells us as a matter of first principle how much to reduce government by telling us, first, what powers the federal government in fact has and, second, how governments at all levels must exercise their powers—by respecting the rights of the people.

That means that if a federal power or federal program is not authorized by the Constitution, it is illegitimate. Given the present size of government, that is a stark conclusion, to be sure. But it flows quite naturally from the Tenth Amendment, the final statement in the Bill of Rights, which says, "The powers not delegated to the United States by the Constitution, nor prohibited by it to the States, are reserved to the States respectively, or to the people." In a nutshell, the Constitution establishes a government of delegated, enumerated, and thus limited powers. As the *Federalist Papers* make clear, the Constitution was written not simply to empower the federal government but to limit it as well.

Since the Progressive Era, however, the politics of government as problem solver has dominated our public discourse. And since the constitutional revolution of the New Deal, following President Franklin Roosevelt's notorious Court-packing scheme, the Supreme Court has abetted that view by standing the Constitution on its head, turning it into a document of effectively unenumerated and hence unlimited powers. (For a fuller discussion of the Constitution and the history of its interpretation, see Chapter 3 of the *Cato Handbook for Congress: 104th Congress.*)

Indeed, limits on government today, when we've had them, have come largely from political and budgetary rather than from constitutional considerations. Thus, it has not been because of any perceived lack of constitutional authority that government in recent years has failed to undertake a program but because of practical limits on the power of government to tax and borrow—and even those limits have failed in times of economic prosperity. That is not the mark of a limited, constitutional republic. It is the mark of a parliamentary system, limited only by periodic elections.

The Founding Fathers could have established such a system, of course. They did not. But we have allowed those marks of a parliamentary system to supplant the system they gave us. To restore truly limited government, therefore, we must do more than define the issues as political or budgetary. We must go to the heart of the matter and raise the underlying constitutional questions. In a word, we must ask the most fundamental question of all: Does the government have the authority, the constitutional authority, to do what it is doing?

How Fast to Reduce Government

As a practical matter, however, before Congress or the courts can relimit government as it was meant to be limited by the Constitution, they need to take seriously the problems posed by the present state of public debate on the subject. It surely counts for something that a substantial number of Americans—to say nothing of the organs of public opinion—have little apprehension of or appreciation for the constitutional limits on activist government. Thus, in addressing the question of how fast to reduce government, we must recognize that the Supreme Court, after over 70 years of arguing otherwise, is hardly in a position, by itself, to relimit government in the far-reaching way a properly applied Constitution requires. But neither does Congress at this point have sufficient moral authority, even if it wanted to, to end tomorrow the vast array of programs it has enacted over the years with insufficient constitutional authority.

For either Congress or the Court to be able to do fully what should be done, therefore, a proper foundation must first be laid. In essence, the climate of opinion must be such that a sufficiently large portion of the American public stands behind the changes that are undertaken. When enough people come forward to ask—indeed, to demand—that government limit itself to the powers the Constitution gives it, thereby freeing individuals, families, and communities to solve their own problems, we will know we are on the right track.

Fortunately, a change in the climate of opinion on such basic questions has been under way for some time now. The debate today is very different from what it was in the 1960s and 1970s. But there is a good deal more to be done before Congress and the courts can move in the right direction in any far-reaching way, much less say that they have restored constitutional government in America. To continue the process, then, Congress should take the lead in the following ways.

Encourage Constitutional Debate in the Nation by Engaging in Constitutional Debate in Congress

Under the leadership of a number of House freshmen, an informal Constitutional Caucus was established in the "radical" 104th Congress. Its purpose was to encourage constitutional debate in Congress and the nation and, in time, to restore constitutional government. Unfortunately, the caucus has been moribund since then. It needs to be revived—along with the spirit of the 104th Congress—and its work needs to be expanded.

The caucus was created in response to the belief that the nation had strayed very far from its constitutional roots and that Congress, absent leadership from elsewhere in government, should begin addressing the problem. By itself, of course, neither the caucus nor the entire Congress can solve the problem. To be sure, in a reversal of all human experience, Congress could agree in a day to limit itself to its enumerated powers and then roll back the countless programs it has enacted by exceeding that authority. But it would take authoritative opinions from the Supreme Court, reversing a substantial body of largely post–New Deal decisions, to embed those restraints in "constitutional law"—even if they have been embedded in the Constitution from the outset, the Court's modern readings of the document notwithstanding.

The Goals of the Constitutional Caucus

The ultimate goal of the caucus and Congress, then, should be to encourage the Court to reach such decisions. But history teaches, as noted above, that the Court does not operate entirely in a vacuum, that to some degree public opinion is the precursor and seedbed of its decisions. Thus, the more immediate goal of the caucus should be to influence the debate in the nation by influencing the debate in Congress. To do that, it is not necessary or even desirable, in the present climate, that every member of Congress be a member of the caucus—however worthy that end might ultimately be—but it is necessary that those who join the caucus be committed to its basic ends. And it is necessary that members establish a clear agenda for reaching those ends.

To reduce the problem to its essence, members of Congress are besieged daily by requests to enact countless measures to solve endless problems. Indeed, listening to much of the recent campaign debate, one might conclude that no problem is too personal or too trivial to warrant the attention of the federal government. Yet most of the "problems" Congress spends most of its time addressing—from health care to mortgages to retirement security to economic competition—are simply the personal and economic problems of life that individuals, families, and firms, not governments, should be addressing. What is more, as a basic point of constitutional doctrine, under a constitution like ours, interpreted as ours was meant to be interpreted, there is little authority for government at any level to address such problems.

Properly understood and used, then, the Constitution can be a valuable ally in the efforts of the caucus and Congress to reduce the size and scope

25

of government. For in the minds and hearts of most Americans, it remains a revered document, however little it may be understood by a substantial number of them.

The Constitutional Vision

If the Constitution is to be thus used, however, the principal misunderstanding that surrounds it must be recognized and addressed. In particular, the modern idea that the Constitution, without further amendment, is an infinitely elastic document that allows government to grow to meet public demands of whatever kind must be challenged. More Americans than presently do must come to appreciate that the Founding Fathers, who were keenly aware of the expansive tendencies of government, wrote the Constitution precisely to check that kind of thinking and that possibility. To be sure, the Founders meant government to be our servant, not our master, but they meant it to serve us in a very limited way—by securing our rights, as the Declaration of Independence says, and by doing those few other things that government does best, as spelled out in the Constitution.

In all else, we were meant to be free—to plan and live our own lives, to solve our own problems, which is what freedom is all about. Some may characterize that vision as tantamount to saying, "You're on your own," but that kind of response simply misses the point. In America, individuals, families, and organizations have never been "on their own" in the most important sense. They have always been members of communities, of civil society, where they could live their lives and solve their problems by following a few simple rules about individual initiative and responsibility, respect for property and promise, and charity toward the few who need help from others. Massive government planning and programs have upset that natural order of things—less so in America than elsewhere, but very deeply all the same.

Those are the issues that need to be discussed, both in human and in constitutional terms. We need, as a people, to rethink our relationship to government. We need to ask not what government can do for us but what we can do for ourselves and, where necessary, for others—not through government but apart from government, as private citizens and organizations. That is what the Constitution was written to enable. It empowers government in a very limited way. It empowers people—by leaving them free—in every other way.

To proclaim and eventually secure that vision of a free people, the Constitutional Caucus should reconstitute itself and rededicate itself to that end at the beginning of the 111th Congress and the beginning of every Congress thereafter. Standing apart from Congress, the caucus should nonetheless be both of and above Congress—as the constitutional conscience of Congress. Every member of Congress, before taking office, swears to support the Constitution—hardly a constraining oath, given the modern Court's open-ended reading of the document. Members of the caucus should dedicate themselves to the deeper meaning of that oath. They should support the Constitution the Framers gave us, as amended by subsequent generations, not as "amended" by the Court's expansive interpretations.

Encouragement of Debate

Acting together, the members of the caucus could have a major effect on the course of public debate in this nation—not least, by virtue of their numbers. What is more, there is political safety in those numbers. As Benjamin Franklin might have said, no single member of Congress is likely to be able to undertake the task of restoring constitutional government on his own, for in the present climate he would surely be hanged, politically, for doing so. But if the caucus hangs together, the task will be made more bearable and enjoyable—and a propitious outcome made more likely.

On the caucus's agenda, then, should be those specific undertakings that will best stir debate and thereby move the climate of opinion. Drawn together by shared understandings, and unrestrained by the need for serious compromise, the members of the caucus are free to chart a principled course and employ principled means, which they should do.

They might begin, for example, by surveying opportunities for constitutional debate in Congress, then making plans to seize those opportunities. Clearly, when new bills are introduced, or old ones are up for reauthorization, an opportunity is presented to debate constitutional questions. But even before that, when plans are discussed in party sessions, members should raise constitutional issues. Again, the caucus might study the costs and benefits of eliminating clearly unconstitutional programs, the better to determine which can be eliminated most easily and quickly.

Above all, the caucus should look for strategic opportunities to employ constitutional arguments. Too often, members of Congress fail to appreciate that if they take a principled stand against a seemingly popular program—and state their case well—they can seize the moral high ground and ultimately prevail over those who are seen in the end as being more politically driven.

27

All of that will stir constitutional debate—which is just the point. For too long in Congress that debate has been dead, replaced by the often-dreary budget debate. This nation was not established by men with green eyeshades. It was established by men who understood the basic character of government and the basic right to be free. That debate needs to be revived. It needs to be heard not simply in the courts—where it is twisted through modern "constitutional law"—but in Congress as well.

Enact Nothing without First Consulting the Constitution for Proper Authority and Then Debating That Question on the Floors of the House and the Senate

It would hardly seem necessary to ask Congress, before it enacts any measure, to cite its constitutional authority for doing so. After all, is that not simply part of what it means, as a member of Congress, to swear to support the Constitution? And if Congress's powers are limited by virtue of being enumerated, presumably there are many things Congress has no authority to do, however worthy those things might otherwise be. Yet so far have we strayed from constitutional thinking that such a requirement is today treated perfunctorily—when it is not ignored altogether.

The most common perfunctory citations—captured ordinarily in consti-tutional boilerplate—are to the general welfare and commerce clauses of the Constitution. It is no small irony that both those clauses were written as shields against overweening government; yet today they are swords of federal power.

The General Welfare Clause

The general welfare clause of Article I, section 8, of the Constitution was meant to serve as a brake on the power of Congress to tax and spend in furtherance of its enumerated powers or ends: the spending that attended the exercise of an enumerated power had to be for the *general* welfare, not for the welfare of particular parties or sections of the nation.

That view, held by Madison, Jefferson, and most others, stands in marked contrast to the view of Hamilton—that the Constitution established an *independent* power to tax and spend for the general welfare. But as South Carolina's William Drayton observed on the floor of the House in 1828, Hamilton's view would make a mockery of the doctrine of enumer-ated powers, the centerpiece of the Constitution, rendering the enumeration of Congress's other powers superfluous: whenever Congress wanted to do something it was barred from doing by the absence of a power to do so, it could simply declare the act to be serving the "general welfare" and get out from under the limits imposed by enumeration.

That, unfortunately, is what happens today. In 1936, the Court came down, almost in passing, on Hamilton's side, declaring that there is an independent power to tax and spend for the general welfare. Then in 1937, in upholding the constitutionality of the new Social Security program, the Court completed the job when it stated the Hamiltonian view not as dicta but as doctrine. It then reminded Congress of the constraints imposed by the word "general," but added that the Court would not police that restraint. Rather, Congress would be left to police itself, the very Congress that was distributing money from the treasury with ever greater particularity. Since that time, the relatively modest redistributive schemes that preceded the New Deal have grown exponentially until today they are everywhere.

The Commerce Clause

The commerce clause of the Constitution, which grants Congress the power to regulate "commerce among the states," was also written primarily as a shield—against overweening *state* power. Under the Articles of Confederation, states had erected tariffs and other protectionist measures that impeded the free flow of commerce among the states. Indeed, the need to break the logjam that resulted was one of the principal reasons for the call for a convention in Philadelphia in 1787. To address the problem, the Framers gave *Congress* the power to regulate—or "make regular"—commerce among the states. It was thus meant to be a power primarily to facilitate free trade.

That functional account of the commerce power is consistent with the original understanding of the power, the 18th-century meaning of "regulate," and the structural limits entailed by the doctrine of enumerated powers. Yet today the functional account is all but unknown. Following decisions by the Court in 1937 and 1942, Congress has been able to regulate anything that even "affects" interstate commerce, which, in principle, is everything. Far from regulating to ensure the free flow of commerce among the states, much of that regulation, for all manner of social and economic purposes, actually frustrates the free flow of commerce.

As the explosive growth of the modern redistributive state has taken place almost entirely under the general welfare clause, so, too, the growth of the modern regulatory state has occurred almost entirely under the

29

commerce clause. That raises a fundamental question, of course: If the Framers had meant Congress to be able to do virtually anything it wanted under those two simple clauses alone, why did they bother to enumerate Congress's other powers, or bother to defend the doctrine of enumerated powers throughout the *Federalist Papers*? Had they meant that, those efforts would have been pointless.

Lopez *and Its Aftermath*

Today, as noted earlier, congressional citations to the general welfare and commerce clauses usually take the form of perfunctory boilerplate. When it wants to regulate some activity, Congress makes a bow to the doctrine of enumerated powers by claiming congressional findings that the activity at issue "affects" interstate commerce—say, by preventing interstate travel. Given those findings, Congress then claims it has authority to regulate the activity under its power to regulate commerce among the states.

Thus, in summer 1996, when the 104th Congress was pressed to do something about what looked at the time like a wave of church arsons in the South, it sought to broaden the already doubtful authority of the federal government to prosecute such acts by determining that church arsons "hinder interstate commerce" and "impede individuals in moving inter-state." Never mind that the prosecution of arson has traditionally been a state responsibility, there being no general federal police power in the Constitution. Never mind that church arsons have virtually nothing to do with interstate commerce, much less with the free flow of goods and services among the states. The commerce clause rationale, set forth in boilerplate language, was thought by Congress to be sufficient to enable it to move forward and enact the Church Arson Prevention Act of 1996—unanimously, no less.

Yet only a year earlier, in the celebrated case of *United States v. Lopez*, the Supreme Court had declared, for the first time in nearly 60 years, that Congress's power under the commerce clause had limits. To be sure, the Court raised the bar against federal regulation only slightly: Congress would have to show that the activity it wanted to regulate "substantially" affected interstate commerce, leading Justice Thomas to note in his concurrence that the Court was still a good distance from a proper reading of the clause. Nevertheless, the decision was widely heralded as a shot across the bow of Congress. And many in Congress saw it as confirming at last their own view that the body in which they served was simply out of control, constitutionally. Indeed, when it passed the act at issue in *Lopez*, the Gun-Free School Zones Act of 1990, Congress had not even bothered to cite any authority under the Constitution. In what must surely be a stroke of consummate hubris—and disregard for the Constitution— Congress simply assumed that authority.

But to make matters worse, despite the *Lopez* ruling—which the Court reinforced in May 2000 when it found parts of the Violence Against Women Act unconstitutional on similar grounds—Congress passed the Gun-Free School Zones Act again in September 1996. This time, of course, the boilerplate was included—even as Sen. Fred Thompson (R-TN) was reminding his colleagues from the floor of the Senate that the Supreme Court had recently told them that they "cannot just have some theoretical basis, some attenuated basis" under the commerce clause for such an act. The prosecution of gun possession near schools—like the prosecution of church arsons, crimes against women, and much else—is very popular, as state prosecutors well know. But governments can address problems only if they have authority to do so, not from good intentions alone. Indeed, the road to constitutional destruction is paved with good intentions.

Congressional debate on these matters is thus imperative: it is not enough for Congress simply to say the magic words—"general welfare clause" or "commerce clause"—to be home free, constitutionally. Not every debate will yield satisfying results, as the examples above illustrate. But if the Constitution is to be kept alive, there must at least be debate. Over time, good ideas tend to prevail over bad ideas, but only if they are given voice. The constitutional debate must again be heard in the Congress of the United States as it was over much of our nation's history, and it must be heard before bills are enacted. The American people can hardly be expected to take the Constitution and its limits on government seriously if their elected representatives do not.

Move toward Restoring Constitutional Government by Carefully Returning Power Wrongly Taken over the Years from the States and the People

If Congress should enact no new legislation without grounding its authority to do so securely in the Constitution, so too should it begin repealing legislation not so grounded, legislation that arose by assuming power that rightly rests with the states or the people. To appreciate how daunting a task that will be, simply reflect again on Madison's observation that the powers of the federal government under the Constitution are "few and defined."

But the magnitude of the task is only one dimension of its difficulty. Let us be candid: many in Congress will oppose any efforts to restore constitutional government for any number of reasons, ranging from the practical to the theoretical. Some see their job as one primarily of representing the interests of their constituents, especially the short-term interests reflected in the phrase "bringing home the bacon." Others simply like big government, whether because of an "enlightened" Progressive Era view of the world or because of a narrower, more cynical interest in the perquisites of enhanced power. Still others believe sincerely in a "living constitution," one extreme form of which—the "democratic" form— imposes no limit whatsoever on government save for periodic elections. Finally, there are those who understand the unconstitutional and hence illegitimate character of much of what government does today but believe it is too late in the day to do anything about it. All those people and others will find reasons to resist the discrete measures that are necessary to begin restoring constitutional government. Yet where necessary, their views will have to be accommodated as the process unfolds.

Maintenance of Support for Limited Government

Given the magnitude of the problem, then, and the practical implications of repealing federal programs, a fair measure of caution is in order. As the nations of Eastern Europe and the former Soviet Union have learned, it is relatively easy to get into socialism—just seize all property and labor and place it under state control—but much harder to get out of it. It is not simply a matter of returning what was taken, for much has changed as a result of the taking. People have died and new people have come along. Public law has replaced private law. And new expectations and dependencies have arisen and become settled over time. The transition to freedom that many of those nations have experienced, to one degree or another, is what we and many other nations around the world today are facing, to a lesser extent, as we too try to reduce the size and scope of our governments.

As programs are reduced or eliminated, then, care must be taken to do as little harm as possible—for two reasons at least. First, there is some sense in which the federal government today, vastly overextended though it is, stands in a contractual relationship with the American people. That is a very difficult idea to pin down, however. For once the genuine contract—the Constitution—has broken down, the "legislative contracts" that arise to take its place invariably reduce, when parsed, to programs under which some people have become dependent on others, although neither side had a great deal to say directly about the matter at the outset. Whatever its merits, that contractual view is held by a good part of the public, especially in the case of so-called middle-class entitlements.

That leads to the second reason that care must be taken in restoring power to the states and the people, namely, that the task must be undertaken, as noted earlier, with the support of a substantial portion of the people—ideally, at the urging of those people. Given the difficulty of convincing people—including legislators—to act against their relatively short-term interests, it will take sound congressional judgment about where and when to move. More important, it will take keen leadership, leadership that can frame the issues in a way that will communicate both the rightness and the soundness of the decisions that are required.

In exercising that leadership, there is no substitute for keeping "on message" and for keeping the message simple, direct, and clear. The aim, again, is both freedom and the good society. We need to appreciate how the vast government programs we have created over the years have actually reduced the freedom and well-being of all of us—and have undermined the Constitution besides. Not that the ends served by those programs are unworthy—few government programs are undertaken for worthless ends. But individuals, families, private firms, and communities could accomplish most of those ends, voluntarily and at far less cost, if only they were free to do so—especially if they were free to keep the wherewithal that is necessary to do so. If individual freedom and individual responsibility are values we cherish—indeed, are the foundations of the good society—we must come to appreciate how our massive government programs have undermined those values and, with that, the good society itself.

Redistributive Programs

Examples of the kinds of programs that should be returned to the states and the people are detailed elsewhere in this *Handbook*, but a few are in order here. Without question, the most important example of devolution to come from the "radical" 104th Congress was in the area of welfare. However flawed the final legislation may have been from both a constitutional and a policy perspective, it was still a step in the right direction. Ultimately, as will be noted later in a more general way, welfare should not even be a state program. Rather, it should be a matter of private responsibility, as it was for years in this nation. But the process of getting the federal government out of the business of charity, for which there is no authority in the Constitution, has at least begun.

Eventually, that process should be repeated in every other "entitlement" area, from individual to institutional to corporate, from Social Security and Medicare to the National Endowment for the Arts to the Department of Agriculture's Market Access Program, and on and on. Each of those programs was started for a good reason, to be sure, yet each involves taking from some to give to others—means that are both wrong and unconstitutional, to say nothing of monumentally inefficient. Taken together, they put us all on welfare in one way or another, and we are all the poorer for it.

Some of those programs will be harder to reduce, phase out, or eliminate than others, of course. Entitlement programs with large numbers of beneficiaries, for example, will require transition phases to ensure that harm is minimized and public support is maintained. Other programs, however, could be eliminated with relatively little harm. Does anyone seriously doubt that there would be art in America without the National Endowment for the Arts? Indeed, without the heavy hand of government grant making, the arts would likely flourish as they did long before the advent of the NEA—and no one would be made to pay, through his taxes, for art he abhorred.

It is the transfer programs in the "symbolic" area, in fact, that may be the most important to eliminate first, for they have multiplier effects reaching well beyond their raw numbers, and those effects are hardly neutral on the question of reducing the size and scope of government. The National Endowment for the Arts, the National Endowment for the Humanities, the Corporation for Public Broadcasting, the Legal Services Corporation, and the Department of Education have all proceeded without constitutional authority—but with serious implications for free speech and for the cause of limiting government. Not a few critics have pointed to the heavy hand of government in those symbolic areas. Of equal importance, however, is the problem of compelled speech: as Jefferson wrote, "To compel a man to furnish contributions of money for the propagation of opinions which he disbelieves is sinful and tyrannical." But on a more practical note, if Congress is serious about addressing the climate of opinion in the nation, it will end such programs not simply because they are without constitutional authority but because they have demonstrated a relentless tendency over the years to evolve in only one direction—

toward even more government. Indeed, one should hardly expect those institutions to be underwriting programs that advocate less government when they themselves exist through government.

Regulatory Redistribution

If the redistributive programs that constitute the modern welfare state are candidates for elimination, so too are many of the regulatory programs that have arisen under the commerce clause. Here, however, care must be taken not simply from a practical perspective but from a constitutional perspective as well, for some of those programs may be constitutionally justified. When read functionally, recall, the commerce clause was meant to enable Congress to ensure that commerce among the states is regular, and especially to counter state actions that might upset that regularity. Think of the commerce clause as an early North American Free Trade Agreement, without the heavy hand of "managed trade" that often accompanies the modern counterpart.

Thus conceived, the commerce clause clearly empowers Congress, through regulation, to override state measures that may frustrate the free flow of commerce among the states. But it also enables Congress to take such affirmative measures as may be necessary and proper for facilitating free trade, such as clarifying rights of trade in uncertain contexts or regulating the interstate transport of dangerous goods. What the clause does not authorize, however, is regulation for reasons other than to ensure the free flow of commerce—the kind of "managed trade" that is little but a thinly disguised transfer program designed to benefit one party at the expense of another.

Unfortunately, most modern federal regulation falls into that final category, whether it concerns employment, health care, insurance, or whatever. In fact, given budgetary constraints on the ability of government to tax and spend—to take money from some, run it through the treasury, then give it to others—the preferred form of transfer today is through regulation. That puts it "off budget." Thus, when an employer, an insurer, a lender, or a landlord is required by regulation to do something he would otherwise have a right not to do, or not do something he would otherwise have a right to do, he serves the party benefited by that regulation every bit as much as if he were taxed to do so, but no tax increase is ever registered on any public record. The temptation for Congress to resort to such "cost-free" regulatory redistribution is of course substantial, and the effects are both far-reaching and perverse. Natural markets are upset as incentives

35

are changed; economies of scale are skewed as large businesses, better able to absorb the regulatory burdens, are advantaged over small ones; defensive measures, inefficient from the larger perspective, are encouraged; and general uncertainty, anathema to efficient markets, is the order of the day. Far from facilitating free trade, redistributive regulation frustrates it. Far from being justified by the commerce clause, it undermines the very purpose of the clause.

Federal Crimes

In addition to misusing the commerce power for the purpose of regulatory redistribution, Congress has misused that power to create federal crimes. Thus, a great deal of "regulation" has arisen in recent years under the commerce power that is nothing but a disguised exercise of a police power that Congress otherwise lacks. As noted earlier, the Gun-Free School Zones Act, the Church Arson Prevention Act, and the Violence Against Women Act are examples of legislation passed nominally under the power of Congress to regulate commerce among the states. But the actions subject to federal prosecution under those statutes—gun possession, church arson, and gender-motivated violence, respectively—are ordinarily regulated under *state* police power, the power of states, in essence, to "police" or secure our rights. The ruse of regulating them under Congress's commerce power is made necessary because there is no federal police power enumerated in the Constitution—except as an implication of federal sovereignty over federal territory or an incidence of some enumerated power.

That ruse should be candidly recognized. Indeed, it is a mark of the decline of respect for the Constitution that when we sought to fight a war on liquor in the last century we felt it necessary to do so by first amending the Constitution—there being no power otherwise for such a federal undertaking. Today, however, when we engage in a war on drugs—with as much success as we enjoyed in the earlier war—we do so without as much as a nod to the Constitution.

The Constitution lists three federal crimes: treason, piracy, and counterfeiting. Yet today there are more than 3,000 federal crimes and perhaps 300,000 regulations that carry criminal sanctions. Over the years, no faction in Congress has been immune, especially in an election year, from the propensity to criminalize all manner of activities, utterly oblivious to the lack of any constitutional authority for doing so. We should hardly imagine that the Founders fought a war to free us from a distant tyranny only to establish a tyranny in Washington, in some ways even more distant from the citizens it was meant to serve.

Policing of the States

If the federal government has often intruded on the police power of the states, so too has it often failed in its responsibility under the Fourteenth Amendment to police the states. Here is an area where federal regulation has been, if anything, too restrained—yet also unprincipled, oftentimes, when undertaken.

The Civil War Amendments to the Constitution fundamentally changed the relationship between the federal government and the states, giving citizens an additional level of protection, not against federal oppression but against state oppression—the oppression of slavery, obviously, but much else besides. Thus, the Fourteenth Amendment prohibits states from abridging the privileges or immunities of citizens of the United States; from depriving any person of life, liberty, or property without due process of law; and from denying any person the equal protection of the laws. Section 1 of the amendment enables the courts to secure those guarantees. Section 5 gives Congress the "power to enforce, by appropriate legislation, the provisions of this article."

As the debate that surrounded the adoption of those amendments makes clear, the privileges or immunities clause was meant to be the principal source of substantive rights in the Fourteenth Amendment, and those rights were meant to include the rights of property, contract, and personal security—in short, our "natural liberties," as Blackstone had earlier understood that phrase. Unfortunately, in 1873, in the notorious Slaughterhouse Cases, a bitterly divided Supreme Court essentially eviscerated the privileges or immunities clause. There followed, for nearly a century, the era of Jim Crow in the South and, for a period stretching to the present, a Fourteenth Amendment jurisprudence that is as contentious as it is confused.

Modern liberals have urged that the amendment be used as it was meant to be used—against state oppression. But they have also urged that it be used to recognize all manner of "rights" that are no part of the theory of rights that stands behind the amendment as understood at the time of ratification. Modern conservatives, partly in reaction, have urged that the amendment be used far more narrowly than it was meant to be used—for fear that it might be misused, as it has been.

The role of the judiciary under section 1 of the Fourteenth Amendment will be discussed later. As for Congress, its authority under section 5—"to enforce, by appropriate legislation, the provisions of this article"—is clear, provided Congress is clear about those provisions. And on that, we may look, again, to the debates that surrounded not only the adoption of the Fourteenth Amendment but the enactment of the Civil Rights Act of 1866, which Congress reenacted in 1868, just after the amendment was ratified.

Those debates give us a fairly clear idea of what the American people thought they were ratifying. In particular, all citizens, the Civil Rights Act declared, "have the right to make and enforce contracts, to sue, be parties and give evidence; to inherit, purchase, lease, sell, hold, and convey real personal property, and to full and equal benefit of all laws and proceedings for the security of persons and property." Such were the privileges and immunities the Fourteenth Amendment was meant to secure.

Clearly, those basic common-law rights, drawn from the reason-based classical theory of rights, are the stuff of ordinary state law. Just as clearly, however, states have been known to violate them, either directly or by failure to secure them against private violations. When that happens, appeal can be made to the courts, under section 1, or to Congress, under section 5. The Fourteenth Amendment gives no power, of course, to secure the modern "entitlements" that are no part of the common-law tradition of life, liberty, and property: the power it grants, that is, is limited by the rights it is meant to secure. But it does give a power to reach even intrastate matters when states are violating the provisions of the amendment. The claim of "states' rights," in short, is no defense for state violations of individual rights.

Thus, if the facts had warranted it, something like the Church Arson Prevention Act of 1996, depending on its particulars, might have been authorized not on commerce clause grounds but on Fourteenth Amendment grounds. If, for example, the facts had shown that state officials were prosecuting arsons of white churches but not arsons of black churches, then we would have had a classic case of the denial of the equal protection of the laws. With those findings, Congress would have had ample authority under section 5 of the Fourteenth Amendment "to enforce, by appropriate legislation, the provisions of this article."

Unfortunately, in the final version of the act, Congress removed citations to the Fourteenth Amendment, choosing instead to rest its authority entirely on the commerce clause. Not only is that a misuse of the commerce clause, inviting further misuse, but, assuming the facts had warranted it, it is a failure to use the Fourteenth Amendment as it was meant to be used, inviting further failures. To be sure, the Fourteenth Amendment has itself been misused, both by Congress and by the courts. But that is no reason to ignore it. Rather, it is a reason to correct the misuses.

In its efforts to return power to the states and the people, then, Congress must be careful not to misunderstand its role in our federal system. Over the 20th century, Congress assumed vast powers that were never its to assume, powers that belong properly to the states and the people. Those need to be returned. But at the same time, Congress and the courts do have authority under the Fourteenth Amendment to ensure that citizens are free from state oppression. However much that authority may have been underused or overused, it is there to be used, and if it is properly used, objections by states about federal interference in their "internal affairs" are without merit.

Reject the Nomination of Judicial Candidates Who Do Not Appreciate That the Constitution Is a Document of Delegated, Enumerated, and Thus Limited Powers

As noted earlier, Congress can relimit government on its own initiative simply by restricting its future actions to those that are authorized by the Constitution and repealing those past actions that were taken without such authority. But for those limits to become "constitutional law," they would have to be recognized as such by the Supreme Court, which essentially abandoned that view of limited government during the New Deal. Thus, for the Court to play its part in the job of relimiting government constitutionally, it must recognize the mistakes it has made over the years, especially following Roosevelt's Court-packing threat in 1937, and rediscover the Constitution—a process it began in *Lopez*, however tentatively, when it returned explicitly to "first principles." (Unfortunately, in 2005, in *Gonzales v. Raich*, the California medical marijuana decision, the Court abandoned the principles it articulated in *Lopez*, so it isn't clear just where the Court now stands in its efforts over the previous decade to revive the doctrine of enumerated powers.)

But Congress is not powerless to influence the Court in the direction of constitutional restoration: as vacancies arise on the Court and on lower courts, it has a substantial say about who sits there through its power to advise and consent. To exercise that power well, however, Congress must have a better grasp of the basic issues than it has shown in recent years during Senate confirmation hearings for nominees for the Court. In particular, the Senate's obsession with questions about "judicial activism" and "judicial restraint," terms that in themselves are largely vacuous, only distracts it from the real issue—the nominee's philosophy of the Constitution. To appreciate those points more fully, however, a bit of background is in order.

From Powers to Rights

The most important matter to grasp is the fundamental change that took place in our constitutional jurisprudence during the New Deal and the implications of that change for the modern debate. The debate today is focused almost entirely on rights, not powers. Indeed, until the 107th Congress and its focus on ideology, the principal concern during Senate confirmation hearings had been with a nominee's views about what rights are "in" the Constitution. That is an important question, to be sure, but it must be addressed within a much larger constitutional framework, a framework too often missing from recent hearings.

Clearly, the American debate began with rights—with the protests that led eventually to the Declaration of Independence. And in that seminal document, Jefferson made rights the centerpiece of the American vision: rights to life, liberty, and the pursuit of happiness, derived from a premise of moral equality, itself grounded in a higher law discoverable by reason, and all to be secured by a government of powers made legitimate through consent.

But when they set out to draft a constitution, the Framers focused on powers, not rights, for two main reasons. First, their initial task was to create and empower a government, which the Constitution did once it was ratified. But their second task, of equal importance, was to limit that government. Here, there were two main options. The Framers could have listed a set of rights that the new government would be forbidden to violate. Or they could have limited the government's powers by enumerating them, then pitting one against the other through a system of checks and balances—the idea being that where there is no power there is, by implication, a right, belonging to the states or the people. They chose the second option, for they could hardly have enumerated all our rights, but they *could* enumerate the new government's powers, which were meant from the outset to be, again, "few and defined." Thus, the doctrine of enumerated powers became our principal defense against overweening government.

Only later, during the course of ratification, did it become necessary to add a Bill of Rights—as a secondary defense. But in so doing, the Framers were still faced with a pair of objections that had been posed from the start. First, it was impossible to enumerate all our rights, which in principle are infinite in number. Second, given that problem, the enumeration of only certain rights would be construed, by ordinary methods of legal construction, as denying the existence of others. To overcome those objections, therefore, the Framers wrote the Ninth Amendment: "The enumeration in the Constitution of certain rights shall not be construed to deny or disparage others retained by the people."

Constitutional Visions

Thus, with the Ninth Amendment making it clear that we have both enumerated and unenumerated rights, the Tenth Amendment making it clear that the federal government has only enumerated powers, and the Fourteenth Amendment later making it clear that our rights are good against the states as well, what emerges is an altogether libertarian picture. Individuals, families, firms, and the infinite variety of institutions that constitute civil society are free to pursue happiness however they wish, in accord with whatever values they wish, provided only that in the process they respect the equal rights of others to do the same. And governments are instituted to secure that liberty and do the few other things their constitutions make clear they are empowered to do.

That picture is a far cry from the modern liberal's vision, rooted in the Progressive Era, which would have government empowered to manage all manner of economic affairs. But it is also a far cry from the modern conservative's vision, which would have government empowered to manage all manner of social affairs. Neither vision reflects the true constitutional scheme. Both camps want to use the Constitution to promote their own substantive agendas. Repeatedly, liberals invoke democratic power for ends that are nowhere in the Constitution. At other times, they invoke "rights" that are no part of the plan, requiring government programs that are nowhere authorized, while ignoring rights that are plainly enumerated. For their agenda, conservatives rely largely on expansive readings of democratic power that were never envisioned, thereby running roughshod over rights that were meant to be protected, including unenumerated rights.

From Liberty to Democracy

The great change in constitutional vision took place during the New Deal, when the idea that galvanized the Progressive Era—that the basic purpose of government is to solve social and economic problems—was finally instituted in law through the Court's radical reinterpretation of the Constitution. As noted earlier, following the 1937 Court-packing threat, the Court eviscerated our first line of defense, the doctrine of enumerated powers, when it converted the general welfare and commerce clauses from shields against power into swords of power. Then in 1938, a cowed Court undermined the second line of defense, our enumerated and unenumerated rights, when it declared that henceforth it would defer to the political branches and the states when their actions implicated ''nonfundamental'' rights like property and contract—the rights associated with ''ordinary commercial affairs.'' Legislation implicating such rights, the Court said, would be given ''minimal scrutiny'' by the Court, which is tantamount to no scrutiny at all. By contrast, when legislation implicated ''fundamental'' rights like voting, speech, and, later, certain ''personal'' liberties, the Court would apply ''strict scrutiny'' to that legislation, probably finding it unconstitutional.

With that, the Constitution was converted, without benefit of amendment, from a libertarian to a largely democratic document. The floodgates were now open to majoritarian tyranny, which very quickly became special-interest tyranny, as public-choice economic theory amply demonstrates should be expected. Once those floodgates were opened, the programs that poured through led inevitably to claims from many quarters that rights were being violated. Thus, the Court in time would have to try to determine whether those rights were ''in'' the Constitution—a question the Constitution had spoken to indirectly, for the most part, through the now-discredited doctrine of enumerated powers. And if it found the rights in question, the Court would then have to try to make sense of its distinction between ''fundamental'' and ''nonfundamental'' rights.

Judicial "Activism" and "Restraint"

It is no accident, therefore, that until very recently the modern debate has been focused on rights, not powers. With the doctrine of enumerated powers effectively dead, with government's power essentially plenary, the only issues left for the Court to decide, for the most part, were whether there might be any rights that would limit that power and whether those rights are or are not ''fundamental.''

Both liberals and conservatives today have largely bought into this jurisprudence. As noted earlier, both camps believe the Constitution gives a wide berth to democratic decisionmaking. Neither side any longer asks the first question, the fundamental question: Do we have authority, constitutional authority, to pursue this end? Instead, they simply assume that authority, take a policy vote on some end before them, and then battle in court over whether there are any rights that might restrict their power.

Modern liberals, fond of government programs, call on the Court to be ''restrained'' in finding rights that might limit their redistributive and regulatory schemes, especially "nonfundamental" rights like property and contract. At the same time, even as they ignore those rights, liberals ask the Court to be "active" in finding other "rights" that were never meant to be among even our unenumerated rights.

But modern conservatives are often little better. Reacting to the abuses of liberal "activism," many conservatives call for judicial "restraint" across the board. Thus, if liberal programs have run roughshod over the rights of individuals to use their property or freely contract, the remedy, conservatives say, is not for the Court to invoke the doctrine of enumerated powers—that battle was lost during the New Deal—nor even to invoke the rights of property and contract that are plainly in the Constitution— that might encourage judicial activism—but to turn to the democratic process to overturn those programs. Oblivious to the fact that restraint in finding rights is tantamount to activism in finding powers, and in disregard of the fact that it was the democratic process that gave us the problem in the first place, too many conservatives offer us a counsel of despair amounting to a denial of constitutional protection.

No one doubts that in recent decades the Court has discovered "rights" in the Constitution that are no part of either the enumerated or unenumerated rights that were meant to be protected by that document. But it is no answer to that problem to ask the Court to defer wholesale to the political branches, thereby encouraging it, by implication, to sanction unenumerated *powers* that are no part of the document either. Indeed, if the Tenth Amendment means anything, it means that there are no such powers. Again, if the Framers had wanted to establish a simple democracy, they could have. Instead, they established a limited, constitutional republic, a republic with islands of democratic power in a sea of liberty, not a sea of democratic power surrounding islands of liberty.

Thus, it is not the proper role of the Court to find rights that are no part of the enumerated or unenumerated rights meant to be protected by the Constitution, thereby frustrating authorized democratic decisions. But neither is it the proper role of the Court to refrain from asking whether those decisions are in fact authorized and, if authorized, whether their implementation violates the rights guaranteed by the Constitution, enumerated and unenumerated alike.

The role of the judge in our constitutional republic is thus profoundly important and oftentimes profoundly complex. "Activism" is no proper posture for a judge, but neither is "restraint." Judges must apply the Constitution to cases or controversies before them, neither making it up nor ignoring it. They must especially appreciate that the Constitution is a document of delegated, enumerated, and thus limited powers. That will get the judge started on the question of what rights are protected by the document, for where there is no power, there is, again, a right, belonging either to the states or to the people. Indeed, we should hardly imagine that, before the addition of the Bill of Rights, the Constitution failed to protect most rights simply because most were not ''in'' it. But reviving the doctrine of enumerated powers is only part of the task before the Court; it must also revive the classical theory of rights if the restoration of constitutional government is to be completed correctly.

Those are the two sides—powers and rights—that need to be examined in the course of Senate confirmation hearings for nominees for the courts of the United States. More important than knowing a nominee's ''judicial philosophy'' is knowing his philosophy of the Constitution. For the Constitution, in the end, is what defines us as a nation.

If a nominee does not have a deep and thorough appreciation for the basic principles of the Constitution—for the doctrine of enumerated powers and for the classical theory of rights that stands behind the Constitution—then his candidacy should be rejected. In recent years, Senate confirmation hearings have become extraordinary opportunities for constitutional debate throughout the nation. Those debates need to move from the ethereal realm of ''constitutional law'' to the real realm of the Constitution. They are extraordinary opportunities not simply for constitutional debate but for constitutional renewal.

Alarmingly, however, in recent Congresses we saw the debate move not from ''constitutional law'' to the Constitution but in the very opposite direction—to raw politics. The demand that judicial nominees pass an ''ideological litmus test''—that they reflect and apply the ''mainstream values'' of the American people, whatever those may be—is tantamount to expecting and asking judges not to *apply* the law, which is what judging is all about, but to *make* the law according to those values, whatever the actual law may require. The duty of judges under the Constitution is to decide cases according to the law, not according to whatever values or ideology may be in fashion. For that, the only ideology that matters is the ideology of the Constitution.

Conclusion

America is a democracy in the most fundamental sense of that idea: authority, or legitimate power, rests ultimately with the people. But the people have no more right to tyrannize one another through democratic government than government itself has to tyrannize the people. When they constituted us as a nation by ratifying the Constitution and the amendments that have followed, our ancestors gave up only certain of their powers, enumerating them in a written constitution. We have allowed those powers to expand beyond all moral and legal bounds—at the price of our liberty and our well-being. The time has come to return those powers to their proper bounds, to reclaim our liberty, and to enjoy the fruits that follow.

Suggested Readings

Bailyn, Bernard. *The Ideological Origins of the American Revolution.* Cambridge, MA: Belknap, 1967.

Barnett, Randy E., ed. *The Rights Retained by the People: The History and Meaning of the Ninth Amendment.* Fairfax, VA: George Mason University Press, 1989.

_____. *The Structure of Liberty: Justice and the Rule of Law.* New York: Oxford University Press, 1998.

_____. *Restoring the Lost Constitution: The Presumption of Liberty.* Princeton, NJ: Princeton University Press, 2004.

Corwin, Edward S. *The "Higher Law" Background of American Constitutional Law.* Ithaca, NY: Cornell University Press, 1955.

Dorn, James A., and Henry G. Manne, eds. *Economic Liberties and the Judiciary.* Fairfax, VA: George Mason University Press, 1987.

Epstein, Richard A. *Takings: Private Property and the Power of Eminent Domain.* Cambridge, MA: Harvard University Press, 1985.

_____. "The Proper Scope of the Commerce Power." *Virginia Law Review* 73 (1987).

_____. *Simple Rules for a Complex World.* Cambridge, MA: Harvard University Press, 1995.

_____. *Principles for a Free Society: Reconciling Individual Liberty with the Common Good.* Reading, MA: Perseus Books, 1998.

_____. *How Progressives Rewrote the Constitution.* Washington: Cato Institute, 2006.

Ginsburg, Douglas H. "On Constitutionalism." *Cato Supreme Court Review, 2002–2003.* Washington: Cato Institute, 2003.

Hamilton, Alexander, James Madison, and John Jay. *The Federalist Papers.* New York: Mentor, 1961.

Lawson, Gary. "The Rise and Rise of the Administrative State." *Harvard Law Review* 107 (1994).

Lawson, Gary, and Patricia B. Granger. "The 'Proper' Scope of Federal Power: A Jurisdictional Interpretation of the Sweeping Clause." *Duke Law Journal* 43 (1993).

Locke, John. "Second Treatise of Government." In *Two Treatises of Government,* edited by Peter Laslett. New York: Mentor, 1965.

Miller, Geoffrey P. "The True Story of Carolene Products." *Supreme Court Review* (1987).

Pilon, Roger. "Freedom, Responsibility, and the Constitution: On Recovering Our Founding Principles." *Notre Dame Law Review* 68 (1993).

_____. "Restoring Constitutional Government." *Cato's Letter,* no. 9 (1995).

_____. "The Purpose and Limits of Government." *Cato's Letter,* no. 13 (1999).

————. "How Constitutional Corruption Has Led to Ideological Litmus Tests for Judicial Nominees." Cato Institute Policy Analysis no. 446, August 8, 2002.

Reinstein, Robert J. "Completing the Constitution: The Declaration of Independence, Bill of Rights and Fourteenth Amendment." *Temple Law Review* 66 (1993).

Shankman, Kimberly C., and Roger Pilon. "Reviving the Privileges or Immunities Clause to Redress the Balance among States, Individuals, and the Federal Government." Cato Institute Policy Analysis no. 326, November 23, 1998.

Siegan, Bernard H. *Economic Liberties and the Constitution.* Chicago: University of Chicago Press, 1980.

Sorenson, Leonard R. *Madison on the "General Welfare" of America.* Lanham, MD: Rowman & Littlefield, 1995.

Warren, Charles. *Congress as Santa Claus: Or National Donations and the General Welfare Clause of the Constitution.* 1932. Reprint, New York: Arno, 1978.

Yoo, John Choon. "Our Declaratory Ninth Amendment." *Emory Law Journal* 42 (1993).

—Prepared by Roger Pilon

Restructuring the Federal Government

4. Cutting Federal Spending

Congress should

- cut federal spending from 21 percent to 16 percent of gross domestic product over 10 years, as detailed in this chapter;
- terminate, privatize, or transfer to state governments more than 100 programs and agencies, including those involved in agriculture, education, housing, and transportation;
- reform Social Security by cutting the growth in government benefits and adding a system of private accounts;
- cut Medicare spending growth and move toward a health care system based on individual savings and choice;
- convert Medicaid into a block grant and freeze federal spending; and
- impose a statutory cap on the annual growth in total federal outlays.

The federal government is spending too much, running large deficits, and heading toward a financial crisis. Total federal outlays increased 68 percent during the eight years of the Bush administration—fiscal years 2001 to 2009—with large increases in defense, education, health care, and other areas. Those increases have come just as the baby boomers begin to retire and the costs of federal entitlement programs are beginning to balloon. Spending on the three main entitlement programs—Social Security, Medicare, and Medicaid—is expected to roughly double from $1.27 trillion in FY08 to $2.42 trillion by FY18.

Where will the money come from? If government spending is not cut, average working families will face huge tax increases that dwarf anything seen in decades. Tax increases would damage the economy and be strongly resisted by the public. As a consequence, policymakers need to begin identifying programs in the federal budget that can be cut, terminated, transferred to the states, or privatized.

49

This chapter provides policymakers and the public with an outline of federal budget reforms. It proposes eliminating more than 100 agencies and programs to reduce federal spending from about 21 percent to 16 percent of the nation's economy. Cutting the $3.1 trillion budget would avert the looming federal financial crisis, while giving Americans a stronger economy and greater individual freedom. The budget data in this chapter were compiled before the hundreds of billions of dollars of financial system bailouts announced in Fall 2008, and thus the need for large cuts to federal programs has become even more acute.

Where Does Taxpayer Money Go?

Figure 4.1 shows what the federal government spent the taxpayers' money on in FY08. The "entitlement" programs, including Social Security, Medicare, and Medicaid, accounted for 53 percent of total spending. These programs are on autopilot, and they will grow each year unless Congress passes laws to limit benefits or to reduce the number of beneficiaries.

Figure 4.1
Federal Outlays in Fiscal Year 2008
(Billions of Dollars)

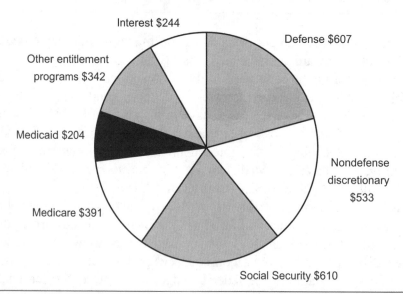

SOURCE: *Budget of the U.S. Government, FY2009.* Medicare is net of offsetting receipts.

''Discretionary'' programs accounted for 39 percent of federal spending. Congress appropriates funds for these programs annually. Discretionary programs cover a huge range of federal activities, including defense, education, energy, environment, foreign aid, housing, labor, science, space, and transportation. Interest represented the remaining 8 percent of the budget.

Figure 4.2 shows changes over time in real, or constant-dollar, spending in major budget categories. Real defense spending fell during the 1990s, but has been rising rapidly since 2001. Defense spending is expected to top Social Security spending in FY09 for the first time since the early 1990s. The category ''all other programs'' includes nondefense discretionary spending and smaller entitlement programs. This category of spending fell slightly during the 1980s, soared during the early 1990s, was flat during the mid-1990s, and started rising again in the late 1990s.

What's Wrong with Federal Spending?

The federal government will spend more than $3.1 trillion in FY09. After taking out the government's core functions of national defense and

Figure 4.2
Federal Outlays by Program

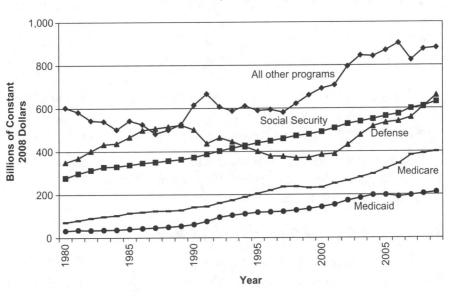

SOURCE: Author calculations based on *Budget of the U.S. Government, FY2009.* FY2008 and FY2009 are estimates. Figure excludes net interest outlays.

justice, it will still spend about $2.4 trillion. That amounts to roughly $21,000 for every household in the United States. Clearly, the federal government has amassed to itself a huge range of spending programs beyond its basic responsibilities.

Indeed, the government is so large that the activities of hundreds of federal agencies are beyond the knowledge and understanding of most citizens. The government has also become too large for our representatives in Congress to adequately oversee and control, as scandal after scandal attests to. Congress has shown itself to be incapable of running a $3 trillion organization with an adequate degree of competence.

Americans would receive more benefit from the federal government if its size and scope were greatly reduced, and they received a limited range of much better quality services. Reforms should begin to shed the noncore functions of the federal government so that members of Congress and the president can focus on delivering high-quality basic services, such as national security.

Table 4.1 at the end of this chapter targets more than 100 programs and agencies for elimination. These programs have one or more of the following failings:

- They are wasteful, which means duplicative, obsolete, mismanaged, ineffective, or subject to high levels of fraud and abuse.
- They benefit special interests at the expense of average citizens and taxpayers.
- They damage society by distorting the economy, by harming the environment, or by creating negative social effects.
- They are activities that should be left to state and local governments.
- They are activities that should be left to private businesses, individuals, and charities.
- They violate the Constitution as serious overreaches of federal power.

Programs with these failings are discussed throughout this *Handbook*, but this chapter tallies the overall savings from an ambitious overhaul of the budget based on these reform criteria.

How to Cut Federal Spending to 16 Percent of GDP

The programs in Table 4.1 should be terminated, privatized, or devolved to state and local governments. Those reforms would save about $440 billion annually in 2008, which equates to savings of about $580 billion annually in 2018 under baseline projections. The proposed cuts are from nearly every federal department, including defense, education, energy, housing, and transportation. This plan includes only a portion of the reforms recommended in other *Handbook* chapters for defense, Social Security, Medicare, and Medicaid.

The reasons for particular cuts are discussed in *Downsizing the Federal Government*. To an economist, some reforms are no-brainers—farm subsidies should be terminated immediately, for example. Other reforms, such as privatizing Amtrak, would require detailed analysis to determine the best way to proceed. Over the long term, as federal involvement in the targeted activities ended, it would be up to state governments, businesses, consumers, and private charities to determine whether those activities were worth sustaining without federal help. Could an entrepreneur make Amtrak succeed in the marketplace? Let's privatize it and find out.

The key to averting a federal fiscal crisis in the years ahead is to cut the three main "entitlement" programs—Social Security, Medicare, and Medicaid. The following are four straightforward reforms that would create annual savings of about $350 billion by 2018 (the first three estimates are based on data in the Congressional Budget Office's "Budget Options"):

- Reduce the growth in Social Security by indexing initial benefits to changes in prices instead of wages to save about $47 billion annually by 2018;
- Increase premiums for Medicare Part B to cover 50 percent of program costs (up from 25 percent today) to save about $68 billion annually by 2018;
- Increase and conform the deductibles and cost sharing for Medicare Part A, Medicare Part B, and Medigap plans to save about $10 billion annually by 2018; and
- Turn Medicaid into a block grant and freeze federal spending to save about $227 billion annually by 2018. Currently, Medicaid funding is split between the federal and state governments in a structure that encourages overspending. This option would turn Medicaid into a block grant and freeze the federal contribution, thus forcing state governments to pursue cost-cutting reforms.

Further reforms to these entitlement programs are discussed in Chapters 12, 13, and 17. But the reforms listed above, combined with the proposed spending cuts in Table 4.1, would balance the federal budget and generate growing surpluses, even with all current tax cuts extended. The plan would reduce the size of the federal government from about 21 percent of gross domestic product today to less than 16 percent by 2018.

Figure 4.3 shows a 10-year projection of federal spending under a business-as-usual scenario and under the reform plan proposed here. Figure 4.4 shows the same projections measured as a share of GDP. The reform plan includes the entitlement cuts proposed here and assumes that the discretionary cuts from Table 4.1 would be phased in over 10 years.

Figures 4.3 and 4.4 also show a projection of federal revenues, based on the Congressional Budget Office forecast of September 2008. The projection assumes that all the tax cuts scheduled to expire by the end of 2010—including individual income tax cuts, business tax breaks, and the estate tax—are made permanent and that the alternative minimum tax is indexed for inflation.

If the reform plan were enacted, the budget would be balanced by 2013, and there would be growing surpluses after that. By 2018, federal spending would be about 30 percent less than it would be under a business-as-usual scenario. The business-as-usual scenario starts with the Congressional Budget Office's baseline projection from September 2008, but assumes that discretionary spending grows as fast as GDP, that troops in Iraq and Afghanistan are drawn down under CBO's optimistic scenario, and that Medicare physician payments are not cut after 2010 as they are under the baseline.

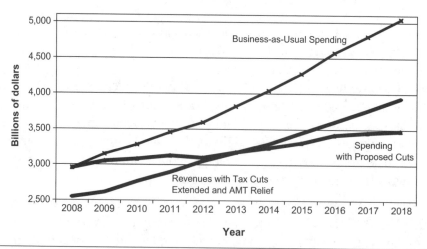

Figure 4.3
Projected Federal Revenues and Spending

SOURCE: Author's estimates based on Congressional Budget Office projections of September 2008. Note: Data are for fiscal years. The "Business as Usual" scenario is the Congressional Budget Office baseline but with discretionary spending growing with GDP. Both spending scenarios include CBO's optimistic option for Iraq troop cuts.

Figure 4.4
Projected Federal Revenues and Spending, Percentage of GDP

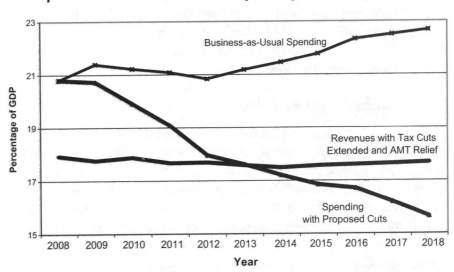

SOURCE: Author's estimates based on Congressional Budget Office projections of September 2008. Note: Data are for fiscal years. The "Business as Usual" scenario is the Congressional Budget Office baseline but with discretionary spending growing with GDP. Both spending scenarios include CBO's optimistic option for Iraq troop cuts.

With the current tax cuts extended and alternative minimum tax relief in place, federal revenues are expected to increase from $2.5 trillion in 2008 to $3.9 trillion in 2018. Under the reform plan, spending would be limited to just $3.5 trillion in 2018 and thus large surpluses would be created. Under the business-as-usual scenario, spending would soar to $5.0 trillion in 2018 and annual deficits of more than $1 trillion would be created.

Measured as a share of GDP, revenues with tax relief in place are projected to decline slightly from 17.9 percent in 2008 to 17.7 percent by 2018. Under the reform plan, spending would fall from 20.8 percent of GDP in 2008 to 15.6 percent by 2018.

The budget savings generated under the spending reform plan could be used to reduce the federal debt, to repeal the alternative minimum tax, or to pursue supply-side tax cuts, as discussed in Chapters 41 and 42. Also, the savings could be used to fund the transition to a Social Security system based on personal accounts, as discussed in Chapter 17.

The cuts included in this plan are not all the budget reforms that should be pursued. Government procurement policies should be reformed to end frequent cost overruns, and additional grant-in-aid programs for the states should be cut. More importantly, further reforms should be made to Social Security, Medicare, and Medicaid. Nonetheless, the cuts listed here provide policymakers with a menu of high-priority reforms. If enacted, they would avert a financial crisis and shrink government in a responsible way, while increasing economic freedom and growth.

How to Reform Budget Rules

This chapter has proposed a range of detailed reductions to the federal budget, but most current members of Congress would find it difficult to make many of these cuts. Their basic instinct is to spend, and that instinct is reinforced by the Capitol Hill culture, by interest groups, and by voices in the media. Thus, part of the reform agenda must be to change federal budget rules to create greater top-down discipline in members of Congress. With tighter budget rules, members would be required to make the needed spending tradeoffs that are often avoided under current rules.

Federal reformers can look to the states for ideas on reforming the budget process, as state policymakers are bound by tighter rules than is Congress. All states except Vermont have statutory or constitutional requirements to balance their budgets. In addition, more than 20 states have some form of overall limitation on taxes or spending. For example, Colorado's constitution limits annual state revenue growth to the sum of population growth plus inflation.

Congress has occasionally bound itself to limits on the overall budget, such as under the 1985 Gramm-Rudman-Hollings Act. That act established a series of declining deficit targets, which, if not met, resulted in an automatic cut, or sequester, to a range of programs. Congress replaced GRH in 1990 with the Budget Enforcement Act. The BEA imposed annual dollar caps on discretionary spending and "pay-as-you-go" rules on entitlement programs, which required that the costs of program expansion be offset elsewhere in the budget.

Bolder efforts to control spending and deficits have been debated in Congress. A balanced-budget amendment (BBA) to the Constitution was introduced as far back as 1936. In 1982, the Senate passed a BBA by a vote of 69–31. In addition to requiring budget balance, the amendment would have limited the annual growth in federal revenues to the growth in national income. Unfortunately, the BBA failed to gain the needed two-thirds approval in the House. At the time, a parallel effort resulted in resolutions being passed in 31 states calling for a constitutional convention to approve a BBA, but that effort came up three states short of the required number. In 1995, Congress again voted on a BBA, and it again narrowly failed. The BBA passed the House by a 300–132 margin, but it fell one vote short of passage in the Senate.

How to Cap Federal Spending

Given the difficulty of amending the Constitution, statutory changes to budget rules can provide a way forward to control spending. In particular, a cap should be placed on the overall annual growth in federal outlays. While the Budget Enforcement Act imposed multiyear caps on discretionary spending, entitlement spending was not capped. Yet it is mainly entitlement spending that is pushing the government toward a financial crisis, and thus entitlements should be included under a federal budget cap.

A simple way to structure a cap is to limit annual spending growth to the growth in an economic indicator, such as gross domestic product. Another possible cap is the sum of population growth plus inflation. In that case, if population grew at 1 percent and inflation was 3 percent, then federal spending could grow by no more than 4 percent. Whichever indicator is used should be smoothed by averaging it over about five years. The principle underlying such a cap is that the government should live within constraints, just as average families do, and it should not consume an increasing share of the nation's economy.

Under a statutory cap, the Office of Management and Budget would provide regular updates on whether spending would likely breach the legal limit, thus allowing Congress time to take corrective actions. If a fiscal year ended and OMB determined that outlays were above the cap, the president would be required to cut spending across the board by the amount needed to meet the cap. Gramm-Rudman-Hollings and the Budget Enforcement Act included such sequester mechanisms that covered various portions of the defense, nondefense, and entitlement budgets. But a better approach would be to cap all spending and subject all departments to a sequester should Congress fail to restrain spending sufficiently.

No statutory cap would ensure that Congress started making large cuts to the budget, such as those proposed in this chapter. But a cap would help lock in whatever spending cuts were achieved because an annual spending cap would prevent excessive growth based on the spending level of the prior year. And a budget growth cap would provide protection for taxpayers against a nightmare scenario of rapid spending increases should the costs of entitlement programs continue to explode.

It is true that Congress could rewrite a statutory spending cap if it didn't want to comply with it at some point in the future. However, with a cap in place, citizens and watchdog groups would have a high-profile symbol of fiscal restraint to rally around and defend. Over time, public awareness and budgetary tradition would aid in the enforcement of a cap.

To sum up, the proposals in this chapter would not only balance the budget but would help defuse the entitlement cost time bomb that threatens to explode on young taxpayers. Making the budget cuts outlined here will be a political challenge, but many cuts that now seem radical to some policymakers will become a policy imperative as entitlement costs rise in coming years.

Besides, policymakers should not view budget cutting as if it were taking bad-tasting medicine. Well-crafted cuts would be positive from many perspectives. They would enlarge personal freedom and responsibility, they would allow the economy to expand more rapidly, and they would leave a positive fiscal legacy to the next generation.

Table 4.1
Proposed Federal Budget Terminations
(FY08 outlays in millions of dollars)

Department of Agriculture	
Economic Research Service	$77
Agricultural Statistics Service	$162
Agricultural Research Service	$1,234
CSREES	$1,193
Agricultural Marketing Service	$636
Risk Management Agency	$4,455
Farm Service Agency	$14,223
Rural Development	$145
Rural Housing Service	$2,326
Rural Business Cooperative Service	$166
Rural Utilities Service	$1,023
Foreign Agricultural Service	$1,192
Food Stamp Program	$38,780
School Lunch and related programs	$14,452
WIC nutrition program	$5,974
Forest Service: state and private	$487
Forest Service: land acquisition	$96
Total proposed cuts	$86,621

Department of Commerce

Economic Development Administration	$352
International Trade Administration	$369
Minority Business Development Agency	$23
Pacific salmon state grants	$74
Fisheries loans and marketing	$7
Technology Administration	$1
Advanced Technology Program	$198
Manufacturing Extension Partnership	$91
Total proposed cuts	$1,115

Department of Defense

A portion of the cuts proposed in Chapter 19	$50,000

Department of Education

Elimination of entire department	$68,046

Department of Energy

General science research	$3,887
Energy supply research	$894
Fossil energy research	$646
Nuclear energy research	$695
Electricity research	$157
Energy Efficiency and Renewable Energy	$1,549
Strategic Petroleum Reserve	$182
Energy Information Administration	$67
Power Marketing Administrations	$474
Total proposed cuts	$8,551

Department of Health and Human Services

Medicare: increase premiums and deductibles; for other reforms, see Chapter 12	
Medicaid: convert to block grant and freeze federal spending; for other reforms, see Chapter 13	
National Institutes of Health: applied R & D	$12,669
Substance Abuse and Mental Health	$3,263
Temporary Assistance for Needy Families	$17,030
State Payments for Family Support	$4,277
Low-Income Home Energy Assistance	$2,522
Promoting Safe and Stable Families	$448

(continued)

59

Table 4.1
(continued)

Child Care Entitlement grants	$2,978
Child Care and Development grants	$2,001
Social Services grants	$1,936
Foster Care and Adoption grants	$6,670
Head Start	$687
Community Services grants	$654
Health professions subsidy	$319
Administration on Aging	$1,389
Total proposed cuts	$56,843
Department of Homeland Security	
State and local programs	$1,651
Assistance to Firefighters grants	$662
Coast Guard: Boat Safety grants	$131
Total proposed cuts	$2,444
Department of Housing and Urban Development	
Elimination of entire department	$52,269
Department of the Interior: Bureau of Reclamation	$1,493
State and Tribal Wildlife grants	$107
Land Acquisition programs	$40
Sport Fish Restoration Fund	$478
Bureau of Indian Affairs	$2,464
Office of Insular Affairs	$374
Indian Gaming Commission	$16
Total proposed cuts	$57,241
Department of Justice	
Antitrust Division	$146
State and local assistance	$1,262
Weed and Seed Program	$52
Community Oriented Policing Services	$480
Juvenile Justice programs	$322
Total proposed cuts	$2,262
Department of Labor	
Employment and Training services	$3,504
Community Service for Seniors	$517
Trade Adjustment Assistance	$834

Job Corps	$1,490
Bureau of International Labor Affairs	$81
Total proposed cuts	$6,426

Social Security
    Cutting of growth in initial benefits by changing from wage indexing
        to price indexing; for other reforms, see Chapter 17

Department of State

Education and Cultural Exchanges	$474
International Organizations, including the United Nations	$1,578
Organisation for Economic Co-operation and Development	$85
International Narcotics Control	$708
Andean Counterdrug Initiative	$312
Total proposed cuts	$3,157

Department of Transportation

Essential Air Service	$62
FAA: air traffic control	$2,440
FAA: grants to airports	$2,970
FAA: facilities and equipment	$2,704
Federal Highway Administration	$37,630
Federal Transit Administration	$6,261
Maritime Administration	$591
Amtrak	$1,397
Total proposed cuts	$54,055

Other Agencies and Activities

Agency for International Development	$3,874
Appalachian, Delta, and Denali Commissions	$99
Army Corps of Engineers	$7,211
Cargo Preference Program	$435
Corporation for National and Community Service	$915
Corporation for Public Broadcasting	$448
Davis Bacon Act	$1,000
District of Columbia fiscal assistance	$97
EPA: state grants	$3,080
Equal Employment Opportunity Commission	$330
Federal Trade Commission: antitrust	$101
International assistance: economic	$3,573

(continued)

61

Table 4.1
(continued)

International assistance: multilateral	$2,093
International Trade Commission	$68
Legal Services Corporation	$350
Millennium Challenge Corporation	$265
NASA	$17,318
National Endowment for the Arts	$132
National Endowment for the Humanities	$146
National Labor Relations Board	$249
National Mediation Board	$12
Neighborhood Reinvestment Corp.	$287
Peace Corps	$333
Presidio Trust	$3
Public Accounting Oversight Board	$139
Service Contract Act	$800
Small Business Administration	$530
Trade and Development Agency	$55
U.S. Postal Service subsidies	$935
Total proposed cuts	$44,878
Grand total annual spending cuts	**$441,639**

SOURCE: Author, based on data in the *Budget of the U.S. Government, FY2009.*

NOTE: CSREES = Comparative State Research, Education, and Extension Service; EPA = Environmental Protection Agency; FAA = Federal Aviation Administration; NASA = National Aeronautics and Space Administration; R & D = research and development; WIC = Women, Infants, and Children.

Suggested Readings

Cato Institute. Downsizing the Federal Government website. www.downsizinggovern ment.org.

Coburn, Tom, with John Hart. *Breach of Trust: How Washington Turns Outsiders into Insiders*. Nashville, TN: WND Books, 2003.

Congressional Budget Office. "Budget Options." February 2007.

————. "The Budget and Economic Outlook: An Update." September 2008.

Edwards, Chris. *Downsizing the Federal Government*. Washington: Cato Institute, 2005.

————. "Federal Aid to the States: Historical Cause of Government Growth and Bureaucracy." Cato Institute Policy Analysis no. 593, May 22, 2007.

Republican Study Committee. "RSC FY2007 Budget: Contract with America Renewed." March 8, 2006. www.house.gov/hensarling/rsc/doc/rsc_2007_budget.pdf.

Slivinski, Stephen. *Buck Wild: How the Republicans Broke the Bank and Became the Party of Big Government*. Nashville, TN: Nelson Current, 2006.

—Prepared by Chris Edwards

5. Fiscal Federalism

> **Congress should**
> - begin terminating the more than 800 federal grant programs that provide state and local governments with about $500 billion annually in subsidies for education, housing, community development, and other nonfederal activities;
> - convert Medicaid from an open-ended matching grant to a block grant, as a first step toward downsizing this massive health subsidy program; and
> - end federal highway and transit funding and repeal the federal gasoline tax that finances these programs.

Under the Constitution, the federal government was assigned specific limited powers and most government functions were left to the states. To ensure that people understood the limits on federal power, the Framers added the Constitution's Tenth Amendment: "The powers not delegated to the United States by the Constitution, nor prohibited by it to the States, are reserved to the States respectively, or to the people."

The Tenth Amendment embodies federalism, the idea that federal and state governments have separate areas of activity and that federal responsibilities were "few and defined," as James Madison noted. Historically, federalism acted as a safeguard of American freedoms. Indeed, President Ronald Reagan noted in a 1987 executive order, "Federalism is rooted in the knowledge that our political liberties are best assured by limiting the size and scope of the national government."

Unfortunately, policymakers and courts have mainly discarded federalism in recent decades. Congress has undertaken many activities that were traditionally reserved to the states and the private sector. Grants-in-aid are a primary mechanism that the federal government has used to extend its power into state and local affairs. Grants are subsidy programs that are combined with federal regulatory controls to micromanage state and local activities.

The Growth in Aid

Federal granting began during the late 19th century, expanded during the early 20th century, and exploded during the 1960s. Under President Lyndon B. Johnson, aid programs were added for housing, urban renewal, education, health care, and many other activities. President Johnson called his policies "creative federalism," but his activism dealt a severe blow to the federalism of the nation's Founders.

The unchallenged optimism of the 1960s about the federal government's ability to solve local problems through grants did not last. In the early 1970s, President Richard M. Nixon argued that federal aid was a "terrible tangle" of overlap and inefficiency. In his 1971 State of the Union address, he lambasted "the idea that a bureaucratic elite in Washington knows best what is best for people everywhere," and said that he wanted to "reverse the flow of power and resources from the states and communities to Washington." For his part, President Jimmy Carter proposed a "concentrated attack on red tape and confusion in the federal grant-in-aid system." Unfortunately, Nixon and Carter made little progress on reforms.

Ronald Reagan had more success at sorting out the "confused mess" of federal grants, as he called it. In a 1981 budget law, dozens of grant programs were eliminated, and many others were consolidated into broader block grants. Reagan's "new federalism" attempted to re-sort federal and state priorities so that each level of government would have responsibility for financing its own programs. However, these efforts to trim the federal aid empire were reversed in subsequent years, although the Republican Congress of the mid-1990s did succeed in turning the federal welfare program into a block grant.

Figure 5.1 shows that there are more than 800 state and local aid programs today, based on my count of programs in the *Catalog of Federal Domestic Assistance*. They range from the giant $225 billion Medicaid program to hundreds of programs that most taxpayers have probably never heard of, such as a $15 million program for "Nursing Workforce Diversity," a $120 million program for "Boating Safety Financial Assistance," and a $150 million program for "Healthy Marriages."

Total federal grant spending in fiscal 2008 was $467 billion. Figure 5.2 shows that real spending on nonhealth grants rose rapidly during the 1960s and 1970s, fell during the 1980s, and soared in the early 2000s.

Figure 5.1
Number of Federal Grant Programs for State and Local Governments, 1879–2006

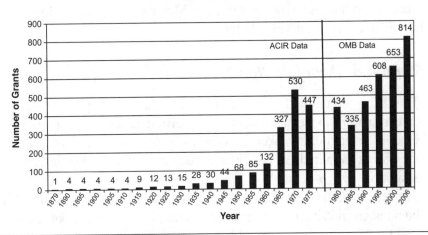

SOURCE: Office of Management and Budget, based on www.cfda.gov.

NOTE: ACIR = Advisory Commission on Intergovernmental Relations; OMB = Office of Management and Budget.

Figure 5.2
Real Federal Grants to State and Local Governments, 1960–2008

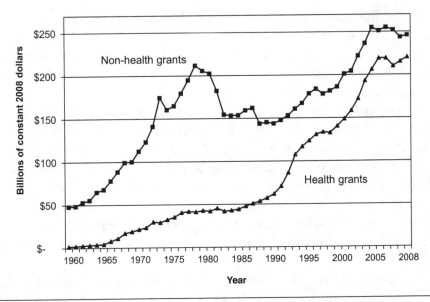

SOURCE: Author's calculations based on *Budget of the U.S. Government, FY2009, Analytical Perspectives*, p. 120. Fiscal years.

Real spending on health care grants has more than quadrupled since 1985, but in recent years spending has been flat. However, that flatness is partly illusory because the new federal prescription drug benefit has shifted billions of dollars of spending from the Medicaid program to Medicare, which is not a grant-in-aid program.

Federal Aid: Theory vs. Reality

The theory behind aid to the states is that the federal government can operate programs in the national interest to efficiently solve local problems. The belief is that policymakers can dispassionately allocate large sums of money across hundreds of activities based on a rational plan designed in Washington.

The federal aid system does not work that way in practice. Most federal politicians are not inclined to pursue broad, national goals, but are consumed by the competitive scramble to secure subsidies for their states. At the same time, federal aid stimulates overspending by state governments and creates a web of complex federal regulations that destroys state innovation. At all levels of the aid system, the focus is on regulatory compliance and the amounts spent, not on delivering quality services. The following are seven reasons why Congress should begin cutting federal grants-in-aid.

1. Grants spur wasteful spending. The basic incentive structure of aid programs encourages overspending by federal, state, and local politicians. The system allows politicians at each level to claim credit for spending on a program, while relying on another level of government to collect part of the tax bill.

Federal politicians design aid regulations that prompt states to increase their own funding of programs. For example, Congress often includes "matching" provisions in programs, which means that the costs of expansion are split between federal and state taxpayers. Under a 50–50 arrangement, for every $2 million a state spends on a program, the federal government chips in $1 million. Matching reduces the "price" to state officials' added spending, thus prompting them to expand programs. Two-thirds of federal aid spending is on grant programs that have matching requirements.

The open-ended federal match under Medicaid, for example, has prompted state governments to continuously expand health benefits and the number of eligible beneficiaries. Indeed, many states have designed complex schemes to artificially raise federal matching payments under Medicaid and to fleece federal taxpayers.

One way to limit the gold rush response of state politicians to matching grants is to convert them to block grants. Block grants provide a fixed sum to states and give them flexibility on program design. For example, the 1996 welfare reform law turned Aid to Families with Dependent Children, an open-ended matching grant, into Temporary Assistance for Needy Families, a lump-sum block grant. Similar block grant reforms should be pursued for Medicaid and other programs. Converting programs to block grants would reduce incentives to overspend and would make it easier for reformers to cut and eliminate programs in the future.

2. Aid allocation is haphazard. The theorists favoring federal grants assume that aid can be rationally distributed to those activities and states with the greatest needs. But in the real world, the aid system has never worked that way. A 1940 article in *Congressional Quarterly* lamented: "The grants-in-aid system in the United States has developed in a haphazard fashion. Particular services have been singled out for subsidy at the behest of pressure groups, and little attention has been given to national and state interests as a whole." A June 1981 report by the Advisory Commission on Intergovernmental Relations concluded, "Regarding national purpose, the record indicates that federal grant-in-aid programs have never reflected any consistent or coherent interpretation of national needs."

Today, for example, states receive varying amounts of highway funding for each dollar of gasoline taxes sent to Washington. While some congested and fast-growing states that need new highways lose out, some slow-growing states get "highways to nowhere" because they have skilled politicians representing them. A major highway law in 2005 included 6,371 "earmarks" directing spending to particular projects that were chosen by individual politicians, not by transportation experts on the basis of merit.

Even if a program could be operated in a rational way, outside of politics, the states can often nullify the policy choices of federal officials. The Department of Education's $15 billion Title I program, for example, is supposed to target aid to the poorest school districts. But evidence indicates that state and local governments use Title I funds to displace their own funding of poor schools, thus putting poor schools no further ahead than without the federal program. In such cases, there is no reason to federalize an activity to begin with, even if one believes in the theory behind federal aid.

3. Grants reduce state policy diversity. Federal grants reduce state innovation because federal money comes with regulations that limit policy flexibility. Grants put the states in a straitjacket of federal rules. Medicaid has perhaps the most complicated top-down rules of any grant program. The 2005 federal budget noted, for example, that the "complex array of Medicaid laws, regulations, and administrative guidance is confusing, overly burdensome, and serves to stifle state innovation and flexibility."

The classic one-size-fits-all federal regulation that defied common sense was the 55-mile-per-hour national speed limit. The limit was enforced between 1974 and 1995 by federal threats of withdrawing state highway grant money. It never made sense that the same speed should be imposed in the wide-open western states and the crowded eastern states, and Congress finally listened to motorists and repealed the law.

However, federal regulations tied to grants are increasing in other areas, such as education. Federal education spending has exploded, and so have federal regulatory controls. The No Child Left Behind law of 2002, for example, mandates that all teachers be "highly qualified," that Spanish-language versions of tests be administered, and that certain children be tutored after school. State officials have complained bitterly about these new federal rules, and 30 state legislatures have passed resolutions attacking NCLB for undermining states' rights.

4. Grant regulations breed bureaucracy. Federal aid is not a costless injection of funding to the states. Its direct cost is paid by federal taxpayers who live in the 50 states. In addition, the system generates an enormous amount of bureaucracy at all three levels of government. Each level of government consumes grant program funding with proposal writing, funding allocations, review, reporting, regulatory compliance, litigation, and many other bureaucratic activities.

State and local agencies must comply with long lists of complex federal regulations, which is one reason why the nation employs an army of 16 million state and local government workers. There are three types of federal aid regulations. The first are the specific rules for each program. Each program may come with hundreds or thousands of pages of rules for grantees to follow. The second are "crosscutting requirements," which are general provisions that apply across aid programs, such as labor market rules. The third are "crossover sanctions," which are the various penalties imposed on the states if certain federal regulatory requirements are not met.

What makes matters worse is that the more than 800 federal grants have overlapping mandates, and each program has unique rules. For example, state and local governments deal with 16 different federal programs that fund first responders, such as firefighters. That complicated federal intrusion has led to fragmented disaster response planning and to much first-responder funding going to projects of little value and to regions with little risk of terrorism.

5. Grants cause policymaking overload. A serious problem caused by the huge scope of federal grant activity is that federal politicians spend their time dealing with local issues, such as public schooling, rather than crucial national issues. The huge array of grant programs generates endless opportunities for federal politicians to earmark projects for their home districts, in a chase for funding that consumes much of their time.

Each new aid program has stretched thinner the ability of policymakers to deal with truly national problems because local spending issues divert their attention. Grants have helped create an "overload" on federal decisionmaking capability. It is hard to quantify this problem, but it is clear that most federal policymakers ignore important national problems, such as they did the increasing threat of terrorism before 9/11. Even after 9/11, a number of investigations have revealed that most members of the House and Senate intelligence committees do not bother, or do not have time, to read crucial intelligence reports. President Calvin Coolidge was right in 1925 when he argued that aid to the states should be cut because it was "encumbering the national government beyond its wisdom to comprehend, or its ability to administer" its proper roles.

6. Grants make government responsibilities unclear. The three layers of government in the United States no longer resemble the tidy layer cake that existed in the 19th century. Instead, they are like a jumbled marble cake with responsibilities fragmented across multiple layers. Federal aid has made it difficult for citizens to figure out which level of government is responsible for particular policy outcomes. All three levels of government play big roles in such areas as transportation and education, thus making accountability difficult. Politicians have become skilled at pointing fingers of blame at other levels of government, as was evident in the aftermath of Hurricane Katrina. When every government is responsible for an activity, no government is responsible.

7. Common problems are not always national priorities. Over the decades, policymakers have argued that various state, local, and private activities needed federal intervention because they had become "national priorities." A June 2005 fact sheet from the secretary of education begins: "The responsibility for K–12 education rests with the states under the Constitution. There is also a compelling national interest in the quality of the nation's public schools. Therefore, the federal government . . . provides assistance to the states and schools in an effort to supplement, not supplant, state support."

Education is, of course, a priority of many people, but that does not mean that the federal government has to get involved. Indeed, there are few activities that the federal government performs that are not also priorities of individuals, businesses, and state and local governments. The states are certainly free to share their policy experiences in areas such as education, but there is no need for top-down control from Washington.

In a 1987 executive order, President Ronald Reagan observed:

> It is important to recognize the distinction between problems of national scope (which may justify federal action) and problems that are merely common to the states (which will not justify federal action because individual states, acting individually or together, can effectively deal with them).

The confusion between problems that are national in scope and those that are merely common to the states even extends to areas such as homeland security. Much "homeland security" funding goes toward items that should be funded locally, such as bulletproof vests for police officers and radio systems for first responders. Federalizing such spending only creates bureaucracy and a tug of war between the states over funding. By contrast, when funding and spending decisions are made together at the state or local levels, policy tradeoffs will better reflect the preferences of citizens within each jurisdiction.

Conclusion

The federal aid system is a roundabout funding system for state and local activities that serves no important economic purpose. During the 1970s and 1980s, government auditors and official commissions pushed for fundamental reforms to the aid system, but those reforms were never made. Ronald Reagan put the system on a diet for a few years, but the core pathologies were not addressed. Since then, hundreds more grant programs have been added, the costs are higher, and the parochial battles over aid are bigger than ever.

The failings of federal aid have long been recognized, but the system has spawned a web of interlocking interests that block reform. Those interests include elected officials in the three levels of government, the hundreds of trade associations representing the recipients of aid, and a large portion of the 16 million state and local workers who depend on federal funding.

The aid system thrives not because it creates good governance, but because it maximizes benefits to politicians. Politicians at each level of government can get involved in spending on a diverse range of programs, while blaming other levels of government for poor service quality and high tax burdens. The federal aid system has been called a "triumph of expenditure without responsibility."

Yet the system desperately needs to be scaled back. With today's large federal budget deficit and the massive cost increases that face entitlement programs, there is little room in the federal budget for state and local activities. Policymakers need to revive federalism and begin to terminate grant programs. If the aid system were shut down, state governments and the private sector would step in and fund those activities that they thought were worthwhile. But by federalizing state and local activities, we are asking Congress to do the impossible—to efficiently plan for the competing needs of a diverse country of more than 300 million people.

Suggested Readings

Advisory Commission on Intergovernmental Relations. From the 1970s to the 1990s, ACIR produced many detailed critiques of federal-state fiscal relations. ACIR reports are available at www.library.unt.edu/gpo/acir/browsetitles.htm.

General Accounting Office. "Federal Assistance: Grant System Continues to Be Highly Fragmented." GAO-03-718T, April 29, 2003.

Government Printing Office. *Catalog of Federal Domestic Assistance.* www.cfda.gov.

Edwards, Chris. *Downsizing the Federal Government.* Washington: Cato Institute, 2005.

_____. "Federal Aid to the States: Historical Cause of Government Growth and Bureaucracy." Cato Institute Policy Analysis no. 593, May 22, 2007. This study has citations for many of the facts in this chapter.

Office of Management and Budget, "Aid to State and Local Governments." *Budget of the United States Government, Fiscal Year 2009, Analytical Perspectives.* Washington: Government Printing Office, 2008.

Ronald Reagan, Executive Order 12612, October 26, 1987. www.reagan.utexas.edu/archives/speeches/1987/102687d.htm.

—Prepared by Chris Edwards

6. Privatization

Congress should

- end subsidies to passenger rail and privatize Amtrak, which would allow the company to innovate, invest, and terminate unprofitable routes;
- privatize the U.S. Postal Service and repeal restrictions on competitive mail delivery;
- privatize the air traffic control system;
- help privatize the nation's airports, while ending federal subsidies;
- help privatize the nation's seaports;
- privatize federal electricity utilities, including the Tennessee Valley Authority and the Power Marketing Administrations;
- privatize portions of the Army Corps of Engineers, such as hydroelectric dams, and transfer the remaining civilian activities to state governments; and
- sell excess federal assets, including buildings, land, and inventory.

In recent decades, governments on every continent have sold state-owned assets, such as airports, railroads, and energy utilities. The privatization revolution has overthrown the belief widely held in the 20th century that governments should own the most important industries in the economy. Privatization has generally led to reduced costs, higher-quality services, and increased innovation in formerly moribund government industries.

The presumption that government should own industry was challenged in the 1980s by British Prime Minister Margaret Thatcher and by President Ronald Reagan, who established a Commission on Privatization. But while Thatcher made enormous reforms in Britain, only a few major federal assets have been privatized in this country. Conrail, a freight railroad, was privatized in 1987 for $1.7 billion. The Alaska Power Administration was privatized in 1996. The federal helium reserve was privatized in 1996 for $1.8 billion. The Elk Hills Petroleum Reserve was sold in 1997 for $3.7 billion. The U.S. Enrichment Corporation, which provides enriched uranium to the nuclear industry, was privatized in 1998 for $3.1 billion.

There remain many federal assets that should be privatized, including businesses such as Amtrak and infrastructure such as the air traffic control system. The government also holds billions of dollars of real estate that should be sold off. The benefits to the federal budget of privatization would be modest, but the benefits to the economy would be large as newly private businesses would improve their performance and innovate.

The Office of Management and Budget has calculated that about half of all federal employees perform tasks that are not "inherently governmental." The Bush administration attempted to contract some of those activities to outside vendors, but such "competitive sourcing" is not privatization. Privatization makes an activity entirely private, with the effect of getting spending completely off the government's books, allowing for greater innovation, and preventing corruption, which is a serious pitfall of government contracting.

Privatization of federal assets makes sense for many reasons. First, sales of federal assets would cut the budget deficit. Second, privatization would reduce the responsibilities of the government so that policymakers could better focus on their core responsibilities, such as national security. Third, there is vast foreign privatization experience that could be drawn on in pursuing U.S. reforms. Fourth, privatization would spur economic growth by opening new markets to entrepreneurs. For example, repeal of the postal monopoly could bring major innovation to the mail industry, just as the 1980s' breakup of AT&T brought innovation to the telecommunications industry.

Some policymakers think that certain activities, such as air traffic control, are "too important" to leave to the private sector. But the reality is just the opposite. The government has shown itself to be a failure at providing efficiency and high quality in services such as air traffic control. Such industries are too important to miss out on the innovations that private entrepreneurs could bring to them.

Stand-Alone Businesses

The federal government operates numerous business enterprises that should be converted into publicly traded corporations, including the U.S. Postal Service, Amtrak, and a number of electric utilities.

- **Postal services.** The mammoth 685,000-person U.S. Postal Service is facing declining mail volume and rising costs. The way ahead is to privatize the USPS and repeal the company's legal monopoly over first-class mail. Reforms in other countries show that there is no good reason for the current mail monopoly. Since 1998, New Zealand's postal market has been open to private competition, with the result that postage rates have fallen and labor productivity at New Zealand Post has risen. Germany's Deutsche Post was partly privatized in 2000, and the company has improved productivity and expanded into new businesses. Postal services have also been privatized or opened to competition in Belgium, Britain, Denmark, Finland, the Netherlands, and Sweden. Japan is moving ahead with postal service privatization, and the European Union is planning to open postal services to competition in all its 27 member nations.

- **Passenger rail.** Subsidies to Amtrak were supposed to be temporary after it was created in 1970. That has not occurred, and Amtrak has provided second-rate rail service for more than 30 years while consuming more than $30 billion in federal subsidies. It has a poor on-time record, and its infrastructure is in bad shape. Reforms elsewhere show that private passenger rail can work. Full or partial rail privatization has occurred in Argentina, Australia, Britain, Germany, Japan, New Zealand, and other countries. Privatization would allow Amtrak greater flexibility in its finances, its capital budget, and the operation of its services—free from costly meddling by Congress.

- **Electric utilities.** The U.S. electricity industry is dominated by publicly traded corporations. However, the federal government owns the huge Tennessee Valley Authority and four Power Marketing Administrations, which sell power in 33 states. These government power companies have become an anachronism as utility privatization has been pursued across the globe. TVA and PMA privatization would eliminate artificially low power rates that cause overconsumption and would increase efficiency in utility operations and capital investment. President Bill Clinton proposed to sell off the four PMAs in his 1996 budget. It is time to dust off those plans and move ahead with reform.

Infrastructure

Before the 20th century, transportation infrastructure was often financed and built by the private sector. For example, there were more than 2,000 companies that built private toll roads in America in the 18th and 19th centuries. Most of those roads were put out of business by the spread of the railroads. Then, during the 20th century, roads and other infrastructure came to be thought of as government activities. By the 1980s, that started to change, and governments around the world began selling off airports, highways, bridges, and other facilities.

Any service that can be supported by consumer fees can be privatized. A big advantage of privatized airports, air traffic control, highways, and other activities is that private companies can freely tap debt and equity markets for capital expansion to meet rising demand. By contrast, modernization of government infrastructure is subject to the politics and uncertainties of government budgeting processes. As a consequence, government infrastructure is often old, congested, and poorly maintained.

- **Air traffic control.** The Federal Aviation Administration has been mismanaged for decades and provides Americans with second-rate air traffic control. The FAA has struggled to expand capacity and modernize its technology, and its upgrade efforts have often fallen behind schedule and gone over budget. For example, the Government Accountability Office found one FAA technology upgrade project that was started in 1983 and was to be completed by 1996 for $2.5 billion, but the project was years late and ended up costing $7.6 billion. The GAO has had the FAA on its watch list of wasteful "high-risk" agencies for years. Air traffic control (ATC) is far too important for such government mismanagement and should be privatized.

   The good news is that a number of countries have privatized their ATC and provide good models for U.S. reforms. Canada privatized its ATC system in 1996. It set up a private, nonprofit ATC corporation, Nav Canada, which is self-supporting from charges on aviation users. The Canadian system has received high marks for sound finances, solid management, and investment in new technologies.

- **Highways.** A number of states are moving ahead with privately financed and operated highways. The Dulles Greenway in Northern Virginia is a 14-mile private highway opened in 1995 that was financed by private bond and equity issues. In the same region, Fluor-Transurban is building and mainly funding high-occupancy toll lanes on a 14-mile stretch of the Capital Beltway. Drivers will pay to use the lanes with electronic tolling, which will recoup the company's roughly $1 billion investment. Fluor-Transurban is also financing and building toll lanes running south from Washington along Interstate 95.

Similar private highway projects have been completed, or are being pursued, in California, Maryland, Minnesota, North Carolina, South Carolina, and Texas. Private-sector highway funding and operation can help pave the way toward reducing the nation's traffic congestion.

- **Airports.** Nearly all major U.S. airports are owned by state and local governments, with the federal government subsidizing airport renovation and expansion. By contrast, airports have been fully or partly privatized in many foreign cities, including Athens, Auckland, Brussels, Copenhagen, Frankfurt, London, Melbourne, Naples, Rome, Sydney, and Vienna. Britain led the way with the 1987 privatization of British Airports Authority, which owns Heathrow and other airports. To proceed with reforms in the United States, Congress should take the lead because numerous federal roadblocks make cities hesitant to privatize. For example, government-owned airports can issue tax-exempt debt, which gives them a financial advantage over potential private airports.

- **Seaports.** Nearly all U.S. seaports are owned by state and local governments. Many operate below world standards because of inflexible union work rules and other factors. A Maritime Administration report in June 2005 noted that "American ports lag well behind other international transportation gateways such as Singapore and Rotterdam in terms of productivity." Dozens of countries around the world have privatized their seaports. One Hong Kong company, Hutchinson Whampoa, owns 30 ports in 15 countries. In Britain, 19 ports were privatized in 1983 to form Associated British Ports. ABP and a subsidiary, UK Dredging, sell port and dredging services in the private marketplace. They earn a profit, pay taxes, and return dividends to shareholders. Two-thirds of British cargo goes through privatized ports, which are highly efficient. Because of the vital economic role played by seaports in international trade, this should be a high priority reform area in the United States.

- **Army Corps of Engineers.** The Corps of Engineers is a federal agency that builds and maintains infrastructure for ports and waterways. Most of the agency's $5 billion annual budget goes toward dredging harbors and investing in locks and channels on rivers, such as the Mississippi. In addition, the corps is the largest owner of hydroelectric power plants in the country, manages 4,300 recreational areas, funds beach replenishment, and upgrades local water and sewer systems.

Congress has used the corps as a pork barrel spending machine for decades. Funds are earmarked for low-value projects in the districts of important members of Congress, while higher-value projects go unfunded. Further, the corps has a history of scandals, including the levee failures in New Orleans and bogus economic studies to justify expensive projects.

To solve these problems, the civilian activities of the corps should be transferred to state, local, or private ownership. A rough framework for reform would be to privatize port dredging, hydroelectric dams, beach replenishment, and other activities that could be supported by user fees and charges. Levees, municipal water and sewer projects, recreational areas, locks, and other waterway infrastructure could be transferred to state governments.

Federal Assets

At the end of fiscal year 2007, the federal government held $1.2 trillion in buildings and equipment, $277 billion in inventory, $919 billion in land, and $392 billion in mineral rights. The federal government owns about one-fourth of the land in the United States.

Many government assets are neglected and abused, and would likely be better cared for in the private sector. It is common to see government property in poor shape, with public housing being perhaps the most infamous government eyesore. The GAO has found that "many assets are in an alarming state of deterioration" and the watchdog agency has put federal property holdings on its list of activities at high risk for waste.

The GAO also notes that the federal government has "many assets it does not need," including billions of dollars worth of excess and vacant buildings. The federal government spends billions of dollars each year maintaining excess facilities of the Departments of Defense, Energy, and Veterans Affairs.

The solution is to sell federal assets that are excess to public needs and to better manage the smaller set of remaining holdings. For example, there are substantial maintenance backlogs on facilities of the Forest Service, Park Service, and Fish and Wildlife Service. The solution is not a larger maintenance budget, but trimming asset holdings to fit limited taxpayer resources. Another part of the solution is to scrap the Davis-Bacon rules, which require that artificially high wages be paid on federal contracts, including maintenance contracts.

Federal asset sales would help reduce the federal deficit and create budget room for improved maintenance of remaining assets. Perhaps more important, economic efficiency and growth would increase as underused assets were put into more productive private hands.

Suggested Readings

Cato Institute. Downsizing the Federal Government website. www.downsizinggovern ment.org.

Edwards, Chris. *Downsizing the Federal Government.* Washington: Cato Institute, 2005. This book provides citations for most of the facts and data in this chapter.

Free and Fair Post Initiative (Europe) website. www.freefairpost.com.

Hudgins, Edward L., ed. *Mail @ the Millennium: Will the Postal Service Go Private?* Washington: Cato Institute, 2000.

Reason Foundation website. www.reason.org/privatization.

Vranich, Joseph, Cornelius Chapman, and Edward Hudgins. ''A Plan to Liquidate Amtrak.'' Cato Institute Policy Analysis no. 425, February 8, 2002.

World Bank. Privatization website. http://psdblog.worldbank.org/psdblog/privatization.

—Prepared by Chris Edwards

GOVERNMENT REFORM

7. The Delegation of Legislative Powers

Congress should

- require all "lawmaking" regulations to be affirmatively approved by Congress and signed into law by the president, as the Constitution requires for all laws; and
- establish a mechanism to force the legislative consideration of existing regulations during the reauthorization process.

Separation of Powers: The Bulwark of Liberty

When the legislative and executive powers are united in the same person, or in the same body of magistrates, there can be no liberty.

—Montesquieu, *The Spirit of the Laws*

Article I, section 1, of the U.S. Constitution stipulates, "All legislative powers herein granted shall be vested in the Congress of the United States, which shall consist of a Senate and House of Representatives." Article II, section 3, stipulates that the president "shall take care that the laws be faithfully executed." Thus, as we all learned in high school civics, the Constitution clearly requires the separation of powers between the branches of government.

The Founders thought concentration of power within a single government body was inimical to a free society. John Adams wrote in 1776 that "a single assembly, possessed of all the powers of government, would make arbitrary laws for their own interest, and adjudge all controversies in their own favor." James Madison in *Federalist* no. 47 justified the Constitution's separation of powers by noting that it was a necessary prerequisite for "a government of laws and not of men." Further, he wrote, "The accumulation of all powers, legislative, executive, and judiciary, in the same hands, whether of one, a few, or many, and whether hereditary, self-appointed, or elective, may justly be pronounced the very definition of tyranny.''

For the first 150 years of the American Republic, the Supreme Court largely upheld the original constitutional design, requiring that Congress rather than administrators make the law. The courts rejected the suggestion that Congress could broadly delegate its lawmaking powers to others, particularly the executive branch. And for good reasons. First, the courts understood the Constitution to be a document of enumerated and thus limited powers, a document that neither explicitly nor implicitly gives Congress the power to delegate. Second, the Supreme Court and Congress both feared power concentrated in any one branch. Third, Americans believed that those who make the law should be directly accountable at the ballot box.

Supported by Congress, the courts, and the people, the separation of powers effectively restrained federal power, just as the Founders had intended. As Alexis de Tocqueville observed, ''The nation participates in the making of its laws by the choice of its legislators, and in the execution of them by the choice of agents of the executive government.'' He also observed that ''it may also be said to govern itself, so feeble and so restricted is the share left to the administrators, so little do the authorities forget their popular origins and the power from which they emanate.''

The New Deal: "Delegation Running Riot"

In his first inaugural address, Franklin Roosevelt compared the effect of the ongoing economic depression to a foreign invasion and argued that Congress should grant him sweeping powers to fight it. Shortly after his taking office in 1933, Congress granted Roosevelt virtually unlimited power to regulate commerce by passing the Agricultural Adjustment Act (which authorized the president to increase agricultural prices via administrative production controls) and the National Industrial Recovery Act, which authorized the president to issue industrial codes to regulate all aspects of the industries they covered. The Supreme Court responded in 1935 in its unanimous opinion in *A.L.A. Schechter Poultry Corp. v. United States.* The Court overturned the industrial code provisions of the NIRA, and, in a separate opinion, Justice Benjamin Cardozo termed the NIRA— and thus the New Deal—''delegation running riot.'' That same year, the Court struck down additional NIRA delegations of power in *Panama Refining Co. v. Ryan.*

Largely because of these decisions, President Roosevelt decried the Court's interference with his political agenda and proposed legislation enlarging the size of the Court so that he could appoint additional justices—the so-called Court-packing plan. He lost that battle but won the war. Although the Court never explicitly reversed its 1935 decisions and continues to articulate essentially the same verbal formulas defining the scope of permissible delegation—indeed, *Schechter* and *Panama Refining* are theoretically good law today—it would be nearly 40 years before the Court again struck down a business regulation on delegation grounds.

As long as Congress articulates some intelligible standard (no matter how vague or arbitrary) to govern executive lawmaking, courts today allow delegation, in Cardozo's words, to run riot. John Locke's admonition that the legislature "cannot transfer the power of making laws to any other hands, for it being but a delegated power from the people, they who have it cannot pass it over to others," recalls an era when individual liberty mattered more than administrative convenience. As Federal District Judge Roger Vinson wrote in *United States v. Mills* in 1989:

> A delegation doctrine which essentially allows Congress to abdicate its power to define the elements of a criminal offense, in favor of an unelected administrative agency such as the [Army] Corps of Engineers, does violence to this time-honored principle. . . . Deferent and minimal judicial review of Congress' transfer of its criminal lawmaking function to other bodies, in other branches, calls into question the vitality of the tripartite system established by our Constitution. It also calls into question the nexus that must exist between the law so applied and simple logic and common sense. Yet that seems to be the state of the law.

Delegation: The Corrosive Agent of Democracy

Delegation does violence, not only to the ideal construct of a free society but also to the daily practice of democracy itself. Ironically, delegation does not help secure "good government"; it helps to destroy it.

Delegation Breeds Political Irresponsibility

Congress delegates power for much the same reason that Congress has run budget deficits for decades. With deficit spending, members of Congress can claim credit for the benefits of their expenditures yet escape blame for the costs. The public must pay ultimately, of course, but largely through taxes levied at some future time by some other officials. Likewise, delegation allows legislators to claim credit for the benefits that a regulatory

85

statute airily promises yet escape the blame for the burdens it will impose, because they do not issue the laws needed to achieve those high-sounding benefits. The public inevitably must suffer regulatory costs to realize regulatory benefits, but the laws will come from an agency that legislators can then criticize for imposing excessive burdens on their constituents. Just as deficit spending allows legislators to appear to deliver money to some people without taking it from others, delegation allows them to appear to deliver regulatory benefits without imposing regulatory costs. It provides, in the words of former Environmental Protection Agency deputy administrator John Quarles, ''a handy set of mirrors—so useful in Washington—by which politicians can appear to kiss both sides of the apple.''

Delegation Is a Political Steroid for Organized Special Interests

As the leading legal scholar John Hart Ely noted, ''One reason we have broadly based representative assemblies is to await something approaching a consensus before government intervenes.'' The Constitution was intentionally designed to curb the ''facility and excess of law-making'' (in the words of James Madison) by requiring that statutes go through a bicameral legislature and the president. Differences in the size and nature of the constituencies of representatives, senators, and the president—and the different lengths of their terms in office—increase the probability that the actions of each will reflect a different balance of interests. That diversity of viewpoint, plus the greater difficulty of prevailing in three forums rather than one, makes it far more difficult for special-interest groups or bare majorities to impose their will on the American people. Hence, the original design effectively required a supermajority to make law as a means of discouraging the selfish exercise of power by well-organized but narrow interests.

Delegation shifts the power to make law from a Congress comprising almost all interests to subgovernments typically representing only a small subset of all interests. The obstacles intentionally placed in the path of lawmaking disappear, to the benefit of organized interests. Diffuse broad interests typically find it even more difficult to press their case before an agency than before a legislature. They often have no direct representation in the administrative process, and effective representation typically requires special legal counsel, expert witnesses, and the capacity to reward or to punish top officials through political organization, press coverage, and close working relationships with members of the appropriate congressional subcommittee. As a result, the general public rarely qualifies as a "stakeholder" in agency proceedings and has little influence over the decision. Delegation thus vitiates Madison's desired check on the "facility and excess of law-making."

Delegation Breeds the Leviathan State

Scarcity of time constrains the growth of government. No matter how many laws Congress would like to pass, there are only so many hours in a session to do so. Delegation dramatically expands potential lawmaking by effectively "deputizing" tens of thousands of bureaucrats, often with broad and imprecise missions to "go forth and legislate." Thus, as journalist Jacob Weisberg has noted: "As a labor-saving device, delegation did for legislators what the washing machine did for the 1950s housewife. Government could now penetrate every nook and cranny of American life in a way that was simply impossible before."

The Threadbare Case for Delegation

Delegation has its defenders. Their arguments are not persuasive.

The Myth of Technical Expertise

Some argue delegation fosters better laws by transferring lawmaking from elected officials, who are beholden to concentrated interests, to experts, who can base their decisions solely on a cool appraisal of the public interest. Yet most agency heads are not scientists, engineers, economists, or other kinds of technical experts; they are political operatives. Since the Environmental Protection Agency's inception in 1970, for example, the overwhelming majority of its administrators and assistant administrators have been lawyers. As MIT professor Michael Golay wrote in *Science*: "Environmental protection policy disagreements are not about what to conclude from the available scientific knowledge; they represent a struggle for political power among groups having vastly differing interests and visions for society. In this struggle, science is used as a means of legitimizing the various positions. . . . Science is a pawn, cynically abused as may suit the interests of a particular protagonist despite great ignorance concerning the problems being addressed."

A lack of agency expertise does not necessarily pose a problem. Government by experts may be worse than government by elected officials. Experts may not possess superior moral knowledge or a better sense of what constitutes the public good. Indeed, specialization often impairs the capacity for moral judgment and breeds professional zealotry. Likewise, specialized expertise provides too narrow a base for the balanced judgments that intelligent policy requires.

Although both agency administrators and legislators often lack the expertise to evaluate technical arguments by themselves, they can get help from agency and committee staff, government institutes (such as the Centers for Disease Control and the Government Accountability Office), and private sources such as medical associations, think tanks, and university scientists. After all, hearings by Congress or agencies are supposed to provide such information.

And only someone naive about modern government would seriously claim that the winds of politics blow any less fiercely in administrative meeting rooms than they do in the halls of Congress. As Nobel laureate economist James Buchanan and others have observed, public officials have many incentives to pursue both private and political ends that often have little to do with their ostensible missions.

Is Congress Too Busy?

New Dealers once argued that "time spent on details [by Congress] must be at the sacrifice of time spent on matters of the broad public policy." But Congress today spends little time on "matters of the broad public policy," largely because delegation forces Congress to spend a large chunk of its time constructing the legislative architecture—sometimes over a thousand pages of it—detailing exactly how various agencies are to decide important matters of policy. Once that architecture is in place, members of Congress find that a large part of their job entails navigating those bureaucratic mazes for special interests jockeying to influence the final nature of the law. Writing such instructions and performing agency oversight to ensure that they are carried out would be unnecessary if Congress made the rules in the first place.

Moreover, delegation often prolongs disputes and keeps standards of conduct murky because pressures from legislators and the complicated procedures imposed on agencies turn lawmaking into an excruciatingly slow process. Agencies typically report that they have issued only a small fraction of the laws that their long-standing statutory mandates require. Competing interests devote large sums of money and many of their best minds to this seemingly interminable process. For example, it took the EPA 16 years to ban lead in gasoline despite the fact that the 1970 Clean Air Act explicitly gave it the authority to do so. Simply making the rules the first time around in the legislative process would take less time than the multiyear regulatory sausage machine requires to issue standards.

Complex Rules for a Complex World

Many believe the complex and technical world of today justifies delegation. As the Supreme Court opined in 1989, "Our jurisprudence has been driven by a practical understanding that in our increasingly complex society, replete with ever changing and more technical problems, Congress simply cannot do its job absent an ability to delegate power under broad general directives."

Yet the vast majority of decisions delegated to the executive branch are not particularly technical in nature. They are instead hotly political, for the reasons mentioned earlier. If Congress must regulate, it could (and probably should) jettison command-and-control regulations that make up the bulk of the *Federal Register* and instead adopt regulations that are less prescriptive and more performance based or market oriented. Most regulatory analysts on both the left and the right agree that this would also have the happy consequences of decreasing regulatory costs, increasing regulatory efficiency, and decreasing the burden on regulators. In addition, a Congress not skewed toward regulation by delegation would rediscover practical reasons for allowing many matters to be left to state and local regulators.

Conclusion

We are today a nation governed not by elected officials, but by unelected bureaucrats. Forcing Congress to vote on every administrative regulation that establishes a rule of private conduct would prove the most revolutionary change in government since the Civil War. The central political issues of the 111th Congress—the complex and heavy-handed array of regulations that entangle virtually all manner of private conduct, the perceived inability of elections to affect the direction of government, the disturbing political power of special interests, the lack of popular respect for the law, the sometimes tyrannical and self-aggrandizing exercise of power by government, and populist resentment of an increasingly unaccountable political elite—are but symptoms of a disease largely caused by delegation. "No regulation without representation!" would be a fitting battle cry for a Congress truly interested in fundamental reform of government. It is a standard that both the left and the right could comfortably rally around, given that many prominent constitutional scholars, policy analysts, and journalists—from Nadine Strossen, former president of the American Civil Liberties Union, to former judge Robert Bork—have supported ending delegation.

Some observers complain that voting on all regulations would overwhelm Congress. Certainly, federal agencies issue thousands of regulations every year. However, the flow of new rules is no argument against congressional responsibility. Congress could bundle relatively minor regulations and vote on the whole package. Both houses could then give major regulations—those that impose costs of more than $100 million annually—close scrutiny.

Of course, forcing Congress to take full and direct responsibility for the law would not prove a panacea. The legislature, after all, has shown itself to be fully capable of violating individual rights, subsidizing special interests, writing complex and virtually indecipherable law, and generally making a hash of things. But delegation has helped to make such phenomena not the exception, but the rule of modern government. No more crucial—and potentially popular—reform awaits the attention of the 111th Congress.

Suggested Readings

Anthony, Robert. "Unlegislative Compulsion: How Federal Agency Guidelines Threaten Your Liberty." Cato Institute Policy Analysis no. 312, August 11, 1998.

DeLong, James. *Out of Bounds, Out of Control: Regulatory Enforcement at the EPA.* Washington: Cato Institute, 2002.

Lawson, Gary. "Delegation and the Constitution." *Regulation*, Summer 1999.

———. "Discretion as Delegation: The 'Proper' Understanding of the Nondelegation Doctrine." *George Washington Law Review* 73 (January 2005).

Lowi, Theodore. *The End of Liberalism: The Second Republic of the United States.* 2nd ed. New York: W. W. Norton, 1979.

———. "Two Roads to Serfdom: Liberalism, Conservatism and Administrative Power." *American University Law Review* 36 (1987).

Schoenbrod, David. *Power without Responsibility: How Congress Abuses the People through Delegation.* New Haven, CT: Yale University Press, 1993.

———. "Politics and the Principle That Elected Legislators Should Make the Laws." *Harvard Journal of Law and Public Policy* 26 (Winter 2003).

—Prepared by Jerry Taylor and John Samples

8. Term Limits

Each member of Congress should

- pledge to be a citizen legislator by limiting his or her time in office to no more than three additional terms in the House of Representatives and no more than two additional terms in the Senate, and
- keep that pledge.

In June 2008, the Gallup Organization reported that just 12 percent of Americans expressed confidence in Congress, the lowest of 16 American institutions, and the worst rating the survey group had found for any institution in the 35-year history of asking this question. About the same time, a *New York Times*/CBS News poll reported that only 24 percent said the government in Washington could be trusted to do what was right just about always or most of the time. This lack of confidence approaches the historical low of 1994 when large numbers of incumbent members of Congress lost their bids for reelection.

These numbers tell us that Americans feel Congress no longer represents their interests and concerns. No wonder. The power of office has virtually put incumbents beyond the reach of the people. But Americans can reclaim their democracy. They can have a government that is accountable to their will, a government for and by the people, in Washington and in every statehouse in America. Restoring democracy requires term limits for incumbents. All members of Congress should pledge to limit their stay on Capitol Hill.

The People Support Term Limits

Voters have spoken loudly and clearly on term limits in virtually all the states that provide an opportunity to do so. Twenty-two states representing nearly half of Congress had term limits for their delegations by 1994. The great majority of those states had opted to limit their representatives to three terms, and all those states had limited their senators to two terms. Only 2 of the 22 states chose six terms for the House. From 1990 to 1995, state legislative term limits passed in 18 states. In November 2000, Nebraska became the 19th state to limit the terms of state legislators. The first 19 states passed term limits by an average vote of 67 percent. Moreover, almost every effort by incumbents to roll back term limits has been defeated by voters. In March 2002, a ballot initiative designed to weaken California's term limits law was soundly defeated at the polls, despite a 10-to-1 spending advantage over term limit defenders. Legislative leaders put another initiative on the ballot in 2008 to extend their terms in office, and voters turned it down again. Voters in Arkansas and Montana also rejected state efforts to lengthen their term limits to 12 years. Critics say term limits deprive Americans of one choice for elected office. Americans do not appear to believe they have been denied a fundamental right to choose their representative.

Members of Congress should listen to the American people on this issue. For years, national polls have found that three of four voters support term limits. In a June 2000 poll by Diversified Research, Inc., 69 percent of Californians said they still approved of the original (1990) term limits initiative. An NBC/*Wall Street Journal* poll in July 2003 found that 67 percent of respondents thought term limits were a good idea. Scholars have concluded that the voters are unlikely to change their minds on this issue. Term limits are here to stay. When will Congress abide by the judgment of the American people?

Take the Pledge

Americans believe term limits would improve Congress. But a Congress controlled by career politicians will never pass a term limits amendment. So the term limits movement, one of the most successful grassroots political efforts in U.S. history, has set out to change Congress from a bastion of careerism into an institution responsive to voters and responsible to our deepest ideals.

Term limits are an important part of the American political tradition. George Washington set the standard. Perhaps the most popular and powerful American in history, Washington nevertheless stepped down after two terms as president. He handed back to the people the immense power and trust they had given him, dramatically making the case that no one should monopolize a seat of power. The tradition of a two-term limit for the president lasted uninterrupted for almost a century and a half. When Franklin D. Roosevelt broke the tradition, Congress moved to codify the term limit by proposing the Twenty-Second Amendment to the Constitution, which the states ratified in just 12 short months. The presidential term limit remains tremendously popular.

We can establish such a tradition in Congress. Since 1994, several dozen new faces have entered the halls of Congress who are serious about changing the culture of Washington, pledging to limit themselves to three terms in the House or two terms in the Senate. Those pledges have resonated with the voters who understand that a lawmaker's career interests do not always coincide with the interests of the people back home. A poll by Fabrizio-McLaughlin and Associates asked, "Would you be more likely to vote for a candidate who pledges to serve no more than three terms in the House, or a candidate who refuses to self-limit?" Seventy-two percent of respondents said they would be more likely to vote for the self-limiter.

Self-limiters serve their constituents well. Former Rep. Matt Salmon (R-AZ) has said term limits gave him the independence to challenge his own party's leadership in favor of the interests of the people of his state. Recent research by Rebekah Herrick and Sue Thomas found that term-limited legislators were less likely than their counterparts to be motivated to run for office for personal goals and more likely to be motivated by issues. This finding implies term-limited legislators are more attentive to making public policy.

Self-limiters also resist Washington's culture of spending. They can vote for spending limits because of the freedom of conscience afforded by their term-limit pledge. The self-limiters' collective experience suggests that self-limitation helps discipline a politician's legislative behavior. Self-limiters exercise greater independence than their non-term-limited peers and appear less fearful of incurring the wrath of either party power brokers or special interest groups. During the past several years, many self-limiters stood out as the most fiscally conservative members of Congress. Not surprisingly, self-limiters have spearheaded opposition to pork-barrel spending and committee budget increases. They have demanded honest accounting and pioneered the political push for real reform of flawed government programs such as Social Security and Medicare—so often used by professional politicians as political footballs.

Term Limits for Committee Chairs

Most laws begin life in congressional committees led by powerful chairs who act as gatekeepers for floor votes on legislation. For decades, the average tenure of a committee chair was about 20 years. The seniority system allowed entrenched politicians from the least competitive districts to wield power over other members, not on the basis of merit but because of their longevity. In the past, the only way to lose a chair was by death, resignation, retirement, or electoral defeat. The seniority system increased the level of pork-barrel spending and blocked much-needed change. For example, in a Cato Institute policy analysis, "Term Limits and the Republican Congress," Aaron Steelman examined 31 key tax and spending proposals in recent Congresses. He found that junior Republicans in Congress were "more than twice as likely to vote for spending or tax cuts as were senior Republicans." Steelman pointed out: "Veteran Republican legislators have proven they are comfortable with big government. It is unlikely that fundamental change in Washington will occur while they continue to control legislative debate and action."

For those reasons, in 1995 the Speaker of the House decided to limit the terms of House committee chairs to three terms, totaling six years. Those limits are an important dent in a corrupt system. Term limits on those powerful positions make the House more responsible and open the way for newer members to influence policy. In 1996, the Republican caucus imposed six-year limits on GOP committee chairs. As a consequence, some changes have occurred on the traditional Senate leadership career path. But the pace of change should be quickened, not slowed down. In the 111th Congress, both parties should impose term limits on Senate committee chairs.

Why We Need Term Limits

Why are term limits so popular? Americans believe that career legislators and professional politicians have created a gaping chasm between themselves and their government. For democracy to work, it must be representative—a government of, by, and for the people. A member of Congress should not be far removed from the private sector. The members of the House of Representatives, in particular, should be close to the people they represent. As Rhode Island's Roger Sherman wrote at the time of our nation's founding: "Representatives ought to return home and mix with the people. By remaining at the seat of government, they would acquire the habits of the place, which might differ from those of their constituents." In the era of year-round legislative sessions, the only way to achieve that objective is through term limits.

What should be the limit on terms? Some observers have proposed as many as six terms (or 12 years) for the House. Three terms for the House is better for several reasons. America is best served by a Congress whose members are there out of a sense of civic duty but who would rather live their lives in the private sector, holding productive jobs in civil society, far removed from government and politics. Such individuals might be willing to spend two, four, or even six years in Washington, but not if the legislative agenda is being set by others who have gained their authority through seniority. Twelve-year "limits," which amount to a minicareer, do little to remove this major obstacle to a more diverse and representative group of Americans seeking office.

We have solid evidence that short, three-term limits enhance the democratic process: Proposition 140 in California, which was passed by the voters there in 1990 and limited the state assembly to three two-year terms. The 1992 assembly elections witnessed a sharp increase in the number of citizens seeking office, with a remarkable 27 freshmen elected to the 80-member lower house of the California legislature. In 2004, Bruce Cain and Thad Kousser concluded from the California experience: "As proponents hoped, women and minorities have been elected to office more frequently, resulting in an increasingly diverse Legislature."

While perhaps not attractive to people seeking to be career politicians, all those developments please the great majority of Americans who favor a return to citizen legislatures. Similarly, a three-term limit for the U.S. House of Representatives would return control of the House—not just through voting but also through participation—to the people. We must make the possibility of serving in Congress a more attractive option for millions more Americans.

A second reason for shorter term limits is that the longer one is in Congress, the more one is exposed to and influenced by the "culture of ruling" that permeates life inside the Beltway. Groups such as the National Taxpayers Union have shown that the longer people serve in Congress, the bigger spenders, taxers, and regulators they become. That is just as true of conservatives as it is of liberals. It is also understandable. Members of Congress are surrounded at work and socially by people who spend other people's money and regulate their lives. It is the unusual individual—although such people do exist—who is not subtly but surely affected by that culture.

Three terms rather than six would better serve as an antidote to the growing "professionalization" of the legislative process. As Mark Petracca has written:

Whereas representative government aspires to maintain a proximity of sympathy and interests between representative and represented, professionalism creates authority, autonomy, and hierarchy, distancing the expert from the client. Though this distance may be necessary and functional for lawyers, nurses, physicians, accountants, and social scientists, the qualities and characteristics associated with being a "professional" legislator run counter to the supposed goals of a representative democracy. Professionalism encourages an independence of ambition, judgment, and behavior that is squarely at odds with the inherently dependent nature of representative government.

Finally, shorter limits for the House would enhance the competitiveness of elections and, as previously noted, increase the number and diversity of Americans choosing to run for Congress. The most competitive races (and the ones that bring out the largest number of primary candidates) are for open seats. Richard Niemi and his colleagues have found that term limits in state legislatures have been associated with increases in open-seat elections and in the number of competitive seats.

Term limits have taken effect all over the country in state legislatures—and they are working. Scholars have found that term limits in the states removed 1,536 legislators from office from 1996 to 2004. Recent studies indicate several desirable changes brought by term limits in the states:

- Term limits remain popular with state electorates long after their introduction.
- Term limits increase turnover in state legislatures.
- Term limits enable nontraditional candidates to run for seats in state legislatures. Hispanic, African-American, and Asian candidates find it easier to enter term-limited legislatures than non-term-limited bodies.
- Term limits weaken seniority systems in state legislatures.
- Lobbyists in term-limited states report that their job has become harder because they cannot establish long-term relationships with legislators.
- Term limits have not strengthened interest groups, state bureaucracies, or legislative staffs as predicted by critics of term limits.

Term limits foster public policies that serve to halt, or at least reduce, the growth in the size and scope of government. Term-limited politicians demonstrate greater respect than their non-term-limited colleagues for taxpayers' money. For example, term-limited legislators place less emphasis on securing projects and pork for their districts.

Clearly, logic and experience make a strong case for term limits. Continued popular support for term limits may be the best indication of their success. Members of Congress should take note.

Conclusion

The term limits movement is not motivated by disdain for the institution of Congress. It is motivated by a sincere desire on the part of the American people to regain control of the most representative part of the federal government. It comes from the democratic hope that we can be governed not by professional politicians but by a citizen legislature. Term limits remain an issue to be reckoned with. Public support is even stronger and deeper for candidates making personal term-limit commitments than for a term-limits amendment. Political leaders who understand the problems created by a permanent ruling elite in Washington—or who simply want to abide by the overwhelming will of their constituents—will pledge to serve no more than three additional terms in the House or two in the Senate.

Suggested Readings

Basham, Patrick. "Assessing the Term Limits Experiment: California and Beyond." Cato Institute Policy Analysis no. 413, August 31, 2001.

———. "Defining Democracy Down: Explaining the Campaign to Repeal Term Limits." Cato Institute Policy Analysis no. 490, September 24, 2003.

Cain, Bruce E., and Thad Kousser. *Adapting to Term Limits: Recent Experiences and New Directions.* Sacramento, CA: Public Policy Institute of California, 2004.

Carey, John M., Richard G. Niemi, and Lynda W. Powell. *Term Limits in the State Legislatures.* Ann Arbor: University of Michigan Press, 2000.

Crane, Edward H., and Roger Pilon, eds. *The Politics and Law of Term Limits.* Washington: Cato Institute, 1994.

Elhauge, Einer. "What Term Limits Do That Ordinary Voting Cannot." Cato Institute Policy Analysis no. 328, December 16, 1998.

Herrick, Rebekah, and Sue Thomas. "Do Term Limits Make a Difference? Ambition and Motivations among U.S. State Legislators." *American Politics Research* 33 (2005).

Kurtz, Karl T., Bruce E. Cain, and Richard G. Niemi. "Conclusions and Implications." In *Institutional Change in American Politics: The Case of Term Limits,* edited by Karl T. Kurtz, Bruce E. Cain, and Richard G. Niemi. Ann Arbor, MI: University of Michigan Press, 2007.

Moncrief, Gary, Lynda W. Powell, and Tim Storey. "Composition of Legislatures." In *Institutional Change in American Politics: The Case of Term Limits,* edited by Karl T. Kurtz, Bruce E. Cain, and Richard G. Niemi. Ann Arbor, MI: University of Michigan Press, 2007.

Niemi, Richard G., Lynda W. Powell, William D. Berry, Thomas M. Carsey, and James M. Snyder Jr. "Competition in State Legislative Elections, 1992–2002." In *The Marketplace of Democracy*, edited by Michael P. McDonald and John Samples. Washington: Brookings Institution Press, 2006.

Owings, Stephanie, and Rainald Borck. "Legislative Professionalism and Government Spending: Do Citizen Legislators Really Spend Less?" *Public Finance Review* 23 (2000).

Steelman, Aaron. "Term Limits and the Republican Congress." Cato Institute Briefing Paper no. 41, October 27, 1998.

—Prepared by Edward H. Crane and John Samples

9. Campaign Finance

> ## Congress should
>
> - repeal the prohibition on soft money fundraising in the Bipartisan Campaign Reform Act of 2002,
> - repeal the provisions of BCRA related to electioneering communications,
> - eliminate taxpayer funding of presidential campaigns and reject new proposals for such funding of congressional campaigns,
> - repeal limits on spending coordinated between a political party and its candidates and
> - reject proposals to mandate electoral advertising paid for by the owners of the television networks.

The 107th Congress passed the most sweeping new restrictions on campaign finance in a generation, the Bipartisan Campaign Reform Act of 2002. During the 108th Congress, the Supreme Court endorsed almost all of BCRA. Over the last four years, the tide has begun running toward more liberty and freedom of speech. In 2007, the Supreme Court expanded the realm of free speech in its decision in *Wisconsin Right to Life v. FEC* by restricting the reach of BCRA. In 2008, the Court again invalidated part of BCRA to vindicate the First Amendment. In *Davis v. Federal Election Commission*, the Court stated that the Constitution protects freedom of speech, not equality of electoral opportunity. Congress should follow the Court's lead and further liberalize our campaigns and elections.

Liberty and Corruption

The Constitution prohibits governments from abridging freedom of speech. In the seminal case of *Buckley v. Valeo* (1976), the Supreme Court recognized that restrictions on political spending abridge political speech:

A restriction on the amount of money a person or group can spend on political communication during a campaign necessarily reduces the quantity of expression by restricting the number of issues discussed, the depth of their exploration, and the size of the audience reached. This is because virtually every means of communicating ideas in today's mass society requires the expenditure of money.

Note that the Court did not say, "Money equals speech." It said that political speech requires spending money. Restrictions on money thus translate into restrictions on speech.

Some support such restrictions because they believe there is "too much money" in politics. In 2004, spending on federal elections came to roughly $4 billion. This sum should be seen in context. According to political scientist Ray La Raja, a single company, Wal-Mart, spent that much on advertising during the same period.

If we believe that voters should be informed, we ought to encourage, not restrict, campaign spending. John J. Coleman of the University of Wisconsin found that campaign spending increases public knowledge of the candidates across all groups in the population. Less spending on campaigns is unlikely to increase public trust, involvement, or attention. Implicit or explicit spending limits reduce public knowledge during campaigns. Getting more money into campaigns benefits voters.

Unfortunately, contributions to campaigns do not enjoy the same constitutional protections as spending. In 1974, to prevent "corruption or the appearance of corruption," Congress severely limited campaign contributions. Until recently, those ceilings have governed American elections without being adjusted for inflation. BCRA raised the limits on "hard money" contributions, but their real value remains well below the ceilings enacted in 1974.

The lower protection afforded contributions makes little sense. Political candidates spend money to obtain the means (often television time) to communicate with voters; such spending, as noted earlier, is protected speech. But contributors give to candidates for the same reason—to enable candidates to present their views to the electorate. Moreover, ceilings on contributions complicate raising money and thus inevitably reduce "the quantity of expression by restricting the number of issues discussed, the depth of their exploration, and the size of the audience reached" by the candidate.

Elections after BCRA have shown that contribution limits restrict speech and political participation. An increase in the donation limit for individuals combined with the emergence of the Internet as a fundraising tool led to greatly increased contributions in the 2006 and 2008 election cycles. BCRA revealed that members of Congress understand the effect of limits on donations. Congress enacted the Millionaire's Amendment, which liberalized the limits on donations to opponents of self-funding candidates. Members understood that liberalized limits meant more fundraising and a more competitive elections.

What about corruption? The Supreme Court has said that restrictions on campaign finance are justified to prevent corruption or the appearance of corruption in politics. What is corruption? Bribery is a clear case of corruption. Bribery involves secretly giving public officials something of value (usually money) in exchange for political favors. Officials then spend bribes on private consumption. Campaign contributions also involve giving money to public officials or their agents. However, by law the recipients may spend contributions only for political purposes. Anyone who spends campaign contributions on fancy cars and lavish houses commits a felony. Unlike bribes, contributions are publicly disclosed.

As Chief Justice John Roberts observed in the *Wisconsin Right to Life* decision, the burden of proof in campaign finance matters lies with the censor, not with the speaker. Congress must show that spending money on politics somehow corrupts the government. Many claim that contributors influence the judgment of legislators and receive favors for their donations. The evidence says otherwise. Three leading scholars examined 41 studies of the influence of money on legislative voting. They concluded: "The evidence that campaign contributions lead to a substantial influence on votes is rather thin. Legislators' votes depend almost entirely on their own beliefs and the preferences of their voters and their party. Contributions explain a minuscule fraction of the variation in voting behavior in the U.S. Congress. Members of Congress care foremost about winning reelection. They must attend to the constituency that elects them, voters in a district or state, and the constituency that nominates them, the party."

What about preventing the appearance of corruption? We might first wonder why the mere appearance of illegality should be sufficient reason to restrict First Amendment rights. Proponents argue that campaign contributions appear to corrupt the political process, thereby undermining public confidence in government. Once again, the evidence runs against proponents of campaign finance restrictions. John Coleman found that campaign spending had no effect on public confidence in government. Nathaniel Persily and Kelli Lammie of the University of Pennsylvania discovered that Americans' "confidence in the system of representative government" is associated with individuals' positions in society, their general tendency to trust others, their beliefs about what government should do, and their ideological or philosophical disagreement with the policies of incumbent officeholders. However, they found that our system of campaign finance had no effect on public confidence.

Congressional Conflicts of Interest

Campaign finance regulation brings every member face-to-face with the problem of self-dealing—not only the self-dealing that the regulations are supposed to prevent but, more immediately, the self-dealing that is inherent in writing regulations not simply for oneself but for those who would challenge one's power to write such regulations in the first place. Only one congressional election since 1974 has seen an incumbent reelection rate lower than 90 percent. Even in the "revolution" of 1994, which changed control of the House of Representatives, 90 percent of incumbents were reelected. The last three elections have seen reelection rates of more than 94 percent.

Campaign finance restrictions may not fully explain the lack of competition for incumbents in American politics. But those restrictions encumber entry into the electoral market and thus discourage credible challenges to incumbents. A challenger needs large sums to campaign for public office, especially at the federal level. He needs big money to overcome the manifest advantages of incumbency—name recognition, the power of office, the franking privilege, a knowledgeable staff, campaign experience, and, perhaps most importantly, easy access to the media. Current law limits the supply of campaign dollars: an individual can give no more than $2,300 to a candidate, and a political party or a political action committee can give no more than $5,000. In a free and open political system, challengers could find a few "deep pockets" to get them started, then build support from there, unrestrained by any restrictions save for the traditional prohibitions on vote selling and vote buying.

Problems with BCRA

BCRA made things worse. By banning "soft money"—unregulated contributions given to the political parties—Congress complicated the lives of challengers. Parties have traditionally directed soft money contributions to races in which challengers might have a chance. At the same time, BCRA does not affect donations by political action committees, most of which go to incumbents. Ray La Raja found that after BCRA the financial gap has widened between officeholders and challengers. Incumbent fundraising increased 20 percent between 2002 and 2006, whereas challenger fundraising stayed flat.

BCRA has reduced the resources available to the political parties. Before BCRA, soft money fundraising by the parties had been rising quickly. The parties have made up some of the shortfall caused by the soft money prohibition in BCRA. If we extrapolate the trend before BCRA, however, both parties would have had a great deal more money to spend if the soft money ban had not been enacted. Moreover, according to La Raja, party receipts in off years have diminished for both the Republican National Committee and the Democratic National Committee under BCRA. For the RNC, the drop-off has been significant, falling from a high of $134 million in 2001 (just before BCRA) to $86 million in 2007. For the DNC, which is typically less well-funded, the decline over the same period was from $68 million to $55 million.

Before BCRA, the parties consulted with candidate campaigns to target soft money for advertising and get-out-the-vote efforts. After BCRA, parties may spend limited sums of hard money only in coordination with candidate campaigns. Parties have ended up spending money independently of their candidates to avoid the coordination restrictions. In some cases, parties have run advertising that candidates for Congress did not support. In these situations, voters can hold a party responsible for its advertising only by voting against a candidate who is not responsible for the messages. Congress could end this absurdity by loosening or removing restrictions on party spending in coordination with candidates.

Congress's conflict of interest did not end with the ban on soft money. Before BCRA, interest groups funded aggressive advertising criticizing members of Congress during their reelection campaigns. To be sure, some of those ads were unfair or inaccurate, but the Constitution protects the right to be both. BCRA prohibited such advertising—now called "electioneering communications"—funded by unions and corporations, including nonprofit corporations, if it mentions a candidate for federal office. If such ads are coordinated with a campaign, their funding is subject to federal election law, including contribution limits. Those restrictions meant elections had fewer ads, less debate of public matters, and less criticism of elected officials.

Activists have responded to the soft money ban and electioneering regulations by raising unlimited contributions on behalf of groups organized under Section 527 of the Internal Revenue Code. These efforts are an exercise of First Amendment rights and provide information to voters. Congress should not seek to prohibit 527 activities. Instead of adding more restrictions, Congress should repeal the soft money prohibition and the restrictions on electioneering, thereby removing the rationale for the existence of the 527 groups.

Not surprisingly, BCRA has not increased public confidence in the campaign finance system. When Americans are asked in a Gallup poll about the state of the nation's campaign finance laws, more than 50 percent say they are dissatisfied and only 21 percent say they are satisfied. Those proportions have not changed since before BCRA.

BCRA loosened federal contribution limits for candidates running against self-funding individuals. Apparently, contributions of over $2,300 corrupted politics—unless an incumbent faces a self-funding millionaire. BCRA seems little more than an incumbent protection law, a monument to the dangers of self-dealing. Recently, the Supreme Court struck down that selective liberalization of campaign finance regulation. Congress should respond by liberalizing contribution limits for all participants and not just for candidates who face a self-funder.

Taxpayer Financing of Campaigns

Some people believe the United States can preclude corruption or its appearance only by prohibiting all private contributions, whether designated as campaign contributions, and by moving to a system of taxpayer-financed campaigns. In practice, several states have established partial public financing. Since 1976, federal taxpayers have partially financed primary and general election campaigns for president. Some now propose to extend public financing. Recently, Sens. Richard Durbin (D-IL) and Arlen Specter (R-PA) introduced S. 936, the Fair Elections Now bill, to force taxpayers to fund congressional campaigns.

Compared with the system it replaced, presidential public financing has not increased competition in the party primaries or the general election. The system borders on insolvency because ever-fewer taxpayers check off the contribution box on their income tax return. The declining support for the program makes sense. Polls show that Americans reject public financing as "welfare for politicians." Congress should eliminate this unpopular multibillion-dollar boondoggle. The Durbin-Specter bill inadvertently provides additional evidence of the public's distaste for taxpayer financing. The bill is not funded by general taxation or by a checkoff system of earmarking taxation as is the presidential system. Instead, the bill purports to obtain sufficient funding from the sale of recovered electromagnetic spectrum, excess spectrum user fees, a tax on private broadcasters, and other miscellaneous sources. These choices for funding sources suggest senators know that taxing to fund campaigns would be highly unpopular with their constituents. If public funding offers so many benefits to the nation, why are taxpayers unwilling to pay the costs of the program? Could it be that taxpayer financing actually offers few benefits? In any case, forcing taxpayers to support campaigns for Congress at a time of continuing budget deficits makes little sense.

The Real Problem

As James Madison said in *Federalist* No. 51, a dependence on the people is the primary control on government. That dependence can only have meaning in elections with vigorous competition. By undermining competitive elections, campaign finance laws undermine democracy. Moreover, to the extent that incumbency is correlated with ever-larger government, BCRA exacerbates the very problem it was meant to reduce—corruption. Campaign finance "reform" distracts us from the real issue, the ultimate source of potential corruption—ubiquitous government. Government today fosters corruption because it exercises vast powers over virtually every aspect of life. Is it any wonder that special interests—indeed, every interest but the general—should be trying either to take advantage of that or to protect themselves from it?

Our Constitution does not authorize the kind of redistributive state we have in this nation today (see Chapter 3 for a detailed discussion). The Constitution establishes a government of delegated, enumerated, and thus limited powers. It sets forth powers that are, as Madison put it in *Federalist* No. 45, "few and defined." Thus, it addresses the problem of self-dealing by limiting the opportunities for self-dealing. If Congress has only limited power to control citizens' lives—if citizens are otherwise free to plan and live their own lives—Congress has little influence to sell, whether for cash, for perquisites, or for votes. Before they take the solemn oath of office, therefore, members of Congress should reflect on whether they are swearing to support the Constitution as written and understood by those who wrote and ratified it or the Constitution the New Deal Court discovered in 1937. The contrast between the two could not be greater. One was written for limited government; the other was crafted for potentially unlimited government. As that potential has materialized, the opportunities for corruption have become ever more manifest. It goes with ubiquitous government.

Conclusion

The answer to the corruption that is thought to attend our system of private campaign financing is not more campaign finance regulations but fewer such regulations. The limits on campaign contributions, in particular, should be removed, for they are the source of many of our present problems. More generally, the opportunities for corruption that were so expanded when we abandoned constitutionally limited government need to be radically reduced. Members of Congress can do that by taking the Constitution and their oaths of office more seriously.

Suggested Readings

Ansolabehere, Stephen, John M. de Figueiredo, and James M. Snyder Jr. "Why Is There So Little Money in U.S. Politics?" *Journal of Economic Perspectives* 17 (Winter 2003).

Coleman, John J. "The Benefits of Campaign Spending." Cato Institute Briefing Paper no. 84, September 4, 2003.

La Raja, Raymond J. "From Bad to Worse: The Unraveling of the Campaign Finance System." *The Forum* 6, no. 1 (2008).

————. *Small Change: Money, Political Parties, and Campaign Finance Reform.* Ann Arbor, MI: University of Michigan Press, 2008.

Persily, Nathaniel, and Kelli Lammie. "Perceptions of Corruption and Campaign Finance: When Public Opinion Constitutes Constitutional Law." *University of Pennsylvania Law Review* 153 (December 2004).

Pilon, Roger. "Freedom, Responsibility, and the Constitution: On Recovering Our Founding Principles." *Notre Dame Law Review* 68 (1993).

Samples, John. "The Failures of Taxpayer Financing of Presidential Campaigns." Cato Institute Policy Analysis no. 500, November 25, 2003.

————. *The Fallacy of Campaign Finance Reform.* Chicago: University of Chicago Press, 2006.

Smith, Bradley A. *Unfree Speech: The Folly of Campaign Finance Reform.* Princeton, NJ: Princeton University Press, 2001.

—Prepared by Roger Pilon and John Samples

10. Reclaiming the War Power

> ## Congress should
> - cease trying to shirk its constitutional responsibilities in matters of war and peace,
> - insist that hostilities not be initiated by the executive branch unless and until Congress has authorized such action,
> - rediscover the power of the purse as a means of restricting the executive's ability to wage unnecessary wars, and
> - reform the War Powers Resolution to make it an effective vehicle for restricting unilateral war making by the president.

No constitutional principle is more important than congressional control over the decision to go to war. In affairs of state, no more momentous decision can be made. For that reason, in a democratic republic, it is essential that that decision be made by the most broadly representative body: the legislature. As James Madison put it in 1793: "In no part of the constitution is more wisdom to be found, than in the clause which confides the question of war or peace to the legislature, and not to the executive department. Beside the objection to such a mixture of heterogeneous powers, the trust and the temptation would be too great for any one man."

The Constitutional Framework

The delegates to the Constitutional Convention of 1787 were well aware of those temptations, and sought to minimize them by limiting the president's war powers. At the start of the June 1 debates over the shape of the executive, Charles Pinckney of South Carolina supported "a vigorous executive," but worried that "the Executive powers of the existing Congress might extend to peace & war &c., which would render the Executive a monarchy, of the worst kind, to wit an elective one." His colleague

107

John Rutledge, also from South Carolina, agreed that the executive should not have the powers of war and peace, as, of course, did Madison, who noted that the executive powers "do not include the Rights of war & peace &c, but the powers shd. be confined and defined—if large we shall have the Evils of elective monarchies." The Framers were nearly unanimous on that point. Even Hamilton, who gave a June 18 speech advocating a "supreme Executive" who might serve for life, didn't envision a president with the power to initiate wars; he'd merely have "the direction of war when authorized or begun."

Accordingly, the document that emerged from the convention vests the bulk of the powers associated with military action with Congress, among them the powers "to declare War, [and] grant Letters of Marque and Reprisal." Other important war-making powers include the power "to raise and support Armies, but no Appropriation of Money to that Use shall be for a longer Term than two Years," and "to provide for calling forth the Militia to execute the Laws of the Union, suppress Insurrections and repel Invasions."

Significantly, several of the enumerated powers allocated to Congress involve the decision to initiate military action. For example, with its power to "grant Letters of Marque and Reprisal," Congress could authorize private citizens to harass and capture enemy ships. Since such actions might well lead to full-scale war, the Constitution vests the power to authorize them in Congress. Similarly, the power "to provide for calling forth the Militia" in cases of domestic unrest leaves it to Congress to decide when domestic unrest has reached the point where military action is required.

In contrast, the grant of authority to the executive as "Commander in Chief" of U.S. armed forces is managerial and defensive. The president commands the army and navy, and leads them into battle, should Congress choose to declare war. He commands the militia to suppress rebellions, should the militia be "called into the actual Service of the United States." In this, as Hamilton noted in *Federalist* No. 69, the president acts as no more than the "first General" of the United States. And generals, it should go without saying, are not empowered to decide with whom we go to war. The Constitution leaves that decision to Congress. As Constitutional Convention delegate James Wilson explained to the Pennsylvania ratifying convention: "This system will not hurry us into war; it is calculated to guard against it. It will not be in the power of a single man, or a single body of men, to involve us in such distress; for the important power in declaring war is vested in the legislature at large."

Congressional Abdication

Congress has not always been eager to take responsibility for that power, however. In his 1973 classic, *The Imperial Presidency*, historian Arthur Schlesinger Jr. noted that the erosion of Congress's control of the war power over the course of the 20th century "was as much a matter of congressional acquiescence as of presidential usurpation." The 2002 debate over war with Iraq demonstrates that that pattern has continued into the 21st century.

Although Bush administration lawyers denied that congressional authorization was necessary to launch the Iraq War, the administration eventually sought, and secured, congressional authorization for the use of force. It did so despite the fact that some prominent members of Congress did not want to be burdened with the vast responsibility the Constitution places on their shoulders. The then–Senate minority leader Trent Lott (R-MS), for instance, treated the Democrats' push for congressional authorization as a partisan annoyance rather than a solemn constitutional duty, calling it "a blatant political move that's not helpful."

Indeed, even in authorizing the president to use force, Congress attempted to shirk its responsibility to decide on war. After voting for the resolution, which gave the president all the authority he needed to attack Iraq, prominent members of Congress insisted they hadn't really voted to use force. That was for the president to decide. As the then–Senate majority leader Tom Daschle (D-SD) put it, "Regardless of how one may have voted on the resolution last night, I think there is an overwhelming consensus . . . that while [war] may be necessary, we're not there yet." But it is not for the president to decide whether we are "there yet." The Constitution leaves that question to Congress.

In the rush to get the Iraq War debate behind them, most members couldn't even be bothered with due diligence on the alleged threat—to examine the available intelligence and decide for themselves whether they thought a serious threat existed. Throughout the fall of 2002, copies of the 92-page National Intelligence Estimate on the Iraq threat were kept in two guarded vaults on Capitol Hill—available to any member of the House or Senate who wanted to review it. In March 2004, the *Washington Post* revealed that only six senators and a handful of representatives found it worth the effort to go and read the whole document. Sen. Jay Rockefeller (D-WV) explained that general reluctance to read intelligence briefings by saying that, when you're a senator, "everyone in the world wants to come see you" in your office and getting away to the secure room—

across the Capitol grounds at the Hart Senate Office Building—is "not easy to do." He added that intelligence briefings tend to be "extremely dense reading."

This will not do. When our representatives vote to wage war, it's not too much to ask that they've absorbed the available information and made an informed decision. Too often, however, it seems they'd prefer to punt the decision to the president, and hold him accountable for a decision that the Constitution insists is theirs to make.

Congressional scholar Louis Fisher compares the Iraq vote to the Gulf of Tonkin Resolution that empowered Lyndon Johnson to expand the Vietnam War. As with the Iraq war resolution, the Gulf of Tonkin Resolution was so broadly worded that it allowed the president to make the final decision about war all by himself. Lyndon Johnson compared the resolution to "grandma's nightshirt" because it "covered everything." And as with Iraq, the president did not immediately use the authority granted him. It would be six months later, after Johnson defeated Barry Goldwater in the November election, before the war escalated with a sustained bombing campaign in North Vietnam. In Iraq, President Bush waited five months before launching Operation Iraqi Freedom. As Fisher put it, "In each case, instead of acting as the people's representatives and preserving the republican form of government, [Congress] gave the president unchecked power." In each case, it was easier to dodge the issue than to take responsibility.

Such broad delegations of legislative authority are constitutionally suspect in the domestic arena; surely they are no less so when it comes to questions of war and peace. As Madison put it:

> Those who are to *conduct a war* cannot in the nature of things, be proper or safe judges, whether *a war ought* to be *commenced*, [or] *continued.* . . . *They are barred from the latter functions by a great principle in free government, analogous to that which separates the sword from the purse, or the power of executing from the power of enacting laws* (emphasis in original).

Situational Constitutionalism and Executive Power

As the Gulf of Tonkin example suggests, the growth of the Imperial Presidency cannot be laid at the feet of any one political party. After all, few Democratic presidents have hesitated to push broad theories of executive power. Our most recent Democratic administration, Bill Clinton's, was no exception. As presidential scholar Christopher Kelley puts it, "The

Clinton administration was every bit as important as the Reagan and first Bush administrations in helping the current Bush administration formulate its attitude toward the unitary executive.''

In fact, President Clinton went even further than his Republican predecessors in his exercise of unilateral, extraconstitutional war powers. By carrying out a 78-day war over Kosovo in 1999, Clinton became the first president to violate the War Powers Resolution's 60-day time limit on combat operations that lack explicit congressional approval. Worse still, Clinton ignored several congressional votes denying him authority to conduct the Kosovo campaign. Congress had considered and *rejected* authorizing the war, yet Clinton continued in defiance of congressional will—with the administration's Office of Legal Counsel providing thinly reasoned legal cover.

For far too long, the debate over presidential power has been dominated by what political scientist Norm Ornstein has called ''situational constitutionalism'': the tendency to support enhanced executive power when one's friends hold the executive branch—and to oppose it when they don't.

Blinded by partisanship, too many prominent public figures have lost sight of our Constitution's foundational principle: skepticism toward unchecked power—a skepticism that ought to apply without regard to person or party. Recovering that skepticism will be necessary if constitutional checks on executive power are to be restored.

Righting of the Constitutional Balance

Should it want to restrain executive war making, Congress has a powerful constitutional tool available to it: the power of the purse. No less an advocate of broad presidential power, John C. Yoo points out that if Congress wants to wind down the Iraq War, it could legally ''require scheduled troop withdrawals, [and] shrink or eliminate units'' deployed to Iraq. Congress used the power of the purse to pressure President Nixon to bring the Vietnam War to a close, and some 20 years later, Congress used similar tactics to end our nation-building excursion in Somalia. A month after the Black Hawk Down incident, in the Defense Appropriations Act for fiscal year 1994, Congress used the power of the purse to cut off funding after March 31, 1994, ''except for a limited number of military personnel to protect American diplomatic personnel and American citizens, unless further authorized by Congress.''

Given Congress's historic reluctance to exercise the power of the purse when troops are in harm's way, however, many reformers believe there's a need for a more comprehensive approach to restraining presidential war making. Toward that end, in the midst of the Watergate scandal and public disaffection over the Vietnam War, Congress passed the War Powers Resolution. That measure has proved an abject failure: in the 35 years since the resolution's passage, presidents have put troops in harm's way over 100 times without letting the WPR cramp their style. The WPR's time limit is supposed to kick in when the president reports that he has sent American forces into hostilities or situations where hostilities are imminent. However, the statute is ambiguous enough to allow the president to "report" without starting the clock, and presidents have exploited that ambiguity. Of 111 reports submitted from 1975 to 2003, only one president deliberately triggered the time limit, and that was in a case where the fighting had ended before the report was made.

Several prominent scholars have proposed amendments to the WPR that would give the resolution teeth. John Hart Ely's "Combat Authorization Act" would shorten the current 60-day "free pass" to 20 days and command the courts to hear suits by members of Congress seeking to start the clock. If the court determined that hostilities were imminent, and if Congress did not authorize the intervention, funds would automatically be cut off after the clock runs out.

In the Bush years, WPR reform has taken on new urgency. Disturbed by the Iraq War disaster and the president's conviction that he has all the constitutional power he needs to start a war with Iran, Rep. Walter Jones (R-NC) recently drew up a bill that echoes Professor Ely's Combat Authorization Act. The Constitutional War Powers Resolution would allow the president to use force unilaterally only in cases involving an attack on the United States or U.S. forces, or to protect and evacuate U.S. citizens. As with Ely's Combat Authorization Act, the CWPR would give members of Congress standing to "start the clock," and would cut off funding should Congress refuse to authorize military action.

In 2005, foreign policy luminaries Leslie H. Gelb and Anne-Marie Slaughter proposed an even simpler solution to the problem of presidential war making: "A new law that would restore the Framers' intent by requiring a congressional declaration of war in advance of any commitment of troops that promises sustained combat." Under the Gelb-Slaughter proposal, the president could still, as the Framers contemplated, "repel sudden attacks," but any prolonged military engagement would require a declaration, otherwise "funding for troops in the field would be cut off automatically."

Each of these proposals has the merit of demanding that Congress carry the burden the Constitution places upon it: responsibility for the decision to go to war. The Gelb-Slaughter plan shows particular promise. Although Congress hasn't declared war since 1942, reviving the formal declaration would make it harder for legislators to punt that decision to the president, as they did in Vietnam and Iraq. Hawks should see merit in making declarations mandatory, since a declaration commits those who voted for it to support the president and provide the resources he needs to prosecute the war successfully. Doves too should find much to applaud in the idea: forcing Congress to take a stand might concentrate the mind wonderfully and reduce the chances that we will find ourselves spending blood and treasure in conflicts that were not carefully examined at the outset.

But we should be clear about the difficulties that comprehensive war powers reform entails. Each of these reforms presupposes a Congress eager to be held accountable for its decisions, a judiciary with a stomach for interbranch struggles, and a voting public that rewards political actors who fight to put the presidency in its place. Representative Jones's Constitutional War Powers Resolution, which seeks to draw the judiciary into the struggle to constrain executive war making, ignores the Court's resistance to congressional standing, as well as the 30-year history of litigation under the War Powers Resolution, a history that shows how adept the federal judiciary is at constructing rationales that allow it to avoid picking sides in battles between Congress and the president.

Even if Jones's Constitutional War Powers Resolution or Ely's Combat Authorization Act could be passed today, and even if the courts, defying most past practice, grew bold enough to rule on whether hostilities were imminent, there would be still another difficulty; as Ely put it: ''When we got down to cases and a court remanded the issue to Congress, would Congress actually be able to follow through and face the issue whether the war in question should be permitted to proceed? Admittedly, the matter is not entirely free from doubt.''

It's worth thinking about how best to tie Ulysses to the mast. But the problem with legislative schemes designed to force Congress to ''do the right thing'' is that Congress seems always to have one hand free. Statutory schemes designed to precommit legislators to particular procedures do not have a terribly promising track record. Historically, many such schemes have proved little more effective than a dieter's note on the refrigerator. No mere statute can truly bind a future Congress, and in areas ranging from agricultural policy to balanced budgets, Congress has rarely hesitated to undo past agreements in the pursuit of short-term political advantage.

113

If checks on executive power are to be restored, we will need far less Red Team–Blue Team politicking—and many more legislators than we currently have who are willing to put the Constitution ahead of party loyalty. That in turn will depend on a public willing to hold legislators accountable for ducking war powers fights and ceding vast authority to the president. Congressional courage of the kind needed to reclaim the war power will not be forthcoming unless and until American citizens demand it.

Suggested Readings

Ely, John Hart. *War and Responsibility: Constitutional Lessons of Vietnam and Its Aftermath.* Princeton, NJ: Princeton University Press, 1993.

Fisher, Louis. *Presidential War Power.* Lawrence: University Press of Kansas, 1995.

———. *Congressional Abdication on War and Spending.* College Station, TX: Texas A&M University Press, 2000.

Healy, Gene. *The Cult of the Presidency.* Washington: Cato Institute, 2008.

Levy, Leonard W. *Original Intent and the Framers' Constitution.* New York: Macmillan, 1988.

—Prepared by Gene Healy

11. Tort and Class-Action Reform

State legislatures should

- enact punitive damages reforms,
- eliminate joint and several liability,
- require government to pay all legal costs if it loses a civil case, and
- illegalize contingency fees paid by government to private attorneys.

Congress should

- constrain courts' long-arm jurisdiction over out-of-state defendants,
- enact a federal choice-of-law rule for multistate litigants in product liability cases, and
- implement multistate class-action reforms.

After a Florida jury conjured up punitive damages of $145 billion for a class of smokers, even anti-tobacco advocates were incredulous. Then, two years later, a California jury recommended a $28 billion treasure trove for a single claimant. So it goes. Not just tobacco, but guns, asbestos, and a cross section of American industry have become victims of an unrestrained tort system.

The Pacific Research Institute estimates that the cost of that system in 2006 exceeded $865 billion—less than 15 percent of which was paid to injured claimants. To put the number in perspective, the budget that year for Iraq and Afghanistan was roughly $500 billion—about 58 percent of tort costs. For a family of four, the annual ''tort tax'' was $9,827—

115

mostly reflected in higher prices. In a global marketplace, that means noncompetitive products, lower profits, fewer jobs, and reduced wealth.

When costs explode, proposals for reform are never far behind. As a result, we have been deluged by congressional schemes to ban lawsuits against gun makers and fast-food distributors, cap medical malpractice awards, and otherwise enlist the federal government in the tort reform battle. But no matter how worthwhile a goal may be, if there is no constitutional authority to pursue it, the federal government must step aside and leave the matter to the states or to private citizens.

Can Tort Reform and Federalism Coexist?

In its quest for constitutional authority, Congress often invokes the commerce clause. Yet consider medical malpractice, for example. No doubt we have a nationwide mess. But not every national problem is a federal problem. A majority of states have capped damages, and virtually all states have considered various other reforms. Mississippi is a case in point. Because of "jackpot justice," doctors fled, insurance companies pulled out, and fewer companies opted to maintain in-state facilities. The result: new laws that capped pain-and-suffering, medical malpractice, and punitive damages.

That's an example of tort reform compatible with federalism. Nowhere in the Constitution, however, is there a federal power to set rules that control lawsuits by in-state plaintiffs against in-state doctors for in-state malpractice. The substantive rules of tort law are not commerce and they are not the business of Congress. On those occasions when a state attempts to expand its sovereignty beyond its borders, federal procedural reforms—about which more in a moment—can curb any abuses.

State-Based Tort Reform

With that in mind, here are six remedies that the states can implement without federal involvement. The first three are directed at punitive damage awards; the final three apply to tort reform more broadly.

First, take the dollar decision away from the jury. For instance, the jury might be instructed to vote yes or no on an award of punitive damages. Then a judge would set the amount in accordance with preset guidelines.

Second, limit punitive damages to cases involving actual malice, intentional wrongdoing, or gross negligence. Whatever the heightened standard, the idea is that accidental injuries arising out of ordinary, garden-variety negligence are unlikely to respond to deterrence for which punitive damages are designed.

Third, states could implement procedural guarantees like those available under criminal law. Punitive awards serve the same purposes as criminal penalties, but defendants are not accorded the protections applicable in a criminal case. Among those protections is a higher burden of proof than the usual civil standard, which is preponderance of the evidence. Also, there is no double jeopardy protection in civil cases. Current rules allow punitive damage awards for the same conduct in multiple lawsuits. And there is no protection against coerced self-incrimination, which criminal defendants can avoid by pleading the Fifth Amendment. In civil cases, compulsory discovery can be self-incriminating.

Fourth, states should dispense with joint and several liability. That's the "deep pockets" rule that permits plaintiffs to collect all of a damage award from any one of multiple defendants, even if the paying defendant was responsible for only a small fraction of the harm. The better rule is to apportion damages in accordance with the defendants' degree of culpability.

Fifth, government should pay attorneys' fees when a government unit is the losing party in a civil lawsuit. In the criminal sphere, defendants are already entitled to court-appointed counsel if necessary; they are also protected by the requirement for proof beyond reasonable doubt and by the Fifth and Sixth Amendments to the Constitution. No corresponding safeguards against abusive public-sector litigation exist in civil cases. By limiting the rule to cases involving government plaintiffs, access to the courts is preserved for less affluent, private plaintiffs seeking remedies for legitimate grievances. But defendants in government suits will be able to resist baseless cases that are brought by the state solely to ratchet up the pressure for a large financial settlement.

Sixth, contingency fee contracts between private lawyers and government entities should be prohibited. When private lawyers subcontract their services to the government, they bear the same responsibility as government lawyers. They are public servants beholden to all citizens, including the defendant, and their overriding objective is to seek justice. Imagine a state attorney's receiving a contingency fee for each indictment, or a state trooper's receiving a bonus for each speeding ticket. The potential for corruption is enormous.

Federal Procedural Tort Reform

Aside from state-imposed reforms, there are at least three areas where the federal government can intervene without offending long-established state prerogatives. The guiding principle is that federal legislatures and courts are authorized to act when there is a high risk that states will appropriate wealth from the citizens of other states. One federal reform consistent with that principle is to amend the rules that control state exercise of so-called long-arm jurisdiction over out-of-state businesses.

Congress could, for example, preclude a local court from hearing a case unless the defendant engages directly in business activities within the state. A company's mere awareness that the stream of commerce could sweep its product into a particular state should not be sufficient to confer jurisdiction. Instead, jurisdiction should be triggered only if the company purposely directs its product to the state. A sensible rule like that would give firms an exit option—that is, they could withdraw from a state and thereby avoid the risk of a runaway jury, even if a product somehow ends up in-state. Today, federal limits on long-arm statutes remain lax or ambiguous. For that reason, oppressive state tort laws remain a threat to out-of-state defendants.

There is a second federal reform that is compatible with federalist principles: a federal choice-of-law rule for product liability cases. Here's how that might work.

Basically, choice of law is the doctrine that determines which state's laws control the litigation. Generally, plaintiffs can and will select the most favorable forum state on the basis, in part, of its tort laws. But suppose a federal choice-of-law rule were enacted for cases in which the plaintiff and defendant are from different states. Suppose further that the applicable law were based on the state where the manufacturer was located. A manufacturer could decide where to locate, and its decision would dictate the applicable legal rules. Consumers, in turn, would evaluate those rules when deciding whether to buy a particular manufacturer's product. If a manufacturer were located in a state that did not provide adequate legal remedies for defective products, consumers would buy from rival companies.

Would there be a race to the bottom by manufacturers searching for the most defendant-friendly tort law? Maybe. But more likely, states would balance their interest in attracting manufacturers against the interest of in-state consumers, who want tougher product liability laws. In effect, healthy competition among the states would enlist federalism as part of the solution rather than raise federalism as an excuse for failing to arrive at a solution.

Class-Action Reform

The third set of procedural reforms that Congress can and should enact is aimed at multistate class actions. In the last 20 years, class actions have morphed from a rarely used procedural device, designed to litigate a large number of unusually similar claims, into a commonly used device for coercing a settlement from companies that often have done nothing wrong.

The 108th Congress attempted to address that problem in the Class Action Fairness Act—by giving defendants the power to remove some class suits from state to federal courts. But after three years of experience, it's clear that CAFA is an incomplete solution to the class-action problem. Congress can do more to directly address key problems associated with modern class actions at the state and federal levels. Here are seven suggestions:

First, CAFA says a class action can be removed to federal court so long as at least one-third of the class members reside outside the state where the suit was filed and the amount at stake in the class action exceeds $5 million. CAFA does not explicitly say, however, whether plaintiffs or defendants bear the burden of proving that those requirements have been met. That threshold question is generating an enormous amount of unnecessary litigation. Even worse, many courts have held that CAFA places the burden of meeting those requirements on defendants—creating, in effect, a presumption against removal under CAFA. Congress should enact a presumption *in favor* of removal, by explicitly providing that plaintiffs bear the burden of showing that the conditions for removal *have not* been met.

Second, CAFA does nothing to solve a thorny problem that often occurs after a federal court refuses to certify a class. Imagine that a federal judge decides that a suit doesn't meet the requirements for class treatment. Currently, nothing prevents class members from asking a second court to certify the very same claims as a class action. As a result, one federal court's decision to deny certification doesn't end the cycle of litigation. That's perverse and unnecessary: as the Seventh Circuit has recognized, the Constitution allows a federal court to "enjoin," or bar, efforts to relitigate the merits of certification in another court, so long as class members were adequately represented when the certification question was initially decided against them.

Unfortunately, while the Constitution allows federal courts to stop class members from shopping their failed lawsuit to other courts, Congress hasn't expressly given federal courts a green light to do so. Some courts,

119

therefore, think they are powerless to stop would-be class members from seeking a second bite at the apple. Congress should clarify that federal courts may enjoin putative members of a rejected class, who have been adequately represented, from relitigating the question of whether their claims can be certified.

Third, CAFA doesn't stop plaintiffs' lawyers and defendants from collusive forum shopping. Acting jointly, they can keep suits in state courts that are willing to approve a sweetheart settlement—ensuring that the lawyers get a big payoff, defendants get a slap on the wrist, and absent class members recover little or nothing. Congress can prevent such collusion by giving absent class members, as well as defendants, the right to remove multistate class actions to federal court.

Fourth, Congress should do more than plug gaps in CAFA. It should rethink the class device itself. Currently, class-action rules create a presumption that individuals out of court, who have not affirmed their connection to the class, favor being "represented" by a trial lawyer who files a class action, supposedly on their behalf. That presumption is based on nothing more than the trial lawyer's say-so. Considering that modern class-action lawyers often claim to "represent" the interests of thousands—or even millions—of people, the presumption is a legal fiction. Many litigants have no idea that their interests are being represented in court, and are silent pawns of plaintiffs' lawyers seeking to coerce settlements and line their pockets. The rule should be changed, by requiring would-be litigants to affirmatively "opt in" to a class action (for example, by mailing a consent form to the court) before they can be counted as part of the "class."

Fifth, Congress should prohibit class actions that deprive defendants of their due process right to assert specific defenses against individual plaintiffs. Presently, classes are certified even when a governing statute or common-law rule requires that key elements of proof—such as reliance, causation, or damages—be shown on an individual basis. That means trial lawyers can use the class device to combine tens of thousands of factually dissimilar claims into one proceeding, making it impossible for defendants to adequately smoke out and identify weak or meritless individual claims. Congress should enact a rule stating that, unless a federal statute clearly provides otherwise, liability in class actions arising under federal law requires case-by-case proof of the elements of each class member's claim.

Sixth, Congress must ensure that only meritorious class actions become certified. Class certification decisions are made very early—before plaintiffs have demonstrated that they have evidence to support their allegations.

That allows trial lawyers to game the system by including numerous meritless claims in one lawsuit, in the hope that corporate defendants will settle before the suit goes to trial. That's not a bad strategy, given the stakes involved: even when faced with clearly weak claims—given the enormity of large classes, which can comprise millions of individuals— few corporations want to bet the company that a jury will get the case right. Congress should nip meritless class actions in the bud by providing that classes may be certified only after the class "representative"—the main plaintiff—is able to make a preliminary factual showing that he or she has a reasonable likelihood of success.

Seventh, Congress must deal with class actions that use flawed statistics. Class actions generally must be proved using evidence "common" to all class members, but some federal statutes allow statistical sampling to prove injuries to a large group. Where this is so, plaintiffs have often used shoddy statistics purporting to show that all class members suffered the same injury. Under current law, unreliable expert evidence cannot be submitted to a jury. Even so, a number of courts have held that judges can certify a class without rigorously reviewing the reliability of plaintiffs' statistics. Congress should, at a minimum, provide that plaintiffs' statistical evidence must meet, before a class action can go forward, the same demanding reliability standards imposed on expert evidence sent to a jury.

Conclusion

When a state exercises jurisdiction beyond its borders or discriminates against out-of-state businesses, federal intervention may occasionally be appropriate. For the most part, however, the states have reformed and are continuing to reform their civil justice systems. Under those circumstances, time-honored principles of federalism dictate that each state exercises dominion over its substantive tort law. Congress can then focus on procedural matters. In that regard, we suggest three reforms: (1) tighten long-arm jurisdiction over out-of-state defendants, (2) implement a federal choice-of-law regime, and (3) restructure the rules for multistate class actions.

Suggested Readings

American Tort Reform Foundation. "Judicial Hellholes 2007." www.atra.org/reports/hellholes/report.pdf.

Epstein, Richard A. "Class Actions: Aggregation, Amplification, and Distortion." *University of Chicago Legal Forum* 475 (2003).

Krauss, Michael I. "Product Liability and Game Theory: One More Trip to the Choice-of-Law Well." *Brigham Young University Law Review* 759 (2002).

Levy, Robert A. *Shakedown: How Corporations, Government, and Trial Lawyers Abuse the Judicial Process*. Washington: Cato Institute, 2004.

McQuillan, Lawrence J., and others. "Jackpot Justice: The True Cost of America's Tort System." Pacific Research Institute, 2007. http://liberty.pacificresearch.org/docLib/20070327_Jackpot_Justice.pdf.

Moller, Mark K. "Controlling Unconstitutional Class Actions: A Blueprint for Future Lawsuit Reform." Cato Institute Policy Analysis no. 546, June 27, 2005.

Nagareda, Richard. "Bootstrapping in Choice of Law after the Class Action Fairness Act." *University of Missouri-Kansas City Law Review* 74, no. 661 (2006).

Redish, Martin. "Class Actions and the Democratic Difficulty: Rethinking the Intersection of Private Litigation and Public Goals." *University of Chicago Legal Forum* 71 (2003).

Redish, Martin, and Nathan D. Larsen. "Class Actions, Litigant Autonomy, and the Foundations of Procedural Due Process." *California Law Review* 95, no. 1573 (2007).

Tager, Evan M. "The Constitutional Limitations on Class Actions." *Mealey's Litigation Report: Class Actions,* 2001. www.appellate.net/articles/Tagercom.pdf.

—Prepared by Robert A. Levy and Mark Moller

HEALTH CARE AND ENTITLEMENT REFORM

12. Medicare

Congress should

- establish, in all parts of Medicare, premiums proportionate to lifetime earnings;
- allow seniors to opt out of Medicare completely, without losing Social Security benefits;
- give Medicare enrollees a means-tested, risk-adjusted voucher with which they may purchase the health plan of their choice;
- limit the growth of Medicare vouchers to the level of inflation;
- allow workers to save their Medicare taxes in a personal, inheritable account dedicated to retirement health expenses; and
- fund any "transition costs" by reducing other government spending, not by raising taxes.

Medicare is the federal entitlement program that provides health insurance to the elderly and disabled. Despite its popularity with seniors, the disabled, and those who might otherwise have to care for them, Medicare infringes on the right of workers to control their retirement savings and on the freedom of seniors to control their own health care. Medicare has done enormous damage to the U.S. health care sector and to individual liberty. Absent congressional action, that damage will only increase over time. Medicare reform is the nation's highest health-policy priority.

Rising Costs and Restricted Freedom

Congress created Medicare in 1965 on premises both morally suspect and impractical. (The same legislation created Medicaid; see Chapter 13.) One premise is that government should tax young workers to pay for the health care needs of their elders, many of whom do not need it and many of whom never contributed to the program. The first generation of Medicare beneficiaries essentially got something for nothing, receiving subsidies without having contributed to the program. As if to celebrate this inequity, the first Medicare beneficiary was a man who neither contributed to Medicare nor needed it: former president Harry S. Truman. Since Medicare's enactment, each generation of seniors has demanded that its children and grandchildren pay the debt it is owed by its elders. Yet successive generations of seniors have voted themselves greater subsidies to be financed by younger taxpayers. The most recent example is Medicare Part D, the prescription drug benefit created by Congress and President Bush in 2003. Less expensive benefit expansions occur routinely, without congressional action, every time Medicare approves an expensive new technology for coverage. In 2004, the Bush administration unilaterally announced that Medicare would cover obesity treatments. The growing generosity of Medicare benefits is the principal reason why Medicare has been responsible for at least a dozen tax increases in its 43-year history. Medicare thus enables each generation to extract more from its children and grandchildren than it gave to its parents and grandparents.

Medicare's obligations and financing structure are unsustainable. A number of factors will fuel growth in Medicare spending in the coming years. Demographic trends will reduce the number of workers available to finance Medicare relative to the number of beneficiaries. According to Medicare's trustees, the ratio will fall from about 4 workers per beneficiary in 2003 to about 2.4 workers per beneficiary in 2030 and will continue to fall until there are only 2 workers per beneficiary in 2078. Health care costs will continue to climb. In 2003, the Congressional Budget Office estimated that 30 percent of Medicare's future growth would be due to society's aging, while 70 percent would be due to the rising cost of health care. Existing revenue streams for Medicare are insufficient to keep the promises that Congress has made to future beneficiaries. Medicare's trustees estimate that Congress would need to put over $80 trillion in an interest-bearing account in 2008 to cover those future funding gaps. In 2008, the entire economic output of the United States was less than $15 trillion. The $700 billion bailout of the financial sector enacted by Congress in late 2008 is less than 1 percent of the amount required to bail out Medicare. The Congressional Budget Office estimates that if Congress were to meet that shortfall by raising income taxes, federal individual income tax rates would roughly double by 2050, with the top marginal rate reaching 66 percent. The CBO further estimates that tax increases of that magnitude could suppress national income by as much as 20 percent.

A second suspect premise is that participation in Medicare is voluntary. In fact, Medicare greatly restricts the freedom of workers, seniors, and entrepreneurs. Medicare crowds out other health insurance options for seniors and forces seniors who decline Medicare benefits to forfeit all past and future Social Security benefits. It prohibits participating providers from delivering Medicare-covered services to beneficiaries on a private basis, an affront to the right of patients and doctors to make mutually beneficial exchanges that affect no one else. And of course funding Medicare is hardly voluntary; Americans are required to pay the 2.9 percent Medicare payroll tax and other federal taxes, which finance the program through general revenues.

A third premise is that government can or should devise a one-size-fits-all package of health insurance benefits for tens of millions of senior citizens. To reduce opposition within the health care industry and ensure enactment, Medicare's sponsors modeled Medicare coverage on Blue Cross Blue Shield coverage as it existed in 1965. The industry wanted Medicare to pay physicians on a fee-for-service basis and to have little ability to refuse payment for low-value or inefficient services. That sounds appealing on the surface—few people like the idea of having government ration medical care. Yet Medicare ends up committing the opposite sin—wasting money on useless services—which can be just as harmful as government rationing. There is considerable evidence that Medicare wastes vast sums of money on low-value services and that fee-for-service payment is a prime contributor to such waste. Researchers at Dartmouth Medical School estimate that 30 percent of Medicare spending does nothing to make beneficiaries healthier or happier. That suggests that Medicare spends about $150 billion each year—roughly the entire economic output of South Carolina—on medical services of no discernible value. Political pressure from the industry prevents Congress or the Medicare bureaucracy from dealing with those problems. (Every dollar of wasteful Medicare spending is a dollar of income to *somebody*, and that somebody typically has a lobbyist.) Having locked in a payment system based on fee-for-service reimbursement and a fragmented delivery system, Medicare suppresses competition from alternative payment and delivery systems (see also Chapter 15, "Health Care Regulation").

When Medicare was enacted, it effectively destroyed a large and growing private market for health insurance for seniors that would have enabled greater experimentation and competition. By 1962, an estimated 60 percent of seniors had voluntary health insurance coverage, up from 31 percent in 1952. Today, seniors essentially have only one place to go for health insurance. They may augment their Medicare coverage by enrolling in a private Medicare Advantage health plan or by purchasing Medicare supplemental or "Medigap" coverage. Medigap plans typically make seniors even less price sensitive and more likely to overconsume care. Medicare Advantage plans (previously known as Medicare + Choice plans) tend to provide an unstable alternative to traditional Medicare, as Congress frequently adjusts payment levels and private plans enter and exit the program on the basis of the (perceived) adequacy of those payments.

Supporters claim that Medicare is more efficient than private insurance because it has lower administrative costs. To reach that conclusion, they ignore many of Medicare's administrative costs, in particular the "excess burden" or reduced economic output caused by Medicare taxes. Those costs are estimated at 20 to 100 percent of Medicare's expenditures, dwarfing any administrative costs of private firms. And decades of reports by government watchdogs demonstrate that the main way Medicare avoids administrative costs is by failing to scrutinize claims to prevent fraud or to ensure value. The Government Accountability Office found that in 2004 Medicare call centers answered providers' billing questions accurately and completely only 4 percent of the time. It is no wonder, then, that the Department of Health and Human Services reports improper Medicare payments of $12.1 billion in 2001. Medicare's avoidance of administrative expenses is a vice, not a virtue.

Reform of Priorities

Medicare should be policymakers' top health care priority, and the program demands immediate reform. Congress should focus immediately on two steps. First, it should charge premiums for all parts of Medicare, charging higher premiums to seniors with higher lifetime earnings (i.e., "means-tested" premiums). Generally, seniors pay premiums only for Part B (physician insurance) and Part D (prescription drug coverage), not for Part A (hospital insurance). Those combined premiums currently account for about 13 percent of total Medicare spending. Congress should increase premiums for high earners until premiums cover at least 25 percent of total outlays.

Increasing premiums on high-income earners creates a problem: it discourages high-income seniors from working by penalizing them with higher premiums. Charging higher premiums to seniors with high *lifetime* incomes can mitigate that problem. (If *past* earnings are the primary factor influencing Medicare premiums, strategic behavior becomes more difficult. Seniors would be unable to alter their past earnings, and reducing their current earnings would have less of an effect on their premiums. The Social Security Administration already possesses the data necessary to calculate seniors' lifetime earnings.)

Second, Congress should allow seniors to opt out of Medicare without losing their Social Security benefits.

Broader means-testing and permission for seniors to opt out of Medicare would achieve only modest progress in shoring up the program's finances and restoring seniors' freedom. They would have an enormous effect, however, on the politics of Medicare. As well-to-do seniors see their premiums rise, many will decide that Medicare is a bad deal and will leave the program. If they are allowed to retain their Social Security benefits, even more will exit the program. Today, Medicare covers nearly all seniors, whose medical care is heavily subsidized by younger workers. Reducing those subsidies, and reducing the share of seniors dependent on Medicare, will change the political dynamics of the program and build a constituency among seniors for further and more substantial Medicare reforms.

Critics will object to broader means-testing and permission for seniors to opt out of Medicare for those very reasons. Yet the history of Medicare is one of politically powerful seniors uniting against the interests of younger workers. If such reforms can improve Medicare's financial picture as well as weaken the political coalition that persistently and increasingly raids the paychecks of working Americans, then those are two arguments in their favor.

Next, Congress should end federal micromanagement of the health care sector and replace Medicare with a prefunded system where workers invest their Medicare taxes in personal accounts dedicated to their health needs in retirement. There is no need for Congress to dictate what health insurance benefits seniors should obtain or how physicians, hospitals, and so forth should be paid. Congress should grant all Medicare beneficiaries a voucher that they may use to purchase the health plan of their choice. Overall, the amount that Congress allots to Medicare vouchers should grow no faster—and could grow more slowly—than overall inflation. To enable the poor and sick to obtain a minimum level of coverage, Congress could provide larger vouchers to them, and smaller vouchers to healthy and wealthy beneficiaries. Seniors who desire more expensive health insurance could supplement their vouchers with private funds, just as they do now with

Medicare Advantage and Medigap plans. Medicare vouchers would let the market—rather than the Medicare bureaucracy—determine prices, payment systems, delivery systems, and how to reward quality.

Finally, Congress should stop the looting of the young by the old. Congress should allow workers to put their full 2.9 percent Medicare payroll tax in a personal savings account dedicated to their retirement health needs. Workers could invest those funds in a number of vehicles and augment those funds in retirement with other savings. This proposal for Medicare personal accounts is similar to many Social Security reform proposals (see Chapter 17).

One similarity is that diverting workers' tax payments into personal accounts makes it difficult to pay current benefits. Congress can make up much of those "transition costs" by cutting Medicare outlays. As noted earlier, an estimated 30 percent of Medicare outlays do nothing to improve beneficiaries' health or make them any happier, which suggests that Medicare spending could be reduced by as much without harming seniors' health. Identifying and eliminating those wasteful expenditures will be extremely difficult, and Congress has proved spectacularly inept at the task. Yet competition can achieve what Congress cannot: giving seniors vouchers and the freedom to make their own health care decisions would encourage them to select health plans that eliminate those unnecessary costs. In giving vouchers to seniors, Congress could cut overall Medicare outlays by as much as 30 percent, again with little if any adverse effect on health outcomes. If Congress is unable or unwilling to cover all transition costs by reducing Medicare outlays, it should make up the gap by cutting other government spending (see Chapter 4)—not by raising taxes.

Suggested Readings

Brown, Kent Masterson. "The Freedom to Spend Your Own Money on Medical Care: A Common Casualty of Universal Coverage." Cato Institute Policy Analysis no. 601, October 15, 2007.

Cannon, Michael F. "Bill Gates Doesn't Need Any Help from Younger Workers." In *Should Medicare Be Means-Tested? A Symposium.* Minneapolis: Center of the American Experiment, 2007.

Cannon, Michael F., and Alain Enthoven. "Markets Beat Government on Medical Errors." *American Spectator*, May 13, 2008. http://www.cato.org/pub_display.php?pub_id=9394.

Cannon, Michael F., and Michael D. Tanner. *Healthy Competition: What's Holding Back Health Care and How to Free It.* Washington: Cato Institute, 2007.

Christianson, Jon B., and George Avery. "Prepaid Group Practice and Health Care Policy." In *Toward a 21st Century Health System: The Contributions and Promise of Prepaid Group Practice,* edited by Alain C. Enthoven and Laura A. Tollen. San Francisco: Jossey-Bass, 2004.

Hyman, David A. *Medicare Meets Mephistopheles.* Washington: Cato Institute, 2006.

Kling, Arnold. *Crisis of Abundance: Rethinking How We Pay for Health Care.* Washington: Cato Institute, 2006.

Pauly, Mark V. *Markets without Magic: How Competition Might Save Medicare.* Washington: American Enterprise Institute, 2008.

Saving, Thomas S., and Andrew Rettenmaier. *The Diagnosis and Treatment of Medicare.* Washington: American Enterprise Institute, 2007.

Zycher, Ben. "Comparing Public and Private Health Insurance: Would A Single-Payer System Save Enough to Cover the Uninsured?" Manhattan Institute Medical Progress Report no. 5, October 2007.

—Prepared by Michael F. Cannon

13. Medicaid and SCHIP

State legislators should

- deregulate health care and health insurance, and
- demand that the federal government grant them flexibility, *not* additional funds, to administer their Medicaid and SCHIP programs.

Congress should

- reform Medicare and the tax treatment of health insurance,
- deregulate health care and health insurance,
- eliminate any federal entitlement to Medicaid or SCHIP benefits,
- freeze each state's Medicaid and SCHIP funding at 2009 levels,
- give states total flexibility to use Medicaid and SCHIP funds to achieve a few broad goals, and
- eventually phase out all federal funding of Medicaid and SCHIP.

Americans want to help the needy obtain medical care. Our first obligation to the needy, however, is not to increase their numbers. Thus, the first step lawmakers should take to assist the needy is to eliminate subsidies and regulations that impede market competition. By making medical care of ever-increasing quality available to ever-increasing numbers of people, a free market would reduce the number of people needing assistance.

No matter how well a free market expands quality and access, however, there will always be seriously ill people who cannot afford medical care, or who could have purchased health insurance but chose not to do so. This chapter discusses how the federal and state governments might better address that problem.

The Samaritan's Dilemma

However we choose to help those in need, we confront what economists call "the Samaritan's dilemma": any effort to help the needy will induce others to take advantage of that assistance. Coined by Nobel Prize–winning economist James Buchanan, that term derives from the New Testament story of the Good Samaritan, who came to the aid of a traveler who had been beaten by thieves. Buchanan reasons that if the Samaritan decides to assist more unlucky travelers, travelers would likely take less care to avoid thieves and other hazards. Providing assistance to people can induce them to take less care of themselves.

For a modern manifestation of the Samaritan's dilemma, consider that in 1996 Congress reduced federal welfare benefits and cut millions of recipients from the welfare rolls. At the time, many predicted that cutting welfare would increase poverty. The opposite occurred. When people left the welfare rolls, poverty fell—often dramatically—for every racial category and age group, including children. In every year following 1996, the poverty rate has remained lower than at any point in the 17 years leading up to welfare reform. That fact suggests that the federal government had induced otherwise able-bodied people to become dependent on welfare.

The Samaritan's dilemma calls attention to the certainty that providing too little assistance will result in unnecessary suffering, but providing too much assistance will increase the burden of charity while it reduces society's ability to bear that burden. When assistance becomes more generous, more people will depend on it, and fewer will contribute to the economy and to charity, both public and private.

The Samaritan's dilemma is ubiquitous and unavoidable. It plagues both public and private charity.

To be effective, then, charitable efforts must attempt to distinguish between the truly needy and those who could care for themselves. No entity, public or private, can do that perfectly. Yet some approaches are more effective than others. Private charities, such as Habitat for Humanity, have the incentive and the ability to ensure that their resources assist only the truly needy. If it did not, Habitat could lose funding when donors learn their contributions are going to able-bodied people who don't need assistance.

Government, in contrast, has little ability or incentive to navigate carefully the Samaritan's dilemma. Politicians must craft broad eligibility rules for government welfare programs. Typically, these take the form of a legal entitlement to benefits for anyone who meets certain criteria. The bureaucrats who administer those programs must treat all qualifying individuals equally. If the bureaucracy identifies beneficiaries who technically meet those criteria, but nevertheless need no assistance, the bureaucrats have little ability or incentive to exclude them. In fact, they have the opposite incentive since their careers depend on a thriving welfare program. Even if the bureaucrats were to exclude those non-needy beneficiaries, the beneficiaries could sue the government for withholding benefits to which they are legally entitled. Unlike private charity, public charities rarely see their funding reduced for providing assistance to those who don't need it, because taxpayers don't have the choice to withdraw their "contributions." Either they pay their taxes, or they go to jail. As a result, government charities, such as cash assistance, Medicaid, and the State Children's Health Insurance Program, tend to err on the side of providing too much assistance and subsidizing people who don't need it.

There are ways that government can make medical care and health insurance affordable for low-income Americans that do not involve a Samaritan's dilemma. Federal and state governments can reform Medicare (see Chapter 12) and the tax treatment of health care (see Chapter 14), as well as deregulate medicine (see Chapter 15) and health insurance (see Chapter 16).

Government can better navigate the Samaritan's dilemma, however, by reforming and reducing the size of Medicaid and the State Children's Health Insurance Program.

Medicaid

The federal government and state and territorial governments jointly administer Medicaid—or more precisely, the 56 separate Medicaid programs throughout the United States. Medicaid participation is ostensibly voluntary for states, if not for taxpayers. States that wish to participate (all states do) must provide a federally mandated set of health benefits to a federally mandated population of eligible individuals. In return, each state receives federal funds to administer its program. On average, 57 percent of Medicaid funding comes from the federal government and 43 percent comes from the states. States can make their Medicaid benefits more generous than the federal government requires and can also extend eligibility to more people than the federal government requires. For beneficiaries, Medicaid is an entitlement. So long as they meet the eligibility criteria, they can receive benefits.

According to the Kaiser Family Foundation, in 2005 Medicaid enrollment reached nearly 60 million individuals. Medicaid primarily serves four low-income groups: mothers and their children, the disabled, the elderly, and those needing long-term care. The elderly and disabled comprised 24 percent of beneficiaries, but accounted for 70 percent of expenditures on benefits. Half the enrollees were children, while other adults comprised the remaining 26 percent of enrollees. Those two groups—children and nonelderly, nondisabled adults—comprised 76 percent of enrollees but accounted for 30 percent of expenditures on benefits.

The federal government's method for distributing Medicaid funds to states encourages fraud, creates perverse incentives for state officials, and encourages states to expand their programs to people who don't need assistance. The federal government provides Medicaid funds to each state in proportion to what the state itself spends. The more a state spends on its Medicaid program, the more it receives from the federal government. States receive at least $1 from the federal government for every dollar the state spends. Some states, however, receive as much as $3 for each dollar they put forward. Thus, states can double, triple, or even quadruple their money by spending more on Medicaid. Indeed, states that use fraudulent schemes, such as *pretending* to increase Medicaid spending in order to draw down federal matching funds, can increase their take even further. The federal Medicaid "match" is open-ended; Congress will match any amount a state puts forward.

The availability of matching federal funds creates perverse incentives for state officials to underfund other priorities. Spending $1 on police buys $1 of police protection, but spending $1 on Medicaid buys $2 or more of medical benefits. The federal match also makes lawmakers extremely reluctant to cut Medicaid spending. Cutting $1 of police protection causes $1 of political pain, but results in $1 of budget savings. Obtaining just $1 of budgetary savings through Medicaid cuts requires inflicting $2 to $4 worth of political pain.

Those perverse incentives combine to encourage states to expand their programs to millions of non-needy recipients. For example:

- According to the Urban Institute, about one-fifth of adults and children who are *eligible* for Medicaid nonetheless obtain private coverage. The fact that some 20 percent of those who fall within states' Medicaid eligibility criteria obtain private coverage suggests that many who are enrolled could obtain private coverage as well.
- Middle-class families frequently use Medicaid to pay for nursing-home and other long-term care expenses of their elderly members. A cottage industry of estate planners has emerged to help such

individuals artificially impoverish themselves to become eligible for Medicaid. Many elderly Medicaid enrollees could have purchased private long-term care insurance. Economists Jeffrey Brown of the University of Illinois at Urbana-Champaign and Amy Finkelstein of MIT estimate that Medicaid's long-term care benefits discourage 66 to 90 percent of seniors from purchasing such insurance on the private market.

- The 1996 welfare reform law also cut eligibility to Medicaid for noncitizen immigrants. Harvard economist George Borjas found that, again contrary to expectations, health insurance coverage among noncitizen immigrants *increased* after their eligibility for Medicaid was reduced—an effect that could not be explained by the robust economy of the 1990s. Borjas argues that affected immigrants increased their work effort and found jobs with health benefits.
- Economists Jonathan Gruber of MIT and Kosali Simon of Cornell University estimate that when Medicaid expands eligibility to new groups, "the number of privately insured falls by about 60 percent as much as the number of publicly insured rises." That suggests that many people substitute Medicaid coverage for private coverage.

Medicaid's poor navigation of the Samaritan's dilemma has even permeated popular culture. The 2004 Oscar-winning film *Million Dollar Baby* showcased two forms of Medicaid abuse: One of the film's characters declined the gift of a new house so she could remain eligible for Medicaid (rather than sell the house and purchase her medication herself). Later, the family of a wealthy invalid encouraged the invalid to transfer her assets to the family so that taxpayers (through Medicaid) would pay the wealthy invalid's medical expenses.

Indeed, the more a state expands its Medicaid program, the more difficult it becomes for everyone to afford private insurance. Economists Mark Duggan of the University of Maryland and Fiona Scott Morton of Yale University find Medicaid's drug-pricing controls effectively increase by 13 percent the prices that private purchasers pay for prescription drugs. If grandma's medications cost her $1,000 per year, some $117 of that is a hidden tax attributable to Medicaid.

The State Children's Health Insurance Program

What is true of Medicaid is true of the State Children's Health Insurance Program. Congress created SCHIP in 1997 to expand health insurance coverage among children in families that earned too much to be eligible for Medicaid but too little to afford private health insurance.

The federal government funds state SCHIP programs much as it funds Medicaid, but with two main differences. First, states receive a larger federal match under SCHIP than under Medicaid. Overall, the federal government funds 69 percent of the cost of state SCHIP programs, whereas states forward only 31 percent. Each state can *at least* triple its money by spending on SCHIP. Some states can "pull down" $4 or $5 from the federal government—really, from taxpayers in other states—for each $1 they spend on SCHIP. Second, the federal government limits the overall amount it will contribute to each state's SCHIP program, though that cap is not as binding as it may appear. States such as Georgia sometimes spend all their federal SCHIP funds before the end of the fiscal year, and then petition the federal government for additional funds. Another way to describe those states' behavior is to say that they demand more money and dare Congress to throw sick children off the SCHIP rolls. Congress has repeatedly bailed out such states, effectively rewarding them for committing to spend more federal dollars than they were allowed.

As a result of these perverse incentives, states such as New Jersey have expanded SCHIP eligibility to children in families of four earning as much as $72,000 per year. New York proposed expanding the program to families of four earning $82,000 per year. The Bush administration subsequently refused to provide federal SCHIP funds for families earning over 250 percent of the federal poverty level (about $51,000 for a family of four) unless a state enrolls in Medicaid and SCHIP 95 percent of eligible individuals below that threshold. (The future of that directive is uncertain.) Compared with Medicaid, SCHIP targets families higher up the income scale, who are therefore more likely to have private health insurance. As a result, SCHIP leads to even greater "crowd-out" of private insurance than Medicaid. The Congressional Budget Office reports that by 2006, some 670,000 *adults* had enrolled in the program.

Federal and state politicians devote significant resources to these programs even though expanding coverage may not be the best way to improve the health of targeted populations. Although Medicaid and SCHIP probably do improve health outcomes, economists have found no evidence that these programs produce the greatest possible health improvements for the money spent. Economists Helen Levy and David Meltzer write:

> It is clear that expanding health insurance is not the only way to improve health. . . . Policies could also be aimed at factors that may fundamentally

contribute to poor health, such as poverty and low levels of education. There is no evidence at this time that money aimed at improving health would be better spent on expanding insurance coverage than on any of these other possibilities.

Major reform of Medicaid and SCHIP is long overdue.

Congress Should Reform Medicaid and SCHIP as It Reformed Welfare

It makes little sense for taxpayers to send money to Washington, so those funds can be sent back to their state capitol with strings and perverse incentives attached. Congress should devolve control over Medicaid and SCHIP to the states. The states can then decide whether and how to maintain their own programs, and could learn from the successes and failures of one another's experiments.

In 1996, Congress eliminated the federal entitlement to a welfare check; placed a five-year limit on cash assistance; and froze federal spending on such assistance, which was then distributed to the states in the form of block grants with fewer federal restrictions. The results were unquestionably positive. Welfare rolls were cut in half, and poverty reached the lowest point in a generation.

The federal government should emulate this success by eliminating federal entitlements to Medicaid and SCHIP benefits, freezing federal Medicaid and SCHIP spending at current levels, and distributing those funds to the states as unrestricted block grants. That would eliminate the perverse incentives that favor Medicaid and SCHIP spending over other state priorities, and that encourage states to defraud federal taxpayers. According to Congressional Budget Office projections, freezing Medicaid and SCHIP spending at 2009 levels would produce $979 billion in savings by 2018. That would significantly reduce or even eliminate future federal deficits. In time, the federal government should give the states full responsibility for Medicaid by eliminating federal Medicaid spending while concomitantly cutting federal taxes.

States should hasten these reforms by pressuring the federal government for maximum flexibility in administering their Medicaid programs. With unrestricted Medicaid block grants, states that wanted to spend more on their Medicaid programs would be free to raise taxes to do so, and vice versa.

Suggested Readings

Borjas, George J. "Welfare Reform, Labor Supply, and Health Insurance in the Immigrant Population." *Journal of Health Economics* 22 (November 2003).

Cannon, Michael F. "Medicaid's Unseen Costs." Cato Institute Policy Analysis no. 548, August 18, 2005.

———. "Sinking SCHIP: A First Step toward Stopping the Growth of Government Health Programs." Cato Institute Briefing Paper no. 99, September 13, 2007.

Cannon, Michael F., and Michael D. Tanner. *Healthy Competition: What's Holding Back Health Care and How to Free It.* Washington: Cato Institute, 2007.

Moses, Stephen. "Aging America's Achilles' Heel: Medicaid Long-Term Care." Cato Institute Policy Analysis no. 549, September 1, 2005.

—Prepared by Michael F. Cannon

14. The Tax Treatment of Health Care

> ## State legislators should
>
> - avoid creating special tax breaks for health insurance and medical care, and
> - eliminate existing tax breaks for health insurance and medical care while reducing the overall tax burden.
>
> ## Congress should
>
> - avoid refundable tax credits and other tax reforms that would create new categories of government spending;
> - replace all existing health-related tax breaks with a tax break for "large" health savings accounts; and
> - subsequently eliminate all tax breaks and reduce tax rates, by moving to a tax system that is neutral toward medical care and other forms of consumption.

Many presume the U.S. health care sector to be a free market because the private sector plays a greater role in it than in other advanced countries. It is an error, however, to assume that a market is free because it is private. Government can exert as much control over the private sector as the public sector, simply by ordering private individuals and firms to apply their resources toward the government's goals rather than their own. The fact that the U.S. health care sector is more "private" and less "public" than other nations' therefore tells us little about whether that market is free or unfree. What matters—what determines real as opposed to nominal ownership—is who controls the nation's medical resources.

With Tax Cuts Like This, Who Needs Tax Increases?

One of the most far-reaching and damaging ways that government controls private-sector health care is through tax laws. The federal govern-

141

ment exempts certain health-related uses of income from income and payroll taxes. The largest of these tax breaks is the exclusion of employer-sponsored health insurance from income and payroll taxes.

Workers who obtain health insurance through an employer pay no taxes on the "employer contribution" to the premium, and (thanks to Section 125 plans) many workers pay no taxes on the "employee contribution" either. The tax exclusion for employer-sponsored health insurance is the largest tax break in the federal tax code. In 2007, the revenue loss to the federal government was $147 billion, nearly twice the size of the projected loss from the second-largest revenue loser, the mortgage-interest deduction.

On an individual level, a worker's health insurance premiums and marginal tax rate determine the value of the tax break. Both factors vary across workers. In 2007, the average family premium for job-based coverage was roughly $12,000, to which employers "contributed" an average of roughly $9,000. A worker's overall marginal tax rate is determined by summing her marginal payroll tax rate for Social Security and Medicare (which can be as high as 15.3 percentage points), her marginal federal income tax rate (which may climb to 35 percentage points), and her marginal state income tax rate (which may climb as high as 10 percentage points).

Workers who do not obtain health insurance in an employment setting face a concomitant tax *penalty* when purchasing coverage. They must purchase insurance with income that has already been taxed at marginal rates as high as 50 percent. As a result of the tax break for employer-sponsored insurance, consumers who seek to choose their own health insurance plan must often pay twice as much for less coverage. That hefty tax penalty discourages many workers from seeking insurance on the "individual" market.

Even for workers with employer-sponsored health insurance, this tax break operates more like a tax increase. A survey by economists Michael Morrisey and John Cawley found that 91 percent of health economists agree that *the money that employers use to purchase health insurance comes out of workers' wages*. In other words, if employers were not providing health benefits to workers, they would have to return that $9,000 to workers in the form of higher cash wages. That implies that, rather than encourage employers or shareholders to spend their own money on workers' health benefits, this tax break instead gives employers control over a significant portion of their workers' earnings. As a result, employers effectively control 28 percent of the $2.5 trillion sloshing around America's health care sector. (See Figure 14.1.) Workers who wish to reclaim that money would probably have to find a different job that offers higher cash wages but no health benefits. (Employers seldom "cash out" workers who decline health benefits.) The workers would then have to pay taxes on that money, handing as much as $4,500 of it over to the government.

If government took $9,000 from workers and used it to provide workers with health insurance, we would call that a tax increase. Yet when government drives a wedge between workers and $9,000 of their earnings, we rather curiously call it a tax "cut."

The tax exclusion for employer-sponsored health insurance has made a fine mess of private-sector health care. Even though workers pay for their job-based coverage through lower wages, that cost is not salient to

Figure 14.1
America's $2.5 Trillion Health Care Sector: Who Controls the Money?

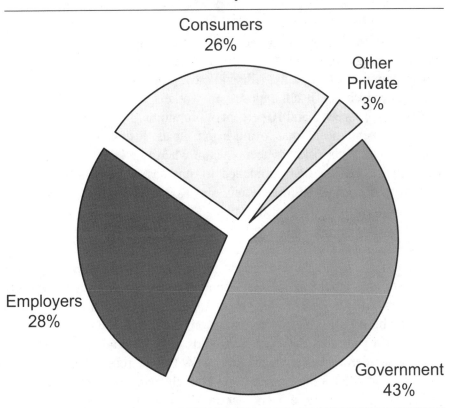

Consumers
26%

Other
Private
3%

Employers
28%

Government
43%

SOURCE: Centers for Medicare & Medicaid Services.

them. Workers feel like they are spending someone else's money. They therefore demand more health insurance than they would if they owned and controlled those dollars. The additional coverage they demand in turn insulates workers from the cost of medical care, which encourages workers to consume many low-value services. Duke University professor Christopher Conover estimates that the exclusion thus imposed a deadweight economic loss on U.S. consumers equal to $106 billion in 2002. It no doubt contributes to Dartmouth Medical School professor Elliot Fisher's conclusion that as much as 30 percent of U.S. medical spending may do nothing to improve health.

The exclusion affects workers negatively. Health insurance premiums persistently rise faster than wages, in part because the exclusion strips workers of any incentive to curb their medical consumption. Rapidly rising health insurance premiums eat into wage increases, but workers have little incentive or ability to do anything about it. When employers try to contain premiums with health plan features that discourage low-value care (such as cost sharing or managed care rules), workers revolt. And why wouldn't they? Stanford economist Alain Enthoven estimates that "less than 5 percent of the insured workforce can both choose a health plan and reap the full savings from choosing economically." The lack of choice hurts, too. Economists Mark Pauly, Allison Percy, and Bradley Herring estimate that reduced choice itself imposes on workers a welfare loss equal to somewhere between 5 and 10 percent of premiums. Tying health insurance to employment means that losing a job means losing health insurance. That leads to "job lock," a phenomenon where workers would prefer to leave their jobs but feel compelled to stay lest they lose their health coverage. According to Mark Pauly and Robert Lieberthal, tying health insurance to employment also doubles the risk that many workers with high-cost medical conditions will end up uninsured.

The exclusion also inhibits competition from potentially higher-value forms of health insurance and health care delivery. As Pauly and Lieberthal note, coverage purchased on the individual market doesn't automatically disappear when a worker changes or loses a job—a feature that offers considerable security. Yet the tax exclusion penalizes that type of insurance. Enthoven argues that the exclusion holds back prepaid group practices like Kaiser Permanente, which have shown great promise in providing high-value care at a reasonable cost. Though many workers prefer such plans, others do not. Employers that offer just one insurance option therefore tend not to offer a prepaid group plan. At the same time, employers often avoid offering more than one plan due to the higher administrative costs. (See also Chapter 15, "Health Care Regulation.")

Reforming of Health Care via the Tax Code

Ideally, government would offer *no* special tax breaks for health care expenses. The purpose of taxes should be solely to raise revenue for the government. If the government must impose a tax, it should distort individuals' economic decisions as little as possible. Creating special tax breaks for certain types of behavior—thereby imposing concomitant tax penalties on other behaviors—is just one more illegitimate tool for controlling the citizenry. If politicians want to subsidize an item like medical care, they should raise general taxes and spend the resulting revenue on that item.

The ultimate goal of tax-based health care reforms should be to eliminate all tax breaks for health-related uses of income, and to tax medical consumption like any other type of consumption. Consumers should make choices about whether, where, and how much health insurance and medical care to purchase based on their values—not on the values that special-interest groups have wormed into the tax code.

Eliminating tax breaks is problematic both in principle and for political reasons. All else being equal, eliminating a tax break brings more revenue into government coffers. That increases government revenues and undoubtedly encourages mischief. In addition, to remove a tax break is to impose a tax on previously untaxed activity. Eliminating the tax break for employer-sponsored insurance would raise taxes on most U.S. workers by requiring them to pay payroll and income taxes on the value of their health insurance premiums. Workers are therefore likely to resist reforms that merely eliminate health-related tax breaks.

A more sensible approach would eliminate those tax breaks and also reduce payroll and income tax rates to a point where the overall amount of revenue raised remains constant or even falls. That would prevent government budgets from growing. Yet even if government revenues remained constant, some individuals would pay lower taxes, while others would face higher tax burdens. The latter group—typically those with the most expensive employer-sponsored health benefits—would still resist reform. In the short term, therefore, it appears politically infeasible to eliminate health-related tax breaks completely.

As a preliminary step, Congress should enact tax reforms that (1) reduce tax-based distortions within the health care sector and (2) prepare consumers and the health care sector for a new tax system with no health-related tax breaks.

Congress took a small step in that direction by creating tax-free health savings accounts (HSAs). HSAs are owned by the individual consumer and follow the account holder from job to job. A worker or her employer can make tax-free contributions to the worker's HSA. If the worker uses those funds to purchase medical care, they remain untaxed. Interest earned on the account is likewise tax-free.

HSAs enable workers to own and control a portion of their health care dollars, because HSA contributions receive the same tax status as employer-sponsored insurance premiums. Workers do not have to surrender those earnings to their employer to obtain the tax break. However, HSAs are only available to consumers who obtain a qualified high-deductible health plan that is rigidly defined by Congress. In addition, HSAs enable workers to control only a small portion of their earnings that their employer otherwise would control. The reason is that HSAs only create tax parity for HSA *contributions*. If workers want to purchase their own health insurance, generally they must still pay the premiums with after-tax dollars. HSAs offer small comfort to a worker whose employer doesn't offer them, or who dislikes the one narrow type of health plan that Congress permits HSA holders to obtain.

HSAs do, however, present an opportunity to reform the tax treatment of health care consistent with the two goals mentioned earlier. Congress should take three steps to expand HSAs:

- Increase HSA contribution limits dramatically, say, from $2,850 to $8,000 for individuals and from $5,500 to $16,000 for families;
- Remove the requirement that HSA holders be covered by a qualified high-deductible health plan, or any type of health plan; and
- Allow HSA holders to purchase health insurance, of any type and from any source, tax-free with HSA funds.

Congress should replace all existing health-related tax breaks with one tax break for these new, "large" HSAs. Large HSAs would reduce distortions within the health care sector and allow workers to purchase the health plan of their choice. Moreover, they would give workers more immediate ownership over that $9,000 that their employer currently controls, and would engender less political opposition than other reforms.

How would Large HSAs work? Suppose a worker currently receives family coverage through her employer. The total premium is $12,000 per

146

year, of which the employer pays $9,000 and the worker pays $3,000. Rather than set aside $9,000 for the worker's health benefits, the employer would add that amount to the worker's salary. The worker would decide how much to contribute to her Large HSA. As with employer-paid health premiums today, those contributions would be exempt from both income and payroll taxes. She could then use those Large HSA funds to purchase health insurance, of any type, from her employer or another source, tax-free. She could stay on the company plan, or choose a policy that would stay with her family when she changes jobs. Her decisions about whether to purchase coverage, where to purchase coverage, what type of coverage to purchase, and whether to pay for medical care out-of-pocket or through insurance would be completely undistorted by the tax code. Unlike today, the worker would *own* every dime she spends on coverage and care, and therefore would seek out health plans and providers who deliver value for the money.

Large HSAs versus Other Proposals

Large HSAs have distinct advantages over other options for reforming the tax treatment of health care, including capping of the exclusion, tax credits (including refundable credits), a standard deduction for health insurance, and full deductibility for all medical spending.

Any reform that achieves tax parity between employer-sponsored health insurance and other forms of insurance (e.g., tax credits, a standard deduction) will cause a certain amount of uncertainty and anxiety. Will healthy workers stay in their employer's health plan? If they leave, will the premiums for the older, sicker workers who remain become unaffordable? Economists agree that if employer plans unravel, employers will return to their workers the money they were spending on health benefits. That will help any workers who are left in the lurch. However, there is also uncertainty about *when* employers will return those funds to workers.

Large HSAs create a very visible moment when employers will be *expected* to add that $9,000 to workers' cash wages—most likely, January 1 of the year that Large HSAs take effect. By ensuring that the shift occurs immediately, and by focusing attention on employers' actions, Large HSAs would do more than other reforms to reduce uncertainty for workers, particularly high-risk workers. Thus, Large HSAs would reduce political opposition to parity in a way that other reforms cannot.

Large HSAs would further mitigate political opposition because fewer workers would face tax increases than would occur under other reforms.

Had Congress enacted Large HSAs in 2006, fewer than 3 percent of workers with employment-based coverage would have seen any reduction in the amount of health benefits exempt from income and payroll taxes. And even those workers would have received a tax cut, because they would have gained *ownership* and *control* over the first $8,000 or $16,000 of their health benefits.

Various estimates have shown that tax reform would reduce the number of Americans who lack health insurance. For example, the Congressional Budget Office projects that a standard tax deduction for health insurance would reduce the number of uninsured by nearly 7 million. Although no estimates have yet been made for Large HSAs, they likely would lead to a comparable reduction in the number of the uninsured.

By comparison, other reforms leave much to be desired. Capping the exclusion has for decades been a political nonstarter, and would neither give workers ownership of their health care dollars nor achieve parity between job-based and other forms of insurance. Uniform tax credits would increase taxes on many workers, yet do nothing to encourage employers to cash out their workers quickly. "Refundable tax credit" is merely code for new government spending and would require even greater (i.e., less politically feasible) tax increases. Full deductibility for all medical spending, as advocated by economists John Cogan, Glenn Hubbard, and Daniel Kessler, would neither give workers ownership nor level the playing field, nor contain the economic distortions due to health-related tax breaks. A standard deduction for health insurance would dramatically reduce the tax code's influence over consumer decisionmaking. Yet even that reform does little to alleviate the uncertainty about what will become of workers' $9,000 when Congress levels the playing field between employment-based and other forms of insurance.

Endgame

Indeed, that uncertainty may be the most significant (if unacknowledged) obstacle to fundamental tax reform. If Congress attempts fundamental tax reform without first giving workers ownership of that $9,000, and giving consumers time to learn how to navigate health insurance markets, opponents will be able to demagogue tax reform to death. To succeed, the demagogues need only frighten a small share of the 180 million Americans with employment-based health insurance.

Large HSAs, however, would allow tax reform to proceed in two steps. First, Large HSAs would give consumers control of the money that employers now spend on their behalf, and would acclimate consumers to making their own health insurance decisions. Consumers are likely to appreciate the option of purchasing health insurance that doesn't disappear when they get sick and lose their jobs. Second, Congress could make the (much smaller) leap to a flat, fair, or national sales tax without having to answer consumers' anxieties about whether they will be able to keep their health insurance, or whether employers will return to workers what's rightly theirs.

Suggested Readings

Cannon, Michael F. "Health Savings Accounts: Do the Critics Have a Point?" Cato Institute Policy Analysis no. 569, May 30, 2006.

————. "Large Health Savings Accounts: A Step toward Tax Neutrality for Health Care." *Forum for Health Economics & Policy* 11, no. 2 (2008).

Cannon, Michael F., and Michael D. Tanner. *Healthy Competition: What's Holding Back Health Care and How to Free It.* Washington: Cato Institute, 2007.

Cochrane, John. "Time-Consistent Health Insurance." *Journal of Political Economy* 103, no. 3 (1995).

Hyman, David A. "Getting the Haves to Come Out Behind." *Journal of Law & Contemporary Problems* 69, no. 4 (2006).

Kling, Arnold. *Crisis of Abundance: Rethinking How We Pay for Health Care.* Washington: Cato Institute, 2006.

Pauly, Mark V., and Robert D. Lieberthal. "How Risky Is Individual Health Insurance?" *Health Affairs* 27, no. 3 (2008).

Pauly, Mark, Allison Percy, and Bradley Herring. "Individual versus Job-Based Insurance: Weighing the Pros and Cons." *Health Affairs* 18, no. 6 (1999)

—Prepared by Michael F. Cannon

15. Health Care Regulation

> ## State governments should
>
> - eliminate licensing of medical professionals or, as a preliminary step, recognize licenses issued by other states;
> - eliminate "corporate-practice-of-medicine" laws;
> - eliminate "certificate-of-need" laws; and
> - enforce private contracts that include medical malpractice reforms.

> ## Congress should
>
> - eliminate states' ability to use licensing laws as a barrier to entry by medical professionals licensed by other states,
> - eliminate the U.S. Food and Drug Administration's efficacy requirement for new drugs, and
> - reject federal medical malpractice reforms.

A widely accepted premise of most health care reform debates is that health and medicine are special areas of the economy where markets are plagued by failure. For example, economists describe medicine as a "credence"—good because it is difficult for consumers to judge its quality before *and even after* they have consumed it. It is also difficult for producers (e.g., doctors, hospitals, etc.) to judge the quality of their services, even after the fact. A doctor might *think* his actions were responsible for a good outcome, or not responsible for a bad outcome, but it is difficult to know for sure. Nevertheless, doctors tend to know more about the need for, and quality of, various services than patients do. That asymmetry of information creates an unequal relationship between patient and physician and causes much concern among health care reformers.

In 1963, Nobel Prize–winning economist Kenneth Arrow penned an influential article for the *American Economic Review* that described government intervention in health care markets as a response to the problems of uncertainty and asymmetric information in medicine. Lobbyists and health care reformers ritually cite Arrow's article as justification for their preferred government interventions.

The reality of health care markets, government intervention, and, indeed, Arrow's article is not that simple. Pulitzer Prize–winning sociologist Paul Starr notes that many government interventions benefit producers of medical care at the expense of consumers and *exacerbate* the problem of uncertainty. Health economist James C. Robinson writes:

> The central proposition of [Arrow's] article, that health care information is imperfect and asymmetrically distributed, has been seized upon to justify every inefficiency, idiosyncrasy, and interest-serving institution in the health care industry. . . . It has served to lend the author's unparalleled reputation to subsequent claims that advertising, optometry, and midwifery are threats to consumer well-being, that nonprofit ownership is natural for hospitals though not for physician practices, that price competition undermines product quality, that antitrust exemptions reduce costs, that consumers cannot compare insurance plans and must yield this function to politicians, that price regulation is effective for pharmaceutical products despite having failed in other applications, that cost-conscious choice is unethical while cost-unconscious choice is a basic human right, that what consumers want is not what they need, and, more generally, that the real is reasonable, the facts are functional, and the health care sector is constrained Pareto-efficient.

Robinson concludes:

> The most pernicious doctrine in health services research, the greatest impediment to clear thought and successful action, is that health care is *different*. . . . To some within the health care community, the uniqueness doctrine is self-evident and needs no justification. After all, health care is essential to health. That food and shelter are even more vital and seem to be produced without professional licensure, nonprofit organization, compulsory insurance, class action lawsuits, and 133,000 pages of regulatory prescription in the *Federal Register* does not shake the faith of the orthodox. . . . The uniqueness doctrine hence proves too much.

Consistent with Robinson's observation, producers have been the driving force behind or have subsequently captured most health care regulations, and have used them to protect themselves from market competition at the expense of consumers. Physicians sought and used licensing and corporate-practice-of-medicine laws to prevent competition from less remunerative prepaid health plans or integrated delivery systems that curtail physician autonomy. Recently, nonphysician clinicians have used licensing, scope-of-practice, and minimum-education requirements to increase their incomes by reducing the supply of, and substitutes for, their services. Hospitals use government regulation to block competition from other, often innovative, medical facilities. Pharmaceutical and medical device manufacturers rely on the U.S. Food and Drug Administration to erect high barriers to entry into those markets.

Perhaps the one area of health care regulation that fails to fit this mold is the courts' refusal to enforce contracts where patients waive some or all of their right to sue for malpractice in return for a reduced price. Nevertheless, the effect of that regulation is the same as all others: lower quality and higher costs.

Medical Professionals

How might markets make medicine better, cheaper, and safer? Harvard Business School professor Clayton Christensen and his colleagues offer this insight: "Many of the most powerful innovations that disrupted other industries did so by enabling a larger population of less-skilled people to do in a more convenient, less-expensive setting things that historically could be performed only by expensive specialists in centralized, inconvenient locations." In medical care, that process of using fewer inputs to achieve greater health outputs would come in large part from allowing less-trained clinicians, such as nurse practitioners and physician assistants, to perform tasks that were once performed only by highly trained (and more costly) physicians.

State licensing of medical professionals allows physicians and others to block that market process. To practice medicine in a state, physicians, nurse practitioners, physician assistants, and other clinicians must obtain a license from that state. To obtain a license, they must satisfy specified minimum-education requirements. For each type of clinician license, each state specifies the tasks the license allows clinicians to perform. That list of tasks is called the clinician's "scope of practice." (Physicians' scope of practice is plenary.)

Licensing allows physicians to restrict entry into their profession and to restrict the supply of substitutes for their services. By lobbying legislatures to restrict the scopes of practice of nurse practitioners and physician assistants, physicians can reserve certain tasks for themselves. Such restrictions increase the demand for physician services and increase physician incomes. They also make medical care more expensive and reduce access.

Licensing also enables midlevel clinicians to do the same. Nurse practitioners, for instance, can restrict entry into their profession (and thereby increase their incomes) by pushing states to increase the education requirements for a nurse practitioner's license. They can block competition from substitutes for their services by lobbying to restrict the scopes of practice of other nonphysician clinicians.

Physicians typically argue that they seek to restrict the scopes of practice of nonphysician clinicians because broader scopes of practice would threaten patient safety. Yet study after study has shown that midlevel clinicians provide a level of quality equal to that of physicians performing the same services. The American Medical Association, the nation's largest lobbying group representing physicians, acknowledges this:

> More than 50 journal articles and reports comparing physician and non-physician services have been reviewed. These were in peer-reviewed journals though not, for the most part, peer-reviewed journals with a physician readership. The articles and reports usually look at one procedure or at the treatment of one kind of patient, usually a patient with an uncomplicated disorder or the need for routine treatment. These studies almost uniformly conclude that in the particular instances studied, a non-physician clinician in defined circumstances can provide an acceptable level of care.

Typically, midlevel clinicians also provide those services at a much lower cost.

Moreover, licensing does little to discipline clinicians who actually harm patients. A study by the consumer watchdog Public Citizen found that between 1990 and 2005, "only 33.26 percent of doctors who made 10 or more malpractice payments were disciplined by their state board—meaning two-thirds of doctors in this group of egregious repeat offenders were not disciplined at all."

There is a limit, of course, to every clinician's competence. Market forces and medical malpractice liability already do much more than licensing to protect patients. In the absence of licensing, private credentialing and the desire to protect brand names and reputations would do even more to safeguard patients from incompetent providers.

The standard, static economic analysis suggests that, on balance, licensing has little if any positive effect on health outcomes. Economists generally agree that licensing increases the quality of medical services *actually delivered*. Economists also agree that licensing increases the cost of medical care and therefore reduces the *quantity* of services delivered. For example, access to care will almost certainly fall if physicians secure regulations that inhibit nurse practitioner–staffed clinics such as MinuteClinic and RediClinic, which provide convenient and affordable access to routine care in retail stores such as CVS and Wal-Mart. Thus, licensing may do nothing to improve overall health.

A more dynamic analysis further suggests that licensing may in fact lead to *worse* health outcomes. Prepaid group practices such as Kaiser Permanente and Group Health Cooperative combine an integrated delivery system with prepayment. These plans make greater use of midlevel clinicians, preventive and primary care, and electronic medical records than other types of insurance or delivery systems. As a result, they have shown remarkable success at increasing the delivery of high-quality services, reducing low-value and harmful services (including medical errors), and making health insurance more affordable. As noted earlier, however, physicians have used licensing to block competition from integrated delivery systems and prepaid health plans, in large part because prepaid group practices are generally less remunerative for physicians and restrict physician autonomy. Thus, licensing may be reducing the overall quality of care by inhibiting higher-quality forms of health care delivery.

Reform is an inadequate response to licensing's pathologies. Whether licensing authority is vested in a legislature or regulatory agency, state or federal, there is no way to insulate that authority from influence by those whose incomes hang in the balance. Even absent political pressure, a government body is inherently unable to strike the proper balance between access and safety for millions of patients across billions of encounters with medical personnel. Such an authority would inevitably restrict access to care and block innovations that make medicine better, cheaper, and safer.

Instead, state governments should eliminate medical licensing. Many things would not change. Hospitals, health plans, and other organizations would continue to rely on board certification, private credentialing organizations, and their own internal processes to evaluate the competence of clinicians. Courts would continue to hold health care organizations and individual clinicians accountable for harm caused by negligence.

What would change is that providers would seek innovative ways to use midlevel clinicians to bring quality care within reach of more low-income Americans. And greater competition between different delivery and payment systems would drive the medical marketplace toward providing greater health for more Americans at a far lower cost.

Medical Facilities

Another way markets might make medical care better, cheaper, and safe is through rigorous competition among medical facilities, including clinics, physician offices, urgent care clinics, ambulatory surgical centers, specialty hospitals, and full-service hospitals. State laws that require government approval of new medical facilities are a leading barrier to competition between medical facilities.

For most of the 20th century, federal and state governments encouraged greater spending on medical care. Medical expenditures—especially by government—truly exploded after the creation of Medicare and Medicaid in 1965. In the 1960s and 1970s, state governments attempted to contain those rapidly growing outlays essentially by engaging in centralized economic planning. Their primary tools were laws requiring hospitals, nursing homes, and even physician offices to obtain a "certificate of need" (CON) from a state planning agency before opening a new facility or investing in new equipment. The rationale behind CON laws was that by restraining the supply of hospital beds, government could restrain medical spending. By 1976, the federal government mandated CON planning nationwide.

CON laws failed to slow the growth of medical spending. In a survey of the empirical literature on CON laws, health economist Michael Morrisey writes that those studies "find virtually no cost-containment effects. . . . If anything, CON programs tended to increase costs." The failure of CON laws to achieve their stated aims led the federal government to lift its CON-planning mandate in 1987 and led many states to eliminate their laws also. Yet other states have maintained and even expanded their CON requirements. Why?

Although CON laws have done nothing to contain spending, they have been a boon for incumbent health care providers. Though the stated purpose of CON laws is cost containment, those regulations also protect existing health care facilities from competition. Morrisey concludes:

> A reasonably large body of evidence suggests that CON has been used to the benefit of existing hospitals. Prices and costs were higher in the presence of CON, investor-owned hospitals were less likely to enter the market, multihospital systems were less likely to be formed, and hospitals were less likely to be managed under for-profit contract. . . . The continued existence of CON and, indeed, its reintroduction and expansion despite overwhelming evidence of its ineffectiveness as a cost-control device suggest that something other than the public interest is being sought. The provider self-interest view is worthy of examination.

CON laws increase health care costs and deny patients the benefits of new forms of health care delivery. There is no justification for these laws, and no place in a market economy for Soviet-style economic planning. States should eliminate CON laws immediately. If state officials are concerned about runaway health expenditures, they should reduce or eliminate the government subsidies that fuel such spending.

Pharmaceutical Regulation

The Food and Drug Administration is the federal agency tasked with implementing the federal Food, Drugs, and Cosmetics Act of 1938, which Congress enacted in response to drug-related poisonings that killed over 100 children. That act requires pharmaceutical manufacturers to demonstrate to the federal government that their products are safe. Originally, if the FDA did not reject the application within 180 days, the firm could proceed to market its product.

Another drug-related tragedy occurred in 1962 when pregnant women taking the tranquilizer thalidomide gave birth to children with severe deformities. Though thalidomide victims numbered over 10,000 worldwide, there were relatively few in the United States, as the FDA had not yet approved thalidomide for marketing. Congress nevertheless responded to this tragedy by enacting the 1962 amendments to the Food, Drugs, and Cosmetics Act. Those amendments require firms to prove to the FDA's satisfaction that their products are efficacious for the indication for which approval is sought and require firms to obtain an affirmative approval from the FDA before marketing a new drug.

Economists have long acknowledged a fundamental tension in the FDA's regulation of pharmaceuticals. According to MIT economist Ernst Berndt and colleagues:

> A central tradeoff facing the FDA involves balancing its two goals—protecting public health by assuring the safety and efficacy of drugs, and advancing the public health by helping to secure and speed access to new innovations.

Failure to meet the first goal—assuring the safety of new drugs—results in what is called a "Type I error." Failure to meet the second goal—speeding access to effective new drugs—results in a "Type II error."

As Table 15.1 illustrates, the FDA succeeds in its mission when it either timely approves an effective drug (quadrant 1) or blocks a harmful drug (quadrant 4). The FDA commits a Type I error when it approves an unsafe

157

Table 15.1
FDA Type I, Type II Error Problem

		Correct Decision	
		Approve	**Delay/Reject**
Approve		(1) **Success** (Helpful drug approved)	(2) **Type I Error** • Harmful drug approved • Patients harmed • Error traced to FDA officials
FDA Decision	**Delay/Reject**	(3) **Type II Error** • Helpful drug withheld • Patients harmed • Error *not* traced to FDA officials	(4) **Success** (Harmful drug withheld)

drug (quadrant 2). Type I errors harm patients by exposing them to dangerous or even deadly products. The FDA commits a Type II error when it delays or denies approval of a beneficial drug (quadrant 3). Type II errors harm patients by withholding products that would protect them from illness or death.

The FDA faces starkly different consequences for Type I and Type II errors. Type I errors bring swift and certain retribution on the agency. The victims of a Type I error are easily identifiable. Victims, their loved ones, the media, and Congress can discipline FDA officials for approving a harmful product. FDA officials know that a Type I error will lead to congressional hearings and public disgrace, and may even end their careers.

In contrast, FDA officials are rarely disciplined for Type II errors. Delaying or denying approval of a beneficial drug harms patients no less than approving an unsafe drug, yet victims of Type II errors are much harder to identify. Neither the Type II victim, nor their loved ones, nor FDA officials know exactly which patients might have been helped by a beneficial drug whose approval was delayed or denied. The patients and their families may never have heard of the drug. Indeed, the FDA may never have heard of the drug either: Type II errors include beneficial drugs that are never developed due to the high cost of winning FDA approval. Because of this information asymmetry, the political system does not— indeed cannot—discipline FDA officials for Type II errors the way it disciplines them for Type I errors.

Dr. Henry Miller, a former FDA official, offers an account of how those incentives affect the behavior of FDA reviewers:

> In the early 1980s, when I headed the team at the FDA that was reviewing the [new drug application, or NDA] for recombinant human insulin, the first drug made with gene-splicing techniques, we were ready to recommend approval a mere four months after the application was submitted (at a time when the average time for NDA review was more than two and a half years). . . . My supervisor refused to sign off on the approval—even though he agreed that the data provided compelling evidence of the drug's safety and effectiveness. "If anything goes wrong," he argued, "think how bad it will look that we approved the drug so quickly." . . . The supervisor was more concerned with not looking bad in case of an unforeseen mishap than with getting an important new product to patients who needed it.

The tradeoff between Type I and Type II errors is unavoidable. Reducing either type of error results in more errors of the other type. The FDA must commit a certain number of each.

The asymmetric information the FDA receives about Type I and Type II errors leads the agency to support policies that *increase* morbidity and mortality. Suppose the FDA were considering a new regulation that would prevent 1,000 deaths due to adverse drug reactions but that would slow down the approval of new drugs such that 10,000 patients would die while waiting for life-extending drugs that otherwise would have been approved. The FDA would implement the new regulation, even though it would result in 9,000 additional deaths.

Every effort to quantify the costs and benefits of FDA regulation supports that conclusion. Economist Sam Peltzman published the first such analysis in 1973. In 2005, Peltzman wrote:

> I found that the unregulated market was very quickly weeding out ineffective drugs prior to 1962. Their sales declined rapidly within a few months of introduction, and there was thus little room for the regulation to improve on market forces. . . . Most of the subsequent academic research reached conclusions similar to mine. . . . I concluded that the proof-of-efficacy requirement was a public health disaster, promoting much more sickness and death than it prevented. Nothing I have seen since has moved me to change that conclusion—the disaster is ongoing.

A study by Tulane University economist Mary K. Olson estimated that when additional revenue from user fees enabled the FDA to review drugs more quickly, the health benefits of quicker access to new drugs were roughly 12 times as great as the costs from additional adverse drug reac-

159

tions. Another study, by University of Chicago economist Tomas Philipson and colleagues, found that quicker reviews brought significant health benefits, but "did not, in fact, have *any* effect on drug safety." That is, there appeared to be no additional adverse drug reactions. Those findings imply that the FDA will tolerate additional deaths due to Type II errors even if doing so were to produce little or no reduction in deaths due to Type I errors. Indeed, despite such research, Congress has in recent years sought to give the FDA additional powers to reduce Type I errors.

Little is to be gained from minor reforms such as user fees. The asymmetry of information available to the FDA guarantees that the agency will always behave in this manner.

Nobel Prize–winning economist Gary Becker advocates eliminating the efficacy standard and returning the FDA to the status quo *ante* 1962. Peltzman suggests, however, that even the safety requirement delivered more harm than benefit. Another Nobel Prize–winning economist, the late Milton Friedman, proposed eliminating the FDA entirely.

At a minimum, Congress should eliminate the FDA's efficacy standard. Eliminating the efficacy standard would not leave patients unprotected. The FDA would still have the power to keep from the market drugs that have not been proved safe to the agency's satisfaction. Moreover, private certification of pharmaceutical safety and efficacy, which already exists informally, would expand. Patients harmed by pharmaceuticals would continue to have recourse to the courts, which (along with liability insurers) would create powerful incentives for pharmaceutical manufacturers to conduct appropriate testing.

The United States already has an essentially unregulated, albeit informal, process for certifying drug efficacy. The FDA approves a drug for one particular use, which goes on the drug's label. Yet physicians may—and do—prescribe drugs for other, "off-label" uses. An example is aspirin. Though designed for pain relief, doctors have long prescribed aspirin to prevent heart attacks.

Lack of FDA certification does not mean such uses are dangerous or unproven. Off-label uses are suggested or discovered by doctors and scientists; tested; and discussed worldwide in medical journals and symposia, and (if validated) appear in medical textbooks, the *U.S. Pharmacopeia Drug Information*, the *American Hospital Formulary Service Drug Information*, and other authoritative sources. Off-label uses often become the standard of care, particularly in fighting cancer and other diseases. Absent the FDA, those private organizations would play a greater role in certifying safety and efficacy.

Moreover, additional organizations would step forward to meet the demand for safety and efficacy certification. Underwriters Laboratories certifies the safety of thousands of consumer products, many inherently dangerous. That organization's charter states that it will certify the safety of any consumer product submitted to it. Underwriters Laboratories or other consumer advocates, such as *Consumer Reports*, could perform that vital function. Most likely, however, integrated and prepaid health plans such as Kaiser Permanente and Group Health Cooperative would perform that function as an agent for their enrollees. Prepaid group plans lead the industry in the use of electronic medical records, which are essential to tracking accurately a drug's effects on patients. When the FDA wanted to study whether the pain reliever Vioxx was causing heart attacks, it turned to Kaiser Permanente of Northern and Southern California.

Market-based certification respects the freedom of doctors and patients to make treatment decisions according to individual circumstances. It also provides them with information more quickly than government certification. Economist J. Howard Beales III found that off-label uses that were later certified by the FDA had been certified by the *U.S. Pharmacopeia Drug Information* an average of 2.5 years sooner. Market-based certification can also do more for patients than government certification can. The FDA is prohibited by law from considering cost-effectiveness as a criterion for approval. In contrast, prepaid group plans face financial incentives to ensure that their enrollees receive maximum value for their money, and can condition their seal of approval on whether a drug provides benefits that are worth the cost.

Two things must be made clear. First, if Congress were to eliminate FDA regulation of pharmaceuticals—or just the agency's efficacy standard—more patients would likely be harmed by new drugs. That unfortunate fact will lead to greater skepticism of new drugs by doctors and patients, as well as innovations that would more quickly detect and stop adverse drug reactions. Second, many more lives would be saved through greater innovation and quicker access to helpful drugs than would be lost to harmful ones.

Medical Liability Reform

The right to sue health care providers for medical malpractice is an important tool for protecting patients from injury due to negligent care. Patients typically have little information about the quality of care. By imposing the costs of negligent care on providers, the medical malpractice "system" can align the incentives of providers with those of patients

Nevertheless, many people complain—with some justification—that the medical liability system in the United States performs poorly. Research suggests that malpractice liability does little to discourage negligent care, that only a small fraction of patients injured by provider negligence actually recover damages from providers, and that many who do recover are not victims of negligence. Many specialists (neurosurgeons and obstetricians, to name two) report that they cannot afford the rising cost of medical liability insurance. Duke University professor Christopher Conover estimates that in 2002, the U.S. medical liability "system" cost Americans $81 billion net of benefits. Physicians and other providers—who have seen often-dramatic increases in malpractice insurance premiums—have intermittently declared the medical liability system to be in "crisis" for over 30 years.

This "crisis" has spawned numerous proposals to reform medical malpractice liability rules. The American Medical Association advocates a nationwide cap on noneconomic damages similar to the $250,000 cap enacted in California. Other proposals include legislative limits on contingency fees for plaintiffs' attorneys; "no-fault" compensation systems for medical injuries, such as the limited programs adopted in Florida and Virginia; alternative forms of dispute resolution, such as arbitration and special medical courts; the English rule of costs; and reform of the collateral source rule.

Each of these reforms would leave some patients better off—typically by reducing prices for medical care—at the cost of leaving other patients worse off. So-called loser pays reforms would often reallocate the costs of frivolous lawsuits to the correct party. However, that rule deters less affluent patients from seeking legal redress for legitimate grievances. A cap on noneconomic damages would reduce health care costs for noninjured patients, but at the expense of leaving some injured patients with uncompensated losses. Limits on contingency fees would reduce costs for noninjured patients, but at the cost of denying compensation to injured patients whose cases plaintiffs' attorneys deem too expensive to pursue.

Many observers have called on the federal government to enact such reforms. As discussed in Chapter 11, Congress is not constitutionally authorized to impose substantive rules of tort law on the states. Although the federal government may enact technical procedural changes, state legislatures are the proper venue for correcting excesses in their civil justice systems. The fact that medical professionals can avoid states with inhospitable civil justice systems gives them significant leverage when advocating state-level medical liability reforms, and gives states incentives to enact such reforms. That some states have done so demonstrates that they have the ability.

Yet state-imposed medical malpractice reforms share two flaws with federally imposed rules. As noted earlier, imposing one set of limits on the right to sue for medical malpractice on all patients and providers will help some patients while hurting others. And the fact that those rules are written into statutes makes harmful rules extremely difficult to remove.

A more patient-friendly and liberty-enhancing approach would allow patients and providers to write their own medical malpractice reforms into legally enforceable contracts. For cases of ordinary negligence, patients could choose the level of protection they desired, rather than have a uniform level of protection (and the resulting price) imposed on them by the courts. Providers could offer discounts to patients who agree to limits on compensation in the event of an injury. If not, the patient could pay the higher price or seek a better deal from another provider. Insurance companies could facilitate such contracts on behalf of their enrollees. Those companies would have strong incentives to ensure that those contracts provide adequate protection, else the insurers could face higher claims from injured patients who could not collect the full extent of their damages. The regular tort rules would continue to apply in cases where patients and providers did not contract around those rules, where patients were subject to duress, or where providers were guilty of intentional wrongdoing or reckless behavior.

Freedom of contract would make medical care more affordable to many low-income patients. It would also enhance quality competition. Providers who know they are less likely to injure patients could offer more expansive malpractice protections, or equivalent malpractice protections at a lower cost. Low-quality providers would not be able to do the same and would face strong financial incentives to improve their processes of care.

Such contracts are not possible today because courts have invalidated them as "against public policy." That policy has restricted the freedom of adults to make mutually beneficial exchanges that hurt no one else. It has also increased the cost of providing medical care to the indigent, which has undoubtedly reduced their access to care.

To remedy this costly restriction on liberty, courts should abandon their current policy and enforce contractual limitations on the right to sue for medical malpractice. If courts refuse, state legislatures should require them to do so. Economist Richard Thaler and law professor Cass Sunstein write:

> In our view, state lawmakers should think seriously about increasing freedom of contract in the domain of medical malpractice, if only to see whether such experiments would reduce the cost of health care without decreasing its quality. Increasing contractual freedom won't solve the health care crisis. But it might well help—and in this domain every little bit of help counts.

As noted earlier, the medical malpractice system does a poor job of providing relief to injured patients, preventing frivolous lawsuits, or discouraging negligence. The remedies for these shortcomings are not obvious. A dynamic marketplace that allows parties to experiment with—and abandon—different malpractice rules is the quickest and surest way to find those solutions.

Suggested Readings

Arrow, Kenneth J. "Uncertainty and the Welfare Economics of Medical Care." *American Economic Review* 53 (1963).

Cannon, Michael F., and Michael D. Tanner. *Healthy Competition: What's Holding Back Health Care and How to Free It.* Washington: Cato Institute, 2007.

Christensen, Clayton M., Richard Bohmer, and John Kenagy. "Will Disruptive Innovations Cure Health Care?" *Harvard Business Review On Point: Curing U.S. Health Care*, 3rd ed., September–October 2000.

Conover, Christopher J. "Health Care Regulation: A $169 Billion Hidden Tax." Cato Institute Policy Analysis no. 527, October 4, 2004.

Enthoven, Alain C., and Laura A. Tollen, eds. *Toward a 21st Century Health System: The Contributions and Promise of Prepaid Group Practice.* San Francisco: Jossey-Bass, 2004.

Epstein, Richard A. "Medical Malpractice: The Case for Contract." *American Bar Foundation Research Journal* 1, no. 1 (1976).

Friedman, Milton. *Capitalism and Freedom.* Chicago: University of Chicago Press, 1962, chapter 9, "Occupational Licensure."

Hamowy, Ronald. "The Early Development of Medical Licensing Laws in the United States, 1875–1900." *Journal of Libertarian Studies* 3, no. 2 (1979).

Kessel, Reuben. "Price Discrimination in Medicine." *Journal of Law and Economics* 1 (1958).

Morrisey, Michael. "State Health Insurance Reform: Protecting the Provider." In *American Health Care: Government, Market Processes, and the Public Interest*, edited by Roger Feldman. New Brunswick, NJ: Transaction, 2000.

Olson, Mary K. "Are Novel Drugs More Risky for Patients than Less Novel Drugs?" *Journal of Health Economics* 23, no. 6 (2004).

Peltzman, Sam. "An Evaluation of Consumer Protection Legislation: The 1962 Drug Amendments." *Journal of Political Economy* 81, no. 5 (1973).

———. *Regulation and the Natural Progress of Opulence.* Washington: AEI Press, 2005.

Philipson, Tomas J., and others. "Assessing the Safety and Efficacy of the FDA: The Case of the Prescription Drug User Fee Acts." National Bureau of Economic Research Working Paper no. 11724, 2005.

Starr, Paul. *The Social Transformation of American Medicine.* New York: Basic Books, 1984.

Svorny, Shirley. "Medical Licensing: An Obstacle to Affordable, Quality Care." Cato Institute Policy Analysis no. 621, September 17, 2008.

Thaler, Richard H., and Cass R. Sunstein. *Nudge: Improving Decisions about Health, Wealth, and Happiness.* New Haven, CT: Yale University Press, 2008, chapter 14, "Should Patients Be Forced to Buy Lottery Tickets?"

—Prepared by Michael F. Cannon

16. Health Insurance Regulation

> **State legislators should**
> - eliminate licensing of health insurance or, as a preliminary step, recognize insurance products licensed by other states.

> **Congress should**
> - eliminate states' ability to use licensing laws as a barrier to trade with out-of-state insurers, and
> - relinquish any role as an insurance regulator.

Every year in the United States, thousands upon thousands of Americans walk or are carried into hospitals. Some are in extreme pain. Some are close to death. Using the tools of modern medicine, doctors routinely heal their pain and save their lives. No less marvelous, however, is the fact that the bill is often paid, voluntarily, *by complete strangers*. These benefactors do not know the patient. They do not know her illness. They may not practice the same religion or speak the same language. Were they to meet the patient, they might not even like her. And yet, without anyone pressuring or forcing them to do so, these people repeatedly purchase life-saving medical care for complete strangers. Indeed, they play a role every bit as important as the doctors and hospitals. By some marvel, this wonderful phenomenon occurs every day in the United States.

That marvel is health insurance. When individuals choose to purchase health insurance, they make an agreement to pay for the medical expenses of those in the insurance pool who become sick or injured. They uphold that agreement by paying a periodic premium to an insurance company. To be sure, it is not compassion for others but self-interest that motivates most insurance purchasers: each wants to have her own medical bills paid in the event of a catastrophe. Yet that only makes health insurance all the more marvelous. Health insurance harnesses the self-interest of millions of strangers to produce an unquestionably compassionate result.

As discussed in Chapter 13 ("Medicaid and the State Children's Health Insurance Program"), that sort of generosity invites opportunistic behavior. If the insurance pool is paying for all their medical care, some patients will consume more medical care than they need. (And why not? Those other people in the pool are just strangers.) Likewise, health care providers will try to sell those patients more medical care than they need. If individuals can tap that generosity whenever they choose, many will not contribute to the pool until they become sick. By the time they join the pool, their medical expenses would well exceed their contributions. Before long, the premiums would spiral out of control, and no one would want to participate. For these reasons, members of the insurance pool hire someone to protect the members' generosity from opportunistic behavior.

Health insurance companies are essentially intermediaries between members of the pool. They charge higher premiums to enrollees who purchase more extensive coverage, because those members will draw more money from the pool. They require members to pay part of the cost of their own medical care (through deductibles, coinsurance, and copayments) to ensure that members aren't careless with other members' money. They look over physicians' shoulders (with managed-care tools like capitation payment, preauthorization, and utilization review) to ensure physicians are being careful with their members' money. They also calibrate each new member's premium to her expected claims. If an individual waits until she is sick to join the pool, her premiums will therefore be much higher than if she joined while healthy. Risk-based premiums thus *promote* compassionate behavior, because they encourage individuals to contribute to the pool while they are still healthy—so their premiums can help save the lives of strangers. Once in the pool, however, insurers don't increase members' premiums when they become ill.

Insurers compete to see who can best manage these features, and provide members the protection they desire at the lowest possible premium. That competition is the market's way of navigating the Samaritan's dilemma, discussed in Chapter 13 ("Medicaid and the State Children's Health Insurance Program").

Do Health Insurance Markets Fail?

Critics claim that unregulated insurance markets do not provide secure access to medical care; that risk-based premiums are unfair; that insurance companies drop people when they get sick; that markets will not provide health insurance to everyone; and that government must create pooling arrangements that correct these alleged market failures.

Evaluating the performance of unregulated health insurance markets is complicated by the fact that most Americans obtain health insurance in markets heavily regulated or distorted by government. For example:

- Nearly all seniors obtain health insurance from government through the federal Medicare program (see Chapter 12).
- Due to large tax preferences for employer-sponsored insurance (see Chapter 14, "The Tax Treatment of Health Care"), about 90 percent of nonelderly Americans with health insurance obtain it through an employer.
- Only 10 percent of the nonelderly insured (about 18 million people) obtain insurance directly from an insurance company, i.e., through the "individual" market.

In addition, many states impose significant regulations on their individual health insurance markets. Even if a state does not, administrative costs and premiums in that market will be higher than necessary because government diverts most consumers into the employment-based market.

Researchers examining America's badly hampered individual health insurance markets nevertheless have found considerable evidence that unregulated markets provide consumers with reliable long-term protection from the cost of illness. For example, University of Pennsylvania economist Mark Pauly and colleagues find as follows:

- "Actual premiums paid for individual insurance are much less than proportional to risk, and risk levels have a small effect on obtaining coverage."
- "Premiums do rise with risk, but the increase in premiums is only about 15 percent of the increase in risk. Premiums for individual insurance vary widely, but that variation is not very strongly related to the level of risk."
- "Guaranteed renewable" policies, which are intended to protect against premium increases if the enrollee becomes sick, "appear to be effective in providing protection against reclassification risks in individual health insurance markets."
- The vast majority of insurance products (75 percent) provided guaranteed renewability *before* they were required to do so by government.

- High-cost individuals who are covered by small employers are nearly twice as likely to end up uninsured as high-cost individuals covered in the individual market.
- "On average, guaranteed renewability works in practice as it should in theory and provides a substantial amount of protection against high premiums to those high-risk individuals who bought insurance before their risk levels changed. The implication is that, although there are some anecdotes about individual insurers trying to avoid covering people who become high risk (for example, by canceling coverage for a whole class of purchasers), the data on actual premium-risk relationships strongly suggest that such attempts to limit risk pooling are the exception rather than the rule."

Similarly, RAND economist Susan Marquis and colleagues find that the individual market protects enrollees with expensive conditions and that risk-based premiums are not as harsh as critics imply:

- "Purchasers derive value from having the range of choices that the individual market offers."
- In the individual market, "a large number of people with health problems do obtain coverage."
- "We also find that there is substantial pooling in the individual market and that it increases over time because people who become sick can continue coverage without new underwriting."
- Regarding enrollees who purchase insurance and later become sick, "in practice they are not placed in a new underwriting class."
- "Our analysis confirms earlier studies' findings that there is considerable risk pooling in the individual market and that high risks are not charged premiums that fully reflect their higher risk."

Recent experience in California shows that insurance companies will sometimes rescind coverage when enrollees provide inaccurate information about preexisting conditions—and perhaps even when enrollees have not done so. California insurers have since reinstated coverage for many enrollees. That episode demonstrates that media scrutiny is an important market mechanism; that government enforcement of insurance contracts can prevent individuals from defrauding strangers and prevent insurers from breaching their contracts; and that both types of consumer protection can spur insurers to change their behavior. All told, free markets provide considerably better health coverage than critics suggest.

Should Markets Provide Universal Coverage?

Critics are correct that markets will not provide health insurance to everyone. Voluntary insurance pools often will not cover medical conditions that are known to exist at the time an individual enrolls.

Health insurance markets are completely justified in not covering preexisting conditions. If they did, few would purchase insurance until they had an expensive medical condition, and the pool would unravel. Thus, there is a very good reason why markets will not deliver universal coverage.

That still leaves a problem. Risk-based premiums will encourage most people to purchase insurance before they become ill. Yet there will always be some people who either did not join a pool while they were still healthy or never had the opportunity because their high-cost condition has been with them since birth.

Assuming they cannot afford medical care, individuals with expensive preexisting conditions require *subsidies*, which is not to say they need *insurance*. Insurance is merely one way—and a very expensive way—of subsidizing preexisting conditions. More than other types of subsidies, insurance resembles a blank check. In general, strangers do not voluntarily give blank checks to other strangers, again with good reason: strangers are difficult to monitor, and the beneficiaries (encouraged by their health care providers) may take more than they need. Other ways of subsidizing the needy include limited amounts of cash, vouchers, or in-kind subsidies from providers, private charities, or government. Compared with the alternatives, the added costs of subsidizing preexisting conditions with insurance outweigh the added benefits.

Exclusions for preexisting conditions do not indicate a lack of compassion by insurance companies or consumers. They are the insurance market's way of telling us that consumers do not want to subsidize people with preexisting conditions *through insurance*. They do not preclude other options for subsidizing the needy, a topic discussed in Chapter 13 ("Medicaid and the State Children's Health Insurance Program").

State Regulation of "Individual" Health Insurance Markets

As a result of the damage it has sustained from federal and state governments, however, the individual market performs well below its potential. As noted earlier, the federal government diverts the vast majority of insurance purchasers into job-based insurance. Moreover, state governments impose countless regulations on their insurance markets. Those

171

regulations include restrictions on insurance pools' ability to limit or refuse coverage, to vary premiums according to risk, and to negotiate price discounts from providers. States also limit enrollees' freedom to purchase only the coverage they wish. Finally, states prohibit their residents from purchasing insurance from states with more consumer-friendly regulation.

The most disastrous state health insurance regulations are known as "guaranteed issue" and "community rating." Guaranteed issue requires insurers to offer coverage to all comers. Supporters claim that requiring insurers to offer coverage to all individuals will increase access to coverage for those with preexisting conditions. States with guaranteed-issue requirements include Idaho, Maine, Massachusetts, New Jersey, New York, Ohio, Rhode Island, and Vermont. Similarly, 31 states and the federal government restrict, to a lesser extent, insurance pools' ability to deny coverage for preexisting conditions.

Guaranteed issue allows individuals to avoid contributing to an insurance pool until they have a high-cost condition, which is akin to letting drivers who cause an accident purchase retroactive auto insurance. Such laws allow people to take advantage of strangers by removing the insurance pool's ability to protect itself from opportunistic behavior. They leave insurance pools smaller and sicker, which puts upward pressure on premiums.

Despite guaranteed-issue requirements, insurance pools can protect themselves somewhat by charging higher premiums to individuals who wait until they are sick to join the pool. As one might expect, many people with preexisting conditions cannot afford those risk-based premiums. Since the very purpose of guaranteed-issue laws is to give those individuals access to health insurance, many states also limit the extent to which insurance pools can price coverage according to risk. In its purest form, "community rating" requires insurance pools to charge the same premium to all members. States with the strictest community-rating laws include Maine, Massachusetts, New Jersey, New York, North Dakota, Oregon, Vermont, and Washington. Some 10 additional states impose lesser limits on insurance pools' ability to adjust premiums according to new enrollees' age and health status.

Community-rating laws try to force insurance pools to provide greater subsidies to people with preexisting conditions. In effect, community rating forces healthy people to pay higher premiums so that irresponsible people can wait until they are sick to purchase insurance. Put differently, community rating prevents insurers from responsibly managing the relationships between members of the pool. When community rating requires insurers to charge healthy 18-year-olds the same premium as 50-year-olds with multiple chronic conditions, it encourages all parties to behave in ways that are harmful to the pool and to society:

- Individuals with preexisting conditions see their premiums fall, and therefore purchase more coverage. That increases claims made against the pool, which increases the community-rated premium.
- Healthy individuals are essentially asked to subsidize sicker members of the pool, who are generally older and (ironically) have higher incomes. As the healthy members see their premiums rise, many will drop out of the pool, safe in the knowledge that they can always return and pay a community-rated (i.e., average) premium. Their departure makes the pool sicker on average, which further increases the community-rated premium. As that premium rises, additional healthy members drop out of the pool, and the cycle repeats itself. Economists and actuaries call that process an "adverse selection death spiral."
- All individuals find that they can no longer reduce their health insurance premiums by engaging in healthy behaviors or avoiding unhealthy behaviors. Thus, fewer individuals will do so, which reduces health and increases claims and premiums.
- Insurers compete to enroll healthy individuals and avoid the sick. Since all enrollees must pay the same premium regardless of their expected claims, healthy members become a gold mine and sick enrollees become a liability. Insurers therefore market their products with benefits (e.g., gym memberships) and advertising (e.g., featuring healthy-looking families) designed to appeal only to healthy people. They may also make enrollment difficult for sicker people, or curtail services that sick people value, hoping that sicker members will choose another insurer.

Community rating contributes to the large number of uninsured. It is one reason why residents of New York and New Jersey face some of the most expensive health insurance premiums in the nation.

For all the damage they cause, community-rating laws appear to offer little benefit. On the basis of his studies of unregulated markets and markets with community rating, Pauly concludes:

> We find that regulation modestly tempers the (already-small) relationship of premium to risk, and leads to a slight increase in the *relative* probability

that high-risk people will obtain individual coverage. However, we also find that the increase in overall premiums from community rating slightly reduces the total number of people buying insurance. All of the effects of regulation are quite small, though. We conjecture that the reason for the minimal impact is that guaranteed renewability already accomplishes a large part of effective risk averaging (without the regulatory burden), so additional regulation has little left to change.

Some 21 states also increase the cost of health insurance with "any-willing-provider" laws. Health insurers frequently negotiate discounts from providers. In exchange, those "preferred" providers receive a greater volume of business as insurers steer enrollees toward them. Any-willing-provider laws, however, require insurers to offer the same payment levels and contract terms to any provider who agrees to those terms. "Any-willing-provider legislation removes the incentive to compete aggressively on a price basis," writes health economist Michael Morrisey. "No one has an incentive to offer much of a discount since discounts will result only in lower prices with little or no expanded volume," he adds. The result is that enrollees pay more for medical care and health insurance.

All states increase the cost of health insurance by requiring consumers to purchase certain types of coverage, whether or not they want the particular coverage. As a result of these "mandated coverage" laws:

- Teetotalers must purchase coverage for alcoholism treatment (45 states).
- Nonsmokers must purchase coverage for smoking-cessation programs (2 states).
- Nondrug users must purchase coverage for drug-abuse treatment (34 states).
- Many consumers must purchase coverage for services they consider quackery, such as acupuncture (11 states), chiropractic (44 states), and naturopathy (4 states).
- Consumers are required to purchase coverage for services that may be more economical to purchase directly, such as various screening exams (mammograms, 50 states; cervical cancer and/or human papillomavirus, 29 states; colorectal cancer, 28 states; newborn hearing, 17 states; ovarian cancer, 3 states; and prostate cancer, 33 states), as well as uncomplicated deliveries (21 states) and well-child care (31 states).
- Ten states require residents to purchase coverage for hairpieces.

- Many consumers must purchase insurance that covers services or people in relationships that they find morally offensive, such as coverage for contraceptives (31 states), human papillomavirus vaccine (16 states), in vitro fertilization (13 states), and domestic partners (13 states).
- States have also required consumers to purchase coverage for medical treatments that later proved *harmful* to health, such as hormone replacement therapy (2 states) and high-dose chemotherapy with autologous bone marrow transplant for breast cancer (at least 1 state, Minnesota).

Eleven states require consumers to purchase 50 or more types of mandated coverage: California (50), Connecticut (51), Maine (53), Maryland (63), Minnesota (64), Nevada (52), New Mexico (51), New York (55), Texas (54), Virginia (55), and Washington (53). Another dozen states require at least 40 types of mandated coverage. State legislatures have enacted a total of 1,961 mandated coverage laws.

Mandated coverage laws are not sought by broad coalitions of consumers. Legislatures impose these requirements on consumers in response to pressure from special-interest groups, such as chiropractors, acupuncturists, massage therapists (four states), and other providers who want to expand the market for their services. Mandated coverage laws are special-interest legislation that harms consumers by reducing choice and increasing both the cost of health insurance and the number of Americans who cannot afford coverage.

States impose many additional regulations on insurance pools, from premium taxes to rules limiting insurers' ability to manage utilization. The Congressional Budget Office estimates that, on average, state regulations increase the cost of health insurance by 15 percent. Moreover, states prohibit individuals (and employers) from avoiding those laws by purchasing health insurance from states with more consumer-friendly regulations.

The Cure: Force Regulators to Compete

The original sin of health insurance regulation is not guaranteed issue, community rating, any-willing-provider laws, or mandated coverage laws. The original sin of health insurance regulation is insurance-licensing laws. Each state uses insurance-licensing laws to require every insurance policy sold to their residents to comply with all other insurance regulations. Insurance-licensing laws prohibit individual insurance purchasers from joining insurance pools with residents of other states. Put differently, they prohibit residents from purchasing out-of-state insurance products that come with a different set of regulatory protections. As a result, insurance-licensing laws erect barriers to trade between the states and prevent individuals from shopping for regulatory protections the same way they shop for other insurance features. In effect, insurance-licensing laws give each state's insurance regulators a monopoly over providing regulatory protections. Those regulators then behave the way all monopolists do: they provide a low-quality product at an excessively high cost.

The best solution would be for states to repeal insurance-licensing laws. Doing so would eliminate government's ability to use regulation to redistribute income, or to shower rents on favored special interests. Government enforcement of contracts would continue to provide the financial solvency protections and other safeguards that insurance purchasers demand. If that is infeasible politically, preliminary steps could provide nearly as much benefit to consumers.

With an approach known as "regulatory federalism" the federal or state governments would leave most health insurance regulations intact but would allow individuals and employers to purchase health insurance from other states, regulated by that second state. If a purchaser is content with her own state's regulations, she could continue to purchase a policy regulated at home. But if her state imposes too many mandates, or prevents the insurance pool from protecting itself from irresponsible and opportunistic behavior, then the purchaser could choose an insurance plan with more consumer-friendly regulations. A recent study by economist Stephen Parente and colleagues estimated the following:

- Letting individuals and employers purchase health insurance from out of state could reduce the number of uninsured Americans by as many as 17 million, or one-third of the most-cited estimate of the number of uninsured.
- When combined with tax reforms (see Chapter 14), this approach could cover as many as 24 million uninsured Americans.

Regulatory federalism would increase competition in health insurance markets. Insurers would face lower barriers to introducing products into new states. As a result, consumers would have much greater choice among cost-saving features (e.g., cost sharing and care management), provider financial incentives (fee-for-service, prepayment, and combinations thereof), and delivery systems (integrated, nonintegrated, and everything in between). Insurance pools would be more stable, and consumers would have much more freedom to obtain coverage that fits their needs.

Perhaps most important, regulatory federalism would force *insurance regulators* to compete against one another to provide the optimal level of regulation. States that impose unwanted regulatory costs on insurance purchasers would see their residents' business—and their premium tax revenue—go elsewhere. The desire to retain premium tax revenue would drive states to eliminate unwanted, costly regulations and retain only those regulations that consumers value. It is likely that one or a handful of states would emerge as the dominant regulators in a national marketplace. Regulatory federalism already exists for corporate chartering, where Delaware has created a niche for itself by offering a hospitable regulatory environment.

Many people, of course, will not want greater competition. Insurance regulators enjoy being monopoly providers. They will oppose threats to their monopoly position, even at the cost of harming consumers. The insurance industry will oppose regulatory federalism, which would subject them to greater competition as well. What insurance company wants to have to look over its shoulder to see if someone else might be doing a better job of managing insurance pools? Those are the very competitive pressures that benefit consumers, yet regulators and insurers will paint competition as a *threat* to consumers.

For example, opponents will claim that regulatory federalism will lead to a "race to the bottom," with some states so eager to attract premium tax revenue that they will eliminate all regulatory protections or skimp on enforcement. In reality, both market and political forces would prevent a race to the bottom. As producers of regulatory protections, states are unlikely to attract or retain customers—insurers, employers, or individual purchasers—by offering an inferior product. Purchasers will avoid states whose regulations prove inadequate, and ultimately, so will insurers. Moreover, the first people to be harmed by inadequate regulatory protections will likely be residents of that state, who will demand that their legislators remedy the problem. The resulting level of regulation would *not* be zero regulation. Rather than a race to the bottom, regulatory federalism would spur a race to equilibrium—or multiple equilibria—between too much and too little regulation. That balance would be struck by consumers' revealing their preferences.

Opponents of regulatory federalism will also claim that consumers would have to travel to another state to have those protections enforced.

On the contrary, those protections can be enforced in the consumer's state of residence. Not only will state courts enforce other states' laws, when appropriate, but another state's regulations can be incorporated into an insurance contract and enforced in the purchaser's home state. Such "choice-of-law" decisions are complicated and often disputed, but are ultimately controlled by extensively developed legal doctrine and case precedents. Insurance regulators can even play a role in policing and enforcing other states' regulatory protections. There is no reason not to allow consumers to choose where they purchase their health insurance.

There are several options for implementing regulatory federalism. Ideally, each state would unilaterally give its residents the right to purchase insurance from out of state. All a legislature need do is deem as licensed in its state any health insurance policy licensed by any of the other 49 states or the District of Columbia.

States could also give their residents a more limited right to purchase coverage out of state. For example, they could allow residents to purchase insurance from select states, or they could enter into reciprocal compacts with other states. These approaches, however, would be less desirable. They would unnecessarily limit competition among insurers and regulators, as well as limit consumer choice. The latter option would condition each consumer's access to affordable health insurance on whether the legislature *of another state* is willing to do the right thing. Lowering this trade barrier unilaterally and completely is the more consumer-friendly option.

The best way to eliminate those trade barriers might be for Congress to do so. The Framers intended the United States to be one large free-trade zone. Article I, section 8, of the Constitution grants Congress the power to regulate commerce among the states, largely so that Congress could prevent states from erecting trade barriers that keep out products from other states. Insurance-licensing laws are a clear example of such trade barriers and a perfect target for congressional elimination. As with state-level reform, Congress need not alter any state's health insurance regulations. All that is necessary is for Congress to require each state to recognize the insurance licenses issued by the other states.

The Constitution, however, does not grant Congress the power to regulate health insurance. Thus, in the same legislation, Congress should relinquish any role as an insurance regulator. Were Congress to do otherwise, the federal government itself would soon emerge as a monopoly provider of regulatory protections, and consumers would be even worse off than they are today. Over time, rent-seeking special interests would storm

Capitol Hill with demands for additional regulation. Once those federal regulations were enacted, they would be even further removed from the people than state regulations, and much more difficult to dislodge. It is crucial, therefore, that any federal law aimed at regulatory federalism do nothing more than allow consumers to purchase health insurance regulated by another state and ensure that those are the only regulations that govern. If Congress uses the opportunity to regulate health insurance itself, reform will not have been worth the effort.

Suggested Readings

Cannon, Michael F., and Michael D. Tanner. *Healthy Competition: What's Holding Back Health Care and How to Free It.* Washington: Cato Institute, 2007.

Hyman, David A. "The Massachusetts Health Plan: The Good, the Bad, and the Ugly." Cato Institute Policy Analysis no. 595, June 28, 2007.

Cochrane, John. "Time-Consistent Health Insurance." *Journal of Political Economy* 103, no. 3 (1995).

Conover, Christopher J. "Health Care Regulation: A $169 Billion Hidden Tax." Cato Institute Policy Analysis no. 527, October 4, 2004.

Herring, Bradley, and Mark V. Pauly. "Incentive-Compatible Guaranteed Renewable Health Insurance Premiums." *Journal of Health Economics* 25, no. 3 (May 2006).

Epstein, Richard A. "Antidiscrimination Principle in Health Care: Community Rating and Preexisting Conditions." In *American Health Care: Government, Market Processes, and the Public Interest,* edited by Roger Feldman. New Brunswick, NJ: Transaction Publishers, 2000.

Miller, Tom. "A Regulatory Bypass Operation." *Cato Journal* 22, no. 1 (Spring–Summer 2002).

Morrisey, Michael. "State Health Insurance Reform: Protecting the Provider." In *American Health Care: Government, Market Processes, and the Public Interest,* edited by Roger Feldman. New Brunswick, NJ: Transaction Publishers, 2000.

Parente, Stephen T., and others. "Consumer Response to a National Marketplace for Individual Insurance." Final report, University of Minnesota Carlton School of Management, June 28, 2008.

Pauly, Mark V., and Bradley Herring. *Pooling Health Insurance Risks.* Washington: AEI, 1999.

———. "Risk Pooling and Regulation: Policy and Reality in Today's Individual Health Insurance Market." *Health Affairs* 26, no. 3 (May–June 2007).

Pauly, Mark V., Allison Percy, and Bradley Herring. "Individual versus Job-Based Health Insurance: Weighing the Pros and Cons." *Health Affairs* 18, no. 6 (November–December 1999).

—Prepared by Michael F. Cannon

17. Social Security

Congress should

- allow workers to privately invest at least half their Social Security payroll taxes through individual accounts.

Although President Bush failed in his efforts to reform Social Security, the problems facing our national retirement system have not gone away. In fact, since the demise of the Bush proposal, Social Security's long-term unfunded liabilities have increased by more than $550 billion, and now total $15.3 trillion. Congress's failure to act is threatening America's economic stability and promises to bury our children and grandchildren under a mountain of debt. Reform is not an option, but a necessity, and Congress should act now.

But all Social Security reforms are not equal. Both raising taxes and cutting benefits have their own economic costs, and they make a bad deal even worse for today's younger workers. However, by allowing younger workers to privately invest their Social Security taxes through individual accounts, we can

- help restore Social Security to long-term solvency, without massive tax increases;
- provide workers with higher benefits than Social Security would otherwise be able to pay;
- create a system that treats women, minorities, and young people more fairly;
- increase national savings and economic growth;
- allow low-income workers to accumulate real, inheritable wealth for the first time in their lives; and
- give workers ownership of and control over their retirement funds.

181

The Financial Crisis

Social Security as we know it is facing irresistible demographic and fiscal pressures that threaten the future retirement benefits of today's young workers. Although Social Security is currently running a surplus, according to the system's own trustees, that surplus will turn into a deficit within the next nine years. That is, by 2017, Social Security will be paying out more in benefits than it takes in through taxes. (See Figure 17.1.)

In theory, Social Security is supposed to continue paying benefits after 2017 by drawing on the Social Security Trust Fund. Furthermore, the trust fund is supposed to provide sufficient funds to continue paying full benefits until 2041, after which it will be exhausted. At that point, *by law,* Social Security benefits will have to be cut by approximately 27 percent.

However, in reality, the Social Security Trust Fund is not an asset that can be used to pay benefits. Any Social Security surpluses accumulated to date have been spent, leaving a trust fund that consists only of government bonds (IOUs) that will eventually have to be repaid by taxpayers. As the Clinton administration's fiscal year 2000 budget explained it:

> These [Trust Fund] balances are available to finance future benefit payments and other Trust Fund expenditures—but only in a bookkeeping sense. . . .
> *They do not consist of real economic assets that can be drawn down in the future to fund benefits.* Instead, they are claims on the Treasury that,

Figure 17.1
Current and Projected Social Security Payouts, 2008–80

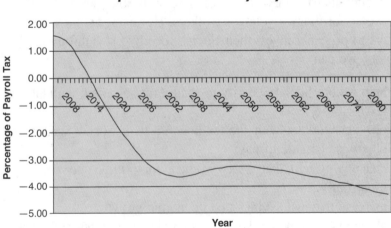

Year

SOURCE: The 2008 Annual Report of the Board of Trustees of the Federal Old-Age and Survivors Insurance and Disability Insurance Trust Funds.

when redeemed, will have to be financed by raising taxes, borrowing from the public, or reducing benefits or other expenditures. The existence of large Trust Fund balances, therefore, does not, by itself, have any impact on the Government's ability to pay benefits.

Even if Congress can find a way to redeem the bonds, the trust fund surplus will be completely exhausted by 2041. At that point, Social Security will need to rely solely on revenue from the payroll tax—but that revenue will not be sufficient to pay all promised benefits. Clearly, Social Security is not sustainable in its current form.

And there are really few options for dealing with the problem. This is not an opinion shared only by supporters of individual accounts. As former President Bill Clinton pointed out, the only ways to keep Social Security solvent are to (1) raise taxes, (2) cut benefits, or (3) get a higher rate of return through private capital investment. Henry Aaron of the Brookings Institution, a leading opponent of individual accounts, agrees. "Increased funding to raise pension reserves is possible only with some combination of additional tax revenues, reduced benefits, or increased investment returns from investing in higher yield assets," he told Congress in 1999.

A Declining Rate of Return

Yes, you could raise taxes and cut benefits enough to bring the system into solvency. That's what Congress has always done in the past. But this time, the tax increases or benefit cuts would have to be enormous. Besides, Social Security taxes are already so high, relative to benefits, that Social Security has quite simply become a bad deal for younger workers, providing a low, below-market rate of return.

This poor rate of return means that many young workers' retirement benefits are far lower than if they had been able to invest those funds privately. However, a system of individual accounts, based on private capital investment, would provide most workers with significantly higher returns. Those higher returns would translate into higher retirement benefits, leading to a more secure retirement for millions of seniors.

Savings and Economic Growth

Social Security operates on a pay-as-you-go basis, with almost all the incoming funds being immediately paid out to current beneficiaries. This system displaces private, fully funded alternatives under which the incoming funds would be saved and invested for the future benefits of today's workers. The result is a large net loss of national savings, which reduces capital investment, wages, national income, and economic growth. Moreover, by increasing the cost of hiring workers, the payroll tax substantially reduces wages, employment, and economic growth as well.

Shifting to a private system, with hundreds of billions of dollars invested in individual accounts each year, would likely produce a large net increase in national savings, depending on how the government financed the transition. This would increase national investment, productivity, wages, jobs, and economic growth. Replacing the payroll tax with private retirement contributions would also improve economic growth because the required contributions would be lower and would be seen as part of a worker's direct compensation, stimulating more employment and output.

Help for the Poor and Minorities

Low-income workers would be among the biggest winners under a system of privately invested individual accounts. Private investment would pay low-income workers significantly higher benefits than Social Security can pay. And that does not take into account the fact that blacks, other minorities, and the poor have below-average life expectancies. As a result, they tend to live fewer years in retirement and collect less in Social Security benefits than do whites. In a system of individual accounts, by contrast, they would each retain control over the funds paid in and could pay themselves higher benefits over their fewer retirement years, or leave more to their children or other heirs.

The higher returns and benefits of a privately invested system would be most important to low-income families, as they most need the extra funds. The funds saved in the individual retirement accounts, which could be left to the children of the poor, would also greatly help families break out of the cycle of poverty. Similarly, the improved economic growth, higher wages, and increased jobs that would result from an investment-based Social Security system would be most important to the poor. Moreover, without reform, low-income workers will be hurt the most by the higher taxes or reduced benefits that will be necessary if we continue on our current course. Averting a financial crisis and its inevitable results would consequently be most important to low-income workers.

In addition, with average- and low-wage workers' accumulating huge sums in their own investment accounts, the distribution of wealth throughout society would become far broader than it is today. That would occur not through the redistribution of existing wealth, but through the creation of new wealth, far more equally held. Because a system of individual accounts would turn every worker into a stockowner, the old division between labor and capital would be eroded. Every laborer would become a capitalist.

Ownership and Control

After all the economic analysis, however, perhaps the single most important reason for transforming Social Security into a system of individual accounts is that it would give American workers true ownership of and control over their retirement benefits.

Many Americans believe that Social Security is an "earned right." That is, because they have paid Social Security taxes they are entitled to receive Social Security benefits. The government encourages this belief by referring to Social Security taxes as "contributions," as in the Federal Insurance Contributions Act. However, the Supreme Court has ruled, in the case of *Flemming v. Nestor*, that workers have no legally binding contractual or property right to their Social Security benefits, and those benefits can be changed, cut, or even taken away at any time.

As the Court stated, "To engraft upon Social Security a concept of 'accrued property rights' would deprive it of the flexibility and boldness in adjustment to ever changing conditions which it demands." That decision built on a previous case, *Helvering v. Davis*, in which the Court had ruled that Social Security was not a contributory insurance program, stating that "the proceeds of both the employer and employee taxes are to be paid into the Treasury like any other internal revenue generally, and are not earmarked in any way."

In effect, Social Security turns older Americans into supplicants, dependent on the political process for their retirement benefits. If they work hard, play by the rules, and pay Social Security taxes their entire lives, they earn the privilege of going hat in hand to the government and hoping that politicians decide to give them some money for retirement.

In contrast, under a system of individual accounts, workers would have full property rights in their private accounts. They would own their accounts and the money in them the same way they own their individual retirement accounts or 401(k) plans. Their retirement benefits would not depend on the whims of politicians.

Simple Rules for Reform

Social Security's problems have led to a growing movement for reform, including proposals to allow younger workers to privately invest some or all of their Social Security taxes through individual accounts.

Unfortunately, however, many of these proposals fell short of what was truly needed to truly fix Social Security. Many proposals contained only tiny accounts, leaving the majority of workers' retirement income subject to government control. Other plans overpromised, pretending that every retiree could become a millionaire with no cost to the taxpayers and no tough decisions.

In developing a plan to reform Social Security, Congress should bear in mind the following simple rules.

Solvency Is Not Enough

The goal of Social Security reform should be to provide workers with the best possible retirement option, not simply to find ways to preserve the current Social Security system. After all, if solvency were the only goal, that could be accomplished with tax increases or benefit cuts, no matter how bad a deal that provided younger workers. A successful Social Security reform will of course result in a solvent system, not just in the short run, but sustainable over time as well. But it will also improve Social Security's rate of return; provide better retirement benefits; treat women, minorities, and low-income workers more fairly; and give workers real ownership and control of their retirement funds.

Size Matters

You don't cut out half a cancer. Many proposals for Social Security reform would allow workers to privately invest only a small portion of their payroll taxes, continuing to rely on the existing pay-as-you-go Social Security system for the majority of Social Security benefits. But small account proposals will not allow low- and middle-income workers to accumulate real wealth or achieve other objectives of reform. Individual accounts should be as large as feasible, ideally at least half of payroll taxes.

There Is No Free Lunch

Individual accounts will create a better, fairer, and more secure retirement system. But they cannot create miracles. They will provide higher retirement benefits than Social Security can pay. But they will not make everyone a millionaire. They will help solve Social Security's financial crisis and save taxpayers trillions of dollars over the long run. But there is no free lunch. There are short-term costs that will require tough choices by the president and Congress.

Some people say that current budget deficits make Social Security reform, and particularly individual accounts, impossible. They point to the "transition cost" of moving to individual accounts. Since current taxes are used to pay current beneficiaries, allowing younger workers to invest their taxes will require a replacement form of revenue to protect current retires. But given Social Security's unfunded liabilities, the transition does not really represent a new cost. It just makes explicit an already implicit debt.

Of course, it would mean paying that debt now rather than later. It is true, therefore, that reforming Social Security will increase short-term budget deficits. But it will save trillions of dollars in the long term. In many ways, it is like refinancing your mortgage. Sure you must pay the points up front, but you save money in the long run.

Although we should not minimize the difficulties of transition financing, it is also important to remember that financing the transition is a one-time event that actually serves to reduce the government's future liabilities. The transition moves the government's need for additional revenue forward in time, but—depending on the transition's ultimate design—it would not increase the amount of spending necessary. In effect, it is a case of "pay a little now or pay a lot later."

Cato's Social Security Plan

- Individuals would be able to privately invest **6.2 percentage points** of their payroll tax through individual accounts. Those who choose to do so will forfeit all future accrual of Social Security benefits.
- Individuals who choose individual accounts will receive **a recognition bond** based on past contributions to Social Security. These zero-coupon bonds will be offered to all workers who have contributed to Social Security, regardless of how long they have been in the system, but will be offered on a discounted basis.
- **Allowable investment options** for the individual accounts will be based on a three-tier system: a centralized, pooled collection and holding point; a limited series of investment options with a lifecycle fund as a default mechanism; and a wider range of investment options for individuals who accumulate a minimum level in their accounts.

- At retirement, individuals will be given an **option of purchasing a family annuity or taking a programmed withdrawal**. Those two options will be mandated only to a level required to provide an income above a minimum level. Funds in excess of the amount required to achieve this level of retirement income can be withdrawn in a lump sum.
- If individuals accumulate sufficient funds within their accounts to allow them to purchase an annuity that will keep them above a minimum income level in retirement, they will be **able to opt out** of the Social Security system entirely.
- **The remaining 6.2 percentage points of payroll taxes** will be used to pay transition costs and to fund disability and survivors benefits. Once, far in the future, transition costs are fully paid for, this portion of the payroll tax will be reduced to the level necessary to pay survivors and disability benefits.
- **The plan should be considered in** the context of payable Social Security benefits. That is, the Social Security system will be **restored to a solvent pay-as-you-go basis** before the development of individual accounts. Workers who choose to remain in the traditional Social Security system will receive whatever level of benefits Social Security can pay with existing levels. The best method for accomplishing this is to change the initial benefit formula from wage indexing to price indexing.
- The Social Security Administration has scored Cato's plan as restoring Social Security to permanent sustainable balance. Indeed, while the transition would initially increase Social Security's short-term deficits, the program would begin to run a permanent surplus by approximately 2048.

Conclusion

Social Security is not sustainable without reform. Simply put, it cannot pay promised future benefits with current levels of taxation. Yet raising taxes or cutting benefits will only make a bad deal worse. At the same time, workers have no ownership of their benefits, and Social Security benefits are not inheritable. This is particularly problematic for low-wage workers and minorities. Perhaps most important, the current Social Security system gives workers no choice or control over their financial future.

It is long past time for Congress to act.

Suggested Readings

Ferrara, Peter, and Michael Tanner. *A New Deal for Social Security.* Washington: Cato Institute, 1998.

Piñera, José. "Empowering Workers: The Privatization of Social Security in Chile." *Cato's Letters* no. 10, May 1996.

Tanner, Michael. "The 6.2 Percent Solution: A Plan for Reforming Social Security." Cato Institute Social Security Paper no. 32, February 17, 2004.

———, ed. *Social Security and Its Discontents: Perspectives on Choice.* Washington: Cato Institute, 2004.

———. "A Better Deal at Half the Cost: SSA Scoring of the Cato Social Security Reform Plan." Cato Institute Briefing Paper no. 92, April 26, 2005.

—Prepared by Michael Tanner

Cutting Federal Departments and Programs

18. Agricultural Policy

Congress should

- phase down and terminate crop subsidies, a process that was supposed to begin with passage of the 1996 Freedom to Farm Act;
- move farmers toward the use of market-based insurance and other financial instruments to protect against adverse prices and weather events;
- eliminate federal controls that create producer cartels in such markets as dairy and sugar; and
- eliminate trade protections on agricultural goods while working through the World Trade Organization to pursue liberalization in global markets.

The U.S. Department of Agriculture distributes between $10 billion and $30 billion in subsidies to farmers and owners of farmland each year. The particular amount depends on the prices of crops, the level of disaster payments, and other factors. More than 90 percent of agricultural subsidies go to farmers of five crops—wheat, corn, soybeans, rice, and cotton. More than a million farmers and landowners receive subsidies, but the payments are heavily tilted toward the largest producers.

In addition to regular cash subsidies, the USDA provides crop insurance, marketing support, and other services for farm businesses. The USDA also performs extensive agricultural research for the industry. These indirect subsidies and services cost taxpayers about $5 billion each year, putting total farm support at between $15 billion and $35 billion annually.

Agriculture has attracted federal government support since the late 19th century, but the subsidies remained modest until the 1930s. New Deal programs included commodity price supports, production controls, marketing orders, import barriers, and crop insurance. The particular structures of federal farm programs have changed over time, but the central planning philosophy behind them has changed little in seven decades.

Agricultural subsidies make no economic sense, but the farm lobby in Washington is powerful and it strongly resists reforms. One strategy of the farm lobby is to co-opt the support of urban legislators, who seek increased subsidies in farm bills for food assistance programs. Legislators who favor environmental subsidies have also been co-opted as supporters of farm bills.

In 1996, Congress enacted some pro-market reforms under the "Freedom to Farm" law. The law allowed farmers greater flexibility in their planting decisions and moved toward reliance on market supply and demand. But Congress reversed course in the late 1990s and passed a series of large supplemental farm subsidy bills. As a result, subsidies that were expected to cost $47 billion over the seven years of the 1996 law ended up costing $121 billion.

In 2002, Congress and the Bush administration passed a farm bill that further reversed the reforms of 1996. The 2002 law increased projected subsidy payments 74 percent over 10 years. It added new crops to the subsidy rolls, and it created a new price guarantee scheme called the "countercyclical" program.

In 2008, Congress overrode a presidential veto to enact farm legislation that continued existing supports and created new subsidy programs. The legislation added an expensive "permanent disaster" program for areas often hit by adverse conditions, and it added a revenue protection program for farm businesses, which is designed to lock in 2008's record-high commodity prices. This Average Crop Revenue Election program might cost taxpayers billions of dollars if prices fall to more typical levels in coming years.

The 2008 farm bill also added a new sugar-to-ethanol program under which the government buys excess imported sugar that might put downward pressure on inflated U.S. sugar prices. The program supports domestic sugar growers' protected 85 percent of the U.S. sugar market, and it provides for the government to sell excess sugar, at a loss if need be, to ethanol producers.

Finally, producers of "specialty crops," including fruits and vegetables, were able to secure new subsidies in the 2008 farm bill, including a marketing support program. Although limited means testing of subsidies was introduced in the 2008 farm bill, a farming household could still earn up to $1.5 million in adjusted gross income before forgoing any farm subsidies.

The federal welfare system for farm businesses is costly to taxpayers, and it damages the economy. Subsidies induce overproduction and inflate land prices in rural America. The flow of subsidies and regulations from Washington hinders farmers from innovating, diversifying their land use, and taking other actions needed to prosper in a competitive global economy.

Eight Types of Federal Farm Subsidies

1. Direct payments. "Direct" payments are cash subsidies for producers of 10 crops: wheat, corn, sorghum, barley, oats, cotton, rice, soybeans, minor oilseeds, and peanuts. Direct payments are based on a historical measure of a farm's acreage used for production, but some payments go to owners of land that is no longer even used for farming. Established in 1996, direct payments were intended to be transitional, a way to wean farmers off old-fashioned price supports. Unfortunately, direct payments have not been phased down as planned even as price supports are continued. Direct payments cost about $5 billion annually.

2. Marketing loans. The marketing loan program is a price support program that began in the New Deal era. The program encourages overproduction by setting a price floor for crops and by reducing the price variability that would otherwise face producers in the free market. The marketing loan program covers the same crops as the direct subsidy program. In addition, the 2002 farm law expanded it to cover wool, mohair, honey, dry peas, lentils, and chickpeas. In recent years, payments under this program have ranged from about $1 billion to $7 billion annually.

3. Countercyclical payments. Although the 1996 farm law moved away from traditional price guarantee subsidies, the 2002 farm bill embraced them with the addition of the countercyclical program. This program covers the same 10 commodities as the direct payments program, and the 2008 farm bill added dry peas, lentils, and chickpeas. In recent years, countercyclical payments have ranged from about $1 billion to $4 billion annually. Like the marketing loan program, the countercyclical program stimulates excess farm production.

4. Conservation subsidies. USDA conservation programs dispense about $3 billion annually to the nation's farmers. The Conservation Reserve Program was created in 1985 to idle millions of acres of farmland. Under the CRP, farmers are paid on a per-acre basis not to grow crops. About one-third of land idled under the CRP is owned by retired farmers, so one does not even have to be a working farmer to get these subsidies.

195

5. Insurance. The Risk Management Agency runs the USDA's farm insurance programs, which are available to farmers to protect against adverse weather, pests, and low market prices. The RMA has annual outlays of about $3 billion. Federal crop insurance policies are sold by 16 private insurance companies, which receive direct federal subsidies. The firms operate like a cartel, earning excess profits from the high premiums they charge. At the same time, the government provides large subsidies for insurance premiums, such that farmers pay only about one-third the full cost of their policies.

6. Disaster aid. The government operates various crop insurance and disaster assistance programs for farmers. In addition, Congress frequently jumps in to declare "disasters" whenever the slightest adverse event occurs, and often distributes special payments to farmers regardless of whether they sustained substantial damage. The 2008 farm bill's new permanent disaster program, intended to reduce ad hoc emergency relief bills, is projected to cost $3.8 billion over the five-year life of the bill.

7. Export subsidies. The USDA operates a range of programs to aid farmers and food companies with their foreign sales. The Market Access Program hands out about $140 million annually to producers in support of activities such as advertising campaigns. Recipients include the Distilled Spirits Council, the Pet Food Institute, the Association of Brewers, the Popcorn Board, and the Wine Institute. Another program, the Foreign Market Development Program, hands out $35 million annually to groups such as the American Peanut Council and the Mohair Council of America.

8. Agricultural research and statistics. Most American industries fund their own research and development programs. The agriculture industry is a notable exception. The USDA spends about $3 billion annually on agricultural research, statistical information services, and economic studies. The USDA carries out research in 108 different locations and provides subsidies to the 50 states for research and education.

Six Reasons to Repeal Farm Subsidies

1. Farm subsidies redistribute wealth. Farm subsidies transfer the earnings of taxpayers to a small group of fairly well-off farm businesses and landowners. USDA figures show that the average income of farm households has been consistently higher than the average of all U.S. households. The average income of farm households in 2006 was $77,654, or 17 percent higher than the $66,570 average for all households.

Although policymakers often discuss the plight of the small farmer, the bulk of federal farm subsidies goes to the largest farms. For example, the largest 10 percent of recipients have received 73 percent of all subsidy payments in recent years. Numerous large corporations and even some wealthy celebrities receive farm subsidies because they are the owners of farmland. It is landowners, not tenant farmers or farm workers, who benefit from subsidies.

2. Farm subsidies damage the economy. The extent of federal micro-management of the agriculture industry is unique. In most industries, market prices balance supply and demand, profit levels signal investment opportunities, and entrepreneurs innovate to provide better products at lower prices. Those market mechanisms are blunted in U.S. agricultural markets. Farm programs variously result in overproduction, overuse of marginal farmland, less efficient planting, excess borrowing by farmers, insufficient attention to cost control, and less market innovation.

3. Farm programs are prone to scandal. Like most federal subsidy programs, farm programs are subject to bureaucratic inefficiencies, recipient fraud, and pork-barrel politics. A 2004 Government Accountability Office study found that as much as half a billion dollars in farm subsidies are paid improperly each year. Farmers create complex organizational structures to get around legal subsidy limits, and many farmers do not pay back their USDA loans, according to the GAO. At the same time, Congress and the USDA tend to distribute payments for farm emergencies carelessly. Disaster payments often go to farmers who have no need for them.

4. Farm subsidies damage U.S. trade relations. Global stability and U.S. security are enhanced when less developed countries achieve stronger economic growth. America can further that end while helping itself by encouraging the expansion of trade by poor nations. However, U.S. and European farm subsidies and import barriers are a serious hurdle to making progress in global trade agreements. U.S. sugar protections, for example, benefit only a very small group of U.S. growers but are blocking broader free trade within the Americas as well as harming U.S. consumers.

The World Trade Organization estimates that even a one-third cut in all tariffs around the world would boost global output by $686 billion, including $164 billion for the United States. Trade liberalization would boost the exports of U.S. goods that are competitive on world markets, including many agricultural products, but U.S. farm subsidies and protections stand in the way of that goal.

197

5. Farm programs damage the environment. Federal farm policies are thought to damage the natural environment in numerous ways. Subsidy programs cause overproduction, which draws marginal farmland into active production. Similarly, trade barriers induce agriculture production on land that is naturally less productive. As a result, marginal lands that might otherwise be used for parks or forests are locked into farm use because farm subsidy payments get capitalized into higher prices for land.

Subsidies are also thought to induce excessive use of fertilizers and pesticides. One reason is that producers on marginal lands that have poorer soils and climates tend to use more fertilizers and pesticides than do other producers. An excessive use of chemicals can contaminate water systems, as Florida sugar growers illustrate. Large areas of wetlands have been converted to sugar cane production because of artificially high U.S. sugar prices. Unfortunately, the phosphorous in fertilizers used by sugar farmers has caused substantial damage to the Everglades.

6. Agriculture would thrive without subsidies. If U.S. farm subsidies were ended and agricultural markets were deregulated, farming would change—different crops would be planted, land usage would change, and some farms would go bankrupt. But it is very likely that a stronger and more innovative industry would emerge that had greater resilience to shocks and downturns.

Interestingly, producers of most U.S. agricultural commodities do not receive regular subsidies from the federal government. In fact, commodities that are eligible for federal subsidies account for about 36 percent of U.S. farm production, whereas commodities that generally survive without subsidies, such as meats and poultry, account for about 64 percent of production. And, of course, most other U.S. industries prosper without the extensive government coddling that many farm businesses receive.

An interesting example of farmers' prospering without subsidies is New Zealand. In 1984, New Zealand ended its farm subsidies, which was a bold stroke because the country is four times more dependent on farming than is the United States. The changes were initially met with fierce resistance, but New Zealand farm productivity, profitability, and output have soared since the reforms. New Zealand farmers have cut costs, diversified land use, sought nonfarm income, and developed niche markets, such as kiwifruit. The Federated Farmers of New Zealand argues that that nation's experience ''thoroughly debunked the myth that the farming sector cannot prosper without government subsidies.'' That myth needs to be debunked in the United States as well.

Suggested Readings

Cato Institute. Center for Trade Policy Studies website. ''Agriculture.'' www.free-trade.org/issues/agriculture.

_____. Downsizing the Federal Government website. U.S. Department of Agriculture. http://www.downsizinggovernment.org.

Edwards, Chris. ''The Sugar Racket.'' Cato Institute Tax & Budget Bulletin no. 46, June 2007.

_____. ''Milk Madness.'' Cato Institute Tax & Budget Bulletin no. 47, July 2007.

Griswold, Daniel, Stephen Slivinski, and Christopher Preble. ''Ripe for Reform: Six Good Reasons to Reduce U.S. Farm Subsidies and Trade Barriers.'' Cato Institute Trade Policy Analysis no. 30, September 14, 2005.

James, Sallie, and Daniel Griswold. ''Freeing the Farm: A Farm Bill for All Americans.'' Cato Institute Trade Policy Analysis no. 34, April 16, 2007.

Lambie, Thomas. ''Miracle Down Under: How New Zealand Farmers Prosper without Subsidies or Protection.'' Cato Institute Free Trade Bulletin no. 16, February 7, 2005.

—Prepared by Chris Edwards and Sallie James

19. The Defense Budget

> *Policymakers should*
>
> - adopt a grand strategy of restraint, which means avoiding state-building missions and eliminating most U.S. defense alliances;
> - redeploy troops in Iraq, South Korea, Europe, and Japan to the United States, lessening the requirement for U.S. forces and allowing reductions in force structure;
> - cut the size of the army to 25–30 brigades and cancel the Future Combat Systems;
> - reduce the size of the Marine Corps to two division equivalents and cancel the Marine Corps Expeditionary Fighting Vehicle program and V-22 Osprey;
> - reduce the navy to 200 ships by cutting the number of carrier battle groups to eight, naval air wings to nine, and expeditionary strike groups to six; and cancel the littoral combat ship program and the DDG-1000 destroyer program;
> - eliminate six fighter air wing equivalents, thereby limiting the air force's procurement of fighters;
> - eliminate roughly one-third of the Pentagon's civilian workforce and identify jobs now done by military personnel that can be done by civilians, who cost less and remain in their jobs longer; and
> - cut the nuclear weapons arsenal to 1,000 warheads based on 8 ballistic nuclear missile submarines (rather than 14), and reduce the number of intercontinental ballistic missiles to 100–200.

In a literal sense, the United States does not have a defense budget. The adjective is wrong. Our military spending is for many purposes: other nations' defense, the purported extension of freedom, the maintenance of hegemony, and the ability to threaten any other nation with conquest. But the relationship between these objectives and the end they purport to serve, the protection of Americans and their welfare, is unclear. In fact, defining the requirements of our defense so broadly is probably counterproductive. Our global military posture and activism drag us into others' conflicts, provoke animosity, cause states to balance our power, and waste resources. We need a defense budget worthy of the name.

The United States faces a benign threat environment. Most wars Americans contemplate fighting could be avoided without harm to U.S. national security. The United States could adopt a far less active defense strategy, a strategy of restraint. This strategy would require far less spending. This chapter describes that defense strategy and budget, even though our current politics preclude its implementation. But before describing that defense budget, we must understand the problems with the current one.

The defense budget increased dramatically in the last eight years (Figure 19.1). A buildup that began in 1998 accelerated dramatically after the 9/11 terrorist attacks. The fiscal year 2009 baseline or nonwar request of $518 billion is $228 billion higher than the FY00 defense budget in current dollars, or about 43 percent higher in real, inflation-adjusted terms. Another $22.8 billion in spending that falls outside the Department of Defense, mostly in the Department of Energy's nuclear weapons management and research programs, is usually counted as defense spending and brings the total to about $541 billion. This will be the highest nonwar budget ever. Including war supplementals, which now include modernization funds scarcely connected to wars in Iraq and Afghanistan, the defense budget in FY09 will likely exceed $700 billion—a total higher in real terms than in any year since World War II. Defense spending now accounts for over 22 percent of federal spending, more than Social Security and more than all other federal discretionary spending. That total still excludes $66 billion for homeland security and $94 billion for veterans planned for FY09, which the Office of Management and Budget does not consider defense spending.

The explosion in defense spending since 2001 results from several factors. First, the cost of personnel has risen far faster than inflation, driven by health care costs and benefits. Second, the services have allowed the cost of procurement programs to spiral out of control in case after case, mostly because they insist on pressing the technological envelope. Third, the wars in Iraq and Afghanistan now approach $200 billion annually and have driven up personnel and operations and maintenance costs. Fourth,

Figure 19.1
Escalating "Emergency" Supplemental War Spending Impedes Accountability of Defense Funding: Defense Expenditures, FY2001–2009

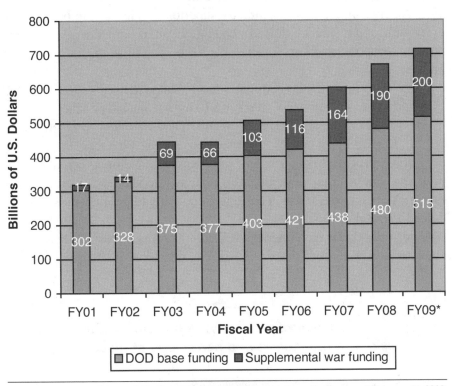

SOURCE: *Congressional Research Service,* "FY2009 Defense Budget: Issues for Congress," February 11, 2008.

*The $200 billion supplemental cost in FY09 is an estimate based on recent history and force levels in Iraq and Afghanistan.

the Pentagon has failed to make sufficient tradeoffs in its force structure choices. Although increased fear of terrorism helped cause the spike in defense spending, little of the base defense budget goes to counterterrorism-related activities.

There are many problems with the current defense budget; this chapter highlights only the three most important. First, it is too large for the threats we face and therefore wasteful. Second, it fails to adhere to a strategy that would force choices among competing means of providing defense. Third, it funds the Iraq War, which detracts from American security at great expense and spends too much to remake the military, particularly the ground forces, into a force meant to fight more wars like Iraq.

A Benign Threat Environment

The United States is one of the most secure nations in history. Invasion and civil war, the troubles that traditionally required militaries, are unthinkable here. Yet our military spending is half the world's, as seen in Figure 19.2. No rival challenges our military superiority. That would be the case even with a far smaller defense budget. Even if larger rivals existed, nuclear weapons and our location far from potential enemies provide great security.

The closest thing the United States has to state enemies—North Korea, Iran, and Syria—together spend about $10 billion annually on their militaries, less than one-sixtieth of what we do. They are local troublemakers, but all lack military means to strike our shores—a tactic that would only invite their destruction in any case. Russia's declining democracy is troubling, but no immediate threat to Americans. Should Russia threaten Europe, the Europeans, with a collective economy larger than ours, should defend themselves.

China may challenge American military supremacy decades hence, but there are several reasons that this possibility does not justify heavy defense

Figure 19.2
U.S. Military Spending vs. the World, 2008
(billions of U.S. dollars and percentage of global total)

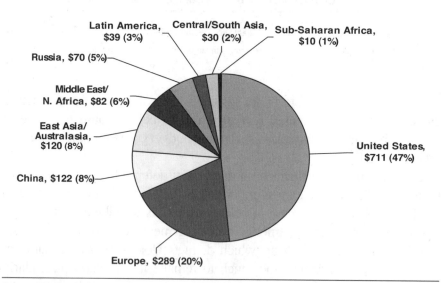

SOURCE: The Center for Arms Control and Non-Proliferation, February 11, 2008.

spending today. First, China's defense spending (estimated by the International Institute for Strategic Studies at $122 billion) goes mostly toward territorial defense. Second, China's ability to become a great military power is hindered by the uncertainty of its continued rapid wealth creation. Third, China and the United States have little reason for a rivalrous military posture akin to the cold war. There is no significant ideological conflict, China's authoritarian system will not spread, and it is no opponent of capitalism. The only possible territorial conflict is Taiwan, which is a problem only so long as we claim to defend it. (See also Chapters 53, "Relations with China, India, and Russia," and 54, "East Asian Security Commitments.")

Nor can terrorism justify our current defense spending. Military forces are useful in destroying well-defended targets. Terrorists are mostly hidden and lightly armed. The trick is finding them, not killing or capturing them, which is relatively simple once they are found. True, where terrorists fight in civil wars or assemble outside the reach of friendly governments, military forces are occasionally useful. But even then our primary weapons are relatively cheap niche capabilities: aerial drones, cruise missiles, or special operations forces—not conventional force structure. Even in rare cases like Afghanistan where ground forces and air support are useful, only a small portion of our conventional force structure is needed.

The defense budget ignores this geopolitical fortune. Absent an enemy like Nazi Germany or the Soviet Union—a great power rival with expansionist intent and capability—there is no justification for cold war–level defense spending. Assessments of defense requirements like the Quadrennial Defense Review and the National Security Strategy offer vague language about uncertainty to justify this massive force structure. There are possible scenarios that might employ our force structure, but remote possibilities can justify any spending. The best hedge against the uncertain future is a prosperous and innovative economy supporting a small, capable military that can be expanded to meet threats.

Today, many defense analysts and officials—most notably Defense Secretary Robert Gates and Chairman of the Joint Chiefs of Staff Mike Mullen—argue that the United States should set a floor for defense spending equal to 4 percent of gross domestic product. This argument makes little sense. Yes, defense spending as a percentage of GDP is near a post–World War II low and military spending consumed larger portions of our wealth during past wars—over 35 percent during World War II and nearly 15 percent during the Korean War. Defense spending has remained between 4 and 5 percent of GDP during the Iraq War, by contrast. But this measure does not account for the fact that the country has grown far wealthier over the past five decades. Our GDP is more than six times bigger than it was in 1950. Defense spending has grown absolutely over this period, but the economy has grown so much that defense is a smaller portion of GDP, as Figure 19.3 demonstrates. The amount of spending devoted to defense should fluctuate with threats, not economic growth, as proponents of fixed-ratio spending would have it. And as we have seen, threats do not justify such spending.

Strategy Should Drive Force Structure

The second problem with the defense budget is its failure to adhere to a strategy. There is no dearth of Pentagon documents using that word, but the real thing is absent. Because resources are limited, strategy is choice—the prioritization of resources among competing demands. In the United States, strategy should prioritize threats, causing choice among the military services and the platform communities within them. For example,

Figure 19.3
Past and Projected Spending for National Defense, 1940–2025

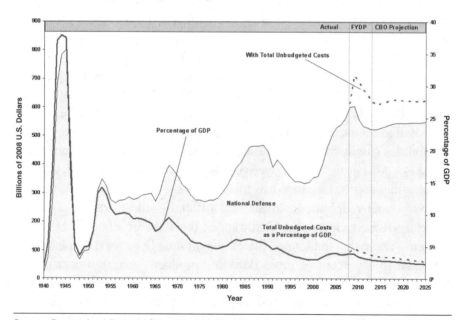

SOURCE: Congressional Budget Office, "The Long-Term Impact of Current Defense Plans," March 2008.
NOTE: CBO = Congressional Budget Office; FYDP = fiscal year defense plan.

the Eisenhower administration's massive retaliation strategy saw the defense of industrial centers in Western Europe and East Asia from communism as the principal American security challenge. To defend these areas at reasonable cost, it threatened nuclear strikes against the Soviet Union in defense of allied states in Europe and Asia. Because bombers delivered nuclear weapons then, this strategy gave the air force roughly half the budget, leaving the army and navy to fight over the remainder. Likewise, today some analysts call for an offshore balancing strategy that would eschew occupations of foreign countries and overseas basing in favor of a navy-dominated strategy that threatens force from the sea. This strategy would give the navy and marines greater shares of the budget, cutting back on allocations going to the air force, and especially the army.

But the Bush administration has avoided such choices in its defense budget. Initially, the administration, led by Secretary of Defense Donald Rumsfeld, advocated a technologically transformed military that might have marginally reduced the role and budget of the army, had peace held. However, the administration's response to 9/11—invading and occupying Afghanistan and Iraq—demanded tremendous manpower for policing duties. If these wars were seen as harbingers of a new reality, as the administration sometimes said, the obvious course was to grow the army and marines budgets and cut spending on the navy and air force, which are less relevant to counterinsurgencies. Capability suited to possible future enemies might have been sacrificed to deal with the current ones.

Instead, the Bush administration and Congress tried to have it all. They chose to pay for the wars through supplemental appropriations that are subject to limited congressional oversight. This mechanism protects regular defense spending mainly intended for conventional combat from being cut to pay for the wars. The air force and navy budgets continue to grow despite their limited relevance to the wars under way, and their procurement priorities have not changed. In fact, excluding supplementals, the Bush administration has essentially kept the budget shares of each service fixed since it took office, following in the footsteps of administrations since Kennedy's. Budget categories less associated with the wars, procurement and research, developing, testing, and evaluation, have each grown by over 50 percent in real terms during the Bush administration. (Most war costs fall in the operations and maintenance account.) This lack of prioritization explains the seeming paradox of having a huge budget that cancels few defense programs (the army's Crusader artillery system and Comanche helicopter are rare exceptions) but will still fall $100 billion a year or so shy of the funds needed to meet its own requirements, according to Congressional Budget Office estimates. (See the dotted line Figure 19.3.)

Only in 2007, when it proposed the expansion of the ground forces, did the Bush administration acknowledge that it had an army-centric approach to defense. Under the expansion plan, which will take at least three years, the marines will grow by 27,000 to 202,000 and the army by 65,000 soldiers to 547,000. According to the Congressional Budget Office, the cost of the expansion will exceed $100 billion and will add $14 billion in annual spending once it has been accomplished. Both the FY08 defense budget and the administration's proposed FY09 defense budget contain funds for this growth. The increased spending, however, is accomplished mainly by topline budget growth rather than coming at the expense of the other services—the army's share of defense spending will grow by only 1–2 percent, once war-related spending is excluded.

Planning of More Iraqs

The problem with this partial effort at aligning the defense strategy with the defense budget is that the administration has the wrong strategy— the third problem. It is true that the ground forces are overstretched. But the solution is doing less, not adding forces for more wars of occupation. The U.S. experiences in Iraq and Afghanistan demonstrate the difficulty and prohibitive cost of reordering foreign societies. Occupying Afghanistan was hard to avoid, but it is an exceptional case. Large-scale counterinsurgency and state-building campaigns are not needed to prevent anti-American terrorism. History is full of failed states, and only a handful gave rise to terrorism. Most are inhospitable to everyone, terrorists included. In those rare instances where terrorists targeting Americans do gather, the U.S. military can prevent havens without running the state. Using only a small portion of our intelligence and strike capability, along with local allies, we can deny terrorists havens. In fact, as political scientists have documented, occupations are likely to provoke terrorism directed at the United States, not prevent it.

New Criteria for Determining the Size of U.S. Forces

U.S. defense planners today suffer from strategic incontinence. They envision the U.S. military as a tool to contain China; transform failed states so they resemble ours; chase terrorists; keep oil cheap; democratize the Middle East; protect European, Asian, and Middle Eastern states from aggression and geopolitical competition that might require them to develop military power independent of ours; popularize the United States via humanitarian missions; respond to natural disasters abroad; and more. The forces needed to accomplish this litany of aspirations can never be enough, so analysts want more of everything, and higher and higher defense spending. Instead, our military budget should defend us. That is a relatively cheap and simple task.

That budget should reflect a strategy befitting our circumstance and strengths: an "island nation" remote from trouble that has the wealth and technical know-how to replace manpower with technology, not an imperial power bent on forcing its way of life on far-off states that we struggle to comprehend. We should avoid the tendency to confuse foreign disorder with foreign threats. We should also reduce our commitments to defend others. The rationale for our cold war alliances has disappeared; the alliances should follow suit. (See "Transatlantic Relations," Chapter 55.)

The need for disengagement is particularly acute in the Middle East. We often hear that U.S. military forces are needed to promote stability and cheap oil in the region. The truth is close to the opposite. Our troops there tend to produce destabilizing nationalist or sectarian backlash, a problem exacerbated in recent years by the burgeoning of communications technology that draws more people into regional or international politics. Oil's price is little affected by U.S. troop presence in supplier nations, except insofar as the wars we participate in or threaten there drive its price up. (See "U.S. Policy in the Middle East," Chapter 52.)

Avoiding civil wars, abandoning cold war alliances, and leaving the Middle East would dramatically reduce the odds of war, allowing considerable reductions in the size and cost of our military. Still, restraint is not pacifism. International relations are unpredictable, and attacks on the United States must be deterred or met with force. Under a strategy of restraint, the United States would retain a powerful military that is dominant in air, land, and naval combat.

According to the latest Quadrennial Defense Review, the U.S. military is designed to conduct two overlapping major combat operations, with the possibility of decisive victory in a prolonged irregular warfare campaign in one theater. A restrained defense strategy requires a force designed to wage only one major conventional campaign. That force could still participate in irregular missions, but the need to preserve the force for other purposes would make leaders less likely to use it recklessly. A smaller force would also encourage the United States to share occupational burdens with allies, as in Afghanistan.

Far from requiring more troops, a strategy of restraint would allow the ground forces to shrink. The army would need only roughly 30 brigade combat teams, as opposed to the current planned 48, and the marines only two division equivalents (or Marine Expeditionary Forces), instead of three. In a land war, the National Guard and reserves would augment these forces. With fewer burdens, the National Guard could focus on homeland security missions. Special operations forces would take the lead in training foreign military forces and hunting terrorists in ungoverned regions in the rare cases where U.S. forces are required.

The navy could shrink to eight carrier battle groups, and six expedition-ary strike groups requiring roughly 200 ships. Today's naval platforms are significantly more capable (and expensive) than the prior generation of naval ships and aircraft, so a smaller force is sufficient given the absence of blue-water rivals. This reduction is more likely to occur if it is implemented gradually as ships retire and are not replaced one to one.

The air force should be reduced to 14 fighter air wing equivalents or fewer from the current 20 and its support and training infrastructure reduced to reflect the change. Three factors permit this reduction. First, the increased range and precision of carrier-based airpower have greatly lessened the need for land-based tactical airpower. Second, the absence of rivals invest-ing in an airpower that can challenge ours lessens force requirements needed to gain air superiority. Third, improvements in airpower, principally precision targeting, make each airframe far more capable than in the past. While buying fewer short-range aircraft, the air force should continue on its current track to buy intelligence, surveillance, and reconnaissance assets in the air and in space, in particular unmanned aerial vehicles. Under restraint, the air force will fly fewer missions, but a higher percentage of its missions will begin in the United States. Hence, a higher portion of the air force budget should go to long-range assets: bombers, air-refueling tankers, and airlift.

Suggested Reforms

Over the next few years, Congress should push the Department of Defense to implement a defense budget based on restraint. These changes, outlined below, should eventually allow reductions in the nonwar defense budget to about $350 billion a year in today's dollars. Even these cuts will leave the U.S. military with a great margin of dominance over all other militaries. Additional reductions are certainly possible. Most of these savings would be achieved by cutting force structure from the services, which reduces the operating cost of the military and ultimately the need for new equipment and manpower.

- Redeploy troops from Iraq, South Korea, Europe, and Japan to the United States. Leaving Iraq would save roughly $130 billion a year. The savings achieved by leaving Europe, South Korea, and Japan would be small because our allies pay some costs. The savings would come largely by lessening the requirement for U.S. forces, allowing reductions in force structure. These changes are discussed below.
- Instead of increasing the size of the army to 48 brigades, cut it to 25–30 brigades, cutting procurement and personnel to match the resized force. This reduction would take several years to accomplish, but upward of $15 billion to $20 billion annually would be saved immediately by avoiding the cost of the expansion alone.
- Cancel the Future Combat Systems. FCS, a family of 14 major systems, down from 18, including vehicles, weapons, and a communications system, relies on many unproved technologies. Its lifetime price tag has grown from $99 billion to $160 billion. It is premised on two bad ideas: that the army must deploy in a great hurry, hence on aircraft, and that the resulting light vehicles can avoid close fights with improved sensors and communications. Recent history shows that the army will have time to deploy via sealift, but will need heavy vehicles once it arrives. Ground forces still find most enemies by contact, and even insurgents can destroy light vehicles and sometimes tanks. Thus, heavy vehicles should remain the principle army combat vehicles and a mix of heavy and Stryker brigades will suffice. The army should break off and retain pieces of FCS that can stand alone.
- Reduce the marines to roughly two division equivalents rather than expanding to three.
- Eliminate the Marine Corps Expeditionary Fighting Vehicle program and cease purchases of the V-22 Osprey tilt-rotor aircraft. The EFV is an armored amphibious vehicle intended for amphibious landings under fire. Such landings are central to the marines' identity, but none have occurred since 1950. The vehicles are also overpriced and unreliable. The tilt-rotor Osprey is a good idea for attacks from the sea, but it has a terrible safety record and is far over budget. It also cannot carry heavy loads, meaning that it would drop off the marines it carries without sufficient means to maneuver under fire.
- Reduce the number of carrier battle groups to eight (and naval air wings to nine) and expeditionary strike groups to six, allowing the

fleet size to fall to 200 as ships retire. This change should be accomplished by speeding retirements of older ships and slowing procurement of new ones. One objection to this reduction in force structure is that it limits the places U.S. forces can be, what the navy refers to as "presence." This complaint has some validity, but there is little evidence that U.S. forces stabilize the regions they patrol.

- Instead of buying more DDG-51s to replace the disastrous DDG-1000 program, as the navy wants, keep the number of planned DDGs at the current level. The navy should also terminate the costly littoral combat ship program and consider a cheaper class of frigates, such as a version of the Coast Guard National Security Cutter or a foreign-built ship.

- Slow submarine procurement to allow a gradual decline in the number of attack submarines to roughly 40. Absent more significant challenges to American command of the seas, more boats are unnecessary. Production might be ramped up should sensor and missile technology threaten to overcome the defenses of surface ships.

- Eliminate six fighter air wing equivalents, thereby limiting the air force's needed procurement of fighters.

- Hold the number of F-22 Raptors to the 183 already purchased and close the production line. The F-22 is the world's preeminent air-to-air fighter, but the F-35 Joint Strike Fighter will be the world's second-best. That is good enough in a world where air-to-air challengers are disappearing. Moreover, the F-35 has substantial air-to-ground capability, a far more useful capability. The air force should fill out its reduced requirements with Joint Strike Fighters or F-18E/Fs, if F-35 development is too slow.

- Close the C-17 production line to limit congressional demand for more of these aircraft.

- The reductions in conventional force structure and U.S. military commitments should allow a matching reduction of roughly one-third in the Pentagon's civilian workforce. Even so, the Pentagon should accelerate efforts to identify jobs now done by military personnel that can be done by civilians, who cost less and remain in their jobs longer.

- Refocus the investment in missile defense programs away from procurement and toward research and development, reducing spending to $2 billion to $3 billion annually. Cancel the components with excessive cost overruns, such as the airborne-laser program.

- Cut the nuclear weapons arsenal to 1,000 warheads based on 8 ballistic nuclear missile submarines (rather than 14), and dramatically reduce the number of intercontinental ballistic missiles. Eliminate bomber-based nuclear weapons, and use all bombers for conventional missions.
- Double nonproliferation funding in the Departments of Energy and Defense.

Conclusion

Our current defense budget achieves the rare feat of being both excessive and insufficient. We spend too much because we choose too little, allowing a series of expensive goals and programs to continue without a means of choosing among them. Congress should push the Pentagon to institute a strategy of restraint that prioritizes national security dangers and cuts national security spending. This budget would encourage our allies to defend themselves. It would lessen our proclivity to occupy foreign countries under the misguided perception that we can and should remake them. It would diminish the destabilizing perception abroad that the United States has become a revolutionary power and would demonstrate that we have returned to spreading liberal values by example, not force. Most important, this defense budget would husband our power rather than waste it preparing for and fighting conflicts that are not ours.

Suggested Readings

Betts, Richard K. "A Disciplined Defense: How to Regain Strategic Solvency." *Foreign Affairs* 86, no. 6 (November–December 2007).

Congressional Budget Office. "The Long-Term Implications of Current Defense Plans." March 2008. www.cbo.gov/ftpdocs/90xx/doc9043/03-28-CurrentDefensePlans.pdf.

Cordesman, Anthony. "A Poisoned Chalice? The Crisis of National Security Planning, Programming, and Budgeting." Center for Strategic and International Studies, April 22, 2008.

Friedman, Benjamin. "The Terrible 'Ifs.'" *Regulation* 30, no. 4 (Winter 2008).

Friedman, Benjamin, Christopher Preble, and Harvey Sapolsky. "Learning the Right Lessons from Iraq." Cato Institute Policy Analysis no. 610, February 13, 2008.

Kanter, Arnold. *Defense Politics: A Budgetary Perspective.* Chicago: University of Chicago Press, 1979.

Kosiak, Steven. "Analysis of the FY 2009 Defense Budget Request." Center for Strategic and Budgetary Assessments, 2008.

Posen, Barry R. "The Case for Restraint." *The American Interest* 3, no. 1 (November–December 2007).

—Prepared by Benjamin Friedman

20. K-12 Education

Ultimately, the proper federal role in education is whichever one would best serve the public in the long run. That does not mean Congress should ignore the Constitution, which plainly leaves authority over education in the hands of the states and the people. What it means is that if a careful review of the evidence demands a federal role that is not currently authorized, the Constitution could and should be amended to allow it. Conversely, if federal education programs have consistently failed to produce results commensurate to their cost, they should be discontinued.

But what does the evidence show? This chapter reviews federal involvement in education to date, assessing the outcomes of federal programs in light of the considerable resources taxpayers have invested in them. It concludes by offering the simple policy recommendations that follow inexorably from that review.

Have Federal Education Programs Worked?

As shown in Figure 20.1, federal revenues constituted less than 1 percent of public school budgets before the 1930s, and grew only imperceptibly until the post–World War II period. That negligible level of spending was matched by a complete lack of federal interest in shaping what went on in America's classrooms. It wasn't until the National Defense Education

215

Figure 20.1
K–12 Revenues per Pupil, by Level of Government, 1920 to 2005

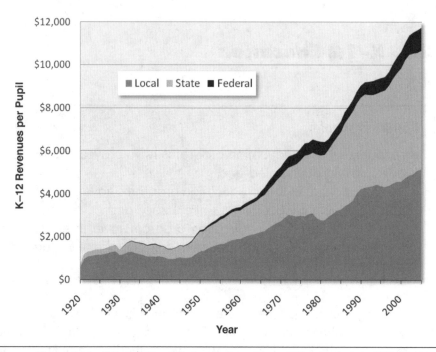

SOURCES: Thomas Snyder, Sally Dillow, and Charlene Hoffman, *Digest of Education Statistics 2007* (Washington: U.S. Department of Education, 2008), Table 162. Missing values are linearly interpolated. Historical consumer price index inflation factors are from http://oregonstate.edu/cla/polisci/faculty-research/sahr/sahr.htm.

Act of 1958, aimed at beefing up math and science instruction after Russia's launch of the satellite Sputnik, that Congress sought to shape public school instruction.

What did the NDEA do, and did it work? Some NDEA funding purchased new equipment for science classrooms, but much of it went toward the development of new math and science curricula by experts in colleges of education, new teacher training programs, and the hiring of experts in these fields as curriculum supervisors within the nation's public school systems. What effect did these expenditures have? That question was addressed in 2006 by the Science and Technology Policy Institute under a federal research contract. According to the STPI study, public school district officials felt that NDEA-funded programs had done some good but that states "found it impossible to identify direct causal links among the myriad of variables influencing public education"—bureaucratese for "who knows?"

Of course the most obvious and meaningful test of the NDEA's effectiveness is to look at academic achievement in math and science before and after the law's passage—something that the STPI study failed to do. Fortunately, nationally representative data for the period are available from the Educational Testing Service, which administered its Preliminary Scholastic Aptitude Test to nationally representative samples of high school juniors periodically between 1955 and 1983. The mathematics results of these little-known "national norm studies" appear in Figure 20.2 (note that the PSAT does not include a science portion).

The results depicted in Figure 20.2 indicate that mathematics performance declined slightly during the latter half of the 1950s, and that this decline actually accelerated from 1960 to 1966, after the NDEA was passed. The avowed belief of school district officials that the law was working is not supported by these results.

Figure 20.2
Math Scores, National Norm PSAT Studies (11th graders),
1955–83

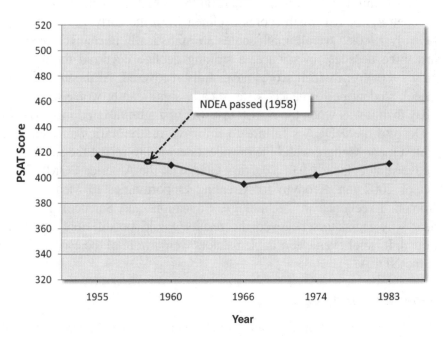

SOURCE: Charles Murray and Richard J. Herrnstein, "What's Really behind the SAT-Score Decline," *Public Interest*, no. 106 (Winter 1992): 32–56.

Looking at the apparent turnaround beginning in 1966, it might be theorized that the new programs and staff put in place by the NDEA did not begin to work until a decade or so after the law was passed. Perhaps, after finally getting their bearings, they contributed to a lasting upward trend in mathematics performance. Whether or not that theory is plausible in principle, it, too, is contradicted by the evidence.

Science and mathematics scores on the Long-Term Trends tests of the National Assessment of Educational Progress became available at the end of the 1960s and beginning of the 1970s. These tests, administered at regular intervals to nationally representative samples of 9-, 13-, and 17-year-old students, offer the best picture of changes in average student achievement over time. The results for younger students are useful for illustrating changes in the relative achievement at different levels of public schooling—how the performance of elementary, middle, and high school children varied over time. But since the goal of the NDEA was to better prepare students for success in challenging college work after high school, it is to the performance of 17-year-olds that we must turn to assess the law's effectiveness.

As the results shown in Figure 20.3 illustrate, the rising math trend on the PSAT through 1983 is not found on the NAEP mathematics test. On the contrary, NAEP math scores declined from the early 1970s through the early 1980s. Overall, math scores are statistically unchanged over the past three decades. In science, a striking decline occurred through the early 1980s from which scores never fully recovered. At the end of high school, student performance is statistically significantly worse in science today than it was when the NAEP test was first administered in 1969–70.

Despite the NDEA's failure to improve mathematics and science achievement, Congress and the president decided to repeat the same ineffective strategy nearly half a century later, with the America COMPETES Act of 2007 (an acronym for Creating Opportunities to Meaningfully Promote Excellence in Technology, Education, and Science). It is not clear why legislators believed the results would be different this time around. It is not even clear that legislators were aware of the earlier failure of the NDEA.

Head Start and ESEA

In 1965, the federal government created two new programs aimed at closing the achievement gaps between high- and low-income children and between white and black children: the Elementary and Secondary

Figure 20.3
NAEP Long-Term Trends Results (17-year-olds), 1969–70 to 2003–04

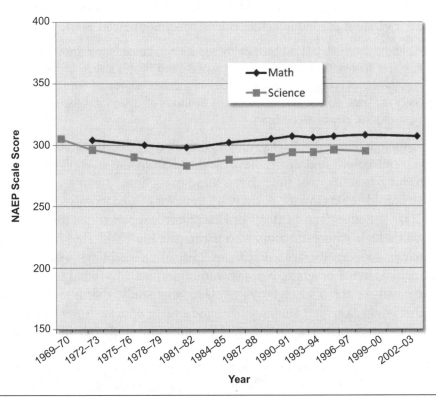

SOURCES: Rebecca Moran and Anthony D. Lutkus, *NAEP 2004 Trends in Academic Progress: Three Decades of Student Performance in Reading and Mathematics* (Washington: U.S. Department of Education, 2005), p. 17; Jay R. Campbell, Catherine M. Hombo, and John Mazzeo, *NAEP 1999 Trends in Academic Progress: Three Decades of Student Performance* (Washington: U.S. Department of Education, 2000), p. 9.

Education Act and a preschool program known as Head Start. As its name implies, Head Start was intended to prepare disadvantaged students to perform better academically once they entered the K–12 system. According to the most recent large-scale study of the program, authored by Michael Puma and others, Head Start has some small positive effects in the early language skills of 3-year-olds, but no effect on their mathematics skills, when compared with a control group of students not receiving Head Start services. Among 4-year-olds, this same federally funded study found fewer language skill improvements and still no mathematics improvements.

These findings are consistent with a comprehensive literature review of the Head Start research released by the Department of Health and

Human Services in 1985. That review described some initial academic gains among preschoolers while they were participating in the program, but a gradual atrophy of such gains as students progressed through the elementary and higher grades. In fact, according to the 1985 study, there were no lasting academic achievement benefits to Head Start:

> Children enrolled in Head Start enjoy significant, immediate gains in cognitive test scores, socioemotional test scores, and health status. In the long run, however, cognitive and socioemotional test scores of former Head Start students do not remain superior to those of disadvantaged children who did not attend Head Start.

Although the 1985 DHHS study reviewed over 200 research papers, a few, both before and since, have deviated from the overall pattern of vanishing benefits over time. Even these exceptional findings, however, have considerable caveats. A study by three UCLA economists published in 2000 ("Longer Term Effects of Head Start") reported that the children of white high school dropouts who participated in Head Start had higher earnings between the ages of 23 and 25 than their siblings who did not participate in the program. No such earnings effect was found for African Americans or for other age ranges. The same study, did, however, find higher graduation rates among whites and among African-American males who had participated in the program (again, compared with siblings who had not).

Head Start represents a relatively small fraction of total federal spending on K–12 education. The bulk of that spending is made under the auspices of the Elementary and Secondary Education Act, which comprises hundreds of different programs. It directs funding to states and school districts for everything from early literacy to dropout prevention, and from "comprehensive school reform" to teacher training. All these programs are collectively intended to advance the law's aim of closing the racial and economic achievement gaps. After more than 40 years of programs providing services from preschool to high school, the most meaningful way to determine the effectiveness of the federal government's interventions is to look at how the achievement gaps have changed over time. Once again, it makes the most sense to look at students at the end of high school to see the cumulative effects of all federal programs (if any).

Figure 20.4 charts scores for black and white 17-year-olds on the three main NAEP tests (reading, mathematics, and science), to get an idea of changes in the racial achievement gap over time. As is evident from these graphs, the overall gap remained essentially unchanged through 1980.

Figure 20.4
NAEP Long-Term Trends Scores for 17-Year-Olds, by Race, 1969–2003

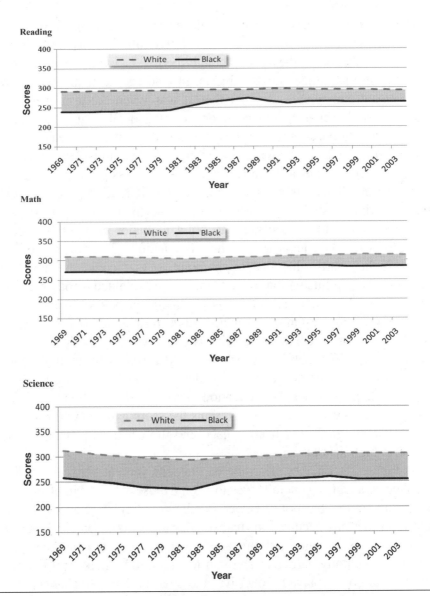

SOURCES: Rebecca Moran and Anthony D. Lutkus, *NAEP 2004 Trends in Academic Progress: Three Decades of Student Performance in Reading and Mathematics* (Washington: U.S. Department of Education, 2005), pp. 33, 42; Jay R. Campbell, Catherine M. Hombo, and John Mazzeo, *NAEP 1999 Trends in Academic Progress: Three Decades of Student Performance* (Washington: U.S. Department of Education, 2000), p. 37.

That is 15 years after the passage of both the ESEA and Head Start, time enough for the children being tested to have passed through all these federal programs from preschool through the end of high school. Nevertheless, the gap had not narrowed.

Then, across subjects, the racial achievement gap among 17-year-olds shrank in the early to mid-1980s. That trend subsequently ceased, and even reversed itself in the 1990s, though the reversal was not uniform in timing or in magnitude across subjects. In reading and mathematics, the achievement gap remains smaller than it was when the tests were first administered. In science, there is no longer a statistically significant difference in the gap between the earliest and most recent test results.

If federal education programs were having their intended effect, we would expect the gaps to have narrowed more or less uniformly over the past 40 years. That has not happened. To credit federal programs with the narrowing of the early 1980s, or to blame them for the subsequent widening, it would be necessary to point to major changes in federal programs in the years leading up to those fluctuations. There are no obvious federal policy shifts that one might point to that could explain these changes. The gap fluctuations must therefore be explained by other factors, whether social, economic, or relating to state-level policy.

What about the gap in performance between rich and poor Americans, the reduction of which was the principal stated aim of both Head Start and the ESEA? Though breakdowns of NAEP scores by family income are unavailable, we can get a rough idea of them by looking at scores according to parental level of education (income and education level being strongly correlated). Figure 20.5 presents the score gaps between students whose parents graduated from college and those whose parents did not complete high school.

As Figure 20.5 makes clear, the gap in achievement between children of college graduates (generally wealthier) and those of high school dropouts (generally poorer) has not narrowed in either reading or science. The gap reduction that has occurred in mathematics amounts to barely 1 percent of the 500-point scale, and fluctuations in that gap are not obviously correlated with any particular shifts in federal policy, making it doubtful that federal policy played a decisive role even in that tiny change.

No Child Left Behind

Disappointed by the ineffectiveness of federal programs despite generations of effort and a massive outlay of taxpayer dollars, Congress and

Figure 20.5
NAEP Long-Term Trends Scores for 17-Year-Olds, by Parents' Level of Education, 1977–2004

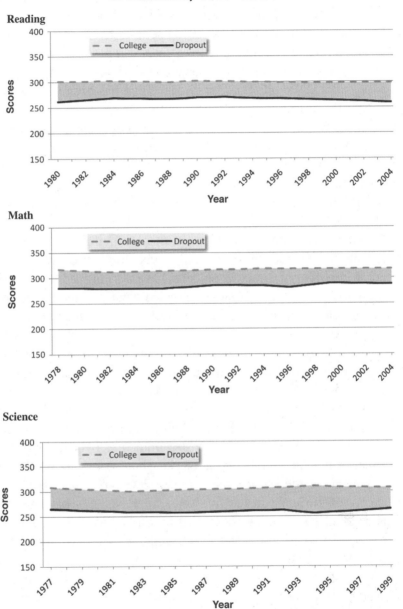

SOURCES: Rebecca Moran and Anthony D. Lutkus, *NAEP 2004 Trends in Academic Progress: Three Decades of Student Performance in Reading and Mathematics* (Washington: U.S. Department of Education, 2005), pp. 37, 46; Jay R. Campbell, Catherine M. Hombo, and John Mazzeo, *NAEP 1999 Trends in Academic Progress: Three Decades of Student Performance* (Washington: U.S. Department of Education, 2000), pp. 50–51.

President Bush decided to shift the emphasis of ESEA programs in 2002, reauthorizing the law under the name No Child Left Behind. In this reconstituted form, states were encouraged to test students in reading and mathematics and to focus their improvement efforts on those schools failing to show adequate progress on those tests from year to year. Has NCLB proved more effective than past federal initiatives?

The National Assessment of Educational Progress has been the one source of nationally representative evidence that has been widely used to assess NCLB's effectiveness. "High-stakes" state-level results are also available, from state tests that are used to judge the performance of schools and school officials, as well as students, but they are not nationally representative and are widely regarded as unreliable measures of changes in student performance over time. Their unreliability is due to reductions in test difficulty over time; narrow teaching to the specific test content; and on occasion, even outright cheating by school officials.

As already discussed, it would be most meaningful to look at trends for students in the final years of public schooling, to observe NCLB's lasting effects (if any). But older students have thus far had little exposure to key NCLB provisions, which are targeted chiefly at the lower grades. Hence, data for elementary and middle school students must be examined for the time being.

According to the NAEP's Nation's Report Card series of tests, 4th-grade reading scores increased by less than one-half of 1 percent of the 500-point scale between 2002 and 2007. As it happens, 4th-grade scores had increased by just over 1 percent between 2000 and 2002, before NCLB was passed. So if NCLB has had an effect at all, it has been to slow the rate of improvement that existed immediately before its passage. The same, incidentally, goes for the black–white score gap, which shrank by 0.8 percent of the score scale between 2000 and 2002, but only by 0.6 percent of the scale in the five years after NCLB's passage. At the 8th grade, students' reading scores fell by one point (0.2 percent of the score scale) between 2002 and 2007, and the black–white score gap remained unchanged.

In mathematics, the story is much the same. In the 4th grade, scores improved by 1 percent between 2003 and 2007, but had improved by nearly 2 percent between 2000 and 2003, before the NCLB could have had any effect. The racial achievement gap shrank by 0.6 percent after NCLB, but by 0.8 percent from 2000 to 2003. Scores for 8th graders rose by 0.4 percent after NCLB, but had improved by 1 percent between 2000 and 2003. The story is once again the same with respect to the achievement gap between black and white students.

It is worth noting that gains in NAEP scores at the 4th- and 8th-grade levels have historically failed to persist through the end of high school, as is evident in the flat trend lines for 17-year-olds shown in the figures earlier. This implies that no additional learning is taking place over the course of children's public schooling, but that some learning has merely shifted to lower grades.

The tiny and likely evanescent post-NCLB gains for younger children, which are smaller than those that occurred immediately before NCLB's passage, represent the good news, such as it is. There is also bad news, which NCLB advocates and the media have uniformly ignored. Two sets of international tests, the Program on International Student Assessment and the Program on International Reading Literacy Survey, offer nationally representative data on trends in U.S. student achievement over the NCLB's lifetime. In every subject, on both tests, the scores of American students have declined.

PISA was first administered to 15-year-olds in 2000, testing them on mathematics, reading, and science. Students in the United States initially earned an overall math score of 493 on the 1,000-point scale, 7 points below average, placing us 18th out of the 27 participating countries. Three years later, PISA results showed no significant change in U.S. math performance. But according to the latest report, the United States suffered a significant decline in mathematics achievement between 2003 and 2006, a period in which an NCLB effect could reasonably have been expected. We now score 474—in 25th place among the 30 participating countries.

PISA also tests students in science, a subject area not specifically targeted by NCLB. Still, it seems reasonable to expect that if the law were actually improving math and reading performance, students might have an easier time with science as a result. As it happens, our overall science score dropped from 499 in 2000 to 489 in 2006, and our ranking fell from 14th out of 27 countries to 21st out of 30 countries. Scores also declined on both the PIRLS and PISA reading tests, but these drops were too small to be statistically significant.

Taken together, the results of NAEP, PISA, and PIRLS indicate that the No Child Left Behind Act has continued the legacy of failure established by its predecessors.

Conclusion and Recommendations

Since the institution of ESEA and Head Start in 1965, federal K–12 programs have cost taxpayers roughly $1.85 trillion in 2008 dollars. To get a feel for how large that number is, 1.85 trillion seconds equals 58,726 years—about 20 times the entire span of recorded human history. After four decades and nearly $2 trillion dollars, after unsuccessfully cycling through an endless series of programs, we have enough evidence and experience to draw a solid conclusion: the federal government cannot significantly improve school performance.

One thing that the federal government could do that would undeniably help American families would be to stop taking vast sums of their money and funneling it into patently ineffective programs. By phasing out futile federal efforts in education, taxpayers would regain control of 70 billion of their hard-earned dollars every year. The effect of this financial windfall on American society would be significant: creating jobs, stimulating investment, and raising the overall standard of living.

It is well within the power of Congress to bring about these benefits. The first step would be to convert all existing federal K–12 education programs into block grants to the states. These grants should then be phased out completely over three years, giving states the time to reallocate their own personnel and resources. As the block grants are phased out, federal income tax rates should be proportionately reduced so that taxpayers retain the money that was previously being spent on ineffective federal programs. At the end of the three-year period, Americans would be enjoying a permanent $70 billion annual tax cut.

The U.S. Constitution delegates the federal government no power to determine the content, methods, testing, or staffing procedures of American schools, but the Constitution is not the word of some supreme being. It is not *right* in some absolute sense, purely by virtue of *being* the Constitution. The wisdom of its exclusion of a federal role in education policymaking must ultimately stand or fall on the basis of the facts. If, as hypothesized in the Introduction, there were compelling evidence that federal government intervention in education would best serve the public's interests, then it would be foolish not to amend the Constitution to allow it. On the basis of the inconceivably expensive failure of federal interventions over more than half a century, it would be foolish not to cease them immediately.

Suggested Readings

Arons, Stephen. *Short Route to Chaos: Conscience, Community, and the Re-Constitution of American Schooling.* Amherst, MA: University of Massachusetts Press, 1997.

Boaz, David, ed. *Liberating Schools: Education in the Inner City.* Washington: Cato Institute, 1991.

Coulson, Andrew J. *Market Education: The Unknown History.* New Brunswick, NJ: Transaction Books, 1999.

Lieberman, Myron. *Public Education: An Autopsy.* Cambridge, MA: Harvard University Press, 1993.

McCluskey, Neal. *Feds in the Classroom: How Big Government Corrupts, Cripples, and Compromises American Education.* Lanham, MD: Rowman & Littlefield, 2007.

Schaeffer, Adam B. "The Public Education Tax Credit." Cato Institute Policy Analysis no. 605, December 5, 2007.

Tooley, James. *E. G. West: Economic Liberalism and the Role of Government in Education.* London: Continuum, 2008.

Walberg, Herbert J. *School Choice: The Findings.* Washington: Cato Institute, 2007.

—Prepared by Andrew J. Coulson

21. Higher Education Policy

Congress should

- phase out federal student aid;
- phase out federal aid to institutions;
- eliminate all grant programs and research unrelated to national security;
- end pork: require that all federal grants to universities be competitively bid; and
- continue to prohibit the U.S. Department of Education from requiring school "outcome measures."

In *Universities in the Marketplace,* former Harvard president Derek Bok observes, "Universities share one characteristic with compulsive gamblers and exiled royalty: there is never enough money to satisfy their desires." This chapter explores the harmful effects of federal involvement in higher education, including distortions wrought by feeding colleges' insatiable financial cravings and efforts to control the ivory tower. When considered in conjunction with the Tenth Amendment dictum that "the powers not delegated to the United States by the Constitution . . . are reserved to the States respectively, or to the people," the message is clear: the federal government should withdraw from higher education.

Where Are We Now?

Unfortunately, neither the 110th Congress nor the president took the Constitution to heart. In July 2008, Congress reauthorized the Higher Education Act, which greatly increased the federal presence in America's ivory tower. The reauthorization came on top of two generous student aid measures that Congress enacted earlier in its session. Moreover, in 2005 the Bush administration started formulating a "national strategy" for higher education, seriously threatening the great independence and flexibility that, despite its problems, have made our higher education system the best in the world.

Since 1965, the federal government has provided an increasingly massive amount of funding for higher education. According to the National Center for Education Statistics, between 1965 and 2007 real federal spending on postsecondary education rose from $7.5 billion to an estimated $36.6 billion. Federal expenditures on university-based research also exploded, increasing from $11.7 billion in 1970 to an estimated $31.4 billion in 2006.

Given the new laws enacted during the 110th Congress, the federal presence is almost certain to keep growing. The College Cost Reduction and Access Act, signed into law in September 2007, sets a five-year schedule to gradually cut interest rates on federally subsidized loans from 6.8 percent to 3.4 percent, encouraging a lot more student borrowing. The Ensuring Continued Access to Student Loans Act of 2008 increases unsubsidized Stafford loan maximums, eases PLUS loan qualifications, and gives the U.S. Department of Education new authority to fund student lending. Finally, the renewed Higher Education Act increases Pell Grant maximums from $5,800 to $8,000 by 2014; authorizes forgiveness of up to $10,000 in federal loans for anyone working in an area of "national need"; adds numerous reporting requirements for colleges and regulations for private lending; and establishes 64 new programs.

The Adverse Effects of Federal Student Aid

According to *The College Cost Crisis,* a 2003 report from the House Subcommittee on 21st Century Competitiveness: "America's higher education system is in crisis. Decades of uncontrolled cost increases are pushing the dream of a college degree further out of reach for needy students." Ironically, student aid is a major force behind the crisis.

It's a simple matter of supply and demand. On the demand side, more and more Americans have sought a college education, pushing prices higher. Ordinarily, the upward pressure would have been restrained by consumers' willingness and ability to pay, but, as economist Richard Vedder explains in *Going Broke by Degree: Why College Costs Too Much,* because third parties like the federal government absorb tuition increases, budget constraints have been diminished. "The shift to the right of the demand curve for students—and the resulting higher tuition," Vedder writes, "[have] been aided and abetted by a large and proliferating number of government assistance programs."

Explaining the supply side is the so-called Bennett hypothesis, put forth in 1987 by the then Secretary of Education William Bennett, who argued that "increases in financial aid . . . have enabled colleges and universities blithely to raise tuitions, confident that Federal loan subsidies would help cushion the increase."

Figures 21.1 through 21.3 bear out this aid effect, showing how student aid (primarily coming through the federal government) diminishes customers' sensitivity to price increases. The tallest bars in each figure are the

Figure 21.1
Private, Four-Year Institution Tuition, Fees, and Room and Board before and after Aid (2006 Dollars)

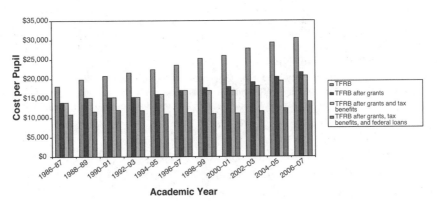

Figure 21.2
Public, Four-Year Institution Tuition, Fees, and Room and Board before and after Aid (2006 Dollars)

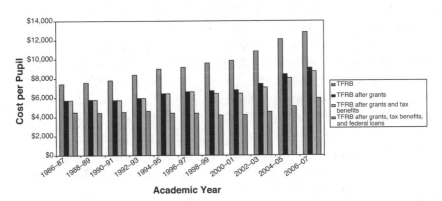

231

Figure 21.3
Public, Two-Year Institution Tuition and Fees before and after Aid (2006 Dollars)

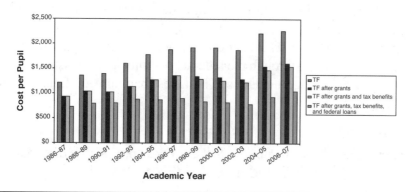

SOURCES: U.S. Department of Education, National Center for Education Statistics, *Digest of Education Statistics 2007,* Table 210; College Board, *Trends in College Pricing 2004,* Tables 4a and 4b; College Board, *Trends in College Pricing 2007,* Tables 3b, 4a, and 4b; and College Board, *Trends in Student Aid 2007,* Table 7 (available upon request from the College Board).

NOTE: TF = tuition and fees; TFRB = tuition, fees, room and board. Aid per student was estimated by calculating enrollment-weighted average TFRB and adjusting average grant, tax benefit, and loan aid proportionate to differing TFRB costs by school type. Numbers also adjusted to estimate aid and costs for undergraduate students only.

published costs of tuition, fees, and room and board (TFRB). (Note that two-year public schools do not usually have room and board charges so only their tuition and fees are shown. Two-year private schools, with relatively tiny enrollments and no available cost data, are omitted.) The middle two bars are the costs after subtracting grants and tax benefits, aid that makes students largely insensitive to the costs it covers because it needn't be paid back. The final bars show TFRB after subtracting federal loans as well as grants and tax benefits. The loans do not completely desensitize students to the costs they cover, but with low interest rates and generous terms, they soften the blow.

These tables show that increasing aid doesn't supply all the fuel for the college-cost skyrocket, but it does furnish a lot. For instance, had students had to pay the full "sticker price" increase at four-year private schools (Figure 21.1), the average cost in real dollars would have risen from $18,122 in 1986–87 to $30,497 in 2006–07, a 68 percent increase. After accounting for average grant and tax-based aid, however, the increase was only 49 percent, and the price to the consumer went from only $13,966 to $20,781. After adding loans, the cost grew from $10,943 to $14,158, just a 29 percent increase.

Even after hugely inflating prices, federal aid has probably helped some students attend college, with enrollment increasing about 48 percent between 1986 and 2006. But it's brought other distortions in addition to inflation. Part of the enrollment increase, for instance, came from increasingly large percentages of students requiring remedial work, students who might not have tried college—which they finish at significantly lower rates than nonremediated students—if they'd had to pay the costs themselves. College also seems to be getting easier as colleges scramble for money: the American Academy of Arts and Sciences reports that from the mid-1960s to the mid-1990s, college grade point averages grew steadily whereas Scholastic Aptitude Test scores declined.

That might be why outcomes have not improved. According to the Population Studies Center at the University of Michigan, within eight years of graduating, 51.1 percent of students in the high school class of 1972 had finished two- or four-year college degrees. In contrast, only 45.3 percent of 1992's high school class had done the same. In addition, while college attendance is up, overall adult literacy has barely budged. A federal assessment found that in 2003 only 13 percent of Americans 16 years old or older were "proficient" in reading prose, understanding written directions, or performing quantitative tasks. This dismal score was down from 1992, when 15 percent of Americans were proficient in prose and document literacy. To a significant extent, it seems a college degree may just be replacing a high school diploma as a sign of minimum competence.

It's difficult to say, of course, exactly how many students would have attended college without federal aid, but it's fairly clear that the poor—those people federal aid is supposed to most help—are hurt worst by aid-driven inflation. According to the National Center for Education Statistics, most students intending to pursue postsecondary education and their parents overestimate the cost of college, but lower-income parents and students overestimate the most, disproportionately dissuading them from pursuing higher education. Moreover, aid has been increasingly skewed toward middle- and even upper-income students. Tax credits and deductions are available only to families with sufficient income to pay taxes, and institutions have been spending more of their own dollars on "merit" aid for high-performing, disproportionately wealthier, students.

With all this in mind, phasing out federal aid probably wouldn't result in diminished accessibility for truly college-ready students. For one thing, even now philanthropists support many promising, low-income college kids; they would have much greater incentive to do so were the federal government not in the aid business. Even better, although it is distorted, the financial value of a college education is still very real. That means private lenders would have a strong incentive to work with qualified, low-income students; both borrower and lender would profit. Most important, ending federal aid would drive prices down. Students and parents would demand only those things for which they themselves were willing to pay, and schools would have to get maximum value out of everything from increasingly underused buildings to bloated staffs to make themselves affordable.

Of course, no school official has ever confessed to setting tuition to capture aid, or to becoming wasteful from an abundance of cash. Several college presidents and administrators have, however, admitted that universities grab every dime they can get. Bok, recall, likened universities' greed to that of exiled royalty and compulsive gamblers. In *Honoring the Trust: Quality and Cost Containment in Higher Education,* former Stanford University Vice President William Massy writes that "universities press their pricing to the limits that markets, regulators, and public opinion will allow." Finally, in a 2006 *New York Times* article, former Emory University President William M. Chace offered "the honest talk" he wanted to give incoming freshmen, explaining that "like the auto industry, we have a sticker price and the price people really pay," and that college "could be cheaper, but . . . you and your parents have made it clear that you want the best . . . more spacious and comfortable student residences . . . gyms with professional exercise equipment, better food of all kinds," and so on.

The Trouble with Institutional Aid and Research Grants

Although the federal government provides about 65 percent of all student aid, states provide the most aid to institutions. But that doesn't make federal institutional aid irrelevant.

Generally, federal aid is given to special classes of schools. The Department of Education *Fiscal Year 2009 Budget Summary* reports that in 2008 Congress appropriated nearly $800 million in institutional aid, primarily for historically black colleges and universities (HBCUs) and other minority institutions. In addition to this amount, Howard University, an HBCU in Washington, received a specific appropriation of $233 million, and Gallaudet University, a school for deaf students also in Washington, received over $113 million.

Although this aid is limited, it still presents problems, the most fundamental being that it takes money from taxpayers and gives it to schools favored by politicians. Moreover, it gives receiving schools unfair advantages over competing institutions. For instance, in 2008 Howard University received almost 60 percent of what all the other HBCUs in the country got combined—$395 million—giving it a clear financial leg up on its HBCU peers.

A much larger problem is federal research funding, which the National Center for Education Statistics estimates totaled $31.4 billion in 2006. Why so much federal investment in research? It is partially for national defense; universities do a great deal of work for the Pentagon and defense-related projects. The other major thrust is "basic" research that promises little or no immediate profit and which, its supporters argue, would not get done without federal financing.

Vedder finds that much of this supposedly basic research is neither necessary nor likely to be undertaken only with federal dollars. He points out that researchers often seek grants after their research is nearly complete, frequently use grant money just to refine research, and undertake projects that industry is willing to do.

In addition to this waste, universities' growing emphasis on research has come at the expense of teaching. "For many institutions, the balance between research and education has tilted too far toward research," declares Massy. "Faculty time represents the university's most important asset . . . [but] there are only so many hours in a day, and even the most highly motivated professors have finite amounts of energy."

Pork

One final source of federal money is described by the *Chronicle of Higher Education* as "directed, noncompetitive appropriations," aka pork. As the *Chronicle* reported in March 2008, these projects are costing taxpayers more money every year, from $528 million in 1998 to at least $2.25 billion in 2008. And what has the barrel produced? According to *Lobbying for Higher Education* by Vanderbilt University professor Constance Ewing Cook, over the years it has included such gems as $8 million to build a planetarium for Delta College in Michigan, a community college that offers no science majors, and $21 million for West Virginia's Wheeling Jesuit College, a bounty almost twice the size of the school's annual budget. In 2008, earmarks included $140,502 "to maintain healthful interscholastic youth-sports programs" at the University of Maine; $98,000 to build a "Student Wellness and Recreation Center" at Heidelberg College in Ohio; and $1,915,934 for the Charles B. Rangel

235

Center for Public Service at the City University of New York, earmarked by Rep. Charles B. Rangel (D-NY).

Still a Pretty Free Market

Even with the significant distortions in American higher education, ours is widely considered the best postsecondary system in the world. Driven by consumer freedom and competition among autonomous institutions, it has an unmatched vibrancy. That's a major reason why in 2007, according to the Organisation for Economic Co-operation and Development, the United States was "by far the most popular destination for international students."

In light of this market-driven strength, arguably the biggest recent threat to America's ivory tower hasn't come directly from rampant price inflation, but from federal efforts to impose new controls on colleges and universities largely justified on the grounds that Washington makes a huge "investment" in higher education. Employing this reasoning, in September 2005, Secretary of Education Margaret Spellings announced the creation of a commission tasked with formulating a "comprehensive national strategy" for American higher education. On the heels of the No Child Left Behind Act—which imposed unprecedented federal control on elementary and secondary education—the commission's charge signaled that the Bush administration was looking to force "standards and accountability" on academia.

The commission's final report stopped short of advocating outright federal imposition of standards and tests, but it did call for the creation of "a national strategy for lifelong learning" and a federal database populated with information on every college student in the country. Worse, after the report's release Spellings tried to impose outcome-measurement requirements on schools through regulation of accreditors, bodies whose stamp of approval is needed for colleges and students to receive federal aid. To be recognized by the federal government, accreditors would need to require schools to have explicit outcome measures, a requirement likely to translate into standardized tests for incoming and outgoing students.

Congress's response to these efforts was on target. In May 2007, Sen. Lamar Alexander (R-TN) threatened to introduce legislation barring the secretary from imposing such regulations. A House subcommittee promptly attached an amendment to a 2008 spending bill prohibiting the Department of Education from promulgating new accreditation rules. Finally, the reauthorized Higher Education Act forbids the department from imposing student achievement standards or creating a "unit record" database.

Removal of the Federal Government from Higher Education

James Madison wrote in *Federalist* No. 45: "The powers delegated by the proposed Constitution to the federal government are few and defined. . . . [They] will be exercised principally on external objects, as war, peace, negotiation, and foreign commerce." Since the Constitution grants the federal government no role in higher education, Washington may only be involved in ways that support legitimate federal concerns. That essentially means maintaining the Senior Reserve Officers' Training Corps, service academies, and national defense-related research, and otherwise withdrawing from higher education.

Washington cannot, however, withdraw immediately. Abruptly ending federal student aid, for instance, would leave millions of students scrambling for funds and would overwhelm private lenders, schools, and charitable organizations that have made plans based on expected levels of federal involvement. What follows is an overview of a six-year plan that would withdraw the federal government gradually while setting a clear path for devolving Washington from higher education.

- **Immediately:** Prohibit pork barrel spending; only federal grants that are competitively bid can be sent to colleges. Award no new research grants unrelated to national security but let projects under way continue to completion.
- **In four years:** End federal aid to institutions. The four-year time frame offers schools an adequate transition period either to economize or find new sources of revenue because federal aid accounts for only a small part of most institutions' overall budgets.
- **In six years:** Eliminate all federal student aid programs. Each year between enactment of federal phaseout legislation and the end of the six-year period, the maximum Pell Grant value, incorporating cost-of-living adjustments pegged to inflation, will be reduced in equal increments. Similarly, maximum loan sizes and government subsidy rates will be reduced for all federal loan programs in equal, six-year increments.

Conclusion

The federal presence in higher education is both unconstitutional and harmful. Federal student aid drives up college prices, creates numerous distortions and inefficiencies, and costs taxpayers ever more. Federal institutional aid, university-based research grants, and academic pork also cost taxpayers billions of dollars each year. Finally, federal efforts to impose "accountability" on the nation's ivory tower threaten to destroy its greatest strengths: institutional autonomy, consumer freedom, and the powerful competition and innovation they create. Washington must get out of higher education.

Top Five Signs of Too Much Money in Higher Education

1. The Bureau of Labor Statistics reports that college students devote 3.2 hours to education on an average *weekday,* versus 3.9 hours to "leisure and sports."

2. "Ever needed a beach getaway in the middle of finals week?" asks the University of Missouri in its description of the school's Tiger Grotto recreation center. The grotto boasts "palm trees and other tropical flora," a "Lazy River" that "allows you to float along without any effort while you watch ZouTV on the big screen," and "sauna and steam shacks."

3. According to *Forbes* magazine, between 1983 and 2007 businesses focused on efficiency and saw their after-inflation energy costs rise 60 percent. Colleges experienced a 124 percent leap.

4. The National Center for Higher Education Management Systems reports that in 2006 the *six-year* graduation rate for bachelor's students was only 56.4 percent.

5. A 2007 National Center on Addiction and Substance Abuse survey found that almost half of full-time college students binge drink or abuse drugs, while the percentage of students who got drunk at least three times per month rose 26 percent between 1993 and 2001.

Suggested Readings

College Board. *Trends in Student Aid 2007* and *Trends in College Pricing 2007*. www.collegeboard.com.

Leef, George. "The Overselling of Higher Education." John William Pope Center Inquiry Paper no. 25, September 5, 2006.

Massy, William F. *Honoring the Trust: Quality and Cost Containment in Higher Education*. Bolton, MA: Anker Publishing Company, Inc., 2003.

Palacios, Miguel. "Human Capital Contracts: 'Equity-Like' Instruments for Financing Higher Education." Cato Institute Policy Analysis no. 462, December 16, 2002.

Singell, Larry D., Jr., and Joe A. Stone. "For Whom the Pell Tolls: The Response of University Tuition to Federal Grants-in-Aid." Working paper. www.uoregon.edu/~lsingell/PellBennett.pdf.

Vedder, Richard. *Going Broke by Degree: Why College Costs Too Much.* Washington: American Enterprise Institute, 2004.

Winter, Greg. "Jacuzzi U: A Battle of Perks to Lure Students." *New York Times,* October 5, 2003.

Wolfram, Gary. "The Threat to Independent Education: Public Subsidies and Private Colleges." Cato Institute Policy Analysis no. 278, August 15, 1997.

—Prepared by Neal McCluskey

22. Housing Policy

Congress should

- turn Fannie Mae and Freddie Mac into fully private organizations, subject to scrutiny by the Securities and Exchange Commission, as it did for Sallie Mae in 1995; and
- reject any proposals to give the Department of Housing and Urban Development, the Environmental Protection Agency, or other agencies regulatory authority over land use in order to promote environmental or other social goals.

State legislators should

- repeal any growth-management laws or other legislation, and refrain from passing new legislation, that give cities authority over land uses of rural areas.

The Real Cause of the Housing Bubble

Deflation of the recent housing bubble has produced the nation's worst recession in more than 25 years and economic repercussions throughout the world. To minimize the damage done by this housing bubble, and to prevent even worse housing bubbles in the future, it is important to understand the true causes of the bubble.

The steep rise in housing prices between 2000 and 2006 has been blamed on the Federal Reserve Bank, unscrupulous lenders, housing speculators, and the repeal of the Glass-Steagall Act. However, none of these factors explains why the growth in housing prices was so different from one region to another.

According to data published by the Office of Federal Housing Enterprise Oversight, housing prices in California and Florida grew by more than

140 percent from the first quarter of 2000. In Georgia and Texas, prices grew by only 45 to 47 percent. From the peak of the market, prices in California and Florida have dropped by an average of 13 to 18 percent. Prices in Georgia and Texas have not declined at all. Since Federal Reserve policies and the other factors listed earlier apply equally to all the states, some other explanation must be found for why housing in California and Florida bubbled whereas housing in Georgia and Texas did not.

The explanation is not that demand for housing is greater in California and Florida. With regard to sheer numbers, Atlanta, Dallas–Ft. Worth, and Houston are the fastest-growing metropolitan areas in the United States, yet they did not experience bubbles after 2000 and have not experienced price declines since 2006.

Instead, the answer is on the supply side of the housing equation. In a free market, the home construction industry can easily meet the demand for new housing resulting from rapid population growth, looser credit, or other changes in the market. If new housing remains affordable, existing home resales will remain affordable as well. If housing prices are not rapidly increasing, then speculators will not be attracted to the housing market.

In most of the regions suffering housing bubbles, the main factors limiting homebuilders' abilities to meet demand for new homes are a variety of land-use regulations that are collectively known as "growth management." Growth management may include urban-growth or urban-service boundaries, large-lot zoning or other restrictions on development of land outside those boundaries, growth limits or growth caps inside the boundaries, and *concurrency* or *adequate public facilities* requirements that limit permits on new development until government financing is available to provide services to those developments.

The key to keeping housing affordable is the presence of large amounts of relatively unregulated vacant land. Historically, city zoning stopped at the city limits. City officials knew that if they imposed too much land-use regulation in the city, developers would go outside the city limits. To prevent this loss of tax revenue, cities kept their regulations flexible. This often led to charges that developers controlled city planning, but because developers would only build what buyers wanted, the truth was that consumers controlled city planning.

Growth-management and other laws that give cities control over rural areas changed the balance of power between consumers and city officials. Officials preferred that all development (and the resulting tax revenues) took place within city boundaries, so they eagerly used growth boundaries and other controls to limit rural development. This resulted in artificial land shortages and dramatic increases in housing costs.

Growth management comes in several flavors, including *slow growth*, which limits the number of building permits issued each year, and *smart growth*, which does not attempt to control growth rates but mandates that growth take place at higher densities instead of in the form of low-density "sprawl." Both kinds of growth management make housing less affordable by creating artificial land shortages.

Hawaii passed the nation's first statewide growth-management law in 1961. Oregon followed in 1973. In addition, California passed a law in 1963 that, while not intended as growth management, effectively gave cities control of all rural areas.

These laws quickly led to housing's becoming unaffordable. A standard measure of housing affordability is the median home price divided by the median family income. A price-to-income ratio of 2 allows a family dedicating 25 percent of its income to a 6 percent mortgage to pay off that mortgage in just 11 years. Twenty-one years are required at a price-to-income ratio of 3, and 53 years at 4.

In the absence of government restrictions on homebuilding, the "natural" price-to-income ratio seems to be about 2. In 1969, price-to-income ratios throughout the United States were about 2—except in Hawaii, where they were 3. By 1979, Hawaiian ratios were well above 5, California's were between 3 and 5, and Oregon's were around 3.

Harvard economist Edward Glaeser notes that housing supply restrictions make prices not only higher but also more volatile. California prices, for example, declined by 10 to 20 percent in the early 1980s. Prices there bubbled again in the late 1980s, then deflated another 20 to 25 percent in the early 1990s. Glaeser also estimates that prices lose only about a third of the gains they make during each bubble, so they get more out of line with the "natural" price-to-income ratio of 2 with each successive bubble.

Few people noted the relationship between growth management and housing affordability problems, so several more states passed growth-management laws in the 1980s and 1990s, including Florida, New Jersey, Connecticut, Rhode Island, Maryland, Washington, Arizona, and Tennessee. In addition, several New England states, including Massachusetts, effectively gave cities control over rural areas by abandoning the county form of government. Finally, a few metropolitan planning organizations, including those for Denver and the Twin Cities, began practicing growth management without the benefit of state legislation.

In almost every case, these laws and plans led to housing bubbles that reduced housing affordability. By 2006, price-to-income ratios ranged between 8 and 12 in most of coastal California and Hawaii; from 5 to 8 in central California and Florida; between 4 and 5 in Arizona, Maryland, Massachusetts, New Jersey, Oregon, Rhode Island, and Washington; and between 3 and 4 in Denver and Minneapolis–St. Paul.

The only state with a statewide growth-management law that did not see high housing prices in the recent bubble was Tennessee, probably because its law was implemented too late to create shortages. The only state to see a major housing bubble without state or local growth-management planning was Nevada. Nevada's prices are high because the federal government owns nearly 90 percent of the land in the state. Before 2000, the sale of federal land to developers in the fast-growth regions around Las Vegas and Reno maintained Nevada's housing affordability. Such sales slowed in 2001, leading to a rapid escalation of land and housing prices. In effect, the federal government, rather than state or local governments, is acting as the growth manager in Nevada.

In sum, the evidence is overwhelming that state and local land-use restrictions—not loose credit, speculators, or Federal Reserve policies—are the real source of the recent housing bubble:

- Housing prices mainly bubbled in states and regions with growth-management plans, whereas they remained stable in regions without such plans.
- Long before the recent changes in the credit market, housing prices previously bubbled in Hawaii, California, and other states with growth-management planning.
- There is a strong correlation between the time when states and regions first implemented growth-management plans and when, soon after, housing prices in those regions first became unaffordable.

Fuel on the Fire

Although loose credit markets did not cause the housing bubble, they did make it worse than it might have been. And one of the main impetuses behind loose credit was, ironically, a federal law designed to reduce the risk to taxpayers of the mortgage market.

The Federal National Mortgage Association (Fannie Mae) and Federal Home Loan Mortgage Corporation (Freddie Mac)—together known as "government-sponsored enterprises" or GSEs—were created to promote affordable homeownership. Since they are implicitly backed by the federal government, Congress worried that they might take unacceptable risks. So in the Housing and Community Development Act of 1992, Congress gave the Department of Housing and Urban Development the mission of overseeing and regulating the GSEs.

That new mission conflicted with HUD's primary mission, however, which "is to increase homeownership, support community development and increase access to affordable housing." Moreover, HUD is far more politicized than the GSEs; while the latter are run as businesses for the benefit of stockholders, HUD is typically run by a politically appointed secretary who is usually a politician and who often has ambitions to return to electoral politics after leaving HUD.

Secretaries of HUD get little political benefit from announcing that, thanks to their oversight, Fannie Mae didn't go bankrupt again this year. Instead, they are rewarded for announcing that homeownership rates have increased. In recent years, Congress has particularly pressured HUD to increase homeownership among blacks and other low-income minorities.

In 1992, when Congress gave HUD oversight over the GSEs, the Census Bureau was finding that homeownership rates had declined from 1980 to 1990. Moreover, rates in California and Oregon had steadily declined since 1960.

HUD today has a program encouraging local planners to promote housing affordability by deregulating land uses. But even if HUD had been aware of the connection between land-use regulation and declining affordability in the 1990s, it had no authority to stop such regulation.

But the 1992 law did give HUD authority to regulate the GSEs. Rather than use this authority to protect taxpayers from risky investments, successive secretaries of HUD used this regulatory power to order the GSEs to accept higher risks in the name of increasing housing affordability. In effect, they tried to use the GSEs to counterbalance the loss of housing affordability resulting from land-use regulation.

First, in 1995, Henry Cisneros ordered that at least 42 percent of the mortgages the GSEs purchased must be for "low- to moderate-income families." In 2000, Andrew Cuomo increased it to 50 percent. These rules led the GSEs to increase their purchases of subprime loans by 10 times. Then, in 2004, Alphonso Jackson increased the requirement to 56 percent, leading the GSEs to further increase their purchases of subprime loans. These purchases turned a previously minor market for subprime borrowers into a major segment of the mortgage market.

The Housing and Economic Recovery Act of 2008 addressed the conflict between HUD's missions by transferring HUD's oversight authority to a new, independent agency, the Federal Housing Finance Agency. In practice, HUD's Office of Federal Housing Enterprise Oversight merely changed its name and its director now reports directly to the president rather than to the secretary of HUD. Yet this leaves open the possibility that the president will direct the FHFA to promote greater risk taking in the name of housing affordability.

The 2008 act also creates an Affordable Housing Trust Fund, derived from an effective tax on the GSEs. In essence, this fund will work to make housing slightly less affordable for most people so as to make housing more affordable for a few people. Although the goal of affordable housing for low-income families is laudable, this is not an effective remedy. Since the real cause of unaffordable housing is land-use regulation, note the comment by economists Edward Glaeser and Joseph Gyourko, "if policy advocates are interested in reducing housing costs, they would do well to start with zoning reform."

Lessons Learned

Fannie Mae and Freddie Mac are nominally private enterprises, but they have the implicit backing of the federal treasury—backing that was affirmed by the September 2008 takeover of the two companies. Critics of the GSEs argue that this backing creates a moral hazard—that is, that GSE managers will take undue risks knowing that taxpayers will back up their losses. Worries about this moral hazard led Congress to give HUD oversight over the GSEs.

Yet Fannie Mae, which was created in 1938, operated successfully for 54 years before such oversight began. Ironically, it was the moral hazard created by giving oversight authority to HUD that proved to be the problem.

While that problem has apparently been corrected by having the director of the Federal Housing Finance Agency report to the president, this still leaves the GSEs open to political interference. To best insulate the GSEs from politics, Congress should relinquish government sponsorship of the GSEs and fully privatize them, as it did for Sallie Mae in 1995. This would hand oversight to the Securities and Exchange Commission and other authorities that regulate and monitor private financial institutions.

America's main housing affordability problems are the result not of market failure (which might justify GSEs) but of state and local land-use regulation that creates artificial housing shortages. The Environmental Protection Agency has proposed that Congress give it or another federal agency authority to impose growth-management policies nationwide in order to reduce greenhouse gas emissions. In fact, there is little evidence that growth management influences greenhouse gas emissions and strong evidence that growth management dramatically reduces housing affordability. Congress should reject any proposals to impose national growth-management planning.

Similarly, state legislatures that have passed growth-management laws or other laws giving cities regulatory control over rural land uses should recognize that these laws are the main impediment to housing affordability. Repeal of these laws (and legislative rejection of similar bills in the states that have not yet passed such laws) will do more to improve housing affordability and homeownership rates than federal programs like the GSEs.

Suggested Readings

O'Driscoll, Gerald P., Jr., "Asset Bubbles and Their Consequences," Cato Institute Briefing Paper no. 103, May 20, 2008.

O'Toole, Randal. "The Planning Tax: The Case against Regional Growth-Management Planning." Cato Institute Policy Analysis no. 606, December 6, 2007.

—Prepared by Randal O'Toole

23. Interior Department and Public Lands

Congress should

- privatize the lands held by the Forest Service and the U.S. Department of the Interior; or, failing that,
- reform the public land agencies by turning individual forests, parks, refuges, and Bureau of Land Management districts, or combinations of those units, into fiduciary trusts;
- allow those trusts to charge a broad range of user fees at market rates;
- fund the trusts exclusively out of a share of those user fees;
- dedicate some or all of the remaining user fees to special stewardship trusts whose goal is to maximize the nonmarket, stewardship values of the land; and
- reform the Endangered Species Act to provide compensation for private landowners for protecting wildlife habitat and to allow privatization of some wildlife to promote recovery efforts.

The Forest Service, Bureau of Land Management, National Park Service, and Fish and Wildlife Service manage 630 million acres of the United States. Representing 28 percent of the country, that is slightly more than the combined land areas of Arizona, California, Hawaii, Idaho, Montana, Nevada, New Mexico, Oregon, Utah, and Washington.

Many Americans are proud of the legacy offered by federal lands for present and future generations, especially the national parks, forests, and other lands that provide significant amounts of recreation. Yet this pride overlooks several problems with public land management:

- Federal land management currently costs taxpayers $7 billion a year.
- Much of that money is spent on things that are not necessarily good for the environment.

249

- A relatively small number of people get most of the benefits while everyone else pays the costs.
- Among the biggest beneficiaries are the bureaucracies themselves, which skillfully manipulate public opinion and members of Congress to increase their budgets.

Several studies from the Cato Institute have endorsed privatization of the public lands, a solution that is strongly opposed by environmentalists, recreationists, and other public land users. A second-best solution that will both enhance the values sought by environmentalists and public land users and correct the fiscal problems of the current system is to turn the public lands into *fiduciary trusts*. In this proposal, the United States would retain title to the lands, but the rules under which they are managed would be very different.

Fiduciary trusts funded out of their own revenues would make federal land managers more responsive to public land users, especially recreationists who would probably be the source of the vast majority of revenues. Besides saving taxpayers billions of dollars per year, trust management would be sustainable and sensitive to a wide range of environmental concerns.

Fiscal Issues

Not counting oil, gas, and coal revenues collected by the Minerals Management Service, Table 23.1 shows that the total revenues collected by the four land-management agencies averaged less than 14 percent of the cost of land management. Moreover, Table 23.2 indicates that the agencies kept most of these revenues for their own operations, returning to the treasury less than 5 cents for every dollar it spent.

The $3.9 billion collected by the Minerals Management Service, 95 percent of which was from oil, gas, and coal, would seem to partly redeem public land management. Yet almost all this revenue came from less than 1 million acres of land. This means the remaining 629 million acres returned less than 5 cents for every tax dollar spent.

To make matters worse, Table 23.2 also shows that Congress gives states or counties most of the funds that agencies return to the treasury. About three-quarters of BLM, all Fish and Wildlife Service, and 285 percent of Forest Service land-management returns to the treasury were paid to counties in 2007. Close to half ($1.62 billion in 2007) the onshore revenues collected by the Minerals Management Service are promised to

Table 23.1
Federal Land Acres, Budgets, and Revenues by Agency, 2007
(millions of acres or dollars)

Agency	Acres	Land Management Appropriations	Land Management Revenues	Returns to Treasury
Forest Service	193	$4,129	$448	$132
National Park Service	84	2,181	346	0
Bureau of Land Management	258	996	239	201
Fish & Wildlife Service	96	398	12	9
Minerals Management Service	—	80	3,935	3,935
Total	631	$7,784	$4,980	$4,277

SOURCES: *2009 Budget Justification for the Forest Service*, pp. D-2 to D-4, F-2; *2009 Budget Justification for the Park Service*, pp. Overview-51 to 52, Overview-70; *2009 Budget Justification for the BLM*, pp. I-11, II-1; *2009 Budget Justification for the Fish & Wildlife Service*, pp. RF-4, RM-11; *2009 Budget Justification for the Minerals Management Service*, p. 45; also see "Reported Royalty Revenue by Category, Fiscal Year 2007," tinyurl.com/5wwnu8.

NOTE: — = not available. "Appropriations" include funds appropriated by Congress out of general funds. "Revenues" include only revenues from land-management user fees. Minerals Management Service data include only onshore revenues and costs.

Table 23.2
Disposition of Land Management Receipts by Agency, 2007
(millions of dollars)

Agency	Total Revenues	Retained by Agencies	Payments to States	Net to Treasury
Forest Service	$448	$316	$377	− $245
National Park Service	346	346	0	0
Bureau of Land Management	239	38	147	54
Fish & Wildlife Service	12	3	9	0
Minerals Management Service	3,935	1,269*	1,620	1,045
Total	$4,980	$1,952	$2,154	$854

SOURCES: *2009 Budget Justification for the Forest Service*, pp. F-2 to F-3; *2009 Budget Justification for the Park Service*, p. Overview-70; *2009 Budget Justification for the BLM*, pp. II-1, IX-14; *2009 Budget Justification for the Fish & Wildlife Service*, pp. RF-4; "Total Disbursement by Fund and Commodity, Fiscal Year 2007," Minerals Management Service, tinyurl.com/5oem7q.

* Reclamation fund, retained by the Department of the Interior for the Bureau of Reclamation.

the states, and most of the rest ($1.27 billion in 2007) are dedicated to a land-reclamation fund.

Ultimately, the treasury retained no more than $854 million in return for the $7.8 billion it spent on public land management in 2007. Practically

251

all of this came from the 1 percent of land that produces oil, gas, and coal; the other 99 percent cost taxpayers more than $7 billion and returned virtually nothing to the treasury.

Most government agencies lose money. Yet the lands and resources managed by these agencies are so valuable that it seems incredible they could be managed at such a huge loss. The basic problem is that Congress has blocked the agencies' ability to make money and, in some cases, has actually given the agencies an incentive to lose money. This in turn leads to other problems, including environmental damage due to misallocations of resources, overproduction of subsidized resources, inequitable distribution of benefits, and unfair competition with private landowners who market many of the same resources.

In 1989, the Forest Service projected that, if the agency was allowed to charge the "market-clearing price" for all resources, it could collect a minimum of $6.7 billion per year in 2005. Nearly three-fourths of this revenue would be from recreation, including hunting and fishing. The agency further estimated that emphasizing recreation over commodity production (which is more or less what has happened since 1989) would boost total revenue to more than $10 billion per year. Similar fees could no doubt be collected on other federal lands.

In other words, federal land user fees would be more than sufficient to pay the costs of managing the national forests if only Congress would allow managers to charge market rates for all forest uses. In addition to saving money, funding forests out of user fees would give managers incentives to protect and produce the resources that users value the most. Moreover, freed from unfair competition from public lands, owners of private land would have an incentive to charge fees for recreation and to alter their management to favor the scenery, wildlife habitat, and other features that recreationists value.

If public lands are as valuable as people say, they should pay their own way. This means:

- Congress should allow public land managers to charge fair market value for all resources,
- Congress should allow managers to keep a fixed share of the receipts for all resources, and
- Congress should reduce appropriations to zero and fund the lands exclusively out of their own receipts.

Wildland Fire

Wildfire is probably the biggest federal land issue today. Paradoxically, though Congress has significantly increased wildfire budgets, more acres are burning than ever before, and wildland fires destroy hundreds of homes and other structures each year.

After the Cerro Grande fire destroyed hundreds of Los Alamos, New Mexico, homes in 2000, Congress asked the Forest Service and the Interior Department to prepare a National Fire Plan. Under this plan, wildfire budgets have more than quadrupled from levels of the early 1990s.

There is little evidence that this huge increase in spending is accomplishing much good.

- Since 2000, an average of twice as many protected acres have burned each year as the average for any decade in recorded history (not counting fires in areas with no forest fire protection).
- Three times as many homes and other structures burned in 2007 as in the average of the 10 previous years.
- Though a postfire analysis of the 2007 Angora fire, near Lake Tahoe, found that recent thinnings had helped minimize damage to the forests, they did not prevent the burning of more than 250 homes.

The Forest Service's explanation for the increased number of acres burned is that excess fuels resulting from decades of fire suppression have left the forests especially vulnerable to fire. This is disputed by numerous studies by fire ecologists. A 2006 article in *Science* magazine, for example, found that recent large fires were mainly a result of drought, not of land-use histories.

A 2002 Forest Service report, *Development of Coarse-Scale Spatial Data for Wildland Fire and Fuel Management*, found that only about 15 percent of federal lands in the West had actually been made more vulnerable to fire as a result of past management. Yet the Forest Service and BLM have taken a one-size-fits-all approach and are applying thinnings and other fuel treatments everywhere.

Even in the 15 percent of forests that suffer from excess fuels, it is unclear that expensive thinnings or other treatments are optimal. Research by Forest Service scientist Jack Cohen concludes, ''Wildland fuel reduction for reducing home losses may be inefficient and ineffective.'' All that is needed to protect homes and other structures from fire, Cohen has found, is to treat the areas within 150 or so feet around the homes. Any treatments outside that perimeter are inefficient because they are unnecessary and ineffective because firebrands or ground fires from fires farther away can easily lead to the destruction of untreated homes.

In short, the Forest Service's own research shows that homes will be protected from fire if and only if the homes and immediately surrounding grounds are treated. Yet Forest Service policy persists in lavishing the most attention on national forest lands that are often many miles away from homes. This strategy, which was adopted in the National Fire Plan without considering any alternatives, has conveniently resulted in huge budget increases for the Forest Service. It also effectively protects current forest managers from the blame for any large fires or houses burned by those fires, because such fires can be blamed instead on past management.

Merger with Interior

The Forest Service is the largest agency in the Department of Agriculture, but its activities more closely resemble agencies in the Department of the Interior. As a result, there is renewed interest in merging the Forest Service into Interior.

Such a merger is neither necessary nor sufficient to correct the serious problems facing the Forest Service. It is unnecessary because the Forest Service already works closely with Interior agencies. As a cost-saving measure, for example, some national forest lands are actually managed by BLM offices and some BLM lands are managed by Forest Service offices. It is unlikely that a merger would result in any greater cost savings. It is insufficient because a merger would not fix the basic structural problems that cause federal land agencies to lose billions of dollars per year. More serious reforms are needed, such as funding federal land managers out of user fees and turning federal lands into fiduciary trusts.

Endangered Species

In addition to managing national wildlife refuges, the Fish and Wildlife Service is responsible for endangered plants, wildlife, and freshwater fish. Congress passed the Endangered Species Act with the noblest of intentions. But the law's methods of carrying out those intentions unfairly places the burden of recovering endangered species populations on any landowner whose land happens to be home to an endangered species.

Landowners naturally resist this burden, so it is no surprise that few species have actually been recovered by the Endangered Species Act.

Even public land managers have been known to resist recovery efforts when those efforts interfere with what the managers perceive to be their primary missions. Efforts by both the Clinton and the Bush administrations to streamline the Endangered Species Act have focused on reducing costs to private landowners, but they have failed to create incentives that would motivate landowners to actually protect species.

To truly reform the act, Congress needs to create a trust fund or funds that can be used to pay landowners to protect wildlife habitat. Second, Congress needs to give the Fish and Wildlife Service the option to privatize some species of wildlife. Private owners are likely to develop innovative ways of protecting and restoring depleted wildlife populations. Anyone who has been to a dog show knows of the huge efforts people are willing to make on behalf of a breed for very little reward. Private ownership of wildlife could harness this energy on behalf of entire species. Such private ownership is common in Britain, but the closest we have come has been the successful efforts by private bird lovers to recover the peregrine falcon.

Fiduciary Trusts

User fees alone will not resolve all the issues and conflicts that face public land managers. For one thing, some resources, such as endangered species habitat and historic and archeological artifacts, are not easily marketed. In addition, land managers motivated by short-term revenues may be tempted to sacrifice the long-run productivity of the land. Fiduciary trusts are an institutional structure that can ensure long-run protection for nonmarketable resources while improving the fiscal management of the lands.

A fiduciary trust is a legal construct based on hundreds of years of British and U.S. common law. A trust consists of four components:

- A *trustor*, the person or entity who creates the trust;
- The *trustee*, the person or people managing the trust;
- The *beneficiary*, the person or people for whom the trust is managed; and
- The *trust instrument*, the legal document that dictates how the trustor wants the trustee to manage the trust.

Trusts are significantly different from the bureaucracies that now manage federal lands. Trust law imposes strong obligations on trustees to preserve the productive capacity of trust resources, produce benefits for the trust beneficiaries, and fully disclose the costs and benefits of their actions. To

255

create a trust, the trustor—Congress—is also obligated to give the trust a clear mission—something that many people would say today's federal land agencies lack.

Conversion of Public Lands into Trusts

Congress should create two types of trusts: one to manage the market resources and the other to manage the nonmarket resources of the public lands. The mission of the market trusts will be to *maximize the revenue from public land management while preserving the productive capacity of the land*. The mission of the nonmarket trusts would be to *maximize the preservation and, as appropriate, restoration of natural ecosystems and cultural resources*. The nonmarket trusts would be a primary method of protecting endangered species, as they could use their funds to give private landowners and public land managers incentives to protect fish and wildlife habitat.

To implement the trusts, Congress could merge or divide the 155 national forests, 59 BLM districts, 390 units of the National Park System, and 548 wildlife refuges into about 60 to 100 different ecoregions and create a pair of market and nonmarket trusts for each ecoregion. Revenues collected by the market trusts would be divided among the market and nonmarket trusts. In areas such as the Powder River Basin, where public lands produce excess revenues, a share would go to the U.S. treasury.

To govern and monitor the trusts, Congress could create a "friends of the trust" association for each ecoregion and allow anyone to join any friends association for a nominal fee of, say, $25 to $30 a year. Members of the friends associations would elect the boards of trustees that oversee the trusts. The trustees, in turn, would hire trust superintendents, approve budgets and user fees, and regulate uses. The friends associations would also monitor the trusts and could vote to recommend to Congress that a particular trust be disbanded and the lands returned to a bureaucracy like one of today's Interior agencies.

With more than 1,000 forests, parks, refuges, and BLM districts, Congress need not choose between adopting or rejecting this program as a whole. Instead, Congress can test the trust idea on selected administrative units. Tests can compare methods of governance, funding mechanisms, alternative geographic sizes, and other aspects of the trust concept.

Conclusion

The 630 million acres managed by the Forest Service and Department of the Interior cost taxpayers $7 billion per year and continually produce major controversies and conflicts among users. Fiduciary trusts offer a way to solve these problems. Congress should test the trust system on selected national parks and other federal lands. If the tests are successful, Congress should reform all federal land agencies into a series of market and nonmarket trusts. The results should satisfy those who care about natural environments and cultural resources, as well as those who care about fiscal responsibility.

Suggested Readings

O'Toole, Randal. *Reforming the Forest Service*. Covelo, CA: Island Press, 1988.
_____. "The Endangered Endangered Species Act." *Different Drummer*, Winter, 1996. http://ti.org/ESATofC.html.
_____. "Should Congress Transfer Federal Lands to the States?" Cato Institute Policy Analysis no. 276, July 3, 1997.
_____. "The Perfect Firestorm: Bringing Forest Service Wildfire Costs under Control." Cato Institute Policy Analysis no. 591, April 30, 2007.
_____. "A Matter of Trust: Why Congress Should Turn Federal Lands into Fiduciary Trusts." Cato Institute Policy Analysis, forthcoming.

—Prepared by Randal O'Toole

24. Surface Transportation Policy

Congress should

- eliminate federal highway, transit, and other surface transportation programs; and
- devolve to the states and local areas full responsibility for highways and transit.

Failing that, Congress should

- fund state highways in block grants based on each state's land area, population, and road mileage;
- fund regional transit in block grants based on each metropolitan area's population and transit fare revenues;
- eliminate any conditions on the use of those funds, such as air pollution mandates or requirements for long-range planning;
- eliminate "flexible funds," that is, funds that can be spent on either highways or transit;
- encourage states and local areas to rely more heavily on user fees to fund all forms of transportation; and
- ensure that any efforts to save energy or reduce greenhouse gas emissions are cost-effective, that is, that state and local governments only invest in projects that can be shown to reduce energy consumption or greenhouse gas emissions at a lower cost than alternative projects.

The Importance of Effective Transportation Policy

Efficient transportation literally provides the wheels that keep the American economy moving. More than 11 percent of our gross domestic product consists of expenditures on personal or for-hire transportation. But without that 11 percent, much of the rest of our economy would grind to a halt as people could not get to work and manufacturers could not get raw materials or deliver their products to consumers.

In 1956, Congress decided to build an Interstate Highway System. Although this system took longer and cost more to build than originally predicted, it led to an extraordinary improvement in American mobility. For example, although interstates make up only 6 percent of state rural highway networks, they provide more than 20 percent of all intercity auto traffic and more than half of all intercity truck traffic.

The key to the success of the Interstate Highway System is that it was a user-pay system, funded exclusively by federal and state gasoline taxes and other highway user fees. This user-pay system helped ensure that interstate highways were built only where they were needed and helped keep construction costs from becoming excessive.

In recent decades, Congress has increasingly departed from user-pay systems, and instead requires users of some forms of transportation—primarily auto drivers—to pay for other forms of transportation—primarily public transit. In addition to being unjust, this policy has led to excessive construction costs and the selection of transportation projects whose costs far outweigh their benefits. One symptom of this misallocation of funds is the growing congestion in America's urban areas.

Proponents of urban transit and intercity high-speed rail are using concerns about energy and global warming to promote the diversion of even more highway user fees to their favored forms of transportation. Yet as will be shown later, these alternative forms of transportation are unlikely to save energy or significantly reduce greenhouse gas emissions.

Brief History

The Federal-Aid Highway Act of 1956 created the Highway Trust Fund to support the construction of the Interstate Highway System, and dedicated a 3-cent-per-gallon federal gasoline tax and other driving-related taxes to that fund. One problem with this law is that a cents-per-gallon gas tax does not automatically adjust for inflation. Congress raised the tax from 3 cents to 4 cents per gallon in 1959, but did not raise it again until 1983. Inflation, combined with higher-than-expected costs of construction, particularly in the 2,300 miles of urban roads that Congress added to the system in 1956, delayed completion of the Interstate System from the original projected date of 1969 to around 1991.

As the Interstate Highway System neared completion in the 1980s, Congress could have phased out the gasoline tax, or at least reduced it to an amount sufficient to maintain the existing system. Instead, the distribution of highway revenues became increasingly politicized. For example, Congress first included earmarks in a transportation bill in 1982. Since then, the number of earmarks has grown exponentially: from 10 in 1982 to 152 in 1987, 538 in 1991, 1,850 in 1998, and 6,373 in 2005. The 2005 earmarks totaled almost 10 percent of the entire six-year authorization.

Further politicization began in 1983 when Congress first diverted highway user fees to mass transit. Even more diversions were permitted in the 1991 Intermodal Surface Transportation Efficiency Act. Among other things, ISTEA allowed metropolitan areas to treat some federal funds as "flexible," that is, spendable on either highways or transit.

Another ISTEA program, New Starts, encouraged transit agencies to build high-cost alternatives to bus transit. Cities that built light rail or other rail projects collected billions in federal funds, while cities satisfied with bus service received a much smaller share of federal transit grants. This circumstance led more cities to propose rail. In turn, it generated a huge rail transit lobby consisting of rail engineering and design firms, railcar manufacturers, and rail contractors.

Technical vs. Behavioral Tools

Passage of the Clean Air Act of 1970 led to a debate that continues to this day: Are technical tools such as catalytic converters or behavioral tools such as disincentives to the automobile the best way to reduce the environmental effects of driving?

Nearly 40 years of experience have shown that technical solutions to air pollution and other auto-related problems can be phenomenally successful. Between 1970 and 2002, U.S. driving increased by 157 percent. Yet thanks largely to catalytic converters and other technical improvements, total auto emissions of carbon monoxide, nitrogen oxides, particulates, and volatile organic compounds declined by more than 50 percent.

In contrast, experience has shown that behavioral tools are extremely costly yet almost completely ineffective at reducing the environmental effects of driving. For example, between 1992 and 2006, federal, state, and local governments spent more than $160 billion (in 2008 dollars) on transit capital improvements—more than one-third of the inflation-adjusted cost of the entire Interstate Highway System. Two-thirds of these transit capital funds, or nearly $110 billion, were spent on rail transit.

In exchange for this huge cost, transit usage grew by less than 15 percent compared with a 45 percent increase in urban driving over the same period. While transit carried about 50 billion passenger miles of travel in 2006, urban interstates alone carried more than three-quarters of a trillion passenger miles.

Despite the mammoth investment in rail transit, transit's share of urban travel declined from 2.0 percent in 1990 to 1.5 percent in 2006. The biggest declines were in urban areas with rail transit, partly because rail transit is so costly that transit agencies are often forced to neglect the bus systems that carry most of their transit patrons.

Nor have land-use policies aimed at creating more compact urban areas proved successful. A 1974 urban-growth boundary compacted the San Jose urbanized area from less than 3,800 people per square mile in 1974 to more than 6,000 today. San Jose also built a 40-mile light-rail system. Yet transit's share of travel declined from 1.2 percent of passenger miles in 1982 (the earliest year for which data are available) to 0.9 percent in 2006, whereas transit's share of commuting trivially increased from 3.1 percent in 1980 to 3.3 percent today.

Similarly dismal results can be found in most other regions that used urban-growth boundaries to become more compact while investing heavily in rail transit. In Portland, Oregon, transit's share of commuting declined from 9.8 percent in 1980 to 7.6 percent today; in San Diego, from 3.5 percent to 3.1 percent; in Sacramento, from 4.1 percent to 2.4 percent; and in Denver, from 6.4 percent to 4.3 percent. Meanwhile, per capita miles of driving have increased in virtually every urban area.

Based on the results, the debate between technical and behavioral tools should be over. Yet Cato's review of long-range transportation plans for the nation's 70 largest metropolitan areas found that one-third of the plans relied primarily on behavioral tools to solve transportation problems, and another one-fifth relied partially on such tools.

The Importance of User Fees

The collapse of the I-35W bridge in Minneapolis led to calls for increased gas taxes to rebuild infrastructure. In fact, preliminary reports indicate that a design flaw, rather than lack of maintenance, may have caused the collapse. But even if more money is needed for highway infrastructure, it would be better to provide that money by ending diversions of federal and state gas taxes to nonhighway activities.

Even better would be a more sensible system of paying for infrastructure out of user fees. Gasoline taxes are not indexed to inflation and fail to account for increases in automobile fuel-efficiency. Road tolls make more sense because they provide transport agencies with accurate information about where people want to go and transport users with accurate information about how much it costs to provide road systems.

User fees such as gas taxes, highway tolls, and transit fares are a fair and equitable way of paying for transportation facilities because they ensure that the people who get the benefits are the ones who pay the costs. User fees also provide signals to users and producers about the costs and value of transportation facilities and services.

Nationally, gas taxes, tolls, and other highway user fees cover 85 to 90 percent of the cost of building, maintaining, and operating highways, roads, and streets. In contrast, transit fares cover only 28 percent of the cost of building and operating the nation's transit systems. On one hand, this means that transit riders have little sense of the real cost of their mode of travel. On the other hand, dependence on taxes encourages many transit agencies to build expensive urban monuments that please politicians, construction companies, and other powerful interests rather than provide high-quality, economical services to actual transit users.

Contrary to popular belief, transit can be funded by user fees. Atlantic City, New Jersey, has a private jitney system that runs 24 hours a day (more than most public transit systems) and is funded entirely by transit fares. In San Juan, Puerto Rico, privately owned jitneys called *públicos* carry more people than the public bus and rail systems combined, yet they are funded entirely by transit fares. Unfortunately, such private transit service is illegal in most cities in the 50 states.

Federal support for transportation, including transit, should be based on performance standards. For example, federal transit funds should be distributed to metropolitan areas based on a formula that includes the transit revenues earned by local systems. That would give transit agencies incentives to boost ridership rather than build urban monuments.

Energy and Greenhouse Gases

Rising gas prices and concerns about greenhouse gases have stimulated calls for the federal government to support more rail transit lines in urban areas and construct a large-scale intercity high-speed rail system. There are two important questions to ask about these policies (or any other programs designed to save energy and reduce greenhouse gas emissions): Do they really work? and If so, are they worth the cost?

The second question is particularly pertinent. McKinsey & Company says that, by 2030, the U.S. can reduce its total greenhouse gas production to well below current levels by investing in technologies that cost less— sometimes substantially less—than $50 per ton of abated carbon dioxide–equivalent emissions. Any program that reduces greenhouse gas emissions at a cost of more than $50 per ton diverts resources away from programs that are more efficient.

Rail Transport Is Not the Answer

A close look at rail transport reveals that it rarely saves energy or reduces greenhouse gas emissions. To the extent that a particular rail line can do so, however, it will cost substantially more than $50 per ton.

This is partly because urban transit and intercity rail are both much more expensive and much more heavily subsidized than flying or driving (Figure 24.1).

The tremendous expense of rail transportation buys few environmental benefits. Contrary to recent media reports, rail transit is not attracting many people out of their cars even in the face of high gas prices. While urban auto usage in the first quarter of 2008 declined by 15.4 billion passenger miles from 2007, transit ridership grew by only about 450 million passenger miles. Transit thus accounted for only about 3 percent of the decline in driving.

Table 24.1
Costs and Subsidies in Cents per Passenger Mile

Mode	Cost	Subsidy
Air	13	0.1
Autos	23	0.5
Amtrak	56	22.0
Transit	85	61.0

SOURCES: *National Transportation Statistics 2008* (Washington: Bureau of Transportation Statistics, 2008), Tables 1-37, 3-07, 3-16, 3-27a, and 3-29a; 2006 National Transit Database, (Federal Transit Administration, 2007) "Capital Use," "Operating Expenses," and "Fares" spreadsheets; *National Economic Accounts* (Washington: National Bureau of Economic Analysis, 2008), Table 2.5.5; *Highway Statistics 2006* (Washington: Federal Highway Administration, 2008), Table HF10; *2006 Annual Report* (Washington: Amtrak, 2007).

NOTE: Subsidies include federal, state, and local support.

Moreover, the biggest decline in driving was in March, but in that month, transit ridership actually declined from March 2007. Transit is clearly not making a difference for most people who are affected by high fuel prices. This is because, even after decades of huge subsidies, transit systems cannot take people where they want to go, when they want to go there—which is especially a problem for inflexible rail systems.

Although rail advocates often lament that the United States is not more like Europe, huge subsidies to European rail transport have not worked there either. Nations in the European Union spend about five times as much as the United States subsidizing urban transit and intercity rail. In 2000, 84.4 percent of U.S. travel was by auto and only 0.6 percent by urban or intercity rail. In Europe, 79.2 percent of travel was by auto and 6.3 percent was by rail. These facts suggest that a quintupling of rail and transit subsidies will, at best, get less than 6 percent of travelers out of their cars and onto trains. Moreover, despite the subsidies, the percentage of European travel by rail is declining, whereas percentages of travel by auto and flying are both increasing. European planners project that the share of travel by rail and bus will continue to decline through 2030.

Even if spending billions on rail transport could attract significant numbers of people out of their cars, it would not save energy or reduce greenhouse gas emissions. Despite the apparent efficiency of steel wheels on steel rails, rail transport is very energy intensive, partly because rail vehicles are, for safety reasons, very heavy.

The Department of Energy reports that the average car on the road today consumes about 3,400 British Thermal Units (BTUs) per passenger mile. Under the Energy Independence and Security Act of 2007, that consumption is expected to decline to just 2,500 BTUs per passenger mile by 2035.

In contrast, urban transit buses use about 4,300 BTUs per passenger mile, about as much as the average sport-utility vehicle. Rail transit uses 2,800 BTUs and Amtrak uses 2,700 BTUs per passenger mile—less than today's average auto but more than the projected usage of an average auto in 2035. Although the rapid turnover of the nation's auto fleet allows auto efficiencies to quickly increase, the long-term nature of rail transit investments means that systems that are inefficient today will remain inefficient for many decades to come. People who ride transit to avoid high gas prices aren't really saving energy; they are merely passing on their energy costs to someone else.

Even when rail operations save some energy, that savings is mitigated by two related energy costs. First, the energy cost of building rail transit

265

is huge. Planners projected that the energy cost of building one light-rail line in Portland, Oregon, would be 172 times the annual energy savings from operating that line. Although highway construction also uses energy, highways are so much more heavily used that the cost per passenger mile is much lower.

Second, new rail transit lines do not replace buses so much as they lead transit agencies to reroute buses into feeder buses serving the rail lines. When taken as a whole, the bus-plus-rail systems often end up consuming more energy, per passenger mile, than the bus systems alone.

Nor does rail transit cost-effectively reduce greenhouse gas emissions. When the electricity needed to power rail transit is generated by fossil fuels, as it is in, for example, Baltimore, Cleveland, Denver, Miami, and Washington, D.C., rail transit often generates more greenhouse gases per passenger mile than the average sport-utility vehicle.

Rail operations generate minimal greenhouse gases where electricity comes from renewable sources, as in the Pacific Northwest. But, once again, this reduction is mitigated by the construction cost. For example, the greenhouse gas emissions from building a proposed light-rail line in Seattle are equal to 45 years of operational savings from that light rail. Cities in such areas would do better installing electric trolley buses than rail transit.

At best, then, the cost of saving a ton of greenhouse gas emissions by building new rail lines is very high. Reducing emissions through rail transit, when it reduces them at all, costs thousands or tens of thousands of dollars per ton. In contrast, making cars more fuel-efficient by using materials that are more lightweight or by improving traffic signal coordination can actually save money for every ton of greenhouse gases abated. Any policies aimed at reducing greenhouse gas emissions should ensure that investments are cost-effective.

Conclusion

Because transportation is so vital to American life, it is important to make transportation investments where they will do the most toward enhancing mobility. The best way to ensure that is to rely on user-pay systems.

There is little reason why a true user-pay system should require federal involvement. But to the extent that Congress remains involved in transportation issues, it should promote user-pay systems at the state and local level and take steps to ensure that state and local use of federal transportation funds is cost-effective. This means, among other things, distributing funds based on performance standards, eliminating earmarks, and streamlining transportation planning.

Suggested Readings

O'Toole, Randal. "A Desire Named Streetcar: How Federal Subsidies Encourage Wasteful Local Transit Systems." Cato Policy Analysis no. 559, January 5, 2006.
_____. "Does Rail Transit Save Energy or Reduce Greenhouse Gas Emissions?" Cato Policy Analysis no. 615, April 14, 2008.
_____. "Roadmap to Gridlock: The Failure of Long-Range Metropolitan Transportation Planning." Cato Policy Analysis no. 617, May 27, 2008.
_____. "Rails Won't Save America." Cato Briefing Paper no. 107, October 7, 2008.
Taylor, Jerry, and Peter Van Doren. "Don't Increase Federal Gasoline Taxes—Abolish Them." Cato Policy Analysis no. 598, August 7, 2007.

—Prepared by Randal O'Toole

25. Cultural Agencies

Congress should

- eliminate the National Endowment for the Arts,
- eliminate the National Endowment for the Humanities, and
- defund the Corporation for Public Broadcasting.

In a society that constitutionally limits the powers of government and maximizes individual liberty, there is no justification for the forcible transfer of money from taxpayers to artists, scholars, and broadcasters. If the proper role of government is to safeguard the security of the nation's residents, by what rationale are they made to support exhibits of paintings, symphony orchestras, documentaries, scholarly research, and radio and television programs they might never freely choose to support? The kinds of things financed by federal cultural agencies were produced long before those agencies were created, and they will continue to be produced long after those agencies are privatized or defunded. Moreover, the power to subsidize art, scholarship, and broadcasting cannot be found within the powers enumerated and delegated to the federal government under the Constitution.

The National Endowment for the Arts, an "independent" agency established in 1965, makes grants to museums, symphony orchestras, individual artists "of exceptional talent," and organizations (including state arts agencies) to "encourage individual and institutional development of the arts, preservation of the American artistic heritage, wider availability of the arts, leadership in the arts, and the stimulation of non-Federal sources of support for the Nation's artistic activities." Among its more famous and controversial grant recipients were artist Andres Serrano, whose exhibit featured a photograph of a plastic crucifix in a jar of his own urine, and the Institute of Contemporary Art in Philadelphia, which sponsored a traveling exhibition of the late Robert Mapplethorpe's homoerotic photo-

269

graphs. (Thanks to an NEA grantee, the American taxpayers once paid $1,500 for a poem, "lighght." That wasn't the title or a typo. That was the entire poem.) The NEA's fiscal year 2008 budget was $144.7 million, up over $20 million from 2004.

The National Endowment for the Humanities, with a FY2008 budget of $141 million, "funds activities that are intended to improve the quality of education and teaching in the humanities, to strengthen the scholarly foundation for humanities study and research, and to advance understanding of the humanities among general audiences." Among the things it has funded are controversial national standards for the teaching of history in schools, the traveling King Tut exhibit, and the documentary film *Rosie the Riveter.*

The 41-year-old Corporation for Public Broadcasting—FY08 budget of $415 million—provides money to "qualified public television and radio stations to be used at their discretion for purposes related primarily to program production and acquisition." It also supports the production and acquisition of radio and television programs for national distribution and assists in "the financing of several system-wide activities, including national satellite interconnection services and the payment of music royalty fees, and provides limited technical assistance, research, and planning services to improve system-wide capacity and performance." Some of the money provided local public radio and television stations is used to help support National Public Radio and the Public Broadcasting Service.

Note that the amount of arts funding in the federal budget is quite small. That might be taken as a defense of the funding, were it not for the important reasons to avoid *any* government funding of something as intimate yet powerful as artistic expression. But it should also be noted how small federal funding is as a percentage of the total arts budget in this country. The NEA's budget is about 1 percent of the $13.7 billion contributed to the arts by private corporations, foundations, and individuals in 2007. According to Americans for the Arts, the nonprofit arts are a $63 billion industry. Surely they will survive without whatever portion of the NEA's budget gets out of the Washington bureaucracy and into the hands of actual artists or arts institutions. Indeed, when the NEA budget was cut in 1995, private giving to the arts rose dramatically.

In 1995, Congress voted to phase out the NEA over three years. The 111th Congress should revive that commitment and also end federal involvement with the National Endowment for the Humanities and the Corporation for Public Broadcasting.

Subsidies by the Poor to the Rich

Since art museums, symphony orchestras, humanities scholarship, and public television and radio are enjoyed predominantly by people of greater-than-average income and education, the federal cultural agencies oversee a fundamentally unfair transfer of wealth from the lower classes up. It's no accident that you hear ads for Remy Martin and "private banking services" on NPR, not for Budweiser and free checking accounts. *Newsweek* columnist Robert J. Samuelson is correct when he calls federal cultural agencies "highbrow pork barrel." As Edward C. Banfield has written, "The art public is now, as it has always been, overwhelmingly middle and upper-middle class and above average in income—relatively prosperous people who would probably enjoy art about as much in the absence of subsidies." Supporters of the NEA often say that their purpose is to bring the finer arts to those who don't already patronize them. But Dick Netzer, an economist who favors arts subsidies, conceded that they have "failed to increase the representation of low-income people in audiences." In other words, lower-income people are not interested in the kind of entertainment they're forced to support; they prefer to put their money into forms of art often sneered at by the cultural elite. Why must they continue to finance the pleasures of the affluent?

Corruption of Artists and Scholars

Government subsidies to the arts and humanities have an insidious, corrupting effect on artists and scholars. It is assumed, for example, that the arts need government encouragement. But if an artist needs such encouragement, what kind of artist is he? Novelist E. L. Doctorow once told the House Appropriations Committee, "An enlightened endowment puts its money on largely unknown obsessive individuals who have sacrificed all the ordinary comforts and consolations of life in order to do their work." Few have noticed the contradiction in that statement. As author Bill Kauffman has commented, Doctorow "wants to abolish the risk and privation that dog almost all artists, particularly during their apprenticeships. 'Starving artists' are to be plumped up by taxpayers. . . . The likelihood that pampered artists will turn complacent, listless, and lazy seems not to bother Doctorow." Moreover, as Jonathan Yardley, the *Washington Post*'s book critic, asked, "Why should the struggling young artist be entitled to government subsidy when the struggling young mechanic or accountant is not?"

271

Politicizing of Culture

James D. Wolfensohn, former chairman of the Kennedy Center for the Performing Arts, decried talk about abolishing the NEA. "We should not allow [the arts] to become political," he said. But it is the subsidies that have politicized the arts and scholarship, not the talk about ending them. Some artists and scholars are to be awarded taxpayers' money. Which artists and scholars? They can't all be subsidized. The decisions are ultimately made by bureaucrats (even if they are advised by artists and scholars). Whatever criteria the bureaucrats use, they politicize art and scholarship. As novelist George Garrett has said: "Once (and whenever) the government is involved in the arts, then it is bound to be a political and social business, a battle between competing factions. The NEA, by definition, supports the arts establishment." Adds painter Laura Main, "Relying on the government to sponsor art work ... is to me no more than subjecting yourself to the fate of a bureaucratic lackey."

Mary Beth Norton, a writer of women's history and a former member of the National Council on the Humanities, argues that "one of the great traditions of the Endowment [for the Humanities] is that this is where people doing research in new and exciting areas—oral history, black history, women's history to name areas I am familiar with—can turn to for funding." When the NEH spent less money in the mid-1980s than previously, Norton complained, "Now, people on the cutting edge are not being funded anymore." But if bureaucrats are ultimately selecting the research to be funded, how cutting-edge can it really be? How can they be trusted to distinguish innovation from fad? And who wants scholars choosing the objects of their research on the basis of what will win favor with government grant referees?

Similar criticism can be leveled against the radio and television programs financed by the CPB. They tend (with a few exceptions) to be aimed at the wealthier and better educated, and the selection process is inherently political. Moreover, some of the money granted to local stations is passed on to National Public Radio and the Public Broadcasting Service for the production of news programs, including *All Things Considered* and the *Newshour with Jim Lehrer.* Why are the taxpayers in a free society compelled to support news coverage, particularly when it is inclined in a statist direction? Robert Coonrod, former president of CPB, defends the organization, saying that "about 90 percent of the federal appropriation goes back to the communities, to public radio and TV stations, which are essentially community institutions." Only 90 percent? Why not leave

100 percent in the communities and let the residents decide how to spend it? Since only 15 percent of public broadcasting revenues now come from the federal government, other sources presumably could take up the slack if the federal government ended the appropriation.

It must be pointed out that the fundamental objection to the federal cultural agencies is not that their products have been intellectually, morally, politically, or sexually offensive to conservatives or even most Americans. That has sometimes, but not always, been the case. Occasionally, such as during the bicentennial of the U.S. Constitution, the agencies have been used to subsidize projects favored by conservatives. The brief against those agencies would be the same had the money been used exclusively to subsidize works inoffensive or even inspiring to the majority of the American people.

The case also cannot be based on how much the agencies spend. In FY08 the two endowments and the CPB were appropriated about $701 million total, a mere morsel in a $3 trillion federal budget. The NEA's budget is about 0.2 percent of the total amount spent on the nonprofit arts in the United States.

No, the issue is neither the content of the work subsidized nor the expense. Taxpayer subsidy of the arts, scholarship, and broadcasting is inappropriate because it is outside the range of the proper functions of government, and as such, it needlessly politicizes, and therefore corrupts, an area of life that should be left untainted by politics.

Government funding of anything involves government control. That insight, of course, is part of our folk wisdom: "He who pays the piper calls the tune." "Who takes the king's shilling sings the king's song."

Defenders of arts funding seem blithely unaware of this danger when they praise the role of the national endowments as an imprimatur or seal of approval on artists and arts groups. Former NEA chair Jane Alexander said: "The Federal role is small but very vital. We are a stimulus for leveraging state, local and private money. We are a linchpin for the puzzle of arts funding, a remarkably efficient way of stimulating private money." Drama critic Robert Brustein asks, "How could the NEA be 'privatized' and still retain its purpose as a funding agency functioning as a stamp of approval for deserving art?"

The politicization of whatever the federal cultural agencies touch was driven home by Richard Goldstein, a supporter of the NEH. Goldstein pointed out:

> The NEH has a ripple effect on university hiring and tenure, and on the
> kinds of research undertaken by scholars seeking support. Its chairman

273

shapes the bounds of that support. In a broad sense, he sets standards that affect the tenor of textbooks and the content of curricula. . . . Though no chairman of the NEH can single-handedly direct the course of American education, he can nurture the nascent trends and take advantage of informal opportunities to signal department heads and deans. He can "persuade" with the cudgel of federal funding out of sight but hardly out of mind.

The cudgel (an apt metaphor) of federal funding has the potential to be wielded to influence those who run the universities with regard to hiring, tenure, research programs, textbooks, and curricula. That is an enormous amount of power to have vested in a government official. Surely, it is the kind of concentration of power that the Founding Fathers intended to thwart.

Separation of Conscience and State

We might reflect on why the separation of church and state seems such a wise idea to Americans. First, it is wrong for the coercive authority of the state to interfere in matters of individual conscience. If we have rights, if we are individual moral agents, we must be free to exercise our judgment and define our own relationship with God. That doesn't mean that a free, pluralistic society won't have lots of persuasion and proselytizing—no doubt it will—but it does mean that such proselytizing must remain entirely persuasive, entirely voluntary.

Second, social harmony is enhanced by removing religion from the sphere of politics. Europe suffered through the Wars of Religion, as churches made alliances with rulers and sought to impose their theology on everyone in a region. Religious inquisitions, Roger Williams said, put towns "in an uproar." If people take their faith seriously, and if government is going to make one faith universal and compulsory, then people must contend bitterly—even to the death—to make sure that the *true* faith is established. Enshrine religion in the realm of persuasion, and there may be vigorous debate in society, but there won't be political conflict—and people can deal with one another in secular life without endorsing the private opinions of their colleagues.

Third, competition produces better results than subsidy, protection, and conformity. "Free trade in religion" is the best tool humans have to find the nearest approximation to the truth. Businesses coddled behind subsidies and tariffs will be weak and uncompetitive, and so will churches, synagogues, mosques, and temples. Religions that are protected from political interference but are otherwise on their own are likely to be stronger and more vigorous than a church that draws its support from government.

If those statements are true, they have implications beyond religion. Religion is not the only thing that affects us personally and spiritually, and it is not the only thing that leads to cultural wars. Art also expresses, transmits, and challenges our deepest values. As the managing director of Baltimore's Center Stage put it: "Art has power. It has the power to sustain, to heal, to humanize ... to change something in you. It's a frightening power, and also a beautiful power. ... And it's essential to a civilized society." Because art is so powerful, because it deals with such basic human truths, we dare not entangle it with coercive government power. That means no censorship or regulation of art. It also means no tax-funded subsidies for arts and artists, for when government gets into the arts funding business, we get political conflicts. Conservatives denounce the National Endowment for the Arts for funding erotic photography and the Public Broadcasting Service for broadcasting *Tales of the City*, which has gay characters. (*More Tales of the City*, which appeared on Showtime after PBS ducked the political pressure, generated little political controversy.) Civil rights activists make the Library of Congress take down an exhibit on antebellum slave life, and veterans' groups pressure the Smithsonian to remove a display on the bombing of Hiroshima. To avoid political battles over how to spend the taxpayers' money, to keep art and its power in the realm of persuasion, we would be well advised to establish the separation of art and state.

Suggested Readings

Banfield, Edward C. *The Democratic Muse.* New York: Basic Books, 1984.

Boaz, David. "The Separation of Art and the State." *Vital Speeches*, June 15, 1995. www.cato.org/speeches/sp-as53.html.

Cowen, Tyler. *In Praise of Commercial Culture.* Cambridge, MA: Harvard University Press, 1998.

Gillespie, Nick. "All Culture, All the Time." *Reason,* April 1999.

Grampp, William. *Pricing the Priceless.* New York: Basic Books, 1984.

Kauffman, Bill. "Subsidies to the Arts: Cultivating Mediocrity." Cato Institute Policy Analysis no. 137, August 8, 1990.

Kostelanetz, Richard. "The New Benefactors." *Liberty,* January 1990.

Lynes, Russell. "The Case against Government Aid to the Arts." *New York Times Magazine,* March 25, 1962.

Samuelson, Robert J. "Highbrow Pork Barrel." *Newsweek,* August 21, 1989.

Subcommittee on Oversight and Investigations of the House Committee on Education and the Workforce. *The Healthy State of the Arts in America and the Continuing*

Failure of the National Endowment for the Arts. 105th Cong., 1st sess., September 23, 1997. Serial no. 105-A.

—Prepared by Sheldon Richman and David Boaz

26. Corporate Welfare and Earmarks

Congress should

- end programs that provide direct grants to businesses;
- end spending that indirectly subsidizes businesses, such as preferential loans and assistance for exporting;
- eliminate trade and regulatory barriers that favor some businesses at the expense of other businesses and consumers;
- eliminate earmarking in spending bills and subject all spending projects—assuming that they are legitimate federal activities—to expert review and competitive bidding;
- expand financial transparency with further Internet disclosures of spending details for proposed and enacted bills; and
- downsize the federal government by terminating programs, reviving federalism, and privatizing activities.

When considering budget issues, federal policymakers are supposed to have the broad public interest in mind. Unfortunately, that is not how the federal budget process usually works in practice. Many federal programs are sustained by special-interest groups working with policymakers seeking narrow benefits at the expense of taxpayers and the general public. This chapter examines how special interests regularly triumph over the general public interest in Washington and focuses on two particular types of spending: corporate welfare and earmarks.

Corporate welfare refers to subsidies and regulatory protections that lawmakers confer on certain businesses and industries. Earmarking refers to the practice of individual lawmakers slipping provisions into bills to fund particular projects in their home states. Earmarks can include subsidies for businesses, nonprofit groups, or state and local governments.

Special Interests' Domination of the General Interest

How can special interests regularly triumph over the broad public interest in our democracy? For one thing, recipients of federal handouts have a strong incentive to create organizations to lobby Congress to keep the federal gravy train flowing. By contrast, average citizens have no strong incentive to lobby against any particular subsidy program because each program costs just a small portion of their total tax bill.

When average citizens do speak out against particular programs, they are usually outgunned by the professionals who are paid to support programs. Those professionals have an informational advantage over citizens because the workings of most federal programs are complex. The lobby groups that defend subsidy programs are staffed by top program experts, and they are skilled at generating media support. One typical gambit is to cloak the narrow private interests of subsidy recipients in public interest clothing, and proclaim that the nation's future depends on increased funding.

Another reason it is hard to challenge spending programs is that lobby groups, congressional supporters, and federal agencies rarely admit that any program is a failure. Washington insiders become vested in the continued funding of programs because their careers, pride, and reputations are on the line, and they will battle against any cuts or reforms.

How do dubious spending programs get enacted in the first place? Table 26.1 shows how Congress can pass special-interest legislation in which the costs outweigh the benefits. The table assumes that legislators vote in the narrow interests of their districts. The hypothetical project shown creates benefits of $40 and costs taxpayers $50, and is thus a loser for the nation. Nonetheless, the project gains a majority vote. The program's

Table 26.1
Majority Voting Does Not Ensure That a Project's Benefits Outweigh Costs

Legislator	Vote	Benefits Received by Constituents	Taxes Paid by Constituents
Clinton	Yea	$12	$10
Cochran	Yea	$12	$10
Collins	Yea	$12	$10
Carper	Nay	$2	$10
Coburn	Nay	$2	$10
Total	Pass	$40	$50

benefits are more concentrated than its costs, and that is the key to gaining political support.

The pro-spending bias of Congress is strengthened by the complex web of vote trading, or logrolling, that often occurs. Table 26.2 shows that because of logrolling, projects that are net losers to society can pass even if they do not have majority support. Because Projects A and B would fail with stand alone votes, Clinton, Cochran, and Collins enter an agreement to mutually support the two projects. That is, they logroll. The result is that the two projects get approved, even though each imposes net costs on society and benefits only a minority of voters.

The popularity of logrolling means that programs that make no economic sense and have only minimal public support are enacted all the time. Earmarked spending and corporate welfare are two manifestations of the problem. It is possible for congressional leaders to counter these pro-spending biases by using party discipline, but in recent years an ''every man for himself'' ethos has permeated Congress, and members have had free rein to grab all the money they can for their narrow causes.

Corporate Welfare

One egregious type of special-interest spending is ''corporate welfare'' or business subsidies. The federal government spends about $90 billion annually on corporate welfare. That includes direct cash payments to businesses, such as subsidies to farmers and grants to automobile compa-

Table 26.2
Logrolling Allows Passage of Subsidies That Benefit Minorities of Constituents

	Project A		Project B		Vote on a Bill Including Projects A and B
Legislator	Benefits Received by Constituents	Taxes Paid by Constituents	Benefits Received by Constituents	Taxes Paid by Constituents	
Clinton	$15	$10	$8	$10	Yea
Cochran	$15	$10	$8	$10	Yea
Collins	$4	$10	$20	$10	Yea
Carper	$3	$10	$2	$10	Nay
Coburn	$3	$10	$2	$10	Nay
Total	$40	$50	$40	$50	Pass

nies. It also includes indirect benefits, such as loans, research, and marketing support for businesses.

In addition to spending programs, corporate welfare comprises barriers to trade designed to protect businesses from foreign competition, and it includes domestic regulations that confer advantages on certain companies at the expense of individual consumers and the general economy.

A Sampler of Corporate Welfare Programs

The following are some corporate welfare programs that are long overdue for repeal. Where provided, spending totals are for fiscal year 2008.

- **Agriculture Department: Market Access Program.** This program hands out more than $200 million annually to exporters of agricultural products to pay for their overseas advertising. Some of the recipients include the Brewers Association, the Pet Food Institute, Sunkist Growers, Welch's Food, and the Wine Institute.
- **Commerce Department: Advanced Technology Program.** This $198 million program gives research grants to high-tech companies.
- **Foreign Military Financing.** U.S. taxpayers fund weapons purchases by foreign governments through this $4.7 billion program.
- **Amtrak.** The federal passenger rail company receives about $1.4 billion in subsidies annually. But Amtrak would be better off privatized so it could cut inefficient routes, maximize profits, and innovate.
- **Export-Import Bank.** This agency uses taxpayer dollars to subsidize the financing of foreign purchases of U.S. goods. It makes billions of dollars of preferential loans to foreigners, guarantees the loans of private institutions, and provides export credit insurance. In 2007, a Dallas television station (WFAA) discovered that the agency provided $243 million in loans to bogus Mexican companies, including drug cartels.
- **Maritime Administration.** This $591 million agency provides subsidies to the commercial shipping and shipbuilding industries. For example, the agency provides loan guarantees for purchases of ships from U.S. shipyards. But the best way to ensure a vigorous U.S.-owned ship industry is to reduce domestic taxes and regulations, which have encouraged the industry to move offshore.
- **Energy Department: Energy Supply Research.** This $894 million program aims to develop new and improved energy technologies.

But the energy industry itself should fund such work, since it will earn profits when breakthroughs are made.

- **Small Business Administration.** This $530 million agency provides subsidized loans and loan guarantees to small businesses. It has a poor record of selecting businesses to support, as its loans have high rates of delinquency.

What Is Wrong with Corporate Welfare?

As the previous examples illustrate, corporate welfare comes in many flavors. Here are six problems that such subsidies create:

1. **Taxpayer cost.** A Cato Institute report in 2007 found that the federal government spends $92 billion annually on corporate welfare. Thus, Congress could provide every household in the nation with an $800 per year tax cut by ending corporate welfare.
2. **Uneven playing field.** By aiding some businesses, corporate subsidies put other businesses without political connections at an unfair disadvantage. When corporate welfare props up failing businesses, it makes no sense because such companies likely have second-rate products or poor managers and are a drag on the economy. At the same time, when corporate welfare supports profitable companies, it also makes no sense because these companies do not need taxpayer help.
3. **Duplication of private activities.** Many federal programs duplicate activities that are routinely provided in private markets, such as insurance, loans, and marketing. If government activities of such a commercial nature are useful, then private markets should be able to carry them out. Consider the Department of Agriculture's $3 billion Risk Management Agency, which says that its mission is to help farmers "manage their business risks through effective, market-based risk management solutions." If the RMA's services really are "market-based," then subsidies are not needed and the agency should be privatized. After all, Wall Street offers a huge array of risk management solutions on which other industries depend.
3. **Harm to consumers and businesses.** When it aids some businesses, the government often damages other businesses and consumers. Consider federal import quotas on sugar, which have pushed up U.S. sugar prices to twice the world level. Those high prices have hurt U.S. candy companies, many of which have moved their production

abroad in recent years to access cheaper sugar. For example, Kraft moved its 600-worker LifeSavers factory from Michigan to Canada in 2002, where sugar is half the U.S. price. Federal regulations in aid of dairy producers are similarly damaging. They push up the costs of milk and cheese for consumers, while hurting U.S. food companies that depend on those products.

4. **A poor track record for picking winners.** Over the decades, many government initiatives have funded new technologies, but most such efforts have been wasteful and ineffective. With regard to energy technologies, for example, the Congressional Budget Office noted in February 2007 that ''federal programs have had a history of funding fossil-fuel technologies that, although interesting technically, have limited practical value, and therefore, little chance of commercial implementation.'' As one particular example, federal ''clean coal'' projects have had a very poor financial and performance track record. We should leave the job of funding innovation to businesses and venture capital firms.

5. **An atmosphere that fosters corruption.** Corporate welfare generates an unhealthy relationship between businesses and the government. One scandal in 2002 involved the Maritime Administration's loan program for shipbuilders. A company called American Classic Voyages received a $1.1 billion loan guarantee from the program to build two cruise ships in former Sen. Trent Lott's (R-MS) hometown. Before completion, the company went bankrupt and left federal taxpayers with a $200 million tab.

6. **A weakened private sector.** Corporate welfare draws talented people into wasteful subsidy activities, and away from more productive pursuits. Companies receiving subsidies often become weaker and less efficient, and they take on riskier projects. Consider, for example, that two federal agencies provided loans of more than $1 billion to Enron Corporation for dubious overseas projects in the 1990s. Many of Enron's foreign projects were duds, and the company may not have pursued them if it had not received federal help. When the company collapsed in scandal, taxpayers lost their investment in Enron's foreign schemes.

Ethanol: A Case Study in Corporate Welfare

Supporters of federal ethanol subsidies claim that ethanol production reduces America's dependence on foreign oil. But that effect is negligible, and it comes at a high cost by distorting the economy and raising food prices.

The federal government subsidizes ethanol—a fuel derived from agricultural products—through a variety of regulatory and tax provisions, including:

- A 9-billion-gallon federal mandate for ethanol usage in vehicles,
- A 51-cent-per-gallon tax credit for ethanol producers,
- A 54-cent-per-gallon tariff on imported ethanol, and
- Subsidies to corn producers, which partly subsidize ethanol production.

As a result of these subsidies, U.S. ethanol production has skyrocketed in recent years, with the effect of transferring much wealth from consumers to farmland owners and agribusinesses. Ethanol subsidies here and abroad are helping to push up food prices worldwide as farmland is converted from food production to fuel production.

As the price of oil has risen in recent years, the prices of agricultural commodities have also risen because of the ethanol link, and that is hurting food consumers everywhere, including many of the world's poorest people. A recent World Bank report concludes that increased biofuel production has been the major factor behind soaring world food prices in recent years.

In 2007, Congress increased the mandated production of ethanol and other renewable fuels to 9 billion gallons in 2008, 11 billion gallons in 2009, and increasing amounts after that. U.S. ethanol is made from corn, and corn producers already receive billions of dollars each year from federal farm subsidy programs. Ethanol subsidies increase the government-generated profits for corn producers and owners of farmland.

Ethanol is damaging to consumers and taxpayers, and it is also not very energy efficient. Studies show varying results, but it appears that the production of ethanol consumes about as much energy as the ethanol itself produces in vehicles, thus providing little net benefit to America's energy needs. Congress should stop fueling the ethanol industry with subsidies and regulations, and let the market decide whether ethanol makes any sense.

Earmarks

The federal budget practice of "earmarking" has exploded during the last 15 years. Earmarks are line items in spending bills inserted by legislators for specific projects in their home states. Some infamous earmarks funded a $50 million indoor rain forest in Iowa and a $223 million "bridge to nowhere'' in Alaska. Earmarks can provide recipients with federal grant money, contracts, loans, or other types of benefits. Earmarks are often referred to as ''pork'' spending.

Figure 26.1 shows that the number of pork projects increased from fewer than 2,000 annually in the mid-1990s to almost 14,000 in 2005. Various scandals and the switch to Democratic control of Congress then slowed the pace of earmarking for a couple of years. But earmarking is on the rise again. The fiscal year 2008 omnibus appropriations bill was bloated with 11,610 spending projects inserted by members of Congress for their states and districts.

Earmarked projects are generally those that have not been requested by the president and have not been subject to expert review or competitive bidding. Thus, if the government had $1 billion to spend on bioterrorism research, it might be earmarked to go to laboratories in the districts of important politicians, rather than to labs chosen by a panel of scientists. Earmarking has soared in most areas of the budget, including defense, education, housing, scientific research, and transportation.

The main problem with earmarking is that most spending projects chosen by earmark are properly the responsibility of state and local governments or the private sector, not the federal government. The rise in earmarks is one manifestation of Congress's growing intrusion into state affairs, as

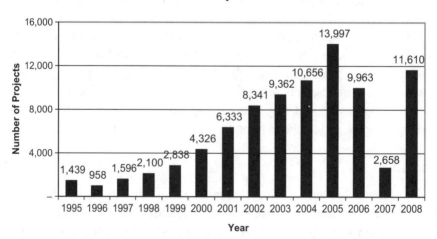

Figure 26.1
Number of Pork Projects, 1995–2008

SOURCE: Citizens Against Government Waste.

discussed in Chapter 5. Consider these earmarks from the FY08 omnibus appropriations bill:

1. $1,648,850 for the private Shedd Aquarium in Chicago, which is also awash with corporate funding;
2. $787,200 for "green design" changes at the Museum of Natural History in Minneapolis;
3. $492,000 for the Rocky Flats Cold War Museum in Arvada, Colorado;
4. $1,950,000 for a library and archives at the Charles B. Rangel Center for Public Service at the City College of New York;
5. $2,400,000 for renovations to Haddad Riverfront Park in Charleston;
6. $500,000 for upgrades to Barracks Row, a swank Capitol Hill neighborhood;
7. $742,764 for fruit fly research, partly conducted in France;
8. $188,000 for the Lobster Institute in Maine; and
9. $492,000 for fuel cell research for Rolls-Royce Group of Canton, Ohio.

Projects 1 to 3 give taxpayer money to groups that should be funding their own activities from admissions fees and charitable contributions. Interestingly, the nonprofit Shedd Aquarium has spent hundreds of thousands of dollars on lobbyists to secure federal earmarks, and its chief executive earned a huge $600,000 salary in 2006. Or consider that the Rock and Roll Hall of Fame in Cleveland has received federal grants, even though there are thousands of music industry millionaires who should be footing the bill.

Projects 4 to 6 are examples of items that state and local governments should fund locally. Unfortunately, state and local officials are increasingly asking Washington for handouts, and lobby groups such as Cassidy and Associates are helping them "mine" the federal budget for grants.

Projects 7 to 9 fund activities that should be left to the private sector. Industries should fund their own research, which is likely to be more cost-effective than government efforts. Besides, successful research leads to higher profits for private businesses, and it makes no sense for taxpayers to foot the bill for such private gains.

Earmarks' Erosion of Fiscal Responsibility

Defenders of earmarks argue that they are no big deal since they represent just a small share of overall federal spending. The problem is that earmarking has contributed to the general erosion in fiscal responsibility in Washington. Earmarks have exacerbated the parochial mindset of most members, who spend their time appeasing state and local interest groups rather than tackling issues of broad national concern. Many politicians complain about the soaring federal deficit, yet their own staff members spend most of their time trying to secure earmarks in spending bills.

The rise in earmarking has encouraged a general spendthrift attitude in Congress. Why should rank-and-file members restrain themselves when their own leaders are usually big recipients of pork? Sen. Tom Coburn (R-OK) is right that the problem with earmarks is "the hidden cost of perpetuating a culture of fiscal irresponsibility. When politicians fund pork projects they sacrifice the authority to seek cuts in any other program." Similarly, Rep. Jeff Flake (R-AZ) concludes that "earmarking . . . has become the currency of corruption in Congress. . . . Earmarks are used as inducements to get members to sign on to large spending measures."

Reforms to Increase Transparency and Downsize the Government

A first step toward eliminating earmarks, corporate welfare, and other special-interest spending is to further increase transparency in the congressional and agency spending processes. Under pressure from reformers, the government has set up a searchable database of federal grants and contracts at www.usaspending.gov. A second step is for citizens to use this website and other tools to research federal spending, and then to call their members of Congress and tell them what programs should be cut.

Citizens should also ask their members to support reforms to the budget process. One idea for cutting corporate welfare is to set up a commission akin to the successful military base–closing commissions of the 1990s. It would draw up a list of current subsidies and present it to Congress, which would vote on the cuts as a package without amendment. To make the package a political winner, all budget savings would go toward immediate tax cuts for families.

Ultimately, earmarking and corporate welfare should be abolished, and spending on activities that are legitimate federal functions should be determined by a system of competitive bidding and expert review. Of course, it will not be easy to reform the spending practices of Congress. Members often feel committed to expanding spending in their districts and on their favored programs. But taxpayers fund all those programs, and they need to do a better job of convincing their members to cut unneeded programs and pass much leaner federal budgets.

Suggested Readings

Carney, Timothy. *The Big Ripoff: How Big Business and Big Government Steal Your Money*. New York: John Wiley & Sons, 2006.

Citizens Against Government Waste website. www.cagw.org.

Congressional Budget Office. "Federal Financial Support of Business." July 1995.

Edwards, Chris. *Downsizing the Federal Government*. Washington: Cato Institute, 2005.

Payne, James L. "Budgeting in Neverland: Irrational Policymaking in the U.S. Congress and What Can Be Done about It." Cato Institute Policy Analysis no. 574, July 26, 2006.

Taxpayers for Common Sense website. www.taxpayer.net.

Slivinski, Stephen. "The Corporate Welfare State: How the Federal Government Subsidizes U.S. Businesses." Cato Institute Policy Analysis no. 592, May 14, 2007.

U.S. Government spending database. www.usaspending.gov. This database provides information on the recipients of federal grants, loans, and contracts.

—Prepared by Chris Edwards and Jeff Patch

Threats to Civil Liberties

27. Civil Liberties and Terrorism

> **Congress should**
> - stop authorizing secret subpoenas, secret arrests, and secret regulations; and
> - repeal the Military Commissions Act and close the Guantánamo prison.

Free societies do not just happen. They must be deliberately created and deliberately maintained. Freedom in America rests on a sophisticated constitutional system of checks and balances. Unfortunately, since 9/11 freedom in America has been under assault by policymakers who repeatedly assert that the "line between liberty and security" must be redrawn. Too many of our policymakers seem to believe that the way to deal with terrorism is to pass more laws, spend more money, and sacrifice more civil liberties. But genuine leadership includes ensuring accountability in government and a willingness to reverse wrongheaded policies. Al Qaeda terrorists do pose a security problem, but it is a problem that should be addressed from within the American constitutional framework.

Say No to the Surveillance State

If policymakers are serious about defending our freedom and our way of life, they must take a sober look at the risks posed by al Qaeda terrorists and wage this war without bypassing the American constitutional framework. Previous Congresses have authorized secret subpoenas, secret arrests, and secret regulations. These policies should be reversed.

Secret Subpoenas

The Fourth Amendment to the Constitution provides, "The right of the people to be secure in their persons, houses, papers, and effects, against unreasonable searches and seizures, shall not be violated, and no Warrants

291

shall issue, but upon probable cause, supported by Oath or affirmation, and particularly describing the place to be searched, and the persons or things to be seized.'' It is important to note that the Fourth Amendment does not ban all government efforts to search and seize private property, but it does limit the power of the police to seize whatever they want, whenever they want.

The warrant application process is the primary check on the power of the executive branch to intrude into people's homes and to seize property. If the police can persuade an impartial judge to issue a search warrant, the warrant will be executed. However, if the judge is unpersuaded, he will reject the application and no search will take place. In the event of a rejection, the police can either drop the case or continue the investigation, bolster their application with additional evidence, and reapply for a warrant. The Bush administration has tried to bypass this constitutional framework by championing the use of secret subpoenas called ''national security letters'' (NSLs).

An NSL is a document that empowers federal agents to demand certain records from businesspeople. Unlike the case with search warrants, executive branch agents do not need to apply to judges to obtain these letters. It is simply some agent's decision that he wants certain information. These letters also threaten citizens with jail should they tell anyone about the government's demands. The Bush administration did not create NSLs, but it pushed to expand the types of business and transactional records for which they could be employed and the frequency with which they are used. When a constitutional challenge was brought against NSLs, Bush's lawyers argued that they were fully consistent with the Bill of Rights. The federal court was not persuaded. Federal Judge Victor Marrero ruled that NSLs violated both the First Amendment and the Fourth Amendment. NSLs violate the First Amendment because they ''operate as an unconstitutional prior restraint on speech.'' NSLs violate the Fourth Amendment because they are written ''in tones sounding virtually as biblical commandments,'' thus making it ''highly unlikely that an NSL recipient would know that he may have a right to contest the NSL, and that a process to do so may exist through a judicial proceeding.'' The Federal Bureau of Investigation reportedly serves more than 30,000 NSLs a year. Congress should abolish NSLs and have the police conduct their searches within the American constitutional framework.

Secret Arrests

In the months following the 9/11 attacks, the federal government, quite properly, launched an aggressive investigation to determine if there were other terrorist cells on U.S. soil. Hundreds of people in the United States were arrested, but the government refused to provide the most basic information regarding the people in its custody. Who were these detainees? Why were they being held? Where could their friends and families find them? We don't know how many of them were citizens—surely most were not—nor how many are still being held, precisely because of the extreme secrecy surrounding the whole operation.

At first, federal officials would release only an overall tally of the number of people arrested and jailed. After several weeks, the Department of Justice announced that it would no longer release even that information. News media organizations and civil rights attorneys subsequently sued the government under the Freedom of Information Act to compel the disclosure of the names, the charges, and other information. Attorneys representing the government insisted that the prisoners had access to counsel and were free to contact anyone they wished, including newspaper reporters. The problem was, of course, that there was no way to verify such assertions. As one federal judge observed, "Just as the government has a compelling interest in ensuring citizens' safety, so do citizens have a compelling interest in ensuring that their government does not, in discharging its duties, abuse one of its most awesome powers, the power to arrest and jail."

In the FOIA litigation, federal officials repeatedly claimed that the information sought would harm "national security." If that claim were valid, FOIA's disclosure requirements would not apply because it would qualify for an exemption. Unfortunately, a federal appellate court declined to "second-guess" the government's assertions to that effect. FOIA anticipates the government's legitimate interest in ongoing investigations. However, to qualify for that exemption, the government must provide an explanation for its stance. The fact that no explanation was supplied in the case of these secret arrests is deeply troubling. Now that the government can evade FOIA with bland assertions of "national security," FOIA has lost much of its vitality. Thus, Congress should revise FOIA to make it crystal clear that the role of the judiciary is to insist that law enforcement agencies meet their disclosure responsibilities and not evade them. In a constitutional republic, the electorate must have information so that it can assess the performance of those in high office. If that information flow is blocked or distorted, the entire system can break down.

Secret Regulations

Under the Constitution, our laws are supposed to be made openly by our elected representatives in the legislative branch. That framework for lawmaking has been bypassed in recent years. Unelected officials are now making secrets laws that they call "security directives." Government officials claim that secrecy is necessary because they do not want to "let the terrorists know what we are doing." Again, it is reasonable to keep some things secret, such as the identity of our spies and informers, but it is startling to behold the transformation of the process by which our laws are made.

When a legal challenge was brought against an aviation security directive concerning passenger identification checks, a government lawyer expressed his confidence in the constitutionality of the secret law—even as he told a federal judge that the judiciary could not see the law itself! Such sweeping claims for secrecy must be rejected. Thus far, these secret laws have mostly affected citizens using mass transit systems (airline and rail passengers), but it would be naive for anyone to believe that the trend will stop there. The prospect of Americans being held accountable for noncompliance with unknowable regulations is outrageous. Congress should reverse this pernicious practice immediately.

Revamp President Bush's Prisoner Policies

The Bush administration's handling of prisoners has been a mess: Guantánamo, secret Central Intelligence Agency prison camps, rendition, denial of habeas corpus, waterboarding and other "alternative interrogation techniques," and military tribunals with special rules of procedure and evidence. With the departure of President Bush and Vice President Cheney, the time is now right to begin anew. The new Congress should begin by moving to restore the writ of habeas corpus and closing the prison facility at Guantánamo Bay.

Detention

The myriad issues surrounding the handling of prisoners can be divided into three subject areas: detention, treatment, and trials. "Detention" is akin to incarceration in a prisoner-of-war camp. There are no criminal charges or trial. POWs are incapacitated during the war and are released afterward. "Treatment" refers to the prisoners' living conditions and to interrogation practices. "Trials" refer to proceedings before military courts and, in this context, to "war crime" allegations. A comprehensive analysis of these issues is beyond the scope of this chapter, but each subject will be briefly addressed.

Perhaps the most important legal issue that has arisen since the 9/11 terrorist attacks has been President Bush's claim that he can arrest anyone in the world and incarcerate that person indefinitely in a POW-style camp. According to the legal papers that Bush's lawyers have filed in the courts, so long as the president has issued an "enemy combatant" order to his secretary of defense, instead of the attorney general, the president can ignore the ordinary constitutional safeguards and procedures.

To fully appreciate the implications of the administration's enemy combatant argument, one must first consider the constitutional procedure of habeas corpus. The Constitution provides, "The Privilege of the Writ of Habeas Corpus shall not be suspended, unless when in Cases of Rebellion or Invasion the public Safety may require it." Notably, the Bush administration has not urged Congress to suspend habeas corpus. Nor has President Bush asserted the claim that he can suspend the writ unilaterally. Bush's lawyers have instead tried to alter the way in which the writ operates when it is not suspended.

By way of background, the writ of habeas corpus is a venerable legal procedure that allows a prisoner to get a hearing before an impartial judge. If the jailer can supply a valid legal basis for the arrest and imprisonment at the hearing, the judge will simply order the prisoner's return to jail. But if the judge discovers that the imprisonment is illegal, he has the power to set the prisoner free. For that reason, the Framers of the U.S. Constitution routinely referred to this legal procedure as the "Great Writ" because it was considered one of the great safeguards of individual liberty.

The government has tried to bypass the writ of habeas corpus in several ways. First, American citizens designated "enemy combatants" were held in solitary confinement in a military brig in the United States. Access to attorneys was denied. According to the government's reasoning, the prisoners could be denied meetings with their attorneys because they were enemy combatants, not accused criminals (who are guaranteed certain constitutional rights). Note the circularity of that argument. The prisoners could not go to court to challenge their "enemy combatant" designation because they were being held in solitary confinement. And if the prisoners could not meet with an attorney to explain their side of the story, it would be virtually impossible for any attorney to rebut the government's enemy combatant allegations in a court hearing.

Second, government attorneys argued that even if an enemy combatant could meet with an attorney and even if a habeas corpus petition could be filed on the prisoner's behalf, the court should summarily throw such petitions out of court. According to Bush's lawyers, the courts should not "second-guess" the president's "battlefield" decisions. But when the government attorneys were pressed about their definition of the term "battlefield," they said they considered the entire world to be the battlefield, including every inch of U.S. territory. Every inch—from Disney World in Florida to Yellowstone Park in the Rockies to the sandy beaches of Hawaii and all the tiny towns in between. They are all on the "battlefield." That is a profoundly disturbing claim because there are *no* legal rights on the battlefield. Military commanders simply exercise raw power. By twisting and redefining the term "battlefield," government attorneys say that because the president is the commander in chief, he can essentially incarcerate whomever he wants.

Congress must repudiate the idea that America is a battlefield. The FBI should, of course, conduct terrorism investigations and surveil and search suspects as necessary and appropriate by following constitutional procedures. If an American is involved, the government can file criminal charges and prosecute.

With respect to non-Americans who are taken prisoner overseas, the legal issues are more complicated. The military has leeway to make the initial decision as to who may be taken into custody, but the military should not have the final word. When the writ of habeas corpus has not been suspended, it means prisoners should be afforded the opportunity to meet with counsel and to file a petition in the event that a mistake has been made. Access to the courts does not mean the judiciary will automatically discharge the prisoners. It means the government must present evidence and supply a good reason for locking up a particular person. If the military can supply a good reason, the court will reject the petition and order the prisoner back to his or her jail cell. If the government will not, or cannot, offer evidence, the court has the power to set the prisoner free. In *Boumediene v. United States*, the Supreme Court properly affirmed the proposition that prisoners can file habeas corpus petitions from the Guantánamo prison. The Court left unresolved whether prisoners from other facilities should have access to the writ. Such uncertainty provides intelligence and military officials with an incentive to hold prisoners elsewhere. The next Congress should move quickly to fully restore habeas corpus by establishing an orderly and transparent prison system. To begin anew, Congress should close the Guantánamo prison. All American prison facilities should fall within the exclusive jurisdiction of a single agency, the Pentagon. The government should not interfere with or eavesdrop on attorney–client communications. And habeas corpus applications should be treated with respect, not disdain.

Treatment

There has been much public discussion about the Bush administration's handling of terror suspects. Although the administration has denied employing torture, it is now apparent that some "new paradigm" was put in place after 9/11. President Bush declared that the Geneva Convention did not apply to "enemy combatants," and he would later admit that secret "alternative interrogation techniques" were used against certain prisoners. It is still hard to believe that the Red Cross was unable to check on the condition of all American prisoners because no complete list was made available. President Bush has admitted to the existence of secret CIA prisons.

Congress must move decisively and take responsibility for all American prisoners. Three steps are essential. First, there must be transparency. All prisoners should be registered with Congress and the Red Cross. A constitutional republic should never "render" individuals to third countries for torture or maintain secret prison facilities for "ghost prisoners."

Second, the chain of command must be clear. Only one government agency, the Pentagon, should be responsible for prisoners. Further, any and all contact with prisoners should be registered in a logbook. And such logbooks should be scrupulously maintained and shared with the defense and intelligence committees of Congress. Such procedures will help ensure prisoner safety and government accountability for mistreatment or other wrongdoing.

Third, until a competent tribunal rules otherwise, the Geneva Convention applies to all American prisoners. During the 1991 Gulf War, the American military held more than 1,000 hearings before such tribunals. Many of the prisoners were determined to be innocent civilians swept up in the fog of war. President Bush waved off this procedure in 2002 by simply declaring that all his prisoners were "enemy combatants" and that enemy combatants were ineligible for Geneva's safeguards. Until the Supreme Court intervened, the prisoners were not afforded any opportunity to contest their status as enemy combatants. Congress must affirm this screening procedure for all prisoners, not just the men presently held at Guantánamo.

If a competent tribunal finds certain prisoners ineligible for Geneva's protective umbrella, American interrogators should not be given carte blanche to employ physical brutality. Instead, various incentives should be used to encourage cooperation and collect intelligence. For example, better food and living conditions can be made available to those who cooperate—while Spartan arrangements will be the rule for those who decline to disclose what they know. In all instances, American commanders should welcome the scrutiny of outside human rights organizations, such as the Red Cross.

Trials

The U.S. Constitution requires certain procedures when the government accuses someone of a crime. The Bill of Rights provides that the accused shall enjoy the right to a speedy and public trial before an impartial jury. The accused is also entitled to the assistance of counsel and must be permitted to confront witnesses against him or her. Shortly after 9/11, President Bush announced that he would personally decide who would receive a trial by jury in civilian court and who would face trial for war crimes before a military tribunal. And Bush would also decide the various rules and procedures that would be followed in the tribunal proceedings.

The Supreme Court struck down Bush's unilateral order establishing a tribunal system in *Hamdan v. Rumsfeld*. Regrettably, Congress subsequently rescued Bush's tribunal plans by enacting the Military Commissions Act. Congress ought to repeal the MCA for two reasons. First, such proceedings will blur the line between our civilian court system and the military court system. Second, such proceedings will set a precedent that other countries can use against the American military in a future conflict.

The U.S. Constitution is a legal charter that empowers and limits government in both peacetime and wartime. The Framers of the Constitution anticipated the necessity of wartime measures, but they were also keenly aware of the need for safeguards against the arbitrary exercise of government power. Article I, section 8, empowers Congress "to define and punish ... Offenses against the Law of Nations." That is, Congress may define the offense and prescribe the punishment for people who are convicted of such offenses. Note, however, that the mode of trial is not left to the discretion of the legislature. The Sixth Amendment says that civilian jury trials are guaranteed in "all criminal prosecutions." There is no exception for "war crimes."

As a matter of history, military commissions have been used in some of our previous wars. Though such precedents were erroneous according to constitutional first principles, those proceedings could at least be cabined by some of the conventions of war between nation-states. Uniforms, for example, made it possible to distinguish combatants from noncombatants. That legal model does not easily apply to terrorists. Since terrorists pose as civilians, the commission system will very likely see a steady influx of cases where the government will be leveling war crime charges against people who appear to be civilians. Except for a handful of cases where the defendant will be known by all to be a member of al Qaeda (Khalid Sheikh Mohammed), the problem of circularity will once again present itself. To take a concrete example, suppose the president accuses a man of aiding a terrorist cell. The accused responds by denying the charge and by insisting on a trial by jury so that he can establish his innocence. The president responds by saying that "enemy combatants" are not entitled to jury trials—whereupon the man is flown to a military prison for his trial.

Even if there was no constitutional problem, special tribunals for war crimes will create a dangerous international precedent. Other states will take note of how the United States deals with war crime allegations. In a future military conflict, U.S. military personnel could find themselves accused of war crimes—and then brought before some unique tribunal that does not operate under the ordinary legal rules of that country. The United States will be hard-pressed to lodge objections to such proceedings if that is how our system operates. Thus, the Military Commissions Act should be repealed.

Conclusion

American institutions tend to look for "quick-fix" solutions to problems. American policymakers must recognize, however, that the danger posed by al Qaeda is not a short-term crisis but a long-term security dilemma for the United States. If Congress rushes to enact anti-terrorism legislation in the aftermath of any terrorist incident, no one can deny that Americans will lose their liberty over the long term. Now that several years have passed since the shock and horror of 9/11, it is time for Congress to reassess the extent of the threat posed by al Qaeda and the powers that have been conferred on the intelligence and law enforcement agents in recent years. Policymakers should not make the mistake of underestimating the American people. Of course, the electorate wants safety, but it wants the federal government to secure that safety by attacking the terrorist base camps, not by using the third degree on disarmed men in secret prisons and not by turning America into a surveillance state.

Suggested Readings

Bovard, James. *Terrorism and Tyranny.* New York: Palgrave, 2003.

Dillard, Thomas W., Stephen R. Johnson, and Timothy Lynch. "A Grand Façade: How the Grand Jury Was Captured by Government." Cato Institute Policy Analysis no. 476, May 13, 2003.

Fisher, Louis. *The Constitution and 9/11.* Lawrence: University of Kansas Press, 2008.

Healy, Gene. *The Cult of the Presidency.* Washington: Cato Institute, 2008.

Heymann, Philip B. *Terrorism, Freedom, and Security.* Cambridge, MA: MIT Press, 2003.

Lynch, Timothy. "Breaking the Vicious Cycle: Preserving Our Liberties while Fighting Terrorism." Cato Institute Policy Analysis no. 443, June 26, 2002.

———. "Power and Liberty in Wartime." *Cato Supreme Court Review, 2003–2004* 23 (2004).

———. "Doublespeak and the War on Terrorism." Cato Institute Briefing Paper no. 98, September 6, 2006.

Mueller, John. *Overblown: How Politicians and the Terrorism Industry Inflate National Security Threats and Why We Believe Them.* New York: Free Press, 2006.

Savage, Charlie. *Takeover: The Return of the Imperial Presidency and the Subversion of American Democracy.* Boston: Little, Brown, 2007.

Schulhofer, Stephen J. *Rethinking the Patriot Act.* New York: Century Foundation Press, 2005.

—Prepared by Timothy Lynch

28. Electronic Surveillance

Congress should

- repeal the FISA Amendments Act of 2008;
- conduct a thorough, public investigation of executive branch surveillance activities over the last three decades;
- require individualized warrants for all eavesdropping conducted on U.S. soil unless both ends of a communication are known to be overseas;
- require prior judicial approval of all domestic intercepts, allowing a 72-hour grace period for emergency foreign intelligence intercepts;
- require that foreign intelligence be the purpose of all FISA intercepts and prohibit coordination between law enforcement and intelligence officials in the choice of FISA eavesdropping targets; and
- reverse the Federal Communications Commission's decisions extending the Communications Assistance for Law Enforcement Act to broadband and Internet telephony providers.

The George W. Bush administration pushed relentlessly for broader domestic eavesdropping powers. In the wake of the 9/11 terrorist attacks, the president persuaded Congress to pass the USA Patriot Act, which included numerous provisions expanding domestic spying authority and limiting judicial oversight. He authorized domestic spying programs that were kept secret for several years before they were revealed by whistle-blower testimony and media reports. When the programs were brought to light, the Bush administration pressured the Foreign Intelligence Surveillance Court—the secret court created to oversee wiretapping activities—to authorize the programs under existing wiretapping rules. When it reportedly refused, the White House turned to Congress, asking it to weaken judicial oversight of domestic surveillance activities. Congress complied with the 2008 FISA Amendments Act.

Don't Overestimate Wiretapping

One effect of the noisy debate over domestic wiretapping has been to greatly exaggerate its importance as a crime-fighting tool. Congress prohibited the federal government from engaging in any wiretapping between 1934 and 1968. In 1968, Congress authorized wiretaps for law enforcement purposes that have come to be known as "Title III" wiretaps. But the use of these wiretaps in investigations of violent crimes continues to be extremely rare. For example, according to the Federal Bureau of Investigation, 17,034 murders, 91,111 rapes, and 855,088 aggravated assaults were committed in 2006, yet the courts authorized only 119 wiretaps in homicide or assault cases. Criminals committed 12 million property crimes in 2006, but the courts authorized only 20 wiretaps in property crime investigations. The vast majority of Title III law enforcement wiretaps—more than 80 percent—are deployed as part of the drug war, an effort that (as discussed in Chapter 33) creates more problems than it solves.

Details on the use of wiretaps for intelligence-gathering and counterterrorism purposes are not available to the public, so it is difficult to judge how crucial wiretaps are in those efforts. But one thing that can safely be said is that technological changes, including the increased flexibility of communications networks and the growing availability of encryption technologies, are making it easier for everyone—law-abiding citizens and terrorists alike—to evade surveillance. Even the most draconian wiretapping laws are unlikely to reverse that trend. A counterterrorism strategy that relies too heavily on wiretapping is a recipe for failure.

Fortunately, government officials have many options for collecting intelligence that do not rely on wiretaps. They include (as permitted by law) installing bugs, intercepting radio communications, subpoenaing relevant business records, infiltrating groups under investigation, and employing confidential informants. The government should be given as much wiretapping authority as is consistent with the protection of civil liberties, but it would be a serious mistake to sacrifice constitutional protections in a futile effort to make wiretapping as easy as it was four decades ago.

Law enforcement and intelligence officials are—properly—focused on catching criminals and terrorists, and they naturally seek the broadest possible powers to do their jobs. But in the process, they have a tendency to lose sight of protecting the rights of innocent Americans. Too often, they seek new powers that will only marginally enhance their investigative powers while significantly eroding constitutional rights. That's why judicial oversight is crucial. We *want* law enforcement to seek every possible advantage in their fight against criminals and terrorists. But we also need independent judges to rein them in when they stray beyond the bounds of the Constitution.

Create a New Church Committee

The erosion of judicial oversight during the Bush administration is troubling because history suggests that judicial oversight is a crucial check on the abuse of executive power. In 1976, a Senate committee headed by Sen. Frank Church (D-ID) released a massive report on abuses of power by federal officials during the preceding half century. It found that the Federal Bureau of Investigation, the National Security Agency, and other government agencies had repeatedly violated the privacy of law-abiding citizens, not to mention federal law. Hundreds of nonviolent political activists, celebrities, journalists, labor leaders, and elected officials were subject to illegal wiretaps, bugs, mail openings, and break-ins during the cold war. The investigation was prompted by the Watergate scandal, but the Church Committee found that abuses of power didn't start with Richard Nixon. Every president since Franklin D. Roosevelt had approved unlawful surveillance programs.

Although the details remain wrapped in secrecy, media reports and the testimony of government whistle-blowers suggest that the George W. Bush administration may have broken the law by spying on law-abiding Americans without a warrant. The *New York Times* reported on one warrantless spying program in December 2005. In March 2006, a retired AT&T technician declared under oath that AT&T had given the NSA unfettered access to its customers' voice and data traffic as that traffic passed through its switching centers in San Francisco and other cities. A May 2006 *USA Today* article revealed another potentially illegal spying program; this one collected the domestic calling records of Americans and attempted to use data-mining software to detect suspicious calling patterns.

The Bush administration took the position that these actions were within the president's inherent authority or were permitted by the Authorization for Use of Military Force passed by Congress. These positions are inconsistent with the history, structure, and text of those documents.

303

Congress cannot craft sensible new eavesdropping rules until it has a clear picture of the government's current domestic spying activities. With the end of the George W. Bush administration, the time is ripe for another in-depth congressional investigation of potentially illegal surveillance by the executive branch. Although Bush administration activities should be a major focus, the investigation should not focus solely on the last eight years. Instead, it should start where the Church Committee left off and investigate domestic spying activities undertaken since the mid-1970s.

Restore FISA Safeguards

In 1978, Congress passed the Foreign Intelligence Surveillance Act, which, for the first time, permitted the use of domestic wiretaps for intelligence-gathering purposes. FISA required judicial oversight of these spying activities, requiring the executive branch to show probable cause that the target was an "agent of a foreign power," and that "the purpose" of the surveillance was foreign intelligence. To ensure that this new, more permissive wiretapping regime was not used for ordinary criminal investigations, the law restricted coordination between officials conducting FISA wiretaps and federal agents involved in ordinary law enforcement. Finally, recognizing that national security could occasionally require the initiation of wiretapping before there was time to seek a court order, FISA created an emergency process whereby the government could begin spying immediately and seek court authorization within 72 hours.

Unfortunately, between 2001 and 2008, Congress crippled the system of judicial oversight it had carefully constructed in 1978. Whereas FISA had originally required that foreign intelligence be "the purpose" of FISA surveillance, the 2001 Patriot Act required that foreign intelligence be only "a significant purpose" of surveillance. The courts interpreted this as a green light for coordination between intelligence and law enforce-ment—even in ordinary criminal cases. That's troubling because the rules for FISA warrants do not require the government to show probable cause that the target has broken the law. Law enforcement and intelligence officials need flexibility to share information about ongoing terrorism investigations, but the FISA process should not be used to spy on Ameri-cans for ordinary law enforcement purposes. (The so-called wall between criminal and intelligence investigators that supposedly prevented full pur-suit of the 9/11 terrorists was a product of bureaucratic incompetence—not the bar on using FISA wiretaps for ordinary crime investigations.)

This danger was greatly enhanced in 2008 when Congress passed the FISA Amendments Act. It allows the government to intercept the international calls of Americans without an individualized warrant. The government need only submit a "certification" to the FISA court describing the general parameters of an eavesdropping program. And the government can begin wiretapping immediately, then drag out the judicial review process for as long as four months.

The new rules include a few provisions ostensibly designed to limit abuses, but those limitations are little more than symbolic. The legislation prohibits the "targeting" of specific Americans and requires that the government adopt "minimization" procedures. However, the legislation places no limits on the breadth of interceptions and places few restrictions on the kinds of information that can be retained and the things that can be done with it. Moreover, it specifically provides that the government is not required to "identify the specific facilities, places, premises, or property" at which interceptions will occur. The details of which communications facilities will be tapped and whose communications will be intercepted will be transmitted directly from the government to telecommunications companies. As a consequence, the judge nominally overseeing the eavesdropping will often lack the information necessary to verify that the law is being followed.

Limit Data Mining

Each of these changes is problematic when viewed in isolation; together, they add up to something even more troubling: the de facto legalization of indiscriminate, or "dragnet," surveillance of Americans' international calls. It appears that the government could, for example, intercept all communications between a particular American city and the Middle East, sifting the traffic for particular words, phrases, or voiceprints. Under such a program, thousands of innocent Americans could have their communications intercepted, reviewed by human analysts, and passed on to other federal agencies, all without meaningful court oversight.

Some advocates contend that such expanded powers are essential to the fight against terrorism. They argue that only by collecting reams of data and feeding it into sophisticated pattern-matching algorithms—often called "data mining"—can we detect terrorist plots in time for law enforcement officials to foil them.

This argument greatly exaggerates the utility of data-mining technologies for counterterrorism efforts. Data-mining techniques work well in business applications such as credit card fraud detection and direct-mail marketing because businesses have thousands of data points with which to tune their algorithms. In contrast, the number of terrorist attacks or instances of terrorism planning on American soil has (thankfully) been far too small to compile a useful profile of the "typical" terrorist. Even the best commercial data-mining applications have a high "false-positive" rate. Using the same algorithms on the terrorist-detection problem would swamp federal agents with the names of innocent Americans. Investigators need fewer leads of higher quality, not many leads of low quality.

Recent history bears this out. In summer 2001, U.S. officials were aware that two men linked to the bombing of the USS *Cole* were in the country. They were not sought, and they became two of the 9/11 hijackers. Casting a broader net for suspects would not have aided the effort to apprehend these two; it would only have given investigators more false leads and distracted them from the real terrorists. However, the British government successfully thwarted a liquid explosives plot in August 2006 using traditional police practices, including an undercover British agent. Dragnet surveillance and data mining would have simply overwhelmed an already overworked law enforcement community. This is a case where liberty and security are not in tension: prohibiting dragnet surveillance and data mining will enhance civil liberties while focusing anti-terrorism efforts. Congress should require individualized warrants for domestic spying even if that precludes the use of these techniques.

Repeal the FISA Amendments Act

Some of the worst provisions of the FISA Amendments Act are due to expire at the end of 2013. However, the nation cannot afford to go that long without adequate judicial oversight. These provisions should be repealed before then. After it has completed its investigation of recent executive eavesdropping activity, Congress should enact more comprehensive legislation that updates surveillance law in a way that will prevent the recurrence of any abuses uncovered by the investigation. At a minimum, it should include individualized warrants, judicial review before the start of eavesdropping (or, in emergency cases, no more than 72 hours after), and restrictions on the use of FISA wiretaps for ordinary law enforcement purposes.

Reform CALEA

In the early 1990s, the FBI began to complain that technological changes in the phone system were impeding wiretaps. Civil liberties groups argued that these complaints were exaggerated. But in 1994, Congress enacted the Communications Assistance for Law Enforcement Act, which required telecom companies to build eavesdropping capabilities into new telephone switches. In 2005, the FCC extended these requirements to broadband service providers and any voice-over-Internet-protocol (VoIP) providers that interconnect with the traditional telephone network.

Deregulate VoIP

Congress should overrule the FCC's ruling because the Internet differs from the telephone network in ways that make complying with CALEA regulations far more burdensome. With traditional landline telephone service, there is invariably a specific company with the ability to intercept all calls to and from a given phone number. Because of the Internet's decentralized architecture, the same is not true of Internet communications. Communications between two VoIP users may travel directly from the sender to the receiver without passing through any servers owned by the software developer. And because someone can log on to the Internet from anywhere in the world, it will often be impossible to predict where to place a wiretap to intercept a given user's calls.

There are two ways that the developers of VoIP applications can comply with CALEA regulations. One is to design their software to use a central server. That would make the software more expensive to deploy (because servers cost money) and would probably degrade its performance. It would also be inconsistent with Congress's intent that vendors not be forced to fundamentally redesign their products to comply with CALEA.

The other option is to add a "back door" to VoIP software that remotely activates an eavesdropping mode when asked to do so by the courts. That solution would create at least two problems. First, there is a risk that the back door could be discovered and exploited by unscrupulous third parties to eavesdrop on unsuspecting users' telephone calls. Second, sophisticated users could detect such eavesdropping by monitoring the network traffic being generated by the software. If the conversation were being transmitted to a third party, it would tip off tech-savvy criminals that they were being monitored.

Both these approaches suffer from an additional weakness: they would almost certainly be discovered and publicized. Because the Internet is a global network, there will always be non-CALEA-compliant communications software available for those who know where to look. Given that criminals and terrorists will gravitate toward this software, there is little point in subjecting only some VoIP providers to CALEA rules. Accordingly, Congress should overrule the FCC and explicitly exempt all Internet-based applications—including VoIP—from CALEA's requirements.

Deregulate Broadband

Congress should do the same for broadband providers. The Internet is still a rapidly changing medium, and requiring every Internet service provider to build eavesdropping into its devices creates a barrier to entry for smaller firms. It is important to remember that exempting ISPs from CALEA would not excuse them from assisting in wiretaps. Providers would still be required to respond to court orders by offering law enforcement technical assistance and access to their facilities. That's how all wiretaps worked before 1994, and in most cases, it will allow law enforcement to obtain a suspect's Internet traffic. But it is overkill to require the installation of eavesdropping equipment in every networking closet in America. Congress should overrule the FCC and make clear that all Internet-based service providers are exempt from CALEA regulations.

Suggested Readings

Diffie, Whitfield, and Susan Landau. *Privacy on the Line: The Politics of Wiretapping and Encryption.* Cambridge, MA: MIT Press, 2007.

Healy, Gene, and Timothy Lynch. "Power Surge: The Constitutional Record of George W. Bush." Cato Institute white paper, May 1, 2006.

Jonas, Jeff, and Jim Harper. "Effective Counterterrorism and the Limited Role of Predictive Data Mining." Cato Institute Policy Analysis no. 584, December 11, 2006.

Lee, Timothy B. "The New FISA Compromise: It's Worse than You Think." *Ars Technica*, July 7, 2008. http://arstechnica.com/articles/culture/fisa-compromise.ars.

—Prepared by Timothy B. Lee

29. National ID Systems

Congress and state leaders should

- resist the establishment of a national identification card and national identification system,
- defund and repeal the REAL ID Act,
- abandon the E-Verify national immigration background system, and
- encourage the development and acceptance of private identification systems.

A national ID has long been regarded as contrary to the American character, and it has been opposed by leading American political figures whenever it has been proposed. For example, when President Ronald Reagan's attorney general William French Smith advocated in a cabinet meeting for support of a national ID card for illegal immigration control, the president reportedly scoffed, "Maybe we should just brand all the babies."

In the same context, Democratic presidential candidate Walter Mondale said: "We've never had citizenship tests in our country before. And I don't think we should have a citizenship card today. That is counterproductive." Democratic Speaker of the House Thomas P. "Tip" O'Neill Jr. (D-MA) called out the ills of national ID systems in a 1987 debate over immigration reform, saying: "Hitler did this to the Jews, you know. He made them wear a dog tag."

A decade before that, Sen. Barry Goldwater (R-AZ) recognized and objected to the surveillance consequences and power shifts caused by national ID systems. In a debate on the Privacy Act of 1974, he said:

> Once the social security number is set as a universal identifier, each person would leave a trail of personal data behind him for all his life which could be immediately reassembled to confront him. Once we can be identified to the administration in government or in business by an exclusive number,

we can be pinpointed wherever we are, we can be more easily manipulated, we can be more easily conditioned and we can be more easily coerced.

One of the first groups to formally consider national ID issues was the Secretary's Advisory Committee on Automated Personal Data Systems within the Department of Health, Education, and Welfare. In 1973, it did an important study of record-keeping practices in the computer age. On national ID systems, the "HEW Report" said: "This Committee believes that fear of a standard universal identifier is justified. . . . Therefore, we take the position that a standard universal identifier should not be established in the United States now or in the foreseeable future."

Members of Congress and state legislators should carry on the American tradition and resist creating or implementing any national identification system. Yet what Senator Goldwater warned of a quarter century ago is now a real threat.

The REAL ID National ID Program

In the wake of the terrorist attacks of September 11, 2001, the idea of a national ID system gained some currency. Among many interests and organizations poring over the problem of terrorism was a group called the Markle Foundation Task Force on National Security in the Information Age. This group of security and technology experts was convened by a New York nonprofit foundation headed by former attorney general nominee Zoë Baird. One of the Markle Task Force's reports contained an appendix titled "Reliable Identification for Homeland Protection and Collateral Gains," which endorsed a national ID system.

The Markle recommendation was cited in a short section of the 9/11 Commission's final report to support the assertion that the federal government should take steps to secure the country's identity systems. Rushing to implement the 9/11 Commission's proposals, Congress adopted a provision of the Intelligence Reform and Terrorism Prevention Act establishing a negotiated rulemaking process and convening a variety of stakeholders to consider how the state driver licensing and identity card systems could be better secured. This group had met twice when a law called the REAL ID Act was passed, repealing this section of IRTPA, disbanding this group, and ending its work.

Passed attached to a military spending bill and without a hearing in either the House or the Senate, the REAL ID Act attempted to create a national ID system. The REAL ID Act sought to coerce states into issuing their driver's licenses and identification cards consistent with national standards and requirements, including distinguishing among citizens and noncitizens. (This combination—nationally uniform standards and indication of citizenship—disposes of the question whether REAL ID is a national identification system. It is.)

The statutory deadline for state compliance with the REAL ID Act was three years from the bill's May 11, 2005, passage. The act threatened states by barring federal agencies from accepting state licenses and IDs for any official purpose unless the state was meeting the requirements of the act. If a state was not complying, its citizens and residents would be inconvenienced and perhaps debarred from certain activities controlled by the federal government, like traveling on commercial aircraft. This risk was intended to cow state officials into turning over their driver-licensing apparatus to the control of the federal government. But on May 11, 2008, not a single state was in compliance with the REAL ID Act.

One of the primary reasons that states refused to implement the law was the massive unfunded mandate it represented. The Department of Homeland Security's own estimates placed the price tag for implementing REAL ID at $17 billion, $11 billion of which would be direct costs to states. Yet the federal government offered piddling financial support, and only to a few states.

The privacy concerns with REAL ID were a second significant motivator of state recalcitrance. State legislators knew that they would be responsible for a sprawling, insecure system of databases housing their constituents' sensitive information—including copies of basic identity documents like birth certificates. The REAL ID card was also supposed to include a "common machine-readable technology," meaning that cards could be scanned and used for data collection and tracking of all citizens—treating even the most law-abiding citizen as a criminal.

These concerns may have been overcome if there were genuine security benefits from a national ID system like REAL ID. But identity-based security against threats like terrorism and illegal immigration is extremely porous. It is subject to both physical and logical avoidance.

Take illegal immigration. Identity-based security against illegal immigration fails when someone can circumvent identity checks, such as at uncontrolled parts of the U.S. border. Once in the country, illegal immigrants can navigate the country relatively easily without ID, and the only solution for this is to check the immigration status of everyone

311

at multiple times and places throughout the nation. Americans reject the idea of living in a ''papers please'' society.

Logical avoidance of identity-based security is when attackers get the identification cards they need to access ID-controlled infrastructure. This is the technique used on 9/11: the hijackers had the identification they needed to get on planes. REAL ID would not prevent future terrorists from obtaining the identification necessary to access planes or other infrastructure. Foreign terrorists with no known history of terror activity would simply have to keep their visas current to get driver's licenses and state-issued ID cards.

Given all the defects of the REAL ID Act, state legislatures across the country passed resolutions and legislation objecting to the law or outright barring their own implementation of the REAL ID Act. With the May 2008 compliance deadline approaching, the Department of Homeland Security gave deadline extensions to states just for the asking. It even gave extensions to states that didn't ask for them, and whose leaders went out of their way to thumb their noses at the DHS.

With states from all parts of the country dead set against implementing REAL ID, it is almost certain not to be implemented, and it should not be. Congress should spend no funds on implementing REAL ID, and it should repeal the REAL ID Act.

The E-Verify Federal Immigration Background Check System

A closely related program with many of the same flaws as REAL ID is the E-Verify federal immigration background check system. In the beginning of the 110th Congress, a national verification system for electronic employment eligibility was treated as a matter of near consensus. Intended to strengthen ''internal enforcement'' of the immigration laws, the idea was to have an Internet-based employee-vetting system that the federal government would have required every employer to use.

But as the debate on verification for electronic employment eligibility continued, the defects of such a system came to light. A mandatory federal background check system would have substantial costs yet would still fail to prevent illegal immigration.

E-Verify would deny a sizable percentage of law-abiding American citizens the ability to work legally. Deemed ineligible by a database with a high percentage of errors, millions each year would go pleading to the Department of Homeland Security and the Social Security Administration for the right to work. The overtaxed bureaucrats in these government offices would hold the livelihoods of law-abiding citizens in their hands, and they would often deny law-abiding citizens the right to earn a living.

Avoidance and attacks on the system would cause more problems. Under-the-table work would increase, and all the illegality associated with it. By increasing the value of identity fraud, a nationally mandated E-Verify system would cause that crime's rates to rise. Illegal immigrants would deepen the minor identity frauds they may commit under the current system.

Creating an accurate and reliable system for verifying employment eligibility under the current immigration laws would require a national identification system, costing about $20 billion to create and hundreds of millions more per year to operate. In fact, the major immigration reform legislation considered in summer 2007 would have required all Americans to have a REAL ID card to get work. This demonstrates the tight link between internal enforcement of immigration law and national ID proposals.

Even if such a system were free and easy to implement, the United States should reject a national ID and background check system like E-Verify. It would cause law-abiding American citizens to lose more of their privacy as government records about them expanded and were converted to untold new purposes. "Mission creep" all but guarantees that the federal government would use a national E-Verify system to extend federal regulatory control over Americans' lives even further, using it to control access to housing, health care, guns, communications, financial services, and whatever else federal authorities wanted to regulate.

Instead of constructing an invasive national immigration background check contraption like E-Verify, Congress should release the immigration law's current tight limits on low-skilled immigration. There is no good alternative to aligning immigration rates with our economic demand for labor and the principle of free trade in labor.

Diverse and Competitive Private Identification and Credentialing

Rather than focus on government-issued ID cards, federal and state policy should encourage and foster the variety of identification and credentialing systems in the private marketplace today, and those that can be developed. People carry many types of privately issued identification cards and credentials that provide as good or greater security and identity assurance than government-issued cards. For example, many people carry credit cards that allow them to pay for goods or services securely. A variety of privately issued access cards allow people entry to buildings or access to automobiles, health care, and so on.

State and federal governments should not insist on particular issuers' cards (i.e., their own "government-issued ID"). Instead, they should accept (and allow acceptance of) any card or device that provides sufficient proof of the information necessary for a given transaction.

For example, many state laws require people buying alcohol to be at least 21 years old. But they don't allow any sufficient proof of age; they require presentment of government-issued ID, including all the data that are extraneous to proving a person's age, like address, weight, eye color, and so on. As cards are scanned more and more often, these policies will needlessly cause tracking of law-abiding citizens and will degrade their privacy.

In a marketplace for identification services, consumers would be able to choose which methods they use to identify themselves or prove relevant credentials like age, how much information they share for this purpose, and whether records are kept of their activities. National ID systems would deprive Americans of such choices.

Suggested Readings

Crews, Clyde Wayne, Jr. "Human Bar Code: Monitoring Biometric Technologies in a Free Society." Cato Institute Policy Analysis no. 452, September 17, 2002.

Harper, Jim. *Identity Crisis: How Identification Is Overused and Misunderstood.* Washington: Cato Institute, 2006.

_____. "Electronic Employment Eligibility Verification: Franz Kafka's Solution to Illegal Immigration." Cato Institute Policy Analysis no. 612, March 6, 2008.

Kopel, David. "You've Got Identity: Why a National ID Is a Bad Idea." *National Review Online*, February 5, 2002. http://www.nationalreview.com/kopel/kopel 020502.shtml.

Lynch, Timothy. "Breaking the Vicious Cycle: Preserving Our Liberties while Fighting Terrorism." Cato Institute Policy Analysis no. 443, June 26, 2002.

_____. "Cooperate, Or Else!" *Reason Online*, June 25, 2004. www.reason.com/hod/ tl062504.shtml.

—Prepared by Jim Harper

30. Regulation of Electronic Speech and Commerce

Congress should

- resist the urge to regulate offensive content on the Web,
- allow the market to address privacy and security concerns,
- let technical solutions have the primary role in suppressing spam and spyware,
- formally disavow authority over the management of Internet addressing,
- reject preemptive regulation of radio frequency identification technology, and
- decline to compel Internet retailers to collect out-of-state sales taxes.

The burst of creativity, communication, and commerce brought forth by the Internet in recent decades is only the beginning of a wave of innovation and progress that the Internet medium will foster. It should be kept an unfettered, entrepreneurial realm so that we can get the maximum benefits from creative, industrious Internet communicators and business-people the world over.

But the Internet regularly comes under assault, as poorly informed lawmakers blame it for the social ills it sometimes reveals. They promise their constituents "protection" from practices that are better cured by new technology, education, choice, and responsible Internet use.

Policymakers must resist intervention in the Internet and the Internet economy. Whether governments act as regulators or promoters of high tech, they will impose needless costs and create unintended consequences. Solutions to problems with the Internet can be found on the Internet itself. The collective intelligence, creativity, and problem-solving ability of technologists and Internet users vastly outstrip those of any government regulator.

Don't Regulate Offensive Content

The Internet contains a lot of frank content relating to sex and eroticism, including content that caters to some quite peculiar interests. Because of the potential exposure of children to material that many people find immoral or offensive, Congress has made repeated attempts to regulate Internet speech.

The Communications Decency Act, passed to ban pornography on the Internet, was struck down by the Supreme Court in 1997. Congress then passed the Child Online Protection Act in 1998 to shield children from online pornography by requiring that website operators verify the ages of visitors. In 2004, the Supreme Court upheld a preliminary injunction barring enforcement of the law on the ground that Internet filters were likely to be a less restrictive means of protecting children from sexually explicit material. The high court remanded the case to the lower courts for a trial, and in July 2008, the U.S. Court of Appeals for the Third Circuit found COPA unconstitutional.

The government should let this ill-considered legislation die, and Congress should not make another attempt to regulate Internet pornography. COPA would have interfered with content that adults have the right to see under the First Amendment. The best and least restrictive defense against unwanted display of sexual content to children is parental supervision. Helpful tools, including filtering software and filtered online services, are available in the private sector. Filtered online services can also limit the receipt of unwanted salacious e-mail, for which COPA is no use.

Leave Privacy and Security to the Market

Many consumers are concerned about what information they reveal when they go online, how that information is protected, and how it will be used. Government regulators have clamored to answer those questions and impose their visions of online commerce. But the best answers will emerge from competition among firms to serve consumers. Because consumers have many options online, and because they can decline to use the Internet entirely, they can reward and punish online businesses on the basis of their privacy and security practices.

Virtually every legitimate online company has voluntarily posted a privacy policy for interested consumers and activists to review and criticize.

The market has converged around "opt-in" e-mail policies because consumers distrust and reject companies that e-mail them without permission. Studies have shown that companies only rarely violate marketing policies. If they do, they risk offending potential customers, drawing adverse publicity, or being sued under breach of contract or other theories of liability.

A good example was the furor over Facebook's announcement of its Beacon program. Under this program, customer activities on third-party websites would have appeared on the consumer's Facebook "news feed." For example, if Amazon.com had participated in the program, a Facebook user's purchases on Amazon.com might have been automatically reported to that user's Facebook friends. The concept outraged many Facebook users. The danger of lost customers forced the company to abandon the plan in a matter of days—much more quickly than government regulators could have responded.

While many users are concerned about companies' use of their private information, many others are relatively unconcerned, and those preferences are rational. With more complete customer information, businesses can offer products and advertisements that are better tailored to individual customers' needs. Consumers rarely suffer any harm from having information about their commercial behavior available to these companies, whether it's called "behavioral tracking," "psychographic profiling," or something else.

It would be counterproductive for regulators to limit such potentially beneficial uses of customer information, and a "do not track" list that has occasionally surfaced as a proposal would be nearly impossible to administer. The risk of governments' accessing information collected by businesses should be controlled by controlling governments, not businesses. Government data retention mandates on Internet businesses should be rejected.

The law should ensure that companies honor the commitments made in their privacy policies but should otherwise leave them free to experiment with new uses for customer data. When they step over the line, they will be swiftly punished by users, who wield considerable influence in the fiercely competitive market for online services.

Market forces similarly dictate appropriate security practices. Companies that have lost or exposed customers' personal information as a result of security breaches have suffered devastating hits in public relations and lost business. There is no need to require companies to use security procedures that are appropriate for them. It is already in their interest to do so.

A California law requiring notice to consumers when a security breach has revealed customer information has been copied by many other states. While openness is often good, excessive notification may needlessly agitate customers over minor breaches that pose little or no danger of harm. A more sensible rule would be to make holders of personal information responsible for reasonably foreseeable harms caused by security breaches. A common-law rule like this would put the burden on the data holder to decide how best to respond to any breach on the basis of the particular facts of each case. It would protect consumers because they could be made whole if a breach harmed them.

Repeal Anti-Spam Legislation, Which Failed

Today, huge quantities of unwanted e-mail travel the Internet, wasting bandwidth, disk space, and recipients' time. Large-scale spamming is a serious nuisance that imposes millions of dollars in costs on third parties. This occurs in the face of anti-spam legislation like the federal CAN-SPAM Act, which passed in late 2003. CAN-SPAM placed several regulations on commercial e-mail and preempted state regulation of e-mail, except for anti-fraud and anti-deception laws. CAN-SPAM went far beyond targeting large-scale spammers and included a variety of broad regulations that impose compliance costs on legitimate businesses while doing little to stop spam.

Ultimately, legal sanctions will be less important than technology in the fight against spam. Most e-mail applications and services now come with powerful spam filters. Although such filters are never perfect, they have become effective enough to make the spam problem manageable. CAN-SPAM and all the laws it preempted are irrelevant and should be repealed.

Don't Enact New Spyware Regulations

Congress should be equally cautious about regulating "spyware," the colloquial term given to software that is installed on a user's computer without the user's knowledge or consent. Government has a legitimate role in prosecuting companies engaged in fraudulent behavior, but it has proved difficult to craft a precise definition of spyware. Overly broad legislation could cause headaches for many legitimate software vendors. Most spyware is already illegal under a variety of laws against fraud and computer hacking, and the Federal Trade Commission has prosecuted several spyware vendors under existing laws. New regulations are unnecessary.

As with spam, the most effective anti-spyware measures will be technical, rather than regulatory. There are already several software producers whose programs search users' computers for spyware. When these programs detect spyware, they remove or quarantine it and reverse unwanted changes to computer settings.

Fully Privatize ICANN

The phrase "Internet governance" is commonly used to describe the responsibilities of the Internet Corporation for Assigned Names and Numbers, but the phrase is misleading. In reality, Internet governance is radically decentralized, with thousands of network owners independently negotiating interconnection agreements. ICANN's primary function is a narrow one: managing the allocation of Internet names and addresses so that no two computers share the same identifier. This is an important task, but it is better described as "coordination" rather than "governance."

ICANN was created by the Clinton administration and placed under the authority of the Department of Commerce. It is officially a private, nonprofit organization, but it has proved susceptible to pressure from the U.S. government. For example, under pressure from the Bush administration, it rejected a proposal for a ".xxx" domain that would have been designated for pornographic materials.

Despite its flaws, ICANN is preferable to the other leading contender for control of Internet addressing. The International Telecommunications Union, acting in conjunction with the United Nations, is seeking to bring the Internet under the control of those international bureaucracies. That would be a mistake. Maintaining the integrity and stability of the Internet's addressing scheme is a technical problem, not a political one. A UN "Internet governance" body would be unlikely to confine itself to the narrow technical issues that are ICANN's bread and butter.

The U.S. government should preempt calls for UN control of Internet addressing by converting ICANN into a fully private, independent organization. ICANN has a complex governance structure designed to ensure that the organization's board includes representatives from a broad spectrum of interested parties and geographic regions. By formally disavowing authority over ICANN, the U.S. government can lay to rest accusations that it is pulling strings behind the scenes. That would take wind out of the sails of those pushing for a UN takeover of ICANN's functions.

Don't Regulate RFID

The last decade saw the emergence of radio frequency identification (RFID) technology, small chips that can be embedded in everyday objects and used for wireless tracking of those objects over relatively short distances. RFID has the potential to increase economic efficiency by rationalizing and streamlining the movement of objects on factory floors, in stores, on trucks and trains, and in warehouses. However, integrating the technology into supply chains has proved more difficult than expected, and it will take many years before the devices are ubiquitous.

Like many new technologies, RFID has attracted criticism from activists who fear that substantial privacy invasions will come from the technology. Although that is certainly possible, their fears have not been borne out so far. Without experience, it is impossible to know how technologies like RFID may be used and what consequences they may have for good or ill. The likely privacy harms from RFID are relatively modest, so it would be counterproductive to enact preemptive regulations before the costs and benefits of the technology are fully understood.

Say No to Internet Taxes

In April 2008, the state of New York announced that it would require Amazon.com and some other online retailers to begin collecting sales taxes on behalf of New York customers. Under federal law, a firm cannot be compelled to collect sales taxes for a state unless it has a physical presence there. Amazon.com is based in the state of Washington and has no physical facilities in New York, but New York officials have argued that the presence of Amazon "affiliates"—third parties that advertise Amazon's products—in New York is sufficient to force Amazon.com to collect New York sales taxes. Amazon.com has vowed to fight the new requirement in court.

New York's initiative is more aggressive than most, but a number of states have banded together to create a "streamlined" sales tax system that would require Internet-based retailers to collect sales taxes from all American customers based on the buyer's location. About 20 states have signed on to the proposal, but it would require congressional action to make it apply nationally.

Advocates of forcing Internet retailers to collect sales taxes for out-of-state customers frame the issue as a matter of fairness, claiming that brick-and-mortar retailers are put at a competitive disadvantage by the need to collect sales taxes from their customers. However, they ignore two important points. First, the sales taxes collected by brick-and-mortar retailers help cover the costs of infrastructure and public services that those retailers use. Traditional retailers benefit from local roads, sewers, police and fire protection, and other public services. The same is not true of Internet retailers who collect sales taxes for out-of-state customers. They pay taxes for the services they receive in their own states, of course, but they receive no benefits from the out-of-state revenues they collect.

More important, any given brick-and-mortar retail store has to be familiar with the tax laws in its own jurisdiction only. In contrast, there are thousands of distinct sales tax jurisdictions in the United States. Not only do these jurisdictions have different tax rates and different lists of items to be taxed, but many have varying definitions of common categories, such as food and clothing. The streamlined sales tax system has made some progress in standardizing such definitions, but its rules are still fiendishly complex and would only get more so as more states joined the project. That means that even the smallest online retailers would be forced to become experts on the minutiae of sales tax law in order to properly classify their products. That would be far more unfair to them than the status quo is to brick-and-mortar firms.

Congress should refuse to sanction any effort to force Internet retailers to collect sales taxes on behalf of out-of-state customers. And in the unlikely event that the courts uphold New York's revenue grab, Congress should step in and make clear that merely allowing third parties in a state to advertise one's products is not sufficient to establish a physical presence there.

Suggested Readings

Bell, Tom W. "Internet Privacy and Self-Regulation: Lessons from the Porn Wars." Cato Institute Briefing Paper no. 65, August 9, 2001.

Corn-Revere, Robert. "Caught in the Seamless Web: Does the Internet's Global Reach Justify Less Freedom of Speech?" Cato Institute Briefing Paper no. 71, July 24, 2002.

Harper, Jim. "Understanding Privacy—And the Real Threats to It." Cato Institute Policy Analysis no. 520, August 4, 2004.

———. "Federal Spyware Legislation: Some Lessons from Antiquity." Cato Institute TechKnowledge no. 89, October 1, 2004.

———. "When Data Security Regulations Fail, There Is an Alternative." Cato Institute TechKnowledge no. 97, March 29, 2005.

———. *Identity Crisis: How Identification Is Overused and Misunderstood*. Washington: Cato Institute, 2006.

Lee, Timothy. "Beacon Lessons." Cato Institute TechKnowledge no. 112, February 8, 2008.

Plummer, James. "'Data Retention': Costly Outsourced Surveillance." Cato Institute TechKnowledge no. 99, January 22, 2007.

Thierer, Adam, and others. Brief of *amici curiae* Center for Democracy and Technology and Adam Thierer of the Progress and Freedom Foundation in the case of *FCC v. Fox Television Stations*. August 8, 2008. http://pff.org/issues-pubs/filings/2008/080808FoxSupremeCourtBrief.pdf.

—Prepared by Timothy B. Lee and Jim Harper

31. Restoring the Right to Bear Arms

Congress should

- compel Washington, D.C., to abide by the principles established in the *Heller* decision;
- repeal the federal ban on interstate purchases of handguns;
- revoke the federal age minimums on buyers and possessors of handguns;
- modernize and improve the operations of the Bureau of Alcohol, Tobacco, Firearms and Explosives;
- restore funding to process "relief from disability" applications to own firearms; and
- rescind the Department of the Interior regulation banning defensive guns in national parks.

For too long, the Second Amendment was consigned to constitutional limbo, all but erased from law textbooks and effectively banished from the nation's courts. But no more. On June 26, 2008, after seven decades without a coherent explanation of the right celebrated during the early Republic as "the true palladium of liberty," the Supreme Court rediscovered the Second Amendment. More than five years after six Washington, D.C., residents challenged the city's 32-year-old ban on all functional firearms in the home, the Court held in *District of Columbia v. Heller* that the gun ban was unconstitutional.

Heller is merely the opening salvo in a series of litigations that will ultimately resolve what weapons and individuals can be regulated and what restrictions are permissible. Near term, the Court must also decide whether Second Amendment rights can be enforced against state and local governments. Despite those remaining hurdles, it's fair to say that the Court's blockbuster decision makes the prospects for reviving the original meaning of the Second Amendment substantially brighter.

Within the *Heller* framework, Congress now has a historic opportunity to begin restoring Americans' right to keep and bear arms. To be sure, Cato Institute scholars have opposed previous congressional meddling in the gun control arena on the ground that most federal regulations of firearms are not authorized under the interstate commerce clause. That clause was intended to ensure the free flow of trade across state lines, not to sanction a federal police power. Regrettably, the battle to limit the interstate commerce power to interstate commerce seems to have been lost in the courts, which have expanded the scope of the commerce clause to cover regulation of nearly anything and everything. But there can be no constitutional objection to repealing laws—or, at a minimum, amending their most egregious provisions—that had no constitutional pedigree ab initio. The same logic applies, of course, to laws that offend the Second Amendment.

Indeed, even if a federal gun law were constitutionally authorized, that does not mean it would be constitutionally mandated. Accordingly, included in what we propose below are recommendations to repeal or amend statutes that are misguided on public policy grounds and that may also be infringements of the Second Amendment.

Compel Washington, D.C., to Abide by the Principles Established in the Heller Decision

No jurisdiction in the United States works as doggedly to disarm citizens as does the District of Columbia, our nation's capital and on-again, off-again murder capital. Until the *Heller* decision, with very few exceptions, no handgun could be registered in D.C. Even those handguns grandfathered before the District's 1976 ban could not be carried from room to room in the home without a license, which was never granted. In addition, all firearms in the home, including rifles and shotguns, had to always be unloaded and either disassembled or bound by a trigger lock. In effect, no one in the District could possess a functional firearm in his or her own residence. And the law applied not just to "unfit" people like felons or the mentally incompetent, but across-the-board to ordinary, honest, responsible citizens. Happily, the Supreme Court has now ruled that all those provisions violate the personal and private right to keep and bear arms that is secured by the Second Amendment.

The D.C. city council was, therefore, on notice to alter the city's gun control regime to comply with the Court's holding. The city's first attempt at revised rules was an abject failure. At least one of the new rules was an obvious attempt to circumvent *Heller*'s directives. Other rules violated the spirit and perhaps the letter of the opinion. At this writing, the city has responded to an avalanche of criticism and passed a second set of temporary rules, which will remain in effect until mid-December 2008, when permanent gun control regulations are due to be enacted. The city's second attempt was better than its first, but the current rules still fall short of *Heller*'s mandate. Nor is there any assurance that the permanent rules will fully comply. Consequently, Congress can and should, under Article I, section 8, of the Constitution, exercise its plenary power over all legislative matters in the nation's capital and compel the city to abide by the principles established in the *Heller* decision. Home rule, arising out of authority delegated by Congress to the D.C. government, is not a license to violate the Constitution.

For starters, Congress should enact legislation to alter how D.C. processes gun registrations. Currently, residents seeking to register a handgun must obtain and complete an application form; submit photographs, proof of residency, and proof of good vision; pass a written test; pay a fee; and be fingerprinted. If approved, the registrant must take the application to a dealer for delivery of the firearm, which is then returned to city officials for ballistics testing. The entire process can take months. Congress should mandate a more streamlined registration process for D.C., based on the congressionally created National Instant Criminal Background Check System, which is mandatory for almost all retail firearm sales in the United States. The NICS uses computerized databases to complete a background check within a few hours in most cases.

Second, with contemptuous disregard for the Supreme Court's decision, D.C. initially sought to continue its ban on virtually all semiautomatic handguns and rifles. The District defined "machine gun" as any gun that could fire 12 or more shots without being manually reloaded. Even guns that did not come with a 12-round magazine were illegal if they were capable of holding 12 rounds. In effect, the only handguns that could be registered were revolvers or single-shot handguns. Semiautomatic handguns constitute about three-quarters of the handguns sold in the United States annually. Banning them all violated *Heller*'s rule against "prohibition of an entire class of 'arms' that is overwhelmingly chosen by American society" for the lawful purpose of self-defense.

Moreover, classifying semiautomatic handguns and rifles as automatic "machine guns" was patently irrational. Semiautomatic guns fire only one round each time the trigger is pulled; they have been available since

325

the 19th century and are used by tens of millions of Americans for hunting, target shooting, and formal competitions, including the Olympics. Perhaps D.C. finally got the message. The city's latest (temporary) rules now permit semiautomatic weapons as long as the actual magazine holds no more than ten rounds of ammunition, even if the weapon is capable of using a larger magazine.

Congress should ensure that the permanent rules ultimately adopted by the District do not constructively ban semiautomatic handguns and rifles. The guidepost should be that a firearm may not be banned unless it is prohibited by federal law or subject to the National Firearms Act, which covers weapons such as automatic machine guns and sawed-off shotguns.

Third, D.C.'s first set of revised rules still required that guns in the home be unloaded and either disassembled, trigger-locked, or kept in a gun safe. An exception was made for a firearm while it was being used against a reasonably perceived threat of immediate harm within the home. That exception was unconstitutionally vague. D.C. residents had no way to determine when the exception would become operative. According to D.C. Attorney General Peter Nickles, a homeowner could not have an unlocked and loaded gun even when investigating the sound of intruders in his or her backyard. Any rule requiring a crime victim to wait until his or her attacker has actually entered the home is unreasonable and shameful.

Once again responding to criticism, the city's second set of revised rules repealed the ban on all loaded firearms in the home, with one exception. If a minor could readily gain access to the loaded firearm without parental consent, then the weapon had to be kept in a secure location. That seems reasonable, but Congress must guarantee that D.C.'s permanent rules are no more restrictive than the rules now in effect on a temporary basis. Here's the controlling principle: D.C. may not prohibit, constructively prohibit, or significantly infringe the ability of individuals to possess and use firearms in their homes for self-protection.

Repeal the Federal Ban on Interstate Purchases of Handguns

Under federal law, a person who is not a licensed dealer—that is, a Federal Firearms Licensee—may acquire a handgun only within the person's own state. The acquirer may, however, purchase the handgun from an out-of-state FFL, providing an arrangement is made for the handgun to be shipped to an FFL in the purchaser's state of residence, where the purchaser can then obtain the handgun after complying with all necessary background checks. That rule does not apply to rifles and shotguns. A buyer may acquire a rifle or shotgun, in person, at a licensee's premises in any state, provided the sale complies with laws applicable in both the state of sale and the state where the purchaser resides. So a person who resides in New Mexico can buy a shotgun from a licensed firearms dealer in South Dakota (who must, by federal law, get prior approval for the sale from the National Instant Criminal Background Check System). The New Mexican can then bring the gun home to New Mexico, in compliance with New Mexico law.

There is no persuasive reason why the framework applicable to rifles and shotguns should not be equally applicable to handguns. No relevant state's laws would be violated, and all background checks would be completed. In short, Congress should repeal the federal restrictions on interstate handgun sales.

The unique situation in Washington, D.C., compels timely action. Because of the District's 1976 ban, there are no stores within the city where a handgun can be obtained, and there is only one FFL willing to take delivery from out-of-city parties, on a limited basis. Thus, for all practical purposes, someone who lives in D.C. cannot acquire a handgun either inside or outside the city. Because it will be months before gun dealers are licensed to do business in the District, residents of the city who do not own a handgun are precluded from exercising the right, guaranteed by the Constitution and affirmed by the Supreme Court, to defend themselves within their homes.

Revoke the Federal Age Minimums on Buyers and Possessors of Handguns

Under current federal law, the minimum age at which prospective buyers can acquire a handgun from an FFL is 21. The minimum age at which anyone can possess a handgun, or purchase a rifle or shotgun from an FFL, is 18. Those restrictions should be repealed.

Assuming that bans on the sale of a handgun to a 20-year-old, or possession of a handgun by a 17-year-old, could survive Second Amendment scrutiny, state, not federal, law should address that topic. Although the federal statute includes some exceptions—for example, a parent may take a child target shooting—it nonetheless usurps traditional state powers, is overbroad, and encroaches on parental rights. Even if a child is under direct and continuous parental supervision, the parent commits a federal crime unless he or she writes a note giving the child permission to target-shoot and the child always carries the note. Congress should abolish federal age limits—leaving the states to set their own policies, with due regard to a paucity of empirical evidence that federal age limits have reduced gun accidents or criminal violence.

Modernize and Improve the Operations of the ATF

Abusive practices by the Bureau of Alcohol, Tobacco, Firearms and Explosives led Congress to enact the Firearms Owners' Protection Act in 1986. Yet much more needs to be done. For example, when the ATF imposes a penalty on a gun store, the store should be able to appeal the case to a neutral administrative law judge. Currently, an employee of the ATF itself hears appeals of ATF penalties.

Appropriations riders have prevented ATF from using gun dealer records to compile a computerized national registration database of gun owners. The prohibition should be part of a permanent statute. Federal law already prohibits the creation of a national gun registry, but ATF has claimed that a computerized database of every sale ever conducted by every retired FFL is not a national gun registry.

Other appropriations riders protect citizen privacy by preventing ATF from disclosing gun-tracing data (e.g., the name and address of a person whose gun is stolen) to the general public. The data can still be disclosed in connection with a bona fide law enforcement investigation. Those disclosure rules should be permanently codified.

The ATF's firearms-testing facility has long been a subject of concern. People who conduct tests on firearms are not required to have expertise in forensics or other procedures appropriate to a crime laboratory. To support prosecutions for machine gun possession, ATF testers have been known to use one ammunition type after another, until they find one that occasionally makes the firearm malfunction by producing two shots from a single trigger pull. The jury then sees an official report from ATF declaring that the gun is a machine gun. Congress should require that all ATF firearms testing be filmed, and the films be preserved.

Restore Funding to Process "Relief from Disability" Applications to Own Firearms

The federal prohibitions on firearms possession are extremely broad, and ex post facto. The Gun Control Act of 1968 banned gun possession by anyone convicted of a felony or dishonorably discharged from the military. Thus, a person who pleaded guilty to a tax offense in 1959, or who was dishonorably discharged in 1965 because of homosexual orientation, is barred for life from possessing a gun. The 1994 ban on gun possession by someone guilty of a domestic violence misdemeanor is also ex post facto—applying to people who might have pleaded guilty decades earlier, although they had done nothing wrong, because they could not afford a lawyer and it was simpler to resolve the case for a $50 fine.

To provide a safety valve for the expansive bans, the Gun Control Act allows "relief from disability." People who can prove they have a long record of law-abiding behavior and good conduct can petition ATF for restoration of their Second Amendment rights. Granting a petition is entirely discretionary on the part of ATF.

Since 1992, appropriations riders have forbidden ATF from processing petitions for restoration of rights. Those riders should end, and ATF should be directed to set up a process in which such petitions are funded by a fee charged the petitioner.

Federal law also bans gun possession by people subject to temporary restraining orders. The law should be clarified so that it applies only to cases where a judge has made a particularized finding that a person has threatened, or constitutes a threat to, another person. Routine orders directing one or both parties in a divorce to stay away from and not harm each other should not be the basis for deprivation of a constitutional right. The change can be effectuated by changing the word "or" to "and" in 18 U.S. Code § 922(d)(8)(B)(i) and in (g)(8)(C)(i).

Rescind the Department of the Interior Regulation Banning Defensive Guns in National Parks

A Department of the Interior regulation bans the possession of loaded guns by all citizens visiting or traveling through national parks. It is unfair to forbid hikers or campers, who may be many miles from law enforcement assistance, from having a means to protect themselves from deadly attack by wild animals or criminals. Although Interior is considering changing the regulation, Congress should ensure that a future administration does not reimpose the old regulation. A federal statute should clearly state that national park visitors may carry firearms outdoors to the extent allowed by the law of the host state.

Conclusion

The Second Amendment secures "the right of the people" by guaranteeing the right of each person. Over the years, our elected representatives have adopted a dangerously court-centric view of the Constitution: a view that decisions about constitutionality are properly left to the judiciary. But members of Congress also swear an oath to uphold the Constitution. Congress can make good on that oath by legislating to restore our right to keep and bear arms.

Suggested Readings

District of Columbia v. Heller, 554 U.S. _____, 128 S. Ct. 2783 (2008).

District of Columbia v. Heller, briefs by the parties and *amici curiae,* see "Case Filings" at www.dcguncase.com.

Doherty, Brian. *Gun Control on Trial: Inside the Supreme Court Battle over the Second Amendment.* Washington: Cato Institute, 2008.

Kleck, Gary. *Targeting Guns: Firearms and Their Control.* Hawthorne, NY: Aldine, 1997.

Korwin, Alan, and David B. Kopel. *The Heller Case: Gun Rights Affirmed!* Scottsdale, AZ: Bloomfield Press, 2008.

Levy, Robert A. "*District of Columbia v. Heller*: What's Next?" *Cato Unbound*, July 14, 2008. www.cato-unbound.org/2008/07/14/robert-a-levy/district-of-columbia-v-heller-whats-next/.

Snyder, Jeffrey R. "Fighting Back: Crime, Self-Defense, and the Right to Carry a Handgun." Cato Institute Policy Analysis no. 284, October 22, 1997.

—Prepared by David B. Kopel and Robert A. Levy

32. Tobacco and the Rule of Law

> **Congress should**
> - enact legislation to abrogate the multistate tobacco settlement, and
> - reject proposed legislation to regulate cigarette manufacturing and advertising.

Enact Legislation to Abrogate the Multistate Tobacco Settlement

The Master Settlement Agreement, signed in November 1998 by the major tobacco companies and 46 state attorneys general, transforms a competitive industry into a cartel, then guards against destabilization of the cartel by erecting barriers to entry that preserve the dominant market share of the tobacco giants. Far from being victims, the big four tobacco companies are at the very center of the plot. They managed to carve out a protected market for themselves—all at the expense of smokers and tobacco companies that did not sign the agreement.

To be sure, the industry would have preferred that the settlement had not been necessary. But given the perverse legal rules under which the state Medicaid recovery suits were unfolding, the major tobacco companies were effectively bludgeoned into negotiating with the states and the trial lawyers. Finding itself in that perilous position, the industry shrewdly bargained for something pretty close to a sweetheart deal.

The MSA forces all tobacco companies—even new companies and companies that were not part of the settlement—to pay "damages," thus foreclosing meaningful price competition. Essentially, the tobacco giants have purchased (at virtually no cost to themselves) the ability to exclude competitors. The deal works like this: Philip Morris, Reynolds, Lorillard, and Brown & Williamson knew they would have to raise prices substantially to cover their MSA obligations. Accordingly, they were concerned that smaller domestic manufacturers, importers, and new tobacco companies that didn't sign the agreement would gain share of market by underpricing cigarettes. To guard against that likelihood, the big four and their state collaborators added three provisions to the MSA.

First, if the aggregate market share of the four majors declined by more than two percentage points, then their "damages" payments would decline by three times the excess over the two-percentage-point threshold. Any reduction would be charged against only those states that did not adopt a "Qualifying Statute," attached as an exhibit to the MSA. Naturally, because of the risk of losing enormous sums of money, all the states have enacted the statute.

Second, the Qualifying Statute requires all tobacco companies that did not sign the MSA to post pro rata damages—based on cigarette sales—in escrow for 25 years to offset any liability that might hereafter be assessed! That's right—no evidence, no trial, no verdict, and no injury, just damages. That was the stick. Then came the carrot.

Third, if a nonsettling tobacco company agreed to participate in the MSA, the new participant would be allowed to increase its market share by 25 percent of its 1997 level without paying damages. Bear in mind that no nonsettling company in 1997 had more than 1.0 percent of the market, which, under the MSA, could grow to a whopping 1.25 percent. Essentially, the dominant companies guaranteed themselves a commanding market share in perpetuity.

Perhaps as troubling, the settlement has led to massive and continuing shifts of wealth from millions of smokers to concentrated pockets of the bar. Predictably, part of that multibillion-dollar booty has started its roundtrip back into the political process. With all that money in hand, trial lawyers have seen their influence grow exponentially. Every day that passes more firmly entrenches the MSA as a fait accompli, and more tightly cements the insidious relationship between trial attorneys and their allies in the public sector. The billion-dollar spigot must be turned off before its corrupting effect on the rule of law is irreversible.

An obvious way to turn off the spigot is to abrogate the MSA. If it is allowed to stand, the MSA will create and finance a rich and powerful industry of lawyers who know how to manipulate the system and are not averse to violating the antitrust laws. At root, the MSA is a cunning and deceitful bargain among the industry, private attorneys, and the states, allowing giant companies to monopolize cigarette sales and foist the cost onto luckless smokers. Indeed, the MSA is the most egregious antitrust violation of our generation—a collusive tobacco settlement that is bilking millions of smokers out of a quarter of a trillion dollars.

Congress should dismantle the MSA to restore competition. That's a tall order, but the stakes are immense.

Reject Proposed Legislation to Regulate Cigarette Manufacturing and Advertising

Under legislation periodically reintroduced in Congress, the Food and Drug Administration would be authorized to regulate cigarette ads and ingredients, including nicotine; set product standards; require new health warnings; and curb marketing to kids. True to form, Philip Morris— the industry leader with the most to gain from restrictions on would-be competitors—quickly chimed in to support many of the proposals. Yet if tobacco is to be regulated as a drug, Congress will simply be guaranteeing a pervasive black market in tobacco products. FDA regulation that makes cigarettes unpalatable, coupled with higher prices, will inevitably foment illegal dealings dominated by criminals and terrorists hooking underage smokers on an adulterated product freed of all constraints on quality that competitive markets usually afford.

The war on cigarettes, like other crusades, may be well-intentioned at the beginning, but as zealotry takes hold, the regulations become foolish and ultimately destructive. Consider the provisions in the current bill that would grant FDA control over tobacco advertising. Not only are the public policy implications harmful, but there are obvious First Amendment violations that should concern every American who values free expression.

Here are the constitutional ground rules: In *Central Hudson Gas & Electric Corp. v. Public Service Comm'n* (1980), the Supreme Court concluded that nonmisleading commercial speech about a lawful activity cannot be regulated unless (a) the government has a substantial interest in doing so, (b) the regulation directly and materially serves that interest, and (c) the regulation is reasonable and no more extensive than necessary to achieve the desired objective. Sixteen years later, the Court affirmed that even vice products like alcoholic beverages are entitled to commercial speech protection. More recently, the Court threw out Massachusetts regulations banning selected cigar and smokeless tobacco ads.

Even if hard facts proved that the demise of specified ads might dissuade some children from smoking, prohibiting generic forms of advertisements—such as those containing cartoon characters—would not meet the

333

final directive of the *Central Hudson* test. When a prohibition is overbroad and unreasonably inhibiting, it is more extensive than necessary to achieve the desired objective. As the Court has stated, the government must not "reduce the adult population . . . to reading only what is fit for children"; alternative and less intrusive means are surely available.

For example, the sale of cigarettes to underage smokers is illegal in every state. Those laws should be vigorously enforced. Retailers found to have violated the law should be prosecuted. A proof-of-age requirement for the purchase of tobacco products is acceptable as long as it is reasonably drafted and objectively administered; and a prohibition on vending machines is not excessively invasive if limited to areas frequented primarily by children (e.g., schools, arcades, and perhaps recreation centers).

However unpopular the tobacco industry, and however repugnant the thought that children may become addicted to smoking, there are countervailing values that sustain a free society. We need not sacrifice our fundamental liberties in order to reduce tobacco consumption by minors. "If there is a bedrock principle underlying the First Amendment," cautions Justice William J. Brennan, "it is that government may not prohibit the expression of an idea simply because society finds the idea itself offensive or disagreeable."

Moreover, if advertising were deregulated, newer and smaller tobacco companies would vigorously seek to carve out a bigger market share by emphasizing health claims that might bolster brand preference. Regrettably, in 1950 the Federal Trade Commission foreclosed health claims—like "less smoker's cough"—as well as tar and nicotine comparisons for existing brands. To get around that prohibition, aggressive companies created *new* brands, which they supported with an avalanche of health claims. Filter cigarettes grew from roughly 1 percent to 10 percent of domestic sales within four years.

Then in 1954, the FTC tightened its restrictions by requiring scientific proof of health claims, even for new brands. The industry returned to promoting taste and pleasure; aggregate sales expanded. By 1957, scientists had confirmed the benefit of low-tar cigarettes. A new campaign of "Tar Derby" ads quickly emerged with tar and nicotine levels collapsing 40 percent in two years. To shut down the flow of health claims, the FTC next demanded that they be accompanied by epidemiological evidence, of which none existed. The commission then negotiated a "voluntary" ban on tar and nicotine comparisons.

Not surprisingly, the steep decline in tar and nicotine ended in 1959. Seven years later, apparently alerted to the bad news, the FTC reauthorized tar and nicotine data but continued to proscribe associated health claims. Finally, in 1970 Congress banned all radio and television ads. Fast-forward more than three decades. In a lawsuit filed against the tobacco industry by the Justice Department, the government argued that ads promoting "light" or low-tar cigarettes as a healthier alternative to regular smokes were fraudulent. Yet Congress is now considering a bill that would authorize the FDA to mandate less nicotine and tar—the same practices condemned as worse than useless because smokers would compensate by puffing harder, consuming more cigarettes, and smoking them closer to the filter.

Today, the potential gains from health-related ads are undoubtedly greater than ever—for both aggressive companies and health-conscious consumers. If, however, government regulation expands, those gains will not be realized. Instead of "healthy" competition for market share, we will be treated to more imagery and personal endorsements—the very ads that anti-tobacco partisans decry.

Mired in regulations, laws, taxes, and litigation, we look to Congress to extricate us from the mess it helped create. Yet if Congress authorizes the FDA to regulate cigarette ads and control the content of tobacco products, it will exacerbate the problem. Equally important, Congress will have delegated excessive and ill-advised legislative authority to an unelected administrative agency.

Of course, the machinery of regulation, once set in motion, will not stop with ameliorative changes. As former Commissioner David A. Kessler stated, outlining his concept of FDA oversight: "Only those tobacco products from which the nicotine had been removed or, possibly, tobacco products approved by FDA for nicotine-replacement therapy would then remain on the market." In other words, cigarettes as we know them would cease to exist.

In 1919, Americans understood that Congress could not prohibit the sale of alcoholic beverages, so Prohibition was effectuated by constitutional amendment. Today, when it comes to tobacco, our lifestyle police argue that we require neither a constitutional amendment nor even an intelligible statute—just an amorphous delegation to an unelected administrative agency, which can ban ingredients it doesn't think "uninformed" citizens should consume. So much for limited government. We are left with the executive state—return of the king.

Just as bad, assigning quasi-legislative authority to the FDA will drive another nail into the coffin of personal responsibility. A federal agency will be empowered to dictate the form and composition of a legal product about which consumers have exhaustive knowledge. Throughout the past century, incessant warnings about the risks of tobacco have come from doctors, public health sources, and thousands of scientific and medical publications. By the 1920s, 14 states had prohibited the sale of cigarettes. A warning has appeared on every pack of cigarettes lawfully sold in the United States for almost four decades. Nicotine content by brand has been printed in every cigarette ad since 1970.

That isn't enough for the anti-tobacco crowd, for whom cigarettes are only the first in a long list of products that the nanny state will monitor. If we know anything at all about government, it is that bureaucrats are likely to have an expansive view of their mission. So what comes next— coffee, soft drinks, red meat, dairy products, sugar, fast foods, automobiles, and sporting goods? The list is endless—all in pursuit of so-called public health.

But smoking is a private, not a public, health question. The term "public," if it is to have any substantive content, cannot be used to describe all health problems that affect numerous people. Instead, "public" should refer only to those cases requiring collective action, when individual harms cannot be redressed without a general societal solution. Smoking, for example, would be a public health problem if it were contagious. But it isn't. Similarly, cigarettes do not infect us as they cross state borders. Nor has nicotine shown up in biological or chemical weapons.

An adult's decision to smoke is a voluntary, private matter. It's time to rein in the administrative state and restore a modicum of individual liberty.

Suggested Readings

Bulow, Jeremy, and Paul Klemperer. "The Tobacco Deal." In *Brookings Papers on Economic Activity: Microeconomics 1998*. Edited by Clifford Winston, Martin N. Bailey, and Peter C. Reiss. Washington: Brookings Institution Press, 1999.

Calfee, John E. "The Ghost of Cigarette Advertising Past." *Regulation*, November–December, 1986.

Levy, Robert A. "Tobacco-Free FDA." *Administrative Law & Regulation News* 2, no. 3 (Winter 1998).

———. *Shakedown: How Corporations, Government, and Trial Lawyers Abuse the Judicial Process*. Washington: Cato Institute, 2004.

O'Brien, Thomas C. "Constitutional and Antitrust Violations of the Multistate Tobacco Settlement." Cato Institute Policy Analysis no. 371, May 18, 2000.

—Prepared by Robert A. Levy

33. The War on Drugs

> **Congress should**
> - repeal the Controlled Substances Act of 1970,
> - repeal the federal mandatory minimum sentences and the federal sentencing guidelines,
> - direct the administration not to interfere with the implementation of state initiatives that allow for the medical use of marijuana, and
> - shut down the Drug Enforcement Administration.

Ours is a federal republic. The federal government has only the powers granted to it in the Constitution. And the United States has a tradition of individual liberty, vigorous civil society, and limited government. Identification of a problem does not mean that the government should undertake to solve it, and the fact that a problem occurs in more than one state does not mean that it is a proper subject for federal policy.

Perhaps no area more clearly demonstrates the bad consequences of not following such rules than does drug prohibition. The long federal experiment in prohibition of marijuana, cocaine, heroin, and other drugs has given us crime and corruption combined with a manifest failure to stop the use of drugs or reduce their availability to children.

In the 1920s, Congress experimented with the prohibition of alcohol. On February 20, 1933, a new Congress acknowledged the failure of alcohol prohibition and sent the Twenty-First Amendment to the states. Congress recognized that Prohibition had failed to stop drinking and had increased prison populations and violent crime. By the end of 1933, national Prohibition was history, though many states continued to outlaw or severely restrict the sale of liquor.

Today, Congress confronts a similarly failed prohibition policy. Futile efforts to enforce prohibition have been pursued even more vigorously since the 1980s than they were in the 1920s. Total federal expenditures for the first 10 years of Prohibition amounted to $88 million—about $1 billion in 2008 dollars. Drug enforcement costs about $19 billion a year now in federal spending alone.

Those billions have had some effect. Total drug arrests are now more than 1.5 million a year. Since 1989, more people have been incarcerated for drug offenses than for all violent crimes combined. There are now about 480,000 drug offenders in jails and prisons, and about 50 percent of the federal prison population consists of drug offenders.

Yet, as was the case during Prohibition, all the arrests and incarcerations haven't stopped the use and abuse of drugs, or the drug trade, or the crime associated with black-market transactions. Cocaine and heroin supplies are up; the more our Customs agents interdict, the more smugglers import. And most tragic, the crime rate has soared. Despite the good news about crime in recent years, crime rates remain at high levels.

As for discouraging young people from using drugs, the massive federal effort has largely been a dud. Every year from 1975 to 2006, at least 82 percent of high school seniors said they found marijuana ''fairly easy'' or ''very easy'' to obtain. During that same period, according to federal statistics of dubious reliability, teenage marijuana use fell dramatically and then rose significantly, suggesting that cultural factors have more effect than the ''war on drugs.''

The manifest failure of drug prohibition explains why more and more political leaders, such as Governors Jesse Ventura and Gary Johnson and Rep. Barney Frank (D-MA), have argued that drug prohibition actually causes more crime and other harms than it prevents. Senator Jim Webb (D-VA) has also been outspoken in his criticism of federal drug policies. In his 2008 book, *A Time to Fight*, Webb wrote: ''Drug addiction is not in and of itself a criminal act. It is a medical condition, indeed a disease, just as alcoholism is, and we don't lock people up for being alcoholics.''

Repeal the Controlled Substances Act

The United States is a federal republic, and Congress should deal with drug prohibition the way it dealt with alcohol prohibition. The Twenty-First Amendment did not actually legalize the sale of alcohol; it simply repealed the federal prohibition and returned to the several states the authority to set alcohol policy. States took the opportunity to design diverse liquor policies that were in tune with the preferences of their citizens.

After 1933, three states and hundreds of counties continued to practice prohibition. Other states chose various forms of alcohol legalization.

The single most important law that Congress must repeal is the Controlled Substances Act of 1970. That law is probably the most far-reaching federal statute in American history, since it asserts federal jurisdiction over every drug offense in the United States, no matter how small or local in scope. Once that law is removed from the statute books, Congress should move to abolish the Drug Enforcement Administration and repeal all the other federal drug laws.

There are a number of reasons why Congress should end the federal government's war on drugs. First and foremost, the federal drug laws are constitutionally dubious. As previously noted, the federal government can exercise only the powers that have been delegated to it. The Tenth Amendment reserves all other powers to the states or to the people. However misguided the alcohol prohibitionists turned out to have been, they deserve credit for honoring our constitutional system by seeking a constitutional amendment that would explicitly authorize a national policy on the sale of alcohol. Congress never asked the American people for additional constitutional powers to declare a war on drug consumers. That usurpation of power is something that few politicians or their court intellectuals wish to discuss.

Second, drug prohibition creates high levels of crime. Addicts commit crimes to pay for a habit that would be easily affordable if it were legal. Police sources have estimated that as much as half the property crime in some major cities is committed by drug users. More dramatically, because drugs are illegal, participants in the drug trade cannot go to court to settle disputes, whether between buyer and seller or between rival sellers. When black-market contracts are breached, the result is often some form of violent sanction, which usually leads to retaliation and then open warfare in the streets.

Our capital city, Washington, D.C., became known as the "murder capital" even though it is the most heavily policed city in the United States. Make no mistake about it, the annual carnage that accounts for America's still high murder rates has little to do with the mind-altering effects of a marijuana cigarette or a crack pipe. It is instead one of the grim and bitter consequences of an ideological crusade whose proponents will not yet admit defeat.

Third, since the calamity of September 11, 2001, U.S. intelligence officials have repeatedly warned us of further terrorist attacks. Given that

339

danger, it is a gross misallocation of law enforcement resources to have federal police agents surveilling marijuana clubs in California when they could be helping to discover sleeper cells of terrorists on U.S. territory. The Drug Enforcement Administration has 10,000 agents, intelligence analysts, and support staff members. Their skills would be much better used if those people were redeployed to full-time counterterrorism investigations.

Fourth, drug prohibition is a classic example of throwing money at a problem. The federal government spends some $19 billion to enforce the drug laws every year—all to no avail. For years, drug war bureaucrats have been tailoring their budget requests to the latest news reports. When drug use goes up, taxpayers are told the government needs more money so that it can redouble its efforts against a rising drug scourge. When drug use goes down, taxpayers are told that it would be a big mistake to curtail spending just when progress is being made. Good news or bad, spending levels must be maintained or increased.

Fifth, drug prohibition channels more than $40 billion a year into a criminal underworld that is occupied by an assortment of criminals, corrupt politicians, and, yes, terrorists. Alcohol prohibition drove reputable companies into other industries or out of business altogether, which paved the way for mobsters to make millions in the black market. If drugs were legal, organized crime would stand to lose billions of dollars, and drugs would be sold by legitimate businesses in an open marketplace.

Drug prohibition has created a criminal subculture in our inner cities. The immense profits to be had from a black-market business make drug dealing the most lucrative endeavor for many people, especially those who care least about getting on the wrong side of the law.

Drug dealers become the most visibly successful people in inner-city communities, the ones with money and clothes and cars. Social order is turned upside down when the most successful people in a community are criminals. The drug war makes peace and prosperity virtually impossible in inner cities.

Students of American history will someday ponder the question of how today's elected officials could readily admit to the mistaken policy of alcohol prohibition in the 1920s but recklessly pursue a policy of drug prohibition. Indeed, the only historical lesson that recent presidents and Congresses seem to have drawn from Prohibition is that government should not try to outlaw the sale of booze. One of the broader lessons that they should have learned is this: prohibition laws should be judged according to their real-world effects, not their promised benefits. If the 111th Congress will subject the federal drug laws to that standard, it will recognize that the drug war is not the answer to problems associated with drug use.

Respect State Initiatives

The failures of drug prohibition are becoming obvious to more and more Americans. A particularly tragic consequence of the stepped-up war on drugs is the refusal to allow sick people to use marijuana as medicine. Prohibitionists insist that marijuana is not good medicine, or at least that there are legal alternatives to marijuana that are equally good. Those who believe that individuals should make their own decisions, not have their decisions made for them by Washington bureaucracies, would simply say that that's a decision for patients and their doctors to make. But in fact there is good medical evidence of the therapeutic value of marijuana— despite the difficulty of doing adequate research on an illegal drug. A National Institutes of Health panel concluded that smoking marijuana may help treat a number of conditions, including nausea and pain. It can be particularly effective in improving the appetite of AIDS and cancer patients. The drug could also assist people who fail to respond to traditional remedies.

More than 70 percent of U.S. cancer specialists in one survey said they would prescribe marijuana if it were legal; nearly half said they had urged their patients to break the law to acquire the drug. The British Medical Association reports that nearly 70 percent of its members believe marijuana should be available for therapeutic use. Even President George Bush's Office of National Drug Control Policy criticized the Department of Health and Human Services for closing its special medical marijuana program.

Whatever the actual value of medical marijuana, the relevant fact for federal policymakers is that 12 states have authorized physicians licensed in those states to recommend the use of medical marijuana to seriously ill and terminally ill patients residing in the states, without being subject to civil and criminal penalties.

The Bush administration paid lip service to the importance of federalism, but its actions in Congress and at the state and local levels undermined that principle. Federal police agents and prosecutors continue to raid medical marijuana clubs—especially in California and Arizona. And both of the president's drug policy officials, drug czar John Walters and DEA chief Karen Tandy, used their offices to meddle in state and local politics.

If it is inappropriate for governors and mayors to entangle themselves in foreign policy—and it is—it is also inappropriate for federal officials to entangle themselves in state and local politics. In the 110th Congress, Reps. Barney Frank (D-MA), Dana Rohrabacher (R-CA), and Ron Paul (R-TX) jointly proposed the States' Rights to Medical Marijuana Act, which would have prohibited federal interference with any state that chose to enact a medical marijuana policy. The 111th Congress should enact a similar bill without delay.

One of the benefits of a federal republic is that different policies may be tried in different states. One of the benefits of our Constitution is that it limits the power of the federal government to impose one policy on the several states.

Repeal Mandatory Minimums

The common law in England and America has always relied on judges and juries to decide cases and set punishments. Under our modern system, of course, many crimes are defined by the legislature, and appropriate penalties are defined by statute. However, mandatory minimum sentences and rigid sentencing guidelines shift too much power to legislators and regulators who are not involved in particular cases. They turn judges into clerks and prevent judges from weighing all the facts and circumstances in setting appropriate sentences. In addition, mandatory minimums for nonviolent first-time drug offenders result in sentences grotesquely disproportionate to the gravity of the offenses.

Rather than extend mandatory minimum sentences to further crimes, Congress should repeal mandatory minimums and let judges perform their traditional function of weighing the facts and setting appropriate sentences.

Conclusion

Drug abuse is a problem for those involved in it and for their families and friends. But it is better dealt with as a moral and medical problem than as a criminal problem—"a problem for the surgeon general, not the attorney general," as former Baltimore mayor Kurt Schmoke puts it.

The United States is a federal republic, and Congress should deal with drug prohibition the way it dealt with alcohol prohibition. The Twenty-First Amendment did not actually legalize the sale of alcohol; it simply repealed the federal prohibition and returned to the several states the authority to set alcohol policy. States took the opportunity to design diverse liquor policies that were in tune with the preferences of their citizens. After 1933, three states and hundreds of counties continued to practice prohibition. Other states chose various forms of alcohol legalization.

Congress should repeal the Controlled Substances Act of 1970, shut down the Drug Enforcement Administration, and let the states set their own policies with regard to currently illegal drugs. They would do well to treat marijuana, cocaine, and heroin the way most states now treat alcohol: It should be legal for stores to sell such drugs to adults. Drug sales to children, like alcohol sales to children, should remain illegal. Driving under the influence of drugs should be illegal.

With such a policy, Congress would acknowledge that our current drug policies have failed. It would restore authority to the states, as the Founders envisioned. It would save taxpayers' money. And it would give the states the power to experiment with drug policies and perhaps devise more successful rules.

Repeal of prohibition would take the astronomical profits out of the drug business and destroy the drug kingpins who terrorize parts of our cities. It would reduce crime even more dramatically than did the repeal of alcohol prohibition. Not only would there be less crime; reform would also free federal agents to concentrate on terrorism and espionage and free local police agents to concentrate on robbery, burglary, and violent crime.

The war on drugs has lasted longer than Prohibition, longer than the Vietnam War. But there is no light at the end of this tunnel. Prohibition has failed, again, and should be repealed, again.

Suggested Readings

Balko, Radley. *Overkill: The Rise of Paramilitary Police Raids in America*. Washington: Cato Institute, 2006.

Benjamin, Daniel K., and Roger Leroy Miller. *Undoing Drugs: Beyond Legalization*. New York: Basic Books, 1991.

Boaz, David. "A Drug-Free America—Or a Free America?" *U.C. Davis Law Review* 24 (1991).

————, ed. *The Crisis in Drug Prohibition*. Washington: Cato Institute, 1991.

Buckley, William F., Jr., and others. "The War on Drugs Is Lost." *National Review,* February 12, 1996.

Luna, Erik. "The Misguided Guidelines: A Critique of Federal Sentencing." Cato Institute Policy Analysis no. 458, November 1, 2002.

Lynch, Timothy, ed. *After Prohibition: An Adult Approach to Drug Policies in the 21st Century*. Washington: Cato Institute, 2000.

Masters, Bill. *Drug War Addiction*. St. Louis: Accurate Press, 2002.

McNamara, Joseph. "The Defensive Front Line." *Regulation*, Winter 2001.

Nadelmann, Ethan A. "Legalize It: Why It's Time to Just Say No to Prohibition." *Foreign Policy*, September–October 2007.

Ostrowski, James. "The Moral and Practical Case for Drug Legalization." *Hofstra Law Review* 18 (1990).

Pilon, Roger. "The Medical Marihuana Referendum Movement in America: Federalism Implications." Testimony before the House Crime Subcommittee, October 1, 1997.

—Prepared by David Boaz and Timothy Lynch

34. Property Rights and the Constitution

Congress should

- enact legislation, to guide federal agencies and to provide notice by the courts, that outlines the constitutional rights of property owners under the Fifth Amendment's Takings Clause;
- follow the traditional common law in defining "private property," "public use," and "just compensation";
- treat property taken through regulation the same as property taken through physical seizure; and
- provide a single forum in which property owners may seek injunctive relief and just compensation promptly.

America's Founders understood clearly that private property is the foundation not only of prosperity but of freedom itself. Thus, through the common law, state law, and the Constitution they protected property rights—the rights of people to freely acquire, use, and dispose of property. With the growth of modern government, however, those rights have been seriously compromised. Unfortunately, the Supreme Court has yet to develop a principled, much less comprehensive, theory for remedying those violations. That failure has led to the birth of the property rights movement in state after state. It is time now for Congress to step in—to correct its own violations and to set out a standard that courts might notice as they adjudicate complaints about state violations.

The Constitution protects property rights mainly through the Fifth Amendment's Takings or Just Compensation Clause: "nor shall private property be taken for public use without just compensation." There are two basic ways government can take property: (1) outright, by condemning the property and taking the title; and (2) through regulations that take uses, leaving the title with the owner—so-called regulatory takings. In the first case, the title is all-too-often taken not for a public use but for a private use; and rarely is the compensation received by the owner just. In the second case, the owner is often not compensated at all for his losses, and when he is the compensation is again inadequate.

Over the past two decades, the Supreme Court started chipping away at the problem of uncompensated regulatory takings, requiring compensation in some cases—even if its decisions were largely ad hoc, leaving most owners to bear the losses themselves. Thus, owners today can get compensation when title is actually taken, as just noted; when their property is physically invaded by government order, either permanently or temporarily; when regulation for other than health or safety reasons takes all or nearly all of the value of the property; and when government attaches conditions to permits that are unreasonable, disproportionate, or unrelated to the purpose behind the permit requirement. But despite those modest advances, toward the end of its 2004 term the Court decided three property rights cases in which the owners had legitimate complaints, and in all three the owners lost. One of those cases was *Kelo v. City of New London*, where the city condemned Susette Kelo's property only to transfer it to another private party that the city believed could make better use of it. In so doing, the Court simply brushed aside the "public use" restraint on the power of government to take private property. The upshot, however, was a public outcry across the nation and the introduction of reforms in over 40 states. But those reforms vary substantially. And nearly all leave unaddressed the far more common problem of regulatory takings.

At bottom, then, the Court has yet to develop a comprehensive theory of property rights, much less a comprehensive solution to the problem of government takings. For that, Congress (or the Court) is going to have to turn to first principles, much as the old common-law judges did. The place to begin, then, is not with the public law of the Constitution but with the private law of property.

Property: The Foundation of All Rights

It is no accident that a nation conceived in liberty and dedicated to justice for all protects property rights. Property is the foundation of every right we have, including the right to be free. Every legal claim, after all, is a claim to something—either a defensive claim to keep what one is holding or an offensive claim to something someone else is holding. John Locke, the philosophical father of the American Revolution and the inspiration for Thomas Jefferson when he drafted the Declaration of Independence, stated the issue simply: "Lives, Liberties, and Estates, which I call by the general Name, *Property*." And James Madison, the principal author of the Constitution, echoed those thoughts when he wrote that "as a man is said to have a right to his property, he may be equally said to have a property in his rights."

Much moral confusion would be avoided if we understood that all of our rights—all of the things to which we are "entitled"—can be reduced to property. That would enable us to separate genuine rights—things to which we hold title—from specious "rights"—things to which other people hold title, which we may want. It was the genius of the old common law, grounded in reason, that it grasped that point. And the common-law judges understood a pair of corollaries as well: that property, broadly conceived, separates one individual from another, and that individuals are independent or free to the extent that they have sole or exclusive dominion over what they hold. Indeed, Americans go to work every day to acquire property just so they can be independent.

Legal Protection for Property Rights

It would be to no avail, however, if property, once acquired, could not be used and enjoyed—if rights of acquisition, enjoyment, and disposal were not legally protected. Recognizing that, common-law judges, charged over the years with settling disputes between neighbors, have drawn upon principles of reason and efficiency, and upon custom as well, to craft a law of property that respects, by and large, the equal rights of all.

In a nutshell, the basic rights they have recognized, beyond the rights of acquisition and disposal, are the right of sole dominion—variously described as a right to exclude others, a right against trespass, or a right of quiet enjoyment, which all can exercise equally, at the same time and in the same respect; and the right of active use—at least to the point where such use violates the rights of others to quiet enjoyment. Just where that point is, of course, is often fact dependent—and is the business of courts to decide. But the point to notice, in the modern context, is that the presumption of the common law is on the side of free use. At common law, that is, people are not required to obtain a permit before they can use their property—no more than people today are required to obtain a permit before they can speak freely. Rather, the burden is upon those who object to a given use to show how it violates a right of theirs. That amounts to having to show that their neighbor's use takes something they own free and clear. If they fail, the use may continue.

Thus, the common law limits the right of free use only when a use encroaches on the property rights of others, as in the classic law of nuisance or risk. The implications of that limit, however, should not go unnoticed, especially in the context of such modern concerns as environmental protection. Indeed, it is so far from the case that property rights are opposed to environmental protection—a common belief today—as to be just the opposite: the right against environmental degradation is a *property* right. Under common law, properly applied, people cannot use their property in ways that damage their neighbors' property—defined, again, as taking things those neighbors hold free and clear. Properly conceived and applied, then, property rights are self-limiting: they constitute a judicially crafted and enforced regulatory scheme in which rights of active use end when they encroach on the property rights of others.

The Police Power and the Power of Eminent Domain

But if the common law of property defines and protects private rights—the rights of owners with respect to each other—it also serves as a guide for the proper scope and limits of public law—defining the rights of owners and the public with respect to each other. For public law, at least at the federal level, flows from the Constitution; and the Constitution flows from the principles articulated in the Declaration—which reflect, largely, the common law. The justification of public law begins, then, with our rights, as the Declaration makes clear. Government then follows, not to give us rights through positive law, but to recognize and secure the rights we already have. Thus, to be legitimate, government's powers must be derived from and consistent with those rights.

The two public powers that are at issue in the property rights debate are the police power—the power of government to secure rights—and the power of eminent domain—the power to take property for public use upon payment of just compensation, as set forth, by implication, in the Fifth Amendment's Takings Clause.

The police power—the fundamental power of government—is derived from what Locke called the Executive Power, the power each of us has in the state of nature to secure his rights. Thus, as such, it is legitimate, since it is nothing more than a power we already have, by right, which we gave to government, when we constituted ourselves as a nation, to exercise on our behalf. Its exercise is legitimate, however, only insofar as it is used to secure rights, and only insofar as its use respects the rights of others. Thus, while our rights give rise to the police power, they also limit it. We cannot use the police power for non-police-power purposes. It is a power to secure rights, through restraints or sanctions, not some general power to provide public goods.

A complication arises with respect to the federal government, however, for it is not a government of general powers. Thus, there is no general federal police power, despite modern developments to the contrary (which essentially ignore the principle). Rather, the Constitution establishes a government of delegated, enumerated, and thus limited powers, leaving most powers, including the police power, with the states or the people, as the Tenth Amendment makes clear. (See Chapter 3 for greater detail on this point.) If we are to abide by constitutional principle, then we have to recognize that whatever power the federal government has to secure rights is limited to federal territory, by implication, or is incidental to the exercise of one of the federal government's enumerated powers.

But if the police power is thus limited to securing rights, and the federal government's police power is far more restricted, then any effort to provide public goods must be accomplished under some other power—under some enumerated power, in the case of the federal government. Yet any such effort will be constrained by the Takings Clause, which requires that any provision of public goods that entails taking private property—whether in whole or in part is irrelevant—must be accompanied by just compensation for the owner of the property. Otherwise, the costs of the benefit to the public would fall entirely on the owner. Not to put too fine a point on it, that would amount to plain theft. Indeed, it was to prohibit that kind of thing that the Founders wrote the Takings Clause in the first place.

Thus, the power of eminent domain—which is not enumerated in the Constitution but is implicit in the Takings Clause—is an instrumental power: it is a means through which government, acting under some other power, pursues other ends—building roads, for example, or saving wildlife. Moreover, unlike the police power, the eminent domain power is not inherently legitimate: indeed, in a state of nature, prior to the creation of government, none of us would have a right to condemn a neighbor's property, however worthy our purpose, however much we compensated him. Thus, it is not for nothing that eminent domain was known in the 17th and 18th centuries as "the despotic power." It exists from practical considerations alone—to enable public projects to go forward without being held hostage to holdouts seeking to exploit the situation by extracting far more than just compensation. As for its justification, the best that can be said for eminent domain is this: the power was ratified by those who were in the original position; and it is "Pareto superior," as economists say, meaning that at least one party, the public, is made better off by its use, as evidenced by its willingness to pay, while no one is made worse off, assuming the owner does indeed receive just compensation.

When Compensation Is Required

We come then to the basic question: When does government have to compensate owners for the losses they suffer when regulations reduce the value of their property? The answers are as follows.

First, when government acts to secure rights—when it stops someone from polluting, for example, or from excessively endangering others—it is acting under its police power and no compensation is due the owner, whatever his financial losses, because the use prohibited or "taken" was wrong to begin with. Since there is no right to pollute, we do not have to pay polluters not to pollute. Thus, the question is not whether value was taken by a regulation but whether a *right* was taken. Proper uses of the police power take no rights. To the contrary, they protect rights.

Second, when government acts not to secure rights but to provide the public with some good—wildlife habitat, for example, or a viewshed, or historic preservation—and in doing so prohibits or "takes" some otherwise *legitimate* use, then it is acting, in part, under the eminent domain power and it does have to compensate the owner for any financial losses he may suffer. The principle here is quite simple: the public has to pay for the goods it wants, just like any private person would have to. Bad enough that the public can take what it wants by condemnation; at least it should pay rather than ask the owner to bear the full cost of its appetite. It is here, of course, that modern regulatory takings abuses are most common as governments at all levels try to provide the public with all manner of amenities, especially environmental amenities, "off budget." As noted earlier, there is an old-fashioned word for that practice: it is "theft," and no amount of rationalization about "good reasons" will change that. Even thieves, after all, have "good reasons" for what they do.

Finally, when government acts to provide the public with some good and that act results in financial loss to an owner but takes no right of the owner, no compensation is due because nothing the owner holds free and clear is taken. If the government closes a military base, for example, and neighboring property values decline as a result, no compensation is due those owners because the government's action took nothing they owned. They own their property and all the uses that go with it that are consistent with their neighbors' equal rights. They do not own the value in their property.

Some Implications of a Principled Approach

Starting from first principles, then, we can derive principled answers to the regulatory takings question. And we can see in the process, there is no difference in principle between an "ordinary" taking and a regulatory taking, between taking full title and taking only uses—a distinction that government supporters repeatedly urge, claiming that the Takings Clause requires compensation only for "full" takings. If we take the text seriously, as we should, the clause speaks simply of "private property." As the quote earlier from Madison suggests, "property" denotes not just some "underlying estate" but all the estates—all the uses—that can rightly be made of a holding. In fact, in every area of property law except regulatory takings we recognize that property is a "bundle of sticks," any one of which can be bought, sold, rented, bequeathed, what have you. Yet takings law has clung to the idea that only if the entire bundle is taken does government have to pay compensation.

That view enables government to extinguish nearly all uses through regulation—and hence to regulate nearly all value out of property—yet escape the compensation requirement because the all-but-empty title remains with the owner. And it would allow a government to take 90 percent of the value in year one, then come back a year later and take title for a dime on the dollar. Not only is that wrong, it is unconstitutional. It cannot be what the Takings Clause stands for. The principle, rather, is that property is indeed a bundle of sticks: take one of those sticks and you take something that belongs to the owner. The only question then is how much his loss is worth.

Thus, when the Court in 1992 crafted what is in effect a 100 percent rule, whereby owners are entitled to compensation only if regulations restrict uses to a point where all value is lost, it went about the matter backwards. It measured the loss to determine whether there was a taking. As a matter of first principle, the Court should first have determined whether there was a taking, then measured the loss. It should first have asked whether otherwise legitimate uses were prohibited by the regulation. That addresses the principle of the matter. It then remains simply to measure the loss in value and hence the compensation that is due. The place to start, in short, is with the first stick, not the last dollar.

The principled approach requires, of course, that the Court have a basic understanding of the theory of the matter and a basic grasp of how to resolve conflicting claims about use in a way that respects the equal rights of all. That is hardly a daunting task, as the old common-law judges demonstrated. In general, the presumption is on the side of active use, as noted earlier, until some plaintiff demonstrates that such use takes the quiet enjoyment that is his by right—and the defendant's right as well. At that point the burden shifts to the defendant to justify his use: absent some defense like the prior consent of the plaintiff, the defendant may have to cease his use—or, if his activity is worth it, offer to buy an easement or buy out the plaintiff. Thus, a principled approach respects equal rights of quiet enjoyment—and hence environmental integrity. But it also enables active uses to go forward—though not at the expense of private or public rights. Users can be as active as they wish, provided they handle the "externalities" they create in a way that respects the rights of others.

What Congress Should Do

The application of such principles is often fact dependent, as noted earlier, and so is best done by courts. But until the courts develop a more principled and systematic approach to takings, it should fall to Congress to draw at least the broad outlines of the matter, both as a guide for the courts and as a start toward getting its own house in order.

In this last connection, however, the first thing Congress should do is recognize candidly that the problem of regulatory takings begins with regulation. Doubtless the Founders did not think to specify that regulatory takings are takings too, and thus are subject to the Just Compensation Clause, because they did not imagine the modern regulatory state: they did not envision our obsession with regulating every conceivable human activity and our insistence that such activity—residential, business, what have you—take place only after a grant of official permission. In some areas of business today, we have almost reached the point at which it can truly be said that everything that is not permitted is prohibited. That is the opposite, of course, of our founding principle: everything that is not prohibited is permitted—where "permitted" means "freely allowed," not allowed "by permit."

Homeowners; developers; farmers and ranchers; mining and timber companies; and businesses large and small, profit making and not for profit, all have horror stories about regulatory hurdles they confront when they want to do something, particularly with real property. Many of those regulations are legitimate, of course, especially if they are aimed, preemptively, at securing genuine rights. But many more are aimed at providing some citizens with benefits at the expense of other citizens. They take rights from some to benefit others. At the federal level, such transfers are not likely to find authorization under any enumerated power. But even if constitutionally authorized, they need to be undertaken in conformity with the Takings Clause. Some endangered species, to take a prominent modern example, may indeed be worth saving, even if the authority for doing so belongs to states, and even if the impetus comes from a relatively small group of people. We should not expect a few property owners to bear all the costs of that undertaking, however. If the public truly wants the habitat for such species left undisturbed, let it buy that habitat or, failing that, pay the costs to the relevant owners of their leaving their property unused.

In general, then, Congress should review the government's many regulations to determine which are and are not authorized by the Constitution. If not authorized, they should be rescinded, which would end quickly a large body of regulatory takings now in place. But if authorized under some constitutionally enumerated power of Congress, the costs now imposed on owners, for benefits conferred on the public generally, should be placed "on budget." Critics of doing that are often heard to say that if we did go on budget, we couldn't afford all the regulations we want. What they are really saying, of course, is that taxpayers would be unwilling to pay for all the regulations the critics want. Indeed, the great fear of those who oppose taking a principled approach to regulatory takings is that once the public has to pay for the benefits it now receives "free," it will demand fewer of them. It should hardly surprise that when people have to pay for something they demand less of it.

It is sheer pretense, of course, to suppose that such benefits are now free, that they are not already being paid for. Isolated owners are paying for them, not the public. As a matter of simple justice, then, Congress needs to shift the burden to the public that is demanding and enjoying the benefits. Among the virtues of doing so is this: once we have an honest, public accounting, we will be in a better position to determine whether the benefits thus produced are worth the costs. Today, we have no idea about that because all the costs are hidden. When regulatory benefits are thus "free," the demand for them, as we see, is all but infinite.

But in addition to eliminating, reducing, or correcting its own regulatory takings—in addition to getting its own house in order—Congress needs to enact general legislation on the subject of takings that might help to restore respect for property rights and reorient the nation toward its own first principles. To that end, Congress should do the following.

Congress Should Enact Legislation That Specifies the Constitutional Rights of Property Owners under the Fifth Amendment's Takings Clause

As already noted, legislation of the kind here recommended would be unnecessary if the courts were doing their job correctly and reading the Takings Clause properly. Because they are not, it falls to Congress to step in. Still, there is a certain anomaly in asking Congress to do the job. Under our system, after all, the political branches and the states represent and pursue the interests of the people within the constraints established by the Constitution, and it falls to the courts, and the Supreme Court in particular, to ensure that those constraints are respected. To do that, the Court interprets and applies the Constitution as it decides cases brought before it—cases often brought against the political branches or a state, as here, where an owner seeks either to enjoin a government action on the ground that it violates his rights or to obtain compensation under the Takings Clause, or both. Thus, it is somewhat anomalous to ask or expect Congress to right wrongs that Congress itself may be perpetrating. After all, is not Congress, in its effort to carry out the public's will, simply doing its job?

The answer, of course, is yes, Congress is doing its job, and thus this call for reform—against the "natural" inclination of Congress, if you will—is somewhat anomalous. But that is not the whole answer. For members of Congress take an oath to uphold the Constitution, which requires them to exercise independent judgment about the meaning of its terms. In doing that, they need to recognize that we do not live in anything like a pure democracy. The Constitution sets powerful and far-reaching restraints on the powers of all three branches of the federal government and, since ratification of the Civil War Amendments, on the states as well. Thus, the simple-minded majoritarian view of our system—whereby Congress simply enacts whatever some transient majority of the population wants enacted, leaving it to the Court to determine the constitutionality of the act—must be resisted as a matter of the oath of office. The oath is taken on behalf of the people, to be sure, but through and in conformity with the Constitution. When the Court fails to secure the liberties of the people, there is nothing in the Constitution to prevent Congress from exercising the responsibility entailed by the oath of office. In fact, that oath requires Congress to step into the breach.

There is no guarantee, of course, that Congress will do a better job of interpreting the Constitution than the Court. In fact, given that Congress is an "interested" party, it could very well do a worse job, which is why the Founders placed "the judicial Power"—entailing, presumably, the power ultimately to say what the law is—with the Court. But that is no reason for Congress to ignore its responsibility to make its judgment known, especially when the Court is clearly wrong, as it is here. Although nonpolitical in principle, the Court does not operate in a political vacuum—as it demonstrated in 1937, unfortunately, after Franklin Roosevelt's notorious Court-packing threat. If the Court can be persuaded to undo the centerpiece of the Constitution, the doctrine of enumerated powers, one imagines it can be persuaded to restore property rights to their proper constitutional status.

Thus, in addition to rescinding or correcting legislation that now results in uncompensated regulatory takings, and enacting no such legislation in the future, Congress should also enact a more general statute that specifies the constitutional rights of property owners under the Fifth Amendment's Takings Clause, drawing upon common-law principles to do so. That means that Congress should do the following.

Congress Should Follow the Traditional Common Law in Defining "Private Property," "Public Use," and "Just Compensation"

As we saw earlier, property rights in America are not simply a matter of the Fifth Amendment—of positive law. Indeed, during the more than two years between the time the Constitution was ratified and took effect and the time the Bill of Rights was ratified, property rights were protected not only against private but against public invasion as well. That protection stemmed, therefore, not from any explicit constitutional guarantee but from the common law. Thus, the Takings Clause was meant simply to make explicit, against the new federal government, the guarantees that were already recognized under the common law. (Those guarantees were implicit in the new Constitution, of course, through the doctrine of enumerated powers, for no uncompensated takings were therein authorized.) With the ratification of the Civil War Amendments—and the Fourteenth Amendment's Privileges or Immunities Clause in particular—the common-law guarantees against the states were constitutionalized as well. Thus, because the Takings Clause takes its inspiration and meaning from the common law of property, it is there that we must look to understand its terms.

355

Those terms begin with "private property": "nor shall private property be taken for public use without just compensation." As every first-year law student learns, "private property" means far more than a piece of real estate. Were that not the case, property law would be an impoverished subject indeed. Instead, the common law reveals the many significations of the concept "property" and the rich variety of arrangements that human imagination and enterprise have made of the basic idea of private ownership. As outlined earlier, however, those arrangements all come down to three basic ideas—acquisition, exclusive use, and disposal—the three basic property rights, from which more specifically described rights may be derived.

With regard to regulatory takings, however, the crucial thing to notice is that, absent contractual arrangements to the contrary, the right to acquire and hold property entails the right to use and dispose of it as well. As Madison said, people have "a property" in their rights. If the right to property did not entail the right of use, it would be an empty promise. People acquire property, after all, only because doing so enables them to use it, which is what gives it its value. Indeed, the fundamental complaint about uncompensated regulatory takings is that, by thus eliminating the uses from property, government makes the title itself meaningless, which is why it is worthless. Who would buy "property" that cannot be used?

The very concept of "property," therefore, entails all the legitimate uses that go with it, giving it value. And the uses that are legitimate are those that can be exercised consistent with the rights of others, private and public alike, as defined by the traditional common law. As outlined above, however, the rights of others that limit the rights of an owner are often fact dependent. Thus, legislation can state only the principle of the matter, not its application in particular contexts. Still, the broad outlines should be made clear in any congressional enactment: the term "private property" includes all the uses that can be made of property consistent with the common-law rights of others, and those uses can be restricted without compensating the owner only to secure such rights, not to secure public goods or benefits.

The "public use" requirement also needs to be tightened, not least because it is a source of private-public collusion against private rights. As noted earlier, eminent domain was known in the 17th and 18th centuries as "the despotic power" because no private person would have the power to condemn, even if he had a worthy reason and did pay just compensation. Yet we know that public agencies often do condemn private property for such private uses as auto plant construction, casino parking lots, and tax-enhancing commercial development. Those are rank abuses of the public use principle: they amount to implicit grants of private eminent domain—and invitations to public graft and corruption. Every private use has spill-over benefits for the public, of course. But if that were the standard for defining "public use," then every time someone wanted to expand his business over his neighbor's property, he could go to the relevant public agency and ask that the neighbor's property be condemned since the expansion would arguably benefit the public through increased jobs, business, taxes, what have you. He would no longer need to bargain with his neighbor but could simply ask—even "pay," as has happened—the agency to condemn the property "for the public good."

Because it is a despotic power, even when the compensation paid actually is just, eminent domain should be used sparingly and only for a truly *public* use. That means for a use that is broadly enjoyed by the public, rather than by some narrow part of the public, and in the case of the federal government, it means for a constitutionally authorized use. In defining "public use," however, there is no bright line. Nevertheless, certain general considerations can help. To begin, provided the compensation is just, no problem arises when title is transferred to the public—to build a military base, for example, or a public highway. Nor is there a genuine problem when, to avoid the holdout situation that might arise with, for example, laying cable or telephone lines, title is transferred to a *private* party—provided the subsequent use is open to all on a nondiscriminatory basis, often to be regulated in the public interest. Were eminent domain available only when the public kept title, the public would be deprived of the relative efficiencies of private ownership in cases like those.

Beyond such cases, however, the "public use" restriction on employing eminent domain looms ever larger. Condemnation for "blight reduction," for example, sweeps too broadly: private uses that constitute nuisances can be enjoined under the police power, after all, without transferring title. And a close cousin, the "economic development" rationale for condemnation, as in the *Kelo* case, should never be allowed, whatever the "public *benefit*" of such transfers. Thus, condemnation for building a sports stadium may be authorized under some state's constitution, but if the stadium is then owned and managed by and for the benefit of private parties, the "public use" standard has been abused, whatever the spillover "public" benefits may be. Here, title settles the matter. Yet even if the public keeps the title, but the effect of the transfer is to benefit a small portion of the public rather than the public generally, the condemnation is also likely to be illegitimate because it is not truly for a "public" use. If some small group wants the benefits provided by the condemnation, private markets provide ample opportunities for obtaining them—the right way. To avoid abuse and the potential for corruption, then, Congress needs to define "public use" rigorously, with reference to titles, use, and control.

Finally, Congress should define "just compensation" with reference to its function: it is a remedy for the wrong of taking someone's property. That the Constitution implicitly authorizes that wrong does not change the character of the act, of course. As noted ealier, eminent domain is "justified" for practical reasons, and because "we" authorized it originally, although none of us today, of course, was there to do so. Given the character of the act, then, the least the public can do is make the victim whole. That too will be a fact-dependent determination. But Congress should at least make it clear that "just" compensation means compensation for all losses that arise from the taking, plus an added measure to acknowledge the fact that the losses arise not by mere accident, as with a tort, but from a deliberate decision by the public to force the owner to give up his property.

It should be noted, however, that not every regulatory taking will require compensation for an owner. Minimal losses, for example, may be difficult to prove and not worth the effort. Moreover, some regulatory restrictions may actually enhance the value of property or of particular pieces of property—say, if an entire neighborhood is declared "historic." Finally, that portion of "just compensation" that concerns market value should reflect value before, and with no anticipation of, regulatory restrictions. In determining compensation, government should not benefit from reductions in value its regulations bring about. Given the modern penchant for regulation, that may not always be easy. But in general, given the nature of condemnation as a forced taking, any doubt should be resolved to the benefit of the owner forced to give up his property.

If Congress enacts general legislation that outlines the constitutional rights of property owners by following the common law in defining the terms of the Takings Clause, it will abolish, in effect, any real distinction between full and partial takings. Nevertheless, Congress should be explicit about what it is doing. Any legislation it enacts should do the following.

Congress Should Treat Property Taken through Regulation the Same As Property Taken through Physical Seizure

The importance of enacting a unified and uniform takings law cannot be overstated. Today, we have one law for "full takings," "physical seizures," "condemnations"—call them what you will—and another for "partial takings," "regulatory seizures," or "condemnations of uses." Yet there is overlap, too: thus, as noted above, the Court has said that if regulations take all uses, compensation is due—perhaps because eliminating all uses comes to the same thing, in effect, as a "physical seizure," whereas eliminating most uses seems not to come to the same thing.

That appearance is deceptive, of course. In fact, the truth is much simpler—but only if we go about discovering it from first principles. If we start with an owner and his property, then define "property," as done earlier, as including all legitimate uses, it follows that any action by government that takes any property is, by definition, a taking—requiring compensation for any financial losses the owner may suffer as a result. The issue is really no more complicated than that. There is no need to distinguish "full" from "partial" takings: *every* condemnation, whether "full" or "partial," is a taking. Indeed, the use taken is taken "in full." Imagine that the property were converted to dollars—100 dollars, say. Would we say that if the government took all 100 dollars there was a taking, but if it took only 50 of the 100 dollars there was not a taking? Of course not. Yet that is what we say under the Court's modern takings doctrine because, as one justice recently put it, "takings law is full of these 'all-or-nothing' situations."

That confusion must end. Through legislation specifying the rights of property owners, Congress needs to make it clear that compensation is required whenever government eliminates common-law property rights and an owner suffers a financial loss as a result—whether the elimination results from regulation or from outright condemnation.

The promise of the common law and the Constitution will be realized, however, only through procedures that enable aggrieved parties to press their complaints. Some of the greatest abuses today are taking place because owners are frustrated at every turn in their efforts to reach the merits of their claims. Accordingly, Congress should do the following.

Congress Should Provide a Single Forum in Which Property Owners May Seek Injunctive Relief and Just Compensation Promptly

In its 1998 term, the Supreme Court decided a takings case that began 17 years earlier, in 1981, when owners applied to a local planning commission for permission to develop their land. After having submitted numerous proposals, all rejected, yet each satisfying the commission's recommendations following a previously rejected proposal, the owners finally sued, at which point they faced the hurdles the courts put before them. Most owners, of course, cannot afford to go through such a long and expensive process, at the end of which the odds are still against them. But that process today confronts property owners across the nation as they seek to enjoy and then to vindicate their rights. If it were speech or voting or any number of other rights, the path to vindication would be smooth by comparison. But property rights today have been relegated to a kind of second-class status.

The first problem, as noted earlier, is the modern permitting regime. We would not stand for speech or religion or most other rights to be enjoyed only by permit. Yet that is what we do today with property rights, which places enormous, often arbitrary, power in the hands of federal, state, and local "planners." Driven by political goals and considerations—notwithstanding their pretense to "smart growth"—planning commissions open the application forum not only to those whose *rights* might be at stake but to those with *interests* in the matter. Thus is the common-law distinction between rights and interests blurred and eventually lost. Thus is the matter transformed from one of protecting rights to one of deciding whose "interests" should prevail. Thus are property rights effectively politicized. And that is the end of the matter for most owners because that is as far as they can afford to take it.

When an owner does take it further, however, he finds the courts are often no more inclined to hear his complaint than was the planning commission. Federal courts routinely abstain from hearing federal claims brought against state and local governments, requiring owners to litigate their claims in state courts before they can even set foot in a federal court on their federal claims. Moreover, the Supreme Court has held that an owner's claim is not ripe for adjudication unless (a) he obtains a final, definitive agency decision regarding the application of the regulation in question, and (b) he exhausts all available state compensation remedies. Needless to say, planners, disinclined to approve applications to begin with, treat those standards as invitations to stall until the "problem" goes away. Then, if an owner does spend years and extraordinary expense going through those hoops and is able to get into federal court, he faces the *res judicata* restriction of the federal Full Faith and Credit Act: the court will say that the case has already been adjudicated by the state courts. Finally, if the claim is against the federal government, the owner faces the so-called Tucker Act Shuffle: he cannot get injunctive relief and compensation from the same court but must instead go to a federal district court for an injunction and to the Federal Court of Claims for compensation.

The 105th and 106th Congresses tried to address those procedural hurdles through several measures, none of which passed both houses. They must be revived and enacted if the unconscionable way we treat owners, trying simply to vindicate their constitutional rights, is to be brought to an end. This is not a matter of "intruding" on state and local governments. Under the Fourteenth Amendment, properly understood and applied, those governments have no more right to violate the constitutional rights of citizens than the federal government has to intrude on the legitimate powers of state and local governments. Federalism is not a shield for local tyranny. It is a brake on tyranny, whatever its source.

Conclusion

The Founders would be appalled to see what we did to property rights over the course of the 20th century. One would never know that their status, in the Bill of Rights, was equal to that of any other right. The time has come to restore respect for these most basic of rights, the foundation of all of our rights. Indeed, despotic governments have long understood that if you control property, you control the media, the churches, the political process itself. We are not at that point yet. But if regulations that provide the public with benefits continue to grow, unchecked by the need to compensate those from whom they take, we will gradually slide to that point—and in the process will pay an increasingly heavy price for the uncertainty and inefficiency we create. The most important price, however, will be to our system of law and justice. Owners are asking simply that their government obey the law—the common law and the law of the Constitution. In reducing their request to its essence, they are saying simply this: Stop stealing our property; if you must take it, do it the right way—pay for it. That hardly seems too much to ask.

Suggested Readings

Bethell, Tom. *The Noblest Triumph: Property and Prosperity through the Ages.* New York: St. Martin's, 1998.

Coyle, Dennis J. *Property Rights and the Constitution: Shaping Society through Land Use Regulation.* Albany: State University of New York Press, 1993.

DeLong, James V. *Property Matters: How Property Rights Are under Assault—And Why You Should Care.* New York: Free Press, 1997.

Eagle, Steven J. *Regulatory Takings*. Charlottesville, VA: Michie Law Publishers, 1996.

Ely, James W. Jr. *The Guardian of Every Other Right: A Constitutional History of Property Rights*. 2d ed. New York: Oxford University Press, 1998.

———. "Poor Relation Once More: The Supreme Court and the Vanishing Rights of Property Owners." *2004–2005 Cato Supreme Court Review*, 2005.

Epstein, Richard A. *Takings: Private Property and the Power of Eminent Domain*. Cambridge, MA: Harvard University Press, 1985.

———. *Supreme Neglect: How to Revive Constitutional Protection for Private Property*. New York: Oxford University Press, 2008.

Farah, Joseph, and Richard Pombo. *This Land Is Our Land: How to End the War on Private Property*. New York: St. Martin's, 1996.

Locke, John. "Second Treatise of Government." In *Two Treatises of Government*, edited by Peter Laslett. New York: Mentor, 1965.

Madison, James. "Property." In *National Gazette*, March 29, 1792. Reprinted in *The Papers of James Madison*, vol. 14, *6 April 1791–16 March 1793*, edited by Robert A. Rutland and others. Charlottesville: University of Virginia Press, 1983.

Pilon, Roger. "Are Property Rights Opposed to Environmental Protection?" In *The Moral High Ground: An Anthology of Speeches from the First Annual New York State Conference on Private Property Rights*, edited by Carol W. LaGrasse. Stony Creek, NY: Property Rights Foundation of America, 1995.

———. "Property Rights, Takings, and a Free Society." *Harvard Journal of Law and Public Policy* 6 (1983).

Pipes, Richard. *Property and Freedom: How through the Centuries Private Ownership Has Promoted Liberty and the Rule of Law*. New York: Alfred A. Knopf, 1999.

Sandefur, Timothy. *Cornerstone of Liberty: Property Rights in Twentieth Century America*. Washington: Cato Institute, 2006.

Siegan, Bernard H. *Property and Freedom: The Constitution, the Courts, and Land-Use Regulation*. New Brunswick, NJ: Transaction Press, 1997.

Siegan, Bernard H., ed. *Planning without Prices: The Takings Clause as It Relates to Land Use Regulation without Just Compensation*. Lexington, MA: Lexington Books, 1977.

—Prepared by Roger Pilon

REGULATION

35. The Limits of Monetary Policy

> **Congress should**
> - amend the Federal Reserve Act to make *long-run* price stability the primary goal of monetary policy;
> - recognize that the Federal Reserve cannot fine-tune the real economy but can achieve long-run price stability by its control over the monetary base (currency held by the public plus bank reserves);
> - hold the Fed accountable for safeguarding the purchasing power of the dollar;
> - abolish the Exchange Stabilization Fund—the Fed's role is to stabilize the *domestic* price level, not to peg the foreign exchange value of the dollar; and
> - repeal the tax on privately issued bank notes and allow digital currency and other substitutes for Federal Reserve notes to emerge, so that free-market forces can help shape the future of monetary institutions.

Today, the United States is on a pure fiat money standard with a discretionary central bank: the dollar has no defined value in terms of a commodity or basket of commodities; there is no convertibility principle operating; and there is no monetary rule to ensure long-run price stability. Consequently, the price level has drifted upward without a solid anchor (Figure 35.1).

James Madison, the chief architect of the Constitution, recognized that convertibility is a more certain way to protect the value of money than reliance on a central bank—even if that central bank were tied to a quantity rule. In 1820, he wrote:

> It cannot be doubted that a paper currency, rigidly limited in its quantity to purposes absolutely necessary, may be made equal and even superior

Figure 35.1
U.S. Price Level in a Pure Fiat Money Regime

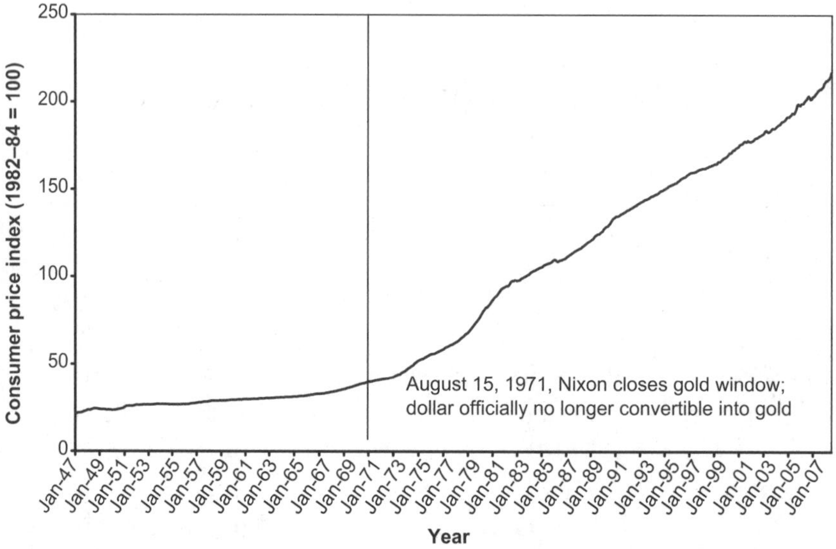

SOURCE: Bureau of Labor Statistics.

in value to specie. But experience does not favor a reliance on such experiments. Whenever the paper has not been convertible into specie, and its quantity has depended on the policy of Government, a depreciation has been produced by an undue increase, or an apprehension of it.

It is ironic that today most policymakers consider the gold standard a relic and any shift away from a pure fiat money regime "an experiment." But policymakers should take Madison's concern about irredeemable paper money seriously and think about monetary rules that could help anchor the future purchasing power of the dollar.

The challenge for Congress is to set the framework for stable money and to recognize that sound money is a prerequisite for financial stability and the efficient operation of a free-market price system. Policymakers should be aware of the limits of monetary policy: the Fed may be able to create money out of thin air but it cannot, by so doing, create goods and services or full employment. Indeed, the opposite is true: inflation distorts price and profit signals and increases uncertainty. As such, there is more likely to be a negative rather than a positive relation between inflation and economic growth (Figure 35.2).

Figure 35.2
Inflation Harms Growth

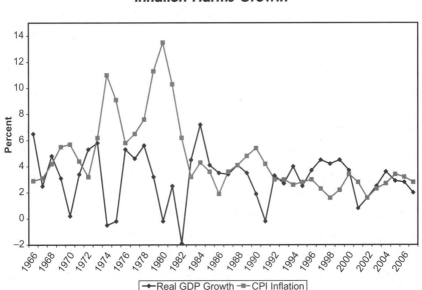

SOURCES: U.S. Department of Commerce: Bureau of Economic Analysis; U.S. Department of Labor: Bureau of Labor Statistics.

Ending the Fed's Dual Mandate

History has shown that monetary stability—money growth consistent with a stable and predictable value of money—is an important determinant of economic stability. Safeguarding the long-run purchasing power of money is also essential for the future of private property and a free society. In the United States, persistent inflation has eroded the value of money and distorted relative prices, making production and investment decisions more uncertain.

In the early 1970s, wage-price controls were imposed—ostensibly aimed at reducing inflationary expectations. Those controls only repressed inflation as money growth accelerated. When the controls were lifted, the excess supply of money became evident. Meanwhile, the controls reduced economic freedom and increased government discretion, thus undermining the rule of law.

Today, we face a growing budget deficit, trillions of dollars of unfunded liabilities, and a mounting federal debt in the wake of the subprime crisis. The danger is that global investors will downgrade U.S. sovereign debt, and that as foreigners buy less of it, the Fed will buy more. Inflation will

367

then reduce the real burden of the debt but only at the cost of slower economic growth and a loss of credibility. We will not become another Zimbabwe, but there will be an increased threat of wage-price controls and a loss of economic freedom. That is why it is essential that the Fed pursue a policy of long-run price stability.

Current law specifies no single objective for monetary policy, which leads to uncertainty. William Poole, former president of the Federal Reserve Bank of St. Louis and a proponent of long-run price stability (that is, zero expected inflation), has pointed to the market disruption caused by the lack of a clear monetary rule to guide Fed policy:

> The fact that markets so often respond to comments and speeches by Fed officials indicates that the markets today are not evaluating monetary policy in the context of a well-articulated and well-understood monetary rule. The problem is a deep and difficult one.

Congress should face that problem by amending Section 2A of the Federal Reserve Act, making long-run price stability the primary aim of monetary policy. If the Fed were held accountable for achieving zero expected inflation, the inflation component of nominal interest rates would vanish and rates would fall to their "natural" level. Increased certainty about the future value of the dollar would also have a beneficial effect on investment and would attract foreign capital, thus promoting output and employment. There would be no need to list "maximum employment" and "moderate long-term interest rates" as separate goals of monetary policy.

The amended Section 2A would read: "The Board of Governors of the Federal Reserve System and the Federal Open Market Committee shall maintain long-run growth of the monetary and credit aggregates so as to maintain long-run price stability." That amendment would not preclude the Fed from acting as a lender of last resort in a liquidity crisis, but it would require a reversion to noninflationary growth of money and credit—and thus ground the public's expectations with regard to the future value of the dollar.

Ending the Fed's dual mandate to achieve both full employment and price stability would recognize the limits of monetary policy and help depoliticize the policymaking process. Rather than having to weigh the short-run tradeoffs between the two goals (lower unemployment at the cost of higher inflation), the Fed could focus on what it can achieve— long-run price stability. The exact monetary rule the Fed adopted to achieve that objective is less important than making policymakers accountable for sound money.

The Price Stability Act of 2008, introduced by Rep. Paul Ryan (R-WI), would be a good template for legislation introduced in the 111th Congress. It would require the Fed to "establish an explicit numerical definition of the term 'price stability'; and maintain a monetary policy that effectively promotes long-term price stability." But the proposed legislation has no teeth: there is nothing in it to penalize the Fed for failing to achieve the stated goal.

Making the Fed Accountable

The Fed's function is not to set interest rates or to target the rate of unemployment or real growth. The Fed cannot control relative prices, employment, or output; it can only directly control the monetary base and thereby affect money growth, nominal income, and the average level of money prices. In the very short run, the Fed can affect output and employment, as well as real interest rates, but it cannot do so in the long run.

Targeting the federal funds rate to achieve the Fed's dual mandate of full employment and price stability assumes that the Fed can correctly forecast the state of the economy. But Fed forecasts are far from perfect, and if the Fed holds the target rate below the market rate by expanding the monetary base, inflation will increase and the Fed will have to put on the brakes.

The self-regulating nature of the classical gold standard is a far cry from today's activist monetary policy. In the choice of monetary rules, the Fed should aim at those that minimize the need for forecasting, such as Carnegie-Mellon economist Bennett McCallum's nominal final demand rule or the variant of that rule proposed by William Niskanen in this *Handbook* (Chapter 36). An even simpler rule is to freeze the monetary base and let private firms supply currency in response to market demand, as proposed by Milton Friedman.

The Fed cannot attain more than one policy target, and it has only one policy instrument. The surest target is long-run price stability, and the only instrument the Fed has direct control over is the monetary base. With a McCallum-type feedback rule, the Fed would adjust the growth of the monetary base to keep nominal gross domestic product (or domestic final sales) on a smooth noninflationary growth path. With an inflation target, the Fed would adjust the monetary base so that the growth rate of the price level was approximately zero in the long run. There would be some rises and falls in the price level due to supply-side shocks, either positive or negative, but expected inflation would remain close to zero (in the 0–2 percent range) over time.

Congress need not dictate the exact rule for the Fed to follow in its pursuit of long-run price stability, but Congress should hold the Fed accountable for achieving that goal—and not require the Fed to respond to supply shocks that would lead to one-time increases or decreases in the price level.

The public's trust and confidence in the future purchasing power of the dollar can be permanently increased by a legal mandate directing the Fed to adopt a monetary rule to achieve long-run price stability. According to Poole:

> The logic, and the evidence, both suggest that the appropriate goal for monetary policy should be price stability, that is, a long-run inflation rate of approximately zero. . . . A central bank's single most important job is preserving the value of the nation's money. Monetary policy has succeeded if the public can reasonably trust that a dollar will buy tomorrow what it will buy today. . . . I am confident that our economy's long-run performance would be enhanced by a monetary policy that aims at, achieves, and maintains a zero rate of inflation.

That institutional change—from a fully discretionary monetary authority to one bound by law to a single target—not only would bolster the Fed's reputation but would enhance the efficiency of the price system and allow individuals to better plan for the future. People's property rights would be more secure as a result.

For a law making price stability the sole aim of monetary policy to be effective, the Fed must be held accountable for failure to meet that target. Consequently, the law must clearly state the price-stability target while letting the Fed choose how best to achieve it. Transparency will make it easier for Congress and the public to monitor the Fed's behavior and to effectively reward or penalize it.

The New Zealand inflation-targeting law is instructive. The Reserve Bank Act of 1989 states that the sole objective of monetary policy is price stability. A target range is set for inflation, as measured by the consumer price index, which the governor of the Reserve Bank must achieve within a specified time horizon, with exceptions made for supply shocks. The governor is required to sign a contract, the Policy Targets Agreement, with the finance minister, in which the governor agrees to a target range for inflation set by the finance minister, the period for achieving it, and the penalty of dismissal for failing to meet the target. That arrangement has served New Zealand well in achieving a low rate of inflation while letting its currency float on the foreign exchange market. Unlike countries with pegged exchange rates and no monetary rule, New Zealand sailed through the Asian financial crisis quite smoothly.

Congress should draw on New Zealand's experience to create a credible monetary law that holds the chairman of the Fed accountable for achieving long-run price stability.

Recognizing the Limits of Monetary Policy

The Fed cannot permanently increase the rate of economic growth or permanently lower the rate of unemployment by increasing money growth, nor can it permanently lower real interest rates. But it can throw the economy off track by policy errors—that is, by creating either too much or too little money to maintain stable expectations about the long-run value of the currency. The most grievous error of discretionary monetary policy, as Milton Friedman and Anna Schwartz have shown in *A Monetary History of the United States*, was the Fed's failure to prevent the money supply from shrinking by one-third between 1929 and 1933, which turned a sharp but otherwise ordinary recession into the Great Depression.

Economics, like medicine, is not an exact science. The guiding principle of economic policy should be the great physician Galen's (A.D. 160) admonition to "first do no harm." Instead of pursuing in vain an activist monetary policy designed to fine-tune the economy and achieve all good things—full employment, economic growth, and price stability—Fed policy ought to be aimed at what it can actually achieve.

Congress must contemplate three questions in its oversight of monetary policy: (1) What can the Fed do? (2) What can't it do? and (3) What should it do?

What Can the Fed Do?

The Fed can

- control the monetary base through open market operations, reserve requirements, and the discount rate;
- provide liquidity quickly to shore up public confidence in banks during a financial crisis;
- influence the level and growth rate of nominal variables, in particular, monetary aggregates, nominal income, and the price level;

371

- control inflation and prevent monetary instability in the long run;
- influence expectations about future inflation and nominal interest rates.

What Can't the Fed Do?

The Fed cannot

- target real variables so as to permanently reduce the rate of unemployment or increase economic growth;
- determine real interest rates;
- peg the nominal exchange rate and at the same time pursue an independent monetary policy aimed at stabilizing the price level, without imposing capital controls;
- fine-tune the economy;
- make accurate macroeconomic forecasts.

What Should the Fed Do?

The Fed should

- keep the growth of nominal GDP (or domestic final sales) on a stable, noninflationary path so that expected inflation is close to zero by controlling the monetary base;
- let market forces determine the dollar's relative price, that is, its foreign-exchange value, which would be more stable in a rules-based monetary regime;
- use forward-looking prices (such as the price of gold, financial assets, and the exchange rate) to help guide monetary policy;
- follow Bagehot's rule during a liquidity crisis and lend only on good collateral at a penalty rate.

Abolishing the Exchange Stabilization Fund

If the Fed is to retain its independence and be held accountable for maintaining the domestic purchasing power of the dollar, it cannot also manage the external value of the dollar, in the absence of capital controls. The dollar should be free to float, capital should be free to move, and the Fed should use its power to control money and credit growth to ensure long-run price stability. Thus, Congress should abolish the Exchange Stabilization Fund, which was created in 1934 by the Gold Reserve Act.

The ESF has been used by the Treasury to try to "stabilize" the external value of the dollar, but without success. It has also been used to make dollar loans to support the currencies of less developed countries. It is time to get rid of this relic of the New Deal, as long recommended by Anna Schwartz.

By abolishing the ESF, Congress would give a clear signal that it supports exchange-rate and capital freedom, and that the primary function of the Fed is to ensure that the future value of the dollar is secure.

Welcoming the Evolution of Alternatives to Government Fiat Money

While Congress should hold the Fed responsible for maintaining the value of money, in terms of its domestic purchasing power, Congress should also welcome the emergence of alternatives to government fiat money, such as digital cash. Monetary institutions should be allowed to evolve as new technology and information become available.

The growth of electronic commerce will increase the demand for new methods of payment, methods that economize on paper currency. As consumers' trust in electronic cash grows, the demand for the Fed's base money may *decrease.* That would actually make the implementation of a monetary rule easier because the Fed need not worry about complications arising from changes in the ratio of currency to deposits, according to monetary economist George Selgin. Indeed, Milton Friedman's simple rule of zero growth of the monetary base may work quite well in the information age, and it may be a step toward private competing currencies, as advocated by F. A. Hayek.

A concrete measure to promote greater monetary choice would be for Congress to repeal the 1 percent tax on bank-issued notes that is still on the books (U.S. Code, Title 12, Section 541), as suggested by economist Kurt Schuler.

Conclusion

Monetary disturbances have been either a major cause of or a key accentuating factor in business fluctuations. Maintaining a money of stable value through institutional reform would be socially beneficial.

It is time for Congress to recognize the limits of activist monetary policy and to focus on long-run price stability as the Fed's primary objective.

Monetary policy should not depend on any one individual or a Federal Open Market Committee of 12 politically appointed people. It should depend on rules that limit discretion and hold the Fed chairman accountable for failing to achieve money of stable value. Financial markets will then show less anxiety upon the release of every Open Market Committee statement.

The major thrust of this chapter has been to call on Congress to make the Fed accountable for maintaining the long-run value of the currency. But Congress should not limit its vision to a monetary system dominated by a government-run central bank, even if that institution is limited by a monetary rule.

Suggested Readings

Dorn, James A. "Public Choice and the Constitution: A Madisonian Perspective." In *Public Choice and Constitutional Economics*, edited by James D. Gwartney and Richard E. Wagner. Greenwich, CT: JAI Press, 1988.

———. "Alternatives to Government Fiat Money." *Cato Journal* 9, no. 2 (Fall 1989).

———, ed. *The Future of Money in the Information Age*. Washington: Cato Institute, 1997.

Dorn, James A., and Anna J. Schwartz, eds. *The Search for Stable Money*. Chicago: University of Chicago Press, 1987.

Friedman, Milton. "The Role of Monetary Policy." *American Economic Review* 58 (1968).

———. "Monetary Policy: Tactics versus Strategy." In *The Search for Stable Money*, edited by James A. Dorn and Anna J. Schwartz. Chicago: University of Chicago Press, 1987.

Gwartney, James, Kurt Schuler, and Robert Stein. "Achieving Monetary Stability at Home and Abroad." *Cato Journal* 21, no. 2 (Fall 2001).

Keleher, Robert E. "A Response to Criticisms of Price Stability." Study for the Joint Economic Committee of the U.S. Congress, September 1997. http://www.house.gov/jec/fed/fed/response.htm.

McCallum, Bennett T. "Choice of Target for Monetary Policy." *Economic Affairs,* Autumn 1995.

Meiselman, David I. "Accountability and Responsibility in the Conduct of Monetary Policy: Mandating a Stable Price Level Rule." Testimony before the Joint Economic Committee of the U.S. Congress on the Humphrey-Hawkins Act. 104th Cong., 1st sess., March 16, 1995.

Niskanen, William A. "A Test of the Demand Rule." *Cato Journal* 21, no. 2 (Fall 2001).

Poole, William. "Monetary Policy Rules?" Federal Reserve Bank of St. Louis *Review* 81 (March–April 1999).

———. "Is Inflation Too Low?" *Cato Journal* 18, no. 3 (Winter 1999).

Reynolds, Alan. "The Fed's Whimsical Monetary Tinkering." *Outlook: Ideas for the Future from Hudson Institute* 1, no. 4 (April 1997).

———. "The Fiscal Monetary Policy Mix." *Cato Journal* 21, no. 2 (Fall 2001).

Schuler, Kurt. "Note Issue by Banks: A Step toward Free Banking in the United States?" *Cato Journal* 20, no. 3 (Winter 2001).

Schwartz, Anna J. "Time to Terminate the ESF and the IMF." Cato Institute Foreign Policy Briefing no. 48, August 26, 1998.

Selgin, George A. "On Foot-Loose Prices and Forecast-Free Monetary Regimes." *Cato Journal* 12, no. 1 (Spring–Summer 1992).

Timberlake, Richard H. *Monetary Policy in the United States: An Intellectual and Institutional History*, especially chaps. 25–27. Chicago: University of Chicago Press, 1993.

———. "Gold Standards and the Real Bills Doctrine in U.S. Monetary Policy." *Independent Review* 11, no. 3 (Winter 2007).

Walsh, Carl E. "Accountability in Practice: Recent Monetary Policy in New Zealand." FRBSF Economic Letter no. 96-25, September 9, 1996.

Warburton, Clark. *Depression, Inflation, and Monetary Policy*. Baltimore: Johns Hopkins University Press, 1966.

White, Lawrence H. *The Theory of Monetary Institutions*. Malden, MA: Blackwell, 1999.

———. "Is the Gold Standard Still the Gold Standard among Monetary Systems?" Cato Institute Briefing Paper no. 100, February 8, 2008.

Yeager, Leland H. "Toward Forecast-Free Monetary Institutions." *Cato Journal* 12, no. 1 (Spring–Summer 1992).

—Prepared by James A. Dorn

36. Monetary Policy and Financial Regulation

Congress should

- amend the Full Employment and Balanced Growth Act of 1978 to clarify the congressional guidance on the conduct of monetary policy,
- repeal the Community Reinvestment Act of 1977,
- encourage the Treasury to use its new powers as a conservator of Fannie Mae and Freddie Mac to liquidate these firms, and
- repeal the $700 billion bailout legislation.

Monetary Policy

For the past 30 years, the Full Employment and Balanced Growth Act of 1978 instructed the Board of Governors of the Federal Reserve to establish a monetary policy to maintain long-term economic growth and minimum inflation. As these two goals are sometimes inconsistent, this congressional guidance has not been very effective. The Federal Reserve has had almost full discretion in the conduct of monetary policy, subject only to the balance of current political concerns.

The intent of Congress would be better served and monetary policy would be more effective if Congress instructed the Federal Reserve to establish a monetary policy that reflects both their concerns in a *single* target. The best such target, I suggest, would be the nominal final sales to domestic purchasers—the sum of nominal gross domestic product plus imports minus exports minus the change in private inventories. First, this is a feasible target: nominal final sales to U.S.-based purchasers are almost completely determined by U.S. monetary policy, whereas the rate of economic growth and the inflation rate are separately affected by a variety of domestic and foreign conditions. Second, this target provides the correct

377

incentives: for any rate of increase in final sales, a reduction of the inflation rate increases the rate of economic growth.

Congress is best advised (1) to specify a target rate of increase of final sales and (2) to instruct the Federal Reserve to minimize the variance around this target rate. The target rate of increase of final sales may best be about 5 percent a year, sufficient to finance a realistic rate of economic growth of 3 percent and an acceptable rate of inflation of about 2 percent. For the past 20 years, actual final sales increased at a 5.4 percent annual rate with an average inflation rate of 2.4 percent, illustrating that a 5 percent annual increase of final sales would be both feasible and a slightly superior target. The primary problem of U.S. monetary policy during this period, as illustrated by Figure 36.1, is that the Federal Reserve overreacted to three financial crises, creating three "bubbles" of aggregate demand—the correction of which caused two subsequent shallow recessions and, most likely, a third.

The first bubble during the past 20 years was a consequence of the Fed's overreaction to the sharp decline in U.S. equity prices in October

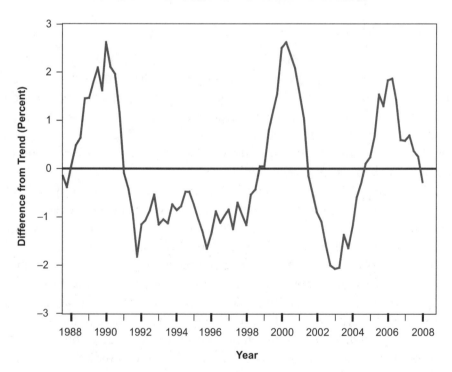

Figure 36.1
Nominal Final Sales to Domestic Purchasers

1987, only two months after Alan Greenspan was confirmed as chairman of the Federal Reserve Board. In turn, the Fed's tightening in response to this demand bubble and the implementation of the first Basel agreement on bank capital standards led to the shallow recession of 1991.

The second unusually large increase in demand was clearly a consequence of the Fed's response to a series of financial crises beginning with the Asian financial crisis of 1997, sustained by the collapse of Long-Term Capital Management and the Russian default in 1998, and the Brazilian devaluation and the anticipated Y2K crisis of 1999. The Fed's easy money policy during this period led to a second bubble in aggregate demand and contributed to the nearly coincident bubble in high-tech stocks. The Fed's tightening to deflate this demand bubble led to the shallow recession of 2001 and contributed to the sharp reduction in equity prices.

The primary cause of the third demand bubble was that the Fed maintained unusually low interest rates for three years following the 2001 recession. This led to the rapid increase in the prices and expenditures for new homes until early 2006. As I write, it is less clear what will happen to this third bubble. The Fed maintained high interest rates through July 2007, contributing to a sharp reduction in real growth through the first quarter of 2008 but as yet without a recession. More important, it is much less clear what will be the effects of the sharp reduction of interest rates since July 2007, the several measures to avoid a collapse of the mortgage market, and the substantial increase in inflation. The rapid increase in consumer and producer prices in summer 2008 should have been ample warning to the Fed not to be diverted from its primary mission. This story is not yet over.

The major lesson from Figure 36.1 is that most of the variation in demand during the past 20 years has been triggered by the Fed's response to financial crises. A second lesson is that the Fed seems to overreact. A reasonable standard by which to judge the Fed's response to a financial crisis would be to avoid a *decline* in the growth of demand relative to the target path. Instead, the Fed's response to financial crises has led demand to increase relative to the target path. A third lesson is that the necessary measures to deflate the demand bubbles caused by overreacting to financial crises should be expected to lead to a recession.

Some of the more important institutional measures that Congress and the Federal Reserve should address are whether and how much the Fed should respond to a financial crisis. The conventional perspective on this issue is that the Fed faces a tradeoff among the potential near-term contagion effects of a financial crisis and the longer-term problem of moral hazard, and that the Fed is biased in favor of reducing the near-term contagion effects. The record of the past 20 years suggests that there is another potential mid-term cost of the Fed's response to a financial crisis— the increased probability of a recession caused by deflating the bubble caused by overreacting to a crisis.

I do not mean to imply that the Fed should never respond to a financial crisis. My objective is to induce more analysis about how to minimize the combined effects of a financial crisis and the Fed's response to it on the Fed's primary mission: how to maintain a steady increase in aggregate demand consistent with a low target rate of inflation.

Financial Regulation

For just over 30 years, the Community Reinvestment Act of 1977 has required commercial and savings banks to offer credit throughout their market area, with the objective of making loans to individuals and small businesses with an income or credit rating that would otherwise deny them access to credit. This act is enforced by requiring a satisfactory record of community service as a condition for approving a bank's application for a merger, an acquisition, or a new branch—a record that is closely monitored by local community organizations. This led to the development of subprime loans, characteristically with a low down payment, a low initial interest rate, and a higher subsequent rate. Changes in the implementing regulations in 1995 allowed the securitization of these subprime loans. Following a 2002 review of the CRA regulations, several regulatory agencies substantially reduced the regulations to which the smaller banks are subject, effective in 2005. The combination of regulatory pressure on the banks to make subprime loans and the increased securitization of subprime loans contributed to some increase in home-ownership rates, especially among those under age 25 and over age 65 and by nonfamily households.

For some years, many politicians and community organizations regarded this process as a successful experiment in political credit allocation, increasing home-ownership rates among those with a poor credit rating without jeopardizing the lenders. But the developments in the financial markets since housing investment peaked early in 2006 should have shattered that illusion. Countrywide, the bank with the largest portfolio of CRA loans, faced bankruptcy until purchased by the Bank of America in early 2008. Bear Stearns was only one of many domestic and foreign securities firms that faced huge losses on their portfolios of mortgage-backed securities.

The several major developments in the mortgage market substantially reduced the incentive of most of the market participants to be concerned about risks. The combination of low down payments and the non-recourse status of most mortgages greatly reduced the risks to the borrower. The mortgage brokers had little reason to be concerned about the risks of the mortgage because they do not hold the loan in their own portfolio; they make their money on the volume of the mortgages they sell to a bank or in a mortgage-backed security. The securities firms that buy the mortgage-backed securities are almost entirely dependent on the few authorized credit-rating firms to rate the risk of these securities. And the home-ownership rates have now dropped below their peak level during the housing boom. In a *New York Times* column, Paul Krugman concludes that "homeownership isn't for everyone. In fact, given the way U.S. policy favors owning over renting, you can make a good case that America already has too many homeowners," a position later endorsed in a *Washington Post* column by Robert Samuelson. The Community Reinvestment Act was a bad idea when it was first approved. The record of the past few years should be sufficient evidence to make the case for its repeal.

In March 2008, following the near collapse of Bear Stearns, the Federal Reserve opened the discount window to make low-interest credit available to securities firms (investment banks) for the first time. This expansion of Federal Reserve credit to the securities firms led to a broad demand to increase the regulation of these firms, which are loosely regulated by the Securities and Exchange Commission. In response, members of the Fed staff were assigned to work with the SEC in the four largest securities firms to increase their information about their financial status, and an information-sharing arrangement was formally approved by a memoran-dum of understanding between the Fed and the SEC in early July. Access to the discount window by the securities firms was initially scheduled to expire in September 2008. In late July, however, Fed Chairman Ben Bernanke extended the broader access to the discount window through January 2009. In mid-July, the Fed also opened the discount window to Fannie Mae and Freddie Mac, as part of a Treasury proposal for authority to prevent the collapse of these two huge government-sponsored mort-gage firms.

In the meantime, there was considerable disagreement on this issue within the government. In a speech in early June, New York Federal Reserve Bank President Tim Geithner remarked:

> We have to recognize that poorly designed regulation has the potential to make things worse. We have to distinguish between problems the markets

will solve on their own and those markets cannot solve. We have to acknowledge not just that regulation comes with costs, but that if not carefully crafted it can distort incentives in ways that make the system less safe. And we have to focus on ways regulation can mitigate the moral hazard risk created by actions central banks and governments have taken and may take in the future to avert systemic financial crises.

In a speech in late June, however, Treasury Secretary Henry Paulson concluded:

We should quickly consider how to most appropriately give the Fed the authority to access necessary information from highly complex financial institutions and the responsibility to intervene to protect the system so they can carry out the role our nation has come to expect—stabilizing the overall system when it is threatened.

The answer is that Congress should *not* add any powers and obligations for the Federal Reserve to regulate the securities firms. Additional regulations are not necessary; the government allowed two large securities firms, Drexel Burnham and Kidder Peabody, to fail in the 1990s without any general financial crisis. Additional regulations would also not be sufficient; about 1,600 commercial banks and about one-third of savings banks failed about 20 years ago despite extensive regulation, because the combination of deposit insurance and access to the discount window created a serious level of moral hazard that reduced the incentive of both depositors and banks to avoid adverse risks. Adding the securities firms and the government-sponsored mortgage firms to the list of financial firms eligible for access to the discount window and subject to regulation by the Federal Reserve would expand the level of moral hazard in the financial system by orders of magnitude.

Allan Meltzer, the leading historian of the Federal Reserve, observes:

In its ninety-five-year history, the Fed has never made a clear statement of its policy for dealing with failures. Sometimes it offered assistance to keep the bank or investment bank afloat. Other times it closed the institution. Troubled institutions have no way to know in advance whether they will be saved or strangled. The absence of a clear policy statement increases uncertainty and encourages problem institutions to demand loans and assistance. Large banks ask Congress to pressure the regulators. Taxpayers pay for the mistakes.

The clear implication of this review is that the government should allow the temporary access to the discount window by the securities firms and the Fed's temporary role to regulate these firms to expire. And, indirectly, that is what happened; after the collapse of Lehman Brothers, the three remaining U.S. securities firms chose to be absorbed by a commercial bank or chose a charter as a bank holding company, choosing more regulation in exchange for continued access to the discount window. More important, to avoid a repetition of the conditions that led to the demand for increased regulation of the securities firms and the government-sponsored mortgage firms, Congress should consider amending the Federal Reserve Act of 1913 to restrict access to the discount window to depositary institutions only.

But the Treasury did not wait, seeking and winning congressional authority to become the conservator of Fannie Mae and Freddie Mac with a potential cost to U.S. taxpayers of up to $200 billion. Paulson described this action as a means to restore these firms to financial health by reducing their most vulnerable mortgage-backed securities over a period of years. But these government-sponsored enterprises are based on a profoundly flawed business model, with their profits owned by their executives and shareholders and their losses a debt of the taxpayers. The Treasury should use its authority to *liquidate* these firms and end the costly experiment with government-sponsored private firms. A direct mortgage subsidy would be a much more efficient policy to increase the homeownership rates among targeted groups if there is a continued political demand for this objective.

And the Treasury's demands exploded in late September when it submitted a three-page bill requesting congressional authority to spend up to $700 billion to purchase mortgage-backed securities from the major domestic and selected foreign banks. The basic structure of this proposal received very little review. In the first round of review, the Senate added several oversight bodies, authorized the additional spending by installment, and set a limit on the compensation of the executives of the banks that sell their mortgage paper to the Treasury, but the Senate did not address the basic structure of the Treasury proposal or any alternative. After a considerable public protest, however, this bill narrowly failed to pass in the House. In response to the House vote, the Senate added a substantially higher limit on insured deposits and more than $100 billion to extend and expand many individual and business tax breaks, including tax credits for the production and use of renewable energy and tax relief to victims of recent floods and storms—changes that were sufficient for approval by the House on October 3.

This bailout plan is almost sure to be a disaster. The Treasury has had no experience in managing a huge portfolio of bad debt. Banks will have an incentive to sell their worst mortgage-backed securities to the Treasury. The Treasury, in turn, will be subject to strong political pressure to defer foreclosures and evictions. And this will probably lead some homeowners to cease paying on their mortgage. After a careful evaluation of the alternatives to this comprehensive bailout plan, Congress should *repeal* the legislation that it approved in October.

Suggested Readings

Benston, George. "The Community Reinvestment Act: Looking for Discrimination That Isn't There." Cato Institute Policy Analysis no. 354, October 6, 1999.

Dorn, James A., and Anna J. Schwartz, eds. *The Search for Stable Money.* Chicago: University of Chicago Press, 1987.

Dowd, Kevin. "Too Big to Fail? Long-Term Capital Management and the Federal Reserve." Cato Briefing Paper no. 52, September 23, 1999.

Kling, Arnold. "Freddie Mac and Fannie Mae: An Exit Strategy for the Taxpayer." Cato Institute Briefing Paper no. 106, September 8, 2008.

Niskanen, William A. "An Unconventional Perspective on the Greenspan Record." *Cato Journal* 26, No. 2 (Spring/Summer 2006).

O'Driscoll, Gerald P., Jr. "Asset Bubbles and Their Consequences." Cato Briefing Paper no. 103, May 20, 2008.

White, Lawrence J. "Fannie Mae, Freddie Mac, and Housing Finance: Why True Privatization Is Good Public Policy." Cato Institute Policy Analysis no. 528, October 7, 2004.

—Prepared by William A. Niskanen

37. Telecommunications, Broadband, and Media Policy

> **Congress should**
> - reject network neutrality regulation of the Internet,
> - reject à la carte regulation of the cable industry,
> - continue the transition to a system of property rights in spectrum,
> - discourage the Federal Communications Commission from imposing nontechnical regulations on the use of privately held spectrum,
> - deregulate the radio and television industries, and
> - end "universal service" and other telecom taxes.

The telecommunications sector is dynamic. Markets and technologies continue to evolve rapidly, but communications policy has not kept pace. The policymaking landscape is encumbered not just with outdated rules and regulations, but also with the same outdated thinking that produced those policies in the first place.

The traditional premises for regulation—a lack of competition and a perceived need to ensure universal service—are vanishing, if not already gone. Telecommunications can be accessed across the nation, and the market for communications services has grown increasingly competitive with each passing year.

Congress last comprehensively revamped telecom law in the Telecommunications Act of 1996. Although that act was widely understood as a liberalization measure, in fact it delegated broad and remarkably ambiguous authority to the Federal Communications Commission and state regulators who have done a poor job of following through with a serious liberalization agenda.

The 1996 Telecom Act's most serious flaw, still unchanged, was that it kept in place increasingly unnatural distinctions that grouped providers into categories, such as "common carriers," cable services, wireless, and mass media and broadcasting. Technological convergence means that many of these formerly distinct industry sectors and companies have already integrated, and the rest are doing so rapidly. A number of firms are already offering telephone, broadband Internet, and pay-television services under a single brand name, for example.

Congress should reform communications policy to end this asymmetry. Placing all telecommunications providers on the same, deregulated playing field should be at the heart of telecommunications policy. Congress should not institute new regulation of telecommunications providers, especially not Internet service providers and their network management practices.

Reject Network Neutrality Regulations

The most-discussed regulatory proposal of recent years—and the proposal that would cause the most long-run harm—is network neutrality regulation. At the moment, Internet service providers operate largely free of the burdensome regulations that afflict the telephone and cable television industries. Network neutrality regulations would open the way for government regulation of the Internet, a danger that greatly outweighs the harms network neutrality regulations are designed to forestall.

Network neutrality is the technical principle holding that network providers should not route packets of data differently based on their destination or contents. It has played an important role in the Internet's spectacular growth over the last decade because it has kept the Internet's barriers to entry low. Network neutrality activists fear that without government regulation, incumbent telecom providers will seek to undermine network neutrality and erect new barriers to entry, speech controls, and the like. They fail to appreciate that neutrality is deeply embedded in the Internet's architecture and cannot be easily changed by network providers. Any efforts to limit customers' online activities are likely to backfire.

For example, when Comcast tried to control congestion by limiting its customers' use of the BitTorrent file-sharing application in 2007, many customers thwarted its efforts by switching to a version of the BitTorrent protocol that used encryption to evade Comcast's filters. Comcast achieved little in the way of congestion control, but it got a lot of bad press in the process. The episode suggests that network owners' ability to control or limit their users' online activities is much more limited than advocates of regulation imagine.

In addition to being unnecessary, network neutrality regulation would also be counterproductive. The proposed definitions of network neutrality all have significant ambiguity, which would lead to years of legal uncertainty. And history is full of examples of industry incumbents' "capturing" the regulatory body ostensibly overseeing them and using it to erect new barriers to entry. The Internet is still a young and dynamic medium; Congress should not risk tying it up in red tape.

Reject "à la Carte" Mandates

Another oft-discussed proposal is "à la carte" cable regulation, which would limit the bundling of channels by cable and satellite television firms. The concept is often presented as enhancing consumer choice by allowing customers to pay for only those channels they really want. This fundamentally misunderstands the economics of the cable industry.

Bundling is a common practice in information industries because it provides consumers with more value for their money. For example, most newspapers bundle their national and local news, business, sports, and opinion sections and provide copies to every customer. It wouldn't be significantly cheaper—and might even be more expensive—to deliver to each customer only the sections he or she reads.

The same dynamic applies in the cable industry. Once they have been produced, television programs can be retransmitted an unlimited number of times. Delivering fewer channels may actually be more expensive because more complex equipment would be needed. In practice, an à la carte mandate would mean significantly higher per-channel prices. Some customers would see their bills go down, while others would see them go up, but every customer would get fewer channels for his or her money.

À la carte regulation would also undermine niche programming. The current bundling approach puts lesser-known channels in millions of homes, allowing customers to sample them and potentially discover new programs they enjoy. An à la carte mandate would discourage this kind of serendipity by only providing customers channels they request in advance.

Create a Free Market in Spectrum

During the 20th century, the FCC managed the nation's electromagnetic spectrum in a manner reminiscent of the Soviet Union. Spectrum licenses were awarded at the whim of FCC commissioners on the basis of vague and arbitrary criteria. Licensees were rarely allowed to deviate from their

387

assigned uses. As a result, some applications have been starved for spectrum, whereas spectrum assigned to other uses have sat idle much of the time.

Congress took a big step toward a free market in spectrum in 1993 when it ordered the FCC to begin assigning new spectrum by using auctions. The auctions the FCC has held over the last 16 years have been very successful. Today's dynamic mobile phone market operates largely on auctioned spectrum, and more spectrum is due to come online with the completion of the digital television transition in February 2009.

The transition to property rights in spectrum should be accelerated in three key ways. First, the de facto property rights that have already been created by auctions over the last 16 years should be formalized. Auction winners should enjoy the same legal protections accorded other kinds of property, and the FCC should encourage the creation of robust secondary markets for spectrum by developing rules for selling, leasing, dividing, and combining spectrum rights.

Second, the FCC should convert more spectrum from limited-use licenses to flexible spectrum ownership. Any spectrum that is currently idle should be reclaimed by the FCC and put up for auction. Private parties who are currently using spectrum under restrictive licenses should have their licenses converted into flexible spectrum-ownership rights. Similarly, state or local governments that hold spectrum licenses should be permitted to use the spectrum for any purpose or lease or sell it to third parties. Some spectrum may need to remain under federal control for military, scientific, or other purposes, but the vast majority of the spectrum should be converted to flexible spectrum ownership.

The FCC should also designate some bands for unlicensed use. In a "spectrum commons," anyone can use spectrum for any purpose provided they meet straightforward technical requirements, such as observing maximum power levels. Unlicensed spectrum enabled the creation of a variety of important short-range communications technologies, including Wi-Fi, Bluetooth, and garage door openers. It is unlikely to prove useful for high-power, long-range communications technologies because of interference problems, so only a limited number of additional unlicensed bands are probably appropriate; most spectrum should be assigned by auction for exclusive use.

Third, the FCC should deregulate the use of spectrum by private parties. The FCC plays a crucial role in developing technical regulations to minimize interference between spectrum holders. But it also enforces a wide variety of regulations that have little to do with preventing interference. Virtually all these regulations are counterproductive and should be repealed.

Reject "Open-Access" Regulations

One example of counterproductive regulation is the FCC's recently imposed "open-access" rules. In 2007, the FCC auctioned off commercial spectrum in the 700-megahertz band that came with strings attached: an open-access rule that required the winner to allow any device or application to interoperate with its network. There are two significant problems with this requirement. First, it deprived the U.S. treasury of revenue. The spectrum almost certainly would have fetched a higher price had it not been encumbered by open-access restrictions. Worse, the open-access rules will give the FCC an ongoing veto over the auction winners' future technical and business decisions, creating an ongoing opportunity for the same kind of rent seeking that now afflicts the wired telecom industry.

The open-access rules were proposed as a remedy for a perceived lack of competition in the wireless marketplace. But a much better way to enhance competition is to put more spectrum into circulation so that more firms can enter the market. More auctions, not more red tape, are the recipe for a dynamic and innovative wireless marketplace.

Deregulate Broadcasting

One area of the electromagnetic spectrum that has been particularly stunted by government regulation is radio and television. The FCC tightly regulates every aspect of broadcasters' activities, leading to wasted spectrum and a slow pace of technological innovation.

The media marketplace is now far more competitive than it was at any time in the 20th century. Television broadcasters face competition from cable and satellite television providers, as well as a variety of new Internet-based services. Terrestrial radio stations compete with satellite radio, MP3 players, and audio streaming to mobile devices. Given this explosion of new options, there is no good policy rationale for singling out television and radio broadcasters for regulation.

Broadcasters should be given flexible licenses that allow them to use their spectrum for any purpose or to sell it to third parties who can put it to better use. Over time, the spectrum is likely to be reallocated to technologies such as cellular data networks that make more efficient use of available spectrum and offer consumers much greater customization. Such networks can continue transmitting the same kind of programming now delivered by broadcast networks, but they could also offer a much wider variety of content, applications, and services. The FCC should have no power to review mergers or spectrum license transfers.

End Arbitrary Media Ownership Regulations

Efforts to reform media ownership rules, which restrict the number of newspapers and television and radio stations that one firm can own, have been bogged down at the FCC for over a decade. In November 2007, the FCC completed its most recent proceedings and announced that it would make just one very minor rule change that would affect only the 20 largest and most competitive media markets. Even this timid decision prompted a firestorm of controversy and legal challenges.

The hysteria over media consolidation is completely unjustified by the empirical evidence. Far from becoming monopolistic, local newspapers and broadcast television stations are being steadily marginalized by new media technologies. Consolidation may help newspapers and television stations continue providing high-quality local coverage in the face of shrinking budgets. In any event, with the explosion of competing communications technologies, there is no longer any good reason for the FCC to micromanage the evolution of the broadcasting industries. The FCC's media concentration rules should be repealed.

Repeal Unconstitutional Indecency Regulations

The growing competition facing traditional broadcasters also undermines the case for "indecency" regulations. In 1978, the Supreme Court upheld censorship of dirty words on the broadcast airwaves against a First Amendment challenge on the ground that broadcasting media "have established a uniquely pervasive presence" in people's lives.

That was a controversial conclusion in 1978; it is plainly false in 2009. The vast majority of households subscribe to paid cable or satellite television services. Traditional broadcast stations are just another option in today's increasingly robust media marketplace. Moreover, technologies such as the V-chip help parents shield their children from objectionable over-the-air programming. The First Amendment demands the repeal of broadcast indecency regulations.

End "Universal Service" and Other Telecom Taxes

As technological convergence brings increased telecom competition, tax policies based on the regulated monopoly model of the past must be comprehensively reformed. The most glaring example is the "temporary" federal 3 percent excise tax on telecommunications put in place in 1898 to fund the Spanish-American War. Recently scaled back, that anachronistic tax should be repealed entirely.

Another for the chopping block is the E-Rate program, which taxes telecommunications services to subsidize some telecommunications users through "universal service" programs. In May 1997, the FCC, in response to the 1996 law, created the E-Rate program, which established a new federal bureaucracy to help wire schools and libraries to the Internet at a beginning cost of $2.25 billion per year in hidden taxes on phone bills. Recent oversight of the E-Rate program has revealed waste and fraud in the program, even as its necessity in the modern telecommunications environment is gone.

Suggested Readings

Gasman, Lawrence. "Who Killed Telecom? Why the Official Story Is Wrong." Cato Institute Policy Analysis no. 533, February 7, 2005.

Harper, Jim. "The 700 MHz Spectrum: How About an 'Open' Auction?" Cato Institute TechKnowledge no. 107, July 30, 2007.

_____. "The Lesson of the XM/Sirius Merger." Cato Institute TechKnowledge no. 119, August 15, 2008.

Lee, Timothy B. "Wu on Wireless: A Simple Solution?" Cato Institute TechKnowledge no. 103, June 1, 2007.

_____. "The Durable Internet: Preserving Network Neutrality without Regulation." Cato Institute Policy Analysis no. 626, November 12, 2008.

Plummer, James. "Public Safety and Public Spectrum." Cato Institute TechKnowledge no. 109, November 6, 2007.

_____. "Low-Power FM: Freedom Is Diversity." Cato Institute TechKnowledge no. 115, May 28, 2008.

Thierer, Adam. "Three Cheers for the FCC Spectrum Task Force Report." Cato Institute TechKnowledge no. 44, November 21, 2002.

_____. "Comments to the Federal Communications Commission Regarding A La Carte and Themed Tier Programming and Pricing Options for Programming Distribution on Cable Television and Direct Broadcast Satellite Systems." Cato Institute filing before the Federal Communications Commission, July 12, 2004. www.cato.org/tech/pubs/fcc-07-12-04.pdf.

—Prepared by Timothy B. Lee, Jim Harper, and James Plummer

38. Copyright and Patent

Congress should

- establish an "orphan works" defense for copyright infringement,
- shorten the term of copyrights,
- repeal the anti-circumvention provisions of the Digital Millennium Copyright Act but preserve the "notice and takedown" safe harbor for Internet service providers,
- reject copy protection mandates such as the "broadcast flag,"
- restore jurisdictional competition in patent law,
- limit forum shopping by plaintiffs in patent cases, and
- establish an "independent invention" defense for patent infringement.

Property rights are the foundation of a free society. They provide a predictable legal framework for the allocation of resources, create incentives for productivity, and limit the arbitrary exercise of power by government officials. Economists have found that nations with secure property rights tend to perform better than nations with weak or unpredictable property rights.

People often describe copyright and patent law collectively as "intellectual property" law, but it's important to remember that, constitutionally and historically, these legal regimes are very different from traditional property rights. Property rights have existed for millennia, but copyright and patent protections are relatively recent developments. Private property is enshrined as a fundamental right by the Fifth Amendment to the Constitution. In contrast, Article I, section 8, of the Constitution empowers Congress to establish patent and copyright protections "for limited times" to the extent that doing so promotes "the progress of science and the useful arts."

Although copyright and patent laws deal with nontraditional kinds of property, the analogy to property rights provides a useful guide for improving these legal regimes, which have faced mounting problems in recent years. Property law has two important characteristics that can guide the reform of patent and copyright policies. First, property law establishes clear, predictable boundaries and straightforward mechanisms for determining who owns what. It ensures that property owners enjoy the fruits of their labor—and that others can determine what rights they need to acquire—with minimum litigation and uncertainty.

Second, the details of American property law have been fleshed out over centuries by a decentralized ''common-law'' process in which judges build on past precedents as they resolve individual disputes. This approach has produced a flexible body of law that adjusts smoothly to social and technological changes. In contrast, the legislative process often creates uncertainty. Newly enacted statutes often create confusion by dislodging long-held expectations and practices, and their meanings do not become clear until the courts have fashioned an accompanying body of case law.

As we will see, many of the changes Congress has made to patent and copyright laws over the last three decades have resulted in unintended consequences. As Congress considers reform proposals, its top priority should be to avoid doing further damage. When in doubt, Congress should take a wait-and-see posture, allowing the courts to flesh out the key issues before it gets involved.

Coping with the Loss of Copyright Formalities

As already noted, clear boundaries and good record-keeping are essential to a well-functioning property system. In real property, a system of surveyors and records at the county courthouse preserves detailed information about property boundaries, allowing anyone to discover who owns any given plot of land. Until recently, copyright had an analogous system of ''formalities'' that helped people determine which works were under copyright and who held the copyrights. To obtain a copyright, an author was required to register his or her work with the Copyright Office, affix a copyright notice to each copy, and renew the copyrights after a fixed period.

This system ensured that the burdens of copyright law fell only on the minority of works that were commercially significant. It also enabled anyone wanting to license a work to find the copyright holder, if one existed. Unfortunately, between 1976 and 1992, Congress dismantled this system of formalities, replacing it with a system of automatic copyright protection for all creative works—whether or not authors want it.

One consequence has been a growing "orphan works" problem: hundreds of thousands of out-of-print works that cannot be used because their copyright holders cannot be found. Many such works have cultural or historical importance but no commercial value. The technology exists to digitize them and place them online, but under current law, anyone doing so would be exposed to enormous liability.

The ideal solution would be to reestablish formalities as a condition for receiving copyright protection. Unfortunately, that would require renegotiating an international agreement called the Berne Convention, which would be extremely difficult.

Creating an Orphan Works Defense

Property law has mechanisms for reclaiming property that has been abandoned by its previous owners; copyright law needs an analogous mechanism. Congress should create a new "orphan works" defense that would permit the use of a work if its copyright holder cannot be found. The courts would conduct a fact-specific inquiry to determine if a diligent search had been conducted, guided by a nonexhaustive list of statutorily defined factors analogous to copyright's four fair-use factors. These factors might include whether there is a notice on the work, whether the user searched databases maintained by the Copyright Office and private parties, and whether the user diligently pursued any clues turned up in the course of the search.

If the rights holder subsequently appeared, the user would not be liable for infringement if he or she could prove that he or she had conducted a diligent search that failed to locate the rights holder. If the court accepted the orphan works defense, the copyright holder would be owed royalties for any unsold copies of the infringing work, but could not seek the draconian "statutory damages" that are ordinarily available to plaintiffs in infringement cases.

Shortening Copyright Terms

The Constitution requires that copyrights be granted "for limited times," but Congress has made a mockery of this requirement (and exacerbated the orphan works problem) by repeatedly and retroactively extending copyright terms. Retroactive extension of copyright terms violates the spirit of the "limited times" restriction. It also does nothing to encourage the creation of new works. Congress should dramatically reduce copyright terms, perhaps to a more traditional 14 or 28 years, which would be more than adequate to reward the production of new works.

Repealing Provisions of The Digital Millennium Copyright Act

In 1998, the same year Congress last extended copyright terms, it also enacted the controversial Digital Millennium Copyright Act. The DMCA made numerous changes to copyright law, but two provisions stand out for their far-reaching consequences. One provision, which established a new safe harbor for Internet service providers, was a rare case in which Congress got it right. It gives ISPs protection from liability for the actions of their customers so long as they promptly remove copyrighted materials from their networks when asked to do so by copyright holders. The rule reduced the legal uncertainty faced by ISPs and created an efficient and fair process for copyright holders to seek the removal of infringing materials. Congress should leave it in place.

The DMCA's other major provision, which prohibits the "circumvention" of copy protection schemes, has not been so beneficial. Courts have long grappled with adapting copyright law to technological change. For example, in a 1984 decision that is widely viewed as a foundation of the modern consumer electronics industry, the Supreme Court rejected Hollywood's contention that Sony should be held responsible for the infringing activities of customers who purchased its Betamax VCR. By 1998, the courts had developed a body of law that struck a careful balance between deterring infringement and promoting technological progress.

The DMCA upset that balance, effectively giving copyright holders veto power over the design of digital media devices. The results have not been good. For example, copy-protected music purchased from the iTunes Music Store cannot be played on non-Apple MP3 players, and the DMCA bans third parties from developing conversion software. Similarly, Hollywood has used its power under the DMCA to limit the development of DVD players, preventing the release of DVD players that can skip commercials or play DVDs purchased abroad and hampering the development of DVD jukeboxes.

Market forces—not congressional edict—should control the evolution of the copy protection marketplace. Congress should repeal the "anti-circumvention" provisions of the DMCA. It should also reject new copy protection mandates. For example, Congress should not require television manufacturers to comply with the ''broadcast flag,'' a copy protection technology championed by Hollywood.

Making Patents Work More like Property

Copyright law has experienced growing pains over the last decade, but those problems have paled in comparison with the crisis facing the patent system. Recent years have seen a massive increase in patent litigation. In *Patent Failure*, Boston University scholars James Bessen and Michael Meurer find that patent litigation exploded during the 1990s. Indeed, they estimate that outside of the pharmaceutical and chemical industries, the costs of patent litigation in 1999 significantly exceeded the profits generated for patent holders. That suggests that today's patent system may actually *discourage* innovation in many high-tech industries.

As with copyright, many problems with the patent system can be traced to the unintended consequences of congressional action. In 1982, Congress created the United States Court of Appeals for the Federal Circuit and gave it jurisdiction over all patent appeals. The theory was that a specialized patent court would improve the quality of patent rulings. Unfortunately, the change has created more problems than it solved. The Federal Circuit has demonstrated a permissive attitude toward patenting, steadily dismantling traditional limitations on patent protection that had made the patent system predictable. It allowed patenting of subject matter that had been considered unpatentable, and upheld patents with broad, vaguely worded claims.

The Federal Circuit's decisions have made it much more difficult for innovators to avoid infringing others' patents. Without the legal certainty that is the hallmark of a well-designed property system, innovators face dramatically reduced incentives to innovate and higher risks from doing so.

Restoring Jurisdictional Competition in Patent Law

A subtler problem with the consolidation of patent jurisdiction was the elimination of competition, which is a crucial part of the common-law process. In most areas of federal law, each of the 12 geographically based appeals courts develops its own distinct body of precedent. When different circuits' precedents begin to diverge—a situation known as a ''circuit split''—it serves as a signal to the Supreme Court that its attention is needed. By the time the Supreme Court takes a case, lower courts will often have developed several distinct bodies of case law, and the Supreme

397

Court need only pick and choose from among the doctrines that the lower courts have already fleshed out.

In contrast, because the Federal Circuit hears all patent appeals, the Supreme Court cannot rely on circuit splits as a signal to intervene in patent law. And when it does overturn a Federal Circuit decision, the high court cannot look to other circuits for ready-made alternatives.

Since 2006, the Supreme Court has begun to rein in the Federal Circuit, deciding four patent cases in three sessions. In each case, the Supreme Court overturned a patent-friendly Federal Circuit decision in favor of a decision that circumscribes patent holders' rights more narrowly. But the lack of competition in patent law makes it difficult for the Supreme Court to quickly bring the Federal Circuit to heel. It cannot look to other circuits for signs that the Federal Circuit has wandered off the reservation, nor can other circuits develop alternatives to the Federal Circuit's patent doctrines.

Therefore, Congress's first step should be to end the experiment with specialization in patent appeals and extend patent jurisdiction to the other 12 federal appeals courts. Restoring jurisdictional competition is an indirect route to fixing the problems with patent law, but if our experience with real property and copyright law is any indication, it's likely to be more effective in the long run.

Congress may still need to intervene at some point to clean up the mess the Federal Circuit has created. For example, the Federal Circuit's de facto legalization of patents on software, business methods, and other abstract concepts was a serious mistake that should be reversed. But the cumbersome, interest-group-driven legislative process is not a good venue for hashing out the details of an intricate body of law like patent law; Congress should give the Supreme Court time to repair patent law before intervening.

If Congress is ultimately forced to step in and overhaul patent law, it will find that competition among circuit courts aids its deliberations. Observing where the circuits differ will give Congress useful information about which areas of law require its attention and which can be safely left alone. And the competing bodies of law developed by the circuits will give Congress the raw material from which to fashion new patent doctrines.

Curtailing Venue Shopping

While it allows competition among courts to improve the substance of patent law, there are a few other steps Congress can take to reduce the harm patent law is currently doing to innovation. One important reform would be to reduce forum shopping by patent plaintiffs. For example, the

Eastern District of Texas has become notorious for its extreme patent-friendliness. As a result, plaintiffs from around the country file lawsuits there even when neither the plaintiff nor the defendant has any real connection to the area. Congress should curtail this abuse by limiting plaintiffs' discretion in choosing a venue for patent lawsuits.

Creating an Independent Invention

Finally, Congress should address the proliferation of broad, vague patents and the resulting rise in inadvertent infringement by creating an "independent invention" defense to charges of patent infringement. Defendants who can prove they developed their products independently without knowledge of the patentee's own technology should not be liable for patent infringement.

Suggested Readings

Bessen, James, and Michael J. Meurer. *Patent Failure: How Judges, Bureaucrats, and Lawyers Put Innovators at Risk.* Princeton, NJ: Princeton University Press, 2008.

Brito, Jerry, and Bridget Dooling. "An Orphan Works Affirmative Defense to Copyright Infringement Actions." *Michigan Telecommunications and Technology Law Review,* vol. 12, p. 75, 2005. http://www.mttlr.org/voltwelve/brito&dooling.pdf.

Jaffe, Erik S. Brief of *amici curiae* Eagle Forum Education and Legal Defense Fund and the Cato Institute in the case of *Eldred v. Ashcroft* before the Supreme Court. December 13, 2001. www.cato.org/pubs/legalbriefs/eldred.pdf.

Lastowka, F. Gregory, and Dan Hunter. "Amateur-to-Amateur: The Rise of a New Creative Culture." Cato Institute Policy Analysis no. 567, April 26, 2006.

Lee, Timothy. "Broadcast Flag Burning." Cato Institute TechKnowledge no. 98, May 12, 2005.

———. "Circumventing Competition: The Perverse Consequence of the Digital Millennium Copyright Act." Cato Institute Policy Analysis no. 564, March 21, 2006.

———. "Bring Appellate Competition Back to Patent Law." Cato Institute TechKnowledge no. 118, July 28, 2008.

Plummer, James. "How Endangered Is Internet Radio?" Cato Institute TechKnowledge no. 102, May 18, 2007.

—Prepared by Timothy B. Lee

39. Health and Safety Policy

Congress should

- eliminate goals of zero risk in statutes governing occupational and environmental health, and
- establish the purpose of safety and health agencies as the identification of opportunities to improve safety and health at costs that are much less than the market value of the benefits.

Before the mid-1960s, the health and safety regulations that we now take for granted were completely absent from the American economy, with the exception of selected regulations for food safety and prescription drugs. The rise of the consumer movement and environmental concerns led to the establishment of the National Highway Traffic Safety Administration in 1966, the Occupational Safety and Health Administration in 1970, the Environmental Protection Agency in 1970, the Consumer Product Safety Commission in 1972, and the Nuclear Regulatory Commission in 1974.

Scholarly assessment of the three decades of experience with regulation and government oversight concludes that health and safety regulations have had no obvious effects on the aggregate trends in accidental deaths. In addition, health and safety statutes and the regulations written to implement them further the incorrect belief that the goal should be zero risk or harm—an impossibly high and costly standard—rather than an efficient or optimal level. And finally, government regulation reduces the incentives for firms to provide their own safety assurances through testing and branding.

Why Should the Government Regulate Risk?

Government action in the health and safety arena can be justified when shortcomings exist in risk information. The goal of regulatory agencies that address health and safety risks should be to isolate instances in which

401

misinformation about health risks prevents people from making their own informed decisions and to isolate instances where health risks are not internalized in the market decisions.

The existence of a health risk does not necessarily imply the need for regulatory action. For example, as long as workers understand the risks they face in various occupations, they will receive wage compensation through normal market forces sufficient to make them willing to bear the risk; the health risk is internalized into the market decision.

In situations in which the risks are not known to workers, as in the case of dimly understood health hazards or situations in which the labor market is not competitive, market forces might not operative effectively to internalize the risk. Those cases, in theory, provide an opportunity for constructive cost-effective government intervention although actual government policy is often neither constructive nor cost-effective.

Zero versus Optimal Risk

Unfortunately, the rationale of correcting market failures has never been a major motivation of regulatory intervention. The simple fact that risks exist has provided the impetus for the legislative mandates of the health and safety regulatory agencies. To this day, very few regulatory impact analyses ever explore in any meaningful way the role of potential market failure in the particular context and the constructive role that market forces may already play in the regulatory situation that is being considered.

The conventional regulatory approach to health and safety risks is to seek a technological solution through capital investments in the workplace, changes in the safety devices in cars, or similar kinds of requirements that entail no additional care on the part of the individual. Stated simply, the conventional view is that the existence of risks is undesirable and with appropriate technological interventions, we can eliminate those risks. This perspective does not recognize the cost tradeoffs involved; the fact that a no-risk society would be so costly as to make risk infeasible does not arise as a policy concern of consequence.

The economic approach to regulating risk is quite different. The potential role of the government is not to eliminate the risk, but rather to address market failures that lead to an inefficient balance between risk reduction and cost. In theory, the task of government regulatory agencies is to identify cases in which regulation can generate more benefits to society than the costs that are incurred and to address the market failures using a cost-effective approach. To achieve those goals, the focus should not simply be on rigid technological standards but on the provision of information or flexible regulatory mechanisms that allow firms to meet performance goals cost-effectively.

Risk Assessment, Statistics, and Value Choices

The discussion so far has presumed that we actually know the level of risk posed by exposure to or use of a product or work in a particular industry. For traditional industrial accidents, time series data exist and the calculation of worker fatality rates is rather straightforward. But for new pharmaceuticals and other products that may have health risks as well as benefits, assessments of the health effects from exposure come from samples of people who represent much larger populations.

In assessing the results from such experiments, researchers must estimate the likelihood that the results from the sample represent the results if the population were studied. The answer depends on the size of the sample and the signal-to-noise ratio in the sample.

The smaller the sample and the smaller the signal-to-noise ratio, the lower the likelihood that the sample result is the population result. Said differently, small sample sizes and noisy data increase the variety of possible population results that are logically possible given a particular sample result. In such small, noisy samples, it becomes more likely that observed effects are the result of chance rather than exposure to products.

And then there is the question that actually has no scientific answer: How confident should we be that a result is not the result of chance? Scientific convention says we should be 95 percent confident that the observed effect is not simply the result of chance, but why 95 percent and not 90 or 85 percent? And should one (on average) keep products on the market knowing that some will have negative health and safety consequences, or restrict many products from being sold knowing that some perfectly acceptable products will not be available?

Which error is worse is not a scientific question and cannot be answered by more or better science. Whether one should worry more about false-positive or false-negative statistical errors is a value rather than a scientific question.

Despite the inability of science to adjudicate value disputes, many health and safety decisions are delegated to bureaucracies, like the Food and Drug Administration, that allegedly use scientific methods to decide what products and practices to allow on the market. In fact, values enter into such decisions in three ways. First, scientists must decide how large the sample sizes should be because that decision, in turn, dictates whether small effects can be differentiated from zero effect. Larger samples allow smaller effects to be differentiated from no effect with greater confidence. Second, scientists must either accept conventional significance tests (95 percent confidence) or propose alternatives, and this choice dictates whether false-positive or false-negative errors are more likely and thus, implicitly, less costly. Third, given the findings of clinical trials and epidemiological studies, scientists and doctors vote using majority rule on whether the benefits are worth the costs, which is obviously an economic rather than strictly scientific decision. In a more libertarian world, the government or preferably multiple private entities would gather and disseminate information but then let individuals decide what to do with it.

How Should Risks Be Evaluated?

Using detailed data on wages and fatality risks across occupations, economists have estimated people's tradeoffs between money and fatality risk, thus establishing a value of statistical lives based on market decisions. The estimates imply that workers receive premiums of about $700 to face an additional annual work-related fatality risk of 1 chance in 10,000. Put somewhat differently, if there were 10,000 such workers facing an annual fatality of 1 chance in 10,000, there would be one actual death on average. In return for that risk, the 10,000 workers would receive total additional wage compensation of $7 million. The compensation establishes the value of a statistical life, based on the workers' wage premiums given the risks they face.

The estimates suggest that in situations in which there is an awareness of the risk, market forces create adequate safety incentives. Thus, we are not operating in a world in which there are no constraints other than regulatory intervention to promote our safety. Rather, market forces already create incentives for safety that should not be overridden by intrusive regulations.

Assessment of Regulatory Performance

Although many agencies use reasonable measures of the value of a statistical life for assessing benefits, the cost per life saved for the regulations actually promulgated often far exceeds the estimated benefits. The restrictive nature of agencies' legislative mandates often precludes consideration of costs in the regulatory decision.

Table 39.1 lists various health and safety regulations and their estimated opportunity cost per life saved (in 2002 dollars). Because the legislative mandate varies across regulations, one sees great variance in the cost per life saved. Indeed, the cost varies even within certain regulatory agencies. For example, EPA's regulation of trihalomethane in drinking water has an estimated cost per statistical life saved of only $300,000, whereas the regulation of sewerage sludge disposal has an estimated cost per life saved of $530 billion. A regulatory system based on sound economic principles would reallocate resources from the high- to the low-cost regulations. That would result in more lives saved at the same cost to society (or equivalently, shifting resources could result in the same number of lives saved at a lower cost to society).

Table 39.1
Opportunity Costs per Statistical Life Saved
(millions of 2002 dollars)

Regulation	Year Issued	Agency	Opportunity Cost per Statistical Life Saved
Childproof lighters	1993	CPSC	$0.1
Unvented space heaters	1980	CPSC	0.2
Trihalomethanes	1979	EPA	0.3
Food-labeling regulations	1993	FDA	0.4
Children's sleepwear flammability	1973	CPSC	2.2
Child restraints	1999	NHTSA	3.3
Grain dust	1988	OSHA	11.0
Benzene	1987	OSHA	22.0
Coke ovens	1976	OSHA	51.0
Asbestos ban	1989	EPA	78.0
DES (cattle feed)	1979	FDA	170.0
Sewage sludge disposal	1993	EPA	530.0
Land disposal restrictions: Phase II	1994	EPA	2,600.0
Drinking water: Phase II	1992	EPA	19,000.0
Formaldehyde	1987	OSHA	78,000.0
Solid waste disposal facility criteria	1991	EPA	$100,000.0

SOURCE: W. Kip Viscusi, "Regulation of Health, Safety, and Environmental Risks," National Bureau of Economic Research Working Paper no. 11934, January 2006.

NOTE: CPSC = Consumer Product Safety Commission; DES = diethylstilbestrol; EPA = Environmental Protection Agency; FDA = Food and Drug Administration; NHTSA = National Highway Traffic Safety Administration; OSHA = Occupational Safety and Health Administration.

Effect of Regulation on Accident Rates

What has been the overall effect of the emergence of health and safety regulations since the early 1970s? One yardstick of performance is to see whether accident rates have declined. Figure 39.1 summarizes fatality rates of various kinds, including motor vehicle accidents, work accidents, home accidents, public non–motor vehicle accidents, and a cumulative category of all accidents.

The basic message of Figure 39.1 is that accident rates have been declining throughout the past 80 years (although that trend has recently stopped). The improvement in our safety is not a new phenomenon that began with the advent of regulatory agencies commissioned to protect the citizenry. There is, for example, no significant downward shift in Figure 39.1's trend for job fatality risk after the establishment of OSHA in 1971. And Figure 39.2 shows that auto fatalities (per 100 million vehicle miles) declined steadily throughout the last 85 years as well. As in the case of the other accident statistics, there is no evidence of a sharp, discontinuous break in the downward trend that occurred with the advent of regulatory policies.

While there may be a beneficial safety-enhancing role played by regulation, the steady decrease in risk throughout the century supports the hypoth-

Figure 39.1
Unintentional Injury Deaths in the United States, 1928–2006

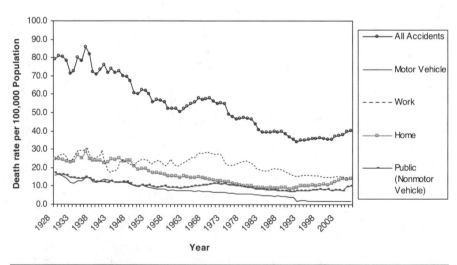

SOURCE: *Injury Facts* (Itasca, IL.: National Safety Council, 2008), pp. 36–37.

Figure 39.2
Motor Vehicle Death Rate in the United States, 1923–2006

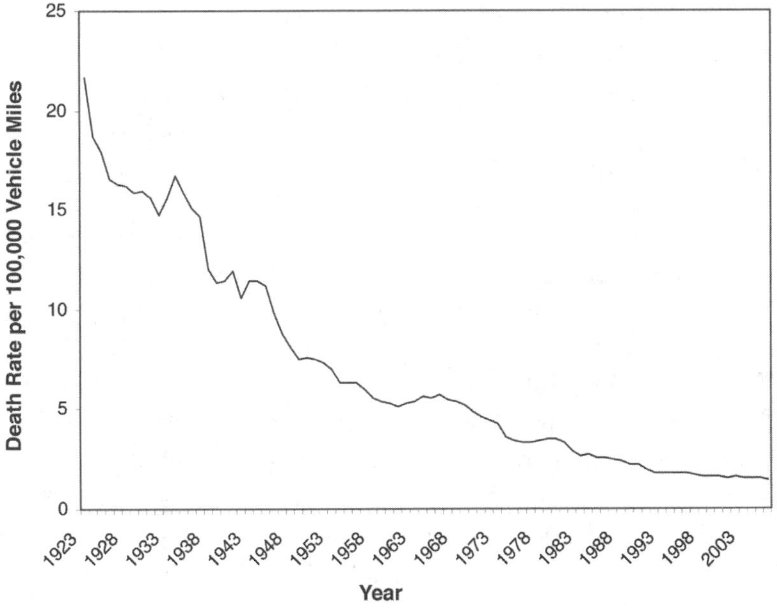

SOURCE: *Injury Facts* (Itasca, IL: National Safety Council, 2008), pp. 110–11.

esis that improvements in societal wealth have greatly increased our demand for safety over time. Coupling that wealth with technological improvements—many of which have been stimulated by the greater demand for safety—has led to dramatic improvements in our individual well-being. Market forces rather than regulatory policy have likely been the most important contributor to safety improvements since early last century.

Recent Policy Controversy

Markets can provide safer products if consumers are willing to pay for them, and some firms credibly commit to provide them and are rewarded for doing so more than the cost of safety provision. Such a state of affairs is called a separating equilibrium: differing degrees of quality and safety are provided at different prices, and consumers choose the package of price and quality level that they prefer.

A market that does not separate is said to "pool." In a pooled market, price and quality variation is not sustainable either because consumers are unwilling to pay for the costs of quality differences (not a market failure) or market characteristics prevent firms from credibly committing to quality and thus consumers have difficulty differentiating good- from poor-quality products.

An impediment to the formation of separating outcomes is the existence of numerous small-scale, anonymous producers whose output is combined without branding. Traditionally, many agricultural products have been marketed this way. In turn, the market pools, and then a safety scandal occurs. The government responds with "regulation" and inspection. Consumers are reassured. But the inspection budgets and systems are inadequate to prevent future safety and health events. New safety incidents occur, and the cycle repeats.

Recently, Congress has responded to two health and safety episodes in predictable fashion. The discovery of lead paint on children's toys imported from China and the salmonella outbreak stemming from Mexican peppers induced Congress to pass new consumer product safety legislation and President George W. Bush to increase the appropriation request for the FDA for fiscal year 2009 by $275 million. Such responses dull both firm and consumer incentives to think about safety and reinforce the mistaken belief that markets are incapable of credibly providing adequately safe products.

Two cases involving food illustrate how markets can transcend the traditional anonymity of agricultural commodities and credibly provide greater quality for a higher price and how regulation can actually interfere in that process. Since the Jack in the Box E. coli outbreak in 1993, branded fast-food outlets and grocery chains have paid a premium for ground beef from Beef Products Incorporated because of the innovative technology and practices that firm uses to reduce the possibility of bacterial contamination. The key to the market separation is that branded fast-food outlets and grocery stores have market value that is greater than their assets. This so-called goodwill would vanish if they were linked to contaminated beef.

The second case involves mad cow disease, U.S. beef producers, and Korean beef consumers. Korea, which used to be the third-largest importer of American beef, has banned American imports since the 2003 mad cow case in the United States. A farm in Kansas wants to test *all* its cattle upon slaughter (at an extra price of $20) to satisfy Korean consumers (and their government) of the meat's safety rather than test 1 in 1,000 randomly as required by the U.S. Department of Agriculture. The USDA has not permitted the firm to use the test because it argues that its standards are adequate. In effect, regulation mandates that the market pool rather than separate.

The toy market also separates rather than pools. U.S. toy manufacturers, the few that remain, emphasize quality and safety in return for a higher price. But consumers deserted such products, often sold in small independent stores, for imports from China sold for less at large chain stores, in part because of the existence of regulation, which they assumed would protect them from risk.

The large importers have responded to the lead-paint scandal by requesting increased regulation through the Consumer Product Safety Commission. Rather than gain consumer trust through their own efforts like the small U.S. manufacturers, the large importers want to use regulation to force the market to pool again—to convince the consumer not to think about price and quality tradeoffs because of government assurance of quality—a clear form of corporate welfare.

Reform Agenda

Almost from its inception, health and safety regulation has been the target of proposed reform. Some policy improvements have occurred, such as elimination of some of the nitpicking of safety standards, the increased use of informational approaches to regulation, and enhanced enforcement efforts. However, health and safety regulations have fallen short of any reasonable standard of performance.

The underlying difficulty can be traced to the legislative mandates of the regulatory agencies. Rather than focus regulations on instances of market failure, the emphasis is on reducing risk irrespective of cost. The regulatory approach has also been characterized by an overly narrow conceptualization of the potential modes of intervention. The emphasis has been on command-and-control regulations rather than information provision or performance-oriented standards.

Defenders of the current regulatory approach have long seized the moral high ground by claiming that their uncompromising efforts protect individual health; less consequential concerns such as cost should not interfere with that higher enterprise. The fallacy of such thinking is that high-cost, low-benefit safety regulations divert society's resources from a mix of expenditures that would be more health enhancing than the allocations dictated by the health and safety regulations. Agencies that make an unbounded financial commitment to safety are frequently sacrificing individual lives in their symbolic quest for a zero-risk society. It is unlikely that this situation will be remedied in the absence of fundamental legislative reform. But as the recent salmonella and lead toy cases illustrate, Congress has great difficulty responding rationally to risk crises.

Suggested Readings

Adams, John. "Cars, Cholera, and Cows: The Management of Risk and Uncertainty." Cato Institute Policy Analysis no. 335, March 4, 1999.

Hahn, Robert W., and Jason K. Burnett. "A Costly Benefit." *Regulation,* Fall 2001.

Hansen, Michael. "Stop the Madness." *New York Times,* June 20, 2008, p. A21.

Kniesner, Thomas J., and John D. Leeth. "Abolishing OSHA." *Regulation,* Winter 1995.

Lipton, Eric, and Louise Story. "Toy Makers Seek Standards for U.S. Safety." *New York Times,* September 7, 2007, p. C1.

Martin, Andrew. "U.S.-Made Toys Benefit from China's Troubles." *New York Times,* August 15, 2007, p. C1.

Miller, Henry I., and Peter Van Doren. "Food Risks and Labeling Controversies." *Regulation,* Spring 2000.

Niskanen, William A. "Arsenic and Old Facts." *Regulation,* Fall 2001.

Scalia, Eugene. "OSHA's Ergonomics Litigation Record: Three Strikes and It's Out." Cato Institute Policy Analysis no. 370, May 15, 2000.

Shin, Annys. "Engineering a Safer Burger." *Washington Post,* June 12, 2008, p. D1.

Viscusi, W. Kip. "Regulation of Health, Safety, and Environmental Risks." National Bureau of Economic Research Working Paper no. 11934, January 2006.

Viscusi, W. Kip, and Ted Gayer. "Safety at Any Price?" *Regulation,* Fall 2002.

Wilson, Richard. "Regulating Environmental Hazards." *Regulation,* Spring 2000.

———. "Underestimating Arsenic's Risk." *Regulation,* Fall 2001.

—Prepared by Peter Van Doren

40. Antitrust

Antitrust is thought by some to be the bulwark of free enterprise. Without the continued vigilance of the Justice Department and the Federal Trade Commission, so the argument goes, large corporations would ruthlessly destroy their smaller rivals and soon raise prices and profits at consumers' expense. When megamergers grab headlines and a federal judge decides that the nation's leading software company should be dismembered, the importance of vigorous antitrust law enforcement seems obvious.

But antitrust has a dark side. The time for modest reform of antitrust policy has passed. Root-and-branch overhaul of what Alan Greenspan referred to a generation ago as a "jumble of economic irrationality and ignorance"—and what modern scholarship has shown repeatedly to be a playground of special pleaders—is called for.

Here are seven reasons why the federal antitrust laws should be repealed.

1. Antitrust Debases the Idea of Private Property

Frequently when government invokes the antitrust laws, it transforms a company's private property into something that effectively belongs to

411

the public, to be designed by government officials and sold on terms congenial to rivals who are bent on the market leader's demise. Some advocates of the free market endorse that process, despite the destructive implications of stripping private property of its protection against confiscation. If new technology is to be declared public property, future technology will not materialize. If technology is to be proprietary, it must not be expropriated. Once expropriation becomes the remedy of choice, the goose is unlikely to continue laying golden eggs.

The principles are these: No one other than the owner has a right to the technology he or she created. Consumers can't demand that a product be provided at a specified price or with specified features. Competitors aren't entitled to share in the product's advantages. By demanding that one company's creation be exploited for the benefit of competitors, or even consumers, government is flouting core principles of free markets and individual liberty.

2. Antitrust Laws Are Fluid, Nonobjective, and Often Retroactive

Because of murky statutes and conflicting case law, companies can never be quite sure what constitutes permissible behavior. If a company cannot demonstrate that its actions were motivated by efficiency, conduct that is otherwise legal somehow morphs into an antitrust violation. Normal business practices—price discounts, product improvements, exclusive contracting—become violations of law. When they're not accused of monopoly price gouging for charging too much, companies are accused of predatory pricing for charging too little or collusion for charging the same.

3. Antitrust Is Based on a Static View of the Market

In real markets, sellers seek to carve out minimonopolies. Profits from market power are the engine that drives the economy. So what might happen in a utopian, perfectly competitive environment is irrelevant to the question of whether government intervention is necessary or appropriate. The proper comparison is with the marketplace that will evolve if the antitrust laws, by punishing success, eliminate incentives for new and improved products. Markets move faster than antitrust laws could ever move. Consumers rule, not producers. And consumers can unseat any product and any company no matter how powerful and entrenched. Just ask WordPerfect, or Lotus, or IBM.

4. Antitrust Remedies Are Designed by Bureaucrats Who Don't Understand How Markets Work

Economic losses from excessive regulation can greatly damage producers and consumers. But government moves forward in the name of correcting market failure, apparently without considering the possibility of government failure. Proponents of antitrust tell us that government planners know which products should be withdrawn from the market, no matter what consumers actually prefer. The problem with that argument is that it leads directly to paternalism, to the idea that an elite corps of experts knows our interests better than we do—and can regulate our affairs to satisfy those interests better than the market does.

The real issue is not whether one product is better than another, but who gets to decide—consumers, declaring their preferences by purchases in the market, or specialists at the Justice Department or the Federal Trade Commission, rating the merits of various goods and services. When we permit government to make such decisions for us, and we allow those decisions to trump the subjective choices of consumers, we abandon any pretense of a free market. In the process, we reduce consumer choice to a formalistic appraisal centering on technical features alone, notwithstanding that products are also desired for quality, price, service, convenience, and a host of other variables.

5. Antitrust Law Is Wielded by Business Rivals and Their Allies in the Political Arena

Instead of focusing on new and better products, disgruntled rivals try to exploit the law—consorting with members of Congress, their staff members, antitrust officials, and the best lobbying and public relations firms that money can buy. Soon enough, the targeted company responds in kind. Microsoft, for example, once conspicuously avoided Washington, politicking—but no longer. And America's entrepreneurial enclave, Silicon Valley, has become the home of billionaire businesspeople who use political influence to bring down their competitors. That agenda will destroy what it sets out to protect. Politicians are mostly order takers. So we'll get the kind of government we ask for—including oppressive regulation. Citizens who are troubled by huge corporations dominating private markets should be even more concerned if those same corporations decide that political clout better serves their interests—politicizing competition to advance the private interests of favored competitors.

6. Barriers to Entry Are Created by Government, Not Private Businesses

Under antitrust law, the proper test for government intervention is whether barriers to entry foreclose meaningful competition. But what is a "barrier"? When a company advertises, lowers prices, improves quality, adds features, or offers better service, it discourages rivals. But it cannot bar them. True barriers arise from government misbehavior, not private power—from special-interest legislation or a misconceived regulatory regimen that protects existing producers from competition. When government grants exclusive licenses to cable, electric, and telephone companies, monopolies are born and nurtured at public expense. When Congress decrees targeted tax benefits, subsidies, insurance guarantees, and loans or enacts tariffs and quotas to protect domestic companies from foreign rivals, that creates the same anti-competitive environment that the antitrust laws were meant to foreclose. The obvious answer, which has little to do with antitrust, is for government to stop creating those barriers at the outset.

7. Antitrust Will Inevitably Be Used by Unprincipled Politicians as a Political Bludgeon

Too often, the executive branch has exploited the antitrust laws to force conformity by "uncooperative" companies. Remember when President Richard M. Nixon wanted to browbeat the three major TV networks, he used the threat of an antitrust suit to extort more favorable media coverage. On a widely publicized tape, Nixon told his aide Chuck Colson: "Our gain is more important than the economic gain. We don't give a goddamn about the economic gain. Our game here is solely political. . . . As far as screwing the networks, I'm very glad to do it." If Nixon were the only culprit, that would be bad enough. But in his 1996 book *Abuse of Power*, former *New York Times* reporter David Burnham shows that presidents from John F. Kennedy through Bill Clinton routinely demanded that the Justice Department bend the rules in pursuit of political ends.

The lesson is clear. The threat of abusive public power is far larger than the threat of private monopoly. It's time for Congress to get rid of the federal antitrust laws. Meanwhile, pending repeal of those laws, Congress must ensure that enforcement by state authorities does not duplicate federal enforcement. Government must not get two bites at the antitrust apple, nor should defendants be exposed to double jeopardy.

Curb the States' Authority to Enforce Federal Antitrust Laws

It's time to rein in the power of state attorneys general (AGs). For most of American history, they did vital, but routine and distinctly unglamorous, legal work for their states. But beginning in the 1980s, some AGs challenged the Reagan administration's policies on antitrust and environmental law, pursuing their own agendas through litigation. In the antitrust context, activist AGs have relied on their so-called *parens patriae* power to sue on behalf of state residents under federal statutes.

The Microsoft case was perhaps the most egregious example of duplicative federal and state antitrust enforcement. Nine states—relying on the same trial, the same facts, the same conclusions of law, and the same injuries to the same people—wanted to override a settlement between Microsoft and the federal government, which 41 of 50 states supported. In a legal brief to a federal judge, the Justice Department offered persuasive reasons why the states should not be allowed an end run around the federal settlement.

First, "the United States is the sole enforcer of the federal antitrust laws on behalf of the American public." Second, the states' remedies would have affected competition and consumers outside their borders—raising "for the very first time the prospect that a small group of states, with no particularized interests to vindicate, might somehow obtain divergent relief with wide-ranging, national economic implications." Third, "the public interest is best served when federal and state antitrust activity is complementary, not duplicative or conflicting." Fourth, the nine holdout states had "neither the authority nor the responsibility to act in the broader national interest, and the plaintiff with that authority and responsibility [that is, the United States] has taken a different course."

Still worse, continued the Justice Department, the relief sought by the nonsettling states "may harm consumers, retard competition, chill innovation, or confound compliance" with the federal settlement. Echoing the Supreme Court, the Justice Department warned that antitrust redress requires a showing of "harm to competition not competitors." Remedies must be crafted for the benefit of the public, not for the private gain of politically favored rivals.

Consider the remarks of respected federal appeals judge Richard Posner, who mediated an abortive Microsoft settlement. Posner offered these recommendations in the *Antitrust Law Journal*: "I would like to see, first, the states stripped of their authority to bring antitrust suits, federal or state, except . . . where the state is suing firms that are fixing the prices of goods or services that they sell to the state. . . . [States] are too subject to influence by . . . competitors. This is a particular concern when the [competitor] is a major political force in that state. A situation in which the benefits of government action are concentrated in one state and the costs in other states is a recipe for irresponsible state action.''

Congress is constitutionally authorized to intervene whenever actual or imminent state practices threaten the free flow of commerce. Congress should use that power and revoke the *parens patriae* authority of the states to enforce federal antitrust laws. Otherwise, some states will continue to abuse their existing authority—exercising it to impose sovereignty beyond their borders and catering to the parochial interests of influential constituents.

Would constraints on state antitrust enforcement powers violate time-honored principles of federalism? Not at all. Federalism isn't simply a matter of states' rights. Nor is it exclusively about devolution of power or promoting efficient government. First and foremost, federalism is about checks and balances based on dual sovereignty. Most often, the states are a counterweight to excessive power in the hands of the federal government. Yet antitrust is an obvious situation where the federal government must curb excessive power in the hands of the states.

Conclusion

More than two centuries ago, Adam Smith observed in the *Wealth of Nations* that ''people of the same trade seldom meet together . . . but the conversation ends in a conspiracy against the public or in some contrivance to raise prices.'' Coming from the father of laissez faire, that warning has often been cited by antitrust proponents to justify all manner of interventionist mischief. Those same proponents, whether carelessly or deviously, rarely mention Smith's next sentence: ''It is impossible indeed to prevent such meetings, by any law which either could be executed, or would be consistent with liberty and justice.''

Antitrust is bad law, bad economics, and bad public policy. It deserves an ignominious burial—sooner rather than later.

Suggested Readings

Armentano, Dominick T. *Antitrust and Monopoly: Anatomy of a Policy Failure.* New York: Wiley, 1982.

DeBow, Michael. ''Restraining State Attorneys General, Curbing Government Lawsuit Abuse.'' Cato Institute Policy Analysis no. 437, May 10, 2002.

Greenspan, Alan. "Antitrust." In *Capitalism: The Unknown Ideal*, edited by Ayn Rand. New York: Signet, 1966.

Levy, Robert A. "Microsoft Redux: Anatomy of a Baseless Lawsuit." Cato Institute Policy Analysis no. 352, September 30, 1999.

———. "The Microsoft Moral: Repeal the Antitrust Laws, for Starters." *American Spectator,* May 2000.

Rockefeller, Edwin S. *The Antitrust Religion.* Washington: Cato Institute, 2007.

Shughart, William F., II. "The Government's War on Mergers: The Fatal Conceit of Antitrust Policy." Cato Institute Policy Analysis no. 323, October 22, 1998.

—Prepared by Robert A. Levy

Tax Policy

41. Federal Tax Reform

Congress should

- extend recent tax rate cuts for individual income, dividends, and capital gains;
- simplify the individual income tax by installing rates of 15 and 25 percent and repealing virtually all deductions and credits;
- cut the federal corporate income tax rate from 35 percent to 15 percent;
- turn Roth individual retirement accounts into all-purpose savings accounts by liberalizing rules on contributions and withdrawals;
- replace business depreciation with capital expensing;
- take these reforms further by replacing the income tax with a consumption-based flat tax at 15 percent;
- repeal the individual and corporate alternative minimum taxes; and
- repeal the estate tax.

At the beginning of the 20th century, federal taxes accounted for 3 percent of the nation's gross domestic product, and federal tax rules filled just a few hundred pages. Today, federal taxes account for about 18 percent of GDP, and federal tax laws and regulations span 67,506 pages, according to CCH Inc.

The federal government extracts about $2.8 trillion in federal taxes from families and businesses each year, which imposes a huge economic cost. The most visible cost is people being left with less money to buy food, clothing, and other needed items, while businesses are left with fewer funds for investment.

The federal tax system imposes other costs. The complexity of federal taxation creates compliance and administrative costs, and it makes financial planning more difficult for individuals and businesses. Furthermore, the hidden nature of many federal taxes imposes a cost in transparency. In particular, it is difficult for citizens to figure out the overall burden of taxes they are paying under the current system.

A final cost of the current tax system is that high rates and the unequal treatment of economic activities create distortions that reduce growth. Given all these problems of the current tax system, tax reforms should aim at three goals: simplification, transparency, and increased economic growth.

Simplification

In 1976, president-to-be Jimmy Carter called for "a complete overhaul of our income tax system. I feel it's a disgrace to the human race." Since that call for reform, the number of pages of federal tax rules has roughly tripled, according to CCH. A recent study by the World Bank found that the United States had the fifth-longest tax code among 20 industrial economies studied. The complexity of the U.S. tax code creates at least five types of costs:

1. **Compliance and enforcement burdens.** Americans spend more than 6 billion hours annually filling out tax forms, keeping records, and learning tax rules, according to the Office of Management and Budget. The paperwork for a tax return of a large corporation can total 10,000 pages. In addition to these costs of tax filing, taxpayers face a burden from audits, notices, liens, levies, seizures, and the millions of penalties assessed each year by the Internal Revenue Service. All in all, a huge public and private tax industry is needed to administer and enforce the complex system, the costs of which are roughly $200 billion annually.
2. **Errors.** Tax complexity causes taxpayers and the IRS to make frequent and costly errors. For example, the IRS has a poor record on answering taxpayer phone inquiries accurately. But don't blame the IRS, blame Congress for larding the tax code with thousands of complex provisions, such as narrow credits and deductions for favored individuals and businesses.
3. **Economic decisionmaking.** Tax complexity impedes efficient deci-sionmaking by families and businesses. For example, the growing number of saving vehicles under the income tax confuses financial planning. If a family chooses the wrong vehicle for its savings, that

decision could result in higher taxes, lower returns, less liquidity, and payment of withdrawal penalties. For businesses, tax complexity injects uncertainty into capital investment and other important decisions.

4. **Inequity and unfairness.** Although equality under the law is a bedrock principle of justice, individuals pay greatly different tax rates under the income tax. For example, IRS data for 2006 show that income taxes averaged 22 percent of adjusted gross income for those earning more than $200,000, but 9 percent for those earning between $50,000 and $100,000. The tax code can also treat people with similar incomes very unequally as a result of the many special exemptions, deductions, and credits. Tax incentives for education, homeownership, alternative fuels, and other items unfairly favor some Americans over others.

5. **Avoidance and evasion.** Tax complexity leads to greater noncompliance with the tax system. Noncompliance stems both from simple confusion over the tax rules and from the aggressive tax planning that complexity makes possible. Taxpayers take more risks on their tax returns when complexity can hide their strategies from the IRS. If the tax code was radically reformed to create simple and transparent rules, taxpayers would focus on productive endeavors rather than designing elaborate avoidance schemes.

Transparency

A simple and transparent tax system would present citizens with a clear picture of the burden of government. If the government imposed only one tax at a flat rate, people could easily compare the cost of government with the costs of other items in their budget, such as food and housing.

Unfortunately, policymakers use various techniques to hide the burden of government, which reduces resistance to high taxes. For example, the introduction of federal income tax withholding in 1943 made paying taxes less painful, and thus helped fuel government growth in subsequent decades.

Another problem is that the government conceals the size of the overall tax load by spreading the burden across numerous types of taxes. Each tax may have multiple rates, deductions, and credits, making it difficult for people to fully understand what share of their overall earnings goes to the government.

Perhaps the most important way that politicians reduce resistance to taxation is to collect taxes from businesses, which generally hides the costs from voters. The biggest hidden tax is the "employer" half of the 15 percent payroll tax that funds Social Security and Medicare. This tax is not reported on worker pay stubs, but economists agree that the burden falls on workers in the form of lower wages.

Another hidden tax is the corporate income tax, which is passed through to individuals in the form of higher prices, lower wages, or reduced returns on savings. Other hidden federal taxes include import duties, unemployment insurance taxes, and excise taxes. All in all, 37 percent of federal taxes are hidden, amounting to about $1 trillion in revenue in fiscal year 2009. The result is that voters perceive the "price" of the government to be artificially low, causing them to "demand" too much of it.

Reforms should make tax structures simple, flat, and visible so that the cost of government is more transparent. For the payroll tax, employers should be encouraged to disclose the entire payroll tax on worker pay stubs and on annual tax forms mailed to employees.

For the income tax, the current mess of multiple rates and narrow breaks should be scrapped in favor of a simple flat tax. All taxpayers should pay an equal share of their income or consumption to the government. Under a flat tax, there would be greater "solidarity" among taxpayers because a proposed tax increase would hit everyone equally. The result would be greater opposition to tax increases, unless citizens believed that their government was giving them good value.

Economic Growth

U.S. output and income levels would be higher if the overall size of the government was reduced. But it is also true that at any particular size of government, the economy would be stronger if the tax system were more efficient. An efficient tax system is one that minimizes distortions that affect working, saving, investing, and entrepreneurship. Unfortunately, the current income tax greatly distorts productive activities and diverts resources into lower-valued uses.

Another way to say this is that the current tax code generates high "deadweight losses." The magnitude of these losses is directly related to marginal tax rates. Indeed, as marginal rates rise, deadweight losses rise more than proportionally. That is why a flatter tax structure with lower rates would be much more efficient than today's graduated, or "progressive," tax structure.

Large reductions in deadweight losses would occur from cutting the highest income tax rates. People with high incomes, such as doctors and executives, often have unique talents. If a skilled surgeon decides to work less because of high tax rates, the biggest losers would be the potential patients who would not benefit from his or her skills.

Another consideration is the high concentration of small businesses in the top income tax brackets. About three-quarters of the top 1 percent of federal taxpayers report some small business income, and these taxpayers have the most flexibility in adjusting their reported taxable income with changes to their working and investing activities.

The bottom line is that every $1 million tax increase costs the economy much more than $1 million because of the losses to efficiency caused by taxpayers' responding to the higher rates. The Congressional Budget Office stated that "typical estimates of the economic cost of a dollar of tax revenue range from 20 cents to 60 cents over and above the revenue raised." Estimates of deadweight losses by Harvard University's Martin Feldstein and others are even higher.

Aside from reducing tax rates, tax reforms should focus on reducing the income tax code's bias against savings and investment. That bias undermines efforts to expand and modernize the nation's capital stock, which in turn reduces long-run economic growth. Also, the income tax system applies different tax burdens to different forms of savings and investment, which further distorts the economy.

Most major tax reform proposals would switch from an income tax base to a consumption tax base to create a neutral system with respect to savings and investment. For businesses, the tax code can be converted to a consumption base by substituting capital "expensing" for depreciation. Under expensing, businesses would immediately deduct the full costs of equipment and structures, rather than deducting the costs over several years.

For individuals, the tax code can be converted to a consumption base by liberalizing Roth individual retirement accounts. Under Roth IRAs, contributions are from after-tax earnings, but account earnings and qualified withdrawals are tax-free. Reforms should liberalize Roth IRA contribution limits, while repealing restrictions on withdrawals. All withdrawals should be made free from taxes and penalties. That would encourage families to build larger nest eggs so that they could enjoy greater economic security free from the government.

Reductions in marginal rates, business capital expensing, and expanded Roth IRAs would move the tax code toward a consumption-based flat tax system built on the design of Hoover Institution senior fellows Robert Hall and Alvin Rabushka. Moving toward a flat tax would make the tax code simpler, more equitable, and more efficient.

Tax Reform Steps

Extend income tax rate cuts. In 2001 and 2003, Congress took some modest tax reform steps, including reducing statutory tax rates on individuals. However, these tax cuts are set to expire at the end of 2010, creating the threat of huge tax increases on taxpayers at all income levels. To avert such a tax hike, Congress should extend the 2001 and 2003 tax cuts permanently.

Cut the dividend tax rate. The maximum individual tax rate on dividends is currently 15 percent, but the rate is scheduled to rise to 40 percent in 2011. Even with today's reduced rate, the combined rate on dividends—taking into account both corporate and individual-level taxes—is the eighth highest of the 30 major industrial countries. If the rate rises in 2011, the United States will have the highest dividend tax rate of all major countries. See *Global Tax Revolution* for details.

Cut the individual capital gains tax rate. The maximum tax rate on individual capital gains is 15 percent, but the rate is scheduled to rise to 20 percent in 2011. As a first reform step, the rate should be maintained at 15 percent because low capital gains tax rates are important to encouraging entrepreneurship and investment. Note that many other advanced nations and jurisdictions have general capital gains tax rates of zero, including Austria, Belgium, the Czech Republic, Greece, Hong Kong, the Netherlands, New Zealand, and Switzerland.

Cut the corporate tax rate to 15 percent. The average statutory corporate tax rate in the European Union was cut from 38 percent in 1996 to 24 percent in 2007. By contrast, the U.S. corporate tax rate is far higher at 40 percent, which includes the 35 percent federal rate plus the average state corporate rate. The federal corporate tax rate should be cut from 35 percent to 15 percent, as discussed further in Chapter 42.

Extend and expand capital expensing. To spur economic growth, Congress has enacted a number of temporary tax cuts in recent years that have allowed companies to expense, or immediately deduct, a portion of the costs of qualified capital purchases. But full capital expensing should be made permanent, which would greatly simplify business taxation while boosting investment and economic growth.

Liberalize Roth IRAs. Roth IRAs should be turned into all-purpose savings accounts that allow withdrawals for any reason, not just for government-specified purposes. Such accounts would encourage families to build up large pools of savings that could be used for any contingency, including medical expenses, home buying, unemployment, college, or unexpected crises. All personal savings—not just retirement savings—create financial stability and should be encouraged. Such all-purpose Roth accounts would also simplify the tax code because the plethora of current special-purpose accounts could be scrapped.

Repeal the estate tax. The tax law of 2001 repealed the federal estate tax, but only through the year 2010. After 2010, the "death tax" is revived in full force with a top tax rate of 55 percent. The death tax raises only about 1 percent of federal revenues, but it is very costly to the economy. It has created a large and wasteful estate-planning industry to help people avoid the tax if they hire enough accountants. Indeed, studies indicate that for every $1 raised by the tax, roughly $1 is lost from avoidance, compliance, and enforcement costs.

In addition, the death tax may not actually raise any money, on net, for the government because it tends to suppress income tax collections. The former chairman of the Council of Economic Advisers, Greg Mankiw, concluded that "estate tax repeal . . . could actually increase total federal revenue," and he has noted that "repeal of the estate tax would stimulate growth and raise incomes for everyone."

Repeal the individual and corporate alternative minimum taxes. The individual alternative minimum tax (AMT) is a parallel income tax system on top of the basic income tax. It has different deductions, exemptions, and tax rates. The AMT is not indexed for inflation, with the result that its burden is expected to grow rapidly in coming years. Without relief from Congress, about 30 million taxpayers will be subject to the AMT by 2010. But there is broad agreement that the AMT should be repealed— America does not need two different income tax systems. The IRS national taxpayer advocate supports repeal, arguing that the AMT is a "poster child for tax-law complexity." The corporate AMT should also be repealed because it distorts business decisionmaking and serves no economic purpose.

Reform the tax policy process. When Congress considers changes to the tax code, the Joint Committee on Taxation estimates the effects on federal revenues. Those estimates are important in policy debates, but they are often erroneous and incomplete, and the process is shrouded in secrecy.

427

One key problem is that estimates do not account for changes that taxes create on the macroeconomy. For example, if marginal tax rates are cut, the economy will grow, generating rising tax revenues to offset government losses from the cut. The tax policy processes at the JCT and the Treasury Department should be reformed so that all analyses of proposed tax policy changes take into account such dynamic effects.

Enact a consumption-based flat tax. In recent decades, proposals to replace the federal income tax with a consumption-based tax have gained support because such reforms would simplify the tax code, increase transparency, and spur economic growth. All the reform steps discussed here would move toward a simpler, flatter consumption-based system. As of 2008, 25 nations and jurisdictions have enacted flat tax systems, as discussed in *Global Tax Revolution*. Most of those systems have low tax rates and favorable treatment of savings and investment. America should join this "flat tax club" to bring fairness to the tax code, to spur investment, and to revitalize the economy.

Suggested Readings

Adams, Charles. *Those Dirty Rotten Taxes: The Tax Revolts That Built America.* New York: Free Press, 1998.

Bradford, David. *Untangling the Income Tax.* Cambridge, MA: Harvard University Press, 1999.

Burton, David. "Reforming the Federal Tax Policy Process." Cato Institute Policy Analysis no. 463, December 17, 2002.

Edwards, Chris. "Simplifying Federal Taxes: The Advantages of Consumption-Based Taxation." Cato Institute Policy Analysis no. 416, October 17, 2001.

———. "Replacing the Scandal-Plagued Corporate Income Tax with a Cash-Flow Tax." Cato Institute Policy Analysis no. 484, August 14, 2003.

———. "Options for Tax Reform." Cato Institute Policy Analysis no. 536, February 24, 2005.

———. "Repealing the Federal Estate Tax." Cato Institute Tax & Budget Bulletin no. 36, June 2006.

———. "The Alternative Minimum Tax: Repeal Not Reform." Cato Institute Tax & Budget Bulletin no. 45, May 2007.

Edwards, Chris, and Dan Mitchell. *Global Tax Revolution.* Washington: Cato Institute, 2008.

Hall, Robert, and Alvin Rabushka. *The Flat Tax.* 2nd ed. Stanford, CA: Hoover Institution Press, 1995.

—Prepared by Chris Edwards

42. International Tax Competition

Congress should

- cut the federal corporate income tax rate from 35 percent to 15 percent;
- take steps toward replacing the individual and corporate income taxes with a low-rate flat tax;
- oppose policies that would make U.S. companies uncompetitive in global markets, such as raising taxes on foreign subsidiaries; and
- oppose efforts to impose global taxes or limit international tax competition.

Globalization is transforming separate national economies into a single world economy. This process is occurring through rising trade and investment flows, greater labor mobility, and rapid transfers of technology. As integration increases, individuals and businesses are gaining freedom to take advantage of foreign economic opportunities. Individuals have more choices about where to work and invest, and businesses have more choices about where to locate their production, research, and headquarters facilities.

Many governments have responded to rising globalization with tax cuts to attract investment and spur growth. Individual income tax rates have plunged in recent decades, and more than two dozen nations have replaced their complex income taxes with simple flat taxes. At the same time, nearly every major country has slashed its corporate tax rate, recognizing that business investment has become highly mobile in today's economy.

That is the good news. The bad news is that some governments and international organizations are trying to restrict tax competition. A battle is unfolding between those policymakers who want to maximize taxation and those who understand that competition is leading to beneficial tax reforms. If plans to stifle tax competition gain ground, growth will be undermined, governments will grow larger, and economic freedom will be curtailed.

Cutting of Tax Rates

High tax rates are difficult to sustain in the competitive global economy. That is particularly true for taxes on capital income, including taxes on dividends, interest, capital gains, business profits, and wealth. High taxation of capital income reduces domestic savings and investment and drives out capital, which reduces a nation's productivity, wages, and income levels over time.

All major industrial nations have cut their income tax rates in recent years. Table 42.1 shows that the average statutory corporate tax rate for the 30-nation Organisation for Economic Co-operation and Development has fallen from 38 percent to 27 percent since the mid-1990s. By contrast, the U.S. corporate tax rate is 40 percent, including the 35 percent federal rate plus the average state corporate tax rate. The U.S. rate is the second highest in the OECD.

Table 42.2 shows that the average top individual income tax rate for the OECD countries fell from 68 percent in 1980 to 42 percent by 2007. The top U.S. rate is about 39 percent, based on a federal rate of 35 percent plus the average of state rates. After 2010, the top federal rate is scheduled to increase from 35 percent to 40 percent. That would push the overall U.S. rate to at least 44 percent, which would be above the average among these nations.

Many countries have also cut their tax rates on dividends, capital gains, estates, and inheritances in recent years. Numerous countries have abolished annual taxes on wealth, which used to be popular in Europe. Further, withholding taxes on cross-border investments have been cut sharply around the world in recent years. All those types of taxes have mobile tax bases, and policymakers have figured out that imposing high rates on mobile tax bases is very counterproductive.

The international tax landscape has become remarkably dynamic. After reforms in 1986, the United States had one of the lowest corporate tax rates. But since then, U.S. policymakers have fallen asleep at the switch on corporate tax reform as other countries have continued to cut. In today's global economy, if a country stands still, it falls behind.

Consider tax rates on dividends. The average tax rate in the OECD— including the burden at both the individual and the corporate levels—fell from 50 percent in 2000 to 43 percent in 2007, according to OECD data.

Table 42.1
Top Corporate Income Tax Rates in the OECD (percent)

Country	1996	1998	2000	2002	2004	2006	2008	Change 1996–2008
Australia	36	36	36	30	30	30	30	−6
Austria	34	34	34	34	34	25	25	−9
Belgium	40	40	40	40	34	34	34	−6
Britain	33	31	30	30	30	30	28	−5
Canada	45	45	45	39	36	36	34	−11
Czech Rep.	39	35	31	31	28	24	21	−18
Denmark	34	34	32	30	30	28	28	−6
Finland	28	28	29	29	29	26	26	−2
France	37	42	37	34	34	33	33	−3
Germany	57	57	52	38	38	38	30	−27
Greece	40	40	40	35	35	29	25	−15
Hungary	33	18	18	18	16	16	16	−17
Iceland	33	30	30	18	18	18	18	−15
Ireland	38	32	24	16	13	13	13	−26
Italy	53	41	41	40	37	37	31	−22
Japan	52	52	42	42	42	41	41	−11
Korea	33	31	31	30	30	28	28	−5
Luxembourg	40	37	38	30	30	30	30	−11
Mexico	34	34	35	35	33	29	28	−6
Netherlands	35	35	35	35	35	30	26	−10
New Zealand	33	33	33	33	33	33	30	−3
Norway	28	28	28	28	28	28	28	0
Poland	40	36	30	28	19	19	19	−21
Portugal	40	37	35	33	28	28	25	−15
Slovakia	n.a.	n.a.	29	25	19	19	19	−10
Spain	35	35	35	35	35	35	30	−5
Sweden	28	28	28	28	28	28	28	0
Switzerland	29	28	25	25	24	21	21	−7
Turkey	44	44	33	33	33	30	20	−24
United States	40	40	40	40	40	40	40	0
Average	38	36	34	31	30	28	27	−11

SOURCE: KPMG, "Corporate and Indirect Tax Rate Survey," 2007. Updated to 2008 by the authors. Data includes both national and subnational taxes. Some numbers have been rounded.

NOTE: n.a. = not applicable.

That means that the U.S. rate of 49 percent is now substantially higher than average as a result of recent tax cuts abroad. Even worse, the U.S. tax rate on dividends is scheduled to rise to 64 percent in 2011, which would be easily the highest rate among major countries.

Table 42.2
Top Individual Income Tax Rates in the OECD (percent)

Country	1980	1985	1990	1995	2000	2005	2007	Change 1980–2007
Australia	62	60	49	47	47	47	45	−17
Austria	62	62	50	50	50	50	50	−12
Belgium	76	76	58	61	60	53	53	−24
Britain	83	60	40	40	40	40	40	−43
Canada	64	57	49	49	48	44	44	−20
Czech Rep.	n.a.	n.a.	n.a.	43	32	32	32	−11
Denmark	66	73	68	64	59	59	59	−7
Finland	68	67	60	57	54	53	52	−16
France	60	65	60	62	61	56	49	−11
Germany	65	65	53	57	56	44	47	−18
Greece	60	63	50	45	43	40	40	−20
Hungary	n.a.	n.a.	50	44	40	38	36	−14
Iceland	63	56	40	47	45	39	36	−27
Ireland	60	65	58	48	42	42	41	−19
Italy	72	81	66	67	51	44	44	−28
Japan	75	70	65	65	50	50	50	−25
Korea	89	65	64	48	44	39	39	−50
Luxembourg	57	57	56	50	47	39	39	−18
Mexico	55	55	40	35	40	30	28	−27
Netherlands	72	72	60	60	52	52	52	−20
New Zealand	62	66	33	33	39	39	39	−23
Norway	75	64	51	42	48	40	40	−35
Poland	n.a.	n.a.	n.a.	45	40	40	40	−5
Portugal	84	69	40	40	40	40	42	−42
Slovakia	n.a.	n.a.	n.a.	42	42	19	19	−23
Spain	66	66	56	56	48	40	39	−27
Sweden	87	80	65	50	55	56	56	−32
Switzerland	38	40	38	37	36	34	34	−4
Turkey	75	63	50	55	45	40	40	−35
United States	73	55	38	43	43	39	39	−34
Average	68	64	52	49	47	43	42	−26

SOURCE: James Gwartney and Robert Lawson, *Economic Freedom of the World* (Vancouver: Fraser Institute, 2007), as updated to 2007 by the authors. Data includes the national and average subnational tax rates.

NOTE: n.a. = not applicable.

Flat Tax Revolution

In the 1980s, the big story in tax competition was the reduction in individual and corporate income tax rates in major industrial countries, such as Britain and the United States. In the 1990s, tax rate cuts intensified and spread to a broader group of countries. In the 2000s, the most exciting tax competition story is the flat tax revolution. By 2008, 25 jurisdictions had adopted single-rate individual income taxes, as shown in Table 42.3.

Ironically, it is the former communist world that is the hotbed of flat tax reforms. From the Czech Republic in the west to Mongolia in the east, 17 nations in the former Soviet bloc have joined the flat tax club. Those nations have adopted flat taxes to spur growth, reduce tax avoidance, and attract foreign investment. Reform leaders, such as Estonia and Slovakia, inspired a broader group of countries to join the flat tax revolu-

Table 42.3
The Flat Tax Club: Income Tax Rates, 2008

Jurisdiction	Year Individual Flat Tax Adopted	Individual Flat Tax Rate	Corporate Tax Rate
Jersey, Channel Islands	1940	20.0%	20.0%
Hong Kong	1947	15.0%	16.5%
Guernsey, Channel Islands	1960	20.0%	20.0%
Jamaica	1986	25.0%	33.3%
Estonia	1994	21.0%	21.0%
Lithuania	1994	24.0%	15.0%
Latvia	1995	25.0%	15.0%
Russia	2001	13.0%	24.0%
Slovakia	2004	19.0%	19.0%
Ukraine	2004	15.0%	25.0%
Iraq	2004	15.0%	15.0%
Romania	2005	16.0%	16.0%
Georgia	2005	12.0%	15.0%
Kyrgyzstan	2006	10.0%	10.0%
Pridnestrovie	2006	10.0%	10.0%
Trinidad	2006	25.0%	25.0%
Iceland	2007	35.7%	18.0%
Kazakhstan	2007	10.0%	30.0%
Mongolia	2007	10.0%	25.0%
Macedonia	2007	10.0%	10.0%
Montenegro	2007	15.0%	9.0%
Albania	2007	10.0%	10.0%
Mauritius	2007	15.0%	15.0%
Czech Rep.	2008	15.0%	21.0%
Bulgaria	2008	<u>10.0%</u>	<u>10.0%</u>
Average of 25 jurisdictions		16.6%	17.9%

SOURCE: Authors. Figures include national and subnational rates. Estonia's corporate rate for retained earnings is zero.

433

tion. In numerous countries, political parties on both the right and the left have supported flat tax reforms.

A "flat tax" generally refers to a direct tax on individuals with a single statutory rate. The flat tax concept also embodies the ideas that special tax preferences should be abolished, people should be treated equally, and income should be taxed only once. Today, the average individual tax rate in the 25 flat tax countries is just 17 percent. Most of the flat tax countries have also cut their corporate tax rates, and the average corporate rate in those nations is just 18 percent.

The flat tax revolution will likely continue to spread, perhaps into western Europe where countries are feeling competitive pressures from the flat tax nations to the east. In the United States, the flat tax has been debated for years but not enacted. Hopefully, further reforms abroad will provide U.S. policymakers the encouragement they need to jump on board the flat tax express.

Corporate Tax Reforms

A key issue for tax policy in the global economy is how to deal with multinational corporations. Corporate taxation is important to investors, but also to the living standards of average Americans. In a globalized economy, the burden of the corporate income tax falls mainly on workers in the form of lower wages. If corporations are not investing in the United States due to high taxes, labor productivity will fall, and that will drag down American wages.

Compared with foreign-based corporations, U.S. multinational corporations are subject to particularly high tax rates and complicated tax rules. The United States taxes corporations on their worldwide income, even though that income may also be subject to taxes in the foreign nations where it is earned. The U.S. tax code provides credits to minimize double-taxation, but this is a complex and uncompetitive method of business taxation. The worldwide system discourages the repatriation of foreign earnings, and it puts U.S. businesses at a disadvantage in foreign markets. By contrast, two-thirds of major nations tax corporations on a territorial basis, which means that they generally do not tax business income earned outside their national borders.

There would be two key advantages of the United States' switching from a worldwide to a territorial system of business taxation. First, it would end the current tax barrier to the repatriation of foreign earnings. Currently, repatriated foreign earnings are subject to the 35 percent federal corporate tax, which suppresses profit repatriation and thus investment in the United States. Under a territorial system, business profits earned abroad would be repatriated free of a U.S. tax burden.

Second, it would help make the United States a good home for the headquarters of multinational corporations. Currently, a high tax rate and the worldwide tax system make the United States a poor choice for locating corporate headquarters. If the United States switched to a territorial system, companies could earn profits abroad without a U.S. tax burden placed on top of the foreign taxes paid. That would make it easier for firms to expand their foreign sales, which in turn would lead to expansion in firms' U.S. headquarters activities, such as management, finance, and research.

Reducing the U.S. corporate tax rate is also a crucial reform because of the mobile nature of the corporate tax base in the globalized economy. Because of the high U.S. tax rate, companies put large efforts into moving their investments and reported profits abroad to low-tax nations, such as Ireland. America's high corporate tax rate is a loser for the U.S. economy, and it is also a loser for the government because it causes the tax base to shrink dramatically.

Recent experience shows that governments lose little, if any, revenue when they cut their corporate tax rates. Corporate tax cuts create strong dynamic responses that offset reductions in revenues. In our book *Global Tax Revolution*, we calculated the average corporate tax rate and average corporate tax revenues as a share of gross domestic product for 19 industrial nations. The average corporate tax rate across countries was 40 percent or more until the mid-1980s. But then tax rates plunged, with the average rate falling from 45 percent in 1985 to 29 percent by 2005. Interestingly, corporate tax revenues did not decline as rates fell. In fact, tax revenues soared from 2.6 percent of GDP in 1985 to 3.7 percent in 2005, which is a 42 percent increase.

Corporate tax revenues have surged in most countries that have cut tax rates. Lower rates generate more real investment and higher incomes in subsequent years. In addition, tax rate cuts result in increases in reported profits as companies reduce their tax avoidance and tax evasion activities. The bottom line is that a corporate tax rate cut is a winner for the economy, for workers, and potentially for the government as well as the tax base expands over time.

Backlash against Tax Competition

The global tax revolution is a supply-side revolution. Supply-side tax cuts are those that reduce the costs of productive activities, such as working, investing, and starting businesses. If the costs of production are reduced, output will increase and incomes will rise. Tax competition creates pressure to cut precisely those taxes that are the most damaging to the economy. More tax competition means more productive economies and higher living standards.

Alas, many politicians and pundits do not see it that way. They claim that tax competition causes distortions in the private sector. The idea is that if investment flows are driven in any way by taxation, it is "inefficient" for the world economy. Ireland is receiving "too much" investment because of its low business taxes, for example. Others argue that tax competition creates distortions in the public sector. Any reduction in government revenue that results from capital and labor emigrating to lower-tax nations is supposed to be an inefficient "fiscal externality." Government revenues will fall below the supposed optimal size as a "race to the bottom" in tax levels ensues.

There are many theoretical flaws in those arguments. For one thing, they are premised on the "public interest theory of government," the idea that government officials always act for the general welfare of citizens. But it is naive to assume that if policymakers had monopoly fiscal power without tax competition, they would set tax rates at the optimal level for the good of the people.

Another mistake of tax competition opponents is to think of tax competition as a zero-sum game. In fact, tax competition drives down tax rates on the most inefficient types of taxes, and thus helps to expand the global economic pie. All nations that enact supply-side tax reforms can generate greater economic growth. Countries are not competing to divide a fixed pie, but to create the least burdensome government and the most prosperity for citizens.

On a practical level, there has not been a race to the bottom in tax revenues around the world, as the critics fear. Fiscal conservatives might wish that there had been, but tax competition has not yet "starved the beast" of bloated government. But looking ahead, tax competition will impose a valuable barrier against government growth. In coming decades, the rising costs of retirement and health programs for the elderly in the United States and elsewhere will generate large pressures to increase taxes. Vigorous tax competition will be a crucial tool to preserve limited government in the 21st century.

Supporters of big government know that expansive welfare states are in jeopardy from tax competition, which is why they are trying to limit it. Their strategy is for governments to impose international agreements to equalize taxes and to share information about each other's taxpayers. Efforts are under way through the European Commission, the United Nations, and the OECD to control tax competition and eliminate downward pressures on tax rates. There are also proposals to create a permanent world tax organization, which would help enforce limits to competition.

Such efforts to restrict tax competition are bad economics, and they also raise privacy and human rights concerns. A goal of tax competition opponents is the adoption of extensive sharing of personal financial information between countries. But governments have a very poor record on keeping personal data private. In one recent British scandal, for example, a low-level tax official lost two computer disks containing the detailed tax, financial, and banking records of 25 million individuals. When less savory governments are involved, the issues can be even more serious. The security of many people will be at risk if governments create a global network of tax police to collect and swap personal financial information.

Tax haven jurisdictions, which have strong privacy laws, are being pressured by groups such as the OECD to make sweeping policy changes to dilute their high standards. But privacy rights are a crucial freedom in the digital age. Tax havens are specialists in privacy, they generally have very high governance standards, and most are economic success stories. It makes no sense for the OECD and other international organizations to run roughshod over their ability to set their own pro-market economic policies.

To defend tax competition, U.S. policymakers should do the following:

- Use American influence to stop the OECD's anti-tax competition project;
- Reject European Union invitations to participate in cartel-like tax initiatives, such as the savings tax directive;
- Block possible schemes of the United Nations to create global taxes, global tax standards, or a global tax organization;
- Oppose efforts to change U.S. policies to reduce tax competition, such as imposing new requirements for the reporting of interest paid to nonresidents; and
- Reject the various efforts of U.S. policymakers to blacklist low-tax nations.

America's Challenge

U.S. tax policy has fossilized, while many other countries are making pro-growth tax reforms. The last major U.S. tax reform was in 1986, which is prehistoric given the fast pace of the modern economy. More bad news is that recent tax cuts enacted in 2001 and 2003 are scheduled to expire at the end of 2010.

America's tax system has both pros and cons compared with other countries. On the plus side, America has:

- A lower overall tax burden than many countries; federal, state, and local taxes are 27 percent of GDP in the United States, compared with an average 36 percent in the 30 OECD nations; and
- No value-added tax; in every other major country, VATs impose a substantial tax burden in addition to income and payroll taxes.

On the minus side, America has:

- The second-highest corporate tax rate in the world at 40 percent, which includes the 35 percent federal rate plus the average state rate;
- The eighth-highest dividend tax rate in the OECD;
- The third-highest estate or inheritance tax rate in the OECD;
- One of the highest tax rates in the world on corporate capital gains;
- Tax rates on individual income, capital gains, dividends, and estates that are scheduled to rise in 2011 when current tax cuts expire; and
- State-level corporate tax rates that have not been cut in decades.

In sum, the overall tax burden in the United States is lower than in many other nations, but our tax system has important negatives, such as high tax rates on savings and investment. Why shouldn't the United States have the simplest and most pro-growth tax system in the world? Ireland has a corporate tax rate of 12.5 percent, and many advanced countries have capital gains and death tax rates of zero. Meanwhile, 25 jurisdictions have installed simple flat taxes. There is no reason why these reforms could not be implemented in the United States.

To that end, Chapter 41 proposes some major tax reform steps. Individual income tax rates should be cut to 15 to 25 percent, and narrow tax breaks abolished. The corporate tax rate should be cut from 35 percent to 15 percent, and the corporate tax system should be made territorial to help U.S. companies compete abroad. These changes would give America a far more competitive tax system. The United States would become a magnet for global investment and would likely enjoy a long-term economic boom. Such reforms would be a big step toward the ultimate goal of enacting a simple, low-rate flat tax that treats taxpayers equally and maximizes growth.

Suggested Readings

De Rugy, Veronique, and Richard Rahn. ''Threats to Financial Privacy and Tax Competition.'' Cato Institute Policy Analysis no. 491, October 2, 2003.

Edwards, Chris. ''Replacing the Scandal-Plagued Corporate Income Tax with a Cash-Flow Tax.'' Cato Institute Policy Analysis no. 484, August 14, 2003.

———. ''Corporate Tax Laffer Curve.'' Cato Institute Tax & Budget Bulletin no. 49, November 2007.

Edwards, Chris, and Daniel J. Mitchell. *Global Tax Revolution.* Washington: Cato Institute, 2008.

Edwards, Chris, and Veronique de Rugy. ''International Tax Competition, A 21st-Century Restraint on Government.'' Cato Institute Policy Analysis no. 431, April 12, 2002.

KPMG. ''Corporate and Indirect Tax Rate Survey.'' 2007. www.kpmgtaxwatch.com/pub/intl/2007_Corporate_and_Indirect_Tax_Rate_Survey.pdf.

Mitchell, Daniel. ''Corporate Taxes: America Is Falling Behind.'' Cato Institute Tax & Budget Bulletin no. 48, July 2007.

Organisation for Economic Co-operation and Development. *Harmful Tax Competition: An Emerging Global Issue.* Paris: OECD, 1998.

———. Tax Database. www.oecd.org/ctp/taxdatabase.

—Prepared by Chris Edwards and Daniel J. Mitchell

ENERGY AND ENVIRONMENT

43. Energy Policy

Congress should

- open up public lands currently off limits to the oil and gas industry in the outer continental shelf and the Arctic National Wildlife Refuge for exploration and drilling;
- repeal Corporate Average Fuel Efficiency standards along with all other energy conservation mandates;
- repeal subsidies for all energy industries, including oil, gas, coal, nuclear, and renewable energies of all kinds;
- repeal fuel consumption mandates for ethanol and resist prospective consumption mandates for other renewable energies;
- eliminate all targeted public energy research and development programs and replace them with a generalized tax credit for private research and development undertakings;
- transfer the maintenance of the nuclear weapons stockpile from the Department of Energy to the Department of Defense and privatize the national laboratories;
- sell the oil from the Strategic Petroleum Reserve and terminate the program;
- eliminate the Department of Energy and all its programs; and
- refuse appeals to impose new taxes and/or regulations on energy producers and manufacturers.

Polling data during the 2008 campaign season found that soaring gasoline prices were, aside from the financial crisis, the most important single issue on the minds of voters. Naturally, politicians have responded with a flurry of legislative proposals designed to reduce fuel prices at the pump. Unfortunately, there is little political agreement on why gasoline prices are at near-historic heights, and this disagreement sets the stage for the arguments about energy policy that now dominate the political landscape.

Understanding of the Price Spiral

The conventional narrative is that changes in gasoline prices can be almost entirely explained over the long run by changes in world crude oil prices. World crude oil prices have increased for six consecutive years—the longest sustained oil price increase in history—because of spectacular global economic growth over that same period. The global economic boom of 2003–08 has increased the demand for all commodities—including crude oil—and this demand shock hit the market at a time when both excess oil production capacity and private oil inventories were at very low levels. Given the fact that neither the demand for nor the supply of crude oil changes very much in the short term in response to price changes, even a modest increase in demand can have a major effect on oil, and thus gasoline, prices. Some economists who study these matters have concluded that the 300 percent increase in global oil prices since 2003 could be entirely explained by a 6 percent increase in global oil demand.

There is room to quibble about the exact mathematical relationship between demand increases and oil price hikes (some data sets, for instance, suggest that a 21 percent increase in global oil demand would be necessary to deliver a 300 percent increase in global oil prices), and, likewise, room to argue about just how one might measure demand (all we can reliably measure is consumption). However, the claim that increased demand for crude oil explains *most* of the price increase since the beginning of the price spiral is widely embraced by most oil economists and oil market analysts.

The conventional narrative holds that whatever *cannot* be explained by the aggregate demand shock can be explained primarily by two additional developments.

First, several modest oil supply disruptions have hit the market over the past few years. When taken as a whole, those disruptions have significantly affected the global oil supply. Civil war in Nigeria, for instance, has taken at various times over the past several years over 1 million barrels of crude oil production a day out of the market. Hurricanes in the Gulf of Mexico have likewise removed over 1 million barrels a day from the market for months at a time. The war in Iraq has reduced oil production and deterred investment in upstream production capacity. Although such events are nothing new to oil markets, an unusually large number of supply disruptions have hit the market in recent years, taking oil out of a market already characterized by growing scarcity and thus exacerbating the price spiral.

Second, global oil production actually *fell* in 2002, 2006, and 2007. While the supply disruptions noted earlier played some role here, declining production from existing reserves (due to both field exhaustion—primarily in the North Sea—and the economic mismanagement of nationally owned oil companies like Mexico's PEMEX) has been the primary driver.

The conventional narrative is informed by a wealth of empirical work and solid data and is almost certainly correct. Hence, "bad" public policy did not cause the increase in retail gasoline prices. The clear implication is that "good" public policy will likewise prove an ineffective remedy.

While the conventional narrative is widely embraced by economists and market analysts, it appears to be a minority perspective within the political class. Both liberals and conservatives offer rather different explanations for the gasoline price spiral. Although both make some allowances for growth in aggregate global oil demand, both liberals and conservatives argue that other factors play a far larger role in the present price spiral than the increase in global economic growth.

Speculators in the Dock

One of the alternative narratives popular among politicians today is that the flow of money into oil futures markets is substantially increasing the demand for crude oil and thus the price of crude oil. Conservatives fond of this claim contend that the market is caught up in an oil price bubble. Liberals argue that speculators and institutional investors are to blame.

Many of those making this argument, however, conflate the purchase of oil delivery contracts with the purchase of oil. The two are not the same. Only about 2 percent of the contracts in futures markets are ever settled in oil. Most of those buying commitments for oil delivery in these "futures" markets in turn sell those commitments to oil refineries or other parties in spot markets when the contract approaches its delivery date. (Spot markets earn their name, by the way, because oil is delivered, figuratively speaking, "on the spot.") If the spot price is higher than the contract price, profits are made; if not, losses are incurred.

Accordingly, the best way to think about futures markets is that they allow people to bet on the price of oil in the future, and most of the bets are about the price of oil for delivery at the end of the following month. For every bet that prices will exceed x, another bet must be made that prices will fall below x because it takes two parties to enter into a contract.

The question, then, is how do bets on the *future* price of oil affect the actual price of oil—present or future? The answer must have something to do with the effect those bets have on either the supply of oil or the demand for oil. Nothing else will do.

Those bets might affect real (spot) prices in two ways. First, if the futures price is higher than the spot price, market actors might buy oil in spot markets, put it in storage, and sell it forward into futures markets, thereby locking in a risk-free profit. Removing oil from spot markets and locking it away in inventories reduces the supply of crude oil available to refiners and increases oil—and thus gasoline—prices. Second, if oil producers notice that the futures price is higher than the spot price, they might reduce production today to increase production tomorrow when prices and thus profits will be higher. Less oil production in the short term equals higher present prices but, of course, lower prices than might otherwise have been the case in the future.

Hence, if the flow of cash into the oil futures market is affecting spot prices, we would expect to see some evidence of oil inventory buildup or strategic production declines. Yet oil inventories have been declining over the course of the oil price spiral, and there is no correlation between futures prices and global oil production trends.

We would also expect to see some evidence that changes of behavior in the futures market preceded higher prices in spot markets. But a rigorous statistical test of that proposition by the Interagency Task Force on Commodity Markets (a task force organized by the Commodity Futures Trading Commission) finds no evidence for that proposition. Between January 2003 and June 2008, the task force found that "there is little evidence that daily position changes by any of the trader sub-categories systematically precede price changes."

"Big Oil" and Price Gouging

Another explanation popular with the political class is that major vertically integrated private oil companies are simply gouging the public with high prices. Evidence of record-high profits by "Big Oil" is marshaled for that proposition.

Yet high profits do not necessarily provide evidence of market power. For instance, if severe weather destroys the Florida citrus crop, citrus growers in California will make above-average profits because the lost supply will drive up price; if it did not, shortages would occur because preweather demand would stay the same but postweather supply could not possibly meet that demand. In this case, evidence that California citrus profits have risen would not constitute evidence that California citrus growers "caused" the high prices. The analogy to the oil sector would hold except for the fact that shortages are the result of economic growth rather than weather.

Nevertheless, profits in the oil and gas sector are greatly overstated. In 2007, oil and gas company profit margins averaged 8.3 percent (defined as net income divided by sales). By comparison, profits in the manufacturing sector as a whole (minus the auto industry) were 8.9 percent in 2007. A better metric of profitability is return on equity. While it's true that industry returns have been 5 to 15 percent better than those available to the manufacturing sector as a whole during the course of this price spiral, that's not particularly striking, because returns on equity were lower than those available to manufacturers during the preceding 20-year period.

The charge that investor-owned oil companies are "causing" oil price increases presupposes that the companies in question are actually capable of increasing global crude oil prices. Although most people seem to believe that Big Oil controls the oil market—or at the very least, has enough power in those markets to manipulate prices—the data tell a different story. ExxonMobil, British Petroleum, Shell, Chevron, and ConocoPhillips combined account for only 15 percent of the oil production coming from the top 100 oil companies in 2007. The largest—ExxonMobil—has only a 3.8 percent share of that market. Moreover, Big Oil controls only 3.9 percent of the global oil reserves held by the world's top 100 oil companies. Hence, arguing that Big Oil controls oil prices is akin to arguing that some collection of small, regional fast-food retailers like Jack in the Box or Hardee's controls fast-food prices nationwide.

The accusation that Big Oil has market power further downstream in the oil business—that is, in the national refining and retail marketing sectors—is on equally shaky ground. Big Oil is losing—not gaining—downstream market share, and the standard metrics employed by economists to measure market power find very little of it in refining markets or wholesale and retail fuel sales.

The Decline of the Dollar

Many have claimed that the decline of the dollar explains much if not most of the oil price spiral. The argument is that the global oil trade is conducted in dollars, so the less valuable the dollar, the less oil the dollar can buy. Moreover, when consumers in other countries buy oil, they must first use their currency (say, euros) to buy dollars. The more valuable those other currencies are relative to the dollar, the more dollars—and

447

thus the more oil—can be bought. Hence, price increases will be felt more lightly by those with stronger currencies than by those with weaker currencies. Accordingly, demand response from consumers trading in relatively "strong" currencies will be less robust than from those trading in weaker currencies.

That claim is largely correct but misleading. From January 2003 to May 2008, the dollar fell, at most, by about 25 percent relative to "all other" currencies, and 75 percent of oil demand is denominated in those other currencies. That implies that world oil demand is 19 percent higher than it otherwise would have been absent the decline of the dollar. Although that might be enough of a change in global demand to explain a large fraction of the oil price increase that occurred over the same period, changes in currency valuation do not "cause" changes elsewhere in the economy. Instead, changes in the economy "cause" changes in currency valuation. For instance, it may well be that changes in oil prices cause changes in currency values! That's because the demand for dollars (and thus the value of dollars) are a reflection of the desire to engage in the trade of goods and services governed by dollars. In short, exchange rates reflect market realities; they do not *change* them.

Is OPEC to Blame?

Many have suggested that production restraint by members of the Organization of the Petroleum Exporting Countries explains the recent oil price increases. Yet there is very little correlation between OPEC production decisions and crude oil price movements over the past several years and little evidence that any significant amount of withholding on the part of OPEC member states is occurring in the market.

A stronger argument is that there would be more oil production and perhaps more excess production capacity were it not for the OPEC cartel. That may well be, but OPEC's production restraint didn't begin in 2003. OPEC has not invested significant funds in oil exploration and development for more than three decades. Hence, no change in OPEC's behavior explains the oil price surge that began in 2003.

Regardless, it is unclear whether there is less oil production with an OPEC cartel than there would be in a hypothetical world without an OPEC cartel. Numerous economists who have attempted to isolate the effect of OPEC on oil production, and thus oil prices, have found no hard evidence that the cartel succeeds in its mission.

The reason for this lack of evidence is partly because of the difficulty in determining whether profit-maximizing private firms would produce more or less oil than is produced by the national oil companies controlled by OPEC. For instance, if one believes that production restraint is a profit-maximizing strategy for Saudi Aramco, then a privately owned Saudi Aramco would likely restrain production as well absent an enforceable government directive to forgo profits and produce at some level dictated by the state (a policy, by the way, that would rob oil from future generations to benefit the present).

While cooperation among privately owned oil companies in the course of establishing production schedules would be illegal in most Western countries, the cartel is a rather ineffective vehicle for producer cooperation. Each member faces strong economic incentives to cheat on production quotas; thus, cheating is the rule rather than the exception, particularly when oil prices are high. Research suggests that cartel members do curtail production at some times to some degree in response to quota allocations, but how often and to what extent is unclear.

Peak Oil

A growing number of market analysts, industry investors, and policy advocates are convinced that conventional crude oil is becoming more scarce, and thus more expensive, as the world consumes ever-larger quantities of something for which there is only a fixed supply. A cottage industry has thus arisen around the proposition that global oil production will soon peak and then begin a slow but rapidly accelerating decline. This approach of "peak oil," according to some, explains the growing scarcity—and thus the rising price—of low-cost crude oil.

Although there is mathematical certainty about the fact that at some point conventional crude oil production will peak, there is little reason to think that day is necessarily on the economic horizon given production data over the past several decades. If oil were growing scarcer, for instance, we should see some evidence of that in rising crude oil prices. But a rigorous analysis of crude oil prices from the first quarter of 1970 through the first quarter of 2008 by economist James Hamilton finds no statistically significant scarcity signal at all. On the contrary, his analysis finds that "the real price of oil seems to follow a random walk without drift." Hence, we cannot say for certain what most people seem to believe—that oil prices have been increasing over time.

Furthermore, Hamilton's analysis suggests that the best predictor of future price (that is, future scarcity) is present price, but the variance is large: 15.28 percent per quarter. That's because small changes in the supply or demand for crude oil have major price impacts in the short run, and any number of minor global events affect the supply or demand for crude oil. Table 43.1, for instance, demonstrates how a forecast for future oil prices made in the first quarter of 2008 grows over time given the observed instability of oil prices.

A conclusion that one can draw from the table is that even if prices rose dramatically in the near future, one could not say with confidence whether that price rise reflected underlying physical scarcities caused by long-term oil field depletions or any number of other short-term supply or demand phenomena commonly seen in the oil industry.

Although peak oilers are correct that new oil discoveries over the last several decades have been smaller and less frequent than in the past, how much crude oil is yet to be discovered is by definition unknown and unknowable. Hence, predictions about "peak oil" in the near term may be correct—or not. We simply don't know enough to say.

There are, however, four reasons for optimism. Together, they suggest that expansion of supply is just as likely—if not likelier—than contraction in the near to mid-term future.

First, high oil prices induce more exploration and more risk taking by oil companies. Economist Klaus Mohn observes: "When the oil price increases, oil companies take on more exploration risk. Consequently,

Table 43.1
95 percent Lower and Upper Bounds on Forecasts for Real Oil Prices

Date	Forecast	Lower	Upper
2008:Q1	$115		
2008:Q2	$115	$85	$156
2008:Q3	$115	$75	$177
2008:Q4	$115	$68	$195
2009:Q1	$115	$62	$212
2010:Q1	$115	$48	$273
2011:Q1	$115	$40	$332
2012:Q1	$115	$34	$391

SOURCE: James D. Hamilton, "Understanding Crude Oil Prices," University of California Energy Institute, 2008.
NOTE: Q = quarter.

discovery rates will fall whereas the average discovery size will increase.'' His examination of exploration and development data off the Norwegian coast suggests that for every 10 percent increase in oil prices, reserves increase by 8.9 percent in the long run.

Second, high prices may likewise induce more production from OPEC countries as well. Claims about depleting reserves may be correct, but there may be many more fields to come.

The Persian Gulf is one of the least explored areas of the world as far as oil and natural gas are concerned. Only about 2,000 exploratory wells have been drilled in the entire Persian Gulf since its emergence as an oil-producing region. The United States, by comparison, has seen more than 1 million such wells. Even today, more than 70 percent of oil exploration activity is concentrated in North America (which holds less than 3 percent of the world's oil reserves), whereas only 3 percent of that activity is occurring in the Middle East (which holds about 70 percent of the world's oil reserves). Moreover, given that most of the exploration in the Persian Gulf occurred decades ago before nationalization of the oil industry, the dramatic advances in exploration technology and know-how have not for the most part been applied to the most promising geological formations in the world. More than a few industry observers argue that, yes, we will almost certainly discover a new Saudi Arabia sometime in the future—but it will likely be in Saudi Arabia.

Will high prices induce substantial new investments in oil exploration in the OPEC countries and Russia, which likewise sits atop very promising but scarcely explored geological formations? Only time will tell, but it is hard to imagine that profit-maximizing oil states would forgo economically promising investments indefinitely, particularly when the oil and gas industry is the primary source of state revenue and prices are on the rise. If new oil is not forthcoming, it will likely be due to political—not geological—constraints.

The upshot is that the observation that major new oil discoveries have declined over the past several decades in both OPEC and non-OPEC countries is problematic because oil prices have likewise been falling over most of that period. Trends in discoveries may historically have more to do with price and politics than with geological scarcity.

Third, major new oil field discoveries are not necessary for major increases in supply. Increasing average field recovery rates from 35 percent to 40 percent, for instance, would increase supply by 300 billion to 600 billion barrels, which is akin to adding a new Saudi Arabia or two to the market. Given that field recovery rates have steadily improved over time—they averaged only 22 percent as recently as 1980—there is reason to hope that high prices will induce new investment in—and corresponding improvement in—low-cost extraction practices and technology.

Unconventional sources of crude oil are another source of potential new supply. The International Energy Agency believes that 6 trillion barrels of crude oil reside in heavy oil and bitumen stocks (primarily tar sands like those in Alberta, heavy oil deposits like those in Venezuela, and oil shale in mineral deposits such as those found in the Rocky Mountain West), of which 2 trillion may be ultimately recoverable. Given that conventional oil reserves worldwide total 1.3 trillion barrels, this suggests that, should conventional crude oil prices rise high enough because of depletion—or alternatively, should extraction costs of unconventional crude oil decline substantially because of technological advance—massive new sources of unconventional oil supply could enter the market.

Beyond unconventional crude oil are even larger possibilities for synthetic oil production from gas-to-liquid technologies, coal-to-liquid technologies, agricultural oils, and methane hydrates found on the seabed and in permafrost Arctic regions. Hydrocarbons for oil production can be harnessed from many sources, and conventional crude oil fields are but one source of many.

Fourth, investments in new field production have followed the oil price spiral and new supply will soon be entering the market. A recent tally in the *Oil & Gas Journal* of publicly known oil development projects under way found that 28 million barrels a day of new supply is coming from 47 countries over the next two decades, a sum that represents approximately one-third of existing daily global production. Although production declines from existing fields will certainly offset that new supply to some degree, the encouraging fact remains that new supplies at the margin are still potentially quite robust.

Policy Responses

Most voters believe that government must do something to reduce gasoline prices. Because gasoline prices over the long run are a manifestation of global crude oil supply and demand, only by increasing the former or reducing the latter can government policy have the desired effect. Unfortunately, there is little scope for government policy to succeed on either front.

Conservatives argue that opening up public lands currently off-limits to the oil industry—primarily the outer continental shelf and the Arctic National Wildlife Refuge—would provide significant price relief for U.S. motorists. This is possible, but unlikely. The U.S. Minerals Management Service (an agency of the U.S. Department of the Interior) estimates that offshore fields that have not yet been exploited will likely yield about 200,000 barrels of crude oil a day once producing at peak capacity and that development of ANWR could add another 780,000 barrels of new crude oil a day. If so, that would mean that government policy could add about 1 million barrels a day to a crude oil market whose size will likely be about 88 million barrels a day in 2020. That implies a reduction in world crude oil prices of no more than 1 percent. Although one can make a strong case that opening up those fields to the oil industry makes good economic sense—economist Robert Hahn, for instance, estimates net benefits of $668 billion for drilling in ANWR and $1.07 trillion for drilling in previously unexploited offshore areas—one cannot argue that what we currently suspect about those fields suggests that a policy of "drill, baby, drill" will reduce gasoline prices in any noticeable way at the pump.

Many, of course, argue that increasing oil supply is either futile or counterproductive. Better, we are told, are policies to increase the supply (and thus to reduce the price) of gasoline alternatives. Accordingly, a blizzard of proposals have been floated to both subsidize and compel the production of plug-in hybrid gasoline-electric-powered vehicles; vehicles propelled by hydrogen-powered fuel cells; and engines that can run on compressed natural gas, corn ethanol, cellulosic ethanol, methanol, and other exotic fuels.

There are three problems with those sorts of policies. First, they presuppose that oil prices will remain high in the future. If oil prices return to prespiral norms (that is, to something less than $30 per barrel), public investment in gasoline alternatives will prove a total economic waste. As noted earlier, those who dismiss the possibility of a price collapse should acquaint themselves with James Hamilton's work. Second, there is no way of knowing which of the many transportation fuel alternatives will prove most economic in the future. Government subsidies and consumption mandates may well go to the "wrong" fuels, particularly because government choices are driven as much—if not more—by political considerations as they are by economic considerations, which means that the emergence of the "best" fuels could well be slowed or even prevented. Third, they

453

are unnecessary. Given the high price of gasoline, tremendous profits are available to those who can commercialize vehicles run by something other than gasoline. If an alternative transportation fuel or technology is promising, then no subsidy is necessary; investors will put their own money on line not out of any sense of public duty but out of a love for profit. Subsidies in this case would allow investors to substitute public resources for their own resources and represent a wealth transfer without any good economic rationale.

Public policy to reduce the demand for crude oil is even less compelling. First, even the most aggressive policies that have been suggested would not change crude oil prices very much. For instance, consider the consequences of a 40 percent improvement in the fuel efficiency of the U.S. auto fleet—an improvement mandated recently by Congress via a tightening of the Corporate Average Fuel Efficiency standard. In two decades, that would reduce U.S. oil consumption by 3.6 million barrels a day. If world crude oil production were at 100 million barrels a day by that time (a reasonable estimate), crude oil prices would likely decline by about 7 percent as a consequence of the policy. Hence, if crude oil prices would otherwise have averaged $100 a barrel at that time, they would instead average $93 a barrel. Motorists would scarcely notice the improvement.

Second, from both a social and an individual perspective, too much conservation can be as bad as too little; an observation easily grasped if we imagine a policy to limit highway speeds to 35 miles per hour nationwide, a prohibition against driving passenger vehicles on certain days of the week, a prohibition against all cars larger than a golf cart, or the like. The "right" tradeoff between fuel consumption and the services rendered by fuel consumption can be made only on a case-by-case basis by motorists themselves. No third party can hope to know enough about the individual tradeoffs in question to make utility-maximizing decisions for millions of people they have not even met.

Accordingly, a necessary (but insufficient) precondition for government policy to reduce oil consumption is evidence that oil consumers are for some reason resisting conservation that would otherwise be in their best interest. That proposition has been tested by Clemson economist Molly Espey and found wanting. In a recent study, she analyzed model year 2001 new car sales to determine if consumers accurately value the savings of improved fuel economy. In theory, new vehicle buyers should be willing to pay for improvements in fuel economy to reflect anticipated savings given the buyers' expectation of future fuel prices and vehicle miles driven. In practice, they do.

Finally, oft overlooked is that other aspects of federal policy—if executed as advertised—would serve to increase rather than decrease fuel prices. For instance, support for "energy independence" is nearly as strong as support for government to "do something" about high gasoline prices. Yet policies to discourage oil imports will by definition raise gasoline prices by preventing relatively lower-cost fuel from entering the U.S. market. If oil imports weren't cheaper than the alternative, after all, then the oil wouldn't be imported in the first place. Similarly, policies to reduce greenhouse gas emissions will necessarily increase oil prices if they are to be effective. That's because the only way to reduce those emissions is to reduce the consumption of carbon-based fuels, and the only way to do that is to increase the price of carbon-based fuels—like gasoline. The relative inelasticity of oil demand along with the relative insensitivity of the atmosphere to modest changes in greenhouse gas emissions implies that a massive increase in oil prices would be necessary to reduce oil consumption enough to make any difference regarding global temperatures.

Broken Markets?

Many have argued that anemic supply-and-demand responses to the oil price spiral are evidence that oil markets are somehow "broken." If high prices (that is, resource scarcity) do not induce significant energy conservation or new oil production, then government must act to do what the market will not. The problem with this argument is that it confuses short-term with long-term market response and misunderstands the reason why supply and demand are so inelastic in the short term.

Sluggish consumer response to high prices reflects the fact that energy conservation often requires expensive capital stock (say, a three-year-old sport-utility vehicle or a house in exurbia far from work and mass transit) to be prematurely sold in favor of new capital investments in more energy-efficient equipment (a Honda Prius or a condo in the city). Consumers do not undertake such decisions lightly, which explains why it often takes several years of high and rising prices to induce robust conservation expenditures and related demand reductions. Once those investments are made, it takes years for them to produce significant energy savings. For example, it takes more than 10 years for the U.S. auto fleet to turn over, so the main way that consumers respond to high prices—buying more fuel-efficient vehicles—will require years to significantly affect demand.

For their part, producers do not willingly invest tens of billions of dollars in excess production capacity that will be used only in case of some sort of supply shock because it would be wildly unprofitable to do so. Likewise, in the early stages of an oil price spiral, producers are often disinclined to immediately invest billions in new production because it is unclear whether those high prices will be there when the new production capacity comes on line—usually 10 or more years later—or even whether prices will be sufficient to cover the cost of the project in question. When producers do respond to price spirals with new investment, they generally find that bottlenecks exist everywhere in the production supply chain. In 2007, for instance, it was reported that all existing offshore rigs were under contract for the next five years. Finally, the threat of higher taxes that always appears during price spirals deters producers from making potentially profitable investments at the margin.

Happily, both the supply and the demand for crude oil are more elastic over the long run. Past experience suggests that a 10 percent increase in price will eventually lead to a 5 percent reduction in demand. While the data necessary to estimate global supply response over the long run do not appear to exist, the best available study on the matter finds: "Outside of North America, on balance non-OPEC countries have a rightward (expanding) shifting supply function. . . . Supply conditions in OPEC countries cannot be depicted by the interaction of conventional supply functions with price; other factors intrude."

Government policy to induce quicker supply or demand response is problematic because the three factors responsible for slow market reaction—uncertainty about future prices, the large capital costs associated with supply-and-demand response, and the lag time between investments in supply and demand and significant changes in the same—cannot be remedied by government. Forcing quicker market response to rising prices threatens to "jump the gun" and mandate expenditures that will prove economically counterproductive.

Market Failure versus Government Failure

Economists agree that, as a general matter, allowing producers to determine what sort and how much energy to produce will lead to more efficient outcomes and lower consumer prices than would vesting those decisions with government. Likewise, leaving to consumers the decision about how much and what kind of energy to consume will prove more economically efficient than the alternative. Only if we find a specific failure in the market—defined as a condition in which mutually beneficial trade between private parties is for some reason difficult or impossible to execute—

will there be room for government improvement over market decisions. Accusations of market failure are usually grounded in evidence that prices are inaccurate, that is, that they do not fully reflect the costs of production or the costs or benefits of consumption.

Several energy market failures have been marshaled to justify intervention in oil markets, but they either fail to convince or imply interventions different from those offered. For instance, energy depletion implies nothing about the inaccuracy of price signals. The environmental costs of oil consumption are best "internalized" in the price mechanism (if they are not already) by an explicit or implicit tax on pollution, not energy per se because the relationship between energy consumption and pollution varies by technology, location, and equipment maintenance. OPEC nations may (individually or jointly) constrain supply, but there is nothing the U.S. government can do about that and the resulting scarcities are fully reflected in oil prices. Developers of new technologies may not be able to capture all the economic gains associated with the commercialization of those technologies, but the proper remedy (if one is necessary) is to make all research and development more attractive to investors, not to vest the government with the power to direct specific R & D activities.

The alleged national security costs associated with oil consumption—perhaps the main rationale offered for intervention since the attacks on 9/11—are nonexistent. The military "oil mission" simply does for oil producers what oil producers can and should do for themselves. Embargoes are ineffective because producers cannot control the destination of the oil they produce once it is released into the market. There is no correlation between oil profits (reflected by prices) and either the number of the acts of or the fatalities from Islamic terrorism. Nor is there a correlation between oil profits secured by anti-American oil producers and "bad acting" by them. And even if there were some clear relationship between oil consumption and terrorism and/or bad acting abroad, we've demonstrated that there is little that the U.S. government could constructively do about it. Global oil supply and demand do not dance to Washington's tune, and the costs of addressing those problems via energy policy rather than through some other foreign policy response are almost certainly prohibitive.

Establishing the existence of a market failure is a necessary but insufficient condition for government intervention. One must further demonstrate that the government is capable of remedying the market failure in question and that intervention will produce more benefits than costs. That is no easy task. Government bureaucrats are hobbled by poor information, political decisionmakers are not experts, and short-term political considerations heavily color government policy. Accordingly, it should not surprise that analysts are very hard-pressed to find any examples when past interventions produced positive economic outcomes. As energy economist Richard Gordon puts it, "The dominant theme of academic writings is that governments have done more harm than good in energy," a view "almost universally supported by academic energy economists, whatever their political outlook."

The Macroeconomic Case for Energy Market Intervention

Some have argued that the relationship between oil price shocks and recession is so well established that government's stewardship of the economy requires it to act to reduce the likelihood and severity of the oil price shocks that the market sometimes delivers. Although that argument is rooted in academic work published over several decades, recent scholarship is not very supportive.

The best summary of what we know about the effect of oil price shocks on the economy comes from economist Lutz Kilian. His survey of the academic literature, combined with his statistical analysis of quarterly economic data from 1970 to 2006, turns "common wisdom" regarding oil price shocks on its head.

Kilian's analysis demonstrates that oil supply disruptions do not correlate well with oil price increases and that the former have virtually no cumulative effect on real oil prices over time. Oil-specific demand shocks (manifest, for instance, by precautionary inventory building in response to international tensions) have the most pronounced effect on oil prices, but oil prices peak in the first month of those shocks and then begin a slow pattern of decline. An aggregate demand shock (the sort we experienced from 2003 to 2008) has only a modest effect on oil prices at first but is more significant over time.

The effect that price shocks have on gross domestic product is mixed. Oil supply shocks that trigger price spirals reduce GDP by about 2 to 3 percent over the first 7 economic quarters of the shock, but most of that loss disappears after 12 economic quarters. Oil-specific demand shocks slowly reduce GDP by almost 5 percent after 12 economic quarters. Aggregate demand shocks increase GDP over the first 4 quarters but then reduce it after the 4th quarter until GDP is reduced by about 5 percent by the 12th economic quarter.

The macroeconomic effect of all three types of oil price shocks is manifested primarily by decreasing demand for automobiles (particularly fuel-inefficient automobiles) and housing. The economy's greater resilience in response to the 2003 aggregate demand shock relative to the 1973 aggregate demand shock is probably best explained by the smaller role the U.S. auto industry plays in the national economy and the fact that consumers have more fuel-efficient domestic cars to switch to than they did in the 1970s. Moreover, the lack of wage and price controls today means that the economy can more quickly and efficiently adjust to rising fuel prices, which was not the case in the 1970s.

The implications of Kilian's analysis are striking. First, government's obsession with oil supply shocks—whether from war, terrorism, bad weather, civil unrest, or political calculation—is unwarranted given past events. Hence, programs like the Strategic Petroleum Reserve, 700 million barrels of federally controlled oil for use in case of some future supply disruption, are expensive and unnecessary insurance policies. Larger, ahistorical disruptions are always possible, but no federal reserve would be large enough to deal with such events in any case.

Second, the most serious macroeconomic damages that follow from price shocks follow from events such as global economic booms and market response to war worries that the government has little (positive) control over. The best that can be hoped for is that the government does not make matters worse by responding with poor monetary policy, the main cause—according to Kilian—of the aggregate demand shock of the early 1970s.

Third, there is no evidence that preemptive intervention in energy markets has reduced the likelihood of, or damage from, price shocks in the past or will do so in the future. While it is a fact that oil markets are volatile and that volatility can have macroeconomic effects, there is nothing that the government can do to affect the underlying supply-and-demand fundamentals that give rise to oil price volatility. Although one might argue that it is more costly to rely on a fuel (oil) that is usually inexpensive but price volatile and occasionally expensive rather than some other fuel that is usually more expensive but less volatile, market actors would provide that "other fuel" if there were public demand for such a tradeoff. Apparently, there is not.

The Economic Wages of Inaction

An increasingly popular argument holds that past public inaction is responsible for the present energy crisis. Had Congress embraced President

Jimmy Carter's energy agenda, we are told, oil demand would be substantially less than it is today and the scarcities that are currently driving oil prices would be far less severe or even nonexistent.

This argument, however, ignores the likelihood that less demand from, say, 1980 through 2003 would likewise have yielded fewer reserve additions over that same period because neither private oil corporations nor nationally owned oil companies would have been inclined to invest billions in upstream production capacity simply to watch it remain idle. Hence, we should not assume that, had Congress embraced Carter's energy agenda and reduced global oil consumption by x million barrels a day below where it is at present, excess production capacity in that hypothetical would be x million barrels a day greater than where it is today. If both markets were in equilibrium, excess production capacity would remain relatively the same in both scenarios. If we then assume that the 2003 aggregate demand shock hits this "Carter-world" scenario, the price impact would be no less than it was in actual practice. In fact, the 2003 aggregate demand shock might actually have done *more* damage in this alternative Carter-world scenario because a unit increase in global demand will have a greater price impact on a smaller oil market than on a larger oil market.

Regardless, how might the existing oil price spiral play out absent government intervention? If past is prologue, high prices will eventually increase supply and reduce demand sufficiently to cause a price collapse and a return to (mean) prespiral oil prices. The relative inelasticity of oil supply and demand in the short run works both ways: even small declines in demand and/or increases in supply can trigger price collapse in the short term. Energy economist Severin Borenstein, for instance, points out that a 7 percent decline in oil demand as consequence of the 1981–83 recession was almost certainly responsible for the resulting oil price collapse in 1985. A similar reduction in demand today—whether from global recession or as a response to high prices—would bring prices down into the $20-per-barrel range if the demand elasticities observed over the past decade continue to govern the market. There is nothing that government can do that would have even a fraction as large an effect on oil prices in the short term.

The record surveyed by Hamilton, however, clearly warns that hard predictions are problematic. Any number of other events could emerge to offset the bust that has always followed the boom. Beyond the usual assortment of transient events that have long affected oil markets are possible endogenous declines in (low-cost) oil production from field deple-tion and structural changes in the global economy stemming from economic growth in the lesser-developed countries, particularly China and India. Either development could conceivably keep prices high even in the face of long-term supply-and-demand response to high prices.

Still, some evidence suggests that oil—which has been run out of electricity generation and industrial application markets as a consequence of earlier price shocks—may well be on the verge of losing its dominant position in transportation markets as a consequence of this latest price shock. Energy economist Samuel Van Vactor demonstrates that, if the current cost estimates for plug-in hybrid electric vehicles (PHEVs) are to be believed, those cars make economic sense for consumers as long as oil prices remain above $55 per barrel over the lifetime of those vehicles. Moreover, PHEV prices will almost certainly come down as the technology matures and companies experience the manufacturing cost declines that usually follow from "learning by doing." Technologists Peter Huber and Mark Mills make a strong argument that long-term trends in energy applications will likely push the transportation sector away from liquid fuel and toward electricity and that PHEVs may be the first step in this direction of many yet to come.

The very uncertainty surrounding the future of oil prices and transporta-tion markets suggests nonintervention. Government simply cannot know the future, meaning that promises to hasten the arrival of this or that energy future are more likely to delay than accelerate the arrival of that day. Bets by market actors regarding future energy prices and technologies may prove little better, but the diffuse employment of private capital ensures that the consequences of those "bad bets" are borne by private investors. "Good bets," however, will produce benefits for all.

Suggested Readings

Adelman, M. A. *The Genie out of the Bottle: World Oil since 1970*. Cambridge, MA: MIT Press, 1995.

Borenstein, Severin. "Cost, Conflict and Climate: U.S. Challenges in the World Oil Market." Working Paper no. 177, Center for the Study of Energy Markets, University of California Energy Institute, June 2008.

Bradley, Robert. *Oil, Gas and Government: The U.S. Experience*. Lanham, MD: Rowman & Littlefield, 1996.

Gordon, Richard. "The Case against Government Intervention in Energy Markets: Revis-ited Once Again." Cato Institute Policy Analysis no. 628, December 1, 2008.

Hahn, Robert, and Peter Passell. "The Economics of Allowing More Domestic Oil Drilling." Working Paper no. 08-121, Center for Regulatory and Market Studies, American Enterprise Institute, August 2008 (revised September 2008).

Hamilton, James. "Understanding Crude Oil Prices." Energy Policy and Economics Working Paper no. 023, University of California Energy Institute, June 2008.

Interagency Task Force on Commodity Markets. "Interim Report on Crude Oil." July 2008.

International Energy Agency. *Resources to Reserves: Oil and Gas Technologies for the Energy Markets of the Future.* Paris: Organisation for Economic Co-operation and Development, 2005.

Kilian, Lutz. "The Economic Effects of Energy Price Shocks." Centre for Economic Policy and Research Discussion Paper no. DP6559, University of Michigan, July 2008.

Maugeri, Leonardo. *The Age of Oil.* Westport, CT: Praeger, 2006.

Robinson, Colin. "Energy Economists and Economic Liberalism." *The Energy Journal* 21, no. 2 (2002).

Smil, Vaclav. *Energy at the Crossroads.* Cambridge, MA: MIT Press, 2003.

Smith, James. "Inscrutable OPEC? Behavioral Tests of the Cartel Hypothesis." *The Energy Journal* 26, no. 1 (2005).

Sutherland, Ronald, and Jerry Taylor. "Time to Overhaul Federal Energy R & D." Cato Institute Policy Analysis no. 424, February 7, 2002.

Taylor, Jerry, and Peter Van Doren. "The Case against the Strategic Petroleum Reserve." Cato Institute Policy Analysis no. 555, November 21, 2005.

———. "Economic Amnesia: The Case against Oil Price Controls and Windfall Profit Taxes." Cato Institute Policy Analysis no. 561, January 12, 2006.

———. "Don't Increase Gasoline Taxes—Abolish Them." Cato Institute Policy Analysis no. 598, August 7, 2007.

Van Vactor, Samuel. "How Oil from the North Went South." Working Paper no. 08-009, United States Association for Energy Economics, July 2008.

Wirl, Franz. *The Economics of Conservation Programs.* Norwell, MA: Kluwer Academic Publishers, 1997.

—Prepared by Jerry Taylor and Peter Van Doren

44. Environmental Policy

Congress should

- Establish a mechanism by which states can apply for regulatory waivers from the Environmental Protection Agency in order to allow states some flexibility in establishing environmental priorities and to facilitate experiments in innovative regulatory approaches;
- replace the Federal Insecticide, Fungicide, and Rodenticide Act and the Toxic Substances Control Act with a consumer products labeling program under the auspices of the Food and Drug Administration;
- repeal the Comprehensive Environmental Response, Compensation, and Liability Act and privatize the cleanup of Superfund sites;
- replace the Resource Conservation and Recovery Act with minimal standards for discharge into groundwater aquifers;
- eliminate federal subsidies and programs that exacerbate environmental damage; and
- replace the Endangered Species Act and section 404 of the Clean Water Act with a federal biological trust fund.

The Theory of Environmental Regulation

Air sheds, watersheds, groundwater, scenic lands, and ecologically important but sensitive ecosystems are widely considered "public goods." That is, in an unregulated marketplace, people who pay to "consume" environmental goods and services (say, those who purchase a conservation easement for an ecologically important wetland) are unable to keep those who don't pay from enjoying the benefits of that purchase. Accordingly,

463

without government regulation, there would be widespread "free riding" and less investment in environmental goods than would be economically and socially desirable.

Moreover, people who might wish to protect their property against polluters via private action will often find that the transaction costs associated with doing so are prohibitive. For instance, if one owned a small lake and discovered that the fertilizer runoff from hundreds if not thousands of homes and agricultural operations was contaminating water quality, the costs associated with tracking down the responsible parties would almost certainly be larger than the costs associated with the pollution itself.

Accordingly, those "market failures" would necessitate government intervention. While there are numerous ways that the government could intervene in environmental marketplaces to address market failure, the method employed by the federal government is public ownership of air, water, and subsurface resources as well as of some sensitive ecosystems. Congress exercises its power over those resources by delegating to executive agencies the authority to determine how resources can and can't be used—that is, by establishing pollution and public land use regulations—usually, but not always, on the basis of assessments of human health risk. The Environmental Protection Agency is further empowered to determine the exact manner in which regulated entities are to go about meeting pollution standards—usually, but not always, dictating the installation of particular control devices or technologies.

Accurate, timely, and accessible information about environmental exposures is also considered by some to be a public good. Absent such laws as the Toxic Substances Control Act and the Federal Insecticide, Fungicide, and Rodenticide Act, individuals, some people think, would be unable to effectively police their exposures to dangerous chemicals. A variation of this argument contends that it is so costly and time-consuming for people to gain access to the environmental health information necessary for intelligent decisionmaking that government must act in the individual's stead and make those decisions for society as a whole.

Debates about the regulation of pollution generally begin with an acceptance of those claims. The political arguments today are over the details:

- Do concentrations of chemical x in the environment truly pose a health risk to the public? If so, we regulate. If not, we don't.
- Should environmental regulations have to pass a cost–benefit test?
- Should government tell firms exactly how to go about meeting federal environmental standards, or should government simply dictate the

permissible concentration of pollutants in a given air shed or water-shed and allow firms some degree of flexibility in complying with those standards?

- How stringently should regulations be enforced, and who should do the enforcing—the EPA, state governments, environmental organizations through third-party lawsuits, or some combination of the three?

The Real Environmental Debate

Although environmental debates sound like they're arguments about science and public health (with a smattering of economics tossed in), they're really debates about preferences and *whose* preferences should be imposed on society. Although participants argue that "sound science" ought to determine whose preferences determine the standards (and that *their* science is better than their opponents'), science cannot referee the debate.

Consider the dispute about the regulation of potentially unhealthy pollutants, the central mission of the EPA. The agency examines toxicological and epidemiological data to ascertain the exposure level at which suspect substances impose measurable human health risks. Even assuming that such analyses are capable of providing the requisite information (a matter, incidentally, that is hotly debated within the scientific and public health community), who is to say whether one risk tolerance is preferable to another?

The amount of resources one is willing to spend on risk avoidance is ultimately subjective. Everyone's risk tolerance is different. Scientists can help inform our decisions, but they cannot point us to the "correct" decision.

Should experts—acting on behalf of regulatory agencies—decide what sort of environmental quality people should or should not have a right to consume? In no other area of the economy do scientists have the power to rule in such a manner. After all, people are allowed to consume all kinds of things—power crystals, magnets, age-defying vitamins, and organic food—that scientists, doctors, and public health officials think are silly or even potentially counterproductive.

Many people, perhaps even a majority of voting Americans, want to secure cleaner air and cleaner water regardless of whether those improvements significantly reduce human health risks. Under the present political regime, however, no such improvements can occur without some alleged scientific justification. That is why people who wish to improve environ-

465

mental quality are forced to embrace whatever science they can—no matter how dubious—to get what they want. They should not, however, have to engage in such scientific gymnastics to secure desired goods or services.

The Case for Preference Neutrality

A government that is fully respectful of the right of individuals to live their lives as they wish (as long as they respect the rights of others to do likewise) would be neutral regarding the subjective preferences of its citizens. People who are more risk tolerant than others should have a right to exercise their preferences, and those who are less risk tolerant than others should have that same right. This reasonable premise has some striking policy implications because the present order is most definitely not neutral regarding environmental preferences.

Preference neutrality works well when it comes to the consumption of private goods, such as those regulated by the Federal Insecticide, Fungicide, and Rodenticide Act and the Toxic Substances Control Act. It does not work well, however, when it comes to the consumption of public environmental goods, which pose a far more difficult problem. Within the same city, for instance, one person cannot exercise his preference for cleaner air without infringing upon another's preference for, say, more entry-level jobs in the manufacturing sector. After all, nothing is free, and people vary (legitimately) in their willingness to trade off environmental goods and services for other goods and services.

A policy founded on preference neutrality requires that we do as little violence to minority preferences as possible. *When it comes to public goods like air and watersheds, some majority will, of necessity, be imposing its preferences on some minority.* The only way to provide safeguards for minority preferences is to require some sort of supermajority consensus before decisions about public goods are made.

Reform of the Clean Air and Clean Water Acts

As noted earlier, within limits, there are no right or wrong air or water quality standards. Political leaders need not constantly war over those issues. Accepting public preferences for cleaner air and water—even without sufficient scientific justification—still leaves a great amount of room for productive reform.

466

The Problem with Command-and-Control Regulation

There is little reason for government to prescribe exactly how firms are to go about complying with pollution standards. Command-and-control regulations, which require regulators to determine exactly which technologies and what manufacturing methods are to be adopted for pollution control in every single facility in the nation, place on public officials informational requirements that are difficult to meet in the real world. This task is complicated by the fact that every air shed and watershed has different carrying capacities for different pollutants.

Command-and-control regulations may often prove more efficient than alternative regulatory arrangements when dealing with a large number of difficult-to-identify pollution sources (for instance, air emissions from automobile tailpipes and water runoff from the application of fertilizers and pesticides). Yet their utility is reduced when targeting identifiable and immobile pollution sources such as manufacturing and electric power facilities. After all, individual plant managers have better incentives to discover the most efficient ways to control pollution at their facilities than do EPA technicians and consultants. That is the case, not only because those managers have more direct knowledge of their facilities and the technology of production, but because competition forces cost minimization, and even the most dedicated EPA official isn't going to lie awake nights searching for new solutions to pollution control problems.

Most regulatory analysts are in agreement that flexible regulatory approaches—such as performance-based regulation (wherein regulators dictate overall emissions levels from a facility but allow facility managers to decide how best to meet those standards), emissions trading, and pollution taxes—are often more efficient and less costly means of meeting environmental standards than are command-and-control alternatives. Unfortunately, those sorts of flexible regulatory strategies are underutilized in the United States for a host of political reasons. That should concern not only economists but environmentalists as well. The less costly it is to "buy" improvements in environmental quality, the greater the public appetite will likely be for additional initiatives to improve environmental quality.

Provision of State Regulatory Waivers

Despite the well-known problems associated with command-and-control environmental regulation, it's unlikely that Congress will find the political capital necessary to reform thousands of pages of counterproductive rules

467

and regulations found in more than a dozen sprawling environmental statutes, given the entrenched special interests that benefit politically and economically from their existence. Accordingly, Congress should take a page from the welfare reform experience and allow states to appeal for waivers from EPA in order to facilitate experiments in regulatory policy.

Case Western law professor Jonathan Adler proposes that Congress adopt a mechanism similar to Section 160 of the 1996 Telecommunications Act to facilitate this reform. Section 160 allows telecommunication companies to submit a request for a regulatory waiver from the Federal Communications Commission. The FCC "shall forebear from applying any regulation or any provision" of the act to a company or class of service providers if the FCC determines upon review of the petition that

- "enforcement of such regulation or provision is not necessary" to ensure that rates "are just and reasonable and are not unreasonably discriminatory,"
- "enforcement of such regulation or provision is not necessary for the protection of consumers," or
- "forbearance from applying such provision or regulation is consistent with the public interest."

The FCC has one year to respond or the petition is deemed granted, and any decision to grant or deny forbearance is subject to judicial review under the Administrative Procedure Act.

Adapting a mechanism akin to Section 160 of the 1996 Telecommunications Act to the environmental arena would mean allowing states to apply for forbearance from any standard or requirement administered by EPA. The state would be expected to submit supporting material detailing the basis for the request and explain why the waiver would serve the public interest. EPA would then provide public notice, seek comment from interested parties, and make a call one way or the other within one year pending judicial review under the aegis of the Administrative Procedure Act.

Some states may wish to experiment with market-oriented emissions trading programs or pollution taxes in lieu of the existing federally imposed command-and-control regimen. Others may well act to tighten existing standards. A few states might even propose reallocation of regulatory efforts in order to concentrate on some relatively more important environmental issues instead of others. A policy of preference neutrality suggests tolerance regarding any such proposals.

Allowing "50 regulatory flowers to bloom" admittedly entails some degree of risk. Although some state experiments will likely bear economic and environmental fruit, others will probably fail to meet expectations. Such risks will certainly engender political opposition to the entire enterprise, but politicians should remember that useful innovations are virtually impossible without the risk of failure. In fact, the risks of failure underscore the value of decentralized policy experiments since localized policy failures would have far less damaging consequences than federal policy failures. Moreover, failed experiments provide useful information, cautioning reformers in other states about problems to avoid. Successful state experiments, on the other hand, could become models for reform elsewhere.

Repeal of FIFRA and TSCA

A policy of preference neutrality would be most easily applicable to consumer preferences that do not directly affect the rights of others to exercise alternative preferences (so-called private goods). TSCA (which governs the use of various chemicals and the abatement of asbestos, indoor radon concentrations, and lead-based paint) and FIFRA (which regulates the use of agricultural chemicals) impose politically derived risk preferences (and their related costs) on individuals without respect for those who are more risk tolerant than the political majority. Accordingly, both statutes should be abolished.

Of course, some people argue that the cost of obtaining good risk information is too great. That's not altogether obvious (a plethora of private, third-party reporting organizations, such as Underwriters Laboratories, Consumers Union, Green Seal, various kosher and halal food certification groups, the Better Business Bureau, and the Good Housekeeping Institute, are well-known and on the job today), and there are remedies available beyond the uniform imposition of politically derived risk tolerances. Mandatory labeling standards—perhaps accompanied by Food and Drug Administration advisories—would address the concern about this alleged market imperfection and do minimal violence to the marketplace and the rights of individual consumers.

Repeal of CERCLA

The Comprehensive Environmental Response, Compensation, and Liability Act, commonly known as "Superfund," addresses the potential risks posed by the past disposal of hazardous wastes. Most scientists and public health officials agree that the risks posed by sites not yet cleaned up under CERCLA are virtually nonexistent. Although those sites might pose a hazard if they were converted to different uses—say, if a school with a dirt playground were built on top of an old Superfund site—such concerns are easily addressed by not converting such sites to problematic uses.

In reality, CERCLA is an extremely expensive land reclamation project, dedicated to turning contaminated land, which at present poses little danger of harm to nearby residents, into land as pure and clean as the driven snow. Congress should acknowledge that some sites are simply not worth reclaiming; containment and isolation should be permitted as an alternative.

Accordingly, CERCLA should be abolished. Abandoned Superfund sites should be privatized in a reverse Dutch auction in which government offers to *pay* potential bidders for assuming ownership of and responsibility for the land. The amount offered escalates until some private party is willing to accept the deal. Owners would then assume full liability for any future damage that might occur. Such a regime would set up the proper incentives for the private remediation or isolation of potentially dangerous environmental contaminants.

Repeal RCRA

The Resource Conservation and Recovery Act regulates the commercial use and disposal of potentially toxic chemicals primarily as a means of protecting groundwater aquifers from contamination. Yet RCRA is not necessary to remedy any traditional environmental market failure.

Groundwater aquifers are not a public good. Ownership is easily created through unitization, the same means employed by owners of oil wells to allocate property rights across geographically disperse fields. Owners of aquifers are quite capable of restricting consumption to people who pay for water and policing the integrity of their aquifers through the tort system.

But even if groundwater resources remain in government hands, there's little reason for such incredibly prescriptive and excessively costly regulations as the kind imposed by RCRA, a statute that stipulates detailed cradle-to-grave management standards for thousands of substances. Better to repeal RCRA and replace it with a minimal discharge standard, that is, prohibit significant discharges of pollutants (as defined by government) into groundwater and impose heavy fines and penalties—perhaps even shutdown orders—on firms discovered to be in violation of the standard.

A requirement that potential dischargers maintain special liability insurance further ensures that firms have strong incentives to minimize the chance of contamination (insurance companies would be reluctant to issue coverage to those whose practices put the insurance company at risk). Public groundwater monitoring costs would be borne by industry, preferably through a special tax levied on the purchase of liability coverage.

End Subsidies for Resource Exploitation

The foremost engine of environmental destruction in America today is not the private sector but federal and state government. A great deal of environmental harm could be alleviated by eliminating the subsidized use of natural resources.

Five "Brownest" Programs in the Budget

- Agricultural subsidies are responsible for excessive pesticide, fungicide, and herbicide use with corresponding increases in non-point-source pollution.
- Sugar import quotas, tariffs, and price-support loans sustain a domestic sugar industry that might not otherwise exist; the destruction of the Everglades is the ecological result.
- Electricity subsidies via the power marketing administrations and the Tennessee Valley Authority artificially boost demand for energy and thereby are responsible for millions of tons of low-level radioactive waste and the disappearance of wild rivers in the West.
- Irrigation subsidies and socialized water services, which generally underwrite half of the cost of consumption, have done incalculable damage to western habitat while artificially promoting uneconomic agriculture with all the attendant environmental consequences. They also lead to tremendous overuse of water resources and worsen periodic shortages.
- Federal construction grant projects—such as the river maintenance, flood control, and agricultural reclamation undertakings of the Army Corps of Engineers—allow uneconomic projects to go forward and cause an array of serious environmental problems.

Repeal the Endangered Species Act

As Chapter 34 argues, compensating property owners for takings meant to secure public goods such as biological diversity is a simple matter of fairness and constitutional justice. But protecting property rights is also a necessary prerequisite for ecological protection. Property owners who expect to experience economic losses if their property is identified as ecologically important have little incentive to exhibit good ecological stewardship.

The Endangered Species Act, which prevents private property owners from making certain uses of their land in order to secure the "public good" of biological diversity, should thus be repealed since it provides no compensation to landowners for public takings. Instead, a federal biological trust should be established that would be funded out of general revenues at whatever level Congress found appropriate. The trust fund would be used to purchase conservation easements (in a voluntary and noncoercive fashion) from private landowners in order to protect the habitat of endangered species.

The virtue of such a reform is that landowners would have incentives rather than disincentives to protect species habitat. Moreover, the cost of biological preservation would become more transparent, which allows better-informed decisionmaking about the use of resources. Finally, such a reform would decriminalize the "ranching" of endangered species for commercial purposes. The ESA prohibits such practices out of a misguided belief that any commercial use of an endangered species inevitably contributes to its decline. Yet the experience of the African elephant and other threatened species belies that concern and strongly suggests that, if private parties are allowed to own and trade animals as commodities, their economic value goes up, not down. That in turn provides better incentives for species protection.

Similarly, section 404 of the Clean Water Act—the provision that ostensibly empowers the EPA to regulate wetlands—should be repealed. Like the ESA, it takes private property out of otherwise inoffensive uses for a public purpose and provides disincentives for wetland conservation. Protection of wetlands habitat should be left to the federal biological trust fund.

The "Greenest" Political Agenda Is Economic Growth

There are a number of reasons why economic growth is perhaps the most important of all environmental policies. First, it takes a healthy, growing economy to afford the pollution control technologies necessitated by environmental protection. A poorer nation, for example, could scarcely have afforded the nearly $200 billion this nation has spent on sewage treatment plants over the past 30 years.

Second, growing consumer demand for environmental goods (parks; recreational facilities; land for hunting, fishing, and hiking; and urban air and water quality) is largely responsible for the improving quantity and quality of both public and private ecological resources. Virtually all analysts agree that, for the vast majority of consumers, environmental amenities are "luxury goods" that are in greatest demand in the wealthiest societies. Economic growth is thus indirectly responsible for improving environmental quality in that it creates the conditions necessary for increased demand for (and the corresponding increase in supply of) environmental quality.

Third, advances in technology, production methods, and manufacturing practices—both a cause and a consequence of economic growth—have historically resulted in less, not more, pollution. Even advances in nonenvironmental technologies and industries have indirectly resulted in more efficient resource consumption and less pollution.

Conclusion

Science can inform individual preferences but cannot resolve environmental conflicts. Environmental goods and services, to the greatest extent possible, should be treated like other goods and services in the marketplace. People should be free to secure their preferences about the consumption of environmental goods such as clean air or clean water regardless of whether some scientists think such preferences are legitimate or not. Likewise, people should be free, to the greatest extent possible, to make decisions consistent with their own risk tolerances regardless of scientific or even public opinion.

Policies that override individual preferences in favor of political preferences are incapable of pleasing a majority of people or resolving subjective disputes. No matter what environmental risk thresholds are set, only those at the political mean will be pleased. The best we can do when it comes to the governance of public goods is to establish mechanisms that allow people the right to secure their preferences to the greatest extent possible.

Given the different circumstances of both communities and environmental media, it makes sense to allow those most directly affected by the pollution issue in question to decide for themselves how best to deal with it. Not only will the tradeoffs associated with differing approaches be more fully appreciated, but, given the fact that people prefer to live amidst those more like them than not, local decisionmaking will almost certainly

473

prove less injurious to minority preferences than decisionmaking at some other level of government.

Suggested Readings

Adler, Jonathan. "Let Fifty Flowers Bloom: Transforming the States into Laboratories of Environmental Policy." Roundtable Paper Series, American Enterprise Institute Federalism Project, September 20, 2001.

Anderson, Terry, and Peter Hill, eds. *Environmental Federalism*. Lanham, MD: Rowman & Littlefield, 1997.

Anderson, Terry, and Donald Leal. *Free Market Environmentalism*. New York: Palgrave, 2001.

DeLong, James. "Privatizing Superfund: How to Clean Up Hazardous Waste." Cato Institute Policy Analysis no. 247, December 18, 1995.

Keohane, Nathaniel, Richard Revesz, and Robert Stavins. "The Choice of Regulatory Instruments in Environmental Policy." *Harvard Environmental Law Review* 22, no. 2 (1998).

Leal, Donald, and Roger Meiners, eds. *Government vs. Environment*. Lanham, MD: Rowman & Littlefield, 2002.

Revesz, Richard, and Robert Stavins. "Environmental Law and Policy." Resources for the Future, Discussion Paper 04-30, June 2004.

Sterner, Thomas. *Policy Instruments for Environmental and Natural Resource Management*. Washington: Resources for the Future, 2002.

Stroup, Richard. *Eco-nomics: What Everyone Should Know about Economics and the Environment*. Washington: Cato Institute, 2003.

Sunstein, Cass. *Risk and Reason*. New York: Cambridge University Press, 2002.

VanDoren, Peter. *Cancer, Chemicals, and Choices: Risk Reduction through Markets*. Washington: Cato Institute, 1999.

Yandle, Bruce, Madhusudan Bhattarai, and Maya Vijaaraghavan. "Environmental Kuznets Curves: A Review of Findings, Methods, and Policy Implications." Political Economy Research Center, Research Study 02-1 Update, April 2004.

Yilmaz, Yesim. "Private Regulation: A Real Alternative for Regulatory Reform." Cato Institute Policy Analysis no. 303, April 20, 1998

—Prepared by Jerry Taylor

45. Global Warming and Climate Change

> **Congress should**
> - pass no legislation restricting emissions of carbon dioxide,
> - repeal current ethanol mandates, and
> - inform the public about how little climate change would be prevented by proposed legislation.

Leading politicians and media figures are insisting that Congress make global warming a very high priority. Global warming is indeed real, and human activity has been a contributor since 1975.

But global warming is also a very complicated and difficult issue that can provoke very unwise policy in response to political pressure. In 2005, for instance, Congress clearly made a very bad decision about climate change when it mandated accelerated production of ethanol. Critics had argued then that corn-based ethanol would actually result in *increased* carbon dioxide emissions. An increasing body of science has since verified this position. Further, corn-based ethanol is responsible in part for the skyrocketing price of corn, soybeans, rice, and wheat since the mandates began.

Although there are many different legislative proposals for substantial reductions in carbon dioxide emissions, there is no operational or tested suite of technologies that can accomplish the goals of such legislation. Fortunately, and contrary to much of the rhetoric surrounding climate change, there is ample time to develop such technologies, which will require substantial capital investment by individuals.

Earth's Temperature History

Although there are several different records of planetary surface temperature, the one most cited is from the United Nations' Intergovernmental Panel on Climate Change.

The IPCC history (Figure 45.1) shows two distinct periods of warming: one roughly from 1910 through 1945 and another that began rather abruptly around 1975 and ended in 1998. The rates of warming of the two periods are statistically indistinguishable. However, they likely resulted from two very different causes. The early warming is more attributable to changes in solar activity, whereas the latter warming has a clear "human" signature, although other "natural" changes also contributed to a minority of that warming.

Has Global Warming "Stopped"?

While it is common knowledge in the climate science community, the public is generally unaware that there has been no net change in the earth's average surface temperature in the last 11 years, as shown in the IPCC history (see Figure 45.2).

Because of a large El Niño climate event, 1998 was an unusually hot year—in fact, it remains the warmest year in IPCC's entire temperature history of almost 150 years. After a strong El Niño warming, there is often a cooling of the relative temperature, which occurred in 1999 and 2000.

Figure 45.1
Average Global Surface Temperature Anomalies, 1900–2007

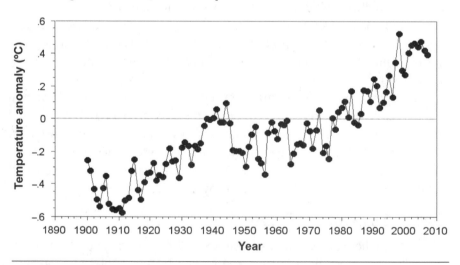

SOURCE: Intergovernmental Panel on Climate Change, 2007 and updates. http://www.cru.uea.ac.uk/cru/data/temperature/.

Figure 45.2
Average Global Surface Temperature Anomalies, 1977–2007

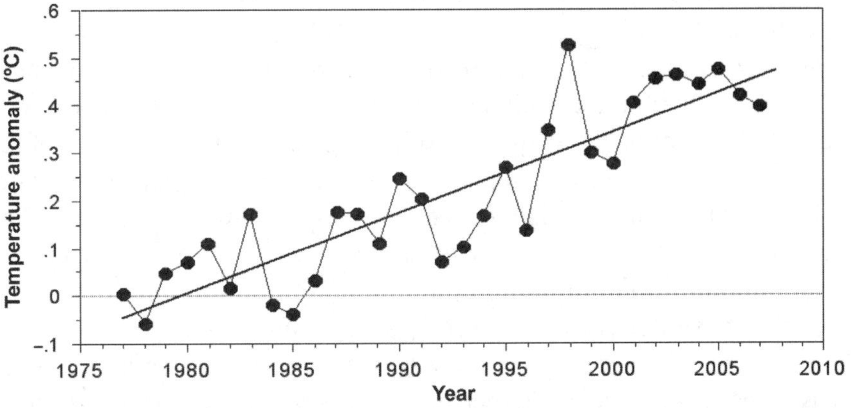

SOURCE: Intergovernmental Panel on Climate Change, 2007 and updates. http://www.cru.uea.ac.uk/cru/data/temperature/.

To begin a study of any trend at a high or a low point is highly dubious. However, if one starts in 2001, after the compensatory cooling, there was still no warming trend through 2007.

A close examination of observed temperatures since 1998 reveals that a combination of tropical oceanic temperatures (as modulated upward and downward by the presence of a warm or cold phase of El Niño) and low solar activity was responsible for the lack of warming, despite increasing concentrations of atmospheric carbon dioxide, the main global-warming gas. Clearly, these two factors could reverse their effects, which would accelerate a warming trend.

However, current indications are that warming may not resume until the middle of the next decade, as shown in a May 2008 article in *Nature* by Noel Keenlyside. Keenlyside's work is based on a projection of two long-term temperature patterns, in the North Atlantic and the tropical Pacific. These patterns will influence the global mean surface temperature—especially over North America and western Eurasia. Keenlyside's work, along with the lack of warming since 1998, has important policy implications.

What Are the Policy Implications?

Scientists and policymakers really have only one set of tools at their disposal for predicting climate change, namely, computer models of how increasing atmospheric carbon dioxide should affect earth's temperature. The thin lines in Figure 45.3 represent individual climate models run by the United Nations' IPCC. They are for IPCC's ''midrange'' scenario for emissions in this century.

Not one of these computer models for climate in the 21st century contains a 20-year period with no warming. So given the lack of warming since 1998, and projections for little or no warming until the middle of the next decade, *there is no scientifically credible model for future warming.*

Further, what warming does occur will likely be lower than the average indicated by all these models. That is because of the nature of carbon dioxide–induced warming.

Carbon dioxide is a ''greenhouse'' gas, meaning that it absorbs energy coming from the earth's surface. When a molecule of carbon dioxide releases that energy, it can either go out to space (where it would have normally gone, absent carbon dioxide) or be reradiated downward, which will result in additional warming.

But the effect is rather small. If carbon dioxide were acting alone, the rise in surface temperature expected this century would be a little more

Figure 45.3
Various Runs of IPCC Computer Models for Its "Midrange" Carbon Dioxide Emissions Scenario

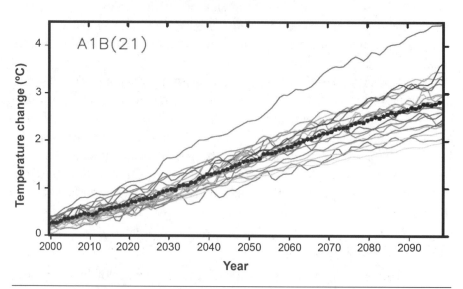

SOURCE: Intergovernmental Panel on Climate Change, 2007, p. 763.

than 1 degree Fahrenheit. However, this increment of warming raises the temperature of the oceans, which means they will naturally send more water vapor into the atmosphere. Water vapor, like carbon dioxide, is a greenhouse gas, and is in fact currently responsible for keeping the earth's surface temperature nearly 30 degrees Centigrade warmer than it would be if there were none.

If, for any reason, warming stops for 20 years (it has already stopped for 11), the "feedback" effect between carbon dioxide and water vapor will also be delayed, as the ocean does not warm up instantaneously. This effect will be further delayed, resulting in less warming than was anticipated, at least in the first half of this century.

This delay gives the political process time to address global warming, time that will allow for the development of technologies that can result in lower emissions of carbon dioxide into the atmosphere. The alternative—precipitously mandating major reductions in emissions without any known acceptable technology—is to be avoided.

Global Warming Perceptions versus Realities

The apocalyptic vision of global warming is driven largely by scenarios of rapid sea-level rise caused by the loss of Greenland's ice, and increasingly strong tropical cyclones (hurricanes and typhoons). These are worth discussing in some detail.

Greenland, the Arctic, and Sea Level

In that vision, Greenland, on which sits 10 percent of the world's ice, will suddenly shed that ice, raising sea levels by 20 feet or so, possibly as soon as 2100. This scenario has been popularized in Al Gore's movie and book, *An Inconvenient Truth*, and has been proselytized largely by one scientist, James Hansen, who heads the Goddard Institute for Space Studies, a branch of the U.S. National Aeronautics and Space Administration.

Both the IPCC and reality paint a much different picture.

The 2007 Fourth Assessment Report of the IPCC (which was awarded the 2007 Nobel Peace Prize along with Gore) projects sea-level rise of between 9 and 19 *inches* in the 21st century, for its "midrange" estimate of carbon dioxide and other greenhouse gas emissions. IPCC notes that this estimate does *not* assume a rapid ice loss from Greenland. Instead, the IPCC wrote that there is no current scientific support for this hypothesis.

479

Indeed, since the IPCC published its report, several scientific papers have been published demonstrating that rapid loss is highly unlikely.

The IPCC's Fourth Assessment Report includes a computer model for Greenland's ice. In the model, the concentration of atmospheric carbon dioxide is four times the preindustrial background, or over 1,100 parts per million, and *that concentration is maintained for 2,000 years.* In that scenario, Greenland loses half its ice approximately a millennium from now.

Clearly, no one can possibly project the energy future of our society 100 years from today, much less 1,000 years.

It is also worth noting that the Eurasian Arctic was several degrees warmer for several *millennia* after the end of the last ice age and that there was no catastrophic loss of Greenland's ice.

The notion that Greenland's temperatures are particularly unusual at this juncture is simply untrue. Figure 45.4 shows Danish Meteorological Institute data dating from the 18th century for southern Greenland coastal temperatures. The data clearly demonstrate that the average temperature for the most recent decade is hardly unusual.

Arctic sea ice reaches its annual minimum at the end of summer, and satellites in orbit since 1979 have detected a significant decline in ice extent at this time of the year.

Note that 1979 is near the end of the *coldest* period in the Arctic since the 1920s (See Figure 45.5). Nowhere in news stories about Arctic ice

Figure 45.4
Summer Coastal Temperatures for Southern Greenland, 1782–2007

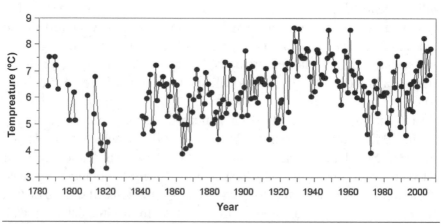

SOURCE: Danish Meteorological Institute, 2008. http://www.dmi.dk/dmi/tr08-04.pdf.

Figure 45.5
IPCC Record of Arctic Temperatures

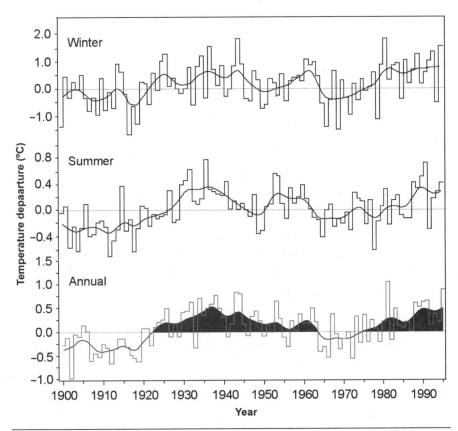

SOURCE: Serreze and others, 2000.

has this fact been noted: in the beginning of the satellite history, sea ice had to have been abnormally expanded. Since then, about half the contraction probably represents a return to more normal conditions for the 20th century, whereas the warming of the most recent years has resulted in another contraction to far below normal, compared to the last century.

The fact that warmer temperatures in the Arctic persisted for *millennia* after the end of the last ice age almost certainly means that the sea ice was depleted far beyond today's level for much of that era, and was perhaps even gone at the end of almost every summer.

We often hear of the "irreversibility" of loss of Arctic sea ice, as the surface changes from white to dark, absorbing (rather than reflecting)

481

radiation, and resulting in additional warming. But if the loss of ice is "irreversible," why did it then return after the warm millennia immediately following the ice age? Clearly, there are several problems with glib projections of any climate disaster in the near future.

Tropical Cyclones and Global Warming

The unusually strong 2004 and 2005 hurricane seasons in the Atlantic basin heightened concern about a relationship between planetary warming and the frequency or severity of tropical cyclones.

On September 16, 2004, in the midst of a hurricane season in which Florida was struck by four major storms, the *Journal of Climate* published an article by Thomas Knutson of the National Oceanic and Atmospheric Administration and Robert Tuleya from Old Dominion University in which computer-generated hurricanes showed a slight increase in strength as carbon dioxide accumulated in the atmosphere. This article received considerable attention, particularly from the *New York Times*, which summarized the work with these words:

> Global warming is likely to produce a significant increase in the intensity and rainfall of hurricanes in coming decades, according to the most comprehensive computer analysis done so far.

This type of press coverage creates a political climate in which policymakers feel compelled to act. In reality, Knutson and Tuleya's article said, "CO_2-induced tropical cyclone intensity changes are unlikely to be detectable in historical observations and will probably not be detectable for decades to come."

It is noteworthy that Knutson's most recent work now calculates that the number of *Atlantic* tropical storms and hurricanes will *decrease* with global warming. In recent decades, as the surface temperature has warmed, the frequency of these storms has dropped in both the eastern North Pacific and Southern oceans.

Nonetheless, alarmist press statements on melting ice, rising seas, and hurricanes cause serious difficulties for policymakers. Further, the proclivity of the media to publicize dramatic interpretations of global warming science should be obvious: stories suggesting that climate change might be more benign are simply not as attractive as those spelling gloom and doom.

482

Past and Future Anthropogenerated Warming and the Policy Response

Most scientists agree that a substantial component of the surface warming that began in the mid-1970s is a result of changes in the earth's greenhouse effect, largely caused by increases in atmospheric carbon dioxide.

It has long been known that atmospheric carbon dioxide must build up at an ever-increasing ("exponential") rate in order to simply support a constant rate of warming. Most future projections for atmospheric carbon dioxide indeed make this assumption. As a result, they tend to predict constant rates of warming, once that warming is established. These are apparent in Figure 45.3. While the rates of the various models differ, the rates for each model are indeed constant.

Figure 45.2 shows IPCC temperatures since the beginning of the recent warming in the mid-1970s. The rate of overall warming also appears to be quite constant, despite the lack of warming since 1998. If this is indeed the rate that has been established as a result of greenhouse gas changes, that should be quite reassuring. It means that warming is modest and will continue to be so. As noted earlier, projections indicating the continued absence of warming in the next few years mean that the IPCC's average warming forecast for this century is most likely an overestimate.

What is a reasonable policy response to such a modest warming? Clearly, an unreasonable response is one that costs a tremendous amount of money while doing nothing about global warming. Legislation to reduce emissions by 70 percent by 2050 is an example. No known technology can accomplish that reduction. Consequently, the policy response is known as "cap-and-trade," where corporations or individuals buy "permits" to emit carbon dioxide above a certain limit, sold by entities that have reduced emissions below that limit. The result is that carbon-based fuels become increasingly expensive as fewer and fewer "permits" are allowed. The most popular version of this legislation is the Lieberman-Warner Climate Security Act (S. 2191), which was debated in the Senate in June 2008. It did not survive a vote for cloture.

Passage of S. 2191 would create an economic disaster. It requires emission reductions to 2005 levels by 2012; 15 percent below 2005 levels by 2020; 33 percent below by 2030; and 66 percent below by 2050. This is an enormously expensive undertaking (with aggregate costs totaling trillions of dollars) with no real climatic gain. Because of growth in emissions since 1990, the actual result of this bill is to lower emissions by only 11 percent from 1990 levels by 2030, and 25 percent by 2050.

The 2030 figure is only a slight increment more than the (unfulfilled) U.S. commitment to the Kyoto Protocol. Assume that the United States adopts Lieberman-Warner and that all other industrial nations meet and keep their obligations under the Kyoto Protocol (only two major countries, Germany and the United Kingdom, will do so, but because of political rather than environmental changes). The net result would be a reduction in warming of 0.08 degrees Centigrade by 2050, an amount far too small to measure. The basis for this calculation was published by the U.S. National Center for Atmospheric Research in 1998.

However, the cost of this bill is enormous, aggregating into trillions of dollars as it goes into effect. Among other things, the costs included the issuance of "credits" for the production of biomass ethanol. Although this cannot yet be achieved on a cost-effective basis, recent research published in *Science* magazine has demonstrated that using existing forested or agricultural land for this process produces *more* carbon dioxide than is emitted by the simple combustion of gasoline for motor fuel.

The lesson to the new Congress must be clear. Observed warming is at or near the low end of the IPCC's projection ranges. The lack of recent warming and projections that this will continue for several years reinforce the notion that warming will be modest, at least in coming decades. Drastic action is unwarranted at this time.

Members of Congress need to ask difficult questions about global warming.

Does the most recent science and climate data argue for precipitous action? (No.) Is there a suite of technologies that can dramatically cut emissions by, say, 2050? (No.) Would such actions take away capital, in a futile attempt to stop warming, that would best be invested in the future? (Yes.) Finally, do we not have the responsibility to communicate this information to our citizens, despite disconnections between perceptions of climate change and climate reality? The answer is surely yes. If not the U.S. Congress, then whom? If not now, when? After we have committed to expensive policies *that do not work* in response to a misperception of global warming?

That is the reality of climate change and the new Congress. It may take courage to resist the political and media demands for drastic action, but the facts point toward caution.

Suggested Readings

Keenlyside, N. S., and others. "Advancing Decadal-Scale Climate Prediction in the North Atlantic Sector." *Nature* 453 (2008).

Knutson, T., and others. "Simulated Reduction in Atlantic Hurricane Frequency under Twenty-First-Century Warming Conditions." *Nature Geoscience* 1 (2008).

Michaels, Patrick J. *Meltdown: The Predictable Distortion of Global Warming by Scientists, Politicians, and the Media.* Washington: Cato Institute, 2004.

Michaels, Patrick J., and Robert C. Balling. *Climate of Extremes: Global Warming Science They Don't Want You to Know.* Washington: Cato Institute, 2009.

—Prepared by Patrick J. Michaels

FOREIGN AND DEFENSE POLICY

46. Countering Terrorism

> **Policymakers should**
>
> - stop using the misleading phrase "war on terrorism";
> - understand that an aim of terrorism is to elicit overreactions that damage the victim state as badly or worse than direct attacks;
> - focus on disrupting al Qaeda senior leadership's ability to plan future terrorist attacks and attract and train new recruits;
> - work with foreign governments to apprehend al Qaeda operatives in other countries, but be prepared to take unilateral action when foreign governments are unable or unwilling to take action themselves and when the diplomatic and strategic risks are low; and
> - recognize that effective strategies for confronting the threat of terrorism rarely involve large-scale military action and that the presence of U.S. ground troops on foreign soil might actually be counterproductive.

Terrorism is best understood as politically motivated violence directed against nonmilitary targets. It is a tactic favored by weak, nonstate actors to raise the costs of a targeted state's policies. Terrorist attacks impose direct costs in lost lives and property, of course, but they produce greater costs to the victim—and corresponding benefits to the terrorists—when they goad the targeted nation into self-injurious overreaction. These overreactions fall into the following categories:

- **Waste of blood and treasure.** Terrorist attacks, or well-placed threats of attack, can prompt the victim to waste its own resources—both the blood of its soldiers and the wealth of its people.
- **Recruitment and sympathy gains.** A strong power victimized by terrorism may respond with violence that is badly directed, or even

489

entirely misdirected, engendering sympathy for terrorist groups and therefore aiding their recruiting and support.

- **Weakened political order and society.** Terrorism may cause victim states to come loose from their ideological moorings, such as the West's traditions of tolerance, individual rights, due process, and the rule of law.

Carefully measured responses deny terrorists the strategic upper hand they seek but cannot achieve on their own. They will deny terrorists the false perception among their target audiences that they are powerful, and they will deny terrorists the moral authority they seek by coaxing wrongdoing from the states they attack.

President George W. Bush did not adopt a careful, strategic approach to terrorism following the 9/11 attacks. Understandably at first, though less so as time passed, he and his administration overreacted to terrorism and clung stubbornly to the "war on terror" metaphor, even as his administration pursued al Qaeda by both military and nonmilitary means.

The members of the new administration will have considerable latitude in shaping policy, but they should begin by formally discarding the phrase "war on terror," which conceals and confuses the nature of U.S. efforts to hunt down violent extremists. The term falsely implies that the challenge is chiefly a military one, and therefore stimulates demand for largely irrelevant, and occasionally counterproductive, military spending. The disastrous invasion of Iraq reflects the problems inherent in construing counterterrorism as a military problem, to be solved by military means. Finally, the loose reference to "terror" is overbroad and inaccurately lumps together disparate groups with often-incompatible objectives. By casting the challenge posed by al Qaeda terrorists as a war, policymakers risk contributing to the already widespread perception that the United States is engaged in a war against all of Islam, thereby playing into the rhetoric of the violent extremists.

In addition to dispensing with the "war on terror," the incoming president and his team can and should focus the government's efforts on those counterterrorism policies that will most likely reduce the threat of mass-casualty attacks. Effective tactics include infiltrating and disrupting terror groups. Targeted, lawful surveillance of terrorists and terror suspects is essential. Controlling access to weapons of mass destruction and their precursors is also vital. Taking reasonable precautions to secure against likely vectors of attack on infrastructure is also important, as is preparing for attacks and their aftermaths. Public communications that more accurately convey risks might quell public demand for overreaction. (For more, see Chapter 47, "Domestic Security.")

Above all, policymakers should aim to counter the strategic logic of terrorism. Specifically, they should take great care not to expend the nation's blood and treasure, avoiding military action if at all possible. They should not give terrorists the gift of overreactions such as violence that injures innocents, as this will aid the terrorists by driving new recruits into their ranks. Finally, they should stand by the foundational Western values of individual rights, due process, tolerance, and the rule of law. In fashioning a proactive strategy to prevent future acts of terrorism, and to mitigate terrorism's harmful effects should prevention fail, policymakers must account for the possibility that short-term reactions might have counterproductive medium- to long-term effects.

The Response to 9/11

Nearly every U.S. president has dealt in some fashion with the threat posed by individuals or groups who wage violence against civilians to advance a political agenda. Rarely, if ever, have past presidents declared war against the group responsible for a specific terrorist act or acts, and none has ever declared war on the tactic "terrorism."

Given the sheer scale of the killing and destruction in the 9/11 attacks and the enormous psychological effect on all Americans, to say nothing of the damage to the U.S. economy, it is understandable that the initial reaction was a desire for revenge. The 19 hijackers were already dead, but Americans wanted to know who financed the operation, who trained the hijackers, and who inspired them to commit mass murder.

We didn't have to look very long, or very hard. Terrorism experts within the White House and elsewhere had correctly fixed on al Qaeda and Osama bin Laden within a matter of a few hours. The administration had already begun executing plans for hunting down bin Laden and his followers by the time President Bush appeared before a joint session of Congress nine days later and declared: "Our war on terror begins with al Qaeda, but it does not end there. It will not end until every terrorist group of global reach has been found, stopped and defeated." The Bush administration adopted a multifaceted approach to fighting terrorism, combining intelligence analysis; traditional law enforcement; and, at times, the use of the U.S. military, including the high-profile missions in Afghanistan and Iraq. But while the actual conduct of the Bush administration's counterterrorism policies implies something different from a traditional war, the Bush White House was extremely reluctant to give up the "war on terror" metaphor. Bush chose to highlight the use of the military as his primary means for combating the most important challenge of his presidency, in part to draw distinctions between himself and his political opponents. Thus was the terminology surrounding the fight against al Qaeda filtered through the lens of partisan politics.

That did not serve us well. As a report by the Defense Science Board notes, evocative phrases such as "global war on terror" and "fighting them there so we don't fight them here" "may have short-term benefits in motivating support at home." But this "polarizing rhetoric," the report went on to say, "can have adverse long-term consequences that reduce the willingness of potential allies to collaborate, and give unwarranted legitimacy and unity of effort to dispersed adversaries."

Indeed, a number of experts have lamented the "war on terror" construct. By declaring a global war on terror, Jeffrey Record wrote in a paper for the Strategic Studies Institute at the U.S. Army War College:

> The [Bush] administration . . . subordinated strategic clarity to the moral clarity it strives for in foreign policy and may have set the United States on a course of open-ended and gratuitous conflict with states and nonstate entities that pose no serious threat to the United States.

"Most of the [global war on terror's] declared objectives," Record concluded, "are unrealistic and condemn the United States to a hopeless quest for absolute security. As such, the [global war on terror's] goals are also politically, fiscally, and militarily unsustainable."

The eminent military historian Michael Howard likewise objected to the term "war." "It implies something finite; a conflict with a clear beginning and an even clearer conclusion," Howard wrote in the journal *Survival*. "Further, 'war' normally is essentially the concern of the military. Today, that is not self-evident," he concluded.

There is also the utter irrationality of declaring war on a tactic. It makes no more sense than it would have for the British and French to have declared war on blitzkrieg in 1939, or for the Americans to have declared war on kamikaze attacks in the Pacific in 1944. Given this flawed formulation, it can be said that the American "war effort" was off the rails from the beginning.

Rhetoric, and the shaping of expectations, are more important in the context of counterterrorism operations than in traditional wars. Victory or defeat in most wars is determined by armies on the battlefield or fleets at sea. By contrast, because terrorists aim specifically at invoking anxiety among the public at large, measures intended to shore up public will are crucial to an effective strategy for countering terrorism.

Our strategy must also be based on reasonable expectations. Terrorism has persisted throughout human history, and it will be with us in some form forever. President Bush candidly conceded this point during the 2004 campaign, when he said to *Today* show host Matt Lauer, "I don't think you can win it." Containing the problem requires a tight focus on the most urgent threats. Of particular concern is the remote, but serious, risk that terrorists might gain control of a nuclear weapon. The scope of destruction from even a single act of nuclear terrorism would be greater than anything ever before witnessed on U.S. soil. It is logical, therefore, for policymakers to pay even more attention, and likely devote more resources, to programs aimed at locking down loose nuclear materials. Diplomacy and cooperation with other countries might include measures to discourage further nuclear proliferation and to enhance security of existing arsenals, but rarely military action.

Many other proposals ostensibly geared toward countering the threat of terrorism, however, will likely be irrelevant and might actually prove harmful. For example, there is strong bipartisan support for expanding the military, especially the army and marines, despite the fact that conventional military forces play only a limited role in combating terrorism. With the exception of the U.S. military operations to depose the Taliban and disrupt al Qaeda camps in Afghanistan, the most successful counterterrorism operations have not involved large numbers of ground troops. The disastrous invasion and occupation of Iraq—cited in a National Intelligence Estimate as the "cause célèbre" for jihadists, "breeding a deep resentment of U.S. involvement in the Muslim world and cultivating supporters for the global jihad movement"—stand in stark contrast to the successful nonmilitary operations that enabled the United States to capture such al Qaeda figures as Ramzi Binalshibh and Khalid Sheikh Mohammed, the key plotters of the 9/11 attacks.

To the extent that our military, and especially our ground forces, have been stretched by the war in Iraq, ending the war in a timely fashion would immediately relieve these stresses. So long as policymakers refuse to end our military involvement and bring U.S. troops home, however, the persistent U.S. presence will likely undermine our wider counterterrorism efforts. A number of experts note that stationing conventional forces in foreign lands is not conducive to fighting terrorism. Indeed, it is often counterproductive. The University of Chicago's Robert Pape links the presence of American troops in the Middle East to the threat of future suicide terrorism against the United States and credits the occupation of Iraq with strengthening al Qaeda. Michael Scheuer, a 22-year veteran of the Central Intelligence Agency who served as head of the agency's bin Laden unit from 1996 to 1999, concurs. Because of the Iraq War, Scheuer told an interviewer in 2006, "there are more people willing to take up arms against the United States, and we have less ability to win hearts and minds in the Arab world."

What Works?

An effective strategy for countering terrorism, and doing so in a manner that does not generate still more terrorism, begins by putting the problem into the proper perspective. The violence and bloodshed that can be unleashed by modern industrial states are several orders of magnitude greater than any caused by international terrorism in the 21st century. This is true even, for example, in the unlikely event that terrorists manage to get their hands on a functioning nuclear device, or build one on their own, and then detonate it in a populated area.

But to portray the terrorists as an existential threat to the United States, or more broadly the West, dramatically exaggerates their power and influence. It is a mistake to repeat al Qaeda's intentions as if they are plausible. Precious few people around the world wish to live under the rule of radical Islamists. Although many Muslims believe that Islam should have a prominent role in political life, solid majorities in many predominantly Muslim countries—including Morocco, Turkey, Indonesia, and Pakistan—worry about Islamic extremism. A National Intelligence Estimate prepared in 2006, titled "The Trends in Global Terrorism," explained, "The jihadists' greatest vulnerability is that their ultimate political solution—an ultraconservative interpretation of shari'a-based governance spanning the Muslim world—is unpopular with the vast majority of Muslims."

Indeed, recent research has concluded that the threat of terrorism is already on the wane. Andrew Mack and Zoe Nielsen analyzed four different data sets and determined that, broadly speaking, the incidences of global terrorism and the human costs of terrorist violence had declined since 2001. Looking to the future, Mack and Nielsen surmised, "In the long term, perhaps sooner, Islamist terror organizations will join the overwhelming majority of other terrorist groups that have failed to achieve their objectives.''

Other empirical studies comport with these findings. Researcher Max Abrahms looked at 28 terrorist organizations and found that they failed to achieve their stated policy objectives 93 percent of the time. Abrahms further concluded that terrorism's ''poor success rate is inherent to the tactic of terrorism itself.'' Because acts of terrorism often kill or injure the very people that terrorists seek to influence, the strategy carries within it the seeds of its own destruction. The *Atlantic Monthly*'s James Fallows concluded that al Qaeda's ''hopes for fundamentally harming the United States . . . rest less on what it can do itself than on what it can trick, tempt, or goad us into doing.'' In short, terrorist aims may be grandiose, but their capacity for achieving those aims is severely limited. The most effective counterterrorism strategies capitalize on our strengths and exploit their weaknesses to let them lose.

A Fresh Start

The intellectual ferment within Islam presents both a challenge and an opportunity for the West. On the one hand, non-Muslims have only a very limited capacity to shape the debate in a positive direction. As the 9/11 Commission report concluded: ''We must encourage reform, freedom, democracy, and opportunity, even though our own promotion of these messages is limited in its effectiveness simply because we are its carriers. . . . The United States can promote moderation, but cannot ensure its ascendancy. Only Muslims can do this.''

On the other hand, and paradoxically, while we cannot ''ensure the ascendancy'' of moderate Muslims, we have a great capacity for influencing the debate within Islam in a negative direction—empowering extremists and marginalizing moderates. As radical Islamism struggles to expand its reach, our words sometimes matter as much as our actions. Thus have our enemies seized on the phrase ''war on terror'' to claim, falsely, that the United States is at war with Islam.

Policymakers should take steps to differentiate their policies from those of the Bush White House and should focus particular attention on those policies that have created ill will within the Muslim community. The leading source of resentment is the U.S. war in Iraq, and policymakers should commit to swiftly ending the U.S. military presence there. Other necessary steps include closing the terrorist holding facilities at Guantánamo Bay, Cuba, and formally renouncing torture, including waterboarding. A series of high-profile public diplomacy and outreach initiatives is also warranted, and might include a particular focus on those predominantly Muslim countries that have managed to maintain working relationships with the United States despite some of the unfortunate excesses of the Bush administration.

Above all else, however, policymakers should approach the problem of terrorism with the necessary perspective. Claims that our national survival hangs in the balance, or that the terrorists pose an existential threat comparable to that of the Nazis or the Soviets, build pressure for policies that do not increase our security but do erode the very liberties that define us as a nation. The new president should begin by recasting the discussion away from that of a war to be won and toward thinking of terrorism as a problem to be confronted and managed.

Suggested Readings

Abrahms, Max. "Why Terrorism Does Not Work." *International Security* 31, no. 2 (Fall 2006).

————. "What Terrorists Really Want: Terrorist Motives and Counterterrorism Strategy." *International Security* 32, no. 4 (Spring 2008).

Fallows, James. "Declaring Victory." *Atlantic Monthly*, September 2006.

Jones, Seth G., and Martin C. Libicki. *How Terrorist Groups End: Lessons for Countering al Qa'ida.* Santa Monica, CA: RAND, 2008.

Mack, Andrew, and Zoe Nielsen. *Human Security Brief, 2007.* Vancouver, BC: Human Security Report Project, School for International Studies, Simon Fraser University, March 2008.

Pape, Robert. "Suicide Terrorism and Democracy: What We've Learned Since 9/11." Cato Institute Policy Analysis no. 582, November 1, 2006.

Record, Jeffrey. "Bounding the Global War on Terror." Strategic Studies Institute, December 2003.

—Prepared by Christopher Preble

47. Domestic Security

Policymakers should

- focus the federal government's efforts on the few areas where it can make a significant contribution to securing the country and eliminate federal security programs that are better performed by other levels of government and the private sector;
- make it clearer to the public that government homeland security efforts cannot make the country absolutely safe against possible terrorist attacks;
- ensure that homeland security efforts are not disproportionately focused on defending against the last attack, such as another 9/11 or the Madrid train bombings, at the expense of other vulnerabilities;
- avoid overreaction or exaggeration of the threat posed by terrorism; and
- ensure that civil liberties are not sacrificed for unneeded and ineffective homeland security measures.

In the wake of the terrorist attacks of September 11, 2001, the U.S. government asserted responsibility for much of the nation's domestic security by creating the Department of Homeland Security. The national government has important security responsibilities, of course, as epitomized by the constitutional power to "provide for the common defense." But a single central authority cannot effectively secure a country as large, diverse, dynamic, and free as the United States. The job of domestic security has too many facets. Instead, the federal government should focus on the security issues that it is uniquely suited to address—the ones that states, localities, and the private sector cannot.

The threat of terrorism, which created the vogue for a national "homeland security" infrastructure, must be understood in a strategic context.

497

Terrorist attacks have direct costs, but they also seek self-injurious overreaction, such as the waste of blood and treasure on the part of the victim state; recruitment and sympathy gains when the victim state misdirects a violent response; and the weakening of the political order in the society attacked so that it is induced to act wrongly. When it does so, it cedes the moral and ideological high ground, making terrorists groups look relatively more legitimate. Policymakers should use risk management to prioritize security efforts, and they should avoid holding out the promise of perfect security, as there is no such thing. Civil liberties must be fully protected, and doing so is consistent with proportionate and well-focused domestic security efforts.

The Limited Federal Role in Domestic Security

The federal government has several important roles in securing against asymmetric threats like terrorism. But it is only one of many institutions arrayed against terrorism, and not the primary or only source of protection.

The federal government's strength is in its traditional international roles: setting a foreign policy that does not exacerbate grievances against the United States or legitimize the use of terrorism against us; developing intelligence information on international terrorist groups; and cooperating with and cajoling foreign governments to assist in pressuring and dismantling foreign terror cells. The federal government can aid state and local agencies that have responsibility for domestic security by disseminating relevant intelligence and vulnerability information within the country; by coordinating multijurisdictional counterterrorism efforts (just as it does with multijurisdictional crime); by maintaining a regularized border environment and interdicting known terrorists, weapons, and harmful materials there; and by providing information that helps state and local actors—public and private—prepare for and mitigate the effects of attacks or disasters.

The federal government cannot secure the thousands of bridges, sports stadiums, airports, bus stations, subways, and shopping malls, or the hundreds of skyscrapers, nuclear power plants, electrical substations, railway lines, food warehouses, water distribution systems, or telecommunications and computing facilities across the country. Responsibility for the security of internal infrastructure should be the responsibility of its owners and of local law enforcement. Since 9/11, the federal government has asserted roles in all these areas and more without regard to whether that level of government is well-suited to the task or whether certain security measures even merit the expenditure of taxpayer dollars.

Use of Risk Management to Focus Security Efforts

The federal government response to the terror threat has been haphazard, oftentimes irrelevant, and occasionally counterproductive because it has been driven chiefly by politics. Instead of being reactive to past attacks and interest group demands, policymakers should focus the security efforts of all governments using risk management. The following questions illustrate a general risk management framework:

- **What are you trying to protect?** Every security program or technology is meant to protect some institution, infrastructure, process, person, or group that may be harmed.
- **What are you trying to protect it from?** Harm to the asset you are trying to protect can come in various ways. The goal here is to describe vulnerabilities and the relevant ways that an asset may be harmed.
- **What is the likelihood of each threat occurring and the consequence if it does?** Each threat has a different likelihood and consequence, and each factor may range from very low to very high. Risk assessment helps target limited resources efficiently by focusing attention on the threats with the greatest combined likelihood and consequence.
- **What kind of action is being taken in response to the threat?** There are four ways of responding to a threat:
  - *Acceptance* of a threat is a rational alternative that is often chosen when the threat has low probability, low consequence, or both.
  - *Prevention* is the alteration of the target or its circumstances to diminish the risk of something bad happening.
  - *Interdiction* is any confrontation with, or influence exerted on, an attacker to eliminate or limit his or her ability to cause harm.
  - *Mitigation* is preparation so that, should something bad happen, its consequences are reduced.
- **Does the response create new risks to the asset or others?** The final step in analyzing the program's efficacy is to be aware of new risks created by the prevention, interdiction, or mitigation of the threats under consideration.

499

These questions help illustrate why localized and decentralized security measures are most effective; a government that is trying to protect everything is protecting nothing. But they also show how the federal government can be helpful to the states, localities, and private-sector entities that actually secure the country.

Consider an example where one of the federal government's intelligence agencies picks up a plan to knock out electrical transmission facilities during a period of particularly cold or hot weather, which could threaten lives and cause economic disruption. This information can be passed along to the owners of the infrastructure so that they can step up the measures that physically secure their facilities (prevention). If the perpetrators are identified in any way, this information can be passed on to state and local law enforcement for possible interdiction. This threat intelligence can also be used to inform states, localities, businesses, and families about the importance of preparing for power loss (mitigation).

Avoidance of Wasteful and Counterproductive Overreaction

It is important to understand terrorism as a strategy. Like our foreign policy, our domestic security policy must be strategic. It must avoid the overreaction that terrorism seeks to engender. Terrorists often have great ambitions, but they lack the means to achieve their goals unless their intended target—be it the government of a nation-state or the citizens of that state—alters its behavior or adopts policies that otherwise redound to the terrorists' benefit.

As discussed in Chapter 46, "Countering Terrorism," terrorism is violence typically used by weak, nonstate actors against states to raise the costs of the victim state's policies. A strong power victimized by terrorism will very likely do violence or take other responses that are badly directed, or even entirely misdirected. This reaction will tend to engender sympathy for the terrorists and aid in their recruiting and support. For example, Paddy Hillyard from Queen's University Belfast has articulated well how British responses to Irish Republican Army terror won sympathy and recruits for the IRA. Lashing out against the communities in which terrorists live, or the places where they hide, forces local neutrals into the wrong camp. And those neutrals are uniquely positioned to undermine those terrorists should they so choose.

Avoiding overreaction is essential for countering the strategic logic of terrorism. Indeed, it is the care given to the measurement of domestic security efforts that will help control terrorism. Huge U.S. government spending on a vast repertoire of dubious security efforts since 2001 has put Osama bin Laden in a position to boast about the large returns on his small investment in the 9/11 attacks, and of his confidence that Americans will continue to expend resources in a vain attempt to chase down every potential terrorist. He crowed in 2004 that it is "easy for us to provoke and bait this administration." Describing his desire to "bleed America to the point of bankruptcy," bin Laden remarked, "All that we have to do is to send two mujahedeen to the furthest point east to raise a piece of cloth on which is written 'al Qaeda,' in order to make generals race there to cause America to suffer human, economic and political losses."

The haphazard and poorly coordinated responses of our federal domestic security agencies are no less a boon to al Qaeda. The Department of Homeland Security and the Transportation Security Administration are basically permanent multibillion-dollar drains on the public fisc. The REAL ID Act and Western Hemisphere Travel Initiative are similarly wasteful, self-destructive programs. These are just a few examples, and they were all prompted by a $500,000 al Qaeda investment.

The Threat to Civil Liberties

A terror-victim government can harm itself in other ways. Terrorists are battling for legitimacy. With little ability to build it on their own, they can at least degrade their opponent's. Terror attacks may cause otherwise liberal and tolerant societies to come somewhat loose from their moorings. Overreaction by the victim state erodes its claim of moral authority to rule; deviating from the rule of law, seeking extraordinary powers, and using mass surveillance all give terrorists legitimacy by admitting their power while undermining the legitimacy of an incumbent government by placing the state at odds with its people. By simply behaving well, the terror-victim government can deliver a devastating blow to terrorism because it causes the bad behavior of terrorists to dominate public perceptions.

In response to the events of 9/11, the Bush administration suspended, eroded, and ignored a range of civil liberties, all the while claiming such steps were legal on the grounds that they were necessary to prevent a future attack. In the course of implementing many of these policies, the Bush administration repeatedly asserted the "state secrets" privilege as grounds for the dismissal of civil cases that challenged the legality of its conduct in the war on terror, specifically with respect to two programs: the rendition of suspected terrorists to foreign countries for interrogation purposes and the National Security Agency's warrantless wiretapping of communications by suspected terrorists.

The veil of secrecy should be lifted, and policymakers should act swiftly to redress civil liberties violations and restore rights that have been lost or diminished over the last several years. Immediate steps include banning trials before military tribunals, closing secret prison facilities, eliminating national security letters, denying authorities the power to jail citizens in the United States as "enemy combatants," ending the practice of extraordinary rendition, banning torture, and ending warrantless wiretapping within the United States.

Emergency Preparedness

Part of avoiding overreaction is recognizing the hard truth: providing absolute and perfect defense against any and all future potential terrorist attacks is impossible. Though they are probably not as endlessly cunning as they are often portrayed, terrorists will bide their time and seek opportunities to stage dramatic attacks. All that can be expected of domestic security is to prevent what can be prevented and to recover well from what cannot. Policymakers who promise perfect security or the elimination of terrorist threats are committing leadership malpractice, just like policymakers who inflate the threat of terrorism.

The country must instead adopt a sound, comprehensive counterterrorism strategy. This begins with understanding terrorism as a strategy and with forcing policymakers to focus on securing the country against both the threat of attack and the threat of overreaction. The government should study how people perceive risk and how they overestimate dramatic but highly unlikely causes of death. A comprehensive counterterrorism strategy, which should include communications planning for reassuring the nation in the event of future attacks, will help ensure that the physical damage from any attack does not metastasize into undue damage to liberty or the economy.

Given the possibility of future attacks, the public should be educated about how to prepare for and respond to terrorist attacks, especially the potential use of chemical, biological, or radiological/nuclear weapons. These communications need not promote fear and could be blended into science curricula in high schools and colleges. Solid, science-based information should be made available about the effects of such weapons and what can be done to mitigate their effects. Resource directories must be published. People need to know where to go and whom to contact in the event of an emergency. And the exaggerated assumptions about what such weapons can do should be debunked.

In short, if there are effective means of providing protection against certain types of possible terrorist attacks (e.g., potassium iodide used to protect the thyroid gland from the effects of exposure to radioactive iodine from a dirty bomb), government officials can let people know exactly what they are, how they work, how to use them, and where to obtain them.

Put in the proper context, it becomes obvious that threat exaggeration is harmful behavior. Pandering to people's fear about terrorism should be a political liability. A public education campaign would force sound estimates of terrorists' capabilities to the surface. Currently, fantastical "movie plot" threats are assumed possible by far too many opinion leaders. Lacking information, they frighten Americans with scheme after scheme. Government authorities are free to cite only the "intentions" of whomever they prosecute, without reference to capability or to the technical feasibility of any plan. Sound threat assessment, therefore, is an essential part of domestic security.

Emergency Response

Emergency response to a terrorist attack (just as with a natural disaster) occurs at the local level. Therefore, instead of it being taxed away to Washington, a large chunk of the money authorized and appropriated for the Department of Homeland Security should be returned to taxpayers for their own use or for state and local response preparation.

Beyond easing public fears through an open, careful, and accurate discussion of threats, and beyond coordinating with state and local agencies, the federal government can take other active measures as part of a comprehensive and effective counterterrorism strategy. For example, there are uses for technology in defeating terrorism. But rather than focusing on mass surveillance, technology should be developed to speed the application of legal processes so that warrants for specific information, meeting legal standards, can be applied for, served, and responded to in short order. Better-organized responsibility for the security of the nation's infrastructure can ensure that knowledge and technology are applied smartly and cost-effectively to secure our infrastructure, to minimize damage should there be future attacks, and to heal injuries to our people and the organs of our society.

Many proposals ostensibly intended to advance domestic security, however, are unnecessary and counterproductive. For example, the United

States should not follow the "English model" by creating a domestic intelligence agency like MI5 and a new "National Security Court System." A National ID card system—whether for "internal enforcement" of immigration law or any other reason—is similarly ill-conceived. Although packaged as an "antiterrorism" measure, determined terrorists will simply bypass the identity-based security system by either bribing the people who are supposed to check the cards or recruiting people with valid cards and "clean" backgrounds to carry out the attacks. And once the system is in place, it will be virtually impossible to dislodge as policymakers are loath to repeal laws and cancel programs—even where there is clear evidence of dysfunction or irrelevance. Thankfully, some states have taken steps to resist federal pressure to establish such a system because of the financial costs associated with implementation. It is disturbing, however, that the United States is still moving toward such a system with so little debate in Washington. Federal policymakers should reverse course and abandon the effort entirely.

Congress correctly responded to the popular backlash against the Bush administration's Total Information Awareness program in 2003 by eliminating the Pentagon office that was responsible for developing the suspect-tracking technology. Unfortunately, there are reports that the federal government seems to be pursuing the same software and other tools that could "mine" millions of public and private records for information about terrorist suspects in secret. If this is indeed the case, it raises disturbing questions not only about the merits of the TIA program itself, but, more generally, about the impervious nature of an emerging surveillance state, a state in which the bureaucracy, not the people, determine which policies will change and which will remain in place. Likewise, the federal government's long-term policy of DNA collection deserves close scrutiny. (For more, see Chapter 29, "National ID Systems.")

The federal government should preserve domestic security, generally, and respond to the problem posed by terrorism, specifically, from within the framework of a free society. In brief, that means having good intelligence, good civil defense, and focused police work. It does not mean secret prisons, torture, military trials, national ID cards, national security letters, secret arrests, suspension of habeas corpus, and warrantless wiretapping. The ultimate outcome is a political climate in which fearmongering is virtually absent and politicians engaging in such behavior are punished at the ballot box. This will occur naturally so long as there is a widespread political consensus on the nature of the threat and general agreement on the approach to that threat that assiduously avoids overreaction.

Suggested Readings

De Rugy, Veronique. "Facts and Figures about Seven Years of Homeland Security Spending." Working Paper no. 08-02, Mercatus Center, George Mason University, March 2008.

Fallows, James. "Success without Victory." *Atlantic Monthly*, January–February 2005.

Friedman, Benjamin. "The Hidden Cost of Homeland Defense." *Audit of the Conventional Wisdom*, 05-12, MIT Center for International Studies, November 2005.

German, Mike. *Thinking Like a Terrorist: Insights of a Former FBI Undercover Agent.* Dulles, VA: Potomac Books, 2007.

Lustick, Ian S. *Trapped in the War on Terror.* Philadelphia: University of Pennsylvania Press, 2006.

Mueller, John. "A False Sense of Insecurity." *Regulation* 27, no. 3 (2004).

Poole, Robert, and Jim Harper. "Transportation Security Aggravation: Debating the Balance between Privacy and Safety in a Post-9/11 Aviation Industry." *Reason*, March 2005.

Shapiro, Jeremy. "Managing Homeland Security: Develop a Threat-Based Strategy." *Opportunity 08*, Brookings Institution, February 2007.

Williams, Cindy. "Strengthening Homeland Security: Reforming Planning and Resource Allocation." *2008 Presidential Transition Series*, IBM Center for the Business of Government, Massachusetts Institute of Technology, 2008.

—Prepared by Jim Harper and Christopher Preble

48. Strengthening the All-Volunteer Military

Policymakers should

- accelerate the pullout of American troops from Iraq;
- improve recruiting programs and enlistment inducements, especially for hard-to-fill occupational specialties;
- continue to change the mix between active and reserve forces to reflect current military commitments, and further reduce the frequency and length of overseas tours;
- consider creating special reserve units designed for garrison duty;
- fully withdraw U.S. forces from outdated cold war deployments in Asia and Europe; and
- drop draft registration and eliminate the Selective Service System.

Thirty-six years ago, the U.S. government inaugurated the All-Volunteer Force. The AVF proved itself an exceptionally proficient and highly adaptable fighting force, capable of deterring superpower competitors and destroying regional powers with relative ease. Now, however, it is under enormous strain. The U.S. military lacks sufficient manpower to satisfy the demands of an imperial foreign policy. The leading source of stress is the war in Iraq. The Iraq conflict alone has taken a heavy toll on the military not only because of the thousands of dead and wounded, but also because of the lengthy and unexpected overseas deployments. Although defenders of the continuing U.S. military presence in Iraq routinely complained that the media were focusing on bad news, the troops lived the bad news.

There is likely to be a sizable U.S. military presence in Iraq for some time, irrespective of the Iraqi government's preferences. But even if troop levels in Iraq begin to drop, those in Afghanistan are likely to increase. Until both wars are concluded, American service personnel will suffer under severe pressure.

The troops nevertheless have performed exceptionally well, and the military has suffered fewer cracks than expected. The United States managed to meet its occupation numbers by turning the Reserves and National Guard into de facto active duty units. The military further met recruiting and retention concerns by imposing "stop-loss," thereby preventing personnel from leaving when their service terms had expired; recalling to active duty many reservists, including members of the rarely used Individual Ready Reserve; increasing recruiting and retention bonuses; and lowering quality standards for new recruits, including accepting older recruits (up to age 42) and issuing more "moral" waivers for once-disqualifying factors, such as criminal convictions.

The military remains worried about the sustainability of the high-quality AVF. Army Chief of Staff General George Casey told Congress: "Our soldiers are deploying too frequently. We can't sustain that." Secretary of the Army Pete Geren worried that "we are consuming readiness as fast as we build it."

Unfortunately, any upcoming relief for the U.S. military will be modest. The Pentagon has had trouble finding sufficient soldiers to man its commitments, and any worsening of the situations in Iraq or Afghanistan or involvement in another conflict would quickly reverse that trend.

Extended deployments place a greater burden on reservists than on active duty forces because the former, who consciously chose not to join the active force, must leave not only family, friends, and community but jobs as well. The burden has been compounded by discrimination against reservists, who often serve longer deployments than active duty soldiers but are last on the list to receive the best equipment, such as Kevlar vests. Nevertheless, the military has pressured reservists to waive the statutory requirement of 12 months at home between overseas deployments.

The military can handle such burdens in a temporary emergency. But speaking only of Afghanistan in March 2002, Secretary Rumsfeld observed: "It's helpful to remember that those who developed the concept for peacekeepers in Bosnia assured everyone that those forces would complete their mission by the end of that year and be home by Christmas. We are now heading into our seventh year of U.S. and international involvement in Bosnia."

America is now in its eighth year of war in Afghanistan and its sixth year of war in Iraq. The treaty being negotiated between Washington and

Baghdad reportedly envisions a continuing U.S. troop presence until 2010, and an American exit from Afghanistan is getting more rather than less distant. How to maintain these deployments?

Adding Marine Corps actives, as the Department of Defense did in spring 2004, helped. At plan's end, in 2012, the Marine Corps will count 202,000 men and women in its ranks, a 16 percent increase over where it was before 9/11. But the marines are a relatively small force that is intended to respond to unexpected contingencies. Warned the Congressional Budget Office, "If all Marine regiments were either deployed, recovering after deployments, or preparing for deployments . . . , DOD's ability to quickly deploy substantial combat power in the early phases of an operation would be degraded." The Marine Corps has had to extend the tours of some personnel stationed in Afghanistan. The U.S. Army's "end strength" will grow to 547,000 in 2012, up from 480,000 before 9/11, but these additional troops cannot solve all the problems that are straining the AVF.

Besides, where can bodies be found? Adding forces takes money and time. The Congressional Budget Office concluded: "Recruiting, training, and equipping two additional divisions would entail up-front costs of as much as $18 billion to $19 billion and would take about five years to accomplish. . . . In the long run, the cost to operate and sustain these new divisions as a permanent part of the Army's force structure would be about $6 billion annually (plus between $3 billion and $4 billion per year to employ them in Iraq)." Such a troop buildup, however, merely pushes the problem one step back. If it is hard to meet today's recruiting goals, how will the military (mainly the army) meet even higher recruiting and retention goals? Creating and training new combat divisions will take time and money, but those can only go so far if the right people are reluctant to join up.

Today, the armed services are having trouble because excessive and unpleasant commitments make it harder for them to attract and keep enough people. The reluctance to serve reflects the attitudes first of those asked to sign up. Those with more of a career orientation toward the military—and especially the army—are likely to hesitate if they fear spending multiple tours in a combat zone. Also critical is the attitude of families of prospective recruits. Army recruiters are finding increasing resistance from parents, especially when they seek to recruit 17-year-olds, who need parental approval to join. In some communities, activists, including parents, have organized to counteract military recruiters.

509

Even more important is the attitude of families for members already in the service. There's an army saying that "we enlist an individual and reenlist a family." Warned retired Army Colonel Robert Maginnis, "Either we find a fix to rotate those troops out and to keep the families content . . . or we're going to suffer what I anticipate is a downturn in retention." So far, the Department of Defense has made most of its manpower targets by adjusting its quality standards. The army and Army Reserve faced the most serious problems. Moreover, admitted Defense Under Secretary David Chu, "Certain high-demand (high-use) units and specialties have experienced higher than normal attrition." By accepting recruits with lower Armed Forces Qualification Test scores, and more recruits who've received general equivalency diplomas rather than high school diplomas and have been in legal trouble, the Pentagon has papered over the problem. Although military efficiency will suffer at the margin, the AVF remains a higher-quality force than the draft military.

In fact, virtually no one who lacks a high school or general equivalency diploma and who doesn't score in the top three of five categories of the Armed Forces Qualification Test can join. This has resulted in a military that is overwhelmingly middle-class; the test scores and educational achievements of recruits exceed those of young people generally. African Americans have traditionally been somewhat overrepresented, but they disproportionately serve in support, not combat arms, and their personnel share has been falling. Hispanics are underrepresented.

Every recent war has sparked proposals for restarting conscription. With the Iraq War, Rep. Charles Rangel (D-NY) and former senator Fritz Hollings (D-SC) introduced legislation to establish a system of conscription-based national service. Sen. John McCain (R-AZ) once supported a draft and national service, but more recently has said it would be needed only during an emergency. What he would do if recruiting became significantly more difficult is unclear.

From a security standpoint, conscription would be foolish. The U.S. military is the finest on earth largely because voluntarism allows the Pentagon to be selective, choosing recruits who are smarter and better educated than their civilian counterparts. Enlistees are also selective; they work to succeed in their chosen career rather than to escape forced service. They serve longer terms and reenlist in higher numbers, increasing the experience and skills of the force.

Although a volunteer military beats a draft force, Washington risks driving down recruiting and retention, which, over the long term, could wreck the AVF. However, the surest barrier to a policy of promiscuous military intervention is not a draft, which allowed the Vietnam War to proceed for years, but the AVF, which empowers average people to say no.

Ironically, while some legislators advocate renewing conscription, other nations—France, Germany, Poland, and Russia, for instance—have moved or are moving to professionalize their forces. In a world where terrorism is a greater threat than a mass attack by the Red Army through Germany's Fulda Gap, the United States has no choice but to build a high-quality force through voluntarism. Indeed, Congress should eliminate draft registration—the list ages rapidly, and a postmobilization sign-up would be available in an emergency—and close down the Selective Service System, an expensive and unnecessary anachronism.

What to do to strengthen the armed services? The obvious place to start is improved pay and benefits, especially for National Guard and Reserve members, who are increasingly being treated like active duty soldiers. One proposal is to extend health insurance for National Guard and Reserve members even when they are not deployed. Also, improved treatment for those deployed overseas, and particularly in battle zones, is imperative. Policymakers should continue programs, such as the rest and recuperation program begun in 2003, in which soldiers are allowed 15 days at home, as well as the program that pays for service personnel's travel to their hometowns from troop arrival points at Dallas–Fort Worth, Atlanta, and Baltimore-Washington airports. Resources also need to be put into recruiting, by increasing signing bonuses, doubling the advertising budget, and developing cyberrecruiting.

The Department of Defense needs to rethink the mix of duties within services as well as shift some billets between active and reserve forces. It should also consider establishing a multitiered reserve force, with some units available for longer-term deployments, others for temporary emergencies, and a number for homeland duties. The Congressional Budget Office suggested creating temporary "constabulary" units made up of members of the Individual Ready Reserve and people who recently left active or Reserve and/or National Guard service. Such units could train for six months, deploy for one year, and then disband. Moreover, the military could offer higher compensation to reservists willing to accept more frequent deployment.

The first priority should be to expeditiously exit Iraq. Lawrence Korb, the assistant secretary of defense for manpower in the Reagan administration, points to Gen. Maxwell Taylor, who observed that we went to

Vietnam to save the country but had to withdraw from Vietnam to save the army. The Baghdad government made clear in the negotiations over a status-of-forces agreement with Washington that the American troops could not stay forever. In 2008, the Bush administration and some presidential candidates apparently hoped to draw out the process as long as possible, if not permanently. But it is in America's interest to pull out U.S. troops as soon as possible. The United States should also drop other unnecessary commitments. We have been slowly drawing down our forces in South Korea and Germany, but far more could be done.

The U.S. military won the cold war, defeated a host of small states with minimal casualties, and could overwhelm any competitor today. But the armed services cannot do everything. Conscription is no answer. Fiddling with military compensation and force structure would help, but would not address the basic problem. Only abandoning a foreign policy of empire will eliminate pressure to create an imperial military.

Suggested Readings

Anderson, Martin, with Barbara Honegger, eds. *The Military Draft: Selected Readings on Conscription.* Stanford, CA: Hoover Institution Press, 1982.

Bandow, Doug. "Fighting the War against Terrorism: Elite Forces, Yes; Conscripts, No." Cato Institute Policy Analysis no. 430, April 10, 2002.

Congressional Budget Office. "The All-Volunteer Military: Issues and Performance." July 2007.

Evers, Williamson, ed. *National Service: Pro & Con.* Stanford, CA: Hoover Institution Press, 1990.

Rostker, Bernard. *I Want You! The Evolution of the All-Volunteer Force.* Santa Monica, CA: RAND Corporation, 2006.

Stiglitz, Joseph E., and Linda J. Bilmes. *The $3 Trillion War: The True Cost of the Iraq Conflict.* New York: W. W. Norton, 2008.

—Prepared by Doug Bandow

49. Iraq

Policymakers should

- withdraw military forces from Iraq by July 1, 2009, leaving behind only a small number of Special Forces personnel to work with Iraqi authorities to disrupt any remaining al Qaeda cells in the country;
- encourage Iraq's neighbors to help contain any postwithdrawal internecine violence in Iraq;
- view the withdrawal from Iraq as the first step toward ending the dangerous and intrusive U.S. military presence in the Persian Gulf region; and
- learn the real lesson of the Iraq experience and avoid future utopian nation-building schemes in the Persian Gulf or any other region.

The U.S. military occupation of Iraq is now well into its sixth year, and the costs of that venture in both treasure and blood have been depressingly high. In October 2008, the financial costs reached $686 billion (in 2008 dollars), thereby exceeding the price tag of the Vietnam War in inflation-adjusted terms. Moreover, the meter continues to run at a rate of at least $120 billion per year. And those are just the direct costs. When one factors in the long-term obligations to America's wounded veterans, adverse economic effects, and other indirect costs, the Iraq War will ultimately cost American taxpayers well in excess of $1 trillion. Some estimates put the figure at more than $3 trillion.

Compared with some previous wars, the number of fatalities for U.S. forces has been relatively modest. Still, more than 4,200 American military personnel have lost their lives, and another 30,000 or more have been wounded, many with horrific, life-altering wounds. And then there are the Iraqis who have perished in this conflict. Estimates of Iraqi fatalities vary wildly, ranging from about 80,000 to more than a million. The most credible estimate—slightly more than 150,000—comes from a World Health Organization study. Whatever the correct total, it is a sizable loss of life.

Supporters of the mission in Iraq have been in high spirits recently. They insist that the "surge" strategy of deploying an additional 30,000 U.S. troops, which President Bush announced in January 2007, has turned around the dire security situation. The United States, they believe, has finally adopted the right strategy for victory in Iraq.

War proponents do have some evidence to back up their assertion that the surge has been successful—at least in the narrow military sense. There is no doubt that the overall security environment in Iraq has improved. Both the number of insurgent attacks and the number of overall fatalities (Iraqi and American) declined noticeably, and by the summer of 2008 were about 70 percent below the levels of 2006 and the first half of 2007. The number of American military fatalities declined even more. The violence in Iraq is no longer the lead story on the network news on most days. Indeed, the media seem to have grown a bit jaded with the Iraq War now that spectacular car bomb explosions in Baghdad and other major cities occur less frequently.

Advocates of the war should be more cautious about proclaiming victory, however. Although the overall extent of violence is significantly lower than it was during the awful period from February 2006 (following the bombing of the Golden Mosque at Samarra) to mid-2007, it is still at about the same level it was in 2004 and early 2005. Very few people considered Iraq during that period to be a stable or peaceful place.

Moreover, war proponents have prematurely proclaimed victory on many occasions before. President Bush's infamous speech under the "Mission Accomplished" banner on the USS *Abraham Lincoln* was only the first of many faulty announcements. The capture of Saddam Hussein, the battle of Fallujah, and the election of the Iraqi parliament (with voters waving their purple ink-stained fingers) were all hailed as decisive turning points in the Iraq conflict. Vice President Cheney's comment in May 2005 that the insurgency was in its "last throes" was yet another erroneous claim of imminent victory. Given that dismal track record, Americans have a right to be skeptical when Iraq War supporters assert that the surge is a definitive success and that "victory" in Iraq is at hand.

If one looks more carefully at the reasons for the improved security environment, the case for caution and skepticism becomes even stronger.

The deployment of additional combat troops undoubtedly had a beneficial effect, but that is not the principal reason for the improvement. Several other factors have played more significant roles.

One reason is especially sobering. In Baghdad, but to some extent in several other cities as well, the decline in killings is largely a result of previous ethnic cleansing efforts that have succeeded all too well. At the beginning of the U.S. occupation, about 45 percent of Baghdad's neighborhoods were predominantly Shiite, about 35 percent were predominantly Sunni, and the remaining 20 percent were thoroughly mixed. Now, about 65 percent of the neighborhoods are overwhelmingly Shiite, about 30 percent are overwhelmingly Sunni, and only about 5 percent are mixed. The last two categories are also heavily dependent on protection from U.S. forces to maintain their precarious status. Hundreds of thousands of people, mostly Sunnis, have fled the city, and in many cases have fled Iraq entirely. With far fewer mixed neighborhoods—and fewer Sunni neighborhoods in proximity to Shiite ones—there are simply not as many opportunities for armed clashes between rival forces or opportunities for the Shiite death squads to practice their deadly trade.

A similar process of ethnic segregation has occurred in other areas of Iraq. Indeed, there are some 2 million internal refugees, most of whom have moved from areas in which they were ethnic or religious minorities to areas in which they and their kin are in the majority. Another 2.4 million people have left Iraq for other countries, in many cases fleeing the effect of ethnic cleansing. The security environment has become more quiescent as a result of those purges, but that should hardly be an occasion for U.S. satisfaction. It also does not bode well for Iraq's long-term prospects as a united country, which remains a key objective of the U.S. mission.

Another factor explaining the decline in violence is the less confrontational role that radical Shiite cleric Moqtada al-Sadr adopted. Frequent clashes had occurred between Sadr's Mahdi Army and both U.S. and Iraqi government forces since the summer of 2003. Even worse, Sadr's followers were apparently some of the most active participants in the Shiite death squads that murdered countless Sunnis. On more than a few occasions, especially during the first two years of the occupation, American military commanders considered arresting Sadr, but they feared that doing so would enrage his followers and lead to full-scale warfare with the Mahdi Army. Moreover, after elections for Iraq's parliament, it became even more difficult to contemplate arresting him, since his faction controlled some

30 seats in the new legislature, and became (nominally at least) a member of the political coalition supporting the U.S.-backed prime minister, Nouri al-Maliki.

This uneasy relationship between the U.S. occupation force and the Mahdi Army persisted until September 2007, when Sadr unexpectedly announced a six-month cease-fire. Although his forces have not entirely honored that truce, there have been noticeably fewer incidents with U.S. and Iraqi government troops, and, perhaps even more importantly, a significant decline in death squad activities.

Sadr's motives for the cease-fire (which he extended in February 2008) are not entirely clear. Perhaps his forces had been weakened by previous skirmishes and needed time to regroup and reequip. In addition, factional rivalries appeared to have begun to undermine the Mahdi Army as a cohesive force, and Sadr used the cease-fire period to purge the organization of so-called rogue elements. Those elements apparently consisted of anyone who challenged Sadr's preeminence.

Whatever the motive, the cease-fire reinforced the decline in overall violence that accompanied the U.S. troop surge. It is uncertain, though, how long that truce will last or what will happen if it comes to an end. In all likelihood, an end to the cease-fire would bring the Mahdi Army back into play as an adversary of the occupation force and lead to an uptick in violence.

Although those various factors played meaningful roles, the most important reason for the improved security environment was the willingness of General David Petraeus and other U.S. military commanders to forge compromises with influential Sunni tribal leaders instead of reflexively regarding them as Saddam "dead enders" and implacable enemies. Many of those leaders signaled a willingness to turn on al Qaeda fighters and cooperate with the United States long before the surge began. Indeed, scattered media reports as early as the summer of 2006 indicated that some Sunni tribes had soured on their alliances with the terrorist organization. That was not too surprising. Foreign al Qaeda operatives were arrogant and abusive. For proud Sunni chieftains, accustomed to exercising power in their regions, being snubbed, bypassed, and bullied by al Qaeda zealots was infuriating. Al Qaeda's strategy of car bombings and other indiscriminate acts of violence against fellow Muslims served to further alienate the organization from its Iraqi allies. Even though most of the victims were Shiites, the spectacle of innocents being slaughtered daily became too much to tolerate.

Unlike their predecessors, Petraeus and his subordinates were shrewd enough to exploit the growing rifts in the insurgency. Indeed, the United States began a strategy to court receptive Sunni leaders even before President Bush announced the surge. Washington has since provided extensive funding to cooperative Sunni tribes and has even helped train the armed fighters of the so-called Awakening Councils. Simply put, the strategy moved from trying to bludgeon the Sunnis to trying to bribe them.

U.S. financial assistance is a crucial lubricant that keeps the Awakening Councils viable and cooperative. Ordinary members typically receive stipends of $300 per month, while higher-ranking figures receive somewhat larger sums. Three hundred dollars might not seem like much to most Americans, but in Iraq that is a sizable amount. It is especially attractive in a country where economic opportunities for the politically dispossessed Sunnis are especially bleak and where the unemployment rate runs well in excess of 20 percent.

In addition to the salaries given to rank-and-file Sunnis, unspecified sums are passed out to tribal leaders, largely in the form of reconstruction grants. At least some of that money does not go to construction projects but goes instead to purchase weapons—most apparently coming from Saudi Arabia—to boost the military capabilities of the Awakening Councils. And, of course, some of the lucre likely goes into the pockets of Sunni tribal elders.

At least in the short term, that approach has worked far better than the previous U.S. strategy. Many, although not all, Sunni leaders have waged open warfare on al Qaeda fighters, and perhaps even more importantly, the new Sunni allies have provided valuable intelligence to the U.S. military about al Qaeda, instead of shielding the organization. As a result, al Qaeda has been marginalized as a political and military player in Iraq.

Yet the strategy of bribing and arming friendly Sunni forces is not without potential peril. If Washington's new Sunni allies do not remain bribed, they could pose a more lethal danger than before to both the Iraqi central government and U.S. forces. As *Washington Post* correspondents Alissa J. Rubin and Damien Cave note, "It is an experiment in counterinsurgency warfare that could contain the seeds of civil war—in which, if the fears come true, the United States would have helped organize some of the Sunni forces arrayed against the central government on which so many American lives and dollars have been spent." In other words, the U.S. strategy may end up funding and equipping both sides for a new, and more intense, phase of Iraq's sectarian warfare.

Lastly, whatever the tactical military successes of the surge, it has not achieved its larger political goal, which President Bush described in his announcement of the surge as giving the Iraqi government "the breathing space it needs to make progress in other critical areas." Getting Iraq's feuding Sunni, Shiite, and Kurdish political leaders to create an effective, united government remains elusive. American optimists highlight such developments as the parliament's passage of de-Baathification reform and a national budget as evidence of great progress. But most Sunnis regard the former as a fraud that will make their precarious status even worse, and when advocates of staying in Iraq cite the mere passage of a national budget as a huge achievement, they are truly grasping at straws.

In reality, the central government remains quarrelsome and largely impotent. The real power lies in the increasingly ethnically homogenous regions. Iraqi Kurdistan is an independent state in all but name, having its own flag, currency, and military—and routinely bypassing Baghdad to cut deals with foreign oil companies and other firms. The predominantly Shiite south is likewise increasingly independent of Baghdad regarding policies that really matter. Despite the decline in violence, the long-term prospects for a stable, united (much less secular and democratic) Iraq are not good.

What the surge did, though, was give the United States a window of opportunity to execute a semigraceful withdrawal. U.S. leaders can claim, quite plausibly, that Washington has gone the extra mile to give the Iraqi people a chance to create a new and effective political system. The United States overthrew Saddam Hussein, presided over the creation of a new constitution, supervised the election of a new government, stabilized the security environment, and dealt severe blows to al Qaeda forces that infiltrated the country. American leaders can, and should, argue that it is now up to Iraqi leaders and the Iraqi people to determine the future of their country. If they are not ready now, when will they be?

Unfortunately, too many U.S. political leaders apparently regard the lull in violence as an excuse to perpetuate the American presence in Iraq indefinitely. As U.S. troop numbers return to presurge levels, it is important to clarify the real strategic choice in Iraq. The choice is not between a U.S. withdrawal in the next 6 to 12 months and a withdrawal some time in the next 5 years or so. It is a choice between promptly withdrawing and trying to stay in Iraq for decades—or, in Senator John McCain's flippant formulation, a century. Unfortunately, the United States' creating numerous "enduring" military bases and building an embassy nearly as large as Vatican City suggests that it intends to stay a very long time.

That would be a serious error. Despite the decline in violence, it is unlikely that the United States will ever achieve the goals that it had when it invaded Iraq in 2003. The notion of post-Saddam Iraq as a secular democratic model for the Middle East was always a chimera. The long-term prospects for even modest unity and stability remain bleak, with or without a U.S. military presence. One must ask how many more American tax dollars should be wasted, and even more important, how many more Americans should die because political leaders are unwilling to admit that they made a mistake. The United States needs a withdrawal strategy—one measured in months, not years. The partial success of the surge provides that opportunity.

Those who want to stay in Iraq insist that we are now on the verge of "victory." Even if that prediction turns out not to be yet another in a long list of false hopes, it is important to understand what form "victory" in Iraq would likely take. Let's consider the best-case scenario that has any realistic prospect of coming true. It would include a democratic Kurdistan in the north that is independent in everything but official international recognition. The rest of Iraq would be run by a quasi-democratic, Shiite-dominated regime that is quite friendly to Iran. Any illusion that Iran does not already have a great deal of influence with the current Iraqi government evaporated in March 2008 when Iranian president Mahmoud Ahmadinejad received a red-carpet welcome in Baghdad.

Moreover, even under the best-case scenario, Iraq's Shiite-led government would still face a persistent, low-grade Sunni insurgency for the foreseeable future (think Northern Ireland from the late 1960s to the mid-1990s). In other words, even the best-case scenario isn't all that great.

As it withdraws its forces, though, Washington should make an effort to try to prevent the worst-case scenario: a regional Sunni-Shiite armed conflict with Iraq as the cockpit. Washington should work with Iraq's neighbors to quarantine the violence in that country. A regional proxy war in Iraq would turn the U.S. mission there into even more of a debacle than it has been already. Worse, Iraq's neighbors could be drawn in as direct participants in the fighting—a development that could create chaos throughout the Middle East.

The best approach would be for the United States to convene a regional conference that includes (at a minimum) Iran, Saudi Arabia, Syria, Jordan, and Turkey. The purpose of such a conference should be to make all parties confront the danger of Iraq's turmoil mushrooming into a regional armed struggle that ultimately would not be in the best interests of any country in the area. Washington should stress the point that Iran, Saudi Arabia, and Iraq's other neighbors risk having events spiral out of control if they do not quarantine the violence and instead seek to exploit it. The U.S. goal should be a commitment by the neighboring states to refrain from meddling—or at least bound the extent of meddling—in that country's sectarian tensions.

Realism about the role of Iraq's neighbors, especially Iran and Syria, is essential. Tehran and Damascus are not about to help the United States out of its dilemmas in Iraq because of a spirit of altruism. Indeed, both governments take a perverse pleasure in Washington's self-inflicted wounds. Our only feasible chance of gaining their cooperation is if we can convince them that overplaying their hand may provoke direct intervention by the Saudis, Turks, and other rivals. There is no guarantee that such a conference would be successful. All of Iraq's neighbors have significant incentives to try to prevent a victory by one Iraqi faction or another. But it is at least worth an attempt to minimize the danger of a wider conflict.

The risk of a proxy war is real, but trying to prevent that outcome does not warrant keeping U.S. forces in Iraq for decades to come. Washington has already worn out its welcome. By a wide and growing margin, the Iraqi people (with the notable exception of the Kurds) want the United States to end the occupation. Even the Iraqi government signaled in July 2008 that it wanted a timeline for the withdrawal of most, if not all, U.S. troops. Washington's decision to invade Iraq was profoundly unwise. Persisting in a costly and problematic mission against the wishes of Iraq's neighbors and the Iraqi people themselves would be even worse. It is time to leave. Indeed, it is long past time to leave.

Equally important, U.S. officials need to learn the right lessons from the bruising Iraq experience. If we merely shift U.S. military personnel from Iraq to another country or countries in the Persian Gulf region, they will still be a lightning rod for Muslim resentment and anger. We need far more than a mere redeployment of forces. America's intrusive military presence in the broader Middle East has been the perfect recruiting poster for al Qaeda and other extremist groups. That presence needs to be greatly reduced even in the short term and then eliminated in stages over the next few years.

Finally, there is a worrisome danger that the Iraq debacle has not eliminated the enthusiasm in America's foreign policy community for nation-building missions. The emerging conventional wisdom seems to be that the failure in Iraq was due to lack of planning and to faulty execution. That is a dangerous delusion. The proper lessons of Iraq are that populations tend to resist being remolded at the point of American bayonets, and that our policymakers do not even begin to understand the political, social, religious, and economic complexities of those societies. Nation-building in almost any context is arrogant international social engineering at its worst. The examples of success (Germany and Japan) that nation-building proponents always cite occurred because of very unusual factors. They were fortuitous exceptions, not templates.

If the new administration assumes that the correct lesson of Iraq is that we need to do Iraq-style missions better in the future, it will be just a matter of time until America finds itself mired in another bloody, frustrating crusade somewhere else in the world. The real lesson of Iraq needs to be that we shouldn't attempt to do Iraq-style missions period.

Suggested Readings

Carpenter, Ted Galen. "Escaping the Trap: Why the United States Must Leave Iraq." Cato Institute Policy Analysis no. 588, February 14, 2007.
_____. *Smart Power: Toward a Prudent Foreign Policy for America*. Washington: Cato Institute, 2008, Chapters 1 and 2.
Carpenter, Ted Galen, and Malou Innocent. "The Iraq War and Iranian Power." *Survival*, Fall 2007.
Cockburn, Patrick. *Moqtada al-Sadr, the Shia Revival, and the Struggle for Iraq*. New York: Scribner, 2008.
Friedman, Benjamin H., Harvey M. Sapolsky, and Christopher Preble. "Learning the Right Lessons from Iraq." Cato Institute Policy Analysis no. 610, February 13, 2008.
Galbraith, Peter W. *The End of Iraq: How American Incompetence Created a War without End*. New York: Simon and Schuster, 2006.
Layne, Christopher. "Who Lost Iraq and Why It Matters: The Case for Offshore Balancing." *World Policy Journal* 24, no. 4 (Fall 2007).

—Prepared by Ted Galen Carpenter

50. U.S. Policy toward Iran

> **Policymakers should**
>
> - press for direct diplomacy with the Iranian leadership;
> - keep diplomatic aims limited to the Iranian nuclear program;
> - evaluate and compose a "Plan B" in the event that diplomacy fails;
> - seek advice from U.S. military leaders about the implications of military action against Iran;
> - educate the public that there is little evidence the Iranian leadership would use nuclear weapons unprovoked; and
> - make clear that the war power rests in the hand of Congress, and that it is not the prerogative of the president to launch military action unauthorized.

Diplomacy with Iran: Low Costs, Potentially High Rewards

On May 31, 2006, Secretary of State Condoleezza Rice held a press conference in the ornate Benjamin Franklin Room at the State Department to announce that the United States would be open to joining the European Union Three (EU3) negotiations on Iran's nuclear program. This was intended to clarify that U.S. policy toward Iran was focused on changing the behavior of the Iranian regime, rather than changing the regime itself, as Tehran had long feared and as many in Washington had long advocated.

Since that time, nearly three years have passed, with no meaningful negotiations between the United States and Iran. The cause for this lost time has been the insistence that Iran suspend uranium enrichment before negotiations take place. The Western powers consider that a good faith gesture from Iran, but the Iranian side has made clear—since before the May 2006 offer—that it views suspension before negotiations as preemptive appeasement. True to form, Iran has refused to suspend enrichment, and has even rebuffed a significantly more generous offer made in summer 2008 of a "freeze for freeze": that the West would not add any new sanctions if Iran would not enhance its enrichment capabilities, attempting to balance the concessions.

Dropping this precondition and entering into talks with Iran would be a low-cost way of determining whether there is space for any diplomatic deal with Tehran. Since May 2006, Washington has insisted on suspension, and has nothing to show for it. Would it not have been better to have been negotiating all this time, even if the result was concluding that Iran was steadfastly opposed to a diplomatic solution?

Instead, Washington has sent a variety of mixed messages, causing the Iranians to wonder whether some U.S. officials were still holding out regime change as a possible option. In 2007 congressional testimony, former National Security Council official Flynt Leverett noted that in joining the EU3 proposal, the United States forced a significant revision: Washington declined to officially sign on "until all language dealing with explicit or implicit security guarantees" for Iran was taken out of the offer. This does not signal a genuine openness to a diplomatic outcome. There must be a candid willingness to "live with" the Iranian government for a deal to take place.

Recent statements from members of the U.S. intelligence community indicate that some in the U.S. government recognize that Iranian concerns over its national security are at the heart of Iran's quest for a nuclear capability. Discussing Iran at a 2008 Center for National Policy event, the chairman of the National Intelligence Council, Thomas Fingar, admitted that Iran's behavior is "certainly explicable in terms of an assessment of their security situation." Accordingly, Fingar noted,

> recognizing that Iran has real security concerns . . . is a useful starting point . . . since we are part of the reason Iran feels insecure, rightly or wrongly.

Some will protest that Iran's truculence demonstrates that no diplomatic resolution is possible. Such speculation is irresponsible when the stakes are so high. Further, though things have changed since the time the offer was made, in 2003 Iran made an effort to reach out to the United States that was rebuffed by the White House. Reeling from the demonstration effect from the destruction of Iraq's military by the United States, Tehran offered to open negotiations on a host of issues, including its nuclear program. This offer was not investigated by the White House, but it could indicate that there is some way to resolve the issue without either a U.S.-Iran war or a nuclear Iran.

Keeping Diplomacy Focused

Many advocates of direct U.S.-Iran diplomacy over the nuclear issue have argued that such engagement must include the range of issues lying between Washington and Tehran, including Iran's (and America's) involvement in Iraq, anti-Israel terrorism, Iran's behavior in the Persian Gulf, and a number of other points of disagreement. This thinking is misguided.

First, Iran continues to create new "facts on the ground" that give it bargaining leverage above what it possessed in 2003 when it probed Washington with its own diplomatic overture. There are many more centrifuges spinning in Natanz, for example, and other refinements in Iran's nuclear program are unknown. Despite the decrease in violence in Iraq, Iran still has very significant leverage there that could be used against the United States. Getting bogged down in issues such as Iran's behavior in the region or its abhorrent treatment of its own citizens, while well-intended, may well allow Iran to run out the clock and acquire either a nuclear capability or a plausible breakout option in which Iran could credibly threaten to withdraw from the Nuclear Nonproliferation Treaty and swiftly move to acquire one.

This development would not help ameliorate any of the ancillary issues that would be inserted into the negotiating process. U.S. policymakers need to ask themselves: If we could ensure a non-nuclear Iran by granting security guarantees and diplomatic recognition, would that be preferable to other likely outcomes? The answer seems clearly to be yes.

And What if Diplomacy Fails?

Policymakers should keep in mind that while diplomacy is a low-cost option, there is still the distinct possibility that even the best-calibrated diplomatic opening to Iran could fail. There is a long history of distrust between the two countries, and recent Iranian statements have tended toward a grandiosity that does not bode well for a mutually agreeable settlement. If negotiations fail, there are no good options. While this is an argument for giving diplomacy the highest priority, it also acknowledges that Washington must choose from a menu of bad choices rather than convincing itself that there is a good one.

While all responsible observers acknowledge that no conceivable military strike could eliminate Iran's nuclear program, supporters of the military option contend that it could retard the program enough to buy time. What

525

is to be done with this additional time, however, is an unanswered question. Considering that U.S. or allied military action against Iran would produce a rally-around-the-flag effect, shoring up the sitting government's legitimacy, it is unclear why this additional time would be beneficial. Iran would no doubt redouble its covert nuclear activities after such an attack and would likely throw out international monitors.

Moreover, the so-called "surgical strike" to which some observers have referred may leave scars more like those of a butter knife rather than a scalpel. According to an August 2008 report from the Institute for Science and International Security, an attack intended to significantly slow Iran's progress on its nuclear program would require "multiple strikes against many sites," and even so, such an attack would be "unlikely to significantly degrade Iran's ability to reconstitute its gas centrifuge program."

At the same time, there is a very serious risk that such strikes, intended as surgical, could precipitate a spiral of escalation that results in full-blown war with Iran. For one thing, in many hypothetical military scenarios, the target set quickly expands from the dozens of sites involved directly in the nuclear program to include Iranian air defenses, suspected chemical or biological weapons sites, and key nodes in Iran's Islamic Revolutionary Guard Corps and other locations. Iran, on the other hand, would no doubt feel compelled to respond, and has more than adequate means to do so, by means that include threatening or attacking U.S. supply lines through southern Iraq, swarming small boats or launching missiles against U.S. naval vessels or oil tankers in the Persian Gulf, or making good on Iran's near-constant threats that, if attacked, one of its first targets would be Israel.

According to numerous press reports, war games simulating a conflict between the United States and Iran always turn out badly. For example, in the 2002 Millennium Challenge game, a crafty marine general, Paul Van Riper, acted as the "red team" and used a variety of asymmetric tactics that wound up killing thousands of U.S. servicemen and sending 16 U.S. naval vessels to the bottom of the gulf. The military's response was to reset the game and prevent Van Riper from using the tactics he'd used before. Van Riper quit his position as commander of the red team, expressing his concern that Iran would certainly use similar tactics in any confrontation.

The U.S. military, in short, is well aware that they have no solution for the problem of Iran's nuclear program. Secretary of Defense Robert Gates summed up the military's view of potential war with Iran as "disastrous on a number of levels.'' But the rhetorical stakes in U.S. policy discussions have been raised to existential heights by a number of commentators who have advanced the idea that the Iranian government's hostile rhetoric and unrelenting defiance of the United States indicates that they are incapable of making decisions based on reasons of state; rather, these commentators insist that Iran is drawing on theological tenets to craft its foreign policy, and is not capable of being deterred from risky, aggressive policies that could lead to nuclear war.

Is the Iranian Government Suicidal?

The op-ed pages of American newspapers have been littered for years with dire proclamations of war, nuclear war, and holocaust in the Middle East if Iran were to acquire a nuclear capability. While there are numerous undesirable aspects to a nuclear-armed Iran, they ought to be examined coldly and in the context of the flawed thinking that led to the Iraq war. Viewed dispassionately, it becomes clear that undesirable as it would be, a nuclear Iran is hardly the searing danger that ubiquitous media commentators have made it out to be.

A number of knowledgeable observers have pointed to the flaws in the Iran-as-suicide-nation thinking, chief among them Israeli observers. It was Reuven Pedatzur of Tel Aviv University who noted that ''past experience shows that the radical Iranian regime, headed by the most extreme of them all, Ayatollah Khomeini, behaved with absolute rationality at the moment of truth.'' And it was Tzipi Livni, then Israel's foreign minister, who made clear in a November 2007 interview in *Haaretz* that she did not view Iranian nuclear weapons as posing an existential threat to Israel. And if they do not pose an existential threat to Israel, they certainly do not pose such a threat to the United States.

The threat that would be posed by Iranian nuclear weapons is not so much a theologically induced nuclear first strike than it is the potential for a nuclear-armed Iran to constrain American foreign policy in the Middle East. Washington fears that if Tehran acquires a nuclear capability, a number of foreign policy options previously available to the United States—including first among them regime change in Iran—would be foreclosed.

This analysis is true, but it is unclear that those foreclosed options would have served U.S. interests in the first place. The most pressing dilemma that could be posed by a nuclear Iran would be the feeling in Iran that it was impervious to American or Israeli retaliation, and that Iran

527

could ramp up its provocative and destabilizing behaviors in the region, such as support for Hezbollah or attempting to expand its influence in Iraq.

These concerns are genuine and serious, but they must be juxtaposed against the policy options that stand before us in the current context of U.S. policy toward Iran. Diplomacy, war, or acquiescence and deterrence are the three policy choices with currency in Washington. The negative consequences of acquiescence and deterrence highlight the importance of at least making a straightforward attempt at diplomacy without preconditions. But the negative consequences of a third U.S. war against a Muslim state in less than a decade make a strong case for deterrence as preferable to war.

Acknowledgment of the Constitutional Assignment of the War Power

Whatever policymakers should decide, it is past time for legislators in both parties to reassert their constitutional prerogative as the rightful holders of the war power. The last country against whom the United States declared war was Romania in World War II, although there have been numerous U.S. wars since that time. The Founders believed that keeping the war power in the hands of Congress as opposed to the president would tie decisions over war and peace more closely to the will of the people.

Since the mid-20th century, however, Congress has abrogated its duty as the institution with the power to make war, in part because of the perverse political calculations that come into play. Politically, the incentives are almost always in favor of war. When a legislator votes to grant the president authorization to use military force, he or she has essentially delegated authority from Congress to the president. If the war goes well, the legislator can claim vindication. If the war goes poorly, he or she can criticize the conduct of the war, and disavow responsibility for the outcome. A formal declaration of war would force legislators to confront the gravity of decisions over war and peace, and create a firm record of their stands on the question that could be used by voters to judge legislative performance.

However difficult the politics of the question, in order to make more prudent decisions about war and peace, and in order to honor their pledge to uphold and defend the Constitution, legislators must face the difficult decisions of war and peace should the question come up in the context of Iran or any other country. If legislators continue to abrogate their powers, their institution will atrophy, and the outcome the Founders were seeking to prevent—a unilateral presidential prerogative to make war at will—will become ever more entrenched in American politics. One hopes the Iran scenario does not come to pass, but regardless, Congress should stand up to retake its rightful role.

Suggested Readings

Albright, David, Paul Brannan, and Jacqueline Shire. "Can Military Strikes Destroy Iran's Gas Centrifuge Program? Probably Not." *ISIS Report*, August 7, 2008.

Carpenter, Ted Galen. "Iran's Nuclear Program: America's Policy Options." Cato Policy Analysis no. 578, September 18, 2006.

Fisher, Louis. *Presidential War Power.* 2nd Revised Edition. Lawrence, KS: University Press of Kansas, 2004.

Hemmer, Christopher. "Responding to a Nuclear Iran." *Parameters,* Autumn 2007.

Logan, Justin. "The Bottom Line on Iran: The Costs and Benefits of Preventive War versus Deterrence." Cato Policy Analysis no. 583, December 4, 2006.

—Prepared by Justin Logan

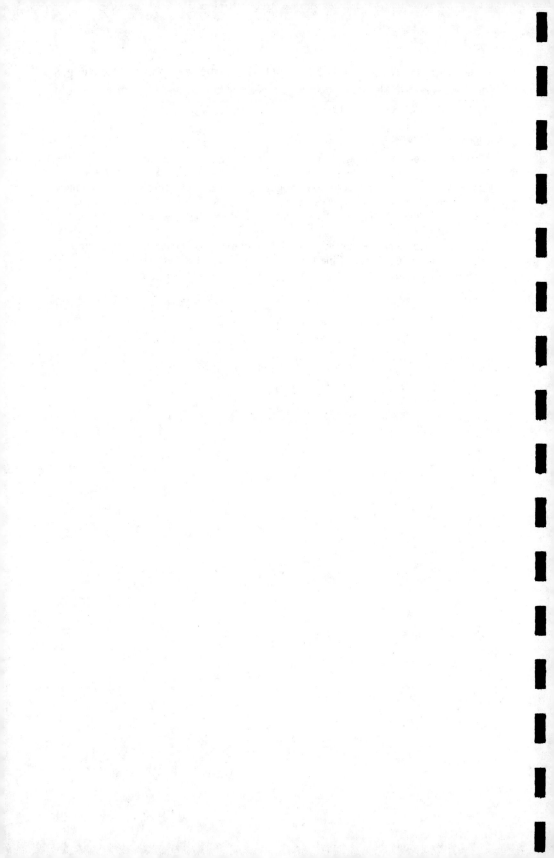

51. U.S. Policy toward Afghanistan and Pakistan

Policymakers should

- make the war in Afghanistan a top priority, as Washington's insufficient military focus has led directly to the Taliban's resurgence in that country's eastern and southern provinces;
- plan for drawing the military mission in Afghanistan to a close, including the withdrawal of most U.S. military personnel within a two- to three-year period;
- develop a comprehensive plan to uproot al Qaeda, Taliban, and other militant safe havens in the tribal belt of western Pakistan, an area used by insurgents to infiltrate neighboring Afghanistan and sabotage U.S.-led North Atlantic Treaty Organization operations;
- recognize that large-scale military action in Pakistan's tribal areas will further radicalize the region's indigenous population and should be deemphasized in favor of low-level clear-and-hold operations, which employ small numbers of U.S. Special Operations Forces and Pakistan's Special Services Group; and
- maintain tighter oversight on the distribution of military aid and the sale of dual-use weapons systems to Pakistan, especially those that have limited utility for counterterrorism operations but instead feed Pakistan's rivalry with India.

Focus on Afghanistan

Shortly after the 2001 invasion of Afghanistan, President George W. Bush decided to pull most of America's Special Operations Forces and Central Intelligence Agency paramilitary operatives off the hunt for Osama bin Laden so they could be reconstituted for war in Iraq. Over the years,

531

the scope of America's commitment in that country took Washington's attention away from the "forgotten war" in Afghanistan. But by summer 2008, the situation in Afghanistan had deteriorated badly.

In June, the deadliest month since the 2001 invasion, a sophisticated Taliban assault on a Kandahar prison freed 1,200 inmates, including 350 Taliban members. Violence in Afghanistan rose 40 percent from the previous year. Ambushes, suicide attacks, and targeted assassinations rose sharply. The Taliban's presence is strongest in the Helmand, Kandahar, Zabol, and Oruzgan provinces in southern Afghanistan, and is either significant or conspicuous in the Paktika, Khowst, Nangarhar, Konar, and Nuristan provinces in eastern Afghanistan. In many of these areas, the Taliban have usurped the traditional functions of a sovereign state, collecting taxes, maintaining order, and providing basic services.

Lessons to Learn

Some U.S. policymakers believe that the war in Afghanistan requires a "surge" of conventional forces similar to that conducted in Iraq in 2007. In 2008, both major party presidential candidates advocated sending two to three additional combat brigades—as many as 15,000 additional troops—to augment the 32,000 U.S. troops already in Afghanistan as part of NATO's 60,000-strong International Security Assistance Force.

But U.S. policymakers should be cautious about deploying more troops to the region. The experience of the Soviet Union's 10-year occupation of Afghanistan should demonstrate to leaders in Washington how easily a modern army can become bogged down in a bloody, frustrating, and protracted guerrilla war.

The anti-Soviet jihad of the 1980s in Afghanistan did not bring about the dissolution of the Soviet system, as some analysts now claim. But the decade-long struggle, once labeled by Soviet President Mikhail Gorbachev as "a bleeding wound," did thoroughly demoralize the USSR.

There are clear differences between what Western coalition forces face today and what the Soviet Union endured during the cold war. First, at least according to open-source information, modern-day militants are not being backed by millions of dollars in covert aid from an opposing superpower. A second critical distinction is that Soviet forces in the early 1980s were not nearly as well equipped as U.S. and NATO forces are today. With force multipliers such as unmanned drones and helicopter gunships, International Security Assistance Force troops are ostensibly better prepared to stabilize the region. But these sorts of technological advantages can go only so far.

The history of the region shows that Afghanistan's fiercely independent and battle-tested Pashtuns are extremely resilient in resisting conventional armies. Time and again, Persian, Greek, Turk, Mughal, British, and Soviet invaders have been unable to subdue a virtually unconquerable people. Like the Soviet Union's ignominious departure from the region, U.S. and NATO troops, despite their sophisticated gadgetry, could easily meet the same fate.

Aside from military operations, and the concomitant difficulty of distinguishing ordinary tribesmen from militant operatives, another reason U.S. leaders should be careful in sending more troops into Afghanistan is the taxing nature of nation-building. Stabilizing and rebuilding a country that lacks government authority and is notoriously resistant to outsiders will be an extensive and daunting undertaking. One central lesson to take away from previous invaders is to forge, first and foremost, a political settlement. But cultivating a political resolution will not be easy, and at least under the current Afghan president, Hamid Karzai, may prove nearly impossible.

Clausewitzian Answers

Legitimacy is the central component of good governance. But presently, the writ of President Karzai is confined largely to the capital, Kabul. Recently, several NATO countries have been highly critical of Karzai's weak leadership, as well as his seeming inability to stamp out government corruption.

One way for Karzai and future Afghan presidents to increase their credibility would be to integrate more of their country's ethnic Pashtuns. Durrani Pashtuns have been Afghanistan's traditional political elite. Karzai himself emerged from the Popalzai clan of the Durrani tribe. However, Ghilzai Pashtuns, unlike their Durrani counterparts, tend to be rural and less educated and were the main foot soldiers for the Taliban. Misgivings about the current government's perceived bias against Ghilzai Pashtuns were compounded shortly after the swift U.S. victory in late 2001, when American forces relied heavily on the Tajik-dominated Northern Alliance to defeat the Pashtun-dominated Taliban. Those kinds of political and social problems cannot be solved simply by boosting U.S. troop levels.

Another reason why U.S. and NATO policymakers must be cautious in their approach toward Afghanistan is that its challenges extend across the border into Pakistan. As long as militants continue to infiltrate the hundreds of unguarded checkpoints along the Afghan-Pakistani border, the security environment in Afghanistan will continue to decline.

Regional Safe Havens

Few places in the world are truly ungoverned. But Pakistan's western frontier with Afghanistan, known as the Federally Administered Tribal Areas, is one such place.

A relic of the 19th century's imperial era, this thin slice of rugged territory was left unconquered by Britain's colonial armies and has been devoid of a governing structure for the past several centuries. After the partition of British India in 1947, the tribal agencies of FATA were absorbed by the independent state of Pakistan, yet remained formally outside the Pakistani constitution.

This vast unpoliced region is now a sanctuary for al Qaeda, the Taliban, and a smattering of other interconnected militant groups. FATA's highly porous border acts as a giant sieve, enabling militants to slip into and out of Afghanistan. Militants also use the area to attack trucks loaded with fuel and supplies for NATO operations in Afghanistan. The 2008 *Annual Threat Assessment of the Director of National Intelligence* reported that "using the sanctuary in the border area of Pakistan, al-Qa'ida has been able to maintain a cadre of skilled lieutenants capable of directing the organization's operations around the world."

Because the Pakistani government has never effectively controlled its autonomous tribal territories, in September 2008 U.S. forces in Afghanistan began to exercise greater latitude in the tribal region, through the escalation of unilateral strikes against militants and incursions onto Pakistani soil.

But like operations in Afghanistan, an overreliance on military force in the tribal areas could just as easily exacerbate regional terrorism. Moreover, military force alone cannot adequately address the political conditions that stimulate radicalism. Over the past several years, the original Afghan Taliban and an indigenous Pakistani version of the Taliban, known as Tehrik-e-Taliban, have operated in FATA and offered themselves as an alternative to the government in Islamabad. Because many Pakistanis, both inside and outside the tribal areas, perceive America's presence in the region to be a central source of regional instability, these groups and their allies are seen by some as a lesser threat.

Given the political, ethnic, and historical complexities of the region, any response from U.S. and NATO forces must be measured, deliberate, and, above all, precise. To confront the region's militancy, Washington must place a greater emphasis on a limited number of Special Operations Forces and human-intelligence operatives, rather than on large-scale battalions and an overwhelming combat presence. A 200-page study by the RAND Corporation, released in July 2008, corroborates this point. In that study titled "How Terrorist Groups End: Lessons for Countering al Qaeda," RAND scholars Seth Jones and Martin Libicki insist that overstated claims such as "shattering" al Qaeda, striking it "major blows," and ensuring terrorists are "on the run" misunderstand the limits of military force. Paraphrasing counterinsurgency expert David Galula, the RAND study asserts:

> Military force is too blunt an instrument to defeat most terrorist groups. Military forces may be able to penetrate and garrison an area that terrorist groups frequent and, if well sustained, may temporarily reduce terrorist activity. But once the situation in an area becomes untenable for terrorists, they will simply transfer their activity to another area, and the problem remains unresolved.

The current struggle for Afghanistan and the borderland of Pakistan would be best waged through law enforcement, intelligence sharing, and as light a military footprint as possible.

Fortunately, the United States and Pakistan appear to be moving in that direction. During late summer 2008, a small number of U.S. Army and Special Operations Forces helped train Pakistan's Special Services Group, a highly specialized organization expected to perform limited ground and air operations in and around FATA. While this limited presence is less than ideal for a region as expansive as FATA, a heavier combat presence risks provoking a hostile response from the region's tribes.

Aside from the military dimension, stabilizing the tribal areas will also require a more effective use of current economic aid. In general, foreign aid tends to be detrimental to a poor country's internal development; it discourages accountability and deters needed domestic reforms. But Washington's motivation is to gain Islamabad's approval for its policies within the region. Because that assistance is a quid pro quo for advancing U.S. policies, stopping aid completely might shut a vital intelligence link needed to neutralize regional terrorism, as well as alienate a Muslim-majority country with a troubling history of nuclear proliferation activities. From counterterrorism to nuclear proliferation to human-intelligence sharing and transporting of supplies for NATO operations, continued cooperation with the Pakistani government is critical for advancing U.S. policies in the region. But the United States must better manage the

535

distribution of aid, which since 9/11 may have totaled nearly $20 billion according to one estimate by the Center for Strategic and International Studies.

The Use of Current Funds

In fact, it is impossible to quantify the exact amount of U.S. aid given to Pakistan. When the Prevention, Conflict Analysis, and Reconstruction Project at the Center for Strategic and International Studies asked nearly 100 former and current U.S. officials how much they thought the United States provided Pakistan annually, replies ranged from $800 million to $5 billion. The problem in fixing on a precise estimate is that the delivery of U.S. aid is highly decentralized within the U.S. government, with different agencies responsible for monitoring only those programs that fall within their respective budgets.

Another problem is that much of the aid evaporates due to widespread corruption and mismanagement in Pakistan. For an eight-month period in 2007, the United States reimbursed Pakistan $55 million for maintenance costs of Vietnam-era Cobra attack helicopters. Later, the United States discovered that Pakistan's army got less than half of that amount from the Pakistani government. That led some Washington lawmakers to believe Islamabad was exaggerating costs in order to acquire more reimbursements and pocket surplus funds. In fact, the Government Accountability Office found that of the over $10.5 billion in unclassified aid given to Pakistan from 2002 through 2007, $5.8 billion was allotted to FATA and the border region, and about 96 percent of that was delivered as reimbursements. For many years, the U.S. government has shoveled billions of dollars in aid to Pakistan without appropriate oversight. Until aid to Pakistan is more properly monitored, prospects for true improvement of the situation in the tribal areas seem dim.

Conclusion

Today, what is missing from the U.S. national security debate is a frank and serious discussion about the strategic consequences of a long-term U.S. presence in Afghanistan. Before committing even more troops to the conflict, policymakers in Washington must recognize that the United States does not have the resources, long-term political interest, or even the proper standing to deal with the entirety of Afghanistan's internal problems. If policymakers intend to rebuild that country from the bottom up, they should prepare for a project that will take years—if not decades—and may not even achieve anything resembling true victory in Afghanistan.

U.S. policy should move in the opposite direction. With regard to Afghanistan, the short-term objective must be to weaken the Taliban and other militants intent on destabilizing the Afghan government. That will require a concerted military campaign and a political effort to wean tribal leaders from those extremist movements they are now inclined to support. The strategy the U.S. military belatedly used in Iraq's Anbar province to split Iraqi Sunnis from al Qaeda may offer some pertinent lessons.

Longer term, though, the United States must develop an exit strategy from Afghanistan. It is not in America's best interest to try to occupy the country for years, much less decades. Unfortunately, Washington seems to have drifted into a vague, open-ended mission. That situation must change.

A similar distinction between short-term and long-term strategy is also necessary regarding Pakistan. Over the next year or two, a greater effort must be made by both Islamabad and Washington to disrupt the Taliban and al Qaeda safe havens in FATA. Without success on that front, the U.S.-NATO mission next door in Afghanistan is likely to fail. However, Washington's longer-term goal needs to be a lower-profile role in Pakistan—not a highly visible military presence. Adopting such an approach means accepting the likelihood that the Taliban–al Qaeda threat centered in Afghanistan and Pakistan cannot be definitively eradicated. U.S. leaders will have to pursue the more modest and realistic goal of merely weakening those movements and keeping them off balance. The alternative is to slog along with expensive, frustrating, and possibly counterproductive campaigns with no end in sight.

Suggested Readings

Abbas, Hassan. *Pakistan's Drift into Extremism: Allah, the Army, and America's War on Terror*. New York: M. E. Sharpe, 2005.

Bennett-Jones, Owen. "U.S. Policy Options toward Pakistan: A Principled and Realistic Approach." Policy analysis brief, Stanley Foundation, February 2008.

Cohen, Craig, and Derek Chollet. "When $10 Billion Is Not Enough: Rethinking U.S. Strategy toward Pakistan." *Washington Quarterly* 30, no. 2 (Spring 2007).

Gregory, Shaun. "The ISI and the War on Terrorism." Pakistan Security Research Unit Brief no. 28, January 24, 2008.

Haqqani, Husain. *Pakistan: Between Mosque and Military*. Washington: Carnegie Endowment for International Peace, 2005.

Innocent, Malou. "Pakistan and the Future of U.S. Policy." Cato Institute Policy Analysis, forthcoming.

Neumann, Ronald. "Borderline Insanity: Thinking Big about Afghanistan." *The American Interest* 3, no. 2 (November–December 2007).

Rashid, Ahmed. *Descent into Chaos: The United States and the Failure of Nation Building in Pakistan, Afghanistan, and Central Asia.* New York: Viking Press, 2008.

Tellis, Ashley J. "Pakistan and the War on Terror: Conflicted Goals, Compromised Performance." Carnegie Endowment Report, January 2008.

—Prepared by Malou Innocent

52. U.S. Policy in the Middle East

Policymakers should

- embrace a policy of "constructive disengagement" from the Middle East by de-emphasizing U.S. alliances in the Middle East, especially with Saudi Arabia and Israel, and by drawing down the American military presence in the region;
- recognize that the current round of peace talks between Israel and Palestine are not expected to yield real results in the short term;
- understand that the Persian Gulf states cannot effectively use the "oil weapon" against the American economy; and
- avoid taking a leading role in resolving regional conflicts given that such efforts have produced an anti-American backlash.

For many decades, successive U.S. administrations have defined U.S. national security interests in the Middle East as ensuring access to Middle East oil, containing any aspiring regional hegemonic powers, and limiting the proliferation of weapons of mass destruction. Washington has tried to achieve this complex set of goals primarily through a network of informal security alliances—especially with Israel, Saudi Arabia, and Egypt. Americans have also attempted to broker peace between the Israelis and the Palestinians; Presidents George H. W. Bush and Bill Clinton both viewed resolution of the conflict as a central component of U.S. policy in the Middle East and attempted to expand the American role in the peace process on the assumption that a resolution of the conflict would reduce the appeal of anti-Americanism and contain the radical forces in the region.

After 9/11, U.S. strategy in the Middle East changed dramatically. George W. Bush came into office intending to make a sharp break from his predecessors, and 9/11 facilitated a shift toward using military might to transform the balance of power in the region. The new administration will likely choose between Bush's example, employing or threatening the use of force to topple obstreperous regimes, or else revert to the policies of his predecessors, cajoling and pleading with the region's leaders to make peace. Given that neither approach has advanced U.S. security and yet has been very costly, the better option would be to chart an entirely new course.

American Security Alliances in the Middle East

Countries in the Middle East receive a disproportionate share of U.S. aid (See Table 52.1). The leading recipient of aid is Israel, but several other countries in the region, including Egypt and Jordan, are awarded hundreds of millions of dollars annually from U.S. taxpayers. The Near East region as a whole, which includes North Africa and the Persian Gulf States, received $5.26 billion in 2008, more than all of Africa ($5.19 billion), and nearly eight times the amount of aid delivered to East Asia.

The costs of U.S. policy in the Middle East are not confined to foreign aid, however. Economists have calculated that the deployment of the U.S.

Table 52.1
Top 10 Recipients of U.S. Foreign Aid in FY08

Country	Total U.S. Aid (millions of U.S. dollars)	Population Mid-2007 (millions)	Average U.S. Aid per Capita (U.S. dollars)
Israel	2,380	7.3	326.02
Egypt	1,706	73.4	23.24
Afghanistan	1,058	31.9	33.16
Pakistan	738	169.3	4.36
Jordan	688	5.7	120.70
Kenya	586	36.9	15.88
South Africa	574	47.9	11.98
Colombia	541	46.2	11.71
Nigeria	491	144.4	3.40
Ethiopia	456	77.1	5.91

SOURCES: U.S. Agency for International Development, "Congressional Budget Justification for Foreign Operations FY 2009 Budget Request," February 29, 2008. Calculations based on FY 2008 estimates and Population Reference Bureau, "2007 World Population Data Sheet."

NOTE: According to USAID estimates, Iraq received a total of only $21 million under three different programs in 2008; most reconstruction assistance to Iraq originates elsewhere, including the Iraq Relief and Reconstruction Fund, and the bulk of those monies were disbursed before 2008.

military to safeguard oil supplies from Saudi Arabia and the rest of the Persian Gulf—particularly since the first Gulf War—costs the United States between $30 billion and $60 billion a year. That calculation does not reflect the costs of the war against Iraq and the continuing occupation of that country. And no statistic can capture the high costs America is paying in the form of extreme anti-Americanism among Arabs and Muslims because of Washington's support for Israel and Saudi Arabia. The stationing of U.S. forces in Saudi Arabia after the first Gulf War is known to have stirred such deep hostility that Osama bin Laden made it the initial focus in his campaign to recruit Muslims from around the globe to attack Americans.

Unfortunately, the Bush administration's move to end the deployment of U.S. troops in Saudi Arabia in August 2003 was not part of an American strategy to disengage from the region, but rather was intended to relieve some of the political pressure on the Saudi royal family. As long as Washington continues to cling to the assumption that it must maintain a dominant military posture in the Persian Gulf, it will be unable to resolve the dilemmas it is currently facing. The alliance with the ruling Arab regimes and the U.S. military presence in the region will continue to foster anti-Americanism and may force the United States into more costly military engagements. Meanwhile, an effort to accelerate "democratization" would likely fail in the near term and could pose a very serious threat to U.S. security in the medium to long term. Given the virulent anti-American sentiments in Saudi Arabia and throughout the Middle East, a government that represented the wishes of the Saudi people could well choose to support al Qaeda or other anti-American terrorist groups.

Redefining of the U.S. Role in the Israeli-Palestinian Peace Process

The first President Bush convened the Madrid Peace Conference in October 1991, while the Clinton administration backed direct negotiations between Israel and Palestine. These negotiations led to the 1993 Oslo Accord between Israel and the Palestinian Liberation Organization, and to a peace accord between Israel and Jordan. However, President Clinton's attempts at mediating a comprehensive peace accord between Israel and the Palestinians during the 2000 Camp David peace summit failed. The core issues—the future of the Jewish settlements in occupied Arab territories, the fate of Jerusalem and its holy sites, and the "right of return" demanded by Palestinian refugees that had left Israel in 1948—remained unresolved. Furthermore, the breakdown of U.S.-led negotiations produced a backlash in Israel where Ariel Sharon was elected prime minister in 2001, and in the Palestinian territories where Hamas gained ground against the more moderate Fatah. This set the stage for a new Palestinian uprising and the continuance of the vicious circle of anti-Israeli terrorism, accompanied by Israeli military retaliation.

The collapse of the Camp David talks and the start of the second intifada, followed by 9/11, demonstrated the high costs Americans would have to pay to maintain a dominant position in the Middle East, both as a military power and as a promoter of the peace process. Thus, in the aftermath of 9/11, policymakers advanced two alternative approaches.

On the one hand, then–secretary of state Colin Powell argued that by reembracing the activist pro-Mideast peace process diplomacy of his predecessors, and by asserting U.S. leadership in a new international effort to revive Israeli-Palestinian negotiations, Washington could counter anti-Americanism and stabilize its position in the region. In particular, Powell promoted the Roadmap for Peace, presented by the "quartet" of the United States, the European Union, Russia, and the United Nations on September 17, 2002. Powell also wanted to provide support for the Arab peace initiative proposed by then–crown prince Abdullah of Saudi Arabia in the Beirut summit on March 28, 2002. The initiative spelled out a "final-status agreement" whereby the members of the Arab League would offer full normalization of relations with Israel in exchange for the withdrawal of its forces from all occupied territories to UN borders established before the 1967 war, and a recognition of an independent Palestinian state with East Jerusalem as its capital.

A competing point of view held that the promotion of Israeli-Palestinian peace should be placed on the policy back burner while American military power would be applied against radical players in the region, including Iraq and Iran. Officials in Washington assumed that the establishment of pro-American democratic governments in Baghdad and other Middle Eastern capitals would create conditions conducive to achieving Israeli-Palestinian peace. This alternative approach gained steam after 9/11. Israel was subjected to Palestinian terrorist attacks during the second intifada, and was considered a strategic ally of the United States in the war on terrorism and against rogue Middle Eastern regimes. Meanwhile, the Palestinian leadership, especially Palestinian Liberation Organization leader Yasser Arafat, was tainted with a stigma of terrorism.

The tilt toward Israel was revealed in 2002 when George W. Bush met several times with Israeli Prime Minister Ariel Sharon, whom he called "a man of peace," and repeatedly refused to meet with Arafat. Bush gave Sharon a green light to launch a large-scale Israeli military operation in the West Bank in March 2002, in response to a terrorist attack in the Israeli coastal city of Netanya. He also backed Tel Aviv's decision to construct a security fence in the West Bank and to withdraw its troops from the Gaza Strip.

The Bush administration's approach combined accelerated democratization and peacemaking, but these goals proved incompatible. While Washington wanted new Palestinian leaders who would make peace with Israel under American supervision, several knowledgeable observers predicted that free elections in the Palestinian territories were likely to elevate anti-Israel forces to power.

And indeed that is exactly what happened with the Palestinian parliamentary elections in January 2006. The radical Islamist Hamas movement, bitterly anti-American and unremittingly hostile toward the peace process, defeated the more moderate but corrupt Fatah movement, winning a majority in the Palestinian Legislative Council. Despite the fact that Washington had pushed Palestinian President Mahmoud Abbas to hold the elections, U.S. policymakers belatedly reversed course. Washington refused to recognize the newly elected government and, together with Israel and the European Union, cut off all funds to the Palestinian Authority, insisting that economic aid to the Palestinians would be resumed only after Hamas ended violence and recognized Israel. The American and Israeli governments also encouraged the Fatah leadership to form a separate Palestinian government in the West Bank in June 2007 while Hamas remained in control of the Gaza Strip, a messy divorce that precipitated frequent violent clashes between Hamas and Fatah forces. Israeli forces and Hamas guerrillas, meanwhile, continued to exchange fire through 2008, although Egyptian mediation helped broker a cease-fire between the two sides in June 2008.

Washington's abortive attempt to implant democracy in Palestine as a means of creating conditions for peace in the Middle East reveals how U.S. policies have often worked at cross-purposes. The ousting of Saddam Hussein and the coming to power of a Shiite-controlled government in Baghdad helped tilt the balance of power in the Persian Gulf to Iran, a country that does not recognize Israel and opposes the peace process. In the Levant, in addition to the Hamas victory in the Palestinian elections in early 2006, a series of other developments that were initially welcomed by the Bush administration (for example, the parliamentary elections in

Lebanon and the 2006 Israel-Hezbollah war), helped strengthen the power of Iran's satellite, the Hezbollah movement. In a way, the road from Baghdad did lead to Jerusalem, but not as the Bush administration expected it would. Instead, Bush's policies eroded U.S. power and influence, and Washington's ability to help bring peace to Israel-Palestine waned even further. This was definitively confirmed at the hastily convened conference held in Annapolis, Maryland, in November 2007, when the Bush administration tried, but failed, to use the perceived common threat from Iran as a way to encourage Israelis and Arabs to overcome their wide differences on the core issues of the Palestinian-Israeli conflict.

Given the manifest failures of the Bush administration's policies, the new president will have a strong incentive to reembrace a variation of the Powell approach, consistent with the policies of the first Bush and Clinton administrations. But a truly different approach is warranted. Trying to maintain a diminishing U.S. position in the Middle East by engaging in the mission impossible of resolving the local conflict there is obviously imprudent. Like other subregional conflicts that pose no direct threat to core U.S. national interests, the situation should be left to those local and regional players with direct interest in these conflicts. A U.S. policy of "benign neglect" would provide incentives for local and regional actors to assume a larger role. These entities could "manage" the situation in the short and medium term, while trying to advance plans for a long-term resolution of the dispute.

That process has already begun. As U.S. diplomatic power has eroded in the region, other regional players have stepped forward. The deals brokered by Egypt for an Israeli-Palestinian cease-fire, Qatar's effort to achieve a compromise between the warring factions in Lebanon, Turkey's mediation between Israel and Syria, and even Iran's aid in mediating between the warring Shiite factions in Iraq should be welcomed. The U.S. government should factor aid from regional actors into the equation as part of a long-term strategy for "constructive disengagement" from the Middle East.

Americans who continue to push for a peace settlement should recognize that the pro-peace factions in both Israeli and Palestinian societies are weak and divided; many Palestinians and Israelis are still ready to pay a high price in blood for what they regard as a fight for survival. A settlement can be possible only when the majority of Israelis and Palestinians recognize that their interests would be best served by negotiation and peaceful resolution of the conflict, and when the minority on both sides who vehemently oppose negotiations can no longer derail the peace process.

In the meantime, many Israelis and Palestinians are interested in keeping the United States entangled in the conflict. Few seem prepared to resolve the conflict on their own. However, the U.S. government does not have to sustain the same level of involvement in the conflict that it maintained during the cold war. No Arab regime can present a serious threat to Israel, whose military is unchallenged in the Middle East. Considerable American military aid to Israel might have been justified in the context of the cold war, but is unnecessary and even harmful under present conditions. U.S. policymakers should withdraw financial assistance to the Palestinians, and phase out aid to Israel. The latter step would create an incentive for Israel to reform its economy, which has become far too dependent on financial support from the United States. Removing this support would also encourage Israel to integrate itself politically and economically into the region.

Meanwhile, U.S. direct involvement in the Israeli-Palestinian conflict does not advance American national interests. Washington should reject demands to internationalize the conflict between Israelis and Palestinians, which implicitly assume that the United States must be responsible for resolving it and paying the costs involved. Instead of complaining about the failure of the United States to make peace in the Middle East, and warning Americans of the dire consequences of failure, the Arab states should recognize that it is in their national interests and that of the long-term stability of the region to do something to resolve the Israeli-Palestinian conflict in a regional context. With its geographic proximity to the Middle East, its dependence on Middle Eastern energy resources, and the large number of Arab immigrants living in major European countries, the European Union also has a clear stake in a more peaceful Middle East. U.S. policymakers should encourage the EU to take a more active role in the region.

A decision to adopt a more low-key approach toward the Israeli-Palestinian conflict makes sense in the context of a wider U.S. strategy of "constructive disengagement" from the Middle East. Had Washington embraced such a policy at the end of the cold war, it could have slowed or reversed the rise of anti-Americanism. Washington's repeated, high-profile failures to deliver a peace agreement spurred continuing opposition to the U.S. military presence in the region and created the environment that gave rise to the terrorist plots of 9/11.

Change in the Long-Term Strategy in the Middle East

Continuing support for American policies in the Middle East, even in the face of the obvious risks and dubious benefits, stems from the erroneous belief that American military involvement in the Middle East protects U.S. access to "cheap" oil. The notion that U.S. policy in the Middle East helps give Americans access to affordable oil makes little sense if one takes account of the military and other costs—including two Gulf Wars—that should be added to the price that U.S. consumers pay for driving.

Many Americans assume that the oil resources in the Persian Gulf would be shut off if American troops were removed from the region. But the U.S. military need not be present in the Persian Gulf to ensure that the region's oil makes it to market. The oil-producing states have few resources other than oil, and if they don't sell it to somebody, they will have little wealth to maintain their power and curb domestic challenges. They need to sell oil more than the United States needs to buy it, and once this oil reaches the market, there is no practical way to somehow punish American consumers. In short, the so-called oil weapon is a dud. Further, if political and military influence were truly required to keep oil flowing, consumers in western Europe and Asia—who are far more likely than Americans to consume oil that originates in the Persian Gulf—should be the ones to bear the cost.

Accordingly, very few economists believe that keeping U.S. troops in the region is a cost-effective strategy. During the cold war, the U.S. policy of actively safeguarding a strategic resource may have made sense with regard to maintaining the unity of the noncommunist alliance under American leadership. At present, however, this policy is badly outdated.

A responsible policy in the Middle East, consistent with American security interests in the region, should be based on de-emphasizing U.S. alliances, especially those with Saudi Arabia and Israel. It should also include a change in popular attitudes toward U.S. dependence on Middle Eastern oil and the necessity for U.S. leadership in the negotiations to end Israeli-Palestinian conflict.

Reshaping U.S. policy in the Middle East would enhance American security and help alter the perception that U.S. policies are guided by double standards. Maintaining a frail balance among all of Washington's commitments in the region is becoming ever more costly, dangerous, and unnecessary. Americans are paying a heavy price to sustain a U.S. military and political presence there. A change is long overdue.

Suggested Readings

Bandow, Doug. "Befriending Saudi Princes: A High Price for a Dubious Alliance." Cato Institute Policy Analysis no. 428, March 20, 2002.

Freedman, Lawrence. *A Choice of Enemies: America Confronts the Middle East*. New York: Public Affairs, 2008.

Gholz, Eugene, and Daryl G. Press. "Energy Alarmism: The Myths That Make Americans Worry about Oil." Cato Institute Policy Analysis no. 589, April 5, 2007.

Hadar, Leon. "Mending the U.S.-European Rift over the Middle East." Cato Institute Policy Analysis no. 485, August 20, 2003.

———. *Sandstorm: American Blindness in the Middle East*. New York: Palgrave Macmillan, 2005.

Miller, Aaron David. *The Much Too Promised Land: America's Elusive Search for Arab-Israeli Peace*. New York: Bantam, 2008.

Shlaim, Avi. *The Iron Wall: Israel and the Arab World*. New York: W. W. Norton, 2001.

Wright, Robin. *Dreams and Shadows: The Future of the Middle East*. New York: Penguin, 2008.

—Prepared by Leon Hadar and Christopher Preble

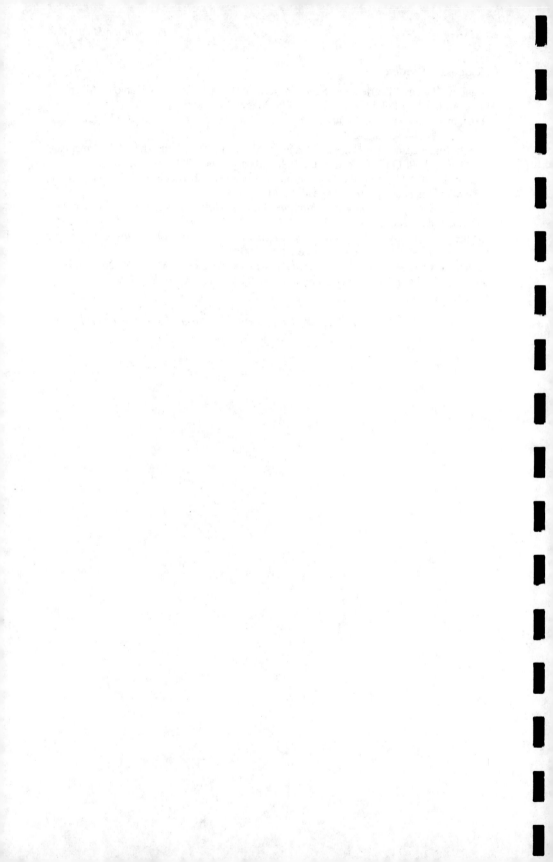

53. Relations with China, India, and Russia

> **Policymakers should**
>
> - maintain a policy of maximum economic and diplomatic engagement with China;
> - adopt a hedging strategy regarding China by encouraging other major powers, especially Japan and India, to play more active security roles;
> - continue attempting to foster closer relations with India;
> - acknowledge that while Washington and New Delhi have some common interests, India is unlikely to become a pliable client state;
> - further acknowledge that the U.S.-India nuclear deal has created additional difficulties in existing nonproliferation institutions;
> - cease efforts toward admitting Ukraine and Georgia into the North Atlantic Treaty Organization;
> - recognize that Russia, like most major powers past and present, will insist on a sphere of influence in its region; and
> - seek ways to sustain cooperation with Moscow on important issues and avoid actions that may trigger a second cold war.

A major challenge for U.S. policymakers in the coming years is to cultivate stable and constructive relations with three especially important—and often difficult—actors in the international system: China, India, and Russia. The first two are rising great powers that have enormous economic and even military potential. Russia, however, is more a reviving great power. As the principal successor state to the defunct Soviet Union (and in reality, the core of the long-standing Russian empire), Russia went through a decade of acute disarray in the 1990s. It has recovered somewhat during this decade, however, and although Moscow is unlikely to regain the superpower status that it claimed during the cold war, it is again a significant factor in both Europe and Central Asia and (to a lesser extent) in other regions as well.

Washington's relations with all three powers can be best described as uneasy. The United States and China maintain an extensive—and growing—economic relationship, but tensions are rising over an assortment of issues. Relations between the United States and India have improved noticeably since the end of the cold war. Throughout America's struggle with the Soviet Union, India ostensibly maintained a nonaligned stance but rather consistently tilted toward the USSR. That position annoyed Washington, which treated India as a de facto Soviet ally. Although relations have become better on multiple fronts, there is still some wariness between the United States and India.

Relations between Washington and Moscow have gone in the other direction. The hope of close, friendly ties, so prominent in the years immediately following the demise of the Soviet Union, has faded badly. Indeed, some experts warn that the two countries are on the brink of a second cold war.

China

American experts who deal with U.S. policy toward the People's Republic of China tend to cluster into two distinct camps. Members of the first faction focus on the growing trade ties between China and the United States and assert with a confidence bordering on certainty that economic progress in China will soon lead to political liberalization and the eventual emergence of a full-blown democracy. By contrast, members of the second faction view China as an ugly, authoritarian—if not totalitarian—power that is already a strategic adversary and may eventually pose a mortal threat to America. Both views contain some elements of truth, but neither is fully accurate.

There are reasons to worry about some aspects of Beijing's behavior both domestically and internationally. Nevertheless, China's rise as a great power seems much less destabilizing than the earlier rise of such malignantly expansionist states as Nazi Germany, Imperial Japan, and the Soviet Union. China is a crucial economic and diplomatic partner of the United States in many respects, and it is a country with important vested interests in the current international system.

In other respects, though, the PRC is a political and even strategic competitor of the United States. It has helped create the Shanghai Cooperation Organization, a strong security partnership linking China to Russia and various Central Asian countries. The SCO has not only conducted joint military exercises, it has also openly advocated trying to exclude the influence of "outside powers" (i.e., the United States) from Central Asia.

Likewise, Beijing has been, at best, marginally helpful in dealing with the Iranian nuclear crisis. A fairly consistent pattern has emerged. The United States and its European allies keep pushing for stronger economic sanctions against Tehran, whereas China (together with Russia) opposes such coercive measures and works to dilute any sanctions that are ultimately imposed. China has been somewhat more helpful in dealing with the North Korean nuclear crisis, but even in that case, Beijing has sometimes tried to fend off pressure on its longtime ally.

Some analysts are worried as well about allegedly fierce resource competition, especially over oil, between China and the United States. There is growing agitation in Washington about China's extensive ties to key oil producers from the Persian Gulf to Africa to Latin America. Likewise, Beijing's increasingly assertive diplomatic position regarding the oil-rich Spratly Islands in the South China Sea, the centerpiece of a massive territorial claim, is drawing hostile scrutiny from American analysts worried about China's intentions. It is more than a remote possibility that the Spratlys could become the focal point of tensions between the United States and China. In addition to their probable oil resources, the islands stand astride key sea-lanes. To put it mildly, Washington is not inclined to recognize Beijing's bold claims to virtually the entire South China Sea, which would give China control over sea-lanes that are crucial to Japan and other key American allies and clients in East Asia.

On the positive side of the ledger, however, is the large and vibrant U.S.-Chinese economic relationship. Sino-American trade exceeded $387 billion in 2007, and China has become an increasingly important arena for U.S. trade and investment.

Yet even the economic ties involve some cause for American apprehension. In particular, China's emergence as the second-largest holder of U.S. treasury debt ($518 billion in 2007)—and probably the largest holder within the next three or four years—is a very significant development. It will become increasingly difficult for Washington to take a strong position on trade or strategic disputes with China if it means angering America's chief banker.

One should not overstate the sources of tension, however, and assume that China and the United States are destined to be enemies, and perhaps even come to blows. As Brookings Institution scholars Richard Bush and Michael O'Hanlon note: "Most hypothetical causes of war between the United States and China turn out, upon inspection, to have little or no basis. The two countries will not duke it out simply to settle the question of who will 'run the world' in the twenty-first century." The economic ties, in particular, create powerful incentives for sensible, cooperative behavior in both capitals.

Even the Taiwan issue, although remaining a dark cloud on the horizon, has become a less acute source of trouble in the short run. The election of Ma Ying-jeou as Taiwan's president has brought to power a government committed to preserving the status quo instead of formalizing permanent political separation from the mainland. Already, economic ties between the mainland and Taiwan are expanding, direct air and sea links have begun, and political talks—suspended since 1999—have resumed. All these steps suggest a period of relative quiescence as long as Ma and his Kuomintang Party retain power. In the long run, though, a confrontation regarding the issue of reunification is still a serious danger.

Although Ma endorses eventual reunification, he also attaches three very important caveats to that goal. First, he has made it clear that reunification can take place only if mainland China evolves into a prosperous, liberal democracy. As he put it, reunification becomes possible once "developments in Mainland China reach a stage when its political democracy, economic prosperity, and social well-being become *congruent* with those of Taiwan." Ma—and most Kuomintang Party members—have no interest in unifying with China in its current, authoritarian incarnation. Second, reunification could take place only with the explicit endorsement of the Taiwanese people. In other words, Taiwan would have a veto. Again, Ma is categorical on that point: "Since Taiwan has become a full-fledged democracy, reunification with Mainland China cannot proceed without the consent of the Taiwanese people." Third, the Kuomintang Party has reluctantly conceded that all options—even independence— must be available to Taiwanese voters when it comes time to make a decision.

All those caveats are an anathema to Beijing. The PRC's political elite has no intention of giving up the Communist Party's monopoly of power and transforming China into a Western-style democracy. Chinese leaders have also emphasized repeatedly that Taiwanese voters cannot have a veto over whether reunification takes place. And Taiwanese independence is an option that Beijing considers utterly illegitimate, even if that is what the island's population might desire.

Beijing expects serious negotiations for reunification at some point. One wonders what will happen if those hopes fail to materialize. One also must wonder how long the status quo will be acceptable to Beijing as China's economic and military power continues to grow. At what point will Chinese leaders find it intolerable to have an upstart, de facto independent country barely 100 miles off China's coast—an upstart island that the overwhelming majority of mainlanders believe is rightfully Chinese territory? Moreover, that upstart island occupies an important strategic location astride the principal sea-lanes in the western Pacific. A clash between Beijing and Taipei remains all too likely in the long run. And given America's implicit defense commitment to Taiwan in the 1979 Taiwan Relations Act (see Chapter 54, "East Asian Security Commitments"), the United States would be caught right in the middle of such a confrontation. That is why Washington should move to sever that defense commitment in an orderly but prompt manner.

Beyond the issue of Taiwan, general U.S. security policy toward China should adhere to the current policy of engagement—with a slight nod toward a hedging strategy. The best course from the standpoint of American interests would be to encourage the emergence of multiple centers of power in Asia. The existence of several significant security actors would complicate the PRC's strategic calculations.

Encouraging the evolution of a multipolar strategic environment is not the same as adopting a U.S.-led containment policy against China. Washington does not have to be the godfather of a vast anti-PRC alliance. If U.S. officials stop smothering Japan and other allies in an effort to perpetuate their security dependence on the United States, and fully accept India as an independent, capable military power, China's neighbors will draw their own conclusions about Beijing's probable strategic behavior and adopt policies accordingly. Washington merely needs to get out of the way of that most normal of processes in the international system.

Encouraging—or at least accepting—the evolution of a balance of power designed to contain any PRC expansionist ambitions is also distinct from regarding China as an implacable foe of the United States. Washington ought to treat China as simply another great power and cultivate a normal relationship, recognizing that the interests of the two countries will sometimes coincide and sometimes conflict. Cooperation needs to be fostered in the first case, and an effort to contain adverse effects must be made in the latter. A normal relationship is inconsistent with attempts to isolate the PRC economically as well as adopt an overt containment policy. Such an approach would be especially unwise. A policy based on the assumption that China will inevitably become an aggressor and a mortal enemy of the United States could easily create a tragic, self-fulfilling prophecy.

Embracing the goal of multipolarity, of course, would mean relinquishing America's own hegemony in East Asia. Washington would have to be content with a status of "first among equals" in the region, and that would entail some loss of control. But a hegemonic role is probably unsustainable over the long term in any case. It is a manifestation of national hubris to think that the United States can forever dominate a region that contains nearly a third of the world's population and is becoming an increasingly sophisticated locus of economic and technological output.

U.S. leaders can adjust gracefully to the emergence of a more normal configuration of power in the region, or they can resist change to the bitter end. If they choose the former course, the United States will be able to influence the nature of the new multipolar strategic environment in Asia and seek the maximum advantage for American interests. The U.S.-PRC relationship would then be merely one component of a complex mosaic of relationships throughout the region, and the United States would have a significant opportunity to pursue a policy that avoided the extremes of viewing the PRC as a strategic partner or a new enemy. Washington would be able to develop a policy toward China that was prudent, sustainable, and beneficial to American interests.

India

Throughout the 1990s, U.S. policy toward India remained rooted in outdated cold war apprehensions. Stemming from India's prominent role in the Non-Aligned Movement, U.S. leaders had long resented New Delhi's role in world affairs, with some viewing the NAM as a fundamentally hostile institution in the context of the cold war. Although India's foremost interest in the NAM was to ally itself with the Soviet Union against China, Washington long misunderstood this reality and saw India as dangerously sympathetic to communism—and with it, the Soviet view of world affairs. Thus, when the Soviet Union collapsed, the linchpin of U.S.-Indian relations—the struggle against communism and India's role in that struggle—was removed and U.S. policy was adrift.

U.S. policymakers were slow to react to this new reality. The traditional U.S. alliance with Pakistan endured through the 1990s and grew in the 2000s, with the Bush administration deeming the government of Pervez Musharraf a "major non-NATO ally" in 2004, granting it expanded access to U.S. military technology. At the same time, the Bush administration maintained a close relationship with Pakistan. However, it attempted to reach out to India.

The centerpiece of the U.S. opening to India was the agreement, announced in 2005 and formally framed in 2007, for American assistance to India's nuclear program in exchange for limited inspections of India's civilian nuclear facilities by the International Atomic Energy Agency. Because India was as a nonsignatory to the nuclear Non-Proliferation Treaty, this development was lauded as a nonproliferation success by the Bush administration.

However, the deal underwent several revisions after having been first introduced, with nearly every round of revisions either expanding existing loopholes for India or creating new ones. Since India only promised to allow IAEA monitoring of its civilian facilities, and maintained the right to define what qualifies as "civilian," the deal wound up providing India significant space to maintain a parallel nuclear weapons program outside the scrutiny of the IAEA.

More important, the ad hoc agreement with India has provided significant rhetorical ammunition to countries like Iran, who regularly operate their nuclear programs at the edge of the IAEA's writ. Iran immediately began comparing U.S. cooperation with non-NPT signatory India, and Iran's own status as a signatory to the NPT. Washington essentially conceded the main thrust of this argument when Assistant Secretary of State Richard Boucher responded in 2006 to a reporter's question about the Iran-India analogy by admitting: "Is there a double-standard? Yeah. There should be." Although this candor may be acceptable among Americans in Washington, it should not be difficult to see how hard a sale such an approach to proliferation is among other world powers.

The nuclear deal has accordingly presented a potential problem for U.S.-Indian relations: the deal is viewed as a cornerstone of a new relationship between the two countries. Should the deal unravel in the future, there will be sour feelings on both sides and the prospect for better relations between the two nations will deteriorate. The important work of improving U.S.-Indian relations would have been better served if the Bush administration had either chosen a different way of bringing the countries together or, at the very least, not sent the president to India with an explicit mandate to sign a deal without having the particulars worked out in advance. This situation was used by India to extract further concessions from Washington in the last minutes of negotiations.

The reason the clumsy handling of the deal is so regrettable is that improved relations with India should be a central component of the U.S. approach to China in the coming years. With over a billion citizens and an annual economic output well over $1 trillion, India should provide constraints on Chinese strategic designs in the coming decades. The point is not to frame a "containment" policy of China, but to recognize that a China surrounded by weaker, poorer states without good relations with the United States is likely to act differently than it would with sturdy, prosperous states in Asia enjoying good relations with Washington. Historical animosity between India and China, while it certainly exists, is not at the level of acrimony of Chinese-Japanese relations, and accordingly, cooperation with India should cause less alarm in Beijing than expanded U.S.-Japanese cooperation would.

Although the objective of cultivating good relations with other major Asian powers is important, Washington ought not to fall into the trap of viewing nations as either friend or foe—with us or against us. On certain issues, particularly its energy cooperation with Iran, India is unlikely to satisfy American objectives. On other issues, including economic and military matters, American and Indian objectives overlap and allow for significant cooperation. Accordingly, U.S. policymakers should take care in the implementation of the Indian nuclear deal to emphasize American unanimity on the importance of expanding relations with India, while disagreeing on the merits of the deal itself. Beyond the nuclear deal, policymakers need to realize that India will conduct a foreign policy driven by its self-interest, and that will drive it toward the U.S. position in some cases and away from it in others.

Russia

Few people want to return to the animosity and tensions that marked relations between Washington and Moscow throughout the cold war. But clumsy policies by both the United States and Russia now threaten to bring back those unhappy days. Washington continues to press for further expansion of NATO to Russia's border and is meddling in parochial disputes between Russia and its small neighbor Georgia. For its part, the

Medvedev-Putin regime shows signs of trying to cause headaches for the United States in the Caribbean.

Both governments need to adopt more cautious policies. Secretary of State Condoleezza Rice once famously dismissed the concept of spheres of influence as an obsolete notion, and that view has become all too common among America's foreign policy elite. But that doctrine is very much alive, and U.S. and Russian leaders ignore that reality at their peril.

If a new cold war emerges, Washington will have done much to invite it. But Russia has become needlessly provocative as well. The dark hints in summer 2008 that it might station bombers in Cuba were reckless. For Americans, even the possibility that Moscow might deploy a nuclear-capable weapon system in Cuba brings back memories of the most night-marish episode of the cold war—the Cuban missile crisis. No American government would tolerate such a move—nor should it. Moscow's growing flirtation with Venezuela's Hugo Chávez, an obnoxious nemesis of the United States, is also creating gratuitous tensions. Moscow's joint air and naval exercises with Venezuelan military forces in September 2008 especially did not improve relations with America.

Those moves likely reflect mounting Russian anger at U.S. policies that seem calculated to undermine Russia's influence in its own backyard and even humiliate Moscow. Washington's "in your face" approach is not a recent development. U.S. officials took advantage of Russia's economic and military disarray during the 1990s to establish a dominant position in central and eastern Europe. Washington successfully engineered the admission of Poland, Hungary, and the Czech Republic to NATO in 1998—over the Yeltsin government's objections. That expansion of the alliance was nonprovocative, though, compared with the second round earlier this decade that incorporated Latvia, Estonia, and Lithuania, entities that had been part of the Soviet Union.

NATO expansion was not the only manifestation of contempt for Russia's interests during the 1990s. So too was Western policy in the Balkans—traditionally a key region of concern to Moscow. In 1995, NATO forces intervened in Bosnia's civil war to the clear disadvantage of the Serbs, Russia's long-standing coreligionists and political allies. And then in 1999, the United States and its allies waged an air war against Serbia, ultimately wrenching away its restive province of Kosovo.

Although Russia's political elite was furious at such behavior, given the weakness of the country, they could do little except issue impotent complaints. But that situation has changed. The country is much stronger both economically and militarily than it was a decade ago, and Moscow has begun to push back. For example, it has emphasized that Washington's attempt to gain NATO membership for Ukraine and Georgia crosses a bright red line and will not be tolerated.

Unfortunately, U.S. policymakers don't seem to grasp that the power relationship is different than it was in the 1990s. The Bush administration has pressed forward with plans to deploy missile defense systems in Poland and the Czech Republic, a move that Russia views as an attempt to degrade the effectiveness of its strategic nuclear forces. In response, Moscow has warned Warsaw and Prague that it will target both countries for retaliation in wartime.

Washington's Balkan policy has also remained shockingly insensitive. In February 2008, the United States and its leading European allies bypassed the United Nations Security Council (and hence Russia's veto) to grant Kosovo independence. Russia responded by rallying other countries that worry about that precedent with regard to their own secessionist-minded minorities and has blocked Kosovo's entry into various international organizations. Thanks in part to Moscow's lobbying, only 50 governments have recognized Kosovo's independence—most of them long-standing U.S. allies and clients.

Russian leaders are also showing Washington that Moscow can exploit the Kosovo precedent for its own purposes. That became all too evident in August 2008, when Russia repulsed an attempt by the government of neighboring Georgia to reestablish military and political control over the secessionist region of South Ossetia. Moscow launched a full-scale military counteroffensive against Georgian forces and penetrated deeply into Georgian territory. The Kremlin followed up that move by recognizing the independence of South Ossetia and Abkhazia, another secessionist region. Unfortunately, instead of beating a graceful diplomatic retreat, the United States has responded with further meddling, dispatching a humanitarian aid mission, providing Georgia with $1 billion in reconstruction aid, and redoubling its lobbying efforts on behalf of admitting Georgia (and Ukraine) to NATO.

One could scarcely imagine an issue with less relevance to genuine American interests than the political status of two obscure regions in a small country on Russia's border. Likewise, it is difficult to imagine what genuine Russian interests justify Moscow's bid to forge closer ties with the likes of Cuba and Venezuela. Both Russia and the United States have engaged in thoroughly immature behavior. We are not yet in a new cold war, but unless the two governments adopt far more responsible policies, they may soon produce that tragic outcome.

Conclusion

It is imperative for U.S. leaders to get the right policy toward these three prickly great powers. China and India could well become economic powerhouses before mid-century, and both countries will likely play increasingly significant geostrategic roles in their regions and beyond. Russia may not regain entry to the ranks of elite powers, but it, too, cannot be ignored or marginalized. Among other factors, Russia is the one country with a nuclear arsenal large enough to extinguish America's civilization. Washington may be able to get away with pursuing unwise or ineffectual policies toward lesser powers (as it has with Cuba, for example). It does not have that luxury regarding policy toward China, India, and Russia.

Suggested Readings

Carpenter, Ted Galen. *America's Coming War with China: A Collision Course over Taiwan.* New York: Palgrave/Macmillan, 2006.

_____. *Smart Power: Toward a Prudent Foreign Policy for America.* Washington: Cato Institute, 2008, Chapters 8 and 9.

_____. "Wild Card: A Democratic Taiwan." *China Security* 4, no. 1 (Winter 2008).

Dormandy, Xenia. "Is India, or Will It Be, a Responsible International Stakeholder?" *International Security* (Summer 2007).

Gvosdev, Nikolas. "Parting with Illusions: Developing a Realistic Approach to Relations with Russia." Cato Policy Analysis no. 611, February 29, 2008.

Kerr, Paul K. "U.S. Nuclear Cooperation with India: Issues for Congress." Congressional Research Service Report RL33016, April 23, 2008.

Kurlantzick, Joshua. *Charm Offensive: How China's Soft Power Is Transforming the World.* New Haven, CT: Yale University Press, 2007.

Lieven, Anatol. "To Russia with Realism." *American Conservative,* March 26, 2007.

Shirk, Susan L. *China: Fragile Superpower.* New York: Oxford University Press, 2007.

—Prepared by Ted Galen Carpenter and Justin Logan

54. East Asian Security Commitments

Policymakers should

- terminate, within three years, all defense treaties with South Korea and the Philippines, and withdraw all American military units from those countries by that deadline;
- rescind, within three years, the informal commitment to defend Taiwan;
- continue the policy of being willing to sell Taiwan conventional weapon systems;
- withdraw all ground forces from Japan within two years;
- reassess whether to continue stationing any air and naval units in Japan; and
- immediately commence discussions with Japan about replacing the U.S.-Japan security treaty with a more informal cooperative security arrangement.

The United States has formal "mutual" defense treaties with Japan, South Korea, and the Philippines, all established during the initial decade of the cold war. Washington also has an implicit commitment to defend Taiwan. That commitment is contained in the 1979 Taiwan Relations Act, which Congress passed at the time the Carter administration recognized the People's Republic of China as the legitimate government of that country. The TRA pledge to sell Taiwan weapons of a defensive nature and to regard any coercion by Beijing to compel Taiwan to reunify with the mainland as a grave breach of the peace replaced the formal defense treaty that Washington had maintained with Taipei.

All those defense commitments have a musty, obsolete quality. They were established at a time when America's allies (in reality, security clients) were poor nations that would have been hard-pressed to defend themselves against any capable adversary. Moreover, the United States undertook defense obligations in East Asia at a time when that region appeared to be a crucial theater in the overall struggle against international communism.

That context has changed beyond recognition in the 21st century. Japan is one of the leading economic powers in the world, and South Korea and Taiwan are among the "Asian Tiger" economic success stories. The Philippines has lagged, but even that country is not as weak and vulnerable as it appeared in the late 1940s or early 1950s. And while South Korea and Taiwan still confront threats to their independence (North Korea and China, respectively), those parochial quarrels do not have the kind of broader strategic significance to the United States that might justify extending security guarantees. To be blunt, with the partial exception of its alliance with Japan, America still incurs major risks for very modest—and largely theoretical—benefits. The defense treaties with South Korea and the Philippines as well as the informal security obligation to Taiwan should be terminated. Even the defense treaty with Japan needs to be reassessed.

South Korea

The U.S. alliance with the Republic of Korea (South Korea) is a cold war anachronism. Washington should have weaned Seoul from the U.S. security bottle years ago. When the security treaty went into effect in 1954, South Korea was a war-ravaged hulk that confronted not only a heavily armed North Korea, but a North Korea strongly backed by both Moscow and Beijing. Under those circumstances, it would have been virtually impossible for South Korea to provide for its own defense. Washington had just waged a bloody war to prevent a communist conquest of the country, and given the cold war context, U.S. leaders regarded the Korean Peninsula as a crucial theater in the effort to contain the power of the Soviet Union and China. Therefore, they deemed it necessary to keep the ROK as a security client. Most South Koreans were extremely grateful for the U.S. protection.

Those circumstances bear no resemblance to the situation in the 21st century. Today, South Korea has twice the population and an economy *40 times* larger than that of its communist nemesis. The ROK is an economic powerhouse with the world's 13th-largest economy, and South Korean firms are competitive in a host of high-tech industries. Meanwhile, North Korea is one of the world's economic basket cases, and there have even been major episodes of famine in that pathetic country. Moscow and Beijing have major economic ties with the ROK and regard North Korea as an embarrassment. They have no interest whatever in backing another bid by Pyongyang to forcibly reunify the peninsula.

Under those conditions, South Korea should certainly be able to defend itself. Yet instead of building military forces sufficient to protect its security, Seoul remains heavily dependent on the United States for key aspects of its defense. Despite its proximity to North Korea, the ROK spends a paltry 2.77 percent of its gross domestic product on the military—less than does the United States, half a world away and located in a peaceful region. There is simply no justification for continuing that free ride.

Equally unpleasant is the growing lack of gratitude on the part of many South Koreans for the exertions the United States has made over the decades on behalf of their security. Public opinion polls show that younger South Koreans regard the United States as a more serious threat than North Korea. Indeed, many South Koreans now believe that Washington is the principal obstacle to better relations with North Korea and to eventual political reunification. The current government of President Lee Myung-bak may be less overtly anti-American than that of his predecessor, but that sentiment has scarcely diminished among the general population.

The ongoing North Korean nuclear crisis illustrates the drawbacks associated with Washington's insistence on micromanaging the security affairs of East Asia. In a normal international system, the East Asian frontline states would be taking the lead in formulating policies to deal with North Korea instead of expecting the United States to negotiate directly with Pyongyang and produce an agreement acceptable to them all. They would decide what risks they were willing to incur to compel Pyongyang to abandon its nuclear program—or in the alternative, whether they were prepared to live with a nuclear-armed North Korea.

That is not to say that the United States has no interests at stake regarding North Korea's nuclear ambitions. Washington understandably wants to prevent the proliferation of nuclear weapons—in East Asia and elsewhere. There is also legitimate concern that North Korea might eventually become a nuclear arms peddler, supplying bombs to other anti-American regimes—and perhaps even to terrorist organizations. Pyongyang's apparent assistance to Syria regarding nuclear technology highlighted the proliferation problem.

Nevertheless, the danger a nuclear-armed North Korea could pose to the United States is more remote and theoretical than the danger to North

Korea's neighbors. Their risk exposure is inherent—imposed by the realities of geography. Even if North Korea acquired only a few nuclear warheads and only modestly increased the range of its current delivery systems, it would pose a plausible threat to the security of South Korea, Japan, China, and Russia.

Conversely, America's risk exposure is largely discretionary. The principal reason Washington is obsessed with the North Korean problem is the presence of more than 27,000 U.S. troops in South Korea. Because of those forces, America has put itself, quite literally, on the frontlines of a potentially explosive crisis.

That approach is precisely the opposite of the course Washington ought to adopt. The new administration should immediately begin to reduce America's risk exposure by ordering a phased withdrawal of U.S. forces from South Korea. Washington should also indicate to the East Asian powers that they bear primary responsibility for dealing with the problem of North Korea's nuclear program, since they have the most at stake.

It is time, indeed it is long past time, to insist that South Korea manage its own security affairs. The United States has drawn down its military forces stationed in that country from approximately 37,000 to 27,000 over the past six years. Washington should implement a complete withdrawal within the next three years and terminate the misnamed mutual security treaty. That commitment was designed for an entirely different era. There is no need and very little benefit today for keeping South Korea as a security client.

Taiwan

Washington's security commitment to Taiwan is more vague and informal than the mutual defense treaty with South Korea. It is contained in provisions of the Taiwan Relations Act, which Congress passed in 1979 in response to the Carter administration's decision to end diplomatic relations with the Republic of China (which still claimed to be the legitimate government of the mainland as well as Taiwan) and recognize the People's Republic of China. The TRA commits the United States to provide defensive arms to Taiwan and to regard any attempt by Beijing to use military coercion against Taiwan as a "grave breach of the peace." That commitment falls short of a pledge to intervene with U.S. forces, but it implies as much.

Washington has implemented its policy regarding Taiwan with an approach that experts have described as "dual deterrence" or "strategic ambiguity." The logic of strategic ambiguity is that the Taiwanese will remain uncertain about the extent of U.S. protection—especially if Taipei engages in provocative conduct. Conversely, Beijing will believe that using military force against the island is too risky, because the United States would probably intervene. Supposedly, this mutual uncertainty should lead to caution and restraint on both sides of the Taiwan Strait.

The chief problem with that policy is that it assumes both governments will interpret Washington's posture in exactly the way U.S. officials desire. Unfortunately, events suggest that Taipei and Beijing may be reading American policy in precisely the opposite way from what U.S. leaders intend. The Taiwanese seem increasingly confident that the United States would never abandon a fellow democracy. China, at the same time, seems ever more skeptical that the United States would disrupt the entire global economy and risk war with a nuclear-armed China just to back a small, upstart secessionist island. Those developments are a warning bell in the night about the danger of miscalculation.

From the standpoint of basic prudence, the defense commitment to Taiwan is unwise. As China's economic leverage and military capabilities grow, it becomes increasingly problematic and dangerous for the United States to act as Taiwan's protector. As noted in Chapter 53, Beijing is not likely to tolerate Taiwan's de facto independence indefinitely, even if future governments in Taipei avoid adopting the kinds of assertive, pro-independence policies that the government of President Chen Shui-bian pursued between 2000 and 2008. The best strategy for the United States would be to limit its risk exposure by confining its role to selling arms to Taipei. The implied obligation contained in the Taiwan Relations Act to intervene with U.S. forces in the event of a crisis should be rescinded.

The Philippines

The United States maintains a defense treaty with the Philippines that was established following the end of Manila's status as a U.S. colony. Until the early 1990s, the United States also maintained a major naval base and a major air base in that country. That direct military presence came to an end when ash from a volcanic eruption rendered the air base unusable and an increasingly nationalistic Philippine government declined to renew the lease to the naval base.

Manila invited Washington to send troops again following the 9/11 terrorist attacks to help combat an Islamic militant organization that had ties to al Qaeda. U.S. forces have continued that mission in a low-key fashion in the intervening years. Public sentiment in the Philippines seems divided about military ties to the United States. Philippine leaders appreciate the assistance against Islamic opponents, but the population does not seem eager to see a new, large-scale U.S. military presence, despite some worries about China's long-term ambitions.

The alliance with the Philippines has even less relevance to genuine American interests in the 21st century than does the alliance with South Korea. Even during the cold war, it was a stretch to argue that the Philippines was central to the struggle against Soviet imperialism. The U.S. bases in the Philippines were "useful" largely to facilitate dubious military ventures in East Asia—especially the war in Vietnam.

Absent the cold war strategic context, there is even less justification for a defense relationship with Manila. It is certainly not in America's best interest to become a party to the murky domestic struggles between the Philippine government and restless Muslim minorities. And although some U.S. Navy and Air Force leaders appear to hunger for the reestablishment of major bases in the Philippines as part of a containment strategy directed against China, that too would be both unnecessary and unwise. The United States should promptly terminate the defense treaty with Manila.

Japan

Washington's most significant security relationship in East Asia is the alliance with Japan. That relationship is enshrined in a mutual defense treaty, first signed in 1951 and later updated. The United States also maintains a substantial air, naval, and marine presence in Japan, and American ships make extensive use of port facilities in the country.

Although U.S. leaders gradually came to view Japan as a useful junior partner in the cold war containment strategy against the Soviet Union, the emphasis was always on "junior." Indeed, American officials seemed to regard the alliance as much a means to prevent the emergence of independent Japanese military power as to thwart communist ambitions in East Asia. As late as 1991, the commander of U.S. Marine forces in Japan stated publicly that the U.S. military presence was the "cork in the bottle" when it came to constraining Japan from developing (and possibly using) military power on an independent basis. Experts and pundits, such as *Washington Post* columnist Charles Krauthammer, fretted that without

Washington's restraining influence, the Japanese navy might grow strong enough to one day prowl the Strait of Malacca. With lingering memories of imperial Japan in the 1930s, they wanted to forestall a resurgence of Japanese influence.

For its part, Japan seemed content with being America's very junior security partner. The relationship spared Tokyo from spending more than a paltry 0.8 to 0.9 percent of its gross domestic product on the military, and equally important, it spared Japanese leaders from addressing security issues that would be contentious among domestic political constituencies and would heighten diplomatic tensions with neighboring countries that still seemed obsessed with Imperial Japan's depredations during the 1930s and 1940s.

In the past decade, though, attitudes have shifted among the governing elites in both Japan and the United States. It began to dawn on Japanese political and military leaders that America's interests and policy preferences might not always be the same as Japan's, and that Tokyo could not always count on Washington to adequately protect Japan's vital interests. That point was driven home in 1998 when North Korea conducted a missile test that included overflying Japan. U.S. leaders responded with a casualness that bordered on indifference, much to the annoyance and frustration of their Japanese counterparts. Not long after that episode, Japan decided to develop its own system of spy satellites instead of relying on the United States for the necessary data. More generally, sentiment has gradually grown in Japan for a more assertive security policy.

American attitudes have also become more favorable to the prospect of a more active role for Japan in the security arena. The report of the so-called Armitage Commission (named after future Deputy Secretary of State Richard Armitage) in the late 1990s proposed that Japan play a more robust security role, albeit still in a supporting capacity to the United States. Not coincidentally, Washington's policy regarding the U.S.-Japan alliance during the Bush administration seemed to adhere rather closely to those recommendations, quite possibly reflecting Secretary Armitage's influence.

Japan is an important security partner of the United States and should play a crucial role in the gradual emergence of a multipolar security environment in East Asia. Tokyo's position is especially pivotal if the United States does not want to be the only power standing in the way of eventual Chinese hegemony in that region. Despite underinvesting in defense, Japan has developed modern, capable naval and air forces, and

567

it is certainly capable of doing even more. Although Japan is relevant to important American interests in East Asia and beyond, we should not simply let the alliance operate as though it were on autopilot. It is time for a comprehensive review of every aspect of Washington's security relations with Tokyo.

We should especially move to terminate obsolete portions of that relationship. Most notably, that means withdrawing all U.S. ground forces from Japan. Most of those forces consist of Marine Corps units stationed in Okinawa. U.S. military bases occupy approximately 20 percent of the island's land mass, including some prime real estate, and the presence has long been a source of extreme irritation to the inhabitants. Keeping the marines there makes sense only if the United States intends to intervene with ground forces in a new Korean war or to wage a land war somewhere else in East Asia. Neither mission makes sense from the standpoint of genuine American interests. Those forces should be withdrawn immediately, and the bases closed.

The future disposition of U.S. air and naval forces is a more complex and difficult decision. Some forces should certainly be withdrawn, and many of them can be relocated to American possessions in the Central Pacific, especially Guam, without having a significant negative effect on U.S. military capabilities in that part of the world. But given the importance of East Asia, both strategically and economically, it is uncertain whether the United States should withdraw all its air and naval forces from Japan. That topic needs to be a crucial aspect of discussions about the future U.S.-Japan security relationship.

Those discussions also need to focus on whether the defense treaty should be retained in its current form. At the very least, Washington should insist that Tokyo now take the lead in addressing the security problems in East Asia instead of expecting the United States to continue its dominant role. It is possible that a more informal and flexible security relationship would serve both countries better than the formal alliance.

In any case, Washington's security commitments in East Asia need to be drastically pruned. The alliances with the Philippines and South Korea (to say nothing of the even more distant and irrelevant pact with Australia) should be abolished. Even before rescinding those treaties, the United States should withdraw all its military forces from such client states. Finally, the informal defense commitment to Taiwan must be eliminated. The alliance with Japan is in a different category since it has far greater relevance to legitimate American security interests. However, even that alliance should not be considered sacrosanct.

Suggested Readings

Bandow, Doug. *Foreign Follies: America's New Global Empire*. Washington: Xulon Press, 2006, chap. 5.

_____. "Instability in the Philippines: A Case Study for U.S. Disengagement." Cato Institute Foreign Policy Briefing no. 64, March 21, 2001.

Carpenter, Ted Galen. *Smart Power: Toward a Prudent Foreign Policy for America*. Washington: Cato Institute, 2008, chaps. 7–8.

Carpenter, Ted Galen, and Doug Bandow. *The Korean Conundrum: America's Troubled Relations with North and South Korea*. New York: Palgrave/Macmillan, 2004.

Logan, Justin, and Ted Galen Carpenter. "Taiwan's Defense Budget: How Taipei's Free Riding Risks War." Cato Institute Policy Analysis no. 600, September 13, 2007.

Oros, Andrew. *Normalizing Japan: Politics, Identity, and the Evolution of Security Practice*. Palo Alto, CA: Stanford University Press, 2008.

Preble, Christopher. "Two Normal Countries: Rethinking the U.S-Japan Strategic Relationship." Cato Institute Policy Analysis no. 566, April 18, 2006.

Samuels, Richard J. *Securing Japan: Tokyo's Grand Strategy and the Future of East Asia*. Ithaca, NY: Cornell University Press, 2007.

—Prepared by Ted Galen Carpenter

55. Transatlantic Relations

Policymakers should

- offer no security guarantees nor other implied defense commitments that they are unable to keep;
- recognize that our allies' limited capabilities, driven by demographic and budgetary constraints, but also a lack of political will, increase the risks and burdens on Americans;
- reorient policy away from the use of military force toward the attraction of American values and act to recover our lost moral authority; and
- commit to following the original transatlantic vision proclaimed in the Atlantic Charter, in particular the focus on reducing armaments as opposed to perpetuating American hegemony.

On August 14, 1941, President Franklin D. Roosevelt and British Prime Minister Winston Churchill issued the Atlantic Charter, in which they proclaimed their vision for the world following the defeat of Nazi Germany. It was an extremely idealistic statement, holding out the hope of a world in which "the crushing burden of armaments" would be removed. "All of the nations of the world," they insisted, "for realistic as well as spiritual reasons must come to the abandonment of the use of force." Following the United States' entry into the war, the Atlantic Charter became the basis of the Declaration by United Nations.

Unfortunately, the hopes for an enduring great alliance proved illusory. As relations between the United States, Great Britain, and the Soviet Union deteriorated, alternative security structures were sought. In 1948, the Western democracies created the North Atlantic Treaty Organization, which was designed to provide an American security guarantee to the threatened countries of Europe. The Soviet Union then created its own security organization, the Warsaw Pact, dividing Europe into two blocs.

To be sure, the balance of power was nothing new in Europe, but this balance had a clear ideological component. With NATO, the idea of a special transatlantic relationship was born, which has come to symbolize countries' sharing a common civilization and value system. Thus, when the cold war ended with the collapse of communism, questions emerged about NATO's future. How could the transatlantic community consolidate and expand the values of democracy, and how could it extend the security and stability that it had brought to Western Europe?

NATO Expansion

Two solutions presented themselves, and both were articulated by Václav Havel, the Czech dissident and playwright who emerged from the cold war as the president of his country. In a speech to the Polish Sejm and Senate in January 1990, Havel proposed abolishing both NATO and the Warsaw Pact so that "the process of pan-European integration could be finally set in motion." But with the formal collapse of the Warsaw Pact in July 1991, he changed his mind and called for dividing Europe along civilization lines. "It is tremendously important that NATO should gradually start to embrace the sphere of civilization that it is called on to defend," he told the Congress of Prague in 1996, "an imperative that includes enlarging by admitting those countries that have belonged to the European-American tradition through their entire history." Russia, Havel explained, could not be admitted into NATO because it belonged to a different civilization.

Those who have not understood Russia's opposition to NATO expansion need to reflect on these words. We now take for granted the West's victory in the cold war, and explain it as a triumph of our skill and power. Russians, on the other hand, see it as an acknowledgment that communism did not work. From their point of view, they ended the cold war and dissolved their empire as a testament of their desire to reunite the world so that it would no longer be divided between communists and capitalists, between East and West.

In the 1990s, the Russians seethed as NATO expanded, but there was little they could do. In recent years, however, their opposition to further expansion has begun to resonate in some NATO countries. Significantly, at the Bucharest summit in April 2008, NATO did not adopt a membership action plan for Ukraine and Georgia, despite the strong support of President George W. Bush. This division reflects underlying strains affecting the transatlantic community as a result of conflicts that are not going as well as expected.

The Strain of War

Following the September 11, 2001, terrorist attack, NATO rallied in support of the United States. For the first time in its history, it invoked Article 5—the famous pledge that an attack on one is an attack on all. When the cold war ended, the mantra for NATO's enduring survival was that it now had to act "out of area," and the war in Afghanistan seemed the perfect venue to prove its continued worth.

But the war has turned out to be more difficult than expected. NATO members anticipated that they would be helping with postwar reconstruction and were unprepared for intense military operations. As casualties have increased, public support has eroded.

Europeans are also increasingly uneasy with the way the United States is conducting the overall "war on terror." "In the artistic imagination of Europeans, America has become associated more with servitude than with freedom," Dominique Moisi, a prominent French commentator, observed in summer 2008. "In the Berlin Opera's latest version of Beethoven's 'Fidelio,' the prisoners seemed to be coming out of Guantanamo prison," he stated. Even the British, America's most loyal allies, are upset that they were misled about American use of their territory—notably the island of Diego Garcia in the Indian Ocean, where the United Kingdom grants the United States permission to operate a military base—in the program of "extraordinary rendition."

In addition, American power has come into question, symbolized by the decline of the dollar against the euro. To the east, Russia has staged a remarkable comeback, and it is making its presence in Europe felt. When the cold war ended, the United States dominated Europe as Russia withdrew from its empire. But American power is now stretched, and the Russians are making it clear that the age of American triumphalism is over.

The Return of Russia

During the 1990s, the United States tried to consolidate its power in Eurasia by influencing the construction of oil and gas pipelines, especially around the Caspian Sea. "The world runs on oil and gas, and those who control it wield commercial and geopolitical power," Sheila Heslin, the director for Russian, Ukrainian, and Eurasian affairs at the National Security Council in 1995 and 1996, explained in the *New York Times* in November 1997. "The United States simply cannot afford to allow Russia and Iran to dominate the energy resources of the Caspian, with the enormous political leverage that would confer in the region and even in Europe," she added.

For Russians who thought their peaceful conclusion of the cold war meant the West would accept them as a partner, that attitude was infuriating. After Vladimir Putin became president, they began to respond to the American challenge, in effect telling Washington: "You want to play pipeline politics? Fine, let's play pipeline politics. Let's see who can play this game better."

By 2008, it became obvious that Russia had outmaneuvered the United States. Rising oil prices and the Kremlin's squeezing out private owners of energy resources enabled Russia to use those resources for political advantage with both eastern and western Europe. American officials may lament Moscow's ability to divide Europe, but the Bush administration exploited the divisions of old and new Europe in the buildup to the Iraq War, and the Russians seem equally inclined to play power politics when they believe it will serve their interests.

Nor is energy the only leverage that Russia can employ to sow division. No longer confident that it can supply its forces in Afghanistan via Pakistan, NATO has turned to Russia for help. At the Bucharest summit, Russia agreed to allow its territory to be used for supplying NATO forces, but it expects its interests to be respected in return. As President Dmitry Medvedev put it in a major speech in Berlin in June 2008: "Does it make sense to jeopardize this cooperation for the sake of a bloc politics approach that continues by inertia?"

In other words, if the United States insists on further NATO expansion or doing other things Moscow believes jeopardizes its security, the Russians could refuse to allow NATO to transit its territory. In that case, access to Afghanistan would depend entirely on the reliability of the Pakistani supply route. If that route is jeopardized, NATO's position in Afghanistan will be threatened, increasing the odds of failure. Would public opinion in America's allies blame Russia for this unexpected outcome, or would it blame the United States? If the latter, it is difficult to see how NATO could survive, at least in any meaningful way.

Empty Promises

In Falls Church, Virginia, there is a shopping center dominated by two large flags: an American flag and a South Vietnamese flag. Shortly after the founding of NATO, which formally committed the United States to the security of Western Europe, the United States made a similar promise to countries in Southeast Asia. South Vietnam was one of the Southeast Asia Treaty Organization signatories, and the United States fought a war, and tens of thousands of Americans lost their lives, in an effort to honor that commitment. But the effort failed. And that flag now flies in Virginia because it can no longer fly in Vietnam.

After the failure in Vietnam, the United States rebuilt its armed forces. Their dramatic success in the 1991 Gulf War while the Warsaw Pact disintegrated gave rise to the idea of American hegemony. American power, it seemed, was irresistible.

But the wars in Iraq and Afghanistan have stretched American power to its limits. As the chairman of the Joint Chiefs of Staff, Admiral Michael Mullen, has repeatedly emphasized, troop levels in Afghanistan depend on troop levels in Iraq: an increase in one requires a decrease in the other. Efforts to encourage the allies to contribute more troops, notably at the Bucharest summit, have been disappointing. Indeed, some of the most loyal allies are similarly stretched.

Significantly, it is going to be difficult to address this shortfall by increasing resources. The U.S. armed forces have met recruiting goals, albeit with some shortfalls, but in part by revising rules that otherwise would have excluded candidates who are now eligible for service. However, the number of high school graduates is peaking and will decline until 2015, which should make for a more challenging recruiting environment, especially if the armed forces attempt to expand.

Yet the challenges facing recruitment in the United States are trivial compared with those facing its major NATO allies. As Table 55.1 demonstrates, the recruitment pool (youth cohort) is flat to declining among the major European alliance members, with the notable exception of Turkey. In view of these realities, it is difficult to imagine how NATO can maintain its force levels, which are already proving inadequate for dealing with out-of-area challenges.

Moreover, even if the other NATO members managed to fill their ranks, there is the question of financing the armed forces. Many NATO members devote less than 2 percent of their gross domestic product to defense (see Table 55.2), and future budgetary pressures will make it even more difficult for them to meet that modest objective. There is a great danger, therefore, that America's NATO allies will allow their military capabilities to erode still further, and become permanent free riders on the backs of American taxpayers.

Table 55.1
Demographic Trends among Major U.S. Allies Showing Cumulative Change between 2005 and 2050

Country	Total Population	Working Age (Age 20–64)	Youth Cohort (Age 15–24)
United States	40%	28%	23%
Turkey	51%	48%	8%
Canada	28%	12%	-3%
France	13%	0%	-1%
United Kingdom	8%	-1%	-12%
Spain	-4%	-25%	-39%
Italy	-14%	-29%	-31%
Germany	-16%	-27%	-37%

SOURCE: *World Population Prospects* (New York: United Nations, 2007).

Table 55.2
Comparison of Defense Budgets, 2006

Country	Total Defense Expenditures (millions of U.S.$)	Spending per Capita (in U.S.$)	Defense Spending as Percentage of GDP
United States	617,100	2,049	4.68
France	54,000	884	2.41
United Kingdom	55,440	912	2.31
Germany	37,770	458	1.31
Italy	30,630	527	1.66
Turkey	11,630	163	2.86
Spain	14,410	356	1.18
Netherlands, The	9,900	597	1.50
Greece	7,280	680	2.36
Norway	5,010	1,083	1.49
Belgium	4,420	425	1.12

SOURCE: *The Military Balance 2008* (London: International Institute for Strategic Studies, 2008).

That is the reality of the transatlantic future: it is written in the numbers. Given that Americans are correctly unwilling to shoulder those burdens, a different arrangement must be sought.

Toward a New Relationship

When the cold war was ending, Soviet President Mikhail Gorbachev spoke of creating a "common European home." In his Berlin speech,

Medvedev spoke of supplanting that vision with what amounted to a common transatlantic home. "The future world order is directly linked to the future of Europe, the whole Euro-Atlantic region, and therefore the future of European civilization in its entirety," he said. "Atlanticism as a sole historical principle has already had its day. We need to talk today about unity between the whole Euro-Atlantic area from Vancouver to Vladivostok," he added.

Will the Western powers accept this vision? If they do not, the world will divide again. Russia has not been sitting still, creating the Shanghai Cooperation Organization with China and increasingly focusing on reinforcing ties with Brazil, China, and India. At the 2008 G-8 summit, the leaders of the four countries met on the sidelines. Russia seemed to be sending a message: if we are excluded from the G-8, as some now threaten, we have other options.

Unfortunately, the August 2008 conflict between Russia and Georgia complicates relations between Russia and NATO. Suspicions on both sides are growing, and the prospect of a new cold war cannot be ruled out.

That would be a tragedy, and we need to do all we can to avoid it. We need to stress that transatlantic values are those of the Atlantic Charter: that they are intended to define goals for humanity, rather than divide the world into different civilizations.

But that means we must come to a better understanding of the relationship between our power and our values. Our efforts to use our power have run into unexpected difficulty, and in the process our devotion to our values has come into question. In its 2007 report on transatlantic trends, the German Marshall Fund reported that only 36 percent of Europeans viewed American leadership as "desirable," compared with 64 percent in 2002.

Can that trend be reversed? Two things would be required. First, we must be more realistic about our capabilities. We should not make promises we are unable to keep; we should not make promises of protection if we have no serious capability of providing that protection. One Vietnam is enough.

Second, we should remember Lord Acton's famous admonition that "power tends to corrupt, and absolute power corrupts absolutely." Global hegemony is not only unattainable, it is undesirable, for it will corrupt our democratic values. U.S. policymakers must choose between America as the dominant power within a military alliance supposedly capable of imposing its will anywhere on the globe, and America as "the city on the hill."

A good place to start would be by commemorating the original proclamation of the Atlantic Charter. Even as they faced great military danger, Churchill and Roosevelt knew that security could not be permanently ensured merely by accumulating armaments. The 70th anniversary of the charter in 2011 should provide a fitting opportunity to review how the transatlantic relationship began and where it should be headed.

Suggested Readings

Carpenter, Ted Galen. "The Bush Administration's Security Strategy: Implications for Transatlantic Relations." *Cambridge Review of International Affairs* 16, no. 3 (October 2003).

Carpenter, Ted Galen, and Barbara Conry. *NATO Enlargement: Illusions and Reality.* Washington: Cato Institute, 1998.

Eisenhower, Susan, ed. *NATO at Fifty: Perspectives on the Future of the Transatlantic Alliance.* Washington: Center for Political and Strategic Studies, 1999.

Kaplan, Lawrence S. *NATO United, NATO Divided: The Evolution of an Alliance.* Westport, CT: Praeger, 2004.

Kober, Stanley. "Cracks in the Foundation: NATO's New Troubles." Cato Institute Policy Analysis no. 608, January 15, 2008.

Layne, Christopher. *Peace of Illusions: American Grand Strategy from 1940 to the Present.* Ithaca, NY: Cornell University Press, 2006.

—Prepared by Stanley Kober

56. U.S. Policy in the Balkans

> **Policymakers should**
>
> - support the transfer of peacekeeping duties in Kosovo to the European Union;
> - mandate the withdrawal of all U.S. ground forces from the Balkans by the end of 2009;
> - eliminate foreign aid for nation-building in Bosnia, Kosovo, and elsewhere in the region;
> - allow Serbs within Bosnia to seek greater autonomy or independence;
> - suspend recognition of an independent Kosovo and promote genuine negotiations between Kosovo and Serbia;
> - support liberalization of economic relations with and political liberalization within Serbia, but end meddling in Serbia's elections;
> - leave developments in the Balkans to the people of the Balkans, backed by the EU;
> - shift responsibility for Balkan security issues to the EU and individual European nations; and
> - establish a future policy of nonintervention in Balkan affairs.

For more than a decade and a half, the Balkans have been a major priority of U.S. foreign policy. Washington initiated military action in Bosnia and full-scale war against Serbia to redraw the Balkan map. The United States has also devoted billions of dollars and enormous diplomatic efforts to reengineering countries and territories to suit Washington's arbitrary preferences. Yet American interests in the Balkans were (and remain) minimal at best. Absent a cold war environment that could turn a local conflict into a global conflagration, the Balkans matter much more to the European Union than to America, and not much even to the EU.

579

Moreover, Washington's policy has been fundamentally misguided, seeking to impose a Western vision of liberal pluralism and federalism on peoples still inclined to order their politics along ethnic lines. The United States, followed a bit more reluctantly by the Europeans, has sought to manage Balkan affairs with little concern for Russian interests, including Moscow's goals of ensuring security in the region and gaining international respect for its position. Washington's Balkan policy was one of many issues that helped spawn the Kremlin's military move into Georgia.

It comes as no surprise, then, that Washington's policy in the Balkans has produced disappointing results. Bosnia remains a largely failed state, run by diktat through the EU a decade after its creation; threatened by internal ethnic separatism; and lacking a viable, independent economic base. Kosovo declared its independence with the Bush administration's support, but has stalled at 47 diplomatic recognitions, and only 20 of 27 EU members.

Serbia is governed by a coalition that is pro-Western in the sense that it is committed to seeking entry into the EU, but opposes an independent Kosovo and that it survives only with the sufferance of Slobodan Milosevic's old Socialist Party. The largest opposition party is the hard-line Serbian Radical Party, formally headed by Vojislav Seselj, currently on trial in The Hague for war crimes. Ethnic tension remains a dangerous undercurrent in Macedonia, where nationalism continues to permeate elections. The region is still divided ethnically, politically, and religiously. While a violent breakdown of the present order seems unlikely, it is not impossible, and even an upsurge in tensions would threaten to pull the United States back into conflicts largely irrelevant to its own security.

The end of the cold war should have led to a rethinking of America's role in the North Atlantic Treaty Organization. After all, the quintessential anti-Soviet alliance had few obvious duties with the breakup of the Soviet Union and dissolution of the Warsaw Pact. However, "out-of-area activities" became the new watchword for the alliance. The Balkans were one of those areas, and policing that region turned into a justification for expanding the alliance and increasing U.S. military commitments. The aftermath of 9/11 has provided a second chance to reconsider U.S. policy. Washington is overburdened with two wars, Afghanistan and Iraq, while continuing to subsidize the defense of populous and prosperous states in Asia and Europe. The United States should begin prioritizing its foreign and military policies by turning responsibility for the Balkans over to Europe. Even if the EU and individual European nations decide to do nothing, that is a decision that, given the fact that the Balkans are far more relevant to European than American security, Washington should respect.

Peacekeeping Operations in the Balkans

The U.S. role in Balkan peacekeeping has been steadily ebbing, with American forces withdrawn from Bosnia and Macedonia, and reduced in Kosovo. The remaining 1,300 soldiers in the latter should be withdrawn forthwith. The Balkan region and the EU have accommodated the steady drawdown and can take over to replace America's final contingent. Although the European states are notable for creating large but largely ineffective militaries, with about 1.7 million personnel in uniform—not counting Turkey, also a member of NATO—the Europeans can come up with another 1,300 troops.

It is not enough to bring those soldiers home, though. The United States must inform its European partners that Washington will be participating in no more Balkan peacekeeping expeditions. America's current priorities include ending the occupation of Iraq, salvaging the increasingly shaky mission in Afghanistan, and strengthening global cooperation against al Qaeda and other transnational terrorist organizations. Washington continues to formally guarantee the security of South Korea and Japan and informally guarantee Taiwan's de facto independence, most obviously against a growing China. Some analysts and politicians would have America confront a reinvigorated Russia. Even if the next administration more sensibly begins shedding rather than acquiring obligations against China and Russia, the United States will remain very busy, far busier than the Europeans and with much more serious security work to do elsewhere.

In fact, abandoning any pretense that the United States has an obligation to patrol the Balkans would set a precedent for Washington policymakers to reconsider security guarantees elsewhere in Europe—and in Asia as well. Although the recent Russian-Georgian war has set the eastern Europeans on edge, they should look to the rest of Europe rather than to America for their security.

Although one can imagine the complaints from Europeans that would accompany U.S. disengagement, the process would be salutary for them. For years, leading European officials have promoted a separate European defense and foreign policy. One reason for the EU consolidation proposed by the Lisbon Treaty is to create a continental framework for just such a system. French President Nicolas Sarkozy made creation of an effective EU rapid-deployment force one of the priorities of his recent EU presidency. Yet those efforts have routinely come to naught, since there was no pressing need for the Europeans to shift funds from expensive welfare states to seemingly unnecessary militaries. With the American safety net withdrawn, the Europeans would have to make a more rigorous and honest calculation of their security requirements—starting in the Balkans.

Bosnia

One of the unfortunate developments of the immediate post–cold war period was the bloody disintegration of Yugoslavia. There was more than a little blame, and more than a few atrocities, to spread around. Rather than opening the way to a negotiated, if complicated, redrawing of political boundaries, the Western allies insisted that the new states created out of the former Yugoslavia stay intact, forcing the inhabitants to slug it out for control. Bosnia soon became the arena of the worst turmoil.

The 1995 Dayton Agreement implementing a cease-fire called for the creation of a unitary Bosnian state, within which the Bosnian-Croatian Federation and Bosnian-Serb Republic could exercise substantial autonomy. The allies essentially created a protectorate, in which the Office of the High Representative ran the territory like an imperial governor of old. The result has been ugly. There is little self-sustaining economic growth, as statist economic policies discourage entrepreneurship and business creation; Bosnia has been ranked 121 in the world on economic freedom, and well below average on business freedom, government size, property rights, corruption, and labor freedom. The West has poured billions of dollars into its nation-building project, but even as $5.1 billion was being "invested" in Bosnia, an astounding $1 billion was being looted.

Political advances, too, have been slow. Freedom House rates Bosnia on a scale of 1 (best) to 7 (worst), giving it an overall democracy score of 4.11 in 2008, only a modest uptick from 5.42 in 1999. Bosnia remains particularly deficient in governance, independent media, and corruption. Elections have usually been dominated by those most adept at playing ethnic politics, resulting in frequent interventions by the high representative to overturn the people's choices. Indeed, most of the allied high representatives gloried in the exercise of their power. Wolfgang Petritsch announced that he "did not hesitate" to use his authority "to impose legislation and dismiss officials."

The Bosnian Serbs have guarded their autonomy most jealously, refusing to integrate their police force with that of the federation. In 2007, the International Crisis Group said that allied policy in Bosnia was "in disarray'' and reported a long list of unfinished reforms. The decision by the United States and a majority of the EU to recognize the independence of Kosovo in February 2008 has led to increased Bosnian Serb interest in independence. Serb leader Milorad Dodik has threatened to hold a referendum on the issue, and former high representative Paddy Ashdown warns that ''the division of Bosnia that was [war crimes suspect Radovan Karadzic's] dream is now more likely than at any time since he became a fugitive.''

Indeed, it is hard to see how Bosnia will work as a real country in anything but the very long term, if then. Its people do not view it as a nation; many, if not most, Croats and Serbs feel more loyalty to neighboring nation-states dominated by their own ethnic groups. The lessons Bosnians have learned from the ''international community'' have not been individual liberty, economic freedom, and political democracy, but top-down, unaccountable, outside rule. Although the allied occupation was able to stop widespread violence and killing, it could not kindle feelings of national comradeship.

Moreover, whatever Bosnia's future, it is of little relevance to the United States. Exactly why Washington should care, let alone insist, that Bosnia's Croats and Serbs remain within a country called Bosnia has never been explained. If the Europeans believe this to be an important goal, then let them pursue what amounts to a colonial project. It is not in America's interest to do so, whether with troops, money, or even diplomacy.

Kosovo

Washington's decision to intervene in 1999 in one of the smaller of many violent conflicts around the globe—a far more violent insurgency then raged in Turkey, for instance, but the United States actually helped arm Ankara in its brutal campaign against the Kurds—had no logical basis. Allied occupation policy has been similarly flawed.

Once the allies defenestrated Serb security personnel, there was no chance that the majority ethnic Albanians in Kosovo would return to Serbian rule. However, exactly what Kosovo would become and what its geographic boundaries should be were not as obvious: despite brutal ''ethnic cleansing'' by the victorious ethnic Albanians after the war, Serbs remained in the majority north of the Iber River, centered on the city of Mitrovica. An obvious compromise based on partition was a possibility, but was ruled out by the allies, encouraging the Albanians to be intransigent and demand independence.

Thus, while formal negotiations ensued, they were doomed to fail, since the ethnic Albanians knew they would receive everything they desired by simply saying no to anything Belgrade proposed. After ensuring an impotent negotiating process, the United States and leading EU states declared that independence had become a practical necessity. In February 2008, the United States helped engineer Kosovo's declaration of independence, legally amputating about 15 percent of Serbia's total territory. Serbia rejected the move, and Russia blocked approval by the UN Security Council. All but one political party in Belgrade attacked allied policy: the main issue in the ensuing parliamentary elections was whether to proceed with applying for EU membership while fighting to maintain control over Kosovo. The election yielded a narrow coalition in favor of the former.

U.S. policy maintained an otherworldly quality. American officials seemed genuinely bewildered by the Serbs' opposition to Kosovo's independence. Even as she worked to dismember Serbia, Secretary Condoleeza Rice asserted, "The United States takes this opportunity to reaffirm our friendship with Serbia." Apparently without realizing the absurdity of his remarks, President George W. Bush declared, "the Serbian people can know that they have a friend in America."

Kosovo has demonstrated even less aptitude for becoming an independent state, at least along European standards, than Bosnia. More than 200,000 Serbs, Roma, and others were forced out of the territory immediately after the allied "victory." Four years ago, another round of violence by ethnic Albanian mobs created more Serb casualties and deaths, along with the destruction of Serb homes, churches, and monasteries.

Freedom House gives Kosovo dismal ratings. In 2008, Kosovo earned an overall 5.21 democracy score, with individual ratings of between 4.0 and 5.75 for electoral process, civil society, independent media, governance, judicial independence, and corruption. Many indicators were no better than in 2004, when Kosovo's democracy score was 5.5.

In November 2007, the European Commission released a report on Kosovo that concluded that "some progress was made in consolidating government," but "working tools for an efficient government" still had "to be enhanced and fully applied." Unsurprisingly, given the level of criminal activity by former guerrillas, the commission reported that "corruption is still widespread and remains a major problem." Indeed, warned the commission: "Overall, little progress has been made in the promotion and enforcement of human rights. The [international] administration is not able to ensure the full implementation of human rights standards."

Since its independence declaration, Kosovo has amassed 47 recognitions, about the same meager number of states that recognize Western Sahara's independence from Morocco. Although Kosovo has more heavyweights, led by the United States and leading European states, in its corner, UN acceptance is impossible without Chinese and Russian approval, and even the role of the EU will remain controversial so long as seven members oppose independence. Indeed, the EU could be embarrassed by an adverse ruling by a recent International Court of Justice case filed by Serbia.

The EU is now seeking to take over policing duties in Kosovo from the UN, but its effort is opposed by Serbia and Russia. So long as Serbs in Kosovo's north resist integration with the ethnic Albanian administration based in Pristina, Kosovo will remain a fragile, incomplete state, only one demonstration away from renewed violence. And unless the allies are willing to forcibly suppress independent Serbian assemblies in Mitrovica— or back their forcible suppression by Albanians—partition will occur de facto if not de jure. Of course, no Western government would like the symbolism of using its military to suppress the self-determination of Serbs and force them to submit to a state from which most of their ethnic brethren were violently driven.

Washington should end the U.S. military mission and suspend its ill-considered recognition of Kosovo's independence. The U.S. government should then propose resumption of negotiations—without a preset outcome this time, however. The parties might still resist territorial compromise, but both would benefit from a formal, agreed-upon separation. For instance, partition at the Iber River would leave both sides dissatisfied but better off. Kosovo would win widespread acceptance and a seat in the United Nations. Serbia would preserve some of its territory in northern Kosovo. Washington should not insist on this outcome but should foster negotiations in which this outcome is possible.

Serbia

Politics in this remnant of the former Yugoslavia remain roiled by the Kosovo controversy. Helping to resolve that issue would be the finest service that Washington could perform to encourage a more liberal political environment in Belgrade. In the future, the United States should forswear open intervention in Serbian politics through government-funded institutes and other nongovernmental organizations. The United States should also reduce trade barriers to Serbian commerce, to encourage greater economic liberalization. Moreover, although EU membership is a decision for Serbia and the Europeans, Washington should offer its full blessings to the process.

Macedonia

This former Yugoslav republic suffered through its own ethnic Albanian insurgency, although greater integration of that ethnic minority, which makes up about one-quarter of the population, has at least temporarily ended most of the violence. However, serious political problems persist. Parliamentary elections in June 2008 led to a large majority by the governing coalition, which emphasized nationalism in its ongoing esoteric dispute with Greece over the name Macedonia. The contest was marred by violence and irregularities, cited by the Organization for Security and Cooperation in Europe. This electoral controversy provides a reminder that the insurgency might be in remission, but is not necessarily cured. And if Kosovo eventually succeeds as an independent state, it might create an even greater draw for ethnic Albanians, who remain spread throughout the region, including in Macedonia, the remainder of Serbia, Montenegro, Greece, and, of course, Albania itself.

Skopje remains locked in a bitter disagreement with Greece over its use of the name Macedonia. Treated as a frivolous objection by outsiders, the issue is viewed seriously in Athens and has been used to block Macedonia's membership in NATO. While the United States should encourage the two neighbors to settle the name issue, it should not further expand NATO into the Balkans, whether to Macedonia; Croatia and Albania, which have begun accession talks; Bosnia, which has initiated an Individual Partnership Action Plan; or Montenegro or Serbia, viewed as longer-term prospects. The region is not a security concern for America, and all these states would be security black holes, adding no notable military assets while bringing along a host of potential disputes and ancient hatreds. If the EU wishes to attempt to pacify the Balkans, it is welcome to do so, since it has more interests at stake.

Future U.S. Policy

Washington's insistence on intervening so deeply in a region that is not even of peripheral security interest to America never made sense. The violent breakup of Yugoslavia was tragic because of the violence, not because of the breakup. The United States should have stayed out. If anyone had an interest in attempting to manage Yugoslavia's dissolution, it was the EU, and if the Europeans didn't believe that objective to be worth military intervention, it certainly did not warrant American support.

Although it is always easier to get into than to get out of a geopolitical tar pit, Washington should take advantage of the region's relative peace today to extricate itself from the region—particularly by bringing home its remaining troops and cutting off aid funds. That doesn't mean the absence of any American involvement: the United States should reduce trade barriers to the Balkan states, conduct necessary intelligence operations in an area where terrorists may operate, and retain the option to strike militarily if necessary to destroy or disable terrorist organizations threatening American people or interests.

However, Washington should make clear to the Europeans that the Balkans are the first arena in which the EU nations need to take over responsibility for their own defense and the security of the continent. In return, the United States should promise not to hector or second-guess the Europeans. The Balkans have never been anything more than a peripheral interest for America. The United States no longer can afford—militarily, economically, or diplomatically—to make frivolous interests such as those in the Balkans a major feature of its foreign policy.

Suggested Readings

Bandow, Doug. *Foreign Follies.* Washington: Xulon Press, 2006, Chapter 6.

Carpenter, Ted Galen, ed. *NATO's Empty Victory: A Postmortem on the Balkan War.* Washington: Cato Institute, 2002.

———. "A New Era of Turbulence in the Balkans?" *Mediterranean Quarterly* 19, no. 3 (Summer 2008).

Chandler, David. *Bosnia: Faking Democracy after Dayton.* 2nd ed. London: Pluto Press, 2000.

Deliso, Christopher. *The Coming Balkan Caliphate: The Threat of Radical Islam to Europe and the West.* Westport, CT: Praeger, 2007.

Dempsey, Gary T., ed. *Exiting the Balkan Thicket.* Washington: Cato Institute, 2002.

Dempsey, Gary T., with Roger W. Fontaine. *Fool's Errands: America's Recent Encounters with Nation Building.* Washington: Cato Institute, 2001.

Judah, Tim. *Kosovo: War and Revenge.* New Haven, CT: Yale University Press, 2000.

Layne, Christopher, and Benjamin Schwarz. "Dubious Anniversary: Kosovo One Year Later." Cato Institute Policy Analysis no. 373, June 10, 2000.

—Prepared by Doug Bandow

57. Relations with Cuba

Congress should

- repeal the Cuban Liberty and Democratic Solidarity (Libertad, or Helms-Burton) Act of 1996,
- repeal the Cuban Democracy (Torricelli) Act of 1992,
- restore the policy of granting Cuban refugees political asylum in the United States,
- eliminate or privatize Radio and TV Marti,
- end all trade sanctions on Cuba and allow U.S. citizens and companies to visit and establish businesses in Cuba as they see fit, and
- move toward normalizing diplomatic relations with Cuba.

On July 26, 2006, Cuban dictator Fidel Castro was rushed to the hospital, leading to what many had yearned for for decades: Castro's official departure from power. He has since been replaced as president by his brother Raúl, who, while promising to defend the regime's socialist revolution, has introduced a limited set of economic reforms with the hope of injecting more vitality and efficiency into the island's dilapidated economy. Despite those measures, political repression still prevails in Cuba; political dissent is not tolerated, and opposition activists face constant harassment from the authorities.

Nobody can know for sure what lies ahead for Cuba in the short or medium term. It is possible that, upon the death of Fidel Castro, an emboldened populace or disaffected groups within Cuban society could bring about the sudden collapse of the regime. A more likely scenario foresees Raúl Castro replicating the "Chinese model" of economic liberalization and one-party rule that could be carried out for years. A far less likely possibility is that the status quo will change little in Cuba, notwithstanding the timid reforms introduced thus far.

In the face of such changing circumstances, U.S. policy toward Cuba has essentially remained the same. Washington insists that economic sanctions against the island will not be lifted unless a new regime allows free elections and releases all political prisoners. Accordingly, the Commission for Assistance to a Free Cuba, set up by President Bush in 2003, has provided a series of recommendations intended to "hasten democratic change in Cuba," some of which have resulted in tightening the sanctions imposed since the early 1960s.

Thus, the U.S. government is adamant in continuing a policy toward Cuba that has consistently failed to bring about a democratic transformation in the island.

A Cold War Relic

Sanctions against Cuba were first authorized under the Foreign Assistance Act of 1961, passed by the 87th Congress. In 1962, President John F. Kennedy issued an executive order implementing the trade embargo as a response to Fidel Castro's expropriation of American assets and his decision to offer the Soviet Union a permanent military base and an intelligence post just 90 miles off the coast of Florida at the height of the cold war. Castro's decision confirmed Cuba as the Soviet Union's main ally in the Western Hemisphere.

For three decades, Cuba was a threat to U.S. national security. Not only did Cuba export Marxist-Leninist revolutions to Third World countries (most notably, Angola and Nicaragua), but more importantly, it served as a base for Soviet intelligence operations and allowed Soviet naval vessels port access rights. However, with the collapse of the Soviet Union and the subsequent end of Soviet subsidies to Cuba in the early 1990s, that threat virtually ceased to exist. Trade sanctions against Cuba, however, were not lifted. The embargo was instead tightened in 1992 with the passage of the Cuban Democracy (Torricelli) Act, a bill that former president George H. W. Bush signed into law.

The justification for that act was not national security interests but the Castro regime's form of government and human rights abuses. That change of focus was reflected in the language of the act, the first finding of which was Castro's "consistent disregard for internationally accepted standards of human rights and for democratic values." In 1996, Congress passed the Cuban Liberty and Democratic Solidarity (Libertad) Act, a bill that President Clinton had threatened to veto but instead signed into law in the aftermath of the downing of two U.S. civilian planes by Cuban fighter jets in international airspace.

The Unintended Consequences of a Flawed Policy

The Libertad Act, better known as the Helms-Burton Act for its sponsors Sen. Jesse Helms (R-NC) and Rep. Dan Burton (R-IN), is an ill-conceived law. It grants U.S. citizens whose property was expropriated by Castro the right to sue in U.S. courts foreign companies and citizens "trafficking" in that property (Title III). That right—not granted to U.S. citizens who may have lost property in other countries—is problematic because it essentially extends U.S. jurisdiction to the results of events that occurred in foreign territory.

By imposing sanctions on foreign companies profiting from property confiscated by the Castro regime, the Helms-Burton Act seeks to discourage investment in Cuba. However, while Helms-Burton may have slowed investment in the island, U.S. allies (in particular Canada, Mexico, and members of the European Union) have not welcomed that attempt to influence their foreign policy by threat of U.S. sanctions. Consequently, they have repeatedly threatened to impose retaliatory sanctions and to take the United States to the World Trade Organization.

In May 1998, the Clinton administration and the European Union reached a tentative agreement that would exclude citizens of EU countries from Titles III and IV (denying entry visas to the executives of companies "trafficking" in confiscated property) of the Helms-Burton Act in exchange for guarantees from the EU not to subsidize investments in expropriated properties. The Bush administration continued the policy of repeatedly waiving Title III of the act. But because only Congress can repeal Titles III and IV, the possibility that the EU will impose retaliatory sanctions or take the United States to the WTO remains. That confrontation has risked poisoning U.S. relations with otherwise friendly countries that are far more important than Cuba to the economic well-being and security of the United States.

Moreover, the embargo continues to be the best—and now the only—excuse that the communist regime has for its failed policies. Cuban officials, who have estimated the cumulative cost of the embargo at more than $40 billion, incessantly condemn U.S. policies for causing the meager existence of their people, even though Cuba accepted more than $100 billion in subsidies and credits from the Soviet Union during their three-decade relationship and has received approximately $12 billion in

591

the form of subsidized oil from Venezuela's Hugo Chávez since 1999. Elizardo Sánchez Santa Cruz, a leading dissident in Cuba, has aptly summed up that strategy: "[Castro] wants to continue exaggerating the image of the external enemy which has been vital for the Cuban Government during decades, an external enemy which can be blamed for the failure of the totalitarian model implanted here."

Ironically, the embargo has also become somewhat of a U.S. security liability itself. A recent report by the Government Accountability Office points out that enforcing the embargo and travel ban diverts limited resources from homeland security that could be used to keep terrorists and criminals out of the United States. The GAO report warned that arrival inspections from Cuba intended to enforce the embargo are "straining Customs and Border Patrol's capacity to inspect other travelers according to its mission of keeping terrorists, criminals, and inadmissible aliens out of the country."

Undermining of Tyranny through Free Exchange

Aiming to increase agricultural productivity, Raúl Castro has introduced reforms such as transferring idle state-owned land to individual farmers and authorizing state stores to sell supplies and equipment directly to private producers. Even before those measures took place, the agricultural productivity of the nonstate sector (comprising cooperatives and small private farmers) was 25 percent higher than that of the state sector. As Cuban farmers increase their efficiency and productivity, normal trade ties with the United States would benefit them directly by opening up a market of 300 million consumers.

Ending the embargo could contribute to democracy in Cuba by empowering a nascent private sector that is increasingly independent of the government. Other recent reforms—such as new licenses for private bus and taxi operators and lifting bans on the consumption of electronic appliances—may encourage this development. As a Hoover Institution study pointed out: "In time, increasing amounts [of expanded tourism, trade, and investment] would go beyond the state, and although economics will not single-handedly liberate Cuba, it may contribute some to that end. This is so, in part, because the repressive Cubans within the state apparatus are subject to influences that can tilt their allegiances in positive ways."

Even though Cuba—unlike other communist countries with which the United States actively trades, such as China or Vietnam—has not undertaken substantial market reforms, an open U.S. trade policy is likely to be more subversive of its system than is an embargo. Proponents of the Cuban embargo vastly underestimate the extent to which increased foreign trade and investment can undermine Cuban communism even if that business is conducted with state entities.

Replacing the all-encompassing state with one that allows greater space for voluntary interaction requires strengthening elements of civil society, that is, groups not dependent on the state. That development is more likely to come about in an environment of increased interaction with outside groups than in an environment of increased isolation and state control. According to Philip Peters, vice president of the Lexington Institute, thousands of independent workers in Cuba "are dramatically improving their standard of living and supplying goods and services while learning the habits of independent actors in competitive markets." And because most of these workers are in the service industries (mostly restaurant and food service), they would greatly benefit from the presence of Americans visiting for business or pleasure. A recent study from the International Trade Commission calculates that between 550,000 and 1 million U.S. citizens would visit the island every year if the travel ban were lifted, compared with 171,000 that did so in 2006, mainly Cuban Americans visiting family.

Cuban officialdom appears to be well aware of the danger of increasing interaction between foreigners and nationals. For example, for many years Cuba's opening of its tourism industry to foreign investment was accompanied by measures that prevented ordinary Cubans from visiting foreign hotels and tourist facilities, a restriction that was only recently scrapped by Raúl Castro. As a result, Cubans came to resent their government for what was known as "tourism apartheid." In recent years, Cuban officials have also issued increased warnings against corruption, indicating the regime's fear that unofficial business dealings, especially with foreigners, may weaken allegiance to the government and may even create vested interests that favor more extensive market openings.

Cuba Must Determine Its Own Destiny

Perhaps the biggest shortcoming of U.S. policy toward Cuba is its false assumption that democratic capitalism can somehow be forcibly exported from Washington to Havana. That assumption is explicitly stated in the Helms-Burton Act, the first purpose of which is "to assist the Cuban people in regaining their freedom and prosperity, as well as in joining the

593

community of democratic countries that are flourishing in the Western Hemisphere.''

But the shift toward democratic capitalism that began in the Western Hemisphere almost three decades ago had little to do with Washington's efforts to export democracy. Rather, it had to do with Latin America's realization that previous policies and regimes had failed to provide self-sustaining growth and increasing prosperity. By the same token, the more recent rise of populism in some Latin-American countries is not the result of U.S. policy toward the region but a result of those countries' failure to implement a coherent set of mutually supportive market reforms. Those outcomes, again, depend entirely on Latin-American countries, not on the United States.

Unfortunately, the Bush administration's Commission for Assistance to a Free Cuba continues in Washington's meddling tradition. The administration adopted the commission's recommendation to tighten the embargo by restricting travel and remittances to the island even further. The commission also endorsed the administration's policy of providing aid to Cuban opposition groups, thus lending a semblance of credibility to Castro's claims that dissident groups are agents of Washington, undermining their standing.

Cuban exiles should be allowed to participate in the transformation of Cuban society. However, their participation need not require the U.S. government's active involvement. Thus, Radio and TV Marti, government entities that broadcast to Cuba, should be privatized or closed down. If the exile community believes that those stations are a useful resource in its struggle against the Castro regime, it has the means—there are no legal impediments—to finance such an operation.

A New Cuba Policy Based on American Principles

Washington's policies toward Cuba should be consistent with traditional American principles. First, the United States should restore the practice of granting political asylum to Cuban refugees. The 1994 and 1995 immigration accords between the Clinton administration and the Cuban government have turned the United States into Havana's de jure partner in oppressing those Cubans who risk their lives to escape repression. The ''wet feet, dry feet'' policy, which grants political asylum to Cuban refugees who make it to the U.S. shore on their own and forces the U.S. Coast Guard to return to Cuba those refugees that it picks up at sea, should be eliminated. Instead, the U.S. government should grant political asylum to all Cubans who escape the island.

There is no reason to believe that Cuban refugees would not continue to help the U.S. economy as they always have. The 1980 boatlift, in which 120,000 Cuban refugees reached U.S. shores, proved a boon to the economy of southern Florida. In addition, since the Cuban-American community has repeatedly demonstrated its ability and desire to provide for refugees until they can provide for themselves, such a policy need not cost U.S. taxpayers.

Second, the U.S. government should protect its own citizens' inalienable rights and recognize that free trade is itself a human right. As James Dorn of the Cato Institute says: ''The supposed dichotomy between the right to trade and human rights is a false one. . . . As moral agents, individuals necessarily claim the rights to liberty and property in order to live fully and to pursue their interests in a responsible manner.'' In the case of Cuba, U.S. citizens and companies should be allowed to decide for themselves—as they are in the case of dozens of countries around the world whose political and human rights records are less than admirable—whether and how they should trade with it.

Third, the U.S. government should also respect the right of its own citizens to travel abroad freely and lift the travel ban to Cuba. Currently, U.S. citizens can travel more or less freely to such countries as Iran and North Korea, but not to Cuba. Government bans on the free movement of people are inconsistent with the values of freedom on which the United States was founded. As Rep. Jeff Flake (R-AZ) puts it, ''If somebody should limit your travel, it should be a Communist. It should be someone other than us.''

Fourth, U.S. policy toward Cuba should focus on national security interests, not on transforming Cuban society or micromanaging the affairs of a transitional government as current law obliges Washington to do. That means lifting the embargo and establishing the types of diplomatic ties with Cuba that the United States maintains with other states, even dictatorial states that do not threaten its national security. Those measures, especially the ending of current sanctions, will ensure a more peaceful and smooth transition in Cuba.

Conclusion

Signs of increasing political dissatisfaction with the embargo show that the tide of opinion is clearly turning. A February 2008 Gallup poll showed

595

that 61 percent of Americans favored reestablishing diplomatic ties with Cuba—a 6 percentage point increase since 2004. Business groups such as agricultural producers have grown increasingly critical of the embargo since it deprives them of a potentially lucrative market. For example, since the enactment of the Trade Sanctions Reform and Export Enhancement Act in 2000, which allows cash-only sales to Cuba of U.S. farm products and medical supplies, U.S. agricultural exports to the island went from zero to $447 million in 2007. The International Trade Commission estimates that lifting the embargo could further increase U.S. farm sales to Cuba by between $175 million and $350 million per year. According to the American Farm Bureau, Cuba could eventually become a $1 billion agricultural export market for U.S. farmers. It is important that, as trade expands and relations normalize, Washington resists calls to provide export credits or other official assistance to U.S. businesses or the Cuban government. Such corporate welfare and foreign aid have a poor record at promoting development.

Support has also been mounting in Congress in favor of relaxing the trade embargo and travel ban. In December 2006, a bipartisan congressional delegation traveled to Cuba and met with government officials there, in one of the highest-ranking visits by U.S. authorities since former president Jimmy Carter traveled to Havana in May 2002. Several bipartisan measures were introduced in the 110th Congress intended to end the trade embargo and travel ban—one of them (H.R. 654) having as many as 120 cosponsors—but they lack broad backing by congressional leaders.

Ending the embargo will not save communism from itself. Only internal reform will bring sustained investment and growth to Cuba. A transition may be forthcoming on the island, and the United States can help by lifting the embargo.

Suggested Readings

Clarke, Jonathan G., and William Ratliff. "Report from Havana: Time for a Reality Check on U.S. Policy toward Cuba." Cato Institute Policy Analysis no. 418, October 31, 2001.

Council on Foreign Relations. "U.S.-Cuban Relations in the 21st Century." Report of an Independent Task Force sponsored by the Council on Foreign Relations, New York, 1999.

Falcoff, Mark. *Cuba the Morning After: Normalization and Its Discontents*. Washington: AEI Press, 2004.

Flake, Jeff. "Will U.S. Trade with Cuba Promote Freedom or Subsidize Tyranny?" Remarks at the Cato Policy Forum, July 25, 2002. www.cato.org-events-020725pf.html.

Griswold, Daniel. "Cuba and the United States in the 21st Century." Speech at Rice University, October 12, 2005. www.freetrade.org/node/433.

Latell, Brian. *After Fidel: Raúl Castro and the Future of Cuba's Revolution*. New York: Palgrave Macmillan, 2007.

Montaner, Carlos A. *Cuba Today: The Slow Demise of Castroism*. Madrid: Fundación para el Análisis y los Estudios Sociales, 1996.

Peters, Philip. "A Policy toward Cuba That Serves U.S. Interests." Cato Institute Policy Analysis no. 384, November 2, 2000.

———. "Cuba's Small Entrepreneurs: Down But Not Out." Lexington Institute Research Study, September 30, 2006.

Ratliff, William, and Roger Fontaine. "A Strategic Flip-Flop on the Caribbean: Lift the Embargo on Cuba." Hoover Institution *Essays in Public Policy,* no. 100, 2000.

U.S. Department of State. "Zenith and Eclipse: A Comparative Look at Socio-Economic Conditions in Pre-Castro and Present Day Cuba." January 12, 1998. www.state.gov/p/wha/ci/14776.htm.

U.S. International Trade Commission. "U.S. Agricultural Sales to Cuba: Certain Economic Effects of U.S. Restrictions." July, 2007. www.usitc.gov/publications/pub3932.pdf.

Vásquez, Ian. "Washington's Dubious Crusade for Hemispheric Democracy." Cato Institute Policy Analysis no. 201, January 12, 1994.

—Prepared by Juan Carlos Hidalgo and Ian Vásquez

58. The International War on Drugs

Policymakers should

- greatly de-emphasize counternarcotics activities in Afghanistan, since they undermine America's much more important struggle against al Qaeda and the Taliban;
- stop pressuring the government of Mexico to escalate the war on drugs, since that policy is leading to a dangerous upsurge in violence that threatens to destabilize the country;
- recognize that the "supply-side" campaign against cocaine and other drugs from the Andean region has produced few lasting gains, an inevitable outcome since global demand for such drugs continues to grow;
- accept the decriminalization and harm-reduction strategies adopted by the Netherlands, Portugal, and other countries as a better model for dealing with the problem of drug abuse; and
- move toward abandoning entirely the failed prohibitionist model regarding drugs.

The global trade in illegal drugs is a vast enterprise, estimated at more than $300 billion a year, with the United States as the largest single retail market. It would be a mistake, though, to assume that the only relevant demand factor is U.S. demand. The American market is actually a relatively mature one with overall consumption not substantially different from what it was a decade or two ago. The main areas of demand growth are in eastern Europe, the successor states of the former Soviet Union, and some portions of Latin America. The bottom line is that demand for illegal drugs on a global basis is robust and will likely remain so.

That sobering reality has ominous implications for the strategy that advocates of a "war" on drugs continue to push. Their strategy has long had two major components. The first is to shut off the flow of drugs from drug-source countries, through various methods of drug crop eradication, developmental aid to promote alternative economic opportunities, the interdiction of drug shipments, and the suppression of money-laundering activities. The second component is to significantly reduce demand in the United States through a combination of criminal sanctions, drug treatment programs, and anti-drug educational campaigns.

At best, efforts at domestic demand reduction have achieved only modest results, and the supply-side campaign has been even less effective. Moreover, with global demand continuing to increase, even if drug warriors succeeded in their goal of more substantially reducing consumption in the United States, it would have little adverse effect on trafficking organizations. There is more than enough demand globally to attract and sustain traffickers who are willing to take the risks to satisfy that demand. And since the illegality of the trade creates a massive black-market premium (depending on the drug, as much as 90 percent of the retail price), the potential profits to drug-trafficking organizations are huge. Thus, the supply-side strategy attempts to defy the basic laws of economics, with predictable results. It is a fatally flawed strategy, and Washington's insistence on continuing it causes serious problems of corruption and violence for drug-source and drug-transiting countries.

Ideally, the United States should lead an international effort to abandon the entire prohibitionist model, which would eliminate the black-market premium and allow legitimate businesses to enter a trade that would then have more "normal" profit margins. If Washington is unwilling to embrace such a far-reaching reform, it should at least stop browbeating and bribing drug-source and drug-transiting countries to try to do the impossible: shut off the supply to a robust global market.

The supply-side campaign continues to cause the most problems in three arenas: Afghanistan, the Andean countries of South America, and Mexico.

Afghanistan

The war on drugs threatens to interfere with the U.S.-led effort to combat al Qaeda and the Taliban in Afghanistan. U.S. officials want to eradicate drugs as well as nurture Afghanistan's embryonic democracy, symbolized by the pro-Western regime of President Hamid Karzai. Under pressure from Washington, Karzai has called on the Afghan people to wage war against narcotics with the same determination and ferocity that they resisted the Soviet occupation in the 1980s. Given the economic and social realities in Afghanistan, that is an unrealistic and potentially very dangerous objective.

There has been some skepticism in U.S. military circles about the wisdom of pursuing a vigorous war on drugs in Afghanistan. U.S. military leaders in that country clearly believe that such an effort complicates their primary mission: eradicating al Qaeda and Taliban forces. That is a legitimate worry.

There is little doubt that al Qaeda and other anti-government elements profit from the drug trade. What drug warriors refuse to acknowledge is that the connection between drug trafficking and terrorism is a direct result of making drugs illegal. Not surprisingly, terrorist groups in Afghanistan and other countries are quick to exploit such a vast source of potential funding. Absent a worldwide prohibitionist policy, the profit margins in drug trafficking would be a tiny fraction of their current levels, and terrorist groups would have to seek other sources of revenue.

In any case, the United States faces a serious dilemma if it conducts a vigorous drug eradication campaign in Afghanistan in an effort to dry up the funds flowing to al Qaeda and the Taliban. Those are clearly not the only factions involved in drug trafficking. Many of Karzai's political allies are warlords who control the drug trade in their respective regions. They use the revenues from that trade to pay the militias that keep them in power in their fiefdoms and give them national political clout. Some of these individuals backed the Taliban when that faction was in power, switching sides only when the United States launched its military offensive in Afghanistan in October 2001. Anti-drug campaigns might cause them to change their allegiance yet again.

In addition to the need to placate cooperative warlords, the U.S.-led coalition relies on poppy growers as spies for information on movements of Taliban and al Qaeda units. Disrupting the opium crop alienates those vital sources of information.

The drug trade is a crucial part of Afghanistan's economy. Afghanistan accounts for more than 90 percent of the world's opium supply, and opium poppies are now grown in most provinces. According to the United Nations, some 509,000 Afghan families are involved in opium poppy cultivation. Even measured on a nuclear-family basis, that translates into about 14 percent of Afghanistan's population. Given the role of extended families and clans in Afghan society, the number of people affected is much greater than that. Indeed, it is likely that at least 35 percent of the population is involved directly or indirectly in the drug trade. For many of those people, opium poppy crops and other aspects of drug commerce are the difference between modest prosperity by Afghan standards and destitution. They do not look kindly on efforts to destroy their livelihood.

Despite those daunting economic factors, the U.S. government is putting increased pressure on the Karzai government to crack down on the drug trade. The Afghan regime is responding cautiously, trying to convince Washington that it is serious about dealing with the problem without launching a full-blown anti-drug crusade that will alienate large segments of the population. It has tried to achieve that balance by focusing on high-profile raids against drug-processing labs—mostly those that are not controlled by warlords friendly to the government in Kabul. The Karzai government has been especially adamant in opposing the aerial spraying of poppy fields—a strategy that Washington has successfully pushed allied governments in Colombia and other South American drug-source countries to do.

Washington's pressure on the Karzai government is a big mistake. The Taliban and their al Qaeda allies are rapidly regaining strength, especially in Helmand and Kandahar provinces, perhaps not coincidentally the areas of the most vigorous anti-drug campaigns. If zealous American drug warriors alienate hundreds of thousands of Afghan farmers, the Karzai government's hold on power could become even more precarious. Washington would then face the unpalatable choice of risking the reemergence of chaos in Afghanistan, including the prospect that radical Islamists might regain power, or sending more U.S. troops to stabilize the situation beyond the reinforcements already contemplated in the summer of 2008.

U.S. officials need to keep their priorities straight. Our mortal enemy is al Qaeda and the Taliban regime that made Afghanistan a sanctuary for that terrorist organization. The drug war is a dangerous distraction in the campaign to destroy those forces. Recognizing that security considerations sometimes trump other objectives would hardly be an unprecedented move by Washington. U.S. agencies quietly ignored drug-trafficking activities of anti-communist factions in Central America during the 1980s when the primary goal was to keep those countries out of the Soviet orbit. In the early 1990s, the United States also eased its pressure on Peru's government regarding the drug eradication issue when President Alberto Fujimori concluded that a higher priority had to be given to winning coca farmers away from the Maoist Shining Path guerrilla movement.

U.S. officials should adopt a similar pragmatic policy in Afghanistan and look the other way regarding the drug-trafficking activities of friendly warlords. And above all, the U.S. military must not become the enemy of Afghan farmers whose livelihood depends on opium poppy cultivation. True, some of the funds from the drug trade will find their way into the coffers of the Taliban and al Qaeda. That is an inevitable side effect of a global prohibitionist policy that creates such an enormous profit from illegal drugs. But alienating pro-Western Afghan factions in an effort to disrupt the flow of revenue to the Islamic radicals is too high a price to pay.

The Andean Region

The major drug-source countries of the Andean region—Colombia, Peru, and Bolivia—have long been an arena for Washington's supply-side initiatives against drugs. Indeed, Washington made the reduction of drugs coming out of that region a major priority during the Reagan administration. More recently, the Clinton administration launched Plan Colombia, which eventually turned into a multiyear program with a price tag exceeding $5 billion.

Some good news has been coming out of the largest of the Andean drug-source countries, Colombia. During the presidency of Álvaro Uribe, the level of violence in that country has declined substantially—a refreshing contrast to the carnage that was so typical during the 1980s and 1990s. One reason for that decline has been Uribe's successful counterinsurgency campaign against radical leftist forces, especially the Revolutionary Armed Forces of Colombia. The FARC is much weaker today than it was even a few years ago, and that weakness is likely to intensify with the death of the organization's longtime leader.

Another reason for the decline in violence is a less ruthlessly competitive environment among drug-trafficking organizations. The battles over market share have subsided, and the ferocious turf battles of the past are noticeably less prominent. Major U.S. cities have experienced similar patterns. The extent of violence typically drops off once the battles over territorial distribution of the trade are (at least temporarily) resolved. (If new entrants emerge, though, violence can surge again with dramatic suddenness.)

The decline in violence in Colombia, however, has not been accompanied by a significant decline in either drug crop cultivation or the overall exports of drugs—especially the most prominent export, cocaine. A June 2008 report by the United Nations' Office on Drugs and Crime indicated that coca cultivation in Colombia in 2007 had surged 27 percent from 2006, to some 245,000 acres.

The data in the UN report reflected a problem that has plagued U.S. drug warriors for more than two decades. Concerted anti-drug campaigns will from time to time lead to a decline in drug cultivation and production in one or two of the Andean countries, but that decline is invariably accompanied by increases in one or more of the others. For example, a strong effort from the late 1980s to the late 1990s caused a decline in drug output in both Peru and Bolivia. But that same period saw an explosion of output in Colombia. (Indeed, panic regarding that surge was a major reason why Congress approved Plan Colombia.) When output then declined in Colombia, it revived in Peru and Bolivia. That is known as the "balloon," or "push-down, pop-up" effect. Moreover, concerted anti-drug efforts in the traditional Andean drug-producing states have led to a greater prominence of the trade in such previously minor players as Ecuador, Brazil, and Venezuela.

The 2008 UN report showed the balloon effect. Cultivation remained relatively flat in Peru and Bolivia, but surged in Colombia, reversing the pattern earlier in the decade. The bottom line was that total cultivation in the region increased by 16 percent. Even the most tenacious drug warriors must have been disappointed at that outcome in the ninth year of a program that has cost American taxpayers $5 billion.

Matters may get even worse for Washington's anti-drug campaign in South America. Bolivia's leftist president, Evo Morales, has been reluctant to cooperate with the United States on the drug issue. Indeed, his core political constituency consists of coca farmers. Ecuador's equally leftist government is even less cooperative than Bolivia's has been. In July 2008, Quito refused to renew Washington's 10-year lease on Manta Air Base, one of the three major U.S. counternarcotics bases in Latin America. The loss of Manta will be a severe blow to drug interdiction efforts.

Washington faces trouble on another front. Venezuela's leftist president, Hugo Chávez, has virtually severed ties with the United States on anti-drug issues. Indeed, there are indications that his regime is actively involved in the drug trade.

U.S. leaders need to face the reality that the Andean supply-side campaign is a failure. That strategy has been tried for more than two decades, and the quantity of drugs coming out of the region is as great as ever.

Mexico

Mexico is a major source of heroin, marijuana, and methamphetamine for the U.S. market, as well as the principal transit and distribution point for cocaine coming in from South America. For years, people both inside and outside Mexico have worried that the country might descend into the maelstrom of corruption and violence that plagued the chief drug-source country in the Western Hemisphere, Colombia, from the early 1980s to the early years of this century. There are growing signs that the "Colombi-anization" of Mexico is now becoming a reality.

That tragic prospect is a direct result of Washington's policy of drug prohibition. The enormous potential profit attracts the most violence-prone criminal elements. It is a truism that when drugs are outlawed, only outlaws will traffic in drugs.

If Mexico goes down the same path that Colombia did, the consequences to the United States will be much more severe. Colombia is relatively far away, but Mexico shares a border with the United States and is closely linked to this country economically through the North American Free Trade Agreement. Chaos in Mexico is already spilling over the border and adversely affecting the United States—especially the southwestern states of Arizona, New Mexico, and Texas.

The prominence of the drug trade in Mexico has mushroomed over the past 15 years. One consequence of the increased prominence of the Mexi-can cartels is a spike in violence. Even supposed victories in the drug war prove to be mixed blessings at best. As Stratfor, a risk-assessment consult-ing organization, notes: "Inter-cartel violence tends to swing upward after U.S. or Mexican authorities manage to weaken or disrupt a given organization. At any point, if rival groups sense an organization might not be able to defend its turf, they will swoop in to battle not only the incumbent group, but also each other for control."

The turf battles have been ferocious. In 2005, more than 1,300 people perished in drug-related violence. By 2007, the yearly total had soared to 2,673. And it continues to get worse. By mid-August 2008, the carnage for that year already exceeded the number of fatalities in all of 2007. The U.S. State Department warned American travelers in June 2008 that battles between drug-trafficking gangs (and between those gangs and Mexican military and police) in portions of northern Mexico were so severe that they constituted "small unit combat operations."

In addition to the extensive violence reminiscent of Colombia in the 1980s and 1990s, another Colombian pattern is also emerging in Mexico—the branching out of the drug gangs into kidnapping and other lucrative sources of revenue. Some reports suggest that the kidnapping problem in Mexico is now more severe than it is in Colombia.

U.S. officials concede that the drug-related violence in Mexico does not respect borders. According to John Walters, the director of the U.S. Office of National Drug Control Policy under President Bush: "The killing of rival traffickers is already spilling across the border. Witnesses are being killed. We do not think the border is a shield." A Dallas narcotics officer reaches a similar conclusion: "We're seeing an alarming number of incidents involving the same type of violence that's become all too common in Mexico, right here in Dallas. We're seeing execution-style murders, burned bodies, and outright mayhem. . . . It's like the battles being waged in Mexico for turf have reached Dallas."

U.S. law enforcement officials along the border are increasingly the targets of violence. A Homeland Security Committee report notes that at one time, smugglers "would drop the drugs or abandon their vehicles when confronted by U.S. law enforcement." That is no longer the case. "In today's climate, U.S. Border Patrol agents are fired upon from across the river and troopers and sheriff's deputies are subject to attacks with automatic weapons while the cartels retrieve their contraband." Some of the attacks have come from Mexicans wearing military uniforms. It is uncertain whether they are smugglers with stolen uniforms or whether rogue elements of the Mexican military are attacking U.S. law enforcement personnel on behalf of traffickers.

U.S. policy seems to be based on an assumption that if the Mexican government can eliminate the top drug lords, their organizations will fall apart, thereby greatly reducing the flow of illegal drugs to the United States. Washington has now backed up that policy with a lucrative aid package, the Merida Initiative, to help fund law enforcement reforms and other anti-drug efforts. In the summer of 2008, Congress approved the first installment ($400 million) of what will likely be a multiyear, multibillion dollar program modeled after Plan Colombia, the initiative that began in 2000 for Colombia and its Andean neighbors.

U.S. officials have rejoiced at the willingness of Mexican President Felipe Calderón's administration to make the drug war—and especially the capture of major drug-trafficking figures—a high priority. Since Calderón took office in 2006, the Mexican government has even given the military a lead role in combating the traffickers. The principal outcome of that strategy, however, has been an even greater level of violence, with military personnel increasingly being targets. The military has also now been exposed to the temptation of financial corruption that had previously compromised Mexico's police forces so thoroughly.

The belief that neutralizing Mexican drug kingpins will achieve a lasting reduction in drug trafficking is the same assumption that U.S. officials made with respect to the crackdown on the Medellín and Cali cartels in Colombia during the 1990s. Subsequent developments proved the assumption to be erroneous. The elimination of those two cartels merely decentralized the Colombian drug trade. Instead of two large organizations controlling the trade, today some 300 much smaller, loosely organized groups do so.

More to the point, the arrests and killings of numerous top drug lords in both Colombia and Mexico over the years have not had a meaningful effect on the quantity of drugs entering the United States. Cutting off one head of the drug-smuggling Hydra merely results in more heads taking its place. Jorge Chabat, a Mexican security and drug policy analyst notes: "For years, the U.S. told Mexico's government, 'The problem is that the narcos are still powerful because you don't dismantle the gangs.' Now they're doing just that . . . and the narcos are more powerful than ever."

Mexico can still avoid going down the path to chaos, but time is growing short. Washington had better pay far more attention to the problem than it has to this point, and U.S. officials need to come up with better answers than the ineffectual and discredited policies of the past. If drug prohibition continues, violence and corruption will become a dominant and permanent feature of Mexico's life. The illicit drug trade has already penetrated the country's economy and society to an alarming degree.

U.S. officials need to ask whether they want to risk a chaotic, embryonic narcostate on America's southern border. If they don't want to deal with the turmoil such a development would create, the new administration needs to abandon the prohibitionist strategy and do so quickly.

A New International Drug Policy Is Needed

When the United States and other countries consider whether to persist in a strategy of drug prohibition, they need to consider all the potential societal costs. Drug abuse is certainly a major public health problem, and its costs are considerable. But as we have seen over the decades in Colombia, Mexico, Afghanistan, and other drug-source countries, banning the drug trade creates economic distortions and an opportunity for some of the most unsavory elements to gain tenacious footholds. Drug prohibition leads inevitably to an orgy of corruption and violence. Those are very real societal costs as well. Indeed, those costs exceed any possible benefits that prohibitionist policies could achieve.

Some countries have apparently begun to understand that reality and adjust their policies accordingly. The Netherlands was one of the first to do so with marijuana consumption. The recreational use of cannabis in Amsterdam and other cities, although technically still illegal, is openly tolerated by Dutch authorities. Portugal has gone even further than the Netherlands, changing its laws to decriminalize the simple possession and use of a wide array of recreational drugs. Both countries have risked the disapproval, and at times the diplomatic wrath, of the United States to institute such reforms. And the results have been encouraging. Both countries have seen a reduction in overall crime, especially violent crime. Cristina Fernández de Kirchner, the president of Argentina, endorsed the decriminalization of drug use in August 2008, as did the second-largest party in Mexico. It is an idea that seems poised to spread.

Washington should respect the right of countries who wish to pursue drug policy reforms and not exert pressure to make them adhere to the prohibitionist model. Indeed, U.S. policymakers might profit from their example.

Suggested Readings

Carpenter, Ted Galen. *Bad Neighbor Policy: Washington's Futile War on Drugs in Latin America*. New York: Palgrave/Macmillan, 2003.

———. "How the Drug War in Afghanistan Undermines America's War on Terror." Cato Foreign Policy Briefing no. 84, November 10, 2004.

———. "Mexico Is Becoming the Next Colombia." Cato Foreign Policy Briefing no. 87, November 15, 2005.

Hafvenstein, Joel. *Opium Season: A Year on the Afghan Frontier*. Guilford, CT: Lyons Press, 2007.

Keefer, Philip, Norman V. Loayza, and Rodrigo Soares. "The Development Impact of the Illegality of Drug Trade." Policy Research Working Paper no. 4543, World Bank, Development Research Group Macroeconomics and Growth Team, March 2008.

MacDonald, David. *Drugs in Afghanistan: Opium, Outlaws, and Scorpion Tales*. London: Pluto Press, 2007.

Mares, David R. *Drug Wars and Coffeehouses: The Political Economy of the International Drug Trade*. Washington: CQ Press, 2005.

Nadelmann, Ethan. "Think Again: Drugs." *Foreign Policy*, September–October 2007.

Thoumi, Francisco. *Illegal Drugs, Economy, and Society in the Andes*. Washington: Woodrow Wilson Center Press and Johns Hopkins University Press, 2003.

—Prepared by Ted Galen Carpenter

International Economic Policy

59. Trade

The Gains from Trade

Voluntary economic exchange is inherently fair and does not justify government intervention. Further, government intervention in voluntary economic exchange on behalf of some citizens at the expense of others is inherently unfair.

Beyond the moral case for free trade is the well-established fact that when people are free to buy from, sell to, and invest with one another as they choose, they can achieve far more than when governments attempt to control economic decisions. Widening the circle of people with whom we transact—including across political borders—brings benefits to consumers in the form of lower prices, greater variety, and better quality, and it allows companies to reap the benefits of innovation, specialization, and economies of scale that larger markets bring. Free markets are essential to prosperity, and expanding free markets as much as possible enhances that prosperity.

When goods, services, and capital flow freely across U.S. borders, Americans can take full advantage of the opportunities of the international marketplace. They can buy the best or least expensive goods and services the world has to offer; they can sell to the most promising markets; they can choose among the best investment opportunities; and they can tap into the worldwide pool of capital. Study after study has shown that countries that are more open to the global economy grow faster and achieve higher incomes than those that are relatively closed.

From an economic perspective, then, the case for unilateral trade liberalization—reducing our own trade barriers and subsidies without preconditions or reciprocal commitments from other countries—is sound. Politically, however, the concentrated and organized beneficiaries of protectionism are powerful relative to the much larger, but diffuse and disorganized, beneficiaries of free trade. Politicians tend to be most responsive to the loudest interest groups and are therefore inclined to view imports unfavorably. Thus, the reduction of import barriers is considered "costly," and therefore must be compensated by the benefits of increased export market access.

This view that exports are good and imports are bad is a central misconception upon which rests the belief that trade negotiations and reciprocity are essential to trade liberalization. Under this formulation, an optimal trade agreement, from the perspective of U.S. negotiators, is one that maximizes U.S. access to foreign markets and minimizes foreign access to U.S. markets. An agreement requiring large cuts to U.S. tariffs, which would thus deliver significant benefits to consumers, would not pass political muster unless it could be demonstrated that even larger export benefits were to be had. This misguided premise that imports are the cost of exports and should be minimized lies at the root of public skepticism about trade.

Most of America's remaining tariffs are particularly taxing on lower-income citizens. Although U.S. tariffs are on average relatively low, they are particularly high on products like shoes, clothing, and food—necessities on which lower-income Americans spend a higher proportion of their incomes and that are produced disproportionately by workers and farmers in poorer countries. A 2007 book by Edward Gresser of the Progressive Policy Institute points out that hotel maids who earn $15,000 per year probably pay the equivalent of a week's pay in tariffs annually, whereas hotel managers, because of the goods they buy as well as their higher incomes, probably lose only a few hours' pay in tariffs each year. The benefits of free trade—lower prices, greater choice, and better quality goods—are precisely what every lawmaker interested in improving the lives of America's less fortunate should welcome.

Top 10 Most Costly U.S. Trade Barriers

The 10 costliest U.S. quota, tariff, and licensing barriers belong to imported
- Textiles and apparel
- Sugar
- Dairy
- Footwear and leather products
- Ethyl alcohol
- Beef
- Tuna
- Glass and glass products
- Tobacco

SOURCE: International Trade Commission.

In an increasingly globalized world, the notion that a company has an exclusive nationality is outmoded. Cross-country investment holdings, integrated supply chains that seek to capitalize on the global division of labor, intraindustry trade, and just-in-time production techniques highlight the interdependence of firms located in different countries, and favor firms that can respond nimbly to the new conditions. Congress can help American firms and consumers take maximum advantage of those conditions and create an environment that encourages job creation and economic growth.

Openness to trade and investment—on paper and in reality—will be a crucial determinant of whether countries prosper in the global economy. Although it is in a country's interest to achieve this state of openness without regard to what other countries do, reciprocal trade agreements can help move countries toward that objective, while providing mechanisms to discourage protectionist backsliding. In that regard, bilateral and regional trade agreements can open markets at home and abroad to more import competition, encourage cross-border integration of industries, and reward economic and political reform in other countries. Although less economically important than a comprehensive multilateral agreement, regional and bilateral deals can mark important steps toward the goal of global free trade.

On a larger scale, the multilateral trading system under the auspices of the World Trade Organization provides a useful forum for expanding trade and preventing protectionist backsliding. The concept of "Most Favored Nation"—a cornerstone of the WTO from the beginning—also ensures that trade diversion (a process whereby exclusive preferential trade deals discourage trade with the most efficient producer) is minimized. The WTO's trade policy review and dispute settlement mechanism have helped defuse potential trade wars. Although the WTO and the concept of multilateral trade rules have been crucial to the liberalization of trade, and are worthy of continued support, they are by no means necessary to secure the gains from free and open trade.

U.S. Trade Policy in Limbo

As the 111th Congress convenes, U.S. trade policy is at a crossroads. The post–World War II, bipartisan, pro-trade consensus, which had been showing signs of fray and fissure during the past decade, appears to have collapsed entirely during the 110th Congress. A continuous stream of anti-trade rhetoric, an American public in fear of international trade and globalization, completed trade agreements left in limbo, and the introduction of dozens of antagonistic trade bills are among the dubious achievements of the 110th Congress.

Unless the current Congress takes real steps to rebuild the consensus that has been crucial to U.S. economic vitality and rising living standards for six decades, history likely will view this period as a trade policy watershed for reasons the country will regret.

During the first session of the 110th Congress, "fast-track" negotiating authority or "trade promotion authority" expired and serious efforts to extend or renew that historically crucial tool of trade diplomacy never materialized. Trade promotion authority enables the executive branch to negotiate agreements with other countries, subject to congressional parameters, and then present those completed agreements to Congress for an up-

or-down vote without amendments. Without trade promotion authority, the United States is unlikely to negotiate any substantive new trade agreements.

The Doha Round of multilateral trade negotiations, launched in 2001 under the auspices of the World Trade Organization, was dealt a potentially fatal blow when ministers failed, once again, to reach accord in Geneva in July 2008. There is plenty of blame to be shared among nations for this failure, but the United States was a prominent obstacle on several fronts.

Despite the fact that rich-country farm subsidies have been a central focus of reform throughout the Doha Round, Congress recently passed (over a presidential veto) the Farm Bill of 2008 (formally The Food Conservation and Energy Act of 2008), which commits U.S. taxpayers to continued, trade-distorting subsidization of the U.S. agricultural sector for the next five years—hardly a demonstration of commitment to the kind of reform a Doha Round agreement would require.

Congress also tied the hands of the U.S. Trade Representative where reform of the trade remedy laws is concerned. Although nearly every WTO member favors substantive reform of the agreements disciplining the use of domestic antidumping and countervailing duty laws, the United States stands virtually alone, defending use of calculation practices and determination methodologies that are slanted in favor of the imposition of duties and in some cases run afoul of WTO dispute settlement outcomes.

In addition to U.S. intransigence on the subjects of agricultural and trade remedies reform, the absence of trade promotion authority is among the reasons for the Doha Round's failure. Without trade promotion authority, the prospects of a concluded agreement's making it through the U.S. legislative process without Congress tinkering with the deal's carefully balanced provisions were and will continue to be perceived as unlikely. Essentially, without trade promotion authority, U.S. negotiators lack the credibility to deliver a truly liberalizing agreement.

In an even worse blow to U.S. credibility, some agreements concluded pursuant to the terms of trade promotion authority were not granted an up-or-down vote by the 110th Congress. Instead, Congress forced the Bush administration to reopen four completed agreements (with Peru, Colombia, Panama, and South Korea) to include enforceable labor and environmental provisions as conditions for congressional consideration of those deals (even though such provisions were not required in the trade promotion authority language under which the agreements were negotiated). Nevertheless, the administration capitulated to Congress's demands in May 2007 and convinced our trade partners to reopen the agreements to insert labor and environmental provisions. Yet Congress only made good on its commitment to consider the Peru agreement, while a series of new objections were raised to block consideration of the deals with Colombia, Panama, and South Korea.

The actions of the 110th Congress reflect a shift in attitudes toward trade. Beyond the refusal to consider completed trade agreements, members introduced a few dozen bills objectively characterized as skeptical of, if not hostile to, trade and U.S. trade partners.

It is difficult to avoid the conclusion that the post–World War II preference for engagement, negotiation, and cooperation between the United States and other nations on trade yielded to a burgeoning desire for isolation, litigation, and enforcement during the 110th Congress. That is a particularly troubling development considering that the justification for this change in attitude rests on a series of assumptions that have no basis in fact.

Persistent Myths and Misperceptions about Trade

Congress often cites the rising antipathy of Americans toward international trade as justification for its strident rhetoric and provocative legislation. The results of several different research surveys all seem to support the conclusion that Americans harbor growing fears about trade and globalization. For example, more Americans believed that free trade leads to job losses, lower wages, higher prices, and a slowing economy in 2008 than was the case in 2006.

It is remarkable that trade and, more broadly, U.S. engagement in the global economy have been so badly maligned in the early 21st century. After all, increasing international trade and investment over the past several decades have been crucial catalysts for the enormous wealth creation and robust economic growth experienced in the United States.

Considering the stellar U.S. economic performance of the last quarter century, a period during which U.S. international commercial engagement (as measured by trade as a share of gross domestic product) nearly doubled, those survey results seem counterintuitive, to say the least.

Most Americans have benefited from sustained U.S. economic growth. Most Americans enjoy the fruits of international trade and globalization every day: driving to work in vehicles with at least some foreign content; talking on foreign-made mobile telephones; having extra disposable income because retailers like Wal-Mart, Best Buy, and Home Depot can pass on cost savings made possible by their own access to a plethora of foreign producers; making lower monthly mortgage payments owing to the availability of foreign capital in the mortgage market; depositing bigger paychecks because of their employers' growing sales to customers in India and Brazil; and enjoying health or vacation benefits provided by an employer that happens to be a foreign-owned company.

It is simply implausible that the degree of antipathy toward trade reflected in survey results is driven by personal experiences or realistic fears about the future. The overwhelming majority of Americans have not lost jobs to import competition or outsourcing, nor do they know someone who has. According to the Bureau of Labor Statistics, about 2 to 3 percent of U.S. job loss is attributable to import competition or outsourcing.

So this all raises a crucial question: Why are Americans harboring unfavorable views about trade? It might have something to do with the fact that Americans are routinely barraged with reports from the media, from the campaign trail, and from Congress that trade is a scourge that threatens their jobs and the economy. These tales usually rely on one or more of three prominent myths.

Myth: Manufacturing Is in Decline . . . and Trade Is to Blame

The first myth is that U.S. manufacturing is in decline, and that import competition and outsourcing explain that decline. But according to every statistic relevant to evaluating the health of the sector, manufacturing is unequivocally thriving. It is true that there are fewer workers in the manufacturing sector today than in years past, but manufacturing employment peaked in 1979. Strong productivity gains and the continuing shift of the U.S. economy toward services explain the decline in manufacturing employment.

It is also true that the manufacturing sector's share of total U.S. gross domestic product is smaller today than in years past, but the sector's share of the economy peaked in 1953. In absolute terms, manufacturing output continues to grow year after year, but in relative terms, it has declined because of the burgeoning U.S. services sector (see Figure 59.1).

In 2006, U.S. manufacturing achieved record highs for output, revenues, profits, return on investment, exports, and imports. In fact, U.S. manufacturers accounted for 55 percent of U.S. import value in 2006. In 2007, new records were set for output, revenues, value added, exports, and imports. Profits and return on investment trailed off because of the rising costs of commodities and transportation.

The U.S. manufacturing sector continues to transition away from labor-intensive production toward a higher value-added orientation, but it is

Figure 59.1
Manufacturing Value Added Percent of GDP and Real Value Added
1947–2006

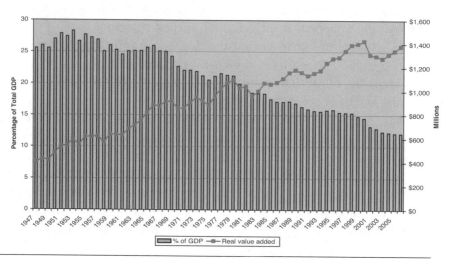

SOURCE: Bureau of Economic Analysis, GDP-by-Industry Accounts, http://www.bea.gov/industry/gpotables/gpo_action.cfm.

certainly not in decline. And access to foreign markets for export sales and access to foreign suppliers for U.S. manufacturing inputs are important parts of the manufacturing sector's success story.

Myth: The Trade Balance Is the Scoreboard

The second myth is that exports are good, imports are bad, and the trade account is the scoreboard. According to this perspective, the United States is losing at trade, as evidenced by its large trade deficit.

But the notion that the trade account should be viewed as a trade policy scoreboard is misguided. First, the trade balance is simply not a function of trade policy. It is a function of fiscal and monetary policy, and of disparate patterns of savings and consumption around the world. Second, the idea that balanced trade or a trade surplus should be an explicit goal of policymakers is folly. Since 1983, the trade deficit has increased from $67 billion to around $800 billion. Yet during that period, real GDP has grown at an average annual rate of 3.2 percent, and employers have added an average of 1.8 million net new jobs to payrolls every year. The unemployment rate has also been in decline for decades: the average rate in the 1980s was 7.3 percent; in the 1990s, it was 5.8 percent; and between

2000 and 2007, it averaged 5.2 percent. The evidence suggests that imports and the trade deficit are pro-cyclical. They both grow as the economy grows, and they both slow and shrink as the economy slows and recedes.

That balanced trade or a trade surplus is even desirable is open to debate. Japan has run a large trade surplus for decades, yet its economy has grown at an anemic 1.2 percent annually since 1991. Germany, another country with a long-standing trade surplus, experienced persistent double-digit unemployment until very recently. What is preferable: balanced trade or robust economic growth?

Myth: Our Trade Partners Cheat

The third myth is that the United States is losing at trade because its trade partners cheat with impunity, and that better enforcement of our current trade agreements would help reverse the first two myths. The most prominent cheater according to those who hold this view is China, which engages in industry subsidization, currency manipulation, intellectual property theft, unfair labor practices, dumping, and other underhanded methods.

Although some of the assertions of rules violations may have merit, the total effect on the trade account is negligible. ''Unfair trade'' constitutes a tiny fraction of overall trade, yet the emphasis that Congress has placed on systematic enforcement confers undue significance on the issue, thereby reinforcing negative perceptions about trade and our trade partners.

Curiously, a study requested of the U.S. International Trade Commission in 2007 by the House Ways and Means Committee about Chinese government policies and their effects on the bilateral trade deficit was abruptly terminated in 2008 by the chairman of that committee. Observers suggested that the committee came to realize that the study might not provide adequate support for the theory that a significant relationship exists.

The 111th Congress would do the country a great service by allowing independent agencies to research and then publish the objective facts about manufacturing, imports, trade agreements, and the trade account. Finding and sharing the truth and letting the ''chips fall where they may'' should be among the first steps toward rebuilding the pro-trade consensus.

Trade Policy for the 21st-Century World Economy

Globalization has changed the way agriculture, manufacturing, and services industries do business. The emergence of previously moribund economies has expanded the labor pool and has permitted a much more diversified and stratified division of labor, which has created scope for elaborate, dispersed, transnational production processes where countries specialize in particular value-added operations.

Yet the politics of U.S. trade policy remain rooted in an outdated conception of trade as an "us versus them" or an "our producers versus their producers" proposition. Though that characterization was never entirely apt, it is a gross mischaracterization today.

Today, it is difficult to distinguish our producers from their producers. Are companies headquartered in Tokyo, Stuttgart, and Stockholm with production facilities in Ohio, South Carolina, and California our producers or theirs? Is Ford's production plant in England or Intel's in China theirs or ours? If we welcome their producers' employing our workers and contributing to our local economies, should U.S. policy treat those producers as adversaries when they sell to U.S. consumers from abroad? Should a "good" American living in Tennessee care more about the success of a U.S. company in the state of Washington or a Tennessee-based subsidiary of a South African company?

The practical, everyday workings of the global economy defy the quaint perceptions held by policymakers and reflected in our outdated, mercantilist trade policy. Collaborations of our producers and their producers compete against other collaborations of our producers and their producers. There is really no practical difference between their producers and our producers, and therefore little utility to trade policy that is premised on the existence of important distinctions.

What is important is how much and what kind of economic activity is occurring in the United States. And that is very much a function of our ability to compete with other countries for talent and investment. To attract investment and talent, the United States must be open to foreign investment, foreign inputs, and foreign workers. And the customs and other administrative procedures that govern movements of goods into and out of the United States must be transparent, predictable, and frictionless.

If our policies are hostile to foreign investment, then value-added activities and the jobs they create will go elsewhere. If we are unaccommodating of foreigners with unique skills—at either end of the economic spectrum—then the investment and value-added activities will go elsewhere. If importing raw materials and components into the United States becomes logistically challenging or unreliable, businesses may see fewer advantages in having production facilities in the United States.

How, then, can Congress work toward rebuilding the pro-trade consensus?

First, Congress should pass the pending free trade agreements with Colombia, Panama, and South Korea, which will help restore U.S. credibility while locking in Americans' duty-free or low-duty access to imports and providing U.S. manufacturers with important new export opportunities.

Second, reauthorizing trade promotion authority for the executive branch would signal the world that the United States has recovered from its bout of self-doubt and stands ready to lead the world toward greater trade openness. Prospective trade agreement partners are more likely to negotiate and conclude agreements if they know the final deal will not be amended or unduly delayed in Congress. The expiration of trade promotion authority in June 2007 contributed to the breakdown in WTO negotiations in 2008.

Third, Congress should acknowledge that U.S. agricultural policy is a constant irritant to international relations, and a costly burden at home (see Chapter 18). American subsidies hurt other agricultural exporting nations, many of which are developing countries, and complicate efforts of U.S. trade negotiators to encourage market openings abroad. Combined with policies promoting the use of biofuels, they have transferred billions of dollars from taxpayers to farmers over the last year: in the last 20 years alone, the opportunity cost of U.S. farm programs to nonfarm U.S. consumers and producers has totaled $1.7 trillion. Transfers to farmers are regressive, too: the average farm household income in 2006 was more than 17 percent higher than the average American household income, according to the Department of Agriculture. The protection of American sugar, dairy, and rice farmers costs American consumers billions of dollars a year and should be removed. Congress can do a great favor to the nation by repealing agricultural supports immediately.

Fourth, Congress should act to ensure that the costs of physically moving goods into and out of the United States—the costs of compliance with customs and other administrative requirements and the cost of transportation and logistics services—are not unduly burdensome to importers and exporters. Accordingly, Congress should exercise its oversight of U.S. Customs and Border Protection to ensure that the agency's cargo security mandate is not suppressing its trade facilitation mandate. Measures to improve the chain of administrative and physical procedures involved in the transport of goods and services across international borders could be more consequential than a new round of multilateral tariff cuts. By World Bank estimates, a one-day reduction in both U.S. import and export clearance processing time could increase U.S. trade by almost $29 billion per year. In that spirit, Congress should finally repeal the anachronistic

Jones Act, which bans foreign shipping between U.S. ports and costs the American economy an estimated $2.8 billion (1996 dollars) annually in higher shipping costs, according to a 1996 U.S. International Trade Commission study. Permitting greater competition in maritime shipping (as well as air and rail transport) would reduce costs and prices, and help the United States remain competitive as a destination for investment.

Fifth, despite its imperfections, the WTO has been an important institution that has served U.S. interests well. Congress should demonstrate its commitment to international trade rules by heeding the recommendations of the Dispute Settlement Body, even when its own laws are impugned by that body. After all, if Congress expects U.S. trade partners to play by the rules and to accept findings that their own laws and regulations may be out of conformity with WTO commitments, then it should stop dragging its feet and comply with the outstanding rulings concerning U.S. trade policies.

Sixth, not only should Congress revise the antidumping law to bring it into conformity with the findings of the WTO Dispute Settlement Body, it should reevaluate its long-standing, bipartisan support for the law. The antidumping law is a vestige of a bygone industrial era, which serves the very narrow interests of a few producers and their representatives in Congress. Although support for antidumping is often cloaked in rhetoric about fair trade and level playing fields, the fact is the law indiscriminately punishes interests that have done nothing wrong. Moreover, that law is used frequently, nowadays, by U.S. companies against other U.S. companies. The globalization of supply chains has rendered antidumping superfluous, if not absurd.

Seventh, Congress should renounce the hyperbole and fearmongering that have come to characterize the trade debate, and instead engage in honest, fact-driven discussion about trade and its effect on the U.S. economy. To that end, Congress should refrain from suppressing the results of objective trade analysis when they don't serve a particular hypothesis.

By any reasonable measure, Americans are better off now than during comparable periods in the past, and expanding engagement in the global economy has played an important role in the ongoing, upward trend in American employment and living standards. To promote further progress for American workers and households, Congress and the administration should pursue policies that expand the freedom of Americans to participate in global markets.

Suggested Readings

Cato Institute. Center for Trade Policy Studies website. www.freetrade.org.

Gresser, Edward. *Freedom from Want: American Liberalism and the Global Economy.* Brooklyn, NY: Soft Skull Press, 2007.

Griswold, Daniel. "Trading Up: How Expanding Trade Has Delivered Better Jobs and Higher Living Standards for American Workers." Cato Institute Trade Policy Analysis no. 36, October 25, 2007.

Ikenson, Daniel. "Leading the Way: How U.S. Trade Policy Can Overcome Doha's Failings." Cato Institute Trade Policy Analysis no. 33, June 19, 2006.

———. "While Doha Sleeps: Securing Economic Growth through Trade Facilitation." Cato Institute Trade Policy Analysis no. 37, June 17, 2008.

Irwin, Douglas. *Free Trade under Fire.* 2nd ed. Princeton, NJ: Princeton University Press, 2005.

James, Sallie. "Maladjusted: The Misguided Policy of 'Trade Adjustment Assistance.'" Cato Institute Trade Briefing Paper no. 26, November 8, 2007.

James, Sallie, and Daniel Griswold. "Freeing the Farm: A Farm Bill for All Americans." Cato Institute Trade Policy Analysis no. 34, April 16, 2007.

Sally, Razeen. *New Frontiers in Free Trade: Globalization's Future and Asia's Rising Role.* Washington: Cato Institute, 2008.

—Prepared by Daniel Ikenson and Sallie James

60. Immigration

Congress should

- expand current legal immigration quotas, especially for employment-based visas;
- repeal the arbitrary and restrictive cap on H1-B visas for highly skilled workers;
- create a temporary worker program for lower-skilled workers to meet long-term labor demand and reduce incentives for illegal immigration; and
- refocus border-control resources to keep criminals and terrorists out of the country.

Immigrants remain a source of economic and social vitality for the United States today as they have throughout our history, even as immigration remains politically controversial. Since the federal government began counting in 1820, more than 73 million immigrants have legally entered the United States to settle and begin new lives. During the Great Migration of the late 19th and early 20th centuries, millions of immigrants helped power America's industrial rise and populate farms in the Midwest and Great Plains. Today, immigrants continue to fill niches in our labor market, at the high and the low end of the skill spectrum, while softening the demographic effect of declining birthrates.

Demographic Effect in Perspective

Critics complain about today's "mass immigration," but when compared with the current U.S. population of more than 300 million, today's immigration numbers are well within the norms of U.S. history. Since 2000, the United States has admitted an average of 1 million legal immigrants per year, or an immigration rate of 3.5 per year per 1,000 U.S. residents. That rate compares with an immigration rate of 9.4 to 10.5 in previous peak decades, as shown in Figure 60.1. In fact, the current legal immigration rate is lower than that of any decade between 1830 and 1930, and is below the average rate of 4.6 during the 19th and 20th centuries. The United States could significantly expand legal immigration and still be well below the immigration rates of previous periods.

The share of the U.S. population that is foreign-born also remains below its historical peaks. According to the U.S. Census Bureau, 12.7 percent of the U.S. population was foreign-born in 2006. That number has been steadily rising since its nadir in 1970, but it is still below the peak of nearly 15 percent in 1910. In other advanced, democratic countries, such as Australia, Canada, and Switzerland, immigrants are a higher share of the population than in the United States.

Immigration has not fueled a population explosion. Instead, it has only partially offset a steep decline in the birthrate and natural growth of the U.S. population and labor force. During the 20th century, the U.S. population grew an average of 1.3 percent per year. Since 2000, the annual growth rate has slipped to just below 1 percent, the slowest rate since the Great Depression. Without immigration, the growth of the U.S. labor force would decline rapidly toward zero during the next two decades. The primary drivers of local population growth remain births and internal migration. Since 2000, 43 percent of U.S. counties have lost population.

Figure 60.1
American Immigration in Perspective

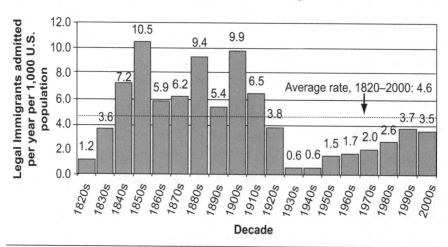

SOURCES: U.S. Census Bureau; *2007 Yearbook of Immigration Statistics,* U.S. Office of Immigration Statistics.

Immigration allows the United States to maintain a healthy if slowing increase in the workforce. Immigration also slows the aging of the U.S. population. According to the Census Bureau, the median age of immigrants who have arrived since 2000 is 28.1 years, compared with 35.6 years for the native-born population. Immigration is helping America avoid the serious demographic problems confronting rapidly aging societies such as Russia, Italy, Japan and, soon, China.

Our Restrictive Immigration System

Immigrating legally to the United States is not easy, despite complaints about "open borders." The United States was almost completely open to immigration from its founding until the 1920s. One of the few exceptions was the Chinese Exclusion Act of 1882, which blocked virtually all immigration from that country. In 1924, Congress imposed quotas on immigration that were designed to preserve the country's existing racial and ethnic composition by severely limiting immigration from southern and eastern Europe. Those quotas remained in effect until 1965.

Most immigrants who gain legal permanent residence status (i.e., a green card) either are closely related to a legal resident in the United States or are sponsored by an employer who must demonstrate a lack of sufficient U.S. workers available for the position. A U.S. citizen can sponsor his or her foreign-born spouse, minor and adult children, brothers and sisters, and parents (if the sponsor is 21 or older). A noncitizen, permanent legal resident can sponsor only his or her spouse, minor children, and adult unmarried children. There is no sponsorship of cousins, aunts, uncles, or other such extended family. A maximum of 50,000 "diversity visas" are also offered each year to immigrants from countries that send relatively few immigrants to the United States. The United States is also open to a limited number of refugees and asylum seekers who fear persecution in their home countries.

Most visa categories are limited by strict quotas. There is no cap on immediate relatives (spouses, minor children, and parents) of U.S. citizens, but all other family preference categories are limited to a total of 226,000 visas per year. In addition, no more than 7 percent of family preference or employment visas (about 26,000) each year can be granted to immigrants from any single country. One result of the quotas is long waiting periods. Spouses of legalized permanent residents can wait as long as 4 years to gain a green card, and siblings of U.S. citizens can wait as long as 20 years. Employment-based visas are capped at 140,000 per year. Most

627

of those visas are set aside for professors and researchers, members of professions such as doctors, and skilled workers such as computer scientists. Only 5,000 permanent residence visas are available each year for low-skilled workers.

In addition to green cards, the U.S. government also allocates nonimmigrant visas that allow foreigners to come to the United States temporarily for study, tourism, business, and diplomacy. Foreigners entering the United States temporarily far outnumber those who are given legal permanent residency. According to the Department of Homeland Security, the United States welcomed 33.7 million temporary visitors during the 2006 fiscal year. Of those, 24.9 million came for pleasure, 5 million for business, 1.7 million for employment, and 1.2 million for study and academic exchanges.

How to Attract Talented and Skilled Workers

To maintain American leadership in the global economy, Congress should raise or abolish the cap on H1-B visas. Congress should also expand the annual quota of employment-based green cards so the most valuable workers can remain in the United States.

Immigrants have played a vital role in the success of America's free-market economy. Some of America's most successful high-tech companies—Google, eBay, Yahoo!, Sun Microsystems, and Intel—were cofounded by immigrants. A 2007 study by the Pratt School of Engineering at Duke University found that one-quarter of all engineering and technology companies launched between 1995 and 2005 had at least one key founder who was foreign-born. Those companies produced $52 billion in sales and employed 450,000 workers in 2005. Most of the immigrant-founded companies were in the software and the innovation and/or manufacturing services sectors. The study also found that foreign nationals living in the United States were listed as inventors or coinventors on almost a quarter of the international patents filed from the United States in 2005.

American companies need to be able to compete for top talent in the world. Our producers must be able to hire the right workers with the right skills to compete in the global marketplace. The Bureau of Labor Statistics projects that the U.S. economy will add a net 1 million new jobs in computers, math, and engineering in the next decade. This expansion of demand occurs during a time when the number of native-born Americans earning degrees in those fields is woefully inadequate. Meanwhile, Canada,

Britain, Australia, and Singapore are competing for the same talent, while China and India become more attractive for returning expatriates.

The main channel for American companies to hire highly skilled foreign-born workers is the H1-B visa program. An H1-B visa allows a worker to enter the United States temporarily for a renewable period of three years. Current law maintains a cap of 65,000 such visas each year, plus another 20,000 for graduates of U.S. universities who have earned at least a master's degree. The 65,000 cap remains at the same level as when it was first imposed in 1990 despite the dramatic growth of America's high-tech sector. In recent years, requests for the visas have exceeded supply months before each fiscal year has begun. *The Economist* magazine was right to call our current H1-B cap "a policy of self-sabotage."

Restricting H1-B visas limits the ability of U.S. companies to expand their activities in the United States. If U.S. companies cannot find the skilled workers they need here at home, they will understandably look abroad to find their workforce through foreign outsourcing and offshoring. It is absurd to scold U.S. companies for hiring skilled workers abroad while denying them the ability to expand their skilled workforce at home.

Highly skilled workers generally complement rather than compete against American-born workers. H1-B workers create employment opportunities for native-born Americans by increasing research and development, production, and exports. Studies have shown that for every H1-B visa requested by an S&P 500 or technology company, the company typically adds five additional workers.

American companies do not hire H1-B workers to replace higher-paid American workers. By law, they cannot pay H1-B workers less than the market rate, and violations of the law have been rare. A competitive labor market makes it difficult for companies to underpay H1-B workers even if they could. If an H1-B worker were being underpaid by his or her current employer, another employer would have an incentive to lure him or her away from its competitor by offering a higher salary. U.S. companies also pay a premium of $6,000 to $10,000 in legal and other fees to hire an H1-B worker.

If what the critics charge were true, we would expect U.S. companies to hire more H1-B workers in difficult times to cut costs. In fact, we've seen the opposite. During the dot-com bust earlier this decade, we saw requests for H1-B visas plunge. U.S. companies apply for an H1-B visa only when they cannot find American workers who are right for the job. By severely restricting H1-B visas, Congress is crippling the ability of U.S.-based companies to compete successfully in the high-tech global market.

Low-Skilled and Illegal Immigration

Any lasting solution to the challenge of illegal immigration must recognize the legitimate needs of American employers to hire the workers necessary to meet the demands of their customers. Reform must also uphold the rule of law and enhance our national security.

According to the most widely accepted estimates, about 12 million foreign-born people are living in the United States without authorization, and that number has been growing by 400,000 to 500,000 annually in recent years. Most illegal immigrants are low-skilled workers, and most come from Mexico and Central America. The continuing inflow of unskilled immigrants to the United States has been driven by two powerful economic and demographic trends.

On the demand side, the U.S. economy continues to create hundreds of thousands of net new jobs each year that require relatively few skills. Although the fastest-growing categories of new jobs being created in our increasingly sophisticated economy require at least some specialized skills, training, and education, jobs are also being created in lower-skilled, mostly service sectors that complement the higher-end jobs.

Meanwhile, the supply of native-born Americans who have traditionally filled such jobs continues to shrink as the typical American worker becomes older and better educated. As recently as the early 1960s, half of the adult Americans in the workforce were high school dropouts; today, fewer than 7 percent of native-born American adults are laboring without a high school diploma. A better-educated labor force is a profoundly positive development, but it also means that fewer workers are willing to claim the still-growing number of jobs in our economy that require few skills and minimal formal education.

Immigrants fill that growing gap in the labor market. Those immigrant workers enable important sectors of the U.S. economy, such as retail, construction, landscaping, restaurants, and hotels, to continue to grow and meet the needs of their customers. Because of low-skilled immigration, those sectors have been able to expand, attract investment, and create middle-class jobs in management, bookkeeping, marketing, and other areas that employ native-born Americans.

Despite those realities, our immigration system contains no legal channel for lower-skilled foreign-born workers to enter the country legally to fill the jobs that an insufficient number of Americans want. As we've seen, visa categories exist for highly skilled foreign-born workers and for close family relatives of immigrants already in the country legally. But a peaceful, hard-working Mexican or Central American who knows of a job in the United States for which no Americans are available has virtually no legal means of entering the United States. The result of this missing channel is wide-scale illegal immigration.

For the past 20 years, the U.S. government has pursued a policy of "enforcement only" in its effort to curb illegal immigration. Since the late 1980s, spending on border enforcement has grown exponentially. The number of Border Patrol officers grew threefold between 1986 and 2002, and doubled again during President Bush's two terms in office. Miles of fencing have been erected through urban border areas and into the surrounding desert. Since 1986, U.S. employers have been subject to fines for knowingly hiring undocumented workers. There is no evidence that more vigorous enforcement has had any long-term effect on the number of illegal workers entering the country. (See Chapter 29, "National ID Systems," for a critique of interior enforcement programs.)

Our current policy has perversely interrupted what had been an established circular pattern of migration from Mexico to the United States. From the mid-1960s to the mid-1980s, during a time of relatively relaxed border enforcement, an estimated 80 percent of Mexicans who entered the United States illegally eventually returned to Mexico. The federal government's ramped-up border enforcement turned a temporary and circular flow into a permanent and growing settlement of illegal immigrants.

The most rational, cost-effective way to reduce illegal immigration is comprehensive immigration reform, including a sufficiently accommodating temporary worker program. Any real hope of reducing illegal immigration will depend on allowing enough foreign-born workers to enter the United States legally to fill the growing gap at the lower rungs of the labor ladder. Without a workable temporary visa program, workers will continue to enter the United States illegally, with all the consequences that flow from a continued influx and stock of illegal workers.

Skeptics of immigration reform point to the 1986 Immigration Reform and Control Act as evidence that reform and legalization cannot work. The 1986 act offered legal permanent resident status to 2.7 million illegal workers who had entered the country before 1982 and to certain agricultural workers, and it significantly ramped up enforcement efforts. Notably missing from the IRCA, however, was any provision to expand the opportunity for low-skilled workers to enter the country legally. The pool of illegal workers was drained temporarily by the amnesty, but it soon began to fill up again as the economic pull of the U.S. labor market overwhelmed even the stepped-up enforcement efforts.

We know from experience that legal immigration, if allowed, will crowd out illegal immigration. In the 1950s, the Bracero program allowed Mexican workers to enter the country temporarily, typically to work on farms in the Southwest. Early in that decade, illegal immigration was widespread because the program offered an insufficient number of visas to meet the labor demands of a growing U.S. economy. Instead of merely redoubling efforts to enforce a flawed law, Congress dramatically increased the number of visas to accommodate demand. As a result, apprehensions of illegal entrants at the border soon dropped by more than 95 percent. Back then, as we can expect now, foreign-born workers rationally chose the legal path to entry when it was available. When the Bracero program was abolished in 1964, illegal immigration began an inexorable rise that continues to this day.

If the goal is to curb illegal immigration, any temporary worker program must offer enough visas to meet the legitimate demands of a growing U.S. labor market. The fact that 400,000 to 500,000 foreign-born workers join the U.S. labor force each year indicates the general magnitude of how much demand exceeds the supply of available, legal workers. A temporary worker program should offer at least that number of visas to allow the revealed demand of American employers to be met legally.

Any temporary worker program must also include complete worker mobility. The best protection for legalized workers remains the freedom to change jobs if pay or conditions are unsatisfactory. A portable visa that allows temporary workers to freely chose whom they work for with a minimum of red tape would enhance their bargaining power in the market-place, improving their pay and working conditions.

Comprehensive reform should also offer legal status to workers already here without authorization. It would be an economic and humanitarian disaster, as well as an administrative nightmare, to round up the 12 million people already here illegally and somehow deport them to their home countries. Most have been in the country for five years or more, and 40 percent have been here for more than a decade. Their contributions to their employers and the U.S. economy should be recognized and weighed against their violation of U.S. immigration laws.

Long-standing critics of comprehensive immigration reform will brand any legalization as an "amnesty." But amnesty means a general pardon, in particular for political offenses. Legalization would not be a pardon or amnesty because, according to the most serious proposals put forward in Congress, undocumented workers would be expected to pay fines and back taxes. They would not be granted the automatic permanent legal status that was a core feature of the IRCA, but only temporary status to remain and work in the United States for a specified period. They would not be given any advantage over applicants currently waiting for permanent status.

Unfounded Fears of Legalization

Expanding legal immigration would not cause a flood of new immigrants, exploding welfare costs, rising crime, lower wages, or compromised security. Legalization would not mean large numbers of new immigrants but rather the replacement of illegal workers with legal workers. Any fears of "chain migration" can be addressed by limiting sponsorships to the "nuclear family" of spouses and minor children. The result would be to allow nuclear families to remain intact, while incrementally moving the U.S. immigration system from one that is primarily family based to one that is employment based.

Only a small and declining share of the American workforce competes against immigrant workers. Studies by the National Research Council and the National Bureau of Economic Research have found that immigration exerts a small negative effect on the wages of the small and declining number of Americans without a high school diploma, while delivering higher real wages to the vast majority of native-born American workers. Enabling and urging young Americans to graduate from high school will do far more to raise the earnings of American workers than barring low-skilled immigrants from the country.

To minimize the effect on taxpayers, immigrant access to welfare and other government payments should be strictly limited. Passage of the 1996 welfare reform act led to a reduction in welfare rolls even as the number of legal and illegal immigrants in the country continued to rise. A 2007 Congressional Budget Office study found that immigration reform would not cause a net loss to the federal government during the decade after its enactment. Studies in Texas, North Carolina, and other states have found a modest negative effect on state and local budgets from low-skilled immigration, but they also noted that those losses were more than offset by economic gains to state residents. Nor do immigrants increase the overall crime rate. Immigrants are actually less likely to commit crimes than native-born Americans. Crime rates have fallen by a third since the early 1990s, while the number of illegal immigrants living in the country has doubled. Policymakers concerned about the fiscal effect of immigration should aim to wall off the welfare state, not our country.

Immigration reform would actually enhance America's border security by bringing more order to the border. Reform would greatly reduce demand for human smuggling, document fraud, and other underground criminal activities. It would encourage millions of undocumented workers to come forward to register and cooperate with law enforcement authorities. It would allow the Homeland Security Department to concentrate its apprehension efforts on violent criminals and terrorists rather than meatpackers and janitors. As Homeland Security Secretary Michael Chertoff told Congress in 2007: "A regulated channel for temporary workers would dramatically reduce the pressure on our borders, aid our economy and ease the task of our law enforcement agents inside the country. There is an inextricable link between the creation of a temporary worker program and better enforcement at the border."

Conclusion

Regulating immigration is the responsibility of the federal government. Enacting economically sound and prudent immigration reform on a national level would bring coherence to the growing patchwork of state and local law enforcement efforts aimed at curbing illegal immigration. There is no substitute for a comprehensive federal immigration system that promotes family cohesion, economic innovation, long-term growth, the rule of law, and secure borders.

Suggested Readings

Anderson, Stuart. "The Impact of Agricultural Guest Worker Programs on Illegal Immigration." National Foundation for American Policy, November 2003.

Griswold, Daniel. "Willing Workers: Fixing the Problem of Illegal Mexican Migration to the United States." Cato Institute Trade Policy Analysis no. 19, October 15, 2002.

――――. "Comprehensive Immigration Reform: Finally Getting It Right." Cato Institute Free Trade Bulletin no. 29, May 16, 2007. www.freetrade.org.

――――. "The Fiscal Impact of Immigration Reform: The Real Story." Cato Institute Free Trade Bulletin no. 30, May 21, 2007.

Legrain, Philippe. *Immigrants: Your Country Needs Them*. Princeton, NJ: Princeton University Press, 2007.

Massey, Douglas S., Jorge Durand, and Nolan J. Malone. *Beyond Smoke and Mirrors: Mexican Immigration in an Era of Economic Integration*. New York: Russell Sage Foundation, 2002.

National Foundation for American Policy. "H1-B Visas and Job Creation." Policy brief, March 2008. www.nfap.net.

National Research Council. *The New Americans: Economic, Demographic, and Fiscal Effects of Immigration*. Washington: National Academy Press, 1997.

Riley, Jason L. *Let Them In: The Case for Open Borders: Six Common Arguments against Immigration and Why They Are Wrong.* New York: Gotham Books, 2008.

—Prepared by Daniel Griswold

61. U.S. Policy toward Latin America

> **Policymakers should**
> - unilaterally open the U.S. market to goods from Latin America,
> - support the Colombia and Panama Free Trade Agreements,
> - end the hemispheric war on drugs, and
> - facilitate dollarization for any country that wishes to adopt the dollar as its national currency.

In limited but important ways, Washington can positively influence economic policy in Latin America. At a time when some countries in the region have seen the rise of populist governments, political turmoil, and a general backlash against free-market reforms that were partially implemented in the 1990s, the United States should exercise its influence by opening its market to the region's goods and by encouraging market reforms.

During most of the time since the passage of the North American Free Trade Agreement with Mexico and Canada in 1993, however, the United States showed no such leadership. Instead, Washington promised to create a hemispheric free trade zone, known as the Free Trade Area of the Americas, but made little effort to promote the idea.

The result was unfortunate, and a window of opportunity was lost. Latin American countries that were eager to enter into a free trade agreement gradually became disillusioned with years of U.S. inaction, and some turned decidedly against the idea of free trade. Worse, as economist Sebastian Edwards points out, Washington's promise of promoting the Free Trade Area of the Americas had the perverse effect of actually halting unilateral trade barrier reductions in Latin America as those countries waited to negotiate reductions as a group with the United States, an expectation that went unfulfilled. Moreover, from the Mexican peso crisis of 1994–95 to the Brazilian currency crisis of 2002, Washington supported massive International Monetary Fund bailouts that encouraged irresponsible behavior by investors and policymakers and surely increased the severity of economic crises in the region.

President Bush emphasized free trade in general and bilateral trade agreements specifically as policy priorities. His administration's initial support for increased steel tariffs and farm subsidies damaged Washington's credibility in a region already wary of U.S. intentions. But the Bush administration quickly regained the initiative, having ushered free trade agreements with Chile, the Dominican Republic, and Peru and with Central America into law and having negotiated free trade agreements with Colombia and Panama. To understand the importance of free trade in Latin America, we must first understand where the region has been.

Latin America since the 1990s

The early 1990s saw the introduction of far-reaching market reforms in many, but not all, Latin American countries, especially in the areas of monetary policy, trade and investment liberalization, and privatization of state-owned enterprises. Countries in the region ended hyperinflation, reduced their tariffs unilaterally, and eventually sold more than $150 billion of state assets. The initial results were high growth and the widespread popularity of the reforms in the countries that did the most to reform. Mexican president Carlos Salinas was the most popular outgoing president in Mexican history in 1994, and presidents Alberto Fujimori of Peru and Carlos Menem of Argentina were reelected by wide margins in the mid-1990s.

By the end of the decade and the beginning of the next one, however, several countries had experienced years of recession, political instability, and economic crises. Even countries that had introduced only timid reforms had that experience. The International Monetary Fund bailed out Argentina, Brazil, Mexico, and Uruguay, some more than once. Most spectacular was the collapse of the Argentine economy in early 2002. That country's default and devaluation sent it into a deep depression, calling into question market reforms in the minds of many Argentines. Latin America's disappointing average annual per capita growth of 1.2 percent in the 1990s was still better than that of the "lost decade" of the 1980s (− 0.2 percent), but it certainly did not live up to expectations and was too often accompanied by economic turmoil.

It is within that context of disillusionment that politicians using populist or demagogic rhetoric have risen to power in Argentina, Bolivia, Ecuador,

Nicaragua, Paraguay, and Venezuela, vilifying the free market as the source of their countries' troubles. Populist politics have influenced the leadership style of more responsible leftist governments, like that of Brazil, and still attract a following among large portions of the populations of countries, like Mexico or Peru, that have chosen not to go down that path. Latin America is thus a divided region between those who wish their countries to become modern democracies based on open markets and those who would opt for various forms of populism based on state-directed development.

But to blame the market is hopelessly wrongheaded. It is important to remember that the regionwide shift to the market occurred because of the failure of past policies, not because governments were committed to free-market principles. For example, the left-leaning ruling party in Mexico, the Peronist Party in Argentina, and Fujimori's upstart party, which campaigned against radical market reforms in Peru, introduced liberalization. By the mid-1990s, with the success of the early reforms, governments lost interest in liberalization. The unfinished reform agenda was extensive and brought diminishing returns in the form of slower growth and negative economic indicators. Argentina, for example, suffered from chronically high unemployment throughout the 1990s because it never reformed its rigid labor laws. Latin America had only begun to embrace economic freedom.

Indeed, a whole range of institutions and policies has been left untouched. The pervasiveness of a vast informal economy in most Latin American countries attests to that fact. The region's citizens have long responded to the high costs of the formal legal and regulatory system by simply operating outside it. They have found the formal system of rules to be prohibitively expensive. The private property rights of the poor in urban and rural areas, for example, are typically not recognized or protected by the state since property titling is complicated or impossible. Yet private property lies at the heart of a market system, and the absence of property titles severely restrains the creation of wealth. Bureaucratic red tape also pushes people into the informal sector. Opening a small business in Latin America legally can cost thousands of dollars in licensing fees and take months or years for approval—a procedure that costs less and takes days in rich countries. The rule of law, another institution essential to the functioning of a market economy, is severely defective or nonexistent in the region. Latin America has received low scores on both the rule of law and its business regulation in *Economic Freedom of the World.*

Other sectors, including health care, education, and public security, have seen virtually no reform although they have continued to deteriorate, often

639

despite increases in spending. That situation has led Argentine economist Ricardo López Murphy to complain that Argentines pay Swedish-level tax rates for public services of African quality.

Thus, Latin America in the 1990s moved partially down the path of economic freedom, but as a region, it still has a long way to travel if it is to sustain growth and avoid financial turmoil. Indeed, the continued adherence to old policy practices in large part explains the region's economic problems since the era of market reforms. The crash of the Mexican peso, for example, resulted from a government-managed exchange rate and expansionary monetary and fiscal policies during an election year, policies thoroughly inconsistent with market economics. Likewise, Brazil has maintained more orthodox macroeconomic policies in recent years alongside some of the world's most burdensome regulations and most wealth inhibiting tax systems, according to the World Economic Forum. Those policies have contributed to an average annual growth rate (3.8 percent) far below that of developing countries as a whole (7.4 percent) during the global economic boom years of 2003–07.

Latin American Success Stories Teach the Real Lessons from the Region

The region's stark ideological divide is most visible along geographic lines. With a couple of exceptions, Latin American countries along the Pacific Rim have signed or are pursuing free trade agreements with the United States and have chosen market democracy as their model. Other countries, led by Venezuela, have chosen various degrees of greater state involvement in economic and social affairs. But not all leftist governments have accepted the populist agenda. Brazil and Uruguay, for example, have tried to maintain sensible macroeconomic policies with the latter country expressing interest in free trade with the United States. Chile, led by a Socialist government, has maintained its status as the freest economy in Latin America.

The most important lessons from the region come from success stories like Chile and from emerging successes that are increasingly setting themselves apart from the rest of Latin America. Chile stands out the most because it has applied and maintained the most far-reaching and coherent set of market-liberal policies for the longest time. The resulting high growth has enabled the country to more than double its per capita income since the late 1980s and to achieve impressive advances in a range of human development indicators. According to the Santiago-based Institute for Liberty and Development, for example, from 1987 to 2006 Chile reduced its poverty rate from 45 percent to 14 percent.

El Salvador has also seen impressive progress under democratic governance. Since the early 1990s, it has been a fast reformer, becoming one of the freest economies in Latin America. There too, growth has transformed the economy, cutting household poverty by about half and extreme poverty by about 60 percent. Peru is another example of a country that implemented and maintained market reforms, thus turning it in recent years into the highest-growth country in the region. Poverty rates have fallen notably, new industries have arisen, nontraditional exports have boomed, and the middle class has grown. Indeed, the growth of the middle class in much of the region is another positive outcome of a stable macroeconomic environment that many countries have achieved. Felipe Calderón's victory over the populist candidate in Mexico's 2006 presidential election was largely due to the middle-class vote. There, free trade played a key role by providing high-quality goods at lower prices to Mexican consumers and, just as important, by helping to spur growth in the Mexican economy. The North American Free Trade Agreement enabled Mexico to begin recovering from its 1994–95 crisis within a year. By contrast, it took Mexico six years to recover from its economic crisis of 1982, a time when its economy was fairly closed.

The policies of the successful countries contrast sharply with those of populist governments, namely, because the region's successes are producing growth based on wealth creation rather than growth based primarily on external factors, such as high world growth or high commodity prices, the earnings of which are then redistributed in the country. Although countries led by populist governments have also enjoyed high growth, their situation is more precarious, and social and economic problems are already emerging there. Uncontrolled spending, scarcity of certain goods, and rising inflation, for example, characterize the Argentine and Venezuelan economies. Populist policies, moreover, are not limited to economics. In Venezuela, President Hugo Chávez has violated the most fundamental principles of democracy, eliminating all checks and balances in government, curtailing freedom of speech and other civil and political liberties, and otherwise ignoring due legislative and legal processes. Because Venezuela is oil rich, the Chávez regime is not just a menace to Venezuelans but also to populations of other Latin American countries, where the regime is spending heavily to try to export its model. That model includes explicit rejections of free trade with the United States in favor of trade agreements between Venezuela and Latin American countries that would receive Venezuelan government subsidies purportedly to promote development.

The divergence in performance between the two models in the region will become even clearer in the coming years. The United States can continue to buttress that demonstration effect by ratifying the free trade agreements with Colombia and Panama. Those free trade agreements would benefit the United States and its trade treaty partners, and they would be yet another signal to the region that the United States is willing to reward countries that implement free-market policies. Nowhere is that more important than in the case of Colombia. That country is properly seen as the ideological opposite of Venezuela, successfully fighting the leftist FARC guerrillas on its own territory; aggressively pursuing free trade with the United States; and denouncing the kinds of populist policies and belligerent foreign policy of its neighbor, Venezuela. Were the United States to deny signing the free trade agreement with Colombia into law, it would not only be a blow to Colombia and Alvaro Uribe, who enjoys the highest popularity ratings of any president in Latin America, it would also be seen throughout the region as a blow to all those in Latin America who favor democratic capitalism.

Washington should likewise continue to pursue free trade with other Latin American countries that have liberalized their economies and are eager to sign a trade treaty with the United States. Independent of free trade negotiations, the United States should immediately reduce its barriers to Latin America's exports, especially textiles and agricultural products. At a time when U.S. credibility is being questioned, such a move would restore some goodwill toward Washington and might help persuade reluctant countries to reduce some of their own trade barriers. At the very least, the United States could then not be blamed for hypocrisy, and the welfare of both the United States and Latin America would improve. Such a unilateral policy of reducing trade barriers, moreover, would not conflict with the goal of negotiating free trade agreements. As Cato Institute scholar Brink Lindsey points out, the United States has regularly signed trade agreements affecting sectors of the U.S. economy that enjoy virtually no protection. For countries that are interested in free trade with the United States, such agreements offer the advantage of "locking in" free trade both at home and abroad. Indeed, the certainty provided by free trade treaties is one of their greatest benefits and explains why they tend to result in increases of both trade and investment.

Dollarization

The United States should support another development in the hemisphere: dollarization. In an effort to eliminate currency risk, including sudden and large devaluations and other manifestations of irresponsible monetary policy, Ecuador and El Salvador joined Panama as countries that use the U.S. dollar as their national currency. Because most of the region's central banks have a poor record of maintaining the value of their currencies, Latin Americans already use the dollar widely, and it has become the currency of choice in many countries. Other countries may wish to replace their currencies with the dollar as well.

The United States should neither discourage nor encourage those moves but should facilitate official dollarization where it occurs. That may mean sharing the dollar's seigniorage—the profit that derives from printing currency—with countries that decide to dollarize. In that way, the United States would neither gain nor lose money as a result of another country's decision to dollarize, but the dollarizing country might more easily dollarize if it could still earn seigniorage from the currency it uses. Dollarization alone cannot solve a country's economic problems, but for countries with poor monetary policies, dollarization would end currency risk, reduce interest rates, and help stimulate investment and growth.

A Constructive Policy toward Latin America

The United States can play a strategic role in promoting economic freedom, stability, and growth in Latin America. In addition to promoting trade, that also means that Washington must end its destructive war on drugs in the region, which works at cross-purposes with important U.S. policy priorities (See Chapter 58, "The International Drug War"). In drug-source and transit countries such as Colombia and Mexico, the drug war is fueling corruption and violence, financing terrorism, undermining the rule of law, and otherwise debilitating the institutions of civil society. In the first nine months of 2008 alone, drug violence killed almost 3,000 people in Mexico as a result of a more aggressive prosecution of the trade. The effect of the U.S.-led war on drugs south of the border has been imperceptible in the United States, but its consequences in Latin America are completely at odds with Washington's stated goal of encouraging free markets and civil society.

The rhetoric of free trade must be followed by policy actions consistent with such language. Congress should support a unilateral reduction of

643

trade barriers to the region's goods and continue to negotiate free trade agreements with countries eager to do so. The United States would thus highlight the success of market reformers in the region by rewarding them without penalizing others. The diverging performances of the countries that embrace economic freedom and the rest can have a powerful effect on the policy direction that Latin American countries subsequently take.

Suggested Readings

Carpenter, Ted Galen. *Bad Neighbor Policy: Washington's Futile War on Drugs in Latin America.* New York: Palgrave/Macmillan, 2003.

Coronel, Gustavo. "Corruption, Mismanagement and Abuse of Power in Hugo Chávez's Venezuela." Cato Institute Development Policy Analysis no. 2, November 27, 2006.

De Althaus, Jaime. *La Revolución Capitalista en el Perú.* Lima, Peru: Fondo de Cultura Económica, 2007.

Fukuyama, Francis, ed. *Falling Behind: Explaining the Development Gap between Latin America and the United States.* New York: Oxford University Press, 2008.

Griswold, Daniel, and Juan Carlos Hidalgo. "A U.S.-Colombia Free Trade Agreement: Strengthening Democracy and Progress in Latin America." Cato Institute Free Trade Bulletin no. 32, February 7, 2008.

Hidalgo, Juan Carlos. "El Salvador: Central American Tiger." Cato Institute Development Policy Analysis, forthcoming.

Mendoza, Plinio Apuleyo, Carlos Alberto Montaner, and Alvaro Vargas Llosa. *Guide to the Perfect Latin American Idiot.* New York: Madison Books, 2001.

Montaner, Carlos Alberto. *Las Raíces Torcidas de América Latina.* Barcelona: Plaza & Janes, 2001.

Reid, Michael. *Forgotten Continent: The Battle for Latin America's Soul.* New Haven, CT: Yale University Press, 2007.

Schuler, Kurt. "Fixing Argentina." Cato Institute Policy Analysis no. 445, July 16, 2002.

Vargas Llosa, Alvaro. *Liberty for Latin America.* New York: Farrar, Straus & Giroux, 2005.

Vargas Llosa, Mario. "Foreword." In *The Other Path,* by Hernando de Soto. New York: Harper and Row, 1989.

Vásquez, Ian. "A Retrospective on the Mexican Bailout." *Cato Journal* 21, no. 3 (Winter 2002).

Véliz, Claudio. *The New World of the Gothic Fox: Culture and Economy in English and Spanish America.* Berkeley: University of California Press, 1994.

—Prepared by Ian Vásquez

62. U.S. Policy toward Sub-Saharan Africa

Congress should

- expand the Africa Growth and Opportunity Act by granting tariff- and quota-free access to all imports from sub-Saharan Africa,
- end U.S. farm subsidies that help undermine African producers and keep food prices in the United States unnecessarily high,
- forgive sub-Saharan African debt on the condition of ending future official lending to governments in the region,
- oppose International Monetary Fund and World Bank lending to sub-Saharan Africa,
- discontinue the U.S. Africa Command that might draw the United States into more African conflicts and be viewed by Africans as a neocolonialist venture, and
- impose "smart" sanctions on leaders under strong suspicion of corruption and human rights abuses.

Sub-Saharan Africa (Africa hereafter) consists of 48 countries, making up an area of 9.4 million square miles and with a population of 782 million people in 2006. Africa is one of the poorest regions in the world. The UN Human Development Index, which measures quality of life around the world on a scale of 0 (low) to 1 (high), scored Africa at 0.493. The scores for the developing world and the United States were 0.691 and 0.951, respectively. Africa lags behind most of the world in practically all indicators of human well-being, including longevity, infant mortality, HIV, malaria and tuberculosis occurrence, nourishment, school enrolment, long-term economic growth, and income per capita.

The ability of the United States to help Africa is limited because most of Africa's development problems are caused by domestic factors requiring domestic solutions. Those problems are extensive and have been aggravated by arbitrary and authoritarian rule, which has been the norm for most of Africa's independence. Centralized political control has undermined political stability, the rule of law, the security of individuals, the protection of private property, and growth.

Indeed, most African governments have imposed central control over their economies, a development strategy not conducive to economic growth. Inflationary monetary policies; price, wage and exchange rate controls; marketing boards (which keep the prices of agricultural products artificially low, thus impoverishing African farmers); and state-owned enterprises and monopolies are commonplace.

Microeconomic policy in the region has also been counterproductive. For example, business regulation in Africa remains much too restrictive. It takes only 2 days for an entrepreneur to start a business in Australia, but 155 days in the Democratic Republic of Congo. No minimum capital is required to start a business in Singapore, but a minimum capital requirement equal to 1,532 percent of the average annual income is needed in Ethiopia. It takes 83 days to enforce a contract in Denmark, but 1,011 days in Angola.

African governments also restrict foreign and domestic investment, and Africa's tariffs are among the highest in the world. According to the World Bank, the average applied tariff on imports to African countries is 14.03 percent. Djibouti, Africa's most protectionist country, implements an average applied tariff of 30.2 percent on imported goods. In contrast, the average tariff of emerging economies like Chile, South Korea, and Taiwan is 5.6 percent.

On the whole, African economies continue to be largely unfree. According to the *Economic Freedom of the World* report, economic freedom in Africa increased at a very sluggish pace in recent decades. On a scale of 0 to 10, where 10 represents the highest measured level of freedom, Africa moved from 4.6 in 1980 to 5.8 in 2006. In contrast, economic freedom in the United States was 8.04 in 2006.

Botswana is a rare exception. Botswana's economic freedom increased from 5.8 in 1980 to 7.0 in 2006. Between 1980 and 2006, Botswana was consistently ranked among Africa's three freest economies. Between 1980 and 2006, its compounded average annual gross domestic product growth rate per capita was 5.4 percent. In Africa, average per capita growth was −0.25 percent. Botswana's GDP per capita adjusted for inflation and purchasing power parity rose from $3,325 in 1980 to $12,121 in 2006.

In Africa as a whole, income stagnated, going from $1,715 in 1980 to $1,727 in 2006.

As long as its economic freedom remains low, Africa's economic performance will continue to disappoint. Similarly, African countries are unlikely to escape poverty as long as their governments remain unaccountable and their actions arbitrary. Unfortunately, there is little the United States can do to positively influence the evolution of Africa's governing institutions and the policies that African countries adopt.

Free Trade

The United States can help by further opening its markets to African exports. Congress has taken a step in the right direction, by adopting the Africa Growth and Opportunity Act in 2000 and later extending it to 2015. With the addition of Togo in April 2008, 40 African countries are now eligible to export to the United States under the terms of the act. In 2007, over 98 percent of U.S. imports from AGOA-eligible countries entered the United States duty-free.

In 2007, AGOA imports totaled $51.1 billion. That amount was more than six times the value of AGOA imports in 2001—the first full year of AGOA provisions. Although petroleum products accounted for most of the AGOA imports, nonoil AGOA imports doubled to $3.4 billion since 2001. Moreover, between 2006 and 2007, U.S. exports to Africa increased by 19 percent to $14.4 billion.

The benefits of free trade are political and economic. First, free trade can be a potent weapon against terror directed against the United States. Apparel trade with the United States alone has created tens of thousands of jobs in the AGOA countries. Such increased economic interconnectedness between the world's trouble spots and the United States may help dissuade potential terrorist sympathizers from harming the United States. National security considerations are clearly relevant to Africa. American lives and assets were targeted in the 1998 embassy bombings in Kenya and Tanzania. Al Qaeda activities have been reported in Somalia and Sudan.

Second, trade increases specialization. Increased specialization leads to increasing productivity. Reductions in the cost of production lead to cheaper goods and services, which, in turn, increase the standard of living for Americans and Africans alike. Unfortunately, Washington limits the economic benefits of AGOA by excluding a variety of products, including those in which Africa could have a comparative trade advantage, from tariff- and quota-free treatment. For example, the United States restricts

647

imports of cotton, sugar, some dairy goods, soft drinks, cocoa products, coffee, tea, tobacco, and peanuts.

Researchers at the World Bank, the IMF, and the University of Maryland found that AGOA yields only 19 to 26 percent of the benefits that it could if it were comprehensive and unconditional. Concerns that further trade opening would negatively affect the number of American jobs are misplaced, especially since AGOA's share of American imports is only 3.3 percent—and it is made up mostly of oil.

While opening U.S. markets to African goods can help Africa, such a move is not sufficient to bring Africa out of poverty. For Africa to prosper, African countries will have to cut their own external and internal trade barriers and undertake wide-ranging economic reforms that will enable Africa's private sector to grow.

Agricultural Subsidies

In addition to making AGOA comprehensive and unconditional, the U.S. government should stop subsidizing the American agricultural sector. The 2008 Farm Bill, which prescribes subsidies and other support for agriculture, will cost U.S. taxpayers $307 billion over the next five years.

Ending farm subsidies would make some agricultural products exported by African countries more competitive, raising farm incomes and reducing poverty in Africa. A recent Oxfam study, for example, found that a complete removal of subsidies to American cotton growers would increase the world price of cotton by between 6 percent and 12 percent, and increase household income in West Africa by between 2.3 percent and 5.7 percent. A richer Africa would provide a more lucrative environment for American firms. Greater economic interdependence and rising prosperity would improve relations between the United States and Africa, and enhance U.S. security.

Foreign Aid

Between 1960 and 2006, U.S. annual official development assistance to Africa increased from $211 million to $5.6 billion in constant 2006 dollars, an increase of an astonishing 2,661 percent. The ratio of U.S. aid to Africa as a percentage of the entire U.S. aid budget rose 17 times, from 1.4 percent in 1960 to 23.8 percent in 2006. Aid to Africa more than tripled under President Bush. Unfortunately, U.S. aid to Africa has done little to promote economic growth.

British economist Peter Bauer once described foreign aid as "taxing poor people in rich countries and passing it on to rich people in poor countries." That is an especially accurate description of aid to Africa. Aid there has increased the size of government to the detriment of the private sector. It has enabled government officials to embezzle large amounts of money and misspend much on loss-making projects. Citizens were left with large debt. Africa has been one of the largest recipients of aid per capita (see Figure 62.1). But, as Figure 62.2 shows, African economic performance has been very poor. Today, most researchers agree that economic growth depends on market-oriented domestic policies.

Countries that follow sound economic policies grow regardless of aid. A comparison between two similarly poor regions, Africa and South Asia (Afghanistan, Bangladesh, Bhutan, India, Maldives, Nepal, Pakistan, and Sri Lanka), may be instructive. As Figure 62.1 shows, between 1981 and 2006, aid to Africa averaged $29 per capita per year (in current dollars). The comparable figure for South Asia was $5. Over those 25 years, South Asian GDP per capita grew at a compounded average annual rate of 3.63 percent. In contrast, growth in Africa hovered around zero.

As Figure 62.2 shows, South Asian GDP per capita grew from $901 in 1981 to $2,215 in 2006. By the same measure, African GDP per capita barely moved—from $1,687 to $1,727.

Figure 62.1
Foreign Aid to Sub-Saharan Africa and South Asia, 1981–2006

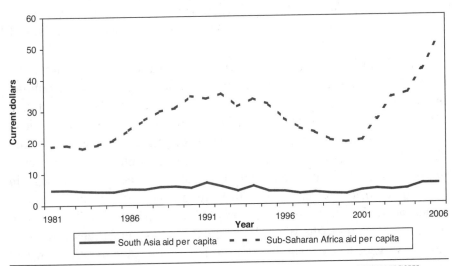

SOURCE: World Bank, *World Development Indicators Online.* http://go.worldbank.org/6HAYAHG8H0.

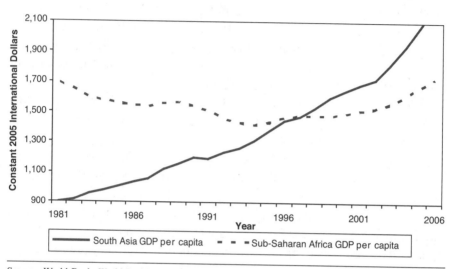

Figure 62.2
Per Capita Income in Sub-Saharan Africa and South Asia,
1981–2006

SOURCE: World Bank, *World Development Indicators Online.* http://go.worldbank.org/6HAYAHG8H0.

The percentage of people in Africa living on less than $1 a day decreased by 5.6 percentage points—from 46.7 percent in 1990 to 41.1 percent in 2004. During the same period, absolute poverty in South Asia declined by 12.2 percentage points—from 43 percent to 30.8 percent. The National Bureau of Economic Research estimated that 1 in 10 people surviving on less than $1 a day in 1970 lived in Africa. In 2004, that number was 1 in 2.

Aside from bilateral aid, Washington also participates in multilateral aid schemes overseen by a variety of international institutions, including the World Bank, the African Development Bank, and the International Monetary Fund. Those multilateral institutions have also backed African regimes that have engaged in gross macroeconomic mismanagement. And although the World Bank's structural adjustment programs and IMF lending were designed to provide credit in exchange for economic reforms in the region, African compliance with lending conditions has been poor or nonexistent. For example, Daniel arap Moi of Kenya "sold" the same package of reforms to the World Bank and the IMF several times. Similarly, Robert Mugabe broke a number of promises to liberalize the Zimbabwean economy. When policy mistakes resulted in Zimbabwe's economic decline,

Mugabe blamed the World Bank and IMF, and their main sponsor, the United States.

The World Bank and IMF do not have the ability to enforce compliance with their loan conditions. Yet both agencies keep lending and Africa's debt continues to accumulate. Out of the 33 countries approved to receive debt relief under the Heavily Indebted Poor Countries Initiative, 27 are African. In 2005, Africa's long-term debt stood at $177 billion, of which $164 billion or 93 percent was public or publicly guaranteed debt (i.e., debt owed by or guaranteed by African governments). That is a dramatic testament to the failure of foreign aid in Africa.

Much of the debt incurred by African governments was misallocated by incompetent government officials or stolen. The people of Africa received few or no benefits. The United States could forgive its share (3.3 percent) of the HIPCs' debt, but debt cancellation will work only if the United States and other official creditors refuse to lend to African governments in the future. Indeed, despite receiving $33 billion in debt relief between 1989 and 1997, HIPCs kept borrowing and falling further into debt. That necessitated another round of debt relief under the auspices of the Multilateral Debt Relief Initiative. In 2005, the year the MDRI came into existence, the debt relief in question was worth an estimated $69 billion in net present value terms.

To break this vicious cycle, HIPCs should rely only on private lenders. Private lenders should be made aware that Western governments will not bail them out in case of a sovereign default. That will make lenders more circumspect when lending money to African countries. Greater scarcity of capital and higher interest rates may encourage African governments to liberalize.

AFRICOM

The U.S. Africa Command began operations on October 1, 2007. The military unit has 600 U.S. personnel currently assigned to it, with plans to expand it to 1,300. AFRICOM is currently stationed in Germany but may soon relocate to an African country, possibly Liberia. In 2008, AFRICOM had a budget of $75.5 million. That was projected to increase to $392 million in 2009. AFRICOM intends to focus on war prevention and to work with African countries to build regional security and crisis-response capacity.

If history is any guide, AFRICOM's mission will expand—as will the number of its personnel. That is partly why most African governments reacted to its creation with apprehension. For example, Nigeria and South Africa, Africa's most powerful nations, have expressed their reservations, claiming that AFRICOM would lead to unwanted expansion of American military influence in Africa and turn the continent into another battleground in the war on terror.

Still others see AFRICOM as a neocolonial adventure necessitated by America's hunger for Africa's natural resources. American decisionmakers should not underestimate African nationalists' continued suspicion of Western motives and their likely perception of AFRICOM's goals as a smoke screen for an American attempt to grab Africa's mineral wealth.

Moreover, most Americans oppose the United States' acting as the world's policeman. Given that African conflicts pose no compelling threat to the vital national interests of the United States, there is little public support for the creation of a new institution to coordinate such activities in Africa.

Smart Sanctions

In cases of gross human rights violations, some form of sanctions may be deemed essential. In the past, few international economic sanctions intended to change the policies of the targeted country have met with success. Global agreement on imposition of sanctions is difficult to reach. Moreover, sanctions tend to harm the poor much more than the ruling elite. They often strengthen the ruling regime and encourage nationalism. The United States could help Africa, however, by targeting those leaders in the region, who are strongly suspected of corruption and abuses of human rights. "Smart sanctions" are unlikely to bring about change in government, but they do make the lives of the ruling elite more difficult.

Measures that should be considered against African dictators and their collaborators include international arrest warrants, freezing of personal assets abroad, prohibitions on travel, and arms embargos. The United States imposed a variety of targeted sanctions on Robert Mugabe of Zimbabwe and his chief lieutenants, which further weakened and isolated the regime in Harare.

Suggested Readings

Baffes, John. "The 'Cotton Problem' in West and Central Africa: The Case for Domestic Reforms." Cato Institute Economic Development Bulletin no. 11, July 10, 2007.

Beaulier, Scott A. "Explaining Botswana's Success: The Critical Role of Post-Colonial Policy." *Cato Journal* 23, no. 2 (Fall 2003).

Easterly, William. *The White Man's Burden: Why the West's Efforts to Aid the Rest Have Done So Much Ill and So Little Good.* New York: Penguin Press, 2006.

Guest, Robert. *The Shackled Continent: Power, Corruption, and African Lives.* Washington: Smithsonian Books, 2004.

Mbeki, Moeletsi. "Underdevelopment in Sub-Saharan Africa: The Role of the Private Sector and Political Elites." Cato Institute Foreign Policy Briefing Paper no. 85, April 15, 2005.

Mwenda, Andrew. "Foreign Aid and the Weakening of Democratic Accountability in Uganda." Cato Institute Foreign Policy Briefing Paper no. 88, July 12, 2006.

Ng, Francis, and Alexander Yeats. *Good Governance and Trade Policy: Are They the Keys to Africa's Global Integration and Growth?* Washington: International Monetary Fund, 1999.

Tupy, Marian. "Trade Liberalization and Poverty Reduction in Sub-Saharan Africa." Cato Institute Policy Analysis no. 557, December 6, 2005.

—Prepared by Marian L. Tupy

63. Foreign Aid and Economic Development

> **Congress should**
>
> - abolish the U.S. Agency for International Development and end government-to-government aid programs;
> - withdraw from the World Bank and the five regional multilateral development banks;
> - not use foreign aid to encourage or reward market reforms in the developing world;
> - eliminate programs, such as enterprise funds, that provide loans to the private sector in developing countries and oppose schemes that guarantee private-sector investments abroad;
> - privatize or abolish the Export-Import Bank, the Overseas Private Investment Corporation, the U.S. Trade and Development Agency, and other sources of international corporate welfare;
> - forgive the debts of heavily indebted countries on the condition that they receive no further foreign aid; and
> - end government support of microenterprise lending and non-governmental organizations.

In 2002, President Bush called for increasing U.S. bilateral development assistance by about 50 percent by fiscal year 2006, gradually raising the aid above the then prevailing level of roughly $10 billion. The Millennium Challenge Account, managed by a new government agency, the Millennium Challenge Corporation, was created in 2004 to direct the additional funds to poor countries with sound policy environments. Likewise in recent years, the World Bank and the United Nations have been advocating a doubling of official development assistance worldwide to about $150 billion. Foreign aid has risen notably. The Bush administration reached its funding goal, and total aid from rich countries is now around $100 billion (see Figure 63.1).

Those calls for significant increases in foreign aid are based on the argument that aid agencies have learned from the failure of past foreign aid programs and that overseas assistance can now be generally effective in promoting growth. But what we know about aid and development provides little reason for such enthusiasm:

- There is no correlation between aid and growth.
- Aid that goes into a poor policy environment doesn't work and contributes to debt.
- Aid conditioned on market reforms has failed.
- Countries that have adopted market-oriented policies have done so because of factors unrelated to aid.
- There is a strong relationship between economic freedom and growth.

A widespread consensus has formed about those points, even among development experts who have long supported government-to-government aid. As developing countries began introducing market reforms in the late 1980s and early 1990s, the most successful reformers also experienced

Figure 63.1
Official Development Assistance, 1960–2007

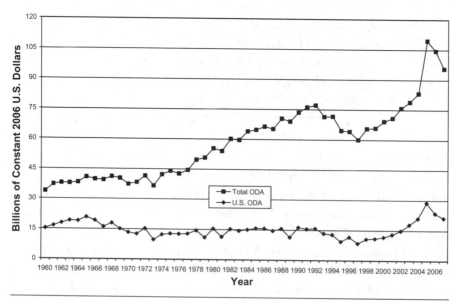

SOURCE: Organisation for Economic Co-Operation and Development, *OECD, Stat Extracts.* http//states.oecd.org.

noticeably better economic performance. As would be expected, the improvement among the successful reformers also improved the apparent performance of foreign aid in those countries—thus, the new emphasis on giving aid to countries that have already adopted good policies. The new approach to aid is dubious for many reasons, not the least of which is the fact that countries with sound policies will already be rewarded with economic growth and do not need foreign aid. In any event, much, if not most, foreign assistance will continue to be awarded without regard to the record of internal reform.

The Dismal Record of Foreign Aid

By the 1990s, the failure of conventional government-to-government aid schemes had been widely recognized and brought the entire foreign assistance process under scrutiny. For example, a Clinton administration task force conceded that, "despite decades of foreign assistance, most of Africa and parts of Latin America, Asia and the Middle East are economically worse off today than they were 20 years ago." As early as 1989, a bipartisan task force of the House Foreign Affairs Committee concluded that U.S. aid programs "no longer either advance U.S. interests abroad or promote economic development."

Multilateral aid has also played a prominent role in the post–World War II period. The World Bank, to which the United States is the major contributor, was created in 1944 to provide aid mostly for infrastructure projects in countries that could not attract private capital on their own. The World Bank has since expanded its lending functions, as have the five regional development banks that have subsequently been created on the World Bank's model: the Inter-American Development Bank, the Asian Development Bank, the African Development Bank, the European Bank for Reconstruction and Development, and the Middle East Development Bank. The International Monetary Fund, also established in 1944, long ago abandoned its original role of maintaining exchange-rate stability around the world and has since engaged in long-term lending on concessional terms to most of the same clients as the World Bank.

Despite record levels of lending, however, the multilateral development banks have not achieved more success at promoting economic growth than has the U.S. Agency for International Development. Numerous self-evaluations of World Bank performance over the years, for example, have uncovered high failure rates of bank-financed projects. In 2000, the bipartisan Meltzer Commission of the U.S. Congress found a 55 to

60 percent failure rate of World Bank projects based on the bank's own evaluations. A 1998 World Bank report concluded that aid agencies "saw themselves as being primarily in the business of dishing out money, so it is not surprising that much [aid] went into poorly managed economies—with little result." The report also said that foreign aid had often been "an unmitigated failure." "No one who has seen the evidence on aid effectiveness," commented Oxford University economist Paul Collier in 1997, "can honestly say that aid is currently achieving its objective."

Although a small group of countries in the developing world (some of which received aid at some point) has achieved self-sustaining economic growth over an extended period, most recipients of aid have not. Rather, as a 1989 USAID report suggested, aid has tended to create dependence on the part of borrower countries.

There are several reasons that massive transfers from the developed to the developing world have not led to a corresponding transfer of prosperity. Aid has traditionally been lent to governments, has supported central planning, and has been based on a fundamentally flawed vision of development.

By lending to governments, USAID and the multilateral development agencies supported by Washington have helped expand the state sector at the expense of the private sector in poor countries. U.S. aid to India from 1961 to 1989, for example, amounted to well over $2 billion, almost all of which went to the Indian state. Ghanaian-born economist George Ayittey complained that, as late as 1989, 90 percent of U.S. aid to sub-Saharan Africa went directly to governments.

Foreign aid has thus financed governments, both authoritarian and democratic, whose policies have been the principal cause of their countries' impoverishment. Trade protectionism, byzantine licensing schemes, inflationary monetary policy, price and wage controls, nationalization of industries, exchange-rate controls, state-run agricultural marketing boards, and restrictions on foreign and domestic investment, for example, have all been supported explicitly or implicitly by U.S. foreign aid programs.

Not only has lack of economic freedom kept literally billions of people in poverty, development planning has thoroughly politicized the economies of developing countries. Centralization of economic decisionmaking in the hands of political authorities has meant that a substantial amount of poor countries' otherwise useful resources has been diverted to unproductive activities, such as rent seeking by private interests or politically motivated spending by the state.

Research by economist Peter Boone of the London School of Economics confirms the dismal record of foreign aid to the developing world. After reviewing aid flows to more than 95 countries, Boone found that "virtually all aid goes to consumption" and that "aid does not increase investment and growth, nor benefit the poor as measured by improvements in human development indicators, but it does increase the size of government." A recent comprehensive study by the IMF also found no relationship between aid and growth.

It has become abundantly clear that as long as the conditions for economic growth do not exist in developing countries, no amount of foreign aid will be able to produce economic growth. Moreover, economic growth in poor countries does not depend on official transfers from outside sources. Indeed, were that not so, no country on earth could ever have escaped from initial poverty. The long-held premise of foreign assistance—that poor countries were poor because they lacked capital—not only ignored thousands of years of economic development history, it also was contradicted by contemporary events in the developing world, which saw the accumulation of massive debt, not development.

Promotion of Market Reforms

Even aid intended to advance market liberalization can produce undesirable results. Such aid takes the pressure off recipient governments and allows them to postpone, rather than promote, necessary but politically difficult reforms. Ernest Preeg, former chief economist at USAID, for instance, noted that problem in the Philippines after the collapse of the Marcos dictatorship: "As large amounts of aid flowed to the Aquino government from the United States and other donors, the urgency for reform dissipated. Economic aid became a cushion for postponing difficult internal decisions on reform. A central policy focus of the Aquino government became that of obtaining more and more aid rather than prompt implementation of the reform program."

A similar outcome is evident in the Middle East, which receives about one-fifth to one-quarter of U.S. economic aid, most of which has historically been received by the governments of Egypt and Israel and, more recently, Iraq. It should not be surprising, then, that the region is notable for its low levels of economic freedom and little economic reform. In 1996, the Institute for Advanced Strategic and Political Studies, an Israeli think tank, complained: "Almost one-seventh of the [gross domestic product] comes to Israel as charity. This has proven to be economically disastrous. It prevents reform, causes inflation, fosters waste, ruins our competitiveness and efficiency, and increases the future tax burden on our children who will have to repay the part of the aid that comes as loans.'' In 2001, the institute again complained that foreign aid has "allowed Israel to avoid a very necessary liberalization of its state-controlled economy.''

Far more effective at promoting market reforms is the suspension or elimination of aid. Although USAID lists South Korea and Taiwan as success stories of U.S. economic assistance, those countries began to take off economically only after massive U.S. aid was cut off. As even the World Bank has conceded, "Reform is more likely to be preceded by a decline in aid than an increase in aid." When India faced Western sanctions in 1998 in response to nuclear tests there, the *International Herald Tribune* reported that ''India approved at least 50 foreign-investment projects to compensate for the loss of aid from Japan and the United States'' and that it would take additional measures to attract capital. In the end, the countries that have done the most to reform economically have made changes despite foreign aid, not because of it.

Still, much aid is delivered on the condition that recipient countries implement market-oriented economic policies. Such conditionality is the basis for the World Bank's structural adjustment lending, which it began in the early 1980s after it realized that pouring money into unsound economies would not lead to self-sustaining growth. But aid conditioned on reform has been ineffective at inducing reform. One 1997 World Bank study noted that there ''is no systematic effect of aid on policy.'' A 2002 World Bank study admitted that ''too often, governments receiving aid were not truly committed to reforms'' and that ''the Bank has often been overly optimistic about the prospects for reform, thereby contributing to misallocation of aid.'' Oxford's Paul Collier explains: ''Some governments have chosen to reform, others to regress, but these choices appear to have been largely independent of the aid relationship. The microevidence of this result has been accumulating for some years. It has been suppressed by an unholy alliance of the donors and their critics. Obviously, the donors did not wish to admit that their conditionality was a charade.''

Lending agencies have an institutional bias toward continued lending even if market reforms are not adequately introduced. Yale University economist Gustav Ranis explains that within some lending agencies, ''ultimately the need to lend will overcome the need to ensure that those [loan] conditions are indeed met.'' In the worst cases, of course, lending agencies do suspend loans in an effort to encourage reforms. When those reforms begin or are promised, however, the agencies predictably respond by resuming the loans—a process Ranis has referred to as a "time-consuming and expensive ritual dance."

In sum, aiding reforming nations, however superficially appealing, does not produce rapid and widespread liberalization. Just as Congress should reject funding regimes that are uninterested in reform, it should reject schemes that call for funding countries on the basis of their records of reform. This includes the Bush administration's Millennium Challenge Corporation. The most obvious problem with that program is that it is based on a conceptual flaw: countries that are implementing the right policies for growth, and therefore do not need foreign aid, will be receiving aid. In practice, the effectiveness of such selective aid has been questioned by a recent IMF review that found "no evidence that aid works better in better policy or geographical environments, or that certain forms of aid work better than others."

The practical problems are indeed formidable. The Millennium Challenge Corporation and other programs of its kind will require government officials and aid agencies—all of which have a poor record in determining when and where to disburse foreign aid—to make complex judgment calls on which countries deserve the aid and when. Moreover, it is difficult to believe that bureaucratic self-interest, micromanagement by Congress, and other political or geostrategic considerations will not continue to play a role in the disbursement of this kind of foreign aid. It is important to remember that the new aid funds administered by the Millennium Challenge Corporation do not actually reform U.S. aid. Rather, they are *in addition to* the much larger traditional aid programs that will continue to be run by USAID—in many cases in the very same countries.

Help for the Private Sector

Enterprise funds are another initiative intended to help market economies. Under this approach, USAID and the Overseas Private Investment Corporation have established and financed venture funds throughout the developing world. Their purpose is to promote economic progress and "jump-start" the market by investing in the private sector.

It was always unclear exactly how such government-supported funds find profitable private ventures in which the private sector is unwilling to invest. Numerous evaluations have now found that most enterprise funds are losing money, and many have simply displaced private investment that otherwise would have occurred. Moreover, there is no evidence that the funds have generated additional private investment, had a positive effect on development, or helped create a better investment environment in poor countries.

Similar efforts to underwrite private entrepreneurs are evident at the World Bank (through its expanding program to guarantee private-sector investment) and at U.S. agencies such as the Export-Import Bank, Overseas Private Investment Corporation, and the Trade and Development Agency, which provide comparable services.

U.S. officials justify those programs on the grounds that they help promote development and benefit the U.S. economy. Yet providing loan guarantees and subsidized insurance to the private sector relieves the governments of underdeveloped countries from creating an investment environment that would attract foreign capital on its own. To attract much-needed investment, countries should establish secure property rights and sound economic policies, rather than rely on Washington-backed schemes that allow avoidance of those reforms.

Moreover, while some corporations clearly benefit from the array of foreign assistance schemes, the U.S. economy and American taxpayers do not. Subsidized loans and insurance programs amount to corporate welfare. Macroeconomic policies and conditions, not corporate welfare programs, affect factors such as the unemployment rate and the size of the trade deficit. Programs that benefit specific interest groups manage only to rearrange resources within the U.S. economy and do so in a very wasteful manner. Indeed, the United States did not achieve and does not maintain its status as the world's largest exporter because of agencies like the Export-Import Bank, which finances less than 2 percent of U.S. exports.

Even USAID claims that the main beneficiary of its lending is the United States because close to 80 percent of its contracts and grants go to American firms. That argument is also fallacious. "To argue that aid helps the domestic economy," renowned economist Peter Bauer explained, "is like saying that a shop-keeper benefits from having his cash register burgled so long as the burglar spends part of the proceeds in his shop."

Debt Relief

Some 41 poor countries today suffer from inordinately high foreign debt levels. Thus, the World Bank and the IMF have devised a $68 billion debt-relief initiative for the world's heavily indebted poor countries. To fund this program, the aid agencies are requesting about half the money from the United States and other donors. The initiative, of course, is an implicit recognition of the failure of past lending to produce self-sustaining growth, especially since an overwhelming percentage of eligible countries' public foreign debt is owed to bilateral and multilateral lending agencies. Indeed, 96 percent of those countries' long-term debt is public or publicly guaranteed (See Table 63.1).

Forgiving poor nations' debt is a sound idea, on the condition that no other aid is forthcoming. Unfortunately, the multilateral debt initiative promises to keep poor countries on a borrowing treadmill, since they will be eligible for future multilateral loans based on conditionality. There is no reason, however, to believe that conditionality will work any better in the future than it has in the past. Again, as a recent World Bank study emphasized, "A conditioned loan is no guarantee that reforms will be carried out—or last once they are."

Nor is there reason to believe that debt relief will work better now than in the past. As former World Bank economist William Easterly has documented, donor nations have been forgiving poor countries' debts since the late 1970s, and the result has simply been more debt. From 1989 to 1997, 41 highly indebted countries saw some $33 billion of debt forgiveness, yet they still found themselves in an untenable position by the time the current round of debt forgiveness began. Indeed, they have been borrowing ever-larger amounts from aid agencies. Easterly notes, moreover, that private credit to the heavily indebted poor countries has been virtually replaced by foreign aid and that foreign aid itself has been lent on increasingly easier terms. Thus, when the World Bank and IMF call for debt forgiveness, it is the latest in a series of failed attempts by rich countries to resolve poor countries' debts.

At the same time, it has become increasingly evident that the debt-relief scheme is a financial shell game that allows the multilaterals to repay their previous loans without having to write down bad debt and thus without negatively affecting their financial status. If official donors wished to forgive debt, they could do so easily. Contributing money to the multilateral debt-relief initiative, however, will do little to promote reform or self-sustaining growth.

Other Initiatives

The inadequacy of government-to-government aid programs has prompted an increased reliance on nongovernmental organizations (NGOs). NGOs, or private voluntary organizations (PVOs), are said to be more effective at delivering aid and accomplishing development objectives

Table 63.1
Heavily Indebted Poor Countries: Amount of Debt Attributable to Official Aid and Other Government-Backed Schemes, 2006

Country	Long-Term Debt (billion US$)	Public and Publicly Guaranteed Debt (billion US$)	Public and Publicly Guaranteed Debt as a Percentage of Long-Term Debt
Afghanistan	1.76	1.76	100.00
Benin	0.78	0.78	100.00
Bolivia	5.06	3.20	63.33
Burkina Faso	1.02	1.02	100.00
Burundi	1.29	1.29	100.00
Cameroon	2.57	2.08	80.94
Central African Republic	0.86	0.86	100.00
Chad	1.69	1.69	100.00
Comoros	0.26	0.26	100.00
Côte d'Ivoire	11.68	10.83	92.75
Democratic Republic of Congo	9.85	9.85	100.00
Eritrea	0.78	0.78	100.00
Ethiopia	2.21	2.21	100.00
Gambia, The	0.69	0.69	100.00
Ghana	1.89	1.89	100.00
Guinea	2.98	2.98	100.00
Guinea-Bissau	0.69	0.69	100.00
Guyana	0.94	0.94	100.00
Haiti	1.03	1.03	100.00
Honduras	3.51	2.99	85.01
Kyrgyz Republic	2.11	1.86	88.13
Liberia	1.12	1.12	100.00
Madagascar	1.24	1.24	100.00
Malawi	0.77	0.77	100.00
Mali	1.41	1.41	100.00
Mauritania	1.40	1.40	100.00
Mozambique	2.51	2.51	100.00
Nepal	3.29	3.29	100.00
Nicaragua	3.71	3.42	92.24
Nigeria	3.80	3.80	100.00
Republic of Congo	5.33	5.33	100.00
Rwanda	0.39	0.39	100.00

Country	Long-Term Debt (billion US$)	Public and Publicly Guaranteed Debt (billion US$)	Public and Publicly Guaranteed Debt as a Percentage of Long-Term Debt
São Tomé and Principe	0.34	0.34	100.00
Senegal	1.86	1.71	91.91
Sierra Leone	1.32	1.32	100.00
Somalia	1.92	1.92	100.00
Sudan	12.10	11.61	95.90
Tanzania	2.93	2.93	99.80
Togo	1.56	1.56	100.00
Uganda	1.11	1.11	100.00
Zambia	1.83	1.00	54.82
Average	2.53	2.39	96.21
Total	103.60	n.a.	n.a.

Source: World Bank, World Development Indicators Online. http://publications.worldbank.org/WDI.

Note: n.a. = not applicable.

because they are less bureaucratic and more in touch with the on-the-ground realities of their clients.

Although channeling official aid monies through PVOs has been referred to as a "privatized" form of foreign assistance, it is often difficult to make a sharp distinction between government agencies and PVOs beyond the fact that the latter are subject to less oversight and are less accountable. Michael Maren, a former employee at Catholic Relief Services and USAID, notes that most PVOs receive most of their funds from government sources.

Given that relationship—PVO dependence on government hardly makes them private or voluntary—Maren and others have described how the charitable goals on which PVOs are founded have been undermined. The nonprofit organization Development GAP, for example, observed that USAID's "overfunding of a number of groups has taxed their management capabilities, changed their institutional style, and made them more bureaucratic and unresponsive to the expressed needs of the poor overseas."

"When aid bureaucracies evaluate the work of NGOs," Maren adds, "they have no incentive to criticize them." For their part, NGOs naturally have an incentive to keep official funds flowing. The lack of proper impact assessments plagues the entire foreign aid establishment, prompting former USAID head Andrew Natsios to acknowledge, "We don't get an objective analysis of what is really going on, whether the programs are working or not." In the final analysis, government provision of foreign assistance through PVOs instead of traditional channels does not produce dramatically different results.

Microenterprise lending, another increasingly popular program among advocates of aid, is designed to provide small amounts of credit to the world's poorest people. The poor use the loans to establish livestock, manufacturing, and trade enterprises, for example.

Many microloan programs, such as the one run by the Grameen Bank in Bangladesh, appear to be highly successful. Grameen has disbursed more than $6.5 billion since the 1970s and achieved a repayment rate of about 98 percent. Microenterprise lending institutions, moreover, are intended to be economically viable, to achieve financial self-sufficiency within three to seven years. Given those qualities, it is unclear why microlending organizations would require subsidies. Indeed, microenterprise banks typically refer to themselves as profitable enterprises. For those and other reasons, Princeton University's Jonathan Morduch concluded in a 1999 study that "the greatest promise of microfinance is so far unmet, and the boldest claims do not withstand close scrutiny." He added that, according to some estimates, "if subsidies are pulled and costs cannot be reduced, as many as 95 percent of current programs will eventually have to close shop." To date, a rigorous assessment of the effectiveness of microenterprise lending has not yet been done due to the lack of reliable data from the lending institutions and the scarcity of proper self-evaluations.

Furthermore, microenterprise programs alleviate the conditions of the poor, but they do not address the causes of the lack of credit faced by the poor. In developing countries, for example, about 90 percent of poor people's property is not recognized by the state. Without secure private property rights, most of the world's poor cannot use collateral to obtain a loan. The Institute for Liberty and Democracy, a Peruvian think tank, found that when poor people's property in Peru was registered, new businesses were created, production increased, asset values rose by 200 percent, and credit became available. Of course, the scarcity of credit is also caused by a host of other policy measures, such as financial regulation that makes it prohibitively expensive to provide banking services for the poor.

In sum, microenterprise programs can be beneficial, but successful programs need not receive aid subsidies. The success of microenterprise programs, moreover, will depend on specific conditions, which vary greatly from country to country. For that reason, microenterprise projects should be financed privately by people who have their own money at stake rather than by international aid bureaucracies that appear intent on replicating such projects throughout the developing world.

Conclusion

Numerous studies have found that economic growth is strongly related to the level of economic freedom. Put simply, the greater a country's economic freedom, the greater its level of prosperity over time (Figure 63.2). Likewise, the greater a country's economic freedom, the faster it will grow. Economic freedom, which includes not only policies, such as free trade and stable money, but also institutions, such as the rule of law and the security of private property rights, increases more than income. It is also strongly related to improvements in other development indicators such as longevity, access to safe drinking water, lower corruption, and

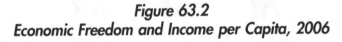

Figure 63.2
Economic Freedom and Income per Capita, 2006

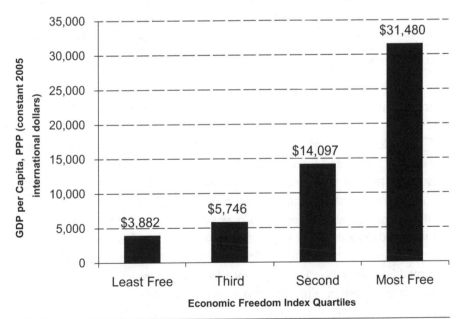

SOURCE: James Gwartney and Robert Lawson, *Economic Freedom of the World: 2008 Annual Report* (Vancouver: Fraser Institute, 2008), p. 18.

NOTE: GDP = gross domestic product; PPP = purchasing power parity.

667

Figure 63.3
Economic Freedom and the Income Level of the Poorest 10 Percent of the Population, 1990–2006

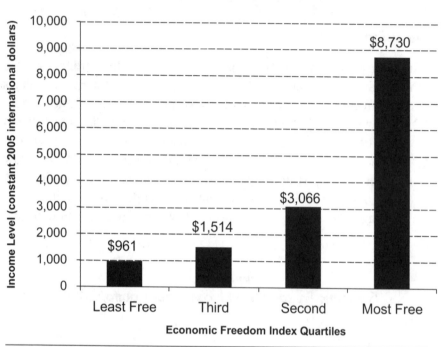

SOURCE: James Gwartney and Robert Lawson, *Economic Freedom of the World: 2008 Annual Report* (Vancouver: Fraser Institute, 2008), p. 20.

dramatically higher incomes for the poorest members of society (Figure 63.3).

Those developing countries, such as Chile, Estonia, and Taiwan, that have most liberalized their economies and achieved high levels of growth have done far more to reduce poverty and improve their citizens' standards of living than have foreign aid programs.

In the end, a country's progress depends almost entirely on its domestic policies and institutions, not on outside factors such as foreign aid. Congress should recognize that foreign aid has not caused the worldwide shift toward the market and that appeals for more foreign aid, even when intended to promote the market, will continue to do more harm than good.

Suggested Readings

Anderson, Robert E. *Just Get Out of the Way: How Government Can Help Business in Poor Countries.* Washington: Cato Institute, 2004.

Ayodele, Thompson, Franklin Cudjoe, Temba Nolutshungu, and Charles Sunwabe. "African Perspectives on Aid: Foreign Aid Will Not Pull Africa out of Poverty." Cato Institute Economic Development Bulletin no. 2, September 14, 2005.

Bandow, Doug, and Ian Vásquez, eds. *Perpetuating Poverty: The World Bank, the IMF, and the Developing World.* Washington: Cato Institute, 1994.

Banerjee, Abhijit. *Making Aid Work.* Cambridge, MA: MIT Press, 2007. Commentary by Ian Vásquez, pp. 47–53.

Bauer, P. T. *Dissent on Development.* Cambridge, MA: Harvard University Press, 1972.

De Soto, Hernando. *The Mystery of Capital: Why Capitalism Triumphs in the West and Fails Everywhere Else.* New York: Basic Books, 2000.

Dichter, Thomas. "Time to Stop Fooling Ourselves about Foreign Aid." Cato Institute Foreign Policy Briefing no. 86, September 12, 2005.

———. "A Second Look at Microfinance: The Sequence of Growth and Credit in Economic History." Cato Institute Development Briefing Paper no. 1, February 15, 2007.

Djankov, Simeon, Jose Montalvo, and Marta Reynal-Querol. "Does Foreign Aid Help?" *Cato Journal* 26, no. 1 (Winter 2006).

Dollar, David, and Aart Kraay. "Trade, Growth and Poverty." World Bank research paper, March 2001.

Easterly, William. *The White Man's Burden: Why the West's Efforts to Aid the Rest Have Done So Much Ill and So Little Good.* New York: Penguin Press, 2006.

———. "Freedom versus Collectivism in Foreign Aid." In *Economic Freedom of the World: 2006 Annual Report,* edited by James Gwartney and Robert Lawson. Vancouver: Fraser Institute, 2006.

Erixon, Fredrik. *Aid and Development: Will It Work This Time?* London: International Policy Network, 2005.

Gwartney, James, and Robert Lawson. *Economic Freedom of the World: 2008 Annual Report.* Vancouver: Fraser Institute, 2008.

Hudson Institute. *The Index of Global Philanthropy: 2008.* Washington: Hudson Institute, 2008.

International Financial Institution Advisory Commission (Meltzer Commission). "Report to the U.S. Congress and the Department of the Treasury." March 8, 2000. www.house.gov/jec/imf/meltzer.htm.

Lal, Deepak. *The Poverty of "Development Economics."* London: Institute of Economic Affairs, 1983, 1997.

Lewis, William W. *The Power of Productivity: Wealth, Poverty, and the Threat to Global Stability.* Chicago: University of Chicago Press, 2004.

Lindsey, Brink. *Against the Dead Hand: The Uncertain Struggle for Global Capitalism.* New York: John Wiley & Sons, 2002.

Lukas, Aaron, and Ian Vásquez. "Rethinking the Export-Import Bank." Cato Institute Trade Briefing Paper no. 15, March 12, 2002.

Maren, Michael. *The Road to Hell: Foreign Aid and International Charity.* New York: Free Press, 1997.

Mwenda, Andrew. "Foreign Aid and the Weakening of Democratic Accountability in Uganda." Cato Institute Foreign Policy Briefing no. 88, July 12, 2006.

Vásquez, Ian. "The Asian Crisis: Why the IMF Should Not Intervene." *Vital Speeches,* April 15, 1998.

———. "The New Approach to Foreign Aid: Is the Enthusiasm Warranted?" Cato Institute Foreign Policy Briefing no. 79, September 17, 2003.

669

Vásquez, Ian, and John Welborn. "Reauthorize or Retire the Overseas Private Investment Corporation." Cato Institute Foreign Policy Briefing no. 78, September 15, 2003.

Walters, Alan. "Do We Need the IMF and the World Bank?" Institute of Economic Affairs Current Controversies no. 10, September 1994.

World Bank. *Doing Business 2009*. Washington: World Bank, 2008.

—Prepared by Ian Vásquez

Index

679

Contributors

Doug Bandow is vice president of policy for Citizen Outreach.

David Boaz is executive vice president of the Cato Institute and author of *Libertarianism. A Primer* and *The Politics of Freedom: Taking on the Left, the Right, and Threats to Our Liberties*.

Michael F. Cannon is director of health policy studies at the Cato Institute and coauthor of *Healthy Competition: What's Holding Back Health Care and How to Fix It*.

Ted Galen Carpenter is vice president for defense and foreign policy studies at the Cato Institute and author of *Smart Power: Toward a Prudent Foreign Policy for America*.

Andrew J. Coulson is director of the Center for Educational Freedom at the Cato Institute and author of *Market Education: The Unknown History*.

Edward H. Crane is president of the Cato Institute.

James A. Dorn is vice president for academic affairs at the Cato Institute and coeditor of *The Future of Money in the Information Age*.

Chris Edwards is director of tax policy studies at the Cato Institute, author of *Downsizing the Federal Government,* and coauthor of *Global Tax Revolution: The Rise of Tax Competition and the Battle to Defend It*.

Benjamin Friedman is a research fellow in defense and homeland security studies at the Cato Institute.

Daniel Griswold is director of the Cato Institute's Center for Trade Policy Studies.

Leon Hadar is a research fellow in foreign policy studies at the Cato Institute and the author of *Sandstorm: American Blindness in the Middle East*.

Jim Harper is director of information policy studies at the Cato Institute and author of *Identity Crisis: How Identification Is Overused and Misunderstood*.

Gene Healy is senior editor at the Cato Institute and author of *The Cult of the Presidency: America's Dangerous Devotion to Executive Power*.

Juan Carlos Hidalgo is project coordinator for Latin America at the Cato Institute's Center for Global Liberty and Prosperity.

Daniel Ikenson is associate director of the Cato Institute's Center for Trade Policy Studies and coauthor of *Antidumping Exposed: The Devilish Details of Unfair Trade Law*.

Malou Innocent is a foreign policy analyst at the Cato Institute.

Sallie James is a policy analyst with the Cato Institute's Center for Trade Policy Studies.

Stanley Kober is a research fellow in foreign policy studies at the Cato Institute.

David B. Kopel is an associate policy analyst at the Cato Institute, research director of the Independence Institute, and coauthor of *The Heller Case: Gun Rights Affirmed!*

Timothy B. Lee is an adjunct scholar at the Cato Institute.

Robert A. Levy is chairman of the Cato Institute and coauthor of *The Dirty Dozen: How Twelve Supreme Court Cases Radically Expanded Government and Eroded Freedom*.

Justin Logan is associate director of foreign policy studies at the Cato Institute.

Timothy Lynch is director of the Cato Institute's Project on Criminal Justice and editor of *After Prohibition: An Adult Approach to Drug Policies in the 21st Century*.

687

director of the Cato Institute's Center for Educational
*Feds in the Classroom: How Big Government Corrupts,
nises American Education.*

professor of environmental sciences at the University of Virginia,
ironmental studies at the Cato Institute, and coauthor of *Climate
al Warming Science They Don't Want You to Know.*

is a senior fellow at the Cato Institute and coauthor of *Global Tax
e Rise of Tax Competition and the Battle to Defend It.*

assistant professor of law at DePaul University and an adjunct scholar
Institute.

Niskanen is chairman emeritus and distinguished senior economist of the
titute and author of *Reflections of a Political Economist.*

J'Toole is a senior fellow at the Cato Institute and author of *The Vanishing
nobile and Other Urban Myths* and *The Best-Laid Plans.*

J. Palmer is vice president for international programs at the Cato Institute.

Patch is a former budget fellow at the Cato Institute.

ger Pilon is vice president for legal affairs, B. Kenneth Simon Chair in Constitutional
Studies, and director of the Center for Constitutional Studies at the Cato Institute.

James Plummer is a former research assistant at the Cato Institute.

Christopher Preble is director of foreign policy studies at the Cato Institute and author
of *Exiting Iraq: Why the U.S. Must End the Military Occupation and Renew the War
against Al Qaeda.*

Sheldon Richman is editor of *The Freeman.*

John Samples is director of the Center for Representative Government at the Cato
Institute and author of *The Fallacy of Campaign Finance Reform.*

Michael Tanner is a senior fellow at the Cato Institute, author of *Leviathan on the
Right: How Big-Government Conservatism Brought Down the Republican Revolution,*
and coauthor of *A New Deal for Social Security.*

Jerry Taylor is a senior fellow at the Cato Institute.

Marian L. Tupy is a policy analyst with the Center for Global Liberty and Prosperity
at the Cato Institute.

Peter Van Doren is editor of Cato's *Regulation* magazine and author of *Chemicals,
Cancer, and Choices.*

Ian Vásquez is director of the Center for Global Liberty and Prosperity at the Cato
Institute and editor of *Global Fortune: The Stumble and Rise of World Capitalism.*